Forgetting

Current Issues in Memory
Series Editor: Robert Logie
Professor of Human Cognitive Neuroscience, University of Edinburgh, UK

Current Issues in Memory is a series of edited books that reflect the state-of-the-art in areas of current and emerging interest in the psychological study of memory. Each volume is tightly focused on a particular topic and consists of seven to ten chapters contributed by international experts. The editors of individual volumes are leading figures in their areas and provide an introductory overview. Example topics include: binding in working memory, prospective memory, memory and ageing, autobiographical memory, visual memory, implicit memory, amnesia, retrieval, memory development.

Other titles in this series:

The Visual World in Memory
Edited by James R. Brockmole

Current Issues in Applied Memory Research
Edited by Graham M. Davies & Daniel B. Wright

Forgetting

Edited by Sergio Della Sala

Psychology Press
Taylor & Francis Group
HOVE AND NEW YORK

Published in 2010
by Psychology Press
27 Church Road, Hove, East Sussex BN3 2FA

Simultaneously published in the USA and Canada
by Psychology Press
270 Madison Avenue, New York, NY 10016

Psychology Press is an imprint of the Taylor & Francis Group, an Informa business

Typeset in Times by RefineCatch Limited, Bungay, Suffolk
Printed and bound in Great Britain by
TJ International Ltd, Padstow, Cornwall
Cover design by Lisa Dynan

This publication has been produced with paper manufactured to strict environmental standards and with pulp derived from sustainable forests.

British Library Cataloguing in Publication Data
A catalogue record for this book is available from the British Library

Library of Congress Cataloging-in-Publication Data
Forgetting / edited by Sergio Della Sala.
p. cm.
Includes bibliographical references and index.
1. Memory. 2. Autobiographical memory. I. Della Sala, Sergio.
BF378.F7.F67 2010
153.1′25—dc22 2009044489

ISBN: 978–1–84872–012–1(hbk)

To Miriam

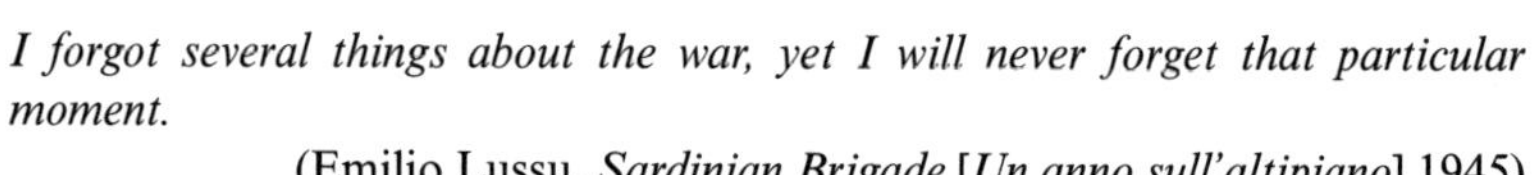

I forgot several things about the war, yet I will never forget that particular moment.

(Emilio Lussu, *Sardinian Brigade* [*Un anno sull'altipiano*] 1945)

Contents

List of contributors ix
Preface xiii

1 **Forgetting: Preliminary considerations** 1
HENRY L. ROEDIGER III, YANA WEINSTEIN, AND POOJA K. AGARWAL

2 **Forgetting: A historical perspective** 23
HANS J. MARKOWITSCH AND MATTHIAS BRAND

3 **A new taxonomy of memory and forgetting** 35
ROBERTO CUBELLI

4 **Forgetting in memory models: Arguments against trace decay and consolidation failure** 49
GORDON D. A. BROWN AND STEPHAN LEWANDOWSKY

5 **Connectionist models of forgetting** 77
JAAP M.J. MURRE

6 **Synaptic plasticity and the neurobiology of memory and forgetting** 101
FLAVIA VALTORTA AND FABIO BENFENATI

7 **The functional neuroimaging of forgetting** 135
BENJAMIN J. LEVY, BRICE A. KUHL, AND ANTHONY D. WAGNER

8 **Sleep and forgetting** 165
PHILIPPE PEIGNEUX, REMY SCHMITZ, AND CHARLINE URBAIN

9 Forgetting due to retroactive interference in amnesia: Findings and implications 185

MICHAELA DEWAR, NELSON COWAN, AND SERGIO DELLA SALA

10 Accelerated long-term forgetting 211

CHRISTOPHER BUTLER, NILS MUHLERT, AND ADAM ZEMAN

11 Aspects of forgetting in psychogenic amnesia 239

MATTHIAS BRAND AND HANS J. MARKOWITSCH

12 Autobiographical forgetting, social forgetting, and situated forgetting: Forgetting in context 253

CELIA B. HARRIS, JOHN SUTTON, AND AMANDA J. BARNIER

13 The role of retroactive interference and consolidation in everyday forgetting 285

JOHN T. WIXTED

Author index 313

Subject index 329

Contributors

Pooja K. Agarwal, Department of Psychology, Washington University, One Brookings Drive, Campus Box 1125, St. Louis, MO 63130–4899, USA.

Amanda J. Barnier, Macquarie Centre for Cognitive Science, Macquarie University, Sydney, NSW 2109, Australia.

Fabio Benfenati, Department of Neuroscience and Brain Technologies, The Italian Institute of Technology, Via Morego 30, 16163 Genova and Department of Experimental Medicine, University of Genova, Viale Benedetto XV, 3, 16132 Genova, Italy.

Matthias Brand, University of Duisburg-Essen, General Psychology: Cognition, Department of Computer Science and Applied Cognitive Science, Faculty of Engineering Sciences, Forsthausweg 2, 47057 Duisburg, Germany and Physiological Psychology, University of Bielefeld, PO Box 100131, D-33501 Bielefeld, Germany.

Gordon D. A. Brown, Department of Psychology, University of Warwick, Coventry CV4 7AL, UK and School of Psychology, University of Western Australia, Crawley, WA 6009, Australia.

Christopher Butler, Department of Clinical Neurology, University of Oxford, Oxford, UK.

Nelson Cowan, Department of Psychological Sciences, 210 McAlester Hall, University of Missouri-Columbia, Columbia, Missouri 65211–2500, USA.

Roberto Cubelli, Department of Cognitive Science and Education, Center for Mind/Brain Sciences, University of Trento, Corso Bettini, 31, I-38068 Rovereto, Trento, Italy.

Sergio Della Sala, Human Cognitive Neuroscience and Centre for Cognitive Ageing and Cognitive Epidemiology, Psychology, University of Edinburgh, UK.

Michaela Dewar, Human Cognitive Neuroscience and Centre for Cognitive

Ageing and Cognitive Epidemiology, Psychology, University of Edinburgh, UK.

Celia B. Harris, Macquarie Centre for Cognitive Science, Macquarie University, Sydney, NSW 2109, Australia.

Brice A. Kuhl, Department of Psychology, University of Stanford, Jordan Hall, Building 420, MC 2130, Stanford, CA 94305, USA.

Benjamin J. Levy, Department of Psychology, University of Stanford, Jordan Hall, Building 420, MC 2130, Stanford, CA 94305, USA.

Stephan Lewandowsky, School of Psychology, University of Western Australia, Crawley, WA 6009, Australia.

Hans J. Markowitsch, Physiological Psychology, University of Bielefeld, PO Box 100131, D-33501 Bielefeld, Germany.

Nils Muhlert, Peninsula Medical School, Barrack Road, Exeter EX2 5DW, UK.

Jaap M. J. Murre, Department of Psychology, University of Amsterdam, Roetersstraat 15, 1018 WB Amsterdam, The Netherlands.

Philippe Peigneux, Neuropsychology and Functional Neuroimaging Research Unit, Université Libre de Bruxelles, Brussels, Belgium and Cyclotron Research Centre, University of Liège, Liège, Belgium.

Henry L. Roediger III, Department of Psychology, Washington University, One Brookings Drive, Campus Box 1125, St. Louis, MO 63130–4899, USA.

Remy Schmitz, Neuropsychology and Functional Neuroimaging Research Unit, Université Libre de Bruxelles, Brussels, Belgium.

John Sutton, Macquarie Centre for Cognitive Science, Macquarie University, Sydney, NSW 2109, Australia.

Charline Urbain, Neuropsychology and Functional Neuroimaging Research Unit, Université Libre de Bruxelles, Brussels, Belgium.

Flavia Valtorta, Division of Neuroscience, S. Raffaele Scientific Institute, Via Olgettina 60, 20132 and International School of Psychotherapy with Imaginative Procedures (SISPI), Corso Concordia 14, 20129 Milan, Italy.

Anthony D. Wagner, Department of Psychology and Neurosciences Program, University of Stanford, Jordan Hall, Building 420, MC 2130, Stanford, CA 94305, USA.

Yana Weinstein, Department of Psychology, Washington University, One Brookings Drive, Campus Box 1125, St. Louis, MO 63130–4899, USA.

John T. Wixted, Department of Psychology, University of California at San Diego, La Jolla, CA 92093–0109, USA.

Adam Zeman, Peninsula Medical School, Barrack Road, Exeter EX2 5DW, UK.

Preface

Because the mountain grass
Cannot but keep the form
Where the mountain hare has lain.
(W. B. Yeats, *Memory*, 1919)

Several books are published each year on various aspects of memory and amnesia. However, little attention has been devoted to the counter aspect of memory, that is, forgetting. Considerable knowledge has been accrued on how healthy people (young and elderly) forget, why forgetting is instrumental to our ability to think and, indeed, to remember. Scientists and clinicians have also gathered knowledge on what happens to brain-damaged people showing pathological forgetting. However, this information is scattered across different disciplines and in highly specialized journals. Hence, the niche for this book, which aims at being a source collating the available interdisciplinary knowledge on forgetting.

Memory and forgetting are inextricably intertwined. In order to understand how memory works we need to understand how and why we forget. Forgetting is usually a term used to refer to a loss, the loss of a memory, due to the decay or overwriting of information. It is a term with a negative connotation, as illustrated by Rowan Atkinson's witty remark: "As I was leaving this morning, I said to myself, 'The last thing you must do is to forget your speech.' And sure enough, as I left the house this morning, the last thing I did was to forget my speech."

However, as Jorge Luis Borges (1942) reminded us in his short story "Funes, the Memorious": "To think is to forget a difference, to generalize, to abstract." That is, forgetting is the other coin of memory: without forgetting, remembering would be impossible, and humans would be like dull computers incapable of creativity. Indeed, Nietzsche maintained that it would be "altogether impossible to live at all without forgetting." Therefore, the importance of the topic should be clear, which, strangely enough, has been neglected in comparison with other features of memory.

This volume addresses various aspects of forgetting, drawing from several disciplines, including experimental and cognitive psychology, cognitive and clinical neuropsychology, behavioural neuroscience, neuroimaging, clinical neurology, and computing modeling. It is by no means an exhaustive review of all the knowledge accrued on forgetting and on how to account for it, but it covers enough material to offer an overview of the topic.

This book could not have seen the light without the work and the insight of several people whom I would like to thank: the series editor, Robert Logie, who invited us to propose this collection of essays; the commisioning editor, Becci Edmondson, and the editorial assistant, Sharla Plant, at Psychology Press; and of course all the authors who kindly contributed to this volume.

Sergio Della Sala
Edinburgh, December 2009

1 Forgetting

Preliminary considerations

Henry L. Roediger III,
Yana Weinstein, and Pooja K. Agarwal
Washington University in St. Louis, USA

> The existence of forgetting has never been proved: we only know that some things do not come to our mind when we want them to.
>
> (Friedrich Nietzsche, 1844–1900)

Of all the common afflictions from which humankind suffers, forgetting is probably the most common. Each of us, every day, forgets something we wish we could remember. It might be something we have done, something we intended to do, a fact, a name of a person or restaurant, and so on ad infinitum. As we age, our incidents of forgetting increase and we worry more about them. A whole industry of books, tapes, and even new mental gymnasia has grown up to deal with the cognitive frailties of old age, the primary one being rampant forgetting. Compared to other nuisances of life, forgetting probably tops the list. The "common cold" is actually quite rare compared to forgetting in all its manifestations. As Underwood (1966) wrote: "Forgetting is a most exasperating and sometimes even painful phenomenon" (p. 542). More recently, Nairne and Pandeirada (2008) maintained that for most people "forgetting is a scourge, a nuisance, a breakdown in an otherwise efficient mental capacity" (p. 179), although they quickly noted that there is often an adaptive value in forgetting too.

Despite the fact that psychologists have been studying learning and memory for 125 years, the current volume is the only one we can find devoted solely to the topic of forgetting. "Forgetting" is a term used in the titles of many works of fiction and even cultural critique (see Markowitsch & Brand, Chapter 2), but this volume is the first scientific one devoted to it. Strange, you might think.

Given the ubiquity of forgetting in our daily lives, the quote by Nietzsche that heads our chapter must seem stranger still. Given its ubiquity, how can the existence of forgetting be doubted? Difficulties of these sorts usually revolve around matters of definition, and that is the case here. We turn to this issue first.

Defining forgetting

According to the authors of the *International encyclopedia of the social sciences*: "It seems quite unnecessary to be concerned with a definition of 'forgetting' " (Sills & Merton, 1968, p. 536). Nonetheless, psychologists have attempted to define forgetting in several different ways. Cubelli (Chapter 3) provides a thorough exploration of the various extant definitions of forgetting, and below we give a general overview. Before undertaking the task of examining these issues, however, we review some preliminary considerations. At least since Köhler (1947, p. 279), psychologists have found it useful to distinguish among three stages in the learning/memory process: acquisition (encoding), storage (maintenance or persistence), and retrieval (utilization of stored information, see too Melton, 1963; Weiner, 1966). Encoding or acquisition is the initial process in learning, although this process may be extended in time as a memory trace (a persisting representation) formed through consolidation. Only events that have been securely encoded or learned in the first place can be said to be forgotten; it makes no sense to say that one has forgotten the 15th name in the Auckland, NZ, telephone book or the capital of Mars, because one never knew these bits of information in the first place. We take Tulving's definition of forgetting – "the inability to recall something now that could be recalled on an earlier occasion" (1974, p. 74) – as our starting point in considering more complex definitions. We consider first the strongest form of the concept of forgetting, the one implicit in the quote from Nietzsche.

Forgetting as complete loss from storage

Davis (2008) defines the strong form of forgetting as "the theoretical possibility that refers to a total erasure of the original memory that cannot be recalled, no matter what techniques are used to aid recall" (p. 317). Given the context of his chapter, we feel sure he would be willing to include not just measures of recall, but any measure (explicit or implicit, direct or indirect) of the prior experience having been encoded in the nervous system. Davis argued that it would only be possible to look for "strong" forgetting in simple organisms (e.g., simple gastropods like slugs) where the entire neural circuitry has been mapped out. "Only when all the cellular and molecular events that occur when a memory is formed return to their original state would I say this would be evidence for true forgetting" (Davis, 2008, p. 317).

To our knowledge, no evidence for this strong form of forgetting has been produced even in simpler organisms; and since all the research in the present volume is about forgetting in organisms more complex than mollusks, it would be practically impossible to obtain evidence for this strong form of forgetting. Even if every test known to psychologists failed to show evidence for any sort of trace of past experience, the possibility remains that a change owing to that prior experience (some latent memory trace) still remains.

Davis (2008) concluded that the strong form of forgetting is not scientifically useful, and we agree with him. We can ask the further question: If the strong form of forgetting can never be proved (as Nietzche's dictum states), does this mean that forgetting in this sense never occurs? We think the answer to this question must be no (although we cannot prove it). Think of all the events and happenings that occurred to you when you were 7 years old, ones you could have easily reported the next day (so they were encoded). Do you still really have traces of all these events lying dormant in your brain, waiting for the right cue to become active again? We strongly doubt it. Probably the many of the millions of events, conversations, facts, people, and so on that are encountered in everyday life and at one point committed to memory do suffer the strong form of forgetting by being obliterated from our nervous systems. However, that is a matter of faith, given that we cannot find proof. As we discuss below, it is possible to entertain a contrary possibility, because powerful cues can bring "forgotten" information back into consciousness. Still, given the huge number of events in one's life, the idea that all would be stored forever (in some form) seems unlikely.

Forgetting as retrieval failure

Another possibility, essentially the obverse of the strong form of forgetting, might be considered a weak form of the concept. In its starkest form, this idea would maintain that all events that have been encoded and stored do somehow persist in the nervous system (including all those from age 7), and the inability to access them now is due to retrieval failure. Although this proposal might seem farfetched, when Loftus and Loftus (1980) surveyed psychologists many years ago, a large percentage (84%) favored something like this view. The percentage today might be lower, but the 1970s were the heyday of studies of retrieval in general and the power of retrieval cues in particular (Tulving & Thomson, 1973; for reviews see Roediger & Guynn, 1996; Tulving, 1983).

The idea of forgetting as retrieval failure is a scientifically useful concept, because (unlike the case with forgetting as storage failure) evidence can be found in its favor. Let us consider one experiment to demonstrate the point. Tulving and Pearlstone (1966) presented high-school students with lists of words to remember. Although there were many conditions, for our purposes consider the condition in which students studied 48 words that were members of 24 common categories, so they heard two words per category. Thus, students heard lists such as "articles of clothing: blouse, sweater; types of birds: blue jay, parakeet." The words were presented at a slow rate (2.5 sec/word) so the encoding of the words was ensured, in the sense that if the experimenter had stopped at any point, the subjects could have successfully recalled the last word presented. Thus, in this sense, all 48 words were learned.

One group of subjects was tested by free recall; they were given a blank sheet of paper and asked to recall the words in any order. They recalled 19.3

words, which means they forgot (failed to retrieve) about 29 others (28.7 to be exact). We can thus ask what happened to the forgotten words. It is logically possible that their representations had completely evaporated and had vanished from storage, but, as already discussed, we can never assume that. On the other hand, it could be that traces of the words were stored, but could not be retrieved with the minimal cues of free recall (people must use whatever cues they can internally generate). Tulving and Pearlstone (1966) found evidence for this latter possibility by giving the students (both the same group that had received a free recall test and a different group that had not had such a test) category names as cues. When the 24 category names (e.g., articles of clothing) were given, students were able to recall 35.9 words (and it did not matter much as to whether or not they had taken the prior free recall test). Thus, with stronger cues, students were able to recall nearly twice as many words as in free recall, showing that some of the forgetting in free recall was due to retrieval failures. Such powerful reversals of forgetting demonstrated in many experiments were probably why the psychologists surveyed in the late 1970s by the Loftuses claimed that forgetting was mostly due to retrieval failures.

Of course, even with the powerful category name cues, students still forgot about 25% of the words (12 of 48). Were these lost from storage? There is no way to know, but probably if the students had been further probed with recognition tests (with strong "copy cues") or with implicit tests (Schacter, 1987), evidence for storage of even more words would have been found. The asymmetry in the logic here – evidence of forgetting as retrieval failure can be obtained, but evidence of forgetting as storage failure cannot – leads back to Nietzsche's dictum. Still, as noted above, we cannot conclude that forgetting never involves elimination of stored traces, just that such a claim cannot be verified scientifically.

Forgetting as loss of information over time

A third way of defining forgetting, the one first used since Ebbinghaus (1885/1964) and many others since his time, is to plot retention of some experiences over time. This definition is complementary to the forgetting-as-retrieval-failure definition, not opposed to it. The typical way to conduct such forgetting experiments is to have (say) seven groups of subjects exposed to the same information (e.g., a list of words). One group would be tested immediately after learning, with other groups tested at varying delays after that point (e.g., 1 hour, 6 hours, 12, hours, 24 hours, 48 hours, and 1 week). Retention would be plotted across the various retention intervals and a forgetting curve would be derived, almost always showing less information recalled or recognized as a function of the time since learning. As Ebbinghaus (1885/1964) put it: "Left to itself every mental content gradually loses its capacity for being revived, or at least suffers loss in this regard under the influence of time" (p. 4). One critical methodological stricture in such experiments is that the type of test be held constant across delays, so that retrieval cues do not differ.

As noted, Ebbinghaus (1885/1964) was the first to plot forgetting over time. He presented his results in a series of tables in his book (see pp. 67–76), but later writers have chosen to show them in a figure and his findings appear in Figure 1.1. Ebbinghaus memorized lists of nonsense syllables so that he could recall them perfectly, and then he tried to relearn the list at varying delays from 19 minutes to 26 days. He measured the number of trials (or the amount of time) needed to learn the list perfectly in the first instance and then, later, he measured the trials or time to relearn the list after varying intervals. The measure shown in Figure 1.1 is percentage of savings in relearning the list, defined as the number of trials needed to learn the list originally (OL, for original learning) minus the number of trials needed for relearning (RL) divided by OL and then multiplied by 100 (to get a percentage). Thus, savings = (OL − RL)/OL × 100. Ebbinghaus noted that the shape of the forgetting curve appeared logarithmic.

This savings method of forgetting is not used much today, but nothing about the forgetting curve much hangs on the exact details of experimental design or the measure used, because nearly all forgetting functions look pretty much alike. Rubin and Wenzel (1996) examined "100 years of forgetting," seeking the best quantitative fit to the hundreds of forgetting curves that had been collected up until that point. They tried 105 different functions and concluded that 4 functions fit the forgetting curves quite well (and pretty much indistinguishably): the logarithmic function, the power function, the exponential in the square root of time, and the hyperbola in the square root of time. More recently, Wixted and Carpenter (2007) have argued that the power function is the correct one to describe the shape of the forgetting curve.

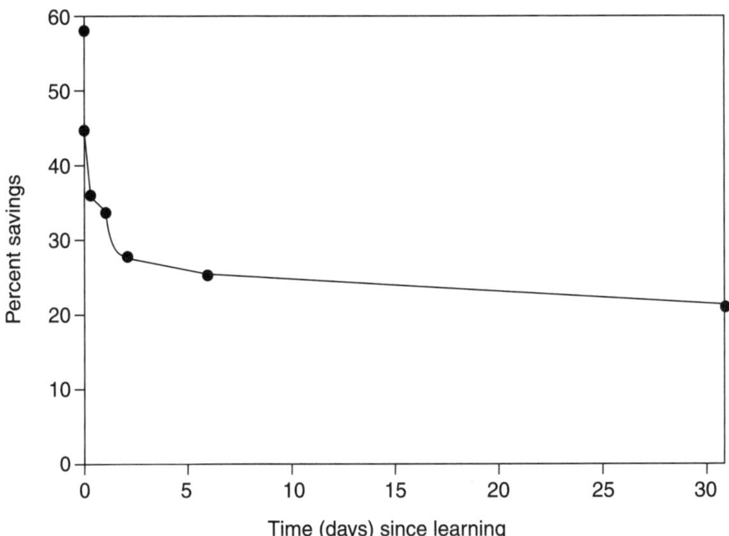

Figure 1.1 Forgetting curve adapted from Ebbinghaus (1885/1964, pp. 67–76).

Although curves like Figure 1.1 are called "forgetting curves," Rubin and Wenzel (1996) pointed out that this is a misnomer. These are retention curves, because the amount retained is plotted. If one really were to plot forgetting, then the curves would increase as a power function over time. True enough, but we will follow the common practice of calling such curves forgetting curves.

Most forgetting curves have been derived from verbal materials over periods of minutes to hours to days. However, even when radically different procedures are used, forgetting functions appear rather similar in that losses occur rapidly at first and then seem to approach an asymptote. The same shape occurs in loss of information from brief visual displays over a couple of seconds (Sperling, 1960), auditory presentations over about 4 seconds (Darwin, Turvey, & Crowder, 1972), holding a few items in short-term memory while distracted by another task (Peterson & Peterson, 1959), remembering a word over some minutes (Rubin, Hinton, & Wenzel, 1999), remembering lists over days (Slamecka & McElree, 1983), and remembering Spanish vocabulary learned in college over many years (Bahrick, 1984). Figure 1.2 shows data from the experiment by Rubin et al. (1999) just mentioned because they used ten measures to produce a more compelling curve than in many such experiments (often only a few data points are obtained).

Given the consistent forgetting effects shown in the literature, theories of forgetting have focused on the inexorable loss of information over time. We review below some of the main contending theories proposed to explain forgetting, but first we deal with a neglected side issue.

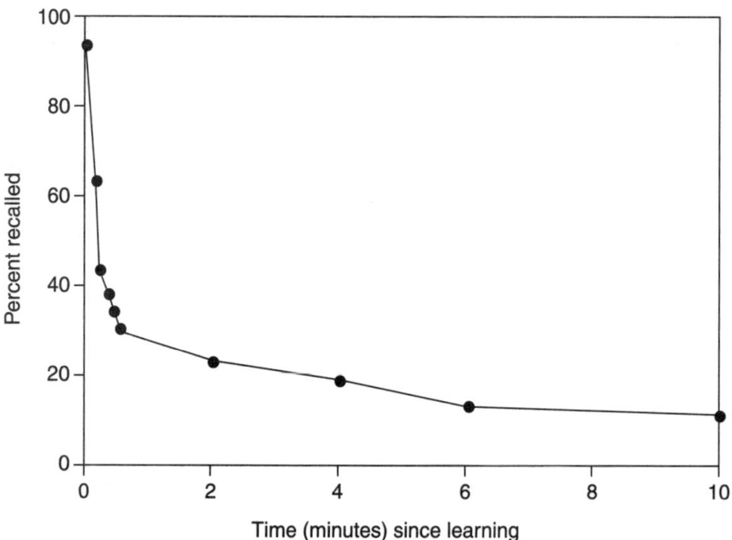

Figure 1.2 Forgetting curve adapted from Rubin, Hinton, and Wenzel (1999, Table A1, p. 1175).

A caveat

Ever since Ebbinghaus, forgetting experiments have employed one of two designs: either separate groups of subjects are exposed to the same material and tested at different points in time (a between-subjects design); or the same group of subjects is given many different sets of materials and the type of material tested at each delay is counterbalanced across subjects (a within-subjects, between-materials design). In both these cases, a particular set of materials is tested only once, because testing material may alter the forgetting curve. In fact, this concern is well founded, because testing does change the forgetting curve – tested material is subject to less forgetting than nontested material (e.g., Roediger & Karpicke, 2006). However, one might question whether the standard way of measuring forgetting, with people assessed only once on material, is particularly representative. After all, in life we all exist in "within-subject, within-materials" situations; for important memories, we recall them repeatedly; we repeatedly retrieve the events of our lives.

These considerations lead to the question of what happens when the same set of events (a list of words or pictures, or any other material) is repeatedly tested over time. Consider an experiment by Erdelyi and Becker (1974, Experiment 2) that meets the usual stricture of forgetting experiments: a set of material (either words or pictures) was presented to subjects and they were tested under the same conditions each time (with no cues provided). The only difference is that the subjects were tested three times, with each recall period occurring relatively soon after the prior recall period in one set of conditions in the experiment. The first test occurred shortly after study and lasted for 7 minutes. After that, the second test occurred for 7 more minutes, and then the third. Thus, as with customary forgetting studies, each successive test occurred after increasingly longer delays. The results are shown in Figure 1.3, where it can be seen that the "forgetting curves" look highly irregular. There was no forgetting of words, and recall of pictures actually improved across repeated tests at greater delays! Many others have replicated these results (e.g., Roediger & Thorpe, 1978) of increases in recall with repeated (and increasingly delayed) tests over time (see Payne, 1987; and Roediger & Challis, 1989, for early reviews of this literature, which actually dates back to early in the 20th century. Erdelyi, 1996 provides a more expansive review).

The pattern in Figure 1.3 indicates that, at the level of individual items, forgetting does not always occur over time because more items were recalled after longer intervals than shortly after learning. Thus, contrary to the quote from Ebbinghaus and much of the literature on forgetting curves, at the level of individual items there is no inexorable decline in "trace strength" or else an item could not be recovered at a later time that was not recalled at an earlier time. This claim is obviously true in the case of pictures from the data in Figure 1.3, but it turns out to be true (at the item level, if not always the list level) in the case of words, too. That is, on a second test, both individual

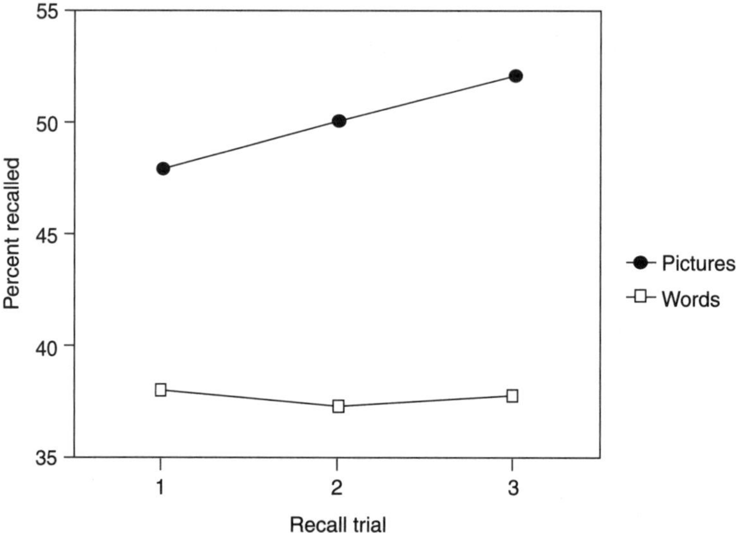

Figure 1.3 Data adapted from Erdelyi and Becker (1974, Figure 1, no interval group, p. 165).

words and pictures that were not recalled on the first test can be recalled on the second test (this phenomenon is called reminiscence; Roediger & Thorpe, 1978). Yet items are also forgotten between tests, and in the case of recall of words in Erdelyi and Becker's (1974) experiment, these two quantities (intertest forgetting and intertest recovery or reminiscence) offset one another for no net increase or decrease. However, in the case of pictures, recovery of items between tests was greater than forgetting, so a net increase occurred. Erdelyi and Becker (1974) labeled this net increase hypermnesia, the improvement in recall over time with repeated tests. Others have reported hypermnesia for words and other sorts of material, too (see Payne, 1987).

Much research has been conducted on the topic of reminiscence and hypermnesia, but this literature has not been incorporated into the study of forgetting for the very good reason that it does not fit. Most writers do not even consider it, but Underwood (1966) at least noted its existence in his chapter on forgetting in his popular textbook. He then went on to say: "We will not be concerned with reminiscence in this chapter" (p. 544), which is one way to deal with the problem (even though not a particularly satisfactory one). Still, it is understandable, because theories of forgetting are mute about improvements in performance with delays from initial learning. Other traditions of work showing such improvements over time exist, too – spontaneous recovery in animal and human learning, reminiscence in motor learning, enhanced performance in motor skill learning after sleep, among others. Wheeler (1995) provided some review and evidence for spontaneous recovery in an interference paradigm.

Although researchers studying forgetting ignore the hypermnesia literature – none of the other authors in this volume touch on the issue – we believe it should be considered. The very facts of reminiscence and hypermnesia point to the importance of retrieval factors and support the definition of forgetting as retrieval failure (Tulving & Pearlstone, 1966). One basic idea is that of a limited capacity retrieval system (Tulving, 1967) in which we know (have stored) much more than we can retrieve at any point in time. Retrieval forms a bottleneck in the system, a fundamental limitation. As discussed below, retrieval of some information often causes forgetting of other information, so that retrieval becomes a self-limiting process (Roediger, 1974, 1978; see too Bjork, Bjork, & Caughey, 2007).

Theories of forgetting: A brief tour

This entire book is about theories of forgetting. Here we set the stage by discussing, quite briefly, the main theories.

Decay theory

This is the oldest and simplest theory, which states that forgetting occurs because of the "wasting effects of time" (McGeoch, 1932). This theory essentially amounts to saying that "forgetting happens." The analogy sometimes made is that memories are like muscles and they atrophy (decay) if they are not used, so they grow ever weaker over time, although this statement merely describes the forgetting curve without explaining why it occurs.

In a classic paper, McGeoch (1932) mounted a withering attack on decay theory from which it has never really recovered. First, he argued that it was improper as a scientific theory because it did not specify a mechanism by which the memory trace would unwind over time. Second, he pointed to data from experiments showing reminiscence (e.g., Brown, 1923) in which items not recalled at one point in time could be recalled later, which is completely inconsistent with decay theory. (This is the point raised in the previous section.) And third, he argued that even when passage of time was controlled, forgetting could be determined by the number or density of events during that time; the more events, the greater forgetting. He pointed to Jenkins and Dallenbach's (1924) experiments showing that greater forgetting of verbal materials occurred after equivalent periods of waking than of sleep. These data are shown in Figure 1.4 (the data were obtained from Dallenbach, 1963). The effects of sleep on retention are a topic of lively interest on the contemporary scene and are discussed in detail by Peigneux, Schmitz, and Urbain in this volume (Chapter 8). Brown and Lewandowsky (Chapter 4) hammer another nail or two into decay theory's coffin.

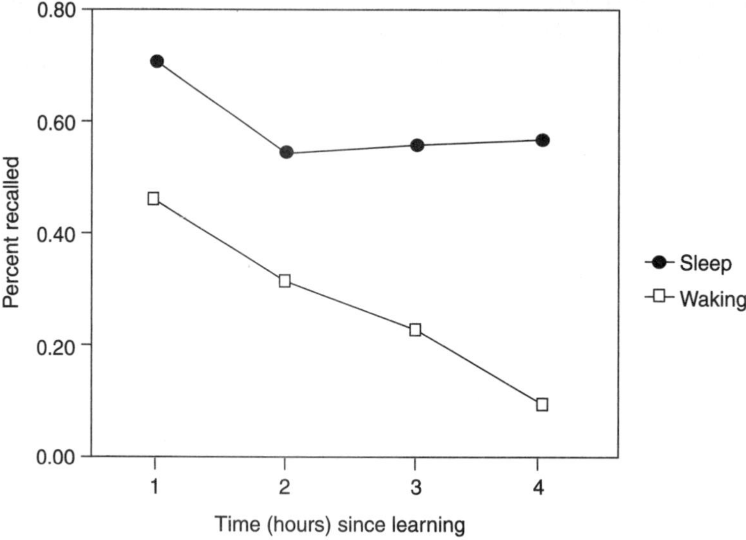

Figure 1.4 Data adapted from Dallenbach (1963, Table 1, p. 701).

Interference theory

While McGeoch (1932) was torching decay theory, he argued that the most important factor in forgetting was actually interference. Interference can arise from anything other than the to-be-remembered information. McGeoch (1942) put it in a straightforward manner in saying that forgetting is often a result of the wrong memory being accessed by a particular cue.

Interference can take many forms, but has been broadly divided into two types: proactive and retroactive. *Proactive interference* refers to the negative effects of prior learning on retention of target information, whereas *retroactive interference* refers to the negative effects of encountering new information after encoding target information. If you drive to work and park in various spots in the same parking lot every day, imagine someone asking you in what spot you parked one week ago. Even if you found your car perfectly that day (thus indicating that you had encoded and stored the information well enough to retrieve it hours later), you would probably have trouble recalling, a week later, where your car was parked on that day. According to interference theorists, the forgetting is due to two sources: all the times you parked in the lot before the critical date create proactive interference, whereas your comings and goings of the past week provide retroactive interference. McGeoch (1932, 1942) argued that retroactive interference was the most potent cause of forgetting.

Retroactive interference

The simplest way to demonstrate retroactive interference is to get subjects to learn a cue–target association (for example, horse–umbrella, or A–B), with the eventual test being to recall B (umbrella) when given A (horse). Two groups of subjects learn a list of A–B pairs to one perfect recitation. Then, in an experimental condition, subjects learn conflicting pairs (A–D, like horse–automobile), again so that they know the pairs perfectly. New responses are paired with the same cues. In a different (control) group subjects learn new pairs after the original A–B learning, so they might learn piano–automobile (C–D learning, where C–D is unrelated to A–B). After both groups have learned their second lists, a delay occurs. The final, criterial task is for both groups to receive the original A cues (horse) with instructions to recall items from the first list. Their task at test is to recall the targets that were paired with the cues in list 1. The finding is that subjects who have experienced the A–B, A–D arrangement recall the responses from the original list less well than those in the A–B, C–D condition. This outcome defines retroactive interference.

Another control condition is sometimes used in which either no activity or a general distracter task (e.g., reading a book or playing a videogame) is employed after A–B learning. Usually this condition produces little forgetting of the A–B pair. The general finding is that, relative to no activity, learning C–D pairs after A–B learning decreases probability of recall of B somewhat, but A–D learning causes much more forgetting. The former type of forgetting is referred to as "nonspecific interference," whereas the latter is caused by "specific interference" (because the A–D pair specifically conflicts with A–B recall).

Two primary processes have been used to explain retroactive interference: unlearning and response competition (Melton & Irwin, 1940). These two comprise the processes of "two factor interference theory." The basic idea for unlearning is that the A–B association is weakened or destroyed when A–D is learned (reminiscent of Nietzsche's definition of forgetting). However, a different view is that the A–B association remains as A–D is learned, but the responses compete with one another during retrieval in response to the cue A–???. This factor endorses the idea of forgetting as retrieval failure.

From the 1940s through the 1960s, researchers used paired associate paradigms to seek evidence for the two factors thought to be responsible for retroactive interference. Crowder (1976, Chapter 8) provides a thorough history of the work through the early 1970s, and Wixted (this volume, Chapter 13) helps to bring the discussion to the present.

Proactive interference

From 1932 through the mid-1950s, proactive interference received short shrift in discussions of forgetting. The discovery that powerful effects of interference from events occurring *prior* to learning some target events can be attributed to Underwood (1957), who set out to solve the conundrum of why subjects in various studies showed remarkably different rates of forgetting over a 24-hour period. He demonstrated that by far the largest factor in forgetting of word lists over a day was the number of word lists studied *before* rather than *after* the target list.

This outcome can be demonstrated using the paradigm described above (often referred to as the A–B, A–D paradigm), whereby the set-up is exactly the same, except that subjects are now tested on list 2 (i.e., they are asked to produce target D when given A) after 24 hours. Underwood (1957) was puzzled by the fact that forgetting in this design differed so dramatically from study to study. However, after some careful scientific detective work (a kind of early meta-analysis), he discovered that the critical variable was the number of prior lists that subjects had learned before the critical list on which they were to be tested the next day. In reviewing the literature, he found that when subjects had learned 15–20 lists prior to learning a last list perfectly, they recalled only 15–20% of the list a day later. However, if subjects learned only one list on the first day, they recalled 80–85% after 24 hours. Of course, according to two-factor theory, proactive interference must be due to response competition, because unlearning does not apply in the proactive case.

Following Underwood's (1957) report, proactive interference became much more studied. However, findings such as those from Jenkins and Dallenbach's (1924) sleep study (described above) and many more studies showed that retroactive interference was still a critical factor in forgetting. In addition, Underwood and Postman (1960) launched a theory arguing that proactive interference from prior linguistic habits was critical to forgetting in laboratory paradigms, but they were later forced to abandon this theory in response to negative evidence (see Crowder, 1976, for a good account of this story).

Wixted (2004) has proposed that the field's concentration on proactive interference was a mistake that possibly led to the "demise" of interference theories of forgetting. He has gone so far as to argue that the whole A–B, A–D list learning paradigm and the tradition surrounding it "may pertain mainly to forgetting in the laboratory and that everyday forgetting is attributable to an altogether different kind of interference" (p. 235). Wixted (Chapter 13) revisits these historical developments and suggests a new role for interference in forgetting that takes into account recent psychological and neuroscientific developments. This chapter can be read alongside Brown and Lewandowsky (Chapter 4) who take a different position. In addition, Dewar, Cowan, and Della Sala (Chapter 9) apply the concept of retroactive interference to explaining anterograde amnesia.

Wixted (2004) may have been hasty in dismissing classic interference theories as irrelevant to forgetting outside the laboratory. It is useful to consider an earlier example of these ideas being written off. In an influential article from several decades ago, Neisser (1978) castigated both learning theory in general and interference theory in particular by saying: "With learning theory out of fashion, the experiments of the interference theorists seem like empty exercises to most of us. Were they ever anything else?" (from p. 8 of Neisser, 1982, which reprinted the 1978 chapter).

Neisser (1978) was arguing that laboratory approaches to studying human memory should be avoided in favor of naturalistic (or at least more realistic) studies. In the same essay (p. 15), he extolled the virtues of Loftus and Palmer's (1974) interesting studies of eyewitness memory (and forgetting). In retrospect, this juxtaposition seems ironic, because the Loftus tradition of studying eyewitness memory actually depends on similar processes to those in classic studies of retroactive interference. In Loftus and Palmer's classic misinformation experiments, which have been repeated in various ways many times, subjects are presented with slides that tell a story about, say, a traffic accident. Following the slide presentation, they are exposed to a test or a passage that contains some inconsistencies with the original story presented in the slides – in other words, misinformation. For instance, in the slide show subjects may have seen a picture of a car driving by a STOP sign, while the text read later refers to a YIELD sign instead. On a final test, subjects are given a choice between the two types of signs and asked to indicate which one they saw in the slides (or they may be asked to recall the type of sign). The outcome is that, relative to a control condition in which the sign was referred to in some neutral way ("a traffic sign"), subjects given the misinformation are much more likely to falsely remember the sign as a YIELD sign (in this example). The misinformation leads to errors in the witness's memory, which has obvious implications for eyewitness testimony in court.

A critical issue is why such errors occur in eyewitness memory: What happens to the original memory for the STOP sign in the slides when subjects incorrectly remember the YIELD sign as a result of the misinformation? Has this memory been inexorably forgotten (although we may never be able to prove it), has it been somehow altered, or is it intact but temporarily inaccessible due to competition from the YIELD sign? These controversies have exact parallels in the retroactive interference literature (see Roediger, 1996). After all, the Loftus paradigm can be considered a species of retroactive interference of the A–B, A–D variety: study sign–STOP, study sign–YIELD, then recall (or recognize) the first kind of sign on a later test.

Loftus and her colleagues originally interpreted their results as showing that the original trace had been changed (from a representation of a stop sign to a yield sign), which is akin to the unlearning interpretation of retroactive interference. However, McCloskey and Zaragoza (1985) later argued that nothing had happened to the original trace, but the interference that occurred in the Loftus misinformation paradigm came about because of competition between responses (STOP and YIELD), the second factor in classic two-factor interference theory. The debate in the misinformation paradigm over the years has recapitulated in many ways the arguments from classic studies of interference from the 1950s and 1960s (Roediger, 1996).

Input and output interference

Although proactive and retroactive interference are well known as possible causes of forgetting, Tulving and Arbuckle (1963) pointed to two other (complementary) sources of forgetting: input and output interference. They discussed these as sources of interference within a single trial. Item 3 in a list of 5 items will be better recalled than item 3 in a list of 10 items; the more events occurring, the less the probability of recalling any one event, which is the operational definition of input interference. Input interference refers to the fact that for larger sets of to-be-learned material, the greater the probability of forgetting any particular item in the set (all other things being equal). This observation forms part of the basis for cue overload theory, discussed below.

The concept of output interference has perhaps enjoyed a more exciting fate as a cause of forgetting than input interference, albeit in a somewhat different incarnation than Tulving and Arbuckle (1963) originally envisioned. Their original idea was that the more items tested before any particular item (the more items "output"), the worse would recall be for the next item. Their experimental situation involved short-term recall, so the act of recall could be considered as a distracter task that eliminated information from primary (or short-term or working) memory. However, the same idea operates in long-term memory (e.g., Brown, 1968; Roediger, 1974) and is now often called retrieval-induced forgetting, due to the influential experimental and theoretical work of Anderson, Bjork, and Bjork (1994) and Anderson and Spellman (1995).

In the retrieval-induced forgetting paradigm introduced by Anderson et al. (1994), subjects were presented with word pairs consisting of category names and exemplars of the category (e.g., furniture–chair; furniture–table; fruit–banana; fruit–apple). Following initial study, they were then given a chance to practice some items from these categories, but only certain exemplars were practiced. In our example, they might practice the furniture category, but they would be repeatedly cued with items like furniture–c______ and retrieve chair. However, other category members (table, in our example) would remain unpracticed. On a later test subjects were given category names and asked to recall all items from the category. The finding is that the items from the practiced category show two effects relative to retrieval from the unpracticed category (from the fruit category, in our example, where no items were practiced). First, the previously practiced items are recalled better than those from the nonpracticed category, in line with work discussed earlier on the effects of testing on retrieval (Roediger & Karpicke, 2006). Second, and more importantly for present purposes, nonpracticed items in the practiced category (like table in our example) were recalled more poorly than items from the nonpracticed category (the fruit items in our example). Thus, active retrieval of some items from the category induced forgetting of the other items, hence the name of the phenomenon: retrieval-induced forgetting.

This ability of our memories to actively inhibit information is crucial for avoiding cognitive overload and producing appropriate responses to the environment. Harris, Sutton, and Barnier (Chapter 12) explore individual differences in retrieval-induced forgetting and how this phenomenon may map onto autobiographical memory.

Retrieval theories

In McGeoch's famous 1932 paper on forgetting, he mentioned (almost in passing) that he believed "altered stimulating conditions" between the context of learning and that of use of information (retrieval) was a cause of forgetting (in addition to retroactive interference). He meant that retention would be better the more the conditions at test matched those during learning and that, conversely, changed conditions between learning and testing would lead to forgetting. In the 1970s, this basic idea attained new adherents as Tulving and Thomson (1973) proposed the encoding specificity principle as governing the effectiveness of retrieval cues. The basic claims are that events are encoded in terms of specific patterns of features; that cues in the retrieval environment also are encoded as feature bundles at the time of retrieval; and (critically) to the extent that features in the cues overlap or match those in the trace, memories for experiences will be evoked (see Flexser & Tulving, 1978, for a formal instantiation of these ideas). These ideas formalize McGeoch's offhand comment and are critical for retrieval analyses of forgetting, which tacitly assume availability of trace information that must be matched by information in cues for retrieval to occur (Tulving, 1983). Forgetting over time may be due to loss of information in the trace or to increasing mismatch between cues and the information in the trace, according to retrieval theories. Much evidence supports these basic ideas (Roediger & Guynn, 1996; Tulving, 1983).

Cue overload

Another theory of forgetting, complementary to interference theory and emphasizing retrieval factors, is cue overload theory (Earhard, 1967; Watkins & Watkins, 1975). The basic idea is straightforward: the more events that are subsumed under a particular cue, the greater the likelihood of forgetting an item associated with a cue. For example, in the A–B, A–D paradigm, two target events are attached to the same cue and hence each is less memorable than if only one were attached. In a different situation, if a list contains many types of furniture, the retrieval cue "furniture" will be less effective at provoking recall of any particular instance of furniture than if a list had presented only one or two types of furniture (e.g., Roediger, 1973). Watkins (1979) provided further examples of this principle in action. The use of the cue overload principle has become ubiquitous in research on forgetting and especially to interference paradigms (see Wixted, Chapter 13). It is useful, if descriptive.

Consolidation

A critical concept in the science of memory is consolidation (e.g., Nadel, 2008). Consolidation may be defined as "the progressive post-acquisition stabilization of the engram" and/or "the memory phase(s) during which [it] takes place" (Dudai, 2002, p. 59). Thus, forgetting may occur because engrams or memory traces are labile; they may last briefly and support retention over the short term, but unless consolidation occurs, the memories will be forgotten.

Related to the issue of forgetting is research on the molecular process of reconsolidation (Sara, 2000, 2008). The idea is that each time a memory is retrieved, it undergoes the same sort of molecular process that happens after initial encoding. Crucially, if this process is interfered with (which can be done by means of chemical inhibitors, see Dudai, 2006), the memory can become altered or, hypothetically, even lost. This basic idea should seem familiar, because we have met it in A–B, A–D interference studies and in the Loftus misinformation work; events coming after a target event may somehow undo or interfere with the target memory. Many chapters in the current volume expand on ideas of lack of consolidation and/or reconsolidation as causes of forgetting (e.g., Wixted, Chapter 13).

Repression

The concept of repression is used to explain some types of forgetting. Freud (1914/1957) popularized the idea that forgetting may be motivated by a need to protect the psyche from threatening memories or thoughts. The idea predates Freud, but he brought it into prominence and adduced many clinical case studies that he thought supported the concept. However, it has had a controversial history. To complicate matters, repression may be defined in several different ways, and Freud changed his theoretical ideas several times during the course of his long career.

At the simplest level, repression is the process of trying to avoid painful memories. So, if a person has bad experiences at work one day and decides to watch a lighthearted movie that evening to put aside (to forget about) the events of the day, that activity would meet this very weak definition of repression. If this were all that were meant by repression, it would not be controversial. Similarly, motivated forgetting of the sort of failing to remember a dentist appointment and thus avoiding pain would fall into this garden variety example of repression.

A second definition of repression holds that ideas and memories may be firmly held in a conscious state, then banished from consciousness into an unconscious state and hence forgotten. This suppression is an active, effortful process, but once the memories become unconscious, they reveal themselves only indirectly (e.g., through Freudian slips or through dreams, the "royal road to the unconscious"). Unconscious memories can also cause unwanted effects on experience and behavior and thus be the source of various mental and even physical problems. We will not discuss the issue of repression as a cause of forgetting further in this context (none of the authors of this volume addresses the idea), but historically the idea of repression has played a central role in certain aspects of psychological theorizing and experimentation (see Erdelyi, 1985).

Adaptive reasons for forgetting

So much angst has been expressed about the erroneous nature of human memory – both in terms of forgetting and, perhaps even worse, the creation of false memories – that we might wonder why our memories have evolved to be so fragile and fallible. However, once we pause to consider the adaptive nature of forgetting and interference, we can see plausible reasons that forgetting exists. For example, if we move to a new city, we must learn a new address and telephone number (among many other things) and not have the old ones constantly intruding. We need to forget them, even though they are well learned. More generally, as our environment changes, so must our memories. People who cannot forget are often plagued with problems, as in Luria's (1968) classic study of S, a mnemonist whose synesthesia empowered (or overpowered) him with a strikingly good recollection of even trivial events from his life. More recently, Parker, Cahill, and McGaugh (2006) reported the case of a woman plagued by the inability to forget the happenings of her life.

In order to understand the value of forgetting, we need to take a step back and consider the function of memory outside the context of attempts to remember autobiographical events or word lists in an experiment. It is likely that our capacity to remember evolved as a tool for navigating the present and planning for the future, rather than for looking back on the past (Nairne & Pandeirada, 2008). To this end, it is not practical or useful to maintain detailed, veridical information of encoded events and information in memory indefinitely. Instead, Bjork and Bjork (1988) have proposed that "disused" memories – those that are retrieved less and less over time, such as the address of your childhood home – become less accessible in order to allow for more relevant information, such as your current address, to take precedence. Crucially, the loss of access to information through disuse is seen not as a failure of the system, but an adaptive feature that facilitates updating (Bjork, 1978).

Anderson and Schooler (1991) provided a more formal analysis of the adaptive nature of forgetting by demonstrating striking parallels between the statistical occurrence of events in the environment and the typical negatively accelerated retention function shown in Figure 1.1. The idea is that events that have been occurring frequently in the recent past are also more likely to occur in the near future. For instance, Anderson analyzed his own email inbox and discovered that on a given day he was more likely to receive an email from someone who had written him recently (and generally more often in the recent past) than someone who had only written a while back. Hence, at any given moment, he was more likely to require access to information about recent senders. The same was true of many other sets of data that Anderson and Schooler examined. While the mathematical analyses involved in Anderson and Schooler's theory are far beyond the scope of this chapter, the take-home message is that forgetting may not be an accident of nature. Rather, the forgetting function may be shaped to mirror the frequency of events in the environment and how they change over time.

Although not usually considered in evolutionary terms, many laboratory phenomena may reveal positive adaptations of forgetting. Retroactive interference can be considered an adaptation if old (unneeded) information is replaced by new, updated information, as in the examples of learning new addresses and telephone numbers.

Conclusion

The aim of this chapter was to provide a brief overview of some key issues in the scientific study of forgetting, but it is by no means complete. Our chapter has focused primarily on the experimental psychologist's approaches to studying forgetting, but, as the remaining chapters in this volume indicate, numerous approaches exist. Although we discussed consolidation and reconsolidation rather tersely, these issues occupy many writers in this book. In fact, as many as six chapters (Brown & Lewandowsky, Chapter 4; Murre, Chapter 5; Levy, Kuhl, & Wagner, Chapter 7; Peigneux et al., Chapter 8; Dewar et al., Chapter 9; and Wixted, Chapter 13) deal extensively with the issue of consolidation in relation to domains ranging from sleep (Chapter 8) to amnesia (Chapter 9). Although we have focused primarily on behavioral data from healthy adults, other chapters in this volume present new and fascinating perspectives on forgetting in patients with Alzheimer's disease (Dewar et al., Chapter 9), epilepsy (Butler, Muhlert, & Zeman, Chapter 10), and psychogenic amnesia (Brand & Markowitsch, Chapter 11), as well as forgetting theories based on alternative techniques including connectionist modeling (Murre, Chapter 5) and neuroimaging (Levy, Kuhl, & Wagner, Chapter 7). Despite the fact that our chapter is incomplete, the issues revolving around the definition and leading theories of forgetting must be borne in mind for all treatments of the topic.

References

Anderson, J. R., & Schooler, L. J. (1991). Reflections of the environment in memory. *Psychological Science*, *2*, 396–408.

Anderson, M. C., Bjork, R. A., & Bjork, E. L. (1994). Mechanisms of inhibition in long-term memory: A new taxonomy. In D. Dagenbach & T. Carr (Eds.), *Inhibitory processes in attention, memory, and language* (pp. 265–325). New York: Academic Press.

Anderson, M. C., & Spellman, B. A. (1995). On the status of inhibitory mechanisms in cognition: Memory retrieval as a model case. *Psychological Review*, *102*, 68–100.

Bahrick, H. P. (1984). Semantic memory content in permastore: Fifty years of memory for Spanish learned in school. *Journal of Experimental Psychology: General, 113*, 1–29.

Bjork, E. L., & Bjork, R. A. (1988). On the adaptive aspects of retrieval failure in autobiographical memory. In M. M. Gruneberg, P. E. Morris, & R. N. Sykes (Eds.), *Practical aspects of memory II* (pp. 283–288). Chichester: Wiley.

Bjork, R. A. (1978). The updating of human memory. In G. H. Bower (Ed.), *The psychology of learning and motivation* (Vol. 12, pp. 235–259). New York: Academic Press.

Bjork, R. A., Bjork, E. L., & Caughey, J. B. (2007). Retrieval as a self-limiting process: Part II. In J. S. Nairne (Ed.), *The foundations of remembering: Essays in honor of Henry L. Roediger, III* (pp. 19–37). New York: Psychology Press.

Brown, J. (1968). Reciprocal facilitation and impairment in free recall. *Psychonomic Science, 10*, 41–42.

Brown, W. (1923). To what extent is memory measured by a single recall? *Journal of Experimental Psychology, 6*, 377–382.

Crowder, R. G. (1976). *Principles of learning and memory*. Hillsdale, NJ: Lawrence Erlbaum Associates, Inc.

Dallenbach, K. M. (1963). Tables vs. graphs as means of presenting experimental results. *American Journal of Psychology, 76*, 700–702.

Darwin, C. J., Turvey, M. T., & Crowder, R. G. (1972). An auditory analogue of the Sperling partial report procedure: Evidence for brief auditory storage. *Cognitive Psychology, 3*, 255–267.

Davis, M. (2008). Forgetting: Once again, it's all about representations. In H. L. Roediger, Y. Dudai, & S. M. Fitzpatrick (Eds.), *Science of memory: Concepts* (pp. 317–320). New York: Oxford University Press.

Dudai, Y. (2002). *Memory from A to Z: Keywords, concepts, and beyond.* Oxford: Oxford University Press.

Dudai, Y. (2006). Reconsolidation: The advantage of being refocused. *Current Opinion in Neurobiology, 16*, 174–178.

Earhard, M. (1967). Cued recall and free recall as a function of the number of items per cue. *Journal of Verbal Learning and Verbal Behavior, 6*, 257–263.

Ebbinghaus, H. (1885/1964). *Memory: A contribution to experimental psychology*. Oxford: Dover.

Erdelyi, M. H. (1985). *Psychoanalysis: Freud's cognitive psychology.* New York: W. H. Freeman.

Erdelyi, M. H. (1996). *The recovery of unconscious memories: Hypermnesia and reminiscence.* Chicago: University of Chicago Press.

Erdelyi, M. H., & Becker, J. (1974). Hypermnesia for pictures: Incremental memory for pictures but not words in multiple recall trials. *Cognitive Psychology, 6*, 159–171.

Flexser, A. J., & Tulving, E. (1978). Retrieval independence in recognition and recall. *Psychological Review, 85*, 153–171.

Freud, S. (1914/1957). The history of the psychoanalytic movement. In J. Strachey (Ed.), *The standard edition of the complete psychological works of Sigmund Freud* (Vol. 14). London: Hogarth Press.

Jenkins, J. G., & Dallenbach, K. M. (1924). Obliviscence during sleep and waking. *American Journal of Psychology, 35*, 605–612.

Köhler, W. (1947). *Gestalt psychology: An introduction to new concepts in modern psychology*. New York: Liveright.

Loftus, E. F., & Loftus, G. R. (1980). On the permanence of stored information in the human brain. *American Psychologist*, *35*, 409–420.

Loftus, E. F., & Palmer, J. C. (1974). Reconstruction of automobile destruction: An example of the interaction between language and memory. *Journal of Verbal Learning and Verbal Behavior*, *13*, 585–589.

Luria, A. R. (1968). *The mind of a mnemonist: A little book about a vast memory*. Cambridge, MA: Harvard University Press.

McCloskey, M., & Zaragoza, M. (1985). Misleading postevent information and memory for events: Arguments and evidence against memory impairment hypotheses. *Journal of Experimental Psychology: General*, *114*, 1–16.

McGeoch, J. A. (1932). Forgetting and the law of disuse. *Psychological Review*, *39*, 352–370.

McGeoch, J. A. (1942). *The psychology of human learning*. Oxford: Longmans, Green, and Company.

Melton, A. W. (1963). Implications of short-term memory for a general theory of memory. *Journal of Verbal Learning and Verbal Behavior*, *2*, 1–21.

Melton, A. W., & Irwin, J. M. (1940). The influence of degree of interpolated learning on retroactive inhibition and the transfer of specific responses. *American Journal of Psychology*, *53*, 173–203.

Nadel, L. (2008). Consolidation: The demise of the fixed trace. In H. L. Roediger, Y. Dudai, & S. M. Fitzpatrick (Eds.), *Science of memory: Concepts* (pp. 177–181). New York: Oxford University Press.

Nairne, J. S., & Pandeirada, J. N. S. (2008). Forgetting. In H. L. Roediger (Ed.), *Learning and memory: A comprehensive reference* (Vol. 2, pp. 179–194). Oxford: Elsevier.

Neisser, U. (1978). Memory: What are the important questions? In M. M. Gruneberg, P. E. Morris, & R. N. Sykes (Eds.), *Practical aspects of memory* (pp. 3–24). London: Academic Press.

Neisser, U. (1982). *Memory observed: Remembering in natural contexts*. San Francisco: W. H. Freeman.

Parker, E. S., Cahill, L., & McGaugh, J. L. (2006). A case of unusual autobiographical remembering. *Neurocase*, *12*, 35–49.

Payne, D. G. (1987). Hypermnesia and reminiscence in recall: A historical and empirical review. *Psychological Bulletin*, *101*, 5–27.

Peterson, L. R., & Peterson, M. J. (1959). Short-term retention of individual verbal items. *Journal of Experimental Psychology*, *58*, 193–198.

Roediger, H. L. (1973). Inhibition in recall from cueing with recall targets. *Journal of Verbal Learning and Verbal Behavior*, *12*, 261–269.

Roediger, H. L. (1974). Inhibiting effects of recall. *Memory & Cognition*, *2*, 261–269.

Roediger, H. L. (1978). Recall as a self-limiting process. *Memory & Cognition*, *6*, 54–63.

Roediger, H. L. (1996). Memory illusions. *Journal of Memory and Language*, *35*, 76–100.

Roediger, H. L., & Challis, B. H. (1989). Hypermnesia: Increased recall with repeated tests. In C. Izawa (Ed.), *Current issues in cognitive processes: The Tulane Flowerree symposium on cognition* (pp. 175–199). Hillsdale, NJ: Lawrence Erlbaum Associates, Inc.

Roediger, H. L., & Guynn, M. J. (1996). Retrieval processes. In E. L. Bjork & R. A. Bjork (Eds.), *Human memory* (pp. 197–236). San Diego: Academic Press.

Roediger, H. L., & Karpicke, J. D. (2006). The power of testing memory: Basic research and implications for educational practice. *Perspectives on Psychological Science*, *1*, 181–210.

Roediger, H. L., & Thorpe, L. A. (1978). The role of recall time in producing hypermnesia. *Memory & Cognition*, *6*, 296–305.

Rubin, D. C., Hinton, S., & Wenzel, A. (1999). The precise time course of retention. *Journal of Experimental Psychology: Learning, Memory, and Cognition*, *25*, 1161–1176.

Rubin, D. C., & Wenzel, A. E. (1996). One hundred years of forgetting: A quantitative description of retention. *Psychological Review*, *103*, 734–760.

Sara, S. J. (2000). Retrieval and reconsolidation: Toward a neurobiology of remembering. *Learning & Memory*, *7*, 73–84.

Sara, S. J. (2008). Consolidation: From hypothesis to paradigm to concept. In H. L. Roediger, Y. Dudai, & S. M. Fitzpatrick (Eds.), *Science of memory: Concepts* (pp. 183–189). New York: Oxford University Press.

Schacter, D. L. (1987). Implicit memory: History and current status. *Journal of Experimental Psychology: Learning, Memory, and Cognition*, *13*, 501–518.

Sills, D. L., & Merton, R. K. (1968). *International encyclopedia of the social sciences*. New York: Macmillan Free Press.

Slamecka, N. J., & McElree, B. (1983). Normal forgetting of verbal lists as a function of their degree of learning. *Journal of Experimental Psychology: Learning, Memory, and Cognition*, *9*, 384–397.

Sperling, G. (1960). The information available in brief visual presentations. *Psychological Monographs: General and Applied*, *74*, 1–30.

Tulving, E. (1967). The effects of presentation and recall of material in free-recall learning. *Journal of Verbal Learning and Verbal Behavior*, *6*, 175–184.

Tulving, E. (1974). Cue-dependent forgetting. *American Scientist*, *62*, 74–82.

Tulving, E. (1983). *Elements of episodic memory*. New York: Oxford University Press.

Tulving, E., & Arbuckle, T. Y. (1963). Sources of intratrial interference in immediate recall of paired associates. *Journal of Verbal Learning and Verbal Behavior*, *1*, 321–334.

Tulving, E., & Pearlstone, Z. (1966). Availability versus accessibility of information in memory for words. *Journal of Verbal Learning & Verbal Behavior*, *5*, 381–391.

Tulving, E., & Thomson, D. M. (1973). Encoding specificity and retrieval processes in episodic memory. *Psychological Review*, *80*, 352–373.

Underwood, B. J. (1957). Interference and forgetting. *Psychological Review*, *64*, 49–60.

Underwood, B. J. (1966). *Experimental psychology*. New York: Appleton-Century-Crofts.

Underwood, B. J., & Postman, L. (1960). Extra-experimental sources of interference in forgetting. *Psychological Review*, *67*, 73–95.

Watkins, M. J. (1979). Engrams as cuegrams and forgetting as cue overload: A cueing approach to the structure of memory. In C. R. Puff (Ed.), *Memory organization and structure* (pp. 347–372). New York: Academic Press.

Watkins, O. C., & Watkins, M. J. (1975). Buildup of proactive inhibition as a cue-overload effect. *Journal of Experimental Psychology: Human Learning and Memory*, *1*, 442–452.

Weiner, B. (1966). Effects of motivation on the availability of memory traces. *Psychological Bulletin*, *65*, 24–37.

Wheeler, M. A. (1995). Improvement in recall over time without repeated testing:

Spontaneous recovery revisited. *Journal of Experimental Psychology: Learning, Memory, and Cognition*, *21*, 173–184.

Wixted, J. T. (2004). The psychology and neuroscience of forgetting. *Annual Review of Psychology*, *55*, 235–269.

Wixted, J. T., & Carpenter, S. K. (2007). The Wickelgren power law and the Ebbinghaus savings function. *Psychological Science*, *18*, 133–134.

2 Forgetting

A historical perspective

Hans J. Markowitsch and Matthias Brand

University of Bielefeld, Germany

Introduction

Memory is viewed as a fundamental and important attribute of human beings. Its significance is concisely captured by the following citation of Ewald Hering (1895): "Memory connects innumerable single phenomena into a whole, and just as the body would be scattered like dust in countless atoms if the attraction of matter did not hold it together so consciousness – without the connecting power of memory – would fall apart in as many fragments as it contains moments" (p. 12). Memory is subsequently seen as a cornerstone of an integrated personality. It is therefore not surprising that nowadays many people strive to improve their memory by buying specific training programs or solving one crossword puzzle after the other. From an evolutionary point of view, however, at times it may be advantageous to forget. As Depue, Curran, and Banich (2007) pointed out, already in the Stone Age it might have been of survival value to forget incidents during hunting when one barely escaped death. (According to this line of thought are the recent attempts to develop "forgetting" drugs for women who were sexually assaulted.) The evolutionary advantage of forgetting might also be suggested from the finding of dissociative behavior in both normal and pathological states (see below). Dissociation as a mechanism of distancing oneself from a previous personal experience can be identified in several autobiographies where the authors write about themselves in the third person (see Günter Grass's 2007 autobiography, *Peeling the onion*, or Reemtsma's 1997 autobiographical description of his kidnapping). Various reports in the literature suggest that individuals with extraordinary extensive memory abilities do not usually experience a feeling of satisfaction as a result of this talent. In 1968, the Soviet Russian neuropsychologist Alexander Luria wrote a book about a mnemonist who was traveling through the country showing his unbelievable memory abilities. Nevertheless, as Luria stated, this man was never happy and later in life gave up his shows and instead used his knowledge of old Hebrew and Armenian to help other people by preparing herbal remedies. A similar case of extraordinary memory abilities is that of a 34-year-old woman who wrote to James McGaugh, a Californian neuroscientist, that since the age of 11 she "had this unbelievable ability to recall my past, but not just recollections." She stated that she "can take a date, between 1974 and today, and tell you what day it falls on, what I was doing that day and if anything of great importance occurred." She further reported in her letter that while most people view her memorizing ability as a gift, she, however, perceives it as "a burden." "I run my entire life through my head every day and it drives me crazy!!!. . . ." (Parker, Cahill, & McGaugh, 2006, p. 35). Other cases of people with extraordinary memory abilities are often accompanied by very specific or limited intellectual and social functioning (e.g., savant syndromes, autism; see Markowitsch, 1992). With its two sides, one of remembering and the other of forgetting, suppressing, or repressing of information, memory may therefore be viewed like a Janus head, with its optimum functioning resulting from the adequate performance of each side as well as the balanced interplay between the two sides.

Memory can be divided into anterograde and retrograde memory (or its corresponding amnesic forms; Figure 2.1) and several content-based long-term memory systems, respectively (Figure 2.2). Among the latter, the episodic-autobiographic memory is the most relevant for our present purposes, as this memory system is most vulnerable to forgetting (Markowitsch, 2003a, 2008).

Origins of investigating forgetting

Harald Weinrich (1997), the author of *Lethe – Kunst und Kritik des Vergessens* [Lethe – Art and critique of forgetting] argued that human beings are, by nature, forgetting creatures (*animal obliviscens*) and that we frequently use the

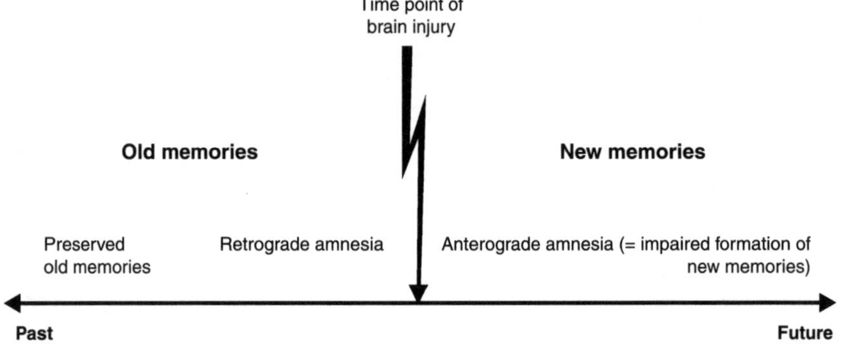

Figure 2.1 Relations between anterograde and retrograde amnesia. The flash symbol represents the time point of a brain infarct or of a major psychic traumatic event, leading to either anterograde or retrograde amnesia or to both. Note that for retrograde amnesia the frequently observed gradient – termed Ribot's law (see Markowitsch, 2009) – is indicated by stating that usually very old memories are preserved in retrograde amnesia, while those close to the point of the event are impaired.

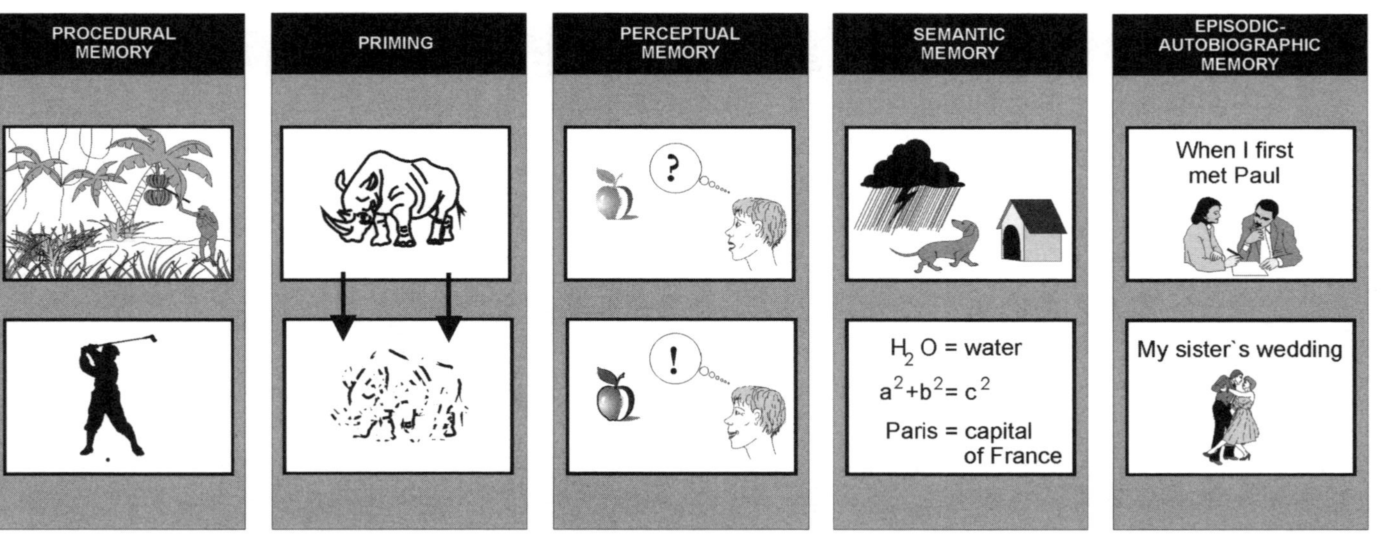

Figure 2.2 The five long-term memory systems and their assumed brain bases (for further description see the text).

word "forgetting" to be reminded not to forget someone or something ("Forget-me-not" has been the flower of loving couples since the 15th century). The title of Weinrich's book refers to the Greek goddess Lethe, who complemented Mnemosyne, the one representing forgetting, and the other memory. As Weinrich's citation of Milton's epic *Paradise Lost* (1667/1674) shows, Lethe is often viewed as the river of forgetting, which enables the souls of the dead to forget, in order to be freed from their previous existence and be subsequently reborn in a new body:

> Far off from these, a slow and silent stream,
> Lethe, the river of oblivion, rolls
> Her wat'ry labyrinth, whereof who drinks,
> Forthwith his former state and being forgets,
> Forgets both joy and grief, pleasure and pain.

The theme of forgetting is also underlined in Weinrich's book by the reference he makes to the meeting between the Greek poet Simonides (originator of "Ars memoriae," the art of memory) and Themistocles. Themistocles, who was able to remember everything instantaneously and apparently throughout his life, reportedly revealed to Simonides that he was rather more interested in an "*ars oblivionis*" (art of forgetting) than in an "*ars memoriae.*" As Weinrich mentions in his book, numerous poets, novelists, and philosophers – from Homer, Ovid, and Plato to Dante, Cervantes, Descartes, Kant, Frederick the Great, Goethe, Sartre, and Borges – emphasized the importance of forgetting over the years. In the scientific realm, however, forgetting became a prominent topic of interest after Freud's writings on the subject (Freud, 1898, 1899, 1901; Freud & Breuer, 1895/1970), although several other scientists of the time, including Freud's teacher Charcot (1892), Pick (1876, 1886, 1905) and Freund (1889), had already written about forgetting in patients with severe memory problems. Other psychoanalysts, such as Carl Jung, followed Freud by writing on forgetting (Jung, 1905a, 1905b); and hysteria was the common denominator for most cases of forgetting (Janet, 1907). Jung (1905a), for example, pointed to the role of "systematic" forgetting, which might trigger the development of Ganser syndrome, a psychogenic amnesic condition discussed below.

Hysteric and psychogenic forgetting

Hysteria and other forms of amnesia, precipitated by stressful or psychotraumatic experiences, have been, since the times of Charcot (1892) and Janet (1907), among the most prominent diagnoses in psychiatry. In addition to these diagnoses of forgetting were those where clinicians assumed that madness was feigned or amnesia simulated (e.g., Heine, 1911; Hey, 1904; Lücke, 1903; Zingerle, 1912). Hysterical amnesia – motivated forgetting (usually of adverse material) – was largely described among women (see, e.g., the case histories of Fräulein Anna O, Frau Emmy v. N, Miss Lucy R, Katharina, and Fräulein Elisabeth v. R, given in Freud & Breuer, 1895/1970). In addition, the condition was identified in war veterans (e.g., Bauer, 1917). The tradition of case reports of females with hysteria may be traced back to "La possession de Jeanne Fèry, religieuse professe du convent des soeurs de la ville de Mons 1584," a description of a "possessed" nun, summarized by Gilles de la Tourette in 1886 (cited in Donath, 1908). In the United States, around the same time, Weir Mitchell (1888) documented a case with some similarities to the medieval nun, namely of Mary Reynolds, an 18-year-old girl who suddenly behaved like a newborn child – "as being for the first time ushered into the world" (cited in Janet, 1907). A closely related case was that of a Bavarian woman with a number of ecstatic religious states (Hoche, 1933; Seidl, 2008).

A detailed review of possible amnesic states – many of which were psychological in nature – was provided by Heine (1911, pp. 55f):

1) epileptic somnolence
2) hysterical somnolence
3) states of unconsciousness and of mnestic activity after traumatic damage to the brain
    a) commotio cerebri
    b) attempt to hang oneself
    c) reanimation after hanging
4) states of somnolence with a relation to physiological sleep
5) hypnotic states
6) migraine-based somnolence
7) affect-based somnolence
8) toxic somnolence, or disturbance of mind
    a) complicated states after intoxication
    b) disease of the mind after CO-inhalation
9) vasomotoric states of somnolence
    a) congestive (transitory mania)
    b) angiospastic (raptus melancholicus)
10) transitory disturbances of mind after infectious diseases
11) paralytic attacks
12) retrograde amnesia without previous disturbances of consciousness
13) Korsakoff's psychosis.

Psychogenic amnesic states, also named functional amnesias (Lundholm, 1932), were usually treated with hypnosis (e.g., Brodmann, 1897; Köhler, 1897) and diagnoses of dissociative personalities were common (e.g., Prince, 1906a, 1906b, 1908, 1929).

The Ganser syndrome

A version of functional amnesia, described in detail already before the turn of the 19th century, was the Ganser syndrome (originally named Ganser symptom; Ganser, 1898/1965, 1904). According to Ganser (1898, 1904) it consisted of a hysterical semi-trance or twilight state, and was characterized by the tendency to give only approximate reactions, and to deny things under high pressure. Impairments of consciousness, amnesia, and the existence of hallucinations were prominent features. After Ganser's original description of the syndrome as "a peculiar hysterical state" it became a well-known (transient) amnesic state that was frequently associated with forensic contexts (e.g., Flatau, 1913; Hey, 1904; Jung, 1902; Lücke, 1903; Matthies, 1908), or traumatic conditions (e.g., Meyer, 1904; Raecke, 1908; Stertz, 1910). The syndrome is still diagnosed today (e.g., Dalfen & Feinstein, 2000; Ladowsky-Brooks & Fischer, 2003), though its definition has suffered several refinements over the years.

Fugues

A special subcategory of psychogenic amnesias were fugue states, defined as retrograde amnesias of autobiographical content (see Figure 2.2), accompanied by leaving the usual home and traveling sometimes far away (Bregman, 1899; Heilbronner, 1903; Schultze, 1903; Stier, 1912; Woltär, 1906). German-language scientists also named this condition "Wanderlust," "Wandertrieb," or poriomania (Donath, 1899, 1907). They sometimes thought that it had a relation to epilepsy (e.g., Burgl, 1900; Kellner, 1898; Mörchen, 1904; Raecke, 1908), and stated that it was not uncommonly of "forensic relevance" (Zingerle, 1912). Fugue states were preponderant in children and young adults (Bregman, 1899; Dana, 1874; Donath, 1908; Heilbronner, 1903; Hey, 1904). Franz (1933) gave a detailed description of a subject with a multiple personality named Jack who ostensibly traveled between Europe, Africa, and the United States and reported being captured and held as a prisoner in East Africa during World War I.

Multiple personality disorders

Other "dissociative reactions" (Janet, 1907) included cases with multiple personalities – with their defining criterion being amnesia for the respective other personality or personality state (Angell, 1906; Azam, 1876; Burnett, 1925; Gordon, 1906; Pick, 1876; Prince, 1906a, 1906b, 1920, 1924; Sidis & Goodhart, 1905; Wilson, 1903) – somnambulism, "fausse reconnaissance," depersonalization, or a state of trance (see, e.g., Abeles & Schilder, 1935; Gillespie, 1937; Heymans, 1904, 1906; Laughlin, 1956). As in other psychogenic amnesias, a link with epilepsy was frequently assumed to exist (Bechterew, 1900; Cowles, 1900; Forel, 1885; Gordon, 1906; Kellner, 1898; Mörchen, 1904).

Various movie versions of the well-known tale of Dr Jekyll and Mr Hyde have provided the public with different artistic views of the pathological spectrum of two souls living within the same body. Both a book (Schreiber, 1973) and a movie – *Sybil* – described the case of Sybil Isabel Dorsett (born in 1923), a young American who, according to her therapist, developed 16 different personalities, whereby – as is typical for this psychiatric condition – her conscious remembering was limited to the actual personality only. As is frequently encountered in such cases, Sybil Isabel Dorsett's diagnosis of dissociative identity disorder was associated with a history of childhood sexual abuse. Laughlin's (1956) book relates a number of "famous" cases, such as that of "Miss Christine Beauchamp," who had three different personality states ("virgin/holy person, woman, prostitute/devil") and "Reverend Mr. Henna," who similarly behaved as a respectable priest during the day and avidly sought the company of prostitutes at night. Altogether, 216 case descriptions can be found in Laughlin's book.

Conclusions

Gordon (1906) stated that "self-consciousness is a *conditio sine qua non* of normal life" (p. 480) and that amnesia is the most typical of all disturbances of consciousness. In persons with multiple personalities, one personality, at least during the first stages of the illness, is unconscious (or totally amnesic) of the other(s). In rare cases, two selves might coexist simultaneously. Gordon's hypothesis is in conformity with the idea that a disturbed self-consciousness typically accompanies states of psychogenic forgetting (Markowitsch, 2003b).

Though it is still debated whether forgetting constitutes an active process (e.g., via interference in the acquisition of new information) or a passive one (decay of information over time) (see Wixted, 2004), descriptions of patients with psychogenic amnesia more readily speak for an active process. It is well known that stressful life conditions lead to cascade-like release of glucocorticoids (stress hormones) and that these interfere with autobiographical memory processing. Stress hormones have the majority of their receptors in the hippocampus and amygdala, which constitute areas that are essential for synchronous binding processes during autobiographical information processing (Markowitsch, 2000). Especially when the stressful events occur in childhood, they may lead to a heightened vulnerability of the individual to later stressful situations and may consequently induce severe and lasting forms of forgetting (Fujiwara et al., 2008; Markowitsch, 1999, 2003a; Markowitsch, Kessler, Weber-Luxenburger, Van der Ven, & Heiss, 2000), or, in rare cases, to anterograde amnesia (Markowitsch, Kessler, Kalbe, & Herholz, 1999).

Similar to Wixted's (2004) suggestions on the general mechanisms of forgetting, forgetting in patients with dissociative amnesias may be seen as an unexpected overload of stressful events that leads to hippocampal-amygdalar dysfunction and consequently impedes the successful activation or reactivation of autobiographical memories. Instead, such memories may become vulnerable and chronically inaccessible to a conscious representation. This may then indeed lead to the decay of memories, as synapses get lost and the interconnectivity between hippocampal and neocortical areas (engaged in memory storage) may shrink. In conclusion, present-day neuroscientific knowledge may facilitate an understanding of the processes of repression and suppression proposed by psychoanalysts at the turn of the last century (Langnickel & Markowitsch, 2006, 2010). Forgetting may be a necessary mechanism of filtering – or in extreme cases of defense, enabling us to perceive ourselves as integrated and robust personalities. Cases of "forgetting" and the current status of dissociative amnesias will be the topic of Chapter 11 (Brand & Markowitsch, 2009).

Acknowledgement

Our research was supported by the German Research Council and the European Commission (FP6 – 043460).

References

Abeles, M., & Schilder, P. (1935). Psychogenic loss of personal identity: amnesia. *AMA Archives of Neurology and Psychiatry*, *34*, 587–604.

Angell, E. B. (1906). A case of double consciousness-amnesic type, with fabrication of memory. *Journal of Abnormal Psychology*, *1*, 155–169.

Azam, M. (1876). Periodical amnesia; or, double consciousness. *Journal of Nervous and Mental Disease*, *3*, 584–612.

Bauer, J. (1917). Hysterische Erkrankungen bei Kriegsteilnehmern [Hysteric diseases in combatants]. *Archiv für Psychiatrie und Nervenkrankheiten*, *57*, 139–168.

Bechterew, W. von (1900b). Ueber periodische Anfälle retroactiver Amnesie [On periodic attacks of retroactive amnesia]. *Monatsschrift für Psychiatrie und Neurologie*, *8*, 353–358.

Brand, M., & Markowitsch, H. J. (2009). Aspects of forgetting in psychogenic amnesia. In S. Della Sala (Ed.), *Forgetting* (pp. 239–251). Hove, UK: Psychology Press.

Bregman, L. E. (1899). Ueber den "Automatisme ambulatoire" ("Fugues", "Dromomania") [On the "automatisme ambulatoire" ("fugues", "dromomania")]. *Neurologisches Centralblatt*, *18*, 776–781.

Brodmann, K. (1897). Zur Methodik der hypnotischen Behandlung [On the methodology of hypnotic treatment]. *Zeitschrift für Hypnotismus, Psychotherapie sowie andere Psychophysiologische und Psychopathologische Forschungen*, *6*, 1–10, 193–214.

Burgl, G. (1900). Eine Reise in die Schweiz im epileptischen Dämmerzustande und die transitorischen Bewusstseinsstörungen der Epileptiker vor dem Strafrichter [A journey to Switzerland done in epileptic somnolence and the transitory disturbances of consciousness before the criminal judge]. *Münchener medizinische Wochenschrift*, *37*, 1270–1273.

Burnett, C. T. (1925). Splitting the mind. *Psychological Monographs*, *34*, 1–132.

Charcot, J. M. (1892). Sur un cas d'amnésie retro-antérograde [On a case with retro- and anterograde amnesia]. *Revue de medicine*, *12*, 81–96.

Cowles, E. (1900). Epilepsy with retrograde amnesia. *American Journal of Insanity*, *56*, 593–614.

Dalfen, A. K., & Feinstein, A. (2000). Head injury, dissociation, and the Ganser syndrome. *Brain Injury*, *14*, 1101–1105.

Dana, C. L. (1874). The study of a case of amnesia or "double consciousness." *Psychological Review*, *1*, 570–580.

Depue, B. E., Curran, T., & Banich, M. T. (2007). Prefrontal regions orchestrate suppression of emotional memories via a two-phase process. *Science*, *317*, 215–219.

Donath, J. (1899). Der epileptische Wandertrieb (Poriomanie) [The epileptic drive to wander (poriomania)]. *Archiv für Psychiatrie und Nervenkrankheiten*, *32*, 335–355.

Donath, J. (1907). Weitere Beiträge zur Poriomanie [Further contributions on poriomania]. *Archiv für Psychiatrie und Nervenkrankheiten*, *42*, 752–760.

Donath, J. (1908). Ueber hysterische Amnesie [On hysterical amnesia]. *Archiv für Psychiatrie und Nervenkrankheiten*, *44*, 559–575.

Flatau, G. (1913). Über den Ganserschen Symptomenkomplex [On the syndrome of Ganser]. *Zeitschrift für die gesamte Neurologie und Psychiatrie*, *15*, 122–137.

Forel, A. (1885). *Das Gedächtnis und seine Abnormitäten* [Memory and its abnormal states]. Zürich: Orell Füssli & Co.

Franz, S. I. (1933). *Persons one and three. A study in multiple personalities*. New York: Whittlesey House.

Freud, S. (1898). Zum psychischen Mechanismus der Vergesslichkeit [On the psychic mechanism of forgetfulness]. *Monatsschrift für Psychiatrie und Neurologie*, *1*, 436–443.

Freud, S. (1899). Ueber Deckerinnerungen [On covered memories]. *Monatsschrift für Psychiatrie und Neurologie*, *2*, 215–230.

Freud, S. (1901). Zur Psychopathologie des Alltagslebens (Vergessen, Versprechen, Vergreifen) nebst Bemerkungen über eine Wurzel des Aberglaubens [On the psychopathology of daily life (forgetting, slips of the tongue, mistakes) together with remarks on the root of superstititon]. *Monatsschrift für Psychiatrie und Neurologie*, *10*, 1–32, 95–143.

Freud, S., & Breuer, J. (1970). *Studien über Hysterie* [Studies on hysteria]. (Enlarged reprint of the 1895 texts of Breuer & Freud.) Frankfurt/M.: Fischer.

Freund, C. S. (1889). Klinische Beiträge zur Kenntnis der generellen Gedächtnisschwäche [Clinical contributions to understanding general memory weakness]. *Archiv für Psychiatrie und Nervenkrankheiten*, *20*, 441–457.

Fujiwara, E., Brand, M., Kracht, L., Kessler, J., Diebel, A., Netz, J., & Markowitsch, H. J. (2008). Functional retrograde amnesia: a multiple case study. *Cortex*, *44*, 29–45.

Ganser, S. J. (1898). Ueber einen eigenartigen hysterischen Dämmerzustand [On a peculiar hysterical state of somnolence]. *Archiv für Psychiatrie und Nervenkrankheiten*, *30*, 633–640

Ganser, S. J. (1904). Zur Lehre vom hysterischen Dämmerzustande [On the theory of the hysterical state of somnolence]. *Archiv für Psychiatrie und Nervenkrankheiten*, *38*, 34–46.

Ganser, S. J. (1965). A peculiar hysterical state (transl. by C. E. Schorer). *British Journal of Criminology, Delinguency, and Deviant Social Behaviour*, *5*, 120–126.

Gillespie, R. D. (1937). Amnesia. *A.M.A. Archives of Neurology and Psychiatry*, *37*, 748–764.

Gordon, A. (1906). On "double ego". *American Journal of the Medical Sciences*, *131*, 480–486.

Grass, G. (2007). *Peeling the onion* (M. H. Heim, trans.). New York: Houghton Mifflin Harcourt.

Heilbronner, K. (1903). Ueber Fugues und fugue-ähnliche Zustände [On fugues and fugue-related states]. *Jahrbücher für Psychiatrie und Neurologie*, *23*, 107–206.

Heine, R. (1911). Die forensische Bedeutung der Amnesie [The forensic significance of amnesia]. *Vierteljahresschrift für gerichtliche Medicin (3. Folge)*, *42*, 51–93.

Hering, E. (1895). *Memory as a general function of organized matter*. Chicago: Open Court.

Hey, J. (1904). *Das Gansersche Symptom und seine klinische und forense Bedeutung* [The Ganser symptom and its clinical and forensic importance]. Berlin: Hirschwald.

Heymans, G. (1904). Eine Enquete über Depersonalisation und "Fausse Reconnaissance" [An inquiry on depersonalization and "fausse reconnaissance"]. *Zeitschrift für Psychologie*, *36*, 321–343.

Heymans, G. (1906). Weitere Daten über Depersonalisation und "Fausse Reconnaissance" [Further data on depersonalization and "fausse reconnaissance"]. *Zeitschrift für Psychologie*, *43*, 1–17.

Hoche, A. E. (1933). *Die Wunder der Therese Neumann von Konnersreuth* [The wonders of Therese Neumann von Konnersreuth]. Munich: Lehmanns Verlag.

Janet, P. (1907). *The major symptoms of hysteria*. New York: Macmillan.

Jung, C. G. (1902). Ein Fall von hysterischem Stupor bei einer Untersuchungsgefangenen [A case of hysteric stupor in a prisoner on trial]. *Journal für Psychologie und Neurologie*, *1*, 110–122.

Jung, C. G. (1905a). Experimentelle Beobachtungen über das Erinnerungsvermögen [Experimental observations on remembrance]. *Centralblatt für Nervenheilkunde und Psychiatrie*, *28*, 653–666.

Jung, C. G. (1905b). Kryptomnesie [Cryptomnesia]. *Die Zukunft*, *13*, 103–115.

Kellner [no first name given] (1898). Ueber transitorische postepileptische Geistesstörungen. *Allgemeine Zeitschrift für Psychiatrie und ihre Grenzgebiete*, *58*, 863–870.

Köhler, F. (1897). Experimentelle Studien auf dem Gebiete des hypnotischen Somnambulismus [Experimental studies in hypnotic somnambulism]. *Zeitschrift für Hypnotismus, Psychotherapie sowie andere psychophysiologische und psychopathologische Forschungen*, *6*, 357–374.

Ladowsky-Brooks, R. L., & Fischer, C. E. (2003). Ganser symptoms in a case of frontal-temporal lobe dementia: Is there a common neural substrate? *Journal of Clinical and Experimental Neuropsychology*, *25*, 761–768.

Langnickel, R., & Markowitsch, H. J. (2006). Repression and the unconsciousness. *Behavioral and Brain Sciences*, *29*, 524–525.

Langnickel, R., & Markowitsch, H. J. (2010). Das Unbewusste Freuds und die Neurowissenschaften. In A. Leitner & H. G. Petzold (Eds.), *Sigmund Freud heute. Der Vater der Psychoanalyse im Blick der Wissenschaft und der psychothera-*

peutischen Schulen [Sigmund Freud today. The father of psychoanalysis viewed from science and psychotherapeutic schools]. Vienna: Krammer Verlag.

Laughlin, H. P. (1956). *The neuroses in clinical practice*. Philadelphia: Saunders.

Lücke [no first name given] (1903). Ueber das Ganser'sche Symptom mit Berücksichtigung seiner forensischen Bedeutung [On the Ganser symptom with consideration of its forensic importance]. *Allgemeine Zeitschrift für Psychiatrie*, *60*, 1–35.

Lundholm, H. (1932). The riddle of functional amnesia. *Journal of Abnormal and Social Psychology*, *26*, 355–366.

Luria, A. R. (1968). *The mind of a mnemonist: A little book about a vast memory*. New York: Basic Books.

Markowitsch, H. J. (1992). *Intellectual functions and the brain. An historical perspective*. Toronto: Hogrefe & Huber.

Markowitsch, H. J. (1999). Neuroimaging and mechanisms of brain function in psychiatric disorders. *Current Opinion in Psychiatry*, *12*, 331–337.

Markowitsch, H. J. (2000). Repressed memories. In E. Tulving (Ed.), *Memory, consciousness, and the brain: The Tallinn conference* (pp. 319–330). Philadelphia, PA: Psychology Press.

Markowitsch, H. J. (2003a). Psychogenic amnesia. *NeuroImage*, *20*, S132–S138.

Markowitsch, H. J. (2003b). Autonoëtic consciousness. In A. S. David & T. Kircher (Eds.), *The self in neuroscience and psychiatry* (pp. 180–196). Cambridge: Cambridge University Press.

Markowitsch, H. J. (2008). Anterograde amnesia. In G. Goldenberg & B. L. Miller (Eds.), *Handbook of clinical neurology (3rd Series, Vol. 88: Neuropsychology and behavioral neurology)* (pp. 155–183). New York: Elsevier.

Markowitsch, H. J., Kessler, J., Kalbe, E., & Herholz, K. (1999). Functional amnesia and memory consolidation. A case of persistent anterograde amnesia with rapid forgetting following whiplash injury. *Neurocase*, *5*, 189–200.

Markowitsch, H. J., Kessler, J., Weber-Luxenburger, G., Van der Ven, C., & Heiss, W.-D. (2000). Neuroimaging and behavioral correlates of recovery from "mnestic block syndrome" and other cognitive deteriorations. *Neuropsychiatry, Neuropsychology, and Behavioral Neurology*, *13*, 60–66.

Matthies (no first name given) (1908). Über einen Fall von hysterischem Dämmerzustand mit retrograder Amnesie [On a case of hysterical somnolence with retrograde amnesia]. *Allgemeine Zeitschrift für Psychiatrie und ihre Grenzgebiete*, *65*, 188–206.

Meyer, A. (1904). The anatomical facts and clinical varieties of traumatic insanity. *American Journal of Insanity*, *60*, 373–441.

Mitchell, S. W. (1888). Mary Reynolds: A case of double consciousness. *Transactions of the College of Physicians of Philadelphia*, *10*, 366–389.

Mörchen [no first name given] (1904). Epileptische Bewusstseinsveränderungen von ungewöhnlicher Dauer und forensischen Folgen. *Monatsschrift für Psychiatrie und Neurologie*, *17*, 15–28.

Parker, E. S., Cahill, L., & McGaugh, J. L. (2006). A case of unusual autobiographical remembering. *Neurocase*, *12*, 35–49.

Pick, A. (1876). Zur Casuistik der Erinnerungstäuschungen [On the casuistry of illusions of remembrance]. *Archiv für Psychiatrie und Nervenkrankheiten*, *6*, 568–574.

Pick, A. (1886). Zur Pathologie des Gedächtnisses [On the pathology of memory]. *Archiv für Psychiatrie und Nervenkrankheiten*, *17*, 83–98.

Pick, A. (1905). Zur Psychologie des Vergessens bei Geistes- und Nervenkranken [The psychology of forgetting in psychiatric and neurological patients]. *Archiv für kriminologische Anthropologie, 18*, 251–261.

Prince, M. (1906a). *The dissociation of a personality*. London: Longmans, Green.

Prince, M. (1906b). Hysteria from the point of view of dissociated personality. *Journal of Abnormal Psychology, 1*, 170–187.

Prince, M. (1908). My life as a dissociated personality. *Journal of Abnormal Psychology, 3*, 240–260, 311–334.

Prince, M. (1920). *The unconscious*. New York: Macmillan.

Prince, M. (1924). *The unconscious* (2nd ed.). New York: Macmillan.

Prince, M. (1929). Miss Beauchamp: The theory of the psychogenesis of multiple personality. *Journal of Abnormal Psychology, 15*, 65–135.

Raecke, J. (1908). Ueber epileptische Wanderzustände (Fugues, Poriomanie) [On epileptic states of wandering (fugues, poriomania)]. *Archiv für Psychiatrie und Nervenkrankheiten, 43*, 398–423.

Reemtsma, J. P. (1997). *Im Keller* [In the cellar]. Hamburg: Hamburg Edition.

Schreiber, F. R. (1973). *Sybil*. New York: Warner Books.

Schultze, E. (1903). Ueber krankhaften Wandertrieb [On poriomania]. *Allgemeine Zeitschrift für Psychologie, 60*, 795–814.

Seidl, O. (2008). Zur Stigmatisierung und Nahrungslosigkeit der Therese Neumann (1898–1962) [On stigmatization and abstinence from eating of Therese Neumann (1898–1962)]. *Nervenarzt, 79*, 836–844.

Sidis, B., & Goodhart, S. P. (1905). *Multiple personality: An experimental investigation into the nature of human individuality*. New York: Appleton.

Stertz, G. (1910). Ueber psychogene Erkrankungen und Querulantenwahn nach Trauma nebst ihrer Bedeutung für die Begutachtungspraxis [On psychogenic diseases and delusions of querulous persons after trauma and their importance for the practice of expert reports]. *Zeitschrift für ärztliche Fortbildung, 7*, 201–211.

Stier, E. (1912). *Wandertrieb und pathologisches Fortlaufen bei Kindern* [Poriomania and pathological running away in children]. Jena: Gustav Fischer.

Weinrich, H. (1997). *Lethe – Kunst und Kritik des Vergessens* [Lethe – Art and critique of forgetting]. Munich: C. H. Beck.

Wilson, A. (1903). A case of double consciousness. *Journal of Mental Science, 49*, 640–658.

Wixted, J. T. (2004). The psychology and neuroscience of forgetting. *Annual Review of Psychology, 55*, 235–269.

Woltär, O. (1906). Über den Bewusstseinszustand während der Fugue [On the state of consciousness during a fugue state]. *Jahrbücher für Psychiatrie und Neurologie, 27*, 125–143.

Zingerle, H. (1912). *Ueber transitorische Geistesstörungen und deren forensische Beurteilung. Juristisch-psychiatrische Grenzfragen* [On transitory mental disturbances and their forensic evaluation. Borderline or minor juridical-psychiatric cases]. Jena: Gustav Fischer.

3 A new taxonomy of memory and forgetting

Roberto Cubelli

University of Trento, Trento, Italy

Forgetting is usually defined as the definitive loss of information or the failure in retrieving it at a certain point in time (Roediger, Dudai, & Fitzpatrick, 2007). It refers to a state whereby people lose the remembrance of events, facts, or habits (Cohen & Conway, 2008).

Etymologically, the word "to forget" derives from the Old English word *forgytan*, which is composed by *for-* (passing by, letting go) and *gietan* (to grasp) and literally means "to lose (one's) grip on" (Hoad, 1996). The two Italian words for "to forget" are *dimenticare*, from the Latin *demens* which means "without mind", and *scordare*, which means "out of mind" (the literal meaning of the original Latin root is "out of heart", reflecting Aristotle's cardiocentric theory of the relationship between mind and body). In most languages, forgetting denotes a defective memory, that is, the inability to retrieve information as a consequence of vulnerable maintenance over time or ineffective recollection.

Forgetting is always referred to in negative terms, as a state or condition where memory does not work normally and appears to be faulty. Indeed, to describe memory errors Schacter (2001) used the term "seven sins" of memory. As stated by Tulving (1974), forgetting is "the inability to recall something now that could be recalled on an earlier occasion" (p. 74). In other words, forgetting is assumed to be the opposite of remembering. This definition of forgetting, however, leaves out some critical points that on the contrary should be accounted for by any theories of memory:

(1) The differences between forgetting in everyday life and amnesia are not clearly outlined. Does only a degree of extent matter? In many textbooks on psychology (e.g., Darley, Gluckberg, & Kinchla, 1991; Nicolas, 2003), or memory (e.g., Radvansky, 2006), amnesia is described as one of the possible causes of forgetting, to be considered as equivalent to decay or interference. No theoretical explanations have been proposed to distinguish the cognitive mechanisms underlying forgetting in neurologically unimpaired individuals and those involved in abnormal performance of patients with organic amnesia. Usually, amnesia is conceived as a more

severe form of forgetting, which differs only in quantitative terms, but this assumption lacks evidential support.

(2) The existence of different components of memory is a well known wisdom. However, forgetting is investigated as a unitary phenomenon rather than specific to each memory system (Wixted, 2007). It is worth noting that different forgetting curves have been observed in different memory tasks. In learning tasks, forgetting is rather rapid initially after learning, but occurs at a relatively slow rate later (e.g., Ebbinghaus, 1885). In contrast, in autobiographical memory, most of the memories are from the recent past, but there is a bump in the curve around the age of 20 (e.g., Rubin, Rahal, & Poon, 1974). Finally, in short-term memory as assessed by means of the Brown–Peterson paradigm, forgetting is very quick and nearly all information is lost after a very brief interval (Keppel & Underwood, 1962). Forgetting appears to be different in the different memory systems. It follows that different cognitive mechanisms should be assumed to explain why information is no longer available when memory is tested.

(3) If forgetting reveals memory failures, remembering should always be desired: the more information remembered, the better functioning is the memory. However, in the so-called *memorists* the exceptional ability to remember details, even irrelevant and unwanted information, is associated with severe difficulties in everyday life. Consider, for instance, the famous case of Shereshevskii described by Luria (1968). He could recall lists of items years after having been presented with them only once. He was so good at memorizing the perceptual details of all environmental stimuli that he found it difficult to grasp abstract ideas. He had trouble in coping with his ability and died in a mental hospital.

The abnormal condition whereby forgetting is absent, masterly described by Jorge Luis Borges in his tale "Funes, the Memorious" (1942/1998), suggests that forgetting is crucial as well as remembering. As Ribot (1881) stated: "Without totally forgetting a prodigious number of states of consciousness, and momentarily forgetting a large number, we could not remember at all. Oblivion, except in certain cases, is thus not a malady of memory, but a condition of its health and its life" (p. 46). Analogously, James (1890) observed: "This peculiar mixture of forgetting with our remembering is but one instance of our mind's selective activity. . . . If we remembered everything, we should on most occasions be as ill off as if we remembered nothing" (p. 680). Currently, despite what was acknowledged by scientists at the end of the 19th century, no models of memory can account for the functional role of forgetting. To go beyond the usual notion of forgetting it is necessary to discuss the relationship between forgetting and memory: the answer to why we forget cannot be found independently from knowing how we remember.

Forgetting is assumed to occur either because of defective retention (the to-be-remembered information is weakly specified, hence susceptible to decay or interference), or unsuccessful recollection (retrieval cues are no longer effective). However, forgetting is not only absence of memory or failure in responding to memory tests; very often it results in memory errors and distortions. Typically, the most employed procedures to assess memory and learning consider only the frequency of the correct responses, while ignoring the unexpected responses and their nature (e.g., Wechsler, 1997). Memory errors have an important heuristic value. They allow testing hypotheses on memory functioning and therefore cannot be disregarded further.

In his famous dialogue the *Theaetetus*, Plato discussed the organization of knowledge and used memory errors as tools to verify the different hypotheses he was taking into consideration. First of all, he provided the metaphor of memory as a wax tablet which holds the impression of each stimulus encountered. Memory is assumed to happen when a new occurrence of the stimulus matches the previously created trace. If the wax is altered or erased, the trace cannot be distinguished from the similar ones or is definitively lost. According to this interpretation, memory errors should result from a mismatch between the imprint on the wax tablet and the actual stimuli, that is, between memory and perception. Therefore, they are expected to occur in recognition tasks only, not in free recall.

Given the unfeasibility of accounting for errors in all tasks, Plato proposed a second metaphor: memory is described as a birdcage, or an aviary, which should contain all learned information, represented in a dynamic form as flying birds. Memory errors are assumed to be the consequence of the difficulty in selecting information and consist in exchanges (a bird is caught instead of), occurring in both recognition and recall tasks. However, following this way of representing memory mechanisms, errors should involve only learned facts or actually experienced events. No false memories should be observed.

In view of that, in the last part of the dialogue Plato proposed the metaphor of writing: information is memorized not as a whole, but as a collection of compounding elements; for example, only the constituent letters of words are memorized. In such a way, to have knowledge refers to the ability to recompose the original information. From this interpretation, it follows that, using the memorized letters, words can be correctly spelled but also nonwords sometimes could be produced. Therefore, when errors occur they can result in false memories, that is, events which never happened or false statements. Assuming memory as a writing system, however, all types of errors can be accounted for but learning remains to be explained. Indeed, if we have to use a fallible operation to rebuild the original information, acquiring new information would appear to be a very hard endeavour. Accurate reproduction could take place gradually over time by progressive "shaping", but this needs external feedbacks to occur or multiple repetitions of the stimulus presentation.

Metaphors are effective tools for advancing knowledge (Draaisma, 1995). They can provide theoretical frameworks for deriving working hypotheses, but they have to be discarded if they fail to account for the whole pattern of the empirical data. Currently, we lack a shared metaphor of memory and forgetting.

To explain the origin of memory errors as evidence of forgetting, models of memory are needed. Memory process comprises three distinct operations: (1) encoding information to be learned; (2) preserving it over time; (3) retrieving and temporarily maintaining it for accomplishing specific tasks or acting in everyday life. Consistent with the dominant spatial metaphor (memory as a store or a library, see for instance Broadbent, 1971), memory can be described as a reproductive process (e.g., Lindsay & Norman, 1977), whereby information is registered, stored, and accessed. On the contrary, if the spatial metaphor is rejected, memory could be conceived as a reconstructive process (Bartlett, 1932), whereby information is interpreted, integrated within existing memories, and recreated.

Assuming the former framework, remembering consists in preserving information exactly as it was at the learning phase, while forgetting should be described as evidence of a defective functioning: memories are either definitively erased or still held but no longer accessible (forgetting as the unavailability or inaccessibility of the stored information). On the contrary, according to the latter, remembering is the accurate reconstruction of the previous interpretation of the stimulus and forgetting should be considered as an intrinsic component of the memory process. Information could be lost in the stimulus-processing stage, as a by-product of normal memory functioning (forgetting as the transformation of the original information).

According to Rubin (2007): "a definitional prerequisite for forgetting is that one has encoded or learned something and so could have a memory for it" (p. 325). This is true only if we conceive memory as a reproductive process. If, on the contrary, we describe memory as reconstructive, then forgetting should occur even in the encoding phase when information is being interpreted on the basis of the previous knowledge and current aims.

Are these two different ways of describing memory and forgetting mutually exclusive? I think they can coexist but we need a new taxonomy of memory components.

To classify the different memory components, several dichotomies have been proposed (Graf & Schacter, 1985; Squire & Zola-Morgan, 1988; Tulving, 1972) and are incorporated in a very influential taxonomy (Squire, 1987). First of all, memory is divided into declarative and nondeclarative memory. Declarative memory includes learned information expressed through recollection and comprises facts (semantic memory) and events (episodic memory). Nondeclarative memory, on the contrary, is a general category including learned skills and habits (procedural memory), priming and perceptual learning, classical conditioning, and nonassociative learning. This taxonomy is mainly based on a biological perspective: It has been proposed to explain the pattern of impaired and preserved memory abilities in amnesia and to associate the different memory systems with distinct cerebral regions (see Squire, 2004). A well-known diagram (see Figure 3.1), quoted in almost all textbooks of cognitive

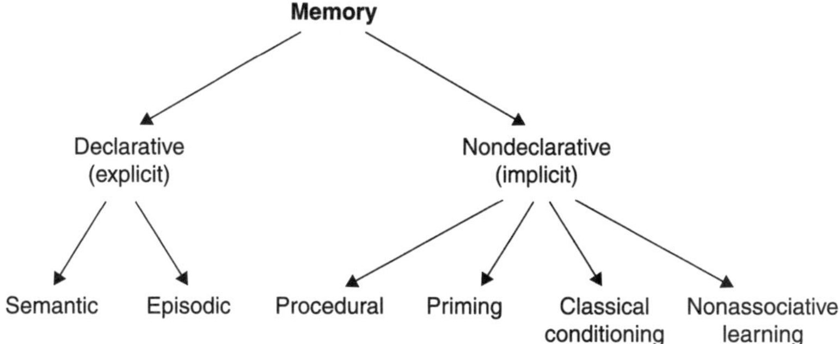

Figure 3.1 Squire's taxonomy of long-term memory systems (from Squire, 2007, modified).

neuroscience (e.g., Gazzaniga, Ivry, & Mangun, 1998), depicts this way of distinguishing the different memory components (Squire, 1987, 2007).

As it stands, however, some weaknesses can be noticed in this taxonomy. First of all, the diagram includes a heterogeneous collection of memory subjects belonging to different categories and levels of analysis: memory contents (semantic, episodic, and procedural), learning type (associative vs. nonassociative), and memory dynamics (priming). This *mélange* of topics can account for the observed performance of the patient HM and other amnesic patients (Squire, 2007), but it is of little use in describing the organization of the memory system and the mechanisms of forgetting.

Further, prospective memory, that is, the memory of intentions (Winograd, 1988), is not included, but it is a very relevant memory component (in dealing with everyday situations, we have to remember the future, not only the past) that is affected in amnesic patients (Parkin, 1997).

Moreover, the distinction between declarative and nondeclarative memory is assumed to be equivalent to the distinction between explicit and implicit memory. It is claimed that while declarative memory consists in the conscious recollection of facts and episodes, nondeclarative memory comprises nonconscious learning capacities and does not provide access to any conscious memory content (Squire & Zola, 1996). Yet, it is not clear why the content of procedural memory should be unconscious. The activation of a learned motor programme and the fast, automatic execution of the correct sequence of movements is not an operation that one performs without consciousness. More correctly, the distinction between explicit and implicit memory refers to the ability to accomplish a memory task with or without any subjective sense of remembering the learning episode (Norman & Schacter, 1996). However, even with this connotation, this distinction does not correspond to declarative and nondeclarative memory. Indeed, historic or geographical information can be retrieved without any reference to the circumstances in which these facts were acquired, as well as learned actions that can be performed remembering the training phase.

In Figure 3.2, the diagram of a new taxonomy is proposed. According to that, long-term memory comprises reproductive and reconstructive memories. Reproductive memory is the kind of memory referred to when the verb "to know" is used. We *know* specific facts or how to do something, that is, we are able to reproduce an information stimulus or target behaviour we have studied (for instance, the name of the European capitals or the motor program to serve in tennis or in volleyball). Learning may occur after a formal study or training phase or by means of practice and repetition. No personal interpretations or substantial variations are admitted in learning facts and procedures.

In contrast, reconstructive memory refers to what is denoted by the verb "to remember". When required, we are able to *remember* what we did in specific circumstances and what we are going to do in the near future. Memory is a creative function, not a mere recording of what happens around us (Cubelli & Della Sala, 2009). At present, using the accrued experience and knowledge, we are able to recreate the past and to imagine the future. Reproductive and reconstructive memory differ in several respects:

(1) By definition, accuracy is high for reproductive memory and low for reconstructive memory.
(2) Reproductive memory is related to studying and education, whereas reconstructive memory concerns everyday activities and supports decisions and actions.
(3) Reconstructive memory is context dependent, with performance depending on contextual information available in both learning and test phase; in contrast, reproductive memory appears to be less influenced by environmental and emotional factors.
(4) Reproductive memory is improved by repetitive stimulus exposition and multiple sessions while reconstructive memory can be distorted when the same event is repeated.
(5) Working memory is crucial in the learning phase of reproductive memory and in the retrieval phase of reconstructive memory.

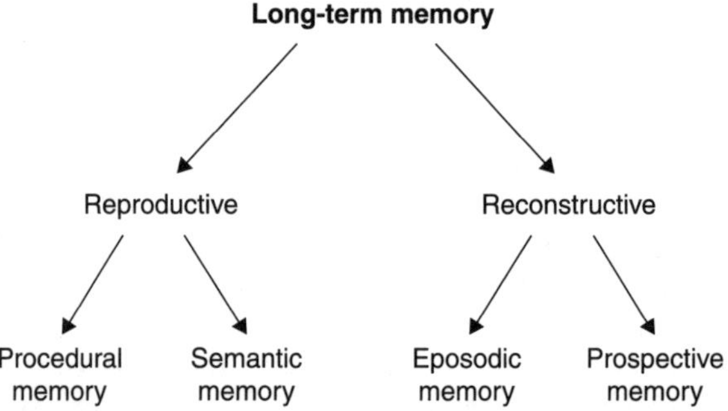

Figure 3.2 A new taxonomy of long-term memory systems.

(6) Within the framework of the Fuzzy Trace Theory (Reyna & Brainerd, 1995), reconstructive memory is based on gist information, whereas reproductive memory also requires verbatim details (i.e., information regarding the surface forms of the experienced items).

This new taxonomy allows us to distinguish between different types of forgetting, both in normal conditions and following acquired brain damage.

In reproductive memory, when learning is completed, memories are persistent, with words (Bahrick, Bahrick, & Wittlinger, 1975) and gestures (Bartolo, Cubelli, & Della Sala, 2008) being maintained over time. Information can temporarily be unavailable; for instance, in the case of blockings, which depend on physical, cognitive, or emotional factors. Exchange and substitution errors may occur in lexical access and they are very useful in depicting models of language production (e.g., Garrett, 1975). Semantic memory is more vulnerable than procedural memory because in retrieval more attentional resources are required (but consider inconsistency of motor performance in athletes, for example; Wrisberg & Anshel, 1989). Also frequency of use can play a causal role in forgetting. If after learning, information is not used again, it appears to be lost, but it can be relearned very rapidly (e.g., the algorithm for computing the root square or the rules for playing bridge), or retrieved when appropriate cues are given (e.g., the names of schoolmates); in behaviouristic terms, spontaneous recovery occurs. In sum, in reproductive memory forgetting consists of information unavailability, but if learning is concluded, that is, the ability to reproduce the target concepts and behaviours is acquired, information is never lost.

The picture is very different following brain damage. First of all, category disorders have been frequently described. Patients with semantic memory disorders can show deficits limited to animals (Crutch & Warrington, 2003; Samson & Pillon, 2003), fruit and vegetables (Caramazza & Shelton, 1998; Hart & Gordon, 1992), or man-made objects (Sacchett & Humphreys, 1992). Similarly, patients with limb apraxia, which reflects an impairment of procedural memory, can show selective deficits affecting transitive (Fukutake, 2003; Heath, Almeida, Roy, Black, & Westwood, 2003) or intransitive (Cubelli, Marchetti, Boscolo, & Della Sala, 2000) gestures. Moreover, learned concepts and behaviour, which in normal conditions are treated as a whole, in these patients result in being disintegrated. For example, patients with semantic memory draw objects from memory with distinctive features omitted, added, or substituted. Cubelli (1995) reported on a patient who drew a goose with four legs, an elephant without trunk and tusks, and a giraffe with two humps. Analogously, patients with ideomotor apraxia produce perseveration, omission, or misordering errors in using objects or imitating well-known symbolic gestures (Rothi, Mack, Verfaellie, Brown, & Heilman, 1988).

Reconstructive memory is characterized by distortion (Schacter, 1995). Monitoring failures (misattribution errors), cognitive and emotional biases, and suggestibility (the tendency to incorporate in memory misleading information coming from different sources) can lead to false memories, either events that never happened or true episodes in the wrong contexts. In the retrieval phase of episodic memory, all information previously acquired concurs in creating new memories. Semantic knowledge and schemata can induce errors in free recall based on plausible inferences (Brewer & Treyens, 1981); invalid cues can also lead to errors in recognition, if consistent with stereotypes and prejudices (Boon & Davies, 1987). Expertise can support memory (e.g., Chase & Simon, 1973; Long & Prat, 2002; Voss, Vesonder, & Spilich, 1980). However, in certain situations it can lead to a defective performance characterized by domain-specific memory errors (Castel, McCabe, Roediger, & Heitman, 2007). Also post-event misinformation can be a powerful source of forgetting by causing retroactive interference (Loftus, 2007). By definition, every memory implies a change; therefore, in episodic memory there is nothing to be learnt or lost. Decay does not matter in reconstructive memory and forgetting has to be considered as the natural consequence of the memory process.

In everyday life, to act relies on remembering past events, even those encountered only once and processed incidentally. Therefore, the encoding phase, which rarely consists in intentional learning, is also involved in forgetting. When faced with a scene or an event, we are able to remember sense and emotions, but we cannot acquire all relevant and irrelevant details, as if memory operated like a video-camera (Clifasefi, Garry, & Loftus, 2007). We remember only what we code and we code on the basis of actual knowledge and purposes, other information being definitely lost. As suggested by Tulving and Thomson (1973): "Specific encoding operations performed on what is perceived determine what is stored, and what is stored determines what retrieval cues are effective in providing access to what is stored" (p. 369). Also prospective memory implies a reconstruction process; it is sensitive to interference and requires reminder cues associated with a previously established intention (Guynn, McDaniel, & Einstein, 1998).

Patients with anterograde amnesia show memory failures and produce confabulations that are akin to the errors produced by normal people (Borsutzkya, Fujiwara, Brand, & Markowitsch, 2008; Dewar, Cowan, & Della Sala, 2007). However, there are phenomena that are specific to amnesia. For example, at variance with control participants, patients with lesions involving the hippocampus show no benefit from conditions with reduced retroactive interference (Cowan, Beschin, & Della Sala, 2004). Further, some confabulating patients produce implausible, incoherent, and internally inconsistent memories that are insensitive to evidence and logical arguments (Moscovitch, 1995).

In conclusion, the study of forgetting cannot be separated from the study of memory. To understand forgetting in normal and pathological conditions, theories of memory and learning are needed. The distinction between reproductive and reconstructive memory can provide a useful framework to investigate forgetting as specific to each memory component and is qualitatively different in the normal population and brain-damaged patients. Normal forgetting in reproductive memory is mainly characterized by omission errors, whereas evidence of forgetting in reconstructive memory is for the most part commission errors (for the distinction between omission and commission errors, see Schacter, 2001). In brain-damaged patients, instead, forgetting may be qualitatively different, and emerges as phenomena which reveal the breakdown of the memory systems and their contents.

With respect to that of Squire (1987), the taxonomy proposed here maintains the idea that memory of the past should include separate components for facts (semantic), events (episodic), and skills and habits (procedural). However, while the original taxonomy is based on how specific contents are attested, the distinction between reproductive and reconstructive memory reflects the assumption that different memory functions correspond to different memory processes. To prove that geographical facts or past events have been memorized, verbal or nonverbal assertions are needed, whereas to prove that one is able to play a musical instrument or to play soccer specific actions must be performed (verbal statements or miming are not definitive evidence of knowledge). Therefore, the separation between declarative and nondeclarative memory refers to how different memory contents are retrieved. This is why procedural memory is considered separately relative to semantic and episodic memory. In contrast, the new taxonomy implies that memory should be split into two separate processes with different functional architecture. Memory contents are not described as different objects stored in different stands, but as the result of different cognitive processes. This is why semantic and procedural memories are thought of as sharing (at least in part) the same learning mechanisms, while episodic memory only is assumed to depend on narrative or creative processes.

The taxonomy proposed by Squire (1987) has a neurobiological rationale. The main purpose is to localize the memory components in the brain; for example, semantic and episodic memories are proposed to lie side by side because they share a dependence on medial temporal lobe structures that procedural memories do not have. However, it is worth noting that semantic and episodic memories are functionally independent and that, while the double dissociation has been frequently reported, very rarely are they simultaneously impaired and only after diffuse brain damage (Tanaka, Miyazawa, Hashimoto, Nakano, & Obayashi, 1999; Wheeler & McMillan, 2001). In contrast, it is well documented that deficits affecting episodic and prospective memories coexist in anterograde amnesia (e.g., Parkin, 1997) and that when acquired knowledge is lost it tends to involve the meaning and attributes of words as well as information about objects and actions (e.g., Dumont, Ska, & Joanette, 2000; Gainotti & Lemmo, 1976). Based on functional and neuropsychological grounds, the taxonomy suggested in this chapter should be considered as a substitute for the standard ones.

In Naccache's (2003) book on Judaism and neuroscience, he discussed the religious commandment to remember. In particular, he reviewed the discussion on the biblical passage "Remember what Amalek did to you on your journey . . . Do not forget" (Deuteronomy, 25, 17–19), where the double injunction seems to be a useless repetition of the commandment in conflict with the "principle of economy" which characterizes the holy text. There is a great debate regarding the meaning of this passage. However, if we consider that forgetting is not the opposite of remembering, we can state that there is no reiteration in the text. Further, we can understand why this precept is strongly related to the ritual of reading the book of Esther twice during the Jewish celebration of Purim. When reconstructing the past, we cannot avoid remembering and at the same time forgetting. In order to remember without forgetting, that is, to maintain facts over time, we need to repeat the past, that is, to reproduce it. Repetition, as well as reading, is essential for learning. The commandment to remember is therefore the commandment to study and learn.

References

Bahrick, H. P., Bahrick, P. O., & Wittlinger, R. P. (1975). Fifty years of memory for names and faces: A cross-sectional approach. *Journal of Experimental Psychology: General*, *104*, 54–75.

Bartlett, F. (1932). *Remembering*. Cambridge: Cambridge University Press.

Bartolo, A., Cubelli, R., & Della Sala S. (2008). Cognitive approach to the assessment of limb apraxia. *Clinical Neuropsychologist*, *22*, 27–45.

Boon, J. C. W., & Davies, G. M. (1987). Eyewitness memory rumors greatly exaggerated: Allport and Postman's apocryphal study. *Canadian Journal of Behavioural Science*, *19*, 430–440.

Borges, J. L. (1942/1998). *Collected fictions*. New York: Viking Penguin.

Borsutzkya, S., Fujiwara, E., Brand, M., & Markowitsch, H. J. (2008). Confabulations in alcoholic Korsakoff patients. *Neuropsychologia*, *46*, 3133–3143.

Brewer, W. F., & Treyens, J. C. (1981). Role of schemata in memory for places. *Cognitive Psychology*, *13*, 207–230.

Broadbent, D. E. (1971). *Decision and stress*. London: Academic Press.

Caramazza, A., & Shelton, J. R. (1998). Domain-specific knowledge systems in the brain: The animate–inanimate distinction. *Journal of Cognitive Neuroscience*, *10*, 1–34.

Castel, A. D., McCabe, D. P., Roediger, H. L. III, & Heitman, J. L. (2007). The dark side of expertise. Domain-specific memory errors. *Psychological Science*, *18*, 3–5.

Chase, W. G., & Simon, H. A. (1973). Perception in chess. *Cognitive Psychology*, *4*, 55–81.

Clifasefi, S. L., Garry, M., & Loftus, E. (2007). Setting the record (or video camera) straight on memory: The video camera model of memory and other memory myths. In S. Della Sala (Ed.), *Tall tales about the mind and brain* (pp. 60–75). New York: Oxford University Press.

Cohen, G., & Conway, M. A. (2008). *Memory in the real world*. Hove, UK: Psychology Press.

Cowan, N., Beschin, N., & Della Sala, S. (2004). Verbal recall in amnesiacs under conditions of diminished retroactive interference. *Brain*, *127*, 825–834.

Crutch, S. J., & Warrington, E. K. (2003). The selective impairment of fruit and vegetable knowledge: A multiple processing channels account of fine-grain category specificity. *Cognitive Neuropsychology, 20*, 355–372.

Cubelli, R. (1995). More on drawing in aphasia therapy. *Aphasiology, 9*, 78–83.

Cubelli, R., & Della Sala, S. (2009). Memories as re-presentations. *Cortex, 45*, 688–692.

Cubelli, R., Marchetti, C., Boscolo, G., & Della Sala, S. (2000). Cognition in action: Testing a model of limb apraxia. *Brain and Cognition, 44*, 144–165.

Darley, J. M., Gluckberg, S., & Kinchla, R. A. (1991). *Psychology*. Englewood Cliffs: New Jersey: Prentice Hall.

Dewar, M. T., Cowan, N. & Della Sala, S. (2007). Forgetting due to retroactive interference: A fusion of Müller and Pilzecker's (1900) early insights into forgetting and recent research on anterograde amnesia. *Cortex, 43*, 616–634.

Draaisma, D. (1995). *Metaphors of memory: A history of ideas about the mind.* Cambridge: Cambridge University Press.

Dumont, C., Ska, B., & Joanette, Y. (2000). Conceptual apraxia and semantic memory deficit in Alzheimer's disease: Two sides of the same coin? *Journal of International Neuropsychological Society, 6*, 693–703.

Ebbinghaus, H. (1885). *Über das Gedchtnis. Untersuchungen zur experimentellen Psychologie*. Leipzig: Duncker & Humblot.

Fukutake, T. (2003). Apraxia of tool use: An autopsy case of biparietal infarction. *European Neurology, 49*, 45–52.

Gainotti, G., & Lemmo, M. (1976). Comprehension of symbolic gestures in aphasia. *Brain and Language, 3*, 451–460.

Garrett, M. F. (1975). The analysis of sentence production. In G. H. Bower (Ed.), *The psychology of learning and motivation*. New York: Academic Press.

Gazzaniga, M. S., Ivry, R. B., & Mangun, G. R. (1998). *Cognitive neuroscience: The biology of the mind.* New York: Norton.

Graf, P., & Schacter, D. L. (1985). Implicit and explicit memory for new associations in normal and amnesic subjects. *Journal of Experimental Psychology: Learning, Memory, and Cognition, 11*, 501–518.

Guynn, M. J., McDaniel, M. A., & Einstein, G. O. (1998). Prospective memory: When reminders fail. *Memory & Cognition, 26*, 287–298.

Hart, J., & Gordon, B. (1992). Neural substrates for object knowledge. *Nature, 359*, 60–64.

Heath, M., Almeida, Q. J., Roy, E. A., Black, S. E., & Westwood, D. (2003). Selective dysfunction of tool-use: A failure to integrate somatosensation and action. *Neurocase, 9*, 156–163.

Hoad, T. F. (1996). *The Concise Oxford Dictionary of English Etymology*. Oxford: Oxford University Press.

James, W. (1890). *Principles of psychology*. New York: Henry Holt.

Keppel, G., & Underwood, B. J. (1962). Proactive inhibition in the short-term retention of single items. *Journal of Verbal Learning and Verbal Behavior, 1*, 153–161.

Lindsay, P. H., & Norman, D. A. (1977). *Human information processing: An introduction to psychology*. New York: Academic Press.

Loftus (2007). Forgetting: The fate of once learned, but "forgotten", material. In H. L. Roediger, Y. Dudai, & S. M. Fitzpatrick (Eds.), *Science of memory: Concepts* (pp. 339–343). Oxford: Oxford University Press.

Long, D. L., & Prat, C. S. (2002). Memory for Star Trek: The role of prior knowledge in recognition revisited. *Journal of Experimental Psychology: Learning, Memory, and Cognition*, *28*, 1073–1082.

Luria, A. R. (1968). *The mind of a mnemonist: A little book about a vast memory*. New York: Basic Books.

Moscovitch, M. (1995). Confabulation. In D. Schacter. (Ed.), *Memory distortion* (pp. 226–251). Cambridge, MA: Harvard University Press.

Naccache, L. (2003). *Quatre exercices de pensée juive pour cerveaux réfléchis. Le judaïsme à la lumière des neurosciences*. Paris: Editions In Press.

Nicolas, S. (2003). *La Psychologie cognitive*. Paris: Armand Colin.

Norman, K. A., & Schacter, D. L. (1996). Implicit memory, explicit memory, and false recollection: A cognitive neuroscience perspective. In L. M. Reder (Ed.), *Implicit memory and metacognition* (pp. 229–257). Hillsdale, NJ: Lawrence Erlbaum Associates, Inc.

Parkin, A. J. (1997). *Memory and amnesia: An introduction* (2nd ed.). Hove, UK: Psychology Press.

Plato (2004). *Theaetetus*. Toronto: Penguin Classic.

Radvansky, G. A. (2006). *Human memory*. Boston: Allyn & Bacon.

Reyna, V. F., & Brainerd, C. J. (1995). Fuzzy-trace theory: Some foundational issues. *Learning and Individual Differences*, *7*, 145–162.

Ribot, T. (1881). *Les Maladies de la mémoire*. Paris: Germer Baillière.

Roediger, H. L., Dudai, Y., & Fitzpatrick, S. M. (2007). *Science of memory: Concepts*. Oxford: Oxford University Press.

Rothi, L. J. G., Mack, L., Verfaellie, M., Brown, P., & Heilman, K. M. (1988). Ideomotor apraxia: Error pattern analysis. *Aphasiology*, *2*, 381–388.

Rubin D. C. (2007). Forgetting: Its role in the science of memory. In H. L. Roediger, Y. Dudai, & S. M. Fitzpatrick (Eds.), *Science of memory: Concepts* (pp. 325–328). Oxford: Oxford University Press.

Rubin D. C., Rahal T. A., & Poon, L. W. (1974). Things learned in early adulthood are remembered best. *Memory & Cognition*, *26*, 3–19.

Sacchett, C., & Humphreys, G. W. (1992). Calling a squirrel a squirrel but a canoe a wigwam: A category-specific deficit for artefactual objects and body parts. *Cognitive Neuropsychology*, *9*, 73–86.

Samson, D., & Pillon, A. (2003). A case of impaired knowledge for fruit and vegetables. *Cognitive Neuropsychology*, *20*, 373–400.

Schacter. D. (1995). *Memory distortion*. Cambridge, MA: Harvard University Press.

Schacter, D. L. (2001). *The seven sins of memory: How the mind forgets and remembers*. Boston, MA: Houghton Mifflin.

Squire, L. R. (1987). *Memory and brain*. New York: Oxford University Press.

Squire, L. R. (2004). Memory systems of the brain: A brief history and current perspective. *Neurobiology of Learning and Memory*, *82*, 171–177.

Squire, L. R. (2007). Memory systems: A biological concept. In H. L. Roediger, Y. Dudai, & S. M. Fitzpatrick (Eds.), *Science of memory: Concepts* (pp. 339–343). Oxford: Oxford University Press.

Squire, L. R., & Zola, S. M. (1996). Structure and function of declarative and non-declarative memory systems. *Proceedings of the National Academic Sciences USA*, *93*, 13515–13522.

Squire, L. R., & Zola-Morgan, S. (1988). Memory: Brain systems and behavior. *Trends in Neuroscience*, *11*, 170–175.

Tanaka, Y., Miyazawa, Y., Hashimoto, R., Nakano, I., & Obayashi, T. (1999). Postencephalitic focal retrograde amnesia after bilateral anterior temporal lobe damage. *Neurology*, *53*, 344–350.

Tulving, E. (1972). Episodic and semantic memory. In E. Tulving & W. Donaldson (Eds.), *Organization of memory* (pp. 381–403). New York: Academic Press.

Tulving, E. (1974). Cue-depending forgetting. *American Scientist*, *62*, 74–82.

Tulving, E., & Thomson, D. M. (1973). Encoding specificity and retrieval processes in episodic memory. *Psychological Review*, *80*, 352–373.

Voss, J. F., Vesonder, G. T., & Spilich, G. J. (1980). Text generation and recall by high-knowledge and low-knowledge individuals. *Journal of Verbal Learning and Verbal Behavior*, *19*, 651–667.

Wechsler, D. (1997). *Wechsler Memory Scale-Third Edition: Administration and scoring manual*. San Antonio, TX: Psychological Corporation.

Wheeler, M. A., & McMillan, C. T. (2001). Focal retrograde amnesia and the episodic–semantic distinction. *Cognitive, Affective & Behavioral Neuroscience*, *1*, 22–36.

Winograd, E. (1988). Some observations on prospective remembering. In M. M. Gruneberg, P. E. Morris, & R. N. Sykes (Eds.), *Practical aspects of memory: Current research and issues* (pp. 348–353). Chichester: Wiley.

Wixted, J. T. (2007). Forgetting: It's not just the opposite of remembering. In H. L. Roediger, Y. Dudai, & S. M. Fitzpatrick (Eds.), *Science of memory: Concepts* (pp. 329–335). Oxford: Oxford University Press.

Wrisberg, C. A., & Anshel, M. H. (1989). The effect of cognitive strategies on free throw shooting performance of young athletes. *Sport Psychologist*, *3*, 95–104.

4 Forgetting in memory models

Arguments against trace decay and consolidation failure

Gordon D. A. Brown

University of Warwick Coventry, UK, and
University of Western Australia, Crawley, Australia

Stephan Lewandowsky

University of Western Australia, Crawley, Australia

Introduction

The chapters in this volume all reference causes of forgetting, but the variety of possible causes (and continued lack of consensus regarding them in different strands of the literature) is striking. Here we examine insights into trace decay, interference, and consolidation that have emerged from recent computational and mathematical models of memory. We suggest that such models: (1) allow rejection of temporal decay as a primary cause of forgetting even in short-term memory tasks; (2) undermine the inference from forgetting data to a distinction between separate short-term and long-term memory systems (STS vs. LTS); (3) offer an alternative explanation, in terms of temporal distinctiveness and interference, for most if not all of the behavioural evidence that has previously been taken as evidence for consolidation.

Two key theoretical issues underpin the present discussion. The first of these concerns the putative distinction between two memory systems that are dedicated to the storage of information over the short and the long term (STS and LTS respectively), and the second concerns the importance of consolidation failure as a cause of forgetting.

STS vs. LTS

Although the utility of a theoretical distinction between STS and LTS has often been questioned (Crowder, 1989; Melton, 1963), only recently have specific models emerged that claim to account for both short-term and long-term memory phenomena within a unified framework. For example, one of our own models (Brown, Neath, & Chater, 2007) asserts that the mechanisms underlying retrieval and forgetting are the same over both short and long timescales, thus questioning the case for a STS–LTS distinction. Here we focus on just one of the traditional arguments for a distinction between memory systems – viz. the assumption of different causes of forgetting from STS (temporal decay) and LTS (proactive and retroactive interference). To anticipate: we conclude that there is no evidence that time-based decay is the sole or even primary cause of forgetting over the short term, thus undermining one piece of evidence from forgetting for the traditional distinction.

Other arguments that are consistent with our perspective can be found elsewhere (e.g., Bhatarah, Ward, & Tan, 2008; Brown, Chater, & Neath, 2008; Brown, Della Sala, Foster, & Vousden, 2007; Neath & Brown, 2006; Tan & Ward, 2000; although see Davelaar, Goshen-Gottstein, Ashkenazi, Haarmann, & Usher, 2005). In particular, we note that interference-based models such as those of Lewandowsky and others (Lewandowsky & Farrell, 2008; Oberauer & Lewandowsky, 2008) and Brown et al. (2007) can account for forgetting data that have previously been assumed to implicate a STS–LTS distinction, and that empirical evidence that has been taken in support of temporal decay can be reinterpreted (Lewandowsky & Brown, 2005; Lewandowsky & Oberauer, 2008; Lewandowsky, Oberauer, & Brown, 2009a).

Consolidation

The second theoretical issue addressed by the present chapter is that of consolidation as a primary factor underpinning memory and forgetting. Consolidation refers to the idea that memories continue to strengthen after they have been formed, and that they thus become more resilient to forgetting over time (e.g., Wixted, 2005). As Wixted (2004b, 2005) notes, consolidation has featured prominently in theorizing on forgetting in the neurosciences for several decades, whereas most cognitive approaches have relied exclusively on alternative notions such as interference or decay. Indeed, not a single recent formal model of memory within a cognitive tradition ascribes an important role to consolidation (e.g., Botvinick & Plaut, 2006; Brown, Neath, et al., 2007; Brown, Preece, & Hulme, 2000; Burgess & Hitch, 1999, 2006; Davelaar et al., 2005; Gillund & Shiffrin, 1984; Henson, 1998; Howard & Kahana, 2002; Oberauer & Lewandowsky, 2008; Page & Norris, 1998; Polyn, Norman, & Kahana, 2009; Raaijmakers & Shiffrin, 1981; Sederberg, Howard, & Kahana, 2008; Shiffrin & Steyvers, 1997). Although these models differ in many respects (e.g., whether forgetting is due primarily to temporal decay, or interference, or encoding failure, or lack of temporal distinctiveness) there is remarkable, albeit implicit, agreement about the unimportance of consolidation. Notwithstanding their omission of consolidation processes, these models can explain a plethora of findings, including a variety of forgetting phenomena. Perhaps not surprisingly, an isolated but notable exception to the models' success is their inability to address data that have been taken as evidence for the importance of consolidation (see Dewar, Cowan, & Della Sala, 2007).

Conversely, models of memory that do emphasize consolidation (McClelland, McNaughton, & O'Reilly, 1995; Meeter & Murre, 2005; Norman & O'Reilly, 2003) handle the data implicating consolidation, but they typically do not address the rich data sets that are traditionally taken as the explananda for cognitive models of memory.

The central question we address, then, is the following: Are current cognitive models deficient because they include no provision for consolidation? Or might the behavioural evidence that has been taken as strong support for consolidation be interpretable in other ways? To foreshadow our principal conclusion, we endorse the latter hypothesis by suggesting that a temporal distinctiveness model of memory can account for data that have hitherto been taken to implicate consolidation.

We proceed as follows. First, we review and reinterpret several sources of evidence for temporal decay, and we conclude that decay is not a primary cause of forgetting in the short term. Second, we consider the form of the forgetting function, and show that (contrary to previous views) it provides support neither for a distinction between STS and LTS nor (as has sometimes been argued, see below) for consolidation. Third, we explore well-known cases where memory *improves* over time (the recency-to-primacy shift) and show that such phenomena not only provide further evidence against trace decay but can also be readily interpreted without recourse to consolidation. In the fourth and final section of the chapter, we directly confront evidence for consolidation in memory and reinterpret the data within a cognitive model that includes no consolidation. Note that owing to space constraints, we restrict consideration to human *behavioural* data only. We do not consider data from imaging studies or lesioning studies involving nonhuman animals. We recognize the potential importance of those sources of data but they are beyond the scope of the present chapter. A case for consolidation as a psychological variable must in any case be supported by behavioural data.

Reinterpreting evidence against forgetting due to time-based decay

There has been a long-standing consensus that decay plays no role in forgetting over the long term (Jenkins & Dallenbach, 1924). Scholars of short-term memory likewise initially eschewed the notion of decay (Atkinson & Shiffrin, 1971), although it gained prominence with Baddeley's phonological loop model (Baddeley, Thomson, & Buchanan, 1975) and decay continues to be central to a number of recent models of short-term memory (e.g., Burgess & Hitch, 1999; Page & Norris, 1998). This theoretical commitment to short-term decay sits alongside a pervasive agreement in the field that long-term forgetting does not involve temporal decay. Parsimony alone implies that a unitary time-invariant forgetting mechanism would be preferable, and we now show that this preference is buttressed by much empirical support.

What empirical evidence could differentiate between time-based decay and other forms of forgetting? At first glance, this issue may appear trivial. One simply extends the amount of time that information resides in memory and observes how much additional forgetting occurs. Alas, closer inspection reveals two problems that render the issue far from trivial. First, it is a priori unclear exactly how much forgetting would be expected on a decay view. Suppose recall declines from .81 to .80 after a few seconds' delay. Is this evidence for decay? What about a decline from .80 to .50? This problem is best resolved by interpreting data only with respect to *quantitative* predictions of the models under consideration (Lewandowsky et al., 2009a; Oberauer & Lewandowsky, 2008). Second, when confronted with unanticipated outcomes, theorists can invoke auxiliary processes to explain the data. For example, if forgetting is absent, decay theorists can appeal to surreptitious compensatory rehearsal that reverses the effects of decay, thus masking its presence (Vallar & Baddeley, 1982). Conversely, an interference view can handle unpredicted forgetting by postulating that some activity during retention interfered with memory (Lewandowsky, Geiger, & Oberauer, 2008a). In order to avoid these interpretative problems, two conditions must be met: (1) rehearsal must be controlled; (2) retention intervals must be kept free of interference. Unfortunately, these two goals are in conflict with each other. To disable rehearsal, there must be some cognitive activity (e.g., the overt recitation of irrelevant material), but this activity could also create interference. Two methodologies have recently emerged that satisfy both goals.

Berman, Jonides, and Lewis (2009) exploited the fact that in short-term recognition, negative probes that were on the preceding trial's study list are generally rejected more slowly than completely novel lures. For example, response latencies to the probe "lion" after study of the list "cat", "table", "truck" are dependent on whether or not "lion" had been studied on the preceding trial – notwithstanding the fact that the preceding list is now irrelevant and rehearsal of those items entirely counterproductive. Berman et al. found that this disadvantage for recently studied lures diminished only negligibly when the inter-trial interval was increased from .3 to 10 s, whereas it was eliminated by insertion of a single intervening study-test trial of equal (10 s) duration. Thus, contrary to what would be expected on a decay view, no longer relevant information lingers in short-term memory undiminished over time unless cleared by intervening cognitive events. This methodology satisfies the two constraints just mentioned because (1) rehearsal of no longer relevant material after its test is counterproductive and hence assuming its presence is difficult to justify; (2) inter-trial intervals were entirely free of interfering activity.

The second methodology was developed by Lewandowsky, Duncan, and Brown (2004) and involved blocking of rehearsal during immediate serial recall by overt articulation of an irrelevant word. Retention time was varied by training participants to recall at different speeds (.4, .8, and 1.6 s/item), thus delaying recall of the last item by over 5 s at the slowest compared to the fastest speed. This added delay reduced performance only negligibly, suggesting that, although compensatory rehearsal was blocked by articulation, there was little manifestation of temporal decay. A similar result was obtained by Cowan et al. (2006) using a related procedure. Children were either asked to recall a list at "whatever speed seemed best" or "as quickly as possible". Recall times decreased from .82 s/item to .5 s/item (a speed-up in excess of 30%) but left recall essentially unchanged. Although rehearsal was not explicitly controlled, it appears unlikely that, when instructed to recall at a comfortable pace, children would have withheld their responses merely to rehearse.

In a recent extension to this methodology, Oberauer and Lewandowsky (2008) added yet another task during retrieval to block possible "attentional" forms of refreshing (e.g., Hudjetz & Oberauer, 2007) that might augment conventional articulatory rehearsal. In addition to overt articulation of an irrelevant word, participants performed a symbolic two-alternative choice task in between recalling list items. Increasing the number of articulations and choice responses from 1 to 4 significantly delayed recall (by up to 14 s for the last list item) but had only a negligible effect on memory (reducing accuracy by .005 per second additional delay). This appears to be a general result, holding across many experiments (Lewandowsky et al., 2009a). Importantly, when all experiments are considered together, the data exhibit considerably less forgetting than the minimum amount that decay models must predict (Lewandowsky et al., 2009a). Intriguingly, these findings mesh well with recent studies of forgetting in amnesia, which also find that memory over intermediate time periods can be substantially improved under conditions where interference is minimized (Cowan, Beschin, & Della Sala, 2004; Della Sala, Cowan, Beschin, & Perini, 2005).

To explain the results from the studies just reviewed, proponents of inexorable temporal decay would need to argue that some form of memory refreshing persisted despite a variety of measures to the contrary. Specifically, decay proponents would need to argue that people continued to rehearse tested and no-longer-relevant material (Berman et al., 2009); they would have to assume that people were rehearsing while articulating irrelevant material out loud (Lewandowsky et al., 2004); and they would have to assume that people were rehearsing while articulating out loud and performing an attention-demanding symbolic choice task (Oberauer & Lewandowsky, 2008). We do not consider those arguments plausible.

How can these recent data that provide evidence against decay in immediate memory be reconciled with the pervasive "word-length effect" (WLE)? The WLE refers to the finding that words that take longer to pronounce (e.g., "hippopotamus", "confederacy") are sometimes remembered more poorly than short words ("buck", "pink"). On a decay hypothesis, the fact that differences in pronunciation durations of only 150–200 ms per word result in poorer recall arises because long words have more time to decay before they can be rehearsed or output. At first glance, the WLE strongly implicates decay and it has been cited as "perhaps the best remaining solid evidence in favour of temporary memory storage" (Cowan, 1995, p. 42).

We offer a different perspective based on arguments recently advanced by Lewandowsky and Oberauer (2008). Their principal argument rests on the fact that the WLE represents a correlation between two measures – articulation duration and memory – and it therefore inherits all interpretative problems that beset correlations. The WLE is correlational irrespective of whether one compares words of different syllabic complexity ("hippopotamus" vs. "gun") or restricts consideration to a purely duration-based WLE involving words of equal syllabic complexity but differing pronunciation durations (e.g., "platoon" vs. "racket"). Articulation duration is, in principle, correlated with many other features that influence a word's memorability. Hence, articulation duration may simply be a proxy variable for something else that determines memorability, and notwithstanding commendably thorough attempts to the contrary (Mueller, Seymour, Kieras, & Meyer, 2003), it is impossible in principle to identify, let alone control, all of these correlated features. This lack of control opens the door for alternative explanations of the WLE not involving decay. Accordingly, a number of studies have found that the WLE arises only with some particular stimuli (Baddeley et al., 1975), is absent in others (Lovatt, Avons, & Masterson, 2000), and sometimes even reversed (i.e., longer words are recalled better) for yet other stimuli (Caplan, Rochon, & Waters, 1992; Lovatt et al., 2000; Lovatt, Avons, & Masterson, 2002; Neath, Bireta, & Surprenant, 2003).[1]

Another recent line of research that has been taken as evidence for trace decay comes from studies of the time-based resource sharing (TBRS) model (Barrouillet, Bernardin, & Camos, 2004; Barrouillet & Camos, 2009). For example, using a complex span task, Portrat, Barrouillet, and Camos (2008) found that memory is reduced when the time taken to complete a between-item processing task is increased while the time available for rehearsal is controlled. Such results have been taken to reflect the operation of time-based decay. However, Lewandowsky and Oberauer (in press) showed instead that the Portrat et al. (2008) results were due to attentional processes occurring after errors on the distractor task, and Lewandowsky, Oberauer, and Brown (2009b) argued more generally against the suggestion that complex-span data implicate decay.

We conclude that a strong case can be made against a role for trace decay in forgetting over the short term.

The form of the forgetting curve

If our preceding arguments against decay are correct, it follows that differential causes of forgetting cannot be used to motivate a distinction between separate STS and LTS systems. However, irrespective of any appeal to short-term decay, forgetting data have been used to argue for a distinction between two memory systems in a different way, based purely on the putative form of the forgetting function. Specifically, it has been argued that the form of the forgetting curve is different over the short term and the long term, consistent with the suggestion that different memory systems are involved at different timescales. In addition, the form of the forgetting curve has been used as evidence for consolidation. Specifically, the fact that when two memories are of equal strength, forgetting appears to be slower for the older of the two (Jost's Second Law: Wixted, 2004a) has been taken to support the idea that older memories are more resistant to forgetting because they have had more time to consolidate (see e.g., Wixted, 2004a, 2004b for a critique of alternative interpretations). In the following, we argue against both of these inferences that have been drawn from the form of the forgetting function.

We begin by highlighting the fact that relatively few recent formal models of memory have been applied to the form of forgetting functions. Although there have been sophisticated and extended empirical attempts to determine the equation that best characterizes the forgetting function (e.g., Rubin & Wenzel, 1994; Wixted & Ebbesen, 1990, 1997), a parallel effort involving process-level or mathematical models has been largely absent (although see Anderson & Schooler, 1991; Sikstrom, 2002). As a first step towards redressing this deficiency, we present a simple temporal distinctiveness model which assumes a single mechanism for forgetting at both short and long timescales. In the model, all forgetting is due to interference and there is no role for consolidation. However, we show that the model nonetheless (a) gives rise to forgetting functions of a variety of forms and (b) handles Jost's Second Law. To foreshadow, we conclude that (a) the search for "the" form of the forgetting function will necessarily remain inconclusive and (b) that the generally agreed characteristics of the forgetting curve – viz. that older memories are forgotten more slowly: Jost's Second Law – does not implicate consolidation.

What are the relevant properties of the forgetting curve? A number of researchers have suggested that the time course of forgetting is well described by a power law (e.g., Anderson & Schooler, 1991; Wixted & Ebbesen, 1990, 1997), while others have argued that it is not (Chechile, 2006; Rubin, Hinton, & Wenzel, 1999; Wickens, 1999). A power function has the form $P = aT^{-b}$ where P is the measure of memory performance, T is time elapsed, and a and b are constants. In contrast to the exponential function ($P = a\, e^{-bT}$) which is characterized by a constant rate of loss, the power function shows initially rapid forgetting that then slows over time. This is a desirable property because, ongoing debate notwithstanding, it is widely accepted that the rate of forgetting slows over time. If you can remember 100 French vocabulary words from your school education 20 years ago, and I can remember 100 French vocabulary words from 200 I learnt yesterday, it seems likely that you will remember more words than I do in a week's time (assuming that neither of us engages in any further learning in the meantime).

We (Brown, Neath, et al., 2007) used a simple temporal distinctiveness model, SIMPLE (for Scale Invariant Memory, Perception, and LEarning), to address the relationship between model architecture and the form of the forgetting function over different timescales. Informally, SIMPLE assumes that the confusability between any two memory traces depends on the ratio of the times that have elapsed between their encodings and the time of recall. The lower that ratio, the lower the confusability among items, and hence the more likely it is that an item is recalled correctly. Hence recent items are less confusable and hence more memorable than are more distant events. For example, items that were encoded 1 s and 2 s ago are less confusable (ratio of .5) than are items from 5 and 6 seconds ago (.83). The mechanism also favours items that were separated in time over others that occurred in close succession. For example, items that occurred 5 s and 10 s ago (ratio .5) are less confusable than items that occurred 7 s and 8 s ago (.88), even though the average retention interval is equal for both pairs of items. It follows that items from further in the past, and items that occurred near each other in time, will be more difficult to recall. As we will see below, this property causes the model to expect slower forgetting of older items without recourse to consolidation.[2]

More formally, the three key assumptions of the model are as follows:

(1) Items are represented by their position within a multidimensional psychological space, with one of those dimensions necessarily devoted to representing time. In the present treatment we would be concerned only with this temporal dimension.
(2) The similarity between any two items in memory is a declining function of the distance separating them in psychological space.
(3) The probability of recalling an item is inversely proportional to that item's summed similarity to all other response alternatives, as illustrated above by the ratios between elapsed times of item pairs.

These assumptions are implemented in the model as follows (the following section may be omitted for readers not interested in the technical details). A more complete specification of the model, including its application to multidimensional memory representations, can be found in Brown, Neath, et al. (2007).

Encoding in multidimensional space

Memory representations are organized along a temporal dimension that reflects the (logarithmically transformed) time since their encoding.

Similarity–distance metric

Following the categorization literature, SIMPLE assumes that the similarity of any two items in memory is a reducing exponential function of the distance between them in psychological space:

$$\eta_{i,j} = e^{-cd_{i,j}},$$

where $\eta_{i,j}$ is the similarity between items i and j and d_{ij} the distance between them (i.e., in this instance, the distance along the temporal axis that separates the two items). Because the timescale is assumed to be logarithmically transformed, the similarity between two items that are differentiated only along the temporal dimension can be equivalently expressed as the ratio of their temporal distances raised to the power c, thus permitting the intuitive analysis presented earlier.

Items that are very close have a similarity approaching unity (i.e., their distance is near 0 and hence the ratio of their temporal distances will be close to 1.0), whereas items that are more psychologically distant have a similarity that, in the extreme, approaches zero. The parameter c governs the rate of decline of similarity with distance. When combined with the logarithmic transformation of the temporal dimension, this similarity metric gives rise to the distinctiveness ratios mentioned earlier.

Similarity determines recall

The distinctiveness and hence discriminability of item i is inversely proportional to its summed similarity to every other potentially recallable item. Specifically, the discriminability of the memory trace for item i, D_i, is given by:

$$D_i = \frac{1}{\sum_{k=1}^{n} (\eta_{i,k})},$$

where n is the number of available response alternatives (normally this is just the number of list items).

In the full version of the model, discriminability translates into recall probability by taking into account the possibility of omissions. Omissions arise from thresholding of low retrieval probabilities by a sigmoid function: If D_i is the discriminability given by the preceding equation, the recall probability P_i is derived as:

$$P_i = \frac{1}{1 + e^{-s(D_i - t)}},$$

where t is the threshold and s determines the slope (or noisiness) of the transforming function. Any D_i that falls below the threshold engenders an omission.

We use the basic assumptions just described to examine forgetting as a function of time in the model. Forgetting in the model occurs over time not because of decay but because of interference – memories become less distinguishable from one another, and hence harder to retrieve, as they retreat into the temporal distance and lose temporal distinctiveness. A more complete account of the model's forgetting behaviour is given in Brown, Neath, et al. (2007); here we merely summarize findings of theoretical interest in the current context.

First of all, we found that small alterations in the parameters of the model, which were intuitively insignificant in terms of its underlying architecture, could change the apparent form of the forgetting curve produced. For example, the forgetting curve might be better described by a logarithmic function than a power law for some parameter settings, while the reverse could hold under different parameter settings (detailed model comparison to take into account the different flexibility of different functional forms was not undertaken, however). This sensitivity to parameter values was taken to suggest that there need be no simple correspondence between a model architecture and the form of the forgetting function that it predicts. It may therefore be that more than a century of effort (Rubin & Wenzel, 1994) of attempting definitively to establish the form of the forgetting curve (without a universally accepted result as yet) may have been misguided in the sense that the inference from the form of a forgetting curve to model architecture, or vice versa, may be far from transparent (see also Wickens, 1999).

Second, despite the above, we found that the model generally obeyed Jost's Second Law in that forgetting slowed over time. In other words, under a range of parameter settings, older memories were forgotten more slowly than younger memories of the same strength. A typical forgetting curve is shown in Figure 4.1 (described below). Reduced rates of forgetting over time occur naturally as a result of the ratio properties of the model. The confusability and hence discriminability in memory of any two items is, in the model, dependent on the ratio of the temporal distances of those items. That ratio will gradually approach unity as the items recede into the past, but the rate at which this happens will slow down over time. For example, consider two items that occurred 1 s ago and 2 s ago. Their confusability is 1/2. When a further 1 s of retention interval was passed, their confusability will have increased to 2/3. Now consider in contrast two items that occurred 100 s and 101 s ago – their confusability will be 100/101. But after a further 1 s of retention has past, the confusability of these items will have increased just to 101/102 – a very small increase. Although these confusabilities will not translate directly into recall probabilities (because confusability with other items and omission error probabilities will also be important), it is nevertheless intuitively clear why the forgetting rate is likely to decrease over time in a temporal ratio model such as SIMPLE. Crucially, this occurs as a natural consequence of the scale-invariant (ratio-like) properties of a model, and makes no reference to consolidation.

Finally, we found that there were situations in which the forgetting curve of the model was most accurately described by an exponential curve over the first 15 s or so of retention, and a power law thereafter. Figure 4.1 shows this behaviour of the model, with a different curve (of different functional form)

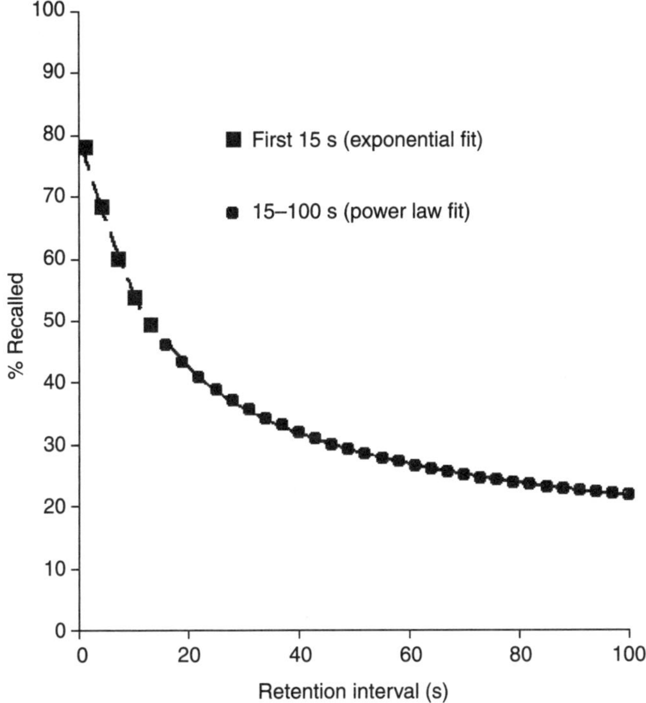

Figure 4.1 A typical forgetting curve produced by the SIMPLE model (see Brown, Neath, & Chater 2007 for details). The dashed line shows the best fitting exponential function to the first 15 s of retention; the unbroken line shows the best fitting power function to the retention function after 15 s.

fitted to the first 15 s of retention of a 5-item list (exponential curve: $R^2 = .99$) and subsequent retention (power function: $R^2 = .999$). Because such behaviour can emerge in a model in which the fundamental mechanism for forgetting remains unchanged with timescale, we suggest that such forgetting data cannot be used to mandate a distinction between different memory systems operating over the short and the long term.

In summary: we have used a temporal distinctness model of memory to show that (a) slower forgetting of older memories can readily be explained without recourse to consolidation; and (b) available forgetting data do not require the assumption of two distinct memory stores with correspondingly different forgetting functions at different timescales.

Recency to primacy shift

We next consider instances in which memory performance actually improves over time. At first glance, such improvements are readily and naturally explained by consolidation, and thus they constitute a particular challenge for alternative models. We focus on one manifestation of performance improvement over time known as the recency to primacy shift. When memory for a short list is tested immediately, the most recent items are almost always advantaged (unless their recall is postponed, as when memory for serial order is required). When a delay intervenes between presentation and test, the recency effect is reduced or abolished. Of greatest interest is the fact that performance on early list items may occasionally be better after a filled retention interval than on an immediate test (e.g., Bjork, 2001).

To clarify, the recency to primacy shift can refer to three different phenomena that are illustrated in Figure 4.2. Line A (identical in both panels) represents a typical pattern of performance on immediate testing – an extended

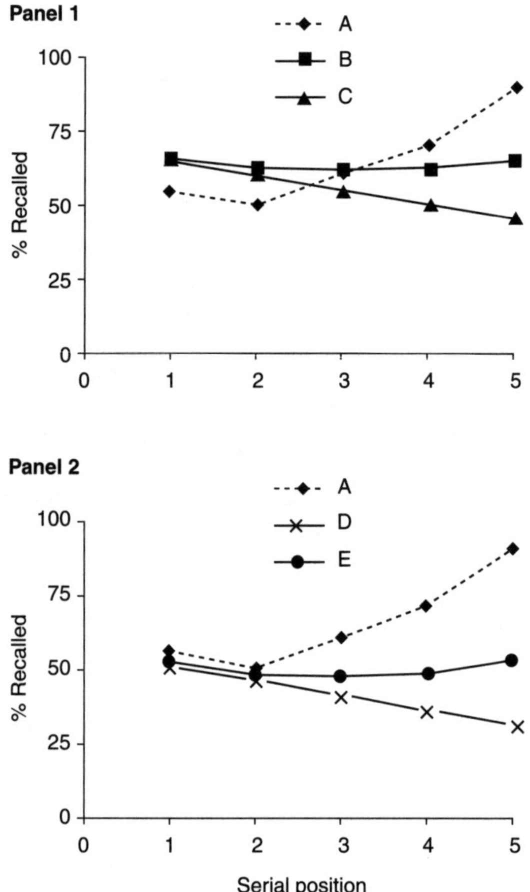

Figure 4.2 Illustration of various types of recency to primacy shift. Panel 1 illustrates increases in absolute performance on the primacy items. Panel 2 illustrates an increase in relative performance on the primacy items (see text for details).

recency gradient is seen. The remaining lines depict possible serial position curves after a filled delay. In all cases the recency effect is reduced. Panel 1 depicts two cases where performance on the primacy item(s) improves in absolute terms relative to their immediate performance. Line B shows the case where performance on the primacy item(s) has improved in absolute terms compared to immediate performance but not relative to later list items, and line C shows the case where primacy is increased in both absolute and relative terms after the delay. In panel 2, line D shows the case where greater relative but not absolute primacy is observed after the delay, and line E shows the case in which performance on the primacy items does not improve after a delay in either absolute or relative terms.

All five patterns have been found in the data. The extent to which patterns C and D occur is controversial, but our main concern here is with any case (such as that seen in B) in which performance on the primacy items improves over time. An initial demonstration of the recency–primacy shift (Wright, Santiago, Sands, Kendrick, & Cook, 1985) has been influential, and the absolute increase over time in performance on the primacy items – that is, patterns B and C in Figure 4.2 – has been found with a number of studies, species, and methodologies (Wright, 2007). We note that in at least some cases, however, the phenomenon has not proved robust. The recency to primacy shift was found by Korsnes et al. (1996) and by Korsnes and Magnussen (1996) in a serial-order memory paradigm (participants were presented with single items and required to respond with the serial position of that item), but Kerr, Ward, and Avons (1998) found that the effect could be explained in terms of response bias. Early findings of the recency to primacy shift in recognition memory (Neath, 1993; Neath & Knoedler, 1994) also failed to be consistently replicated by Kerr, Avons, and Ward (1999). However Knoedler, Hellwig, and Neath (1999) replicated the increase in primacy with a filled delay under a number of conditions, and Bjork (2001) reviews evidence of a shift towards primacy in a range of literatures.

In summary, although the evidence is mixed, we adopt as a working hypothesis the possibility that there are instances in which performance on primacy items increases over time in absolute terms. In free recall, such effects could reflect recall-order phenomena – if early-presented items are recalled first, they will be advantaged over recency items through experiencing less output interference. Many of the relevant data have, however, come from serial memory and recognition tasks (see above). Such data are clearly problematic for the concept of time-based trace decay, for it is hard to see how memory could actually improve over time in such accounts. But could those data not be handled quite naturally by a consolidation view? Although attractive at first glance, we argue against this possibility because, whenever a benefit is observed for primacy items, recent items would have an equal opportunity for consolidation during the increased retention interval. Thus, consolidation could only lead to an increase in either absolute or relative primacy under the (intuitively implausible) assumption that consolidation starts slowly, but then proceeds at an increasing rate after some time has passed (because unless there is an increasing rate of consolidation, the early items could never overtake the later ones).

By contrast, the recency to primacy shift again sits naturally within a temporal distinctiveness framework. Neath and Brown (2006) applied the SIMPLE model to the recency–primacy shift in recognition memory to show how the effect could be understood in terms of relative temporal distinctiveness. Here we illustrate with a more recent temporally extended version of the model. Brown, Chater, and Neath (2008) extended the ratio-rule temporal distinctiveness model of Brown, Neath, et al. (2007) to take account of the fact that items have a temporal extension – that is, they take up a contiguous slice of the temporal axis rather than a single point on it (the initial model made the simplifying assumption that the temporal locations of items could be treated as point sources, and this simplifying assumption is problematic when rehearsal data must be accommodated). The extended model preserves the assumption that memories are represented in terms of their positions along a logarithmically compressed timeline receding into the past, but additionally represents the proportion of the memory timeline taken up by each item. Even if each item has the same actual duration, recent items will occupy more of the timeline than will more temporally distant items, because the latter occupy a more compressed region of the temporal memory dimension. It is assumed that the probability of recalling an item is determined partly by the proportion of the timeline that it occupies. Such an assumption is consistent with a number of scale-invariant memory effects, such as the result of Maylor, Chater, and Brown (2001) showing that memories are retrieved at the same rate whether from the last week, month, or year.

Figure 4.3 shows the compressed timeline for immediate memory for a 4-item list and delayed recall of the same list. If, as just suggested, memorability

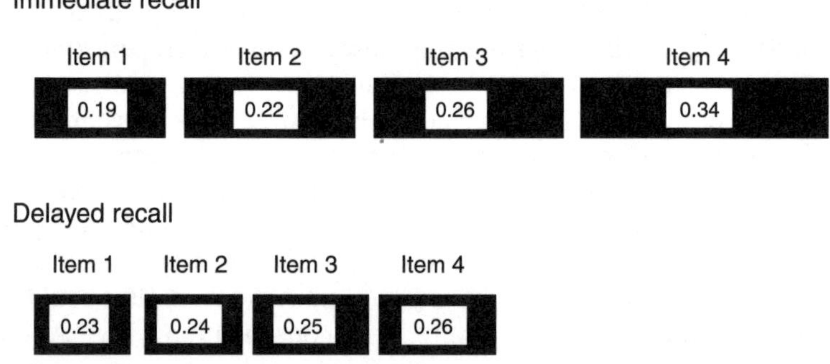

Figure 4.3 Illustration of a compressed timeline in memory for immediate recall (top) and delayed recall (bottom). Each filled black rectangle represents an item, with the width of the item indicating the amount of the memory timeline that it occupies. Numbers within the squares represent the proportion of the timeline occupied by each item.

is determined by the *proportion* of the memory timeline occupied by items, it is readily apparent that performance on the primacy items can increase after the filled retention interval, because the proportion of the timeline occupied by, for example, the first item increases in absolute terms (numbers within black squares denote proportion of total time occupied by an item). In terms of Figure 4.2, the pattern illustrated in panel 1, line B would be produced (see Bjork, 2001, for an alternative account).

In summary, we have argued that the recovery in memory of items over time (a) is problematic for trace decay models of memory, and (b) falls out naturally from a temporal distinctiveness framework without recourse to consolidation mechanisms. We now go on to argue that the same account can shed light on behavioural phenomena that have previously been taken as evidence for consolidation.

Consolidation

We have framed our discussion around the central question of whether cognitive models are deficient through not acknowledging a role for consolidation. Thus far, our critique of indirect evidence for consolidation – viz. the shape of the forgetting function, situations in which performance improves over time – revealed that the data can be equally (or better) accommodated by a distinctiveness model that does not involve consolidation. In this concluding section, we tackle head-on the behavioural data most widely cited in support of consolidation and, for each, offer an alternative theoretical interpretation in terms of temporal distinctiveness.

Temporal gradient of retroactive interference

A key finding is that the effect of retroactive interference is greater when it follows the target material in close temporal proximity. Wixted (2004b) beautifully reviews the relevant literature, much of which dates back almost a century, and we refer the reader to his summary (see also Dewar et al., 2007). The basic paradigm is illustrated schematically in Figure 4.4. The timeline is represented as time moving from left to right; i.e., the present is represented at the right-hand side of the figure. The three solid blocks at the left-hand end of each panel represent material to be learned, the shaded block represents interfering activity (whether similar or dissimilar to the to-be-learned material – the distinction is not needed for the point being made here) and the bar marked "recall" represents the time of retrieval. Thus the retention interval for the to-be-learned material (the solid blocks) is constant in all three panels of the figure. However, the time at which the interfering material occurs varies. In the top panel, the interfering material occurs immediately after the to-be-remembered material has been presented. In the middle panel, the interfering material occurs midway between the to-be-leaned material and the time of recall. In the lowest panel the interfering material occurs

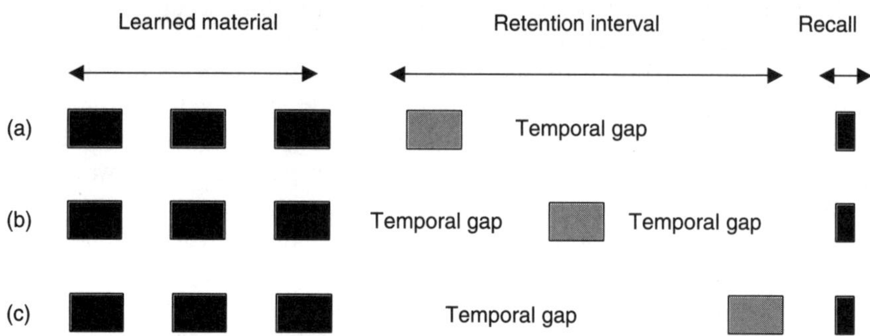

Figure 4.4 Illustration of the changing temporal distinctiveness of to-be-remembered items (filled black rectangles) as a function of the time of presentation of interfering material (filled shaded rectangles).

just before the time of retrieval. Empirically, as summarized by Wixted, the amount of material that is remembered is low when the retroactively interfering material follows on immediately after the to-be-remembered items (panel a), and higher when a long temporal gap intervenes between the learning and the interference (panel b). Performance may drop again when the interfering material immediately precedes retention (panel c), although this pattern is not always seen (e.g., Dewar, Garcia, Cowan, & Della Sala, in press, who find that amnesic patients benefit monotonically from delay of interfering material). The material giving rise to this generalization is dispersed and cannot be reviewed here; we instead take Wixted's summary as our starting point.

The temporal gradient of retroactive interference (RI) is the reducing effect of intervening interference as it becomes more temporally distant from the to-be-remembered material. This gradient sits very naturally with a consolidation account: the consolidation of the original material is assumed to be interrupted by the interfering material to a greater extent if the interfering material follows closely upon it (less time is available for consolidation of the learned items). However, on its own, consolidation is insufficient to explain the inverted-U shape of the temporal effects of RI. A second process is required to explain the impairment that is sometimes associated with interfering material occurring just before retrieval; this process is thought to be the high degree of competition provided by the interfering material at retrieval. Thus, the piece of behavioural evidence most widely cited in support of consolidation actually requires more than consolidation to explain it. By contrast, the entire temporal pattern of interference is naturally, and arguably more parsimoniously, consistent with a temporal-distinctiveness approach to memory. We now sketch how such an account could work.

A key feature of distinctiveness that was implied by our discussion so far, but not made explicit, is that temporally crowded items will be less discriminable, and hence harder to retrieve. Crucially, such interference is local

(Neath, Brown, McCormack, Chater, & Freeman, 2006) – only items that occupy nearby locations along the temporal continuum will interfere with each other. This principle is used in SIMPLE to explain a number of phenomena, such as proactive interference (Keppel & Underwood, 1962; Underwood, 1957) and the release from PI with the passage of time (Loess & Waugh, 1967). Indeed, temporal separation reduces proactive interference in AB–AD paradigms (Keppel, 1964; Underwood & Ekstrand, 1967; Underwood & Freund, 1968) and also over short time periods (Alin, 1968; Kincaid & Wickens, 1970; Peterson & Gentile, 1965). Moreover, there is ample evidence that temporally isolated items (those with longer temporal gaps surrounding them during presentation) are sometimes more easily remembered. Temporal isolation confers a recall advantage in free recall (Brown, Morin, & Lewandowsky, 2006), running memory span (Geiger & Lewandowsky, 2008), and memory for serial order when report order is unconstrained (Lewandowsky, Nimmo, & Brown, 2008b). Forward serial recall presents a clear exception to this pattern, however. Temporally isolated items show little or no advantage in recall in such tasks (e.g., Lewandowsky, Brown, Wright, & Nimmo, 2006).[3]

Temporal distinctiveness models, therefore, predict exactly the pattern noted by Wixted (2004b) – a greater interfering effect of material that is temporally proximal to either study or test – but without any reference to consolidation and on the basis of a single process that is at the heart of distinctiveness. We note that the effect of interference-test proximity is not always observed (Dewar et al., in press); the extent to which interfering material presented just before test will reduce recall may depend on details such as similarity between irrelevant and learned material, but this remains a topic for further research.

Moreover, the timescale-invariant properties of a temporal ratio model like SIMPLE enable it to predict time-based release from the threat of interference at a number of different timescales.

It turns out that the remaining sources of evidence for consolidation cited by Wixted (2004b) are subject to the same parsimonious reinterpretation within the distinctiveness framework.

Effects of sleep on memory

Sleep research has been of central importance in theorizing about consolidation (Meeter & Murre, 2004). It has long been known that a list of words is better remembered if it is followed by a retention interval during which the learner sleeps than if the learning is followed by the same retention interval filled not by sleep but by normal daily activity (Jenkins & Dallenbach, 1924). Sleep is assumed to protect memory from interference (e.g., Ellenbogen, Hulbert, Stickgold, Dinges, & Thompson-Schill, 2006), and it has been suggested that this reflects active consolidation processes that occur during sleep (e.g., Born, Rasch, & Gais, 2006). In support of a consolidation view, sleep's protective benefits are particularly pronounced if it occurs right after study. For example, Ekstrand (1972) showed that retention after a 24-hour retention period that included 8 hours of sleep was better if subjects slept right after study (81% recall) than if they slept right before test (66%). These and related findings are typically taken as evidence for consolidation – it is assumed that the process of consolidation continues during sleep, and that this is particularly beneficial early on during retention, whereas it is partially interrupted by the typical mental activities that otherwise fill the retention interval.

Again, however, the temporal distinctiveness model offers an alternative perspective without recourse to the concept of consolidation. The two conditions are illustrated in Figure 4.5, which follows the same labelling convention as Figure 4.4.

Panel (a) shows the sleep condition; the retention interval that follows learning is unfilled by any new learning activity. Panel (b) shows the potentially interfering material assumed to follow learning when the retention interval is not sleep filled: panels (c) and (d) illustrate the Ekstrand (1972) procedure described above. The superior memory performance in the sleep condition is predicted by temporal distinctiveness models for just the same reason as the temporal gradient of interference is predicted – the to-be-remembered material is rendered temporally isolated, and hence more retrievable, by the following gap during which little or no mental activity occurs. Furthermore, temporal distinctiveness models will predict reduced memory under conditions such as those shown in panel (c), because the learned material is less temporally isolated as a result of the interfering material that immediately follows it. Whether interference will occur when the interfering material immediately precedes test, as illustrated in panel (d), may depend on the similarity of the interfering material to the target material (and hence how strongly it competes for recall).

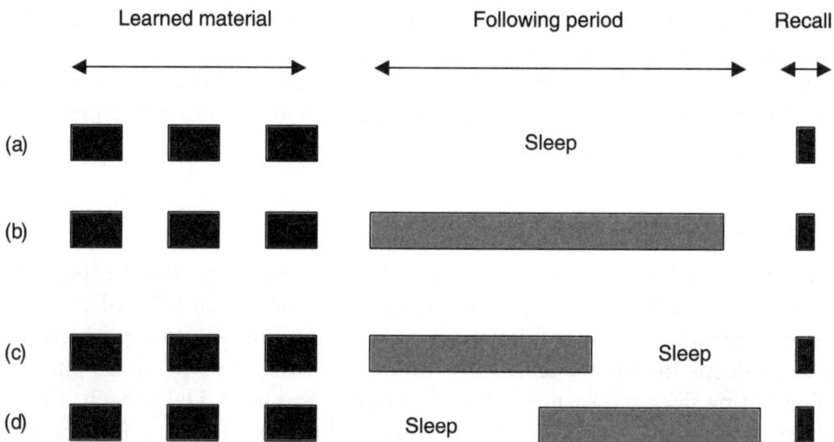

Figure 4.5 Illustration of the changing temporal distinctiveness of to-be-remembered items (filled black rectangles) as a function of the time of sleep relative to the time of learning. Filled shaded rectangles represent interfering activity.

Retrograde amnesia

Perhaps the most widely cited evidence for consolidation comes from the temporal gradient of memory loss associated with retrograde amnesia, which is often known as the Ribot gradient (see, e.g., Meeter & Murre, 2004). The basic phenomenon, associated with damage to the medial temporal lobes, is extensively documented, and involves a loss of memory for past events in a temporally graded manner such that temporally more distant memories are relatively preserved, and more recent memories are lost to a greater extent. Brown (2002) reports a metareview of 247 outcomes from 61 articles, which leads him to conclude that the temporal gradient of memory is monotonic (the impairment gradually and continuously reduces as memories become increasingly temporally distant) and extremely long-lived (extending even up to half a century).[4]

How might this characteristic pattern of data be explained without reference to consolidation? Here we sketch an account according to which (a) access to the temporal dimension in memory is relatively more important for temporally recent memories, and (b) access to the temporal dimension is lost in retrograde amnesia, leading to (c) selective loss of recent memories. We illustrate with a simple simulation.

According to a model like SIMPLE, items can be seen as occupying point locations in multidimensional memory space; the temporal dimension (on which we have focused in the present chapter) is but one of many. Crucially for present purposes, SIMPLE includes the assumption that differential attentional weightings may be given to different dimensions in memory (Brown, Neath, et al., 2007; Lewandowsky et al., 2008b). Specifically, greater attentional weighting will be given to whichever dimension in memory space is most useful for the task in hand. For example, consider a case where memory items are located along just two dimensions: a temporal dimension that becomes compressed as items recede into the past, and a second "item" dimension that acts as a kind of shorthand representation for all the non-temporal dimensions along which an item would be represented. It would make sense for the memory retrieval system to pay relatively greater attention to the temporal dimension when retrieving relatively recent items (which will have quite distinctive locations along the time dimension), and to pay relatively less attention to the temporal dimension and correspondingly greater attention to the other dimension as stimuli recede into the past and the temporal dimension becomes less useful for distinguishing items. This can be seen as akin to the process of a shift from episodic to semantic memory (Brown & McCormack, 2006), and we noted earlier how attention being directed away from the temporal dimension might underlie the selective immunity of immediate serial recall to temporal isolation effects (Lewandowsky et al., 2006) and temporal forgetting (Lewandowsky et al., 2004).

A distinctiveness model augmented with an attentional mechanism offers a potential account of the temporal gradient associated with retrograde amnesia without recourse to the concept of consolidation.

The top curve in Figure 4.6 shows the probability (in SIMPLE) of recalling an item as it recedes into the temporal past (the timescale is arbitrary) under the system just described whereby progressively less weighting is given to the temporal dimension (and more weighting to the other dimension) in memory for older items.[5] It is evident that there is a strong recency gradient, as would be expected, such that more recent memories are more likely to be retrieved. However, what would happen if information about items' locations along the temporal dimension becomes degraded or unavailable? The lower curve shows the temporal retroactive gradient that could result. Because recent memories rely more on availability of temporal information, they suffer more when that information becomes unavailable.[6]

The simple toy model confirms that a temporal-distinctiveness approach may offer an account of temporally graded amnesia without reference to consolidation. Of course, we make no claim to a complete account, and we focus purely on the behavioural data. There is a considerable body of neurobiological evidence consistent with consolidation mechanisms (e.g., Squire, Stark, & Clark, 2004) which remains to be examined, as well as other data that may implicate consolidation processes (see, e.g., Born et al., 2006). However, we do not believe that the neurobiological evidence is necessarily inconsistent with the cognitive-level accounts provided here. In any case, it is perhaps not implausible that a neurobiological underpinning could be given for disruption of time-based retrieval. Many brain regions show signal differences as a function of the temporal distance of memories, such that

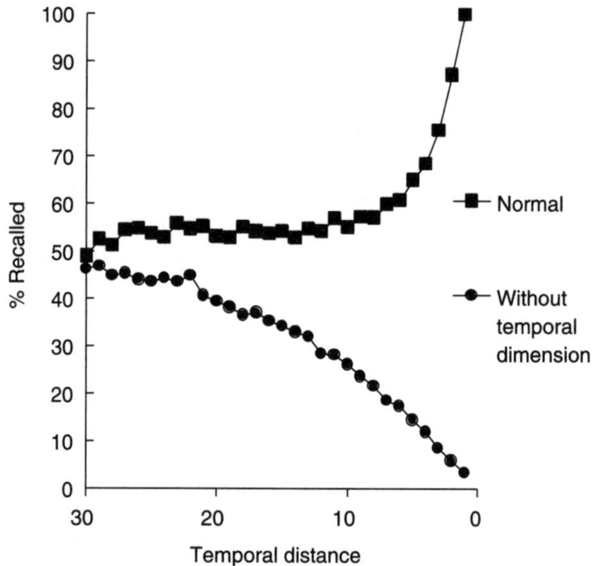

Figure 4.6 Illustration of how a typical recency gradient (top line) may be transformed into temporally graded amnesia (bottom line) if access to a temporal dimension in memory is lost (see text for details).

recent stimuli show greater responses than older stimuli (Woodard et al., 2007). Furthermore, memory for context may become gradually more independent of the hippocampus over time (e.g., Wiltgen & Silva, 2007). The temporal distinctiveness model that we have adopted for present purposes operates at the level of cognitive principle rather than neurobiological process. Recent items are assumed to be more memorable because of their greater temporal distinctiveness. But what gives rise to this greater distinctiveness at a mechanism level? A number of models share the idea that memory involves associating items to a temporal-contextual signal of some kind (Brown et al., 2000; Burgess & Hitch, 1999, 2006; Lewandowsky & Farrell, 2008). One suggestion is, for example, that the signal is made up of a combination of high-frequency and low-frequency oscillators. This signal is assumed to change gradually over time, such that nearby states of the signal are more similar to each other than are more temporally separated states. Thus, if retrieval follows close upon learning, the context signal has had little time to change, and recent items benefit from the overlap between learning context and retrieval context. The benefit that items receive will depend on their recency, with the advantage progressively reducing as items recede further back in time – a recency gradient. Disruption of such a signal – if hippocampal damage were assumed to cause such damage – could lead to retrograde amnesia along the lines discussed above.

In summary, we have suggested that many of the behavioural data that have been taken as evidence for consolidation may be open to explanation in terms of other mechanisms. The mechanism based on distinctiveness that we put forward here clearly represents one candidate worthy of further exploration. However, there are other models that have been identified as promising candidates by recent work on short-term forgetting; for example, the SOB model of Farrell and Lewandowsky and colleagues (Lewandowsky & Farrell, 2008) has been identified in a rigorous model comparison as being best able to handle data on short-term forgetting (Oberauer & Lewandowsky, 2008). It remains to be seen whether it could rival the account of the present phenomena provided by SIMPLE.

Conclusion

We began with the observation that many current cognitive models of memory accord no role to consolidation failure as a cause of forgetting, although they often make reference to trace decay. We have argued that recent progress in memory modelling, combined with a reassessment of the empirical evidence, undermines the case for trace decay as a cause of forgetting. We have also argued that further behavioural evidence is likely to be needed if cognitive modellers are to be convinced to include consolidation mechanisms in their models that currently lack them.

Notes

1 Lewandowsky and Oberauer's (2008) analysis is more extensive, but a full consideration of their arguments is beyond the scope of this chapter.
2 The model as just described predicts time-based forgetting in much the same manner as a decay model and is thus challenged by the data reviewed earlier. Those challenges are overcome by modifications to the model that are not relevant to the current argument (for details, see Lewandowsky et al., 2004).
3 The fact that temporal isolation plays virtually no role in conventional forward serial recall has been taken to imply that people pay no attention to temporal information in those tasks, but use other dimensions such as position instead (Lewandowsky et al., 2006). This is entirely consistent with the observation of Lewandowsky et al. (2004) that there is no temporal forgetting in short-term serial recall. SIMPLE accommodates both results by postulating that items are represented along multiple dimensions, only one of which is temporal, and that people pay no attention to time in many short-term tasks.
4 The fact that consolidation seemingly extends over a time period that exceeds the duration of the average human life span throughout much of human history has been levelled as a criticism against this interpretation (Nadel & Moscovitch, 1997). It is difficult to see how a consolidation process of that duration could have evolved.
5 Specifically, it is assumed that the attentional weight given to the temporal dimension during memory retrieval reduces as a linear function of the temporal distance of the to-be-retrieved memory.
6 This account assumes that the greater weighting given to the temporal dimension for recent items is relatively fixed, i.e., that it is not possible in the absence of access to temporal information to pay correspondingly greater attention to nontemporal dimensions for recent memories.

References

Alin, L. H. (1968). Proactive inhibition as a function of the time interval between the learning of the two tasks and the number of prior lists. *Journal of Verbal Learning & Verbal Behavior*, *7*(6), 1024–1029.

Anderson, J. R., & Schooler, L. J. (1991). Reflections of the environment in memory. *Psychological Science*, *2*, 396–408.

Atkinson, R. C., & Shiffrin, R. M. (1971). Control of short-term memory. *Scientific American*, *225*(2), 82–90.

Baddeley, A. D., Thomson, N., & Buchanan, M. (1975). Word length and the structure of short-term memory. *Journal of Verbal Learning & Verbal Behavior*, *14*, 575–589.

Barrouillet, P., Bernardin, S., & Camos, V. (2004). Time constraints and resource sharing in adults' working memory spans. *Journal of Experimental Psychology: General*, *133*(1), 83–100.

Barrouillet, P., & Camos, V. (2009). Interference: Unique source of forgetting in working memory? *Trends in Cognitive Sciences*, *13*(4), 145–146.

Berman, M. G., Jonides, J., & Lewis, R. L. (2009). In search of decay in verbal short-term memory. *Journal of Experimental Psychology: Learning, Memory and Cognition*, *35*(2), 317–333.

Bhatarah, P., Ward, G., & Tan, L. (2008). Examining the relationship between free recall and immediate serial recall: The serial nature of recall and the effect of test expectancy. *Memory & Cognition*, *36*(1), 20–34.

Bjork, R. A. (2001). Recency and recovery in human memory. In H. L. Roediger III, J. S. Nairne, I. Neath, & A. Surprenant (Eds.), *The nature of remembering: Essays in honor of Robert G. Crowder* (pp. 211–232). Washington, DC: American Psychological Association.

Born, J., Rasch, B., & Gais, S. (2006). Sleep to remember. *Neuroscientist, 12*(5), 410–424.

Botvinick, M. M., & Plaut, D. C. (2006). Short-term memory for serial order: A recurrent neural network model. *Psychological Review, 113*(2), 201–233.

Brown, A. S. (2002). Consolidation theory and retrograde amnesia in humans. *Psychonomic Bulletin & Review, 9*(3), 403–425.

Brown, G. D. A., Chater, N., & Neath, I. (2008). Serial and free recall: Common effects and common mechanisms? A reply to Murdock (2008). *Psychological Review, 115*(3), 781–785.

Brown, G. D. A., Della Sala, S., Foster, J. K., & Vousden, J. I. (2007). Amnesia, rehearsal, and temporal distinctiveness models of recall. *Psychonomic Bulletin & Review, 14*(2), 256–260.

Brown, G. D. A., & McCormack, T. (2006). The role of time in human memory and binding: A review of the evidence. In H. D. Zimmer, A. Mecklinger, & U. Lindenberger (Eds.), *Binding in human memory: A neurocognitive approach* (pp. 251–290). Oxford: Oxford University Press.

Brown, G. D. A., Morin, C., & Lewandowsky, S. (2006). Evidence for time-based models of free recall. *Psychonomic Bulletin & Review, 13*(4), 717–723.

Brown, G. D. A., Neath, I., & Chater, N. (2007). A temporal ratio model of memory. *Psychological Review, 114*(3), 539–576.

Brown, G. D. A., Preece, T., & Hulme, C. (2000). Oscillator-based memory for serial order. *Psychological Review, 107*(1), 127–181.

Burgess, N., & Hitch, G. J. (1999). Memory for serial order: A network model of the phonological loop and its timing. *Psychological Review, 106*, 551–581.

Burgess, N., & Hitch, G. J. (2006). A revised model of short-term memory and long-term learning of verbal sequences. *Journal of Memory and Language, 55*(4), 627–652.

Caplan, D., Rochon, E., & Waters, G. S. (1992). Articulatory and phonological determinants of word-length effects in span tasks. *Quarterly Journal of Experimental Psychology Section A–Human Experimental Psychology, 45*(2), 177–192.

Chechile, R. A. (2006). Memory hazard functions: A vehicle for theory development and test. *Psychological Review, 113*(1), 31–56.

Cowan, N. (1995). *Attention and memory: An integrated framework*. Oxford: Oxford University Press.

Cowan, N., Beschin, N., & Della Sala, S. (2004). Verbal recall in amnesiacs under conditions of diminished retroactive interference. *Brain, 127*, 825–834.

Cowan, N., Elliott, E. M., Saults, J. S., Nugent, L. D., Bomb, P., & Hismjatullina, A. (2006). Rethinking speed theories of cognitive development – Increasing the rate of recall without affecting accuracy. *Psychological Science, 17*(1), 67–73.

Crowder, R. G. (1989). Modularity and dissociations in memory systems. In J. L. Roediger III, & F. I. Craik (Eds.), *Varieties of memory and consciousness: Essays in honor of Endel Tulving* (pp. 271–294). Hillsdale, NJ: Lawrence Erlbaum Associates, Inc.

Davelaar, E. J., Goshen-Gottstein, Y., Ashkenazi, A., Haarmann, H. J., & Usher, M. (2005). The demise of short-term memory revisited: Empirical and computational investigations of recency effects. *Psychological Review, 112*(1), 3–42.

Della Sala, S., Cowan, N., Beschin, N., & Perini, M. (2005). Just lying there, remembering: Improving recall of prose in amnesic patients with mild cognitive impairment by minimising interference. *Memory*, *13*(3–4), 435–440.
Dewar, M. T., Cowan, N., & Della Sala, S. (2007). Forgetting due to retroactive interference: A fusion of Muller and Pilzecker's (1900) early insights into everyday forgetting and recent research on anterograde amnesia. *Cortex*, *43*(5), 616–634.
Dewar, M., Garcia, Y. F., Cowan, N., & Della Sala, S. (in press). Delaying interference enhances memory consolidation in amnesic patients. *Neuropsychology.*
Ekstrand, B. R. (1972). To sleep, perchance to dream: About why we forget. In C. Duncan, P., L. Sechrest, & A. W. Melton (Eds.), *Human memory: Festschrift for Benton J. Underwood* (pp. 59–82). East Norwalk, CT: Appleton-Century-Crofts.
Ellenbogen, J. M., Hulbert, J. C., Stickgold, R., Dinges, D. F., & Thompson-Schill, S. L. (2006). Interfering with theories of sleep and memory: Sleep, declarative memory, and associative interference. *Current Biology*, *16*(13), 1290–1294.
Geiger, S. M., & Lewandowsky, S. (2008). Temporal isolation does not facilitate forward serial recall – or does it? *Memory & Cognition*, *36*(5), 957–967.
Gillund, G., & Shiffrin, R. M. (1984). A retrieval model for both recognition and recall. *Psychological Review*, *91*(1), 1–67.
Henson, R. N. A. (1998). Short-term memory for serial order: The Start–End Model. *Cognitive Psychology*, *36*(2), 73–137.
Howard, M. W., & Kahana, M. J. (2002). A distributed representation of temporal context. *Journal of Mathematical Psychology*, *46*(3), 269–299.
Hudjetz, A., & Oberauer, K. (2007). The effects of processing time and processing rate on forgetting in working memory: Testing four models of the complex span paradigm. *Memory & Cognition*, *35*(7), 1675–1684.
Jenkins, J. G., & Dallenbach, K. M. (1924). Obliviscence during sleep and waking. *American Journal of Psychology*, *35*, 605–612.
Keppel, G. (1964). Facilitation in short- and long-term retention of paired associates following distribution practice in learning. *Journal of Verbal Learning & Verbal Behavior*, *3*(2), 91–111.
Keppel, G., & Underwood, B. J. (1962). Proactive inhibition in short-term retention of single items. *Journal of Verbal Learning & Verbal Behavior*, *1*(3), 153–161.
Kerr, J. R., Avons, S. E., & Ward, G. (1999). Effect of retention interval on serial position curves for item recognition of visual patterns and faces. *Journal of Experimental Psychology: Learning, Memory and Cognition*, *25*(6), 1475–1494.
Kerr, J. R., Ward, G., & Avons, S. E. (1998). Response bias in visual serial order memory. *Journal of Experimental Psychology: Learning, Memory and Cognition*, *24*(5), 1316–1323.
Kincaid, J. P., & Wickens, D. D. (1970). Temporal gradient of release from proactive inhibition. *Journal of Experimental Psychology*, *86*(2), 313–316.
Knoedler, A. J., Hellwig, K. A., & Neath, I. (1999). The shift from recency to primacy with increasing delay. *Journal of Experimental Psychology: Learning, Memory, and Cognition*, *25*(2), 474–487.
Korsnes, M. S., & Magnussen, S. (1996). Age comparisons of serial position effects in short-term memory. *Acta Psychologica*, *94*(2), 133–143.
Korsnes, M. S., Magnussen, S., & Reinvang, I. (1996). Serial position effects in visual short-term memory for words and abstract spatial patterns. *Scandinavian Journal of Psychology*, *37*(1), 62–73.

Lewandowsky, S., & Brown, G. D. A. (2005). Serial recall and presentation schedule: A micro-analysis of local distinctiveness. *Memory*, *13*, 283–292.

Lewandowsky, S., Brown, G. D. A., Wright, T., & Nimmo, L. M. (2006). Timeless memory: Evidence against temporal distinctiveness models of short-term memory for serial order. *Journal of Memory and Language*, *54*, 20–38.

Lewandowsky, S., Duncan, M., & Brown, G. D. A. (2004). Time does not cause forgetting in short-term serial recall. *Psychonomic Bulletin & Review*, *11*(5), 771–790.

Lewandowsky, S., & Farrell, S. (2008). Short-term memory: New data and a model. *Psychology of Learning and Motivation: Advances in Research and Theory*, *49*, 1–48.

Lewandowsky, S., Geiger, S. M., & Oberauer, K. (2008a). Interference-based forgetting in verbal short-term memory. *Journal of Memory and Language*, *59*(2), 200–222.

Lewandowsky, S., Nimmo, L. M., & Brown, G. D. A. (2008b). When temporal isolation benefits memory for serial order. *Journal of Memory and Language*, *58*(2), 415–428.

Lewandowsky, S., & Oberauer, K. (2008). The word-length effect provides no evidence for decay in short-term memory. *Psychonomic Bulletin & Review*, *15*(5), 875–888.

Lewandowsky, S., & Oberauer, K. (in press). No evidence for temporal decay in working memory. *Journal of Experimental Psychology: Learning, Memory and Cognition*.

Lewandowsky, S., Oberauer, K., & Brown, G. D. A. (2009a). No temporal decay in verbal short-term memory. *Trends in Cognitive Sciences*, *13*, 120–126.

Lewandowsky, S., Oberauer, K., & Brown, G. D. A. (2009b). Response to Barrouillet and Camos: Interference or decay in working memory? *Trends in Cognitive Sciences*, *13*(4), 146–147.

Loess, H., & Waugh, N. C. (1967). Short-term memory and intertrial interval. *Journal of Verbal Learning & Verbal Behavior*, *6*(4), 455–460.

Lovatt, P., Avons, S. E., & Masterson, J. (2000). The word-length effect and disyllabic words. *Quarterly Journal of Experimental Psychology Section A–Human Experimental Psychology*, *53*(1), 1–22.

Lovatt, P., Avons, S. E., & Masterson, J. (2002). Output decay in immediate serial recall: Speech time revisited. *Journal of Memory and Language*, *46*(1), 227–243.

McClelland, J. L., McNaughton, B. L., & O'Reilly, R. C. (1995). Why there are complementary learning-systems in the hippocampus and neocortex: Insights from the successes and failures of connectionist models of learning and memory. *Psychological Review*, *102*(3), 419–457.

Maylor, E. A., Chater, N., & Brown, G. D. A. (2001). Scale invariance in the retrieval of retrospective and prospective memories. *Psychonomic Bulletin & Review*, *8*(1), 162–167.

Meeter, M., & Murre, J. M. J. (2004). Consolidation of long-term memory: Evidence and alternatives. *Psychological Bulletin*, *130*(6), 843–857.

Meeter, M., & Murre, J. M. J. (2005). TraceLink: A model of consolidation and amnesia. *Cognitive Neuropsychology*, *22*(5), 559–587.

Melton, A. W. (1963). Implications of short-term memory for a general theory of memory. *Journal of Verbal Learning & Verbal Behavior*, *2*, 1–21.

Mueller, S. T., Seymour, T. L., Kieras, D. E., & Meyer, D. E. (2003). Theoretical implications of articulatory duration, phonological similarity, and phonological complexity in verbal working memory. *Journal of Experimental Psychology: Learning, Memory and Cognition*, *29*(6), 1353–1380.

Nadel, L., & Moscovitch, M. (1997). Memory consolidation, retrograde amnesia and the hippocampal complex. *Current Opinion in Neurobiology*, *7*(2), 217–227.

Neath, I. (1993). Distinctiveness and serial position effects in recognition. *Memory & Cognition*, *21*(5), 689–698.

Neath, I., Bireta, T. J., & Surprenant, A. M. (2003). The time-based word length effect and stimulus set specificity. *Psychonomic Bulletin & Review*, *10*(2), 430–434.

Neath, I., & Brown, G. D. A. (2006). Simple: Further applications of a local distinctiveness model of memory. *Psychology of Learning and Motivation: Advances in Research and Theory*, *46*, 201–243.

Neath, I., Brown, G. D. A., McCormack, T., Chater, N., & Freeman, R. (2006). Distinctiveness models of memory and absolute identification: Evidence for local, not global, effects. *Quarterly Journal of Experimental Psychology*, *59*(1), 121–135.

Neath, I., & Knoedler, A. J. (1994). Distinctiveness and serial position effects in recognition and sentence processing. *Journal of Memory and Language*, *33*(6), 776–795.

Norman, K. A., & O'Reilly, R. C. (2003). Modeling hippocampal and neocortical contributions to recognition memory: A complementary-learning-systems approach. *Psychological Review*, *110*(4), 611–646.

Oberauer, K., & Lewandowsky, S. (2008). Forgetting in immediate serial recall: Decay, temporal distinctiveness, or interference? *Psychological Review*, *115*(3), 544–576.

Page, M. P. A., & Norris, D. (1998). The primacy model: A new model of immediate serial recall. *Psychological Review*, *105*(4), 761–781.

Peterson, L. R., & Gentile, A. (1965). Proactive interference as a function of time between tests. *Journal of Experimental Psychology*, *70*(5), 473–478.

Polyn, S. M., Norman, K. A., & Kahana, M. J. (2009). A context maintenance and retrieval model of organizational processes in free recall. *Psychological Review*, *116*(1), 129–156.

Portrat, S., Barrouillet, P., & Camos, V. (2008). Time-related decay or interference-based forgetting in working memory? *Journal of Experimental Psychology: Learning, Memory and Cognition*, *34*(6), 1561–1564.

Raaijmakers, J. G. W., & Shiffrin, R. M. (1981). Search of associative memory. *Psychological Review*, *88*(2), 93–134.

Rubin, D. C., Hinton, S., & Wenzel, A. (1999). The precise time course of retention. *Journal of Experimental Psychology: Learning, Memory and Cognition*, *25*(5), 1161–1176.

Rubin, D. C., & Wenzel, A. E. (1994). One hundred years of forgetting: A quantitative description of retention. *Psychological Review*, *103*(4), 734–760.

Sederberg, P. B., Howard, M. W., & Kahana, M. J. (2008). A context-based theory of recency and contiguity in free recall. *Psychological Review*, *115*(4), 893–912.

Shiffrin, R. M., & Steyvers, M. (1997). Model for recognition memory: REM – Retrieving Effectively from Memory. *Psychonomic Bulletin & Review*, *4*(2), 145–166.

Sikstrom, S. (2002). Forgetting curves: Implications for connectionist models. *Cognitive Psychology*, *45*(1), 95–152.

Squire, L. R., Stark, C. E. L., & Clark, R. E. (2004). The medial temporal lobe. *Annual Review of Neuroscience*, *27*, 279–306.

Tan, L., & Ward, G. (2000). A recency-based account of the primacy effect in free recall. *Journal of Experimental Psychology: Learning, Memory and Cognition*, *26*(6), 1589–1625.

Underwood, B. J. (1957). Interference and forgetting. *Psychological Review*, *64*(1), 49–60.

Underwood, B. J., & Ekstrand, B. R. (1967). Studies of distributed practice: XXIV. Differentiation and proactive inhibition. *Journal of Experimental Psychology*, *74*(4), 574–580.

Underwood, B. J., & Freund, J. S. (1968). Effect of temporal separation of two tasks on proactive inhibition. *Journal of Experimental Psychology*, *78*(1), 50–54.

Vallar, G., & Baddeley, A. D. (1982). Short-term forgetting and the articulatory loop. *Quarterly Journal of Experimental Psychology Section A: Human Experimental Psychology*, *34*, 53–60.

Wickens, T. D. (1999). Measuring the time course of retention. In C. Izawa (Ed.), *On human memory: Evolution, progress, and reflections on the 30th anniversary of the Atkinson–Shiffrin model* (pp. 245–266). Mahwah, NJ: Lawrence Erlbaum Associates, Inc.

Wiltgen, B. J., & Silva, A. J. (2007). Memory for context becomes less specific with time. *Learning & Memory*, *14*(4), 313–317.

Wixted, J. T. (2004a). On common ground: Jost's (1897) law of forgetting and Ribot's (1881) law of retrograde amnesia. *Psychological Review*, *111*(4), 864–879.

Wixted, J. T. (2004b). The psychology and neuroscience of forgetting. *Annual Review of Psychology*, *55*, 235–269.

Wixted, J. T. (2005). A theory about why we forget what we once knew. *Current Directions in Psychological Science*, *14*(1), 6–9.

Wixted, J. T., & Ebbesen, E. B. (1990). On the form of forgetting. *Psychological Science*, *2*(6), 409–415.

Wixted, J. T., & Ebbesen, E. B. (1997). Genuine power curves in forgetting: A quantitative analysis of individual subject forgetting functions. *Memory & Cognition*, *25*(5), 731–739.

Woodard, J. L., Seidenberg, M., Nielson, K. A., Miller, S. K., Franczak, M., Antuono, P., et al. (2007). Temporally graded activation of neocortical regions in response to memories of different ages. *Journal of Cognitive Neuroscience*, *19*(7), 1113–1124.

Wright, A. A. (2007). An experimental analysis of memory processing. *Journal of the Experimental Analysis of Behavior*, *88*(3), 405–433.

Wright, A. A., Santiago, H. C., Sands, S. F., Kendrick, D. F., & Cook, R. G. (1985). Memory processing of serial lists by pigeons, monkeys, and people. *Science*, *229*(4710), 287–289.

5 Connectionist models of forgetting

Jaap M. J. Murre

University of Amsterdam, Amsterdam, The Netherlands

Introduction

Connectionist models have been around for half a century. Their ability to learn from examples makes them prime candidates as models of human memory. Here, we will review how connectionist models learn and forget. Forgetting can mean many things, from short-term forgetting at the scale of seconds or shorter to very long-term forgetting over several decades. It can be viewed as a side effect of diffuse noise and decay at the level of synapses or as an active process, perhaps to safeguard important memories or to extract high-level abstractions from our daily experiences. Connectionist models can accommodate all of these mechanisms, some of which lie at the heart of the principles by which they work.

In order to understand what connectionist models can do, it is necessary to delve into some of the details of how they work. As we will see, with some very notable exceptions, many of their basic mechanisms immediately translate into psychologically interesting concepts. We have kept the technical details of the models reviewed here down to a bare minimum. Our aim is to give the reader enough background about the structure and functioning of connectionist models to understand their possible relevance for theories of human forgetting.

Activations as STM and weights as LTM

Connectionist models consist of large numbers of artificial neurons[1] that exchange pulse signals (activations) over a dense network of connections (artificial synapses). These models are also known as *neural network models* (Grossberg, 1987) or *parallel distributed processing (PDP) models* (Rumelhart & McClelland, 1986), terms that may be used interchangeably. Connectionist models are inspired by the structure of the brain, which does not necessarily mean that they aim to mimic the neurobiology very closely. Though it is possible to devise highly detailed models of biological neurons, in psychology we typically abstract from the underlying neurobiological complexity, retaining only certain characteristics that are believed to capture the essence of brain mechanisms with respect to explaining behavior. These models are often called *system-level models* to distinguish them from low-level neurobiological models. In the following, we will review the main characteristics of connectionist models and then proceed to discuss mechanisms that may underlie forgetting. As we shall see, there are several ways in which connectionist models may be induced to forget, each of which may capture a specific aspect of human forgetting.

If a given (artificial) neuron A connects to another neuron B, it may send an activation value. In biology neural "firing" tends to be all or none and this is often translated into abstract signals of 0 (no firing) and 1 (firing). An alternative approach is to look at the average rate of firing (say in 1 second) and scale that to a value between 0 and 1. Thus, an activation value of 0.15 signifies a low firing rate and 0.80 a high rate. A neuron that receives many activation pulses will tend to have a high activation value itself and thus in turn induce other neurons to fire. Certain neurons (or connections) are inhibitory, which means here that they will try to prevent other neurons from firing. The interaction between hundreds of neurons, inhibiting or exciting each other at the same time, is extremely complex. It usually defies mathematical analysis and must be simulated on a computer. Fortunately, very fast computers are now everywhere and this has contributed to the popularity of connectionist modeling.

An important concept is the network's activation state. At any given point in time, a neural network will be in a certain activation state: certain neurons will be firing, whereas others will be silent. One can view such an activation state as a form of short-term memory. Changes in the activation state, for example a gradual decay of all activations to zero, are often used as models for short-term forgetting (Grossberg, 1976; Page & Norris, 1998). We will return to this concept of short-term memory in some detail below.

Long-term forgetting is typically modeled by changes in the connections. A connection from neuron A to B will have a certain strength or *weight* that determines how much effect an activation signal fired from A will have on the activation of B. Weights are typically real numbers, e.g., 0.43 or 7.8. If a weight is very low (e.g., 0.001), an activation signal sent to B will have little effect. But if it is high (e.g., 3.1), the signal will contribute to B's tendency to fire activation signals itself. Neuron B, like every neuron, gathers on its input side (i.e., an artificial dendrite) signals received from all neurons connected to B. The activations are weighted on the basis of their connection weights, resulting in the so-called *net input*: the weighted sum of activation signals received. The strength or weight of a connection can also be negative (inhibitory). A strong negative weight implies that an activation signal will reduce the net input of the receiving neuron. Since activation signals are simply numbers, the net input is also a number, for example 8.7 or –10.3 (in the case of strong negative input weights). In some types of networks, if the net input exceeds a certain threshold (often taken as 0), the artificial neuron will fire an activation signal (e.g., the value 1) to all neurons to which it connects. In other types, the net input is translated into a value between 0 and 1, e.g., a net input of –9.4 would give an activation value close to 0, an input value around 0 might lead to an activation of around 0.5. A high net input would drive the neuron's activation to 1.

In many – but not all – types of neural networks, all neurons process their inputs at the same time and also send signals at the same time. Processing is thus distributed over the entire network and occurs in parallel, which is why it is sometimes called parallel distributed processing. This resembles neural processing in the brain, which also occurs in so-called massively parallel fashion.

An important insight from neural network theory in the past decades is that *the structure of a neural network determines its behavior*. Simply put: how neurons are connected determines what the network can do. The insight that the information in the brain is mainly stored in the connections between neurons and not so much in the neuron cell bodies has contributed to the important realization that the brain remains plastic. Even if neuronal cells hardly divide past birth, connections remain prolific and are subject to continuous change, even in adulthood. This leads to a second important insight: *neural networks can change their own connections* on the basis of the patterns to which they are exposed (e.g., pictures of faces). More importantly, the learning rules governing these changes may operate completely locally (e.g., between pairs of neurons) and still lead a globally consistent result (e.g., recognizing a face). How that works we will explain below.

The connections of a neural network model form its long-term memory, which implies that any change in the connections may cause forgetting of the stored memories. Some neural networks models have connections that decay towards zero with time, a process that causes forgetting, but that seems a bit too drastic from a psychological point of view and for which little biological evidence exists. Brain research has revealed that nonuse may weaken synapses, but this happens usually as a result of competition where often-used synapses become stronger at the expense of nonused ones (e.g., Purves, 1988). This mechanism is more akin to interference due to new learning, a paradigm often used to model forgetting in neural networks (discussed below). Instead of constant decay towards zero, it seems more biologically realistic to model forgetting by perturbing the connections, for example by randomly changing weights once every so often. This is often implemented by adding a small random number at each time step or setting a small fraction of the weights to zero randomly. As we shall see, neural network models are very resilient to such perturbations; quite a lot of noise needs to be injected into the neural connections before any effects can be observed in the network behavior.

Learning in neural networks

Two approaches to learning dominate the field of neural networks, and these have their roots in two learning principles: the Hebb rule (Hebb, 1949) and the error-correcting rule (Rosenblatt, 1958). The *Hebb rule* says that if two neurons fire together frequently, the connection weights between them must be increased; if they rarely fire together their interconnecting weights should be weakened.

The *error-correcting rule* (Rosenblatt, 1958) assumes that one is explicitly teaching a neural network to generate a specific (target) output with a given input. It says that if a neuron has a higher activation than prescribed by the target signal, the weights to that neuron should be decreased, or if the activation is too low, its weights should be increased.

What has interested connectionist researchers is that quite basic principles of activation exchange and weight change give rise to very interesting and complex behavior that in many respects resembles human learning and forgetting. As in the brain, signal exchange and weight updates operate at a local scale (i.e., within neurons and connections). Yet they give rise to a global organization of information processing throughout the entire network. To get a grasp of this, let us look at some examples of neural network models. We will first review network models that use Hebbian learning and then turn our attention to networks that are based on error-correcting learning.

Hebbian learning

Donald Hebb (1949) was not the first author to postulate that neural processes become more strongly associated when they are activated simultaneously (e.g., James, 1892/2001), but he was the first to write it down concisely and in terms of neural connections. Indeed, his formulation can easily be turned into a mathematical formula that in its simplest form says: increase a weight proportionally to the product of the activations of the pre- and post-synaptic neuron. In this way, neurons that are active together frequently will develop strong interconnections: neurons that fire together, wire together. To illustrate how this works in practice, we will first discuss Willshaw networks in some detail, followed by a more general discussion of other types of networks, so-called attractor networks.

Willshaw model

The Hebb rule found an early implementation in a model by David Willshaw and colleagues (Willshaw, Buneman, & Longuet-Higgins, 1969). This model has an input layer of artificial neurons and an output layer where each input neuron can be connected to each output neuron. Initially, there are no connections; these emerge through learning. When an input pattern (e.g., a black-and-white image of a face) and an output pattern (e.g., information associated with this person's face, such as a name) are presented, weights can "grow" from the input to the output neurons. If the same face is presented again later, the name of the person can be retrieved.

Like most neural network models, Willshaw networks can handle incomplete input. For example, if only a portion of the face is visible on the input image or if the face is somewhat distorted, the correct output can usually still be retrieved. From the perspective of memory psychology, the input pattern is the retrieval cue. If this cue is too impoverished (e.g., only a small part of the face is visible), the output pattern can no longer be retrieved correctly. Like human memory, an impoverished retrieval cue will often lead some of the output to be retrieved correctly, for example some letters of the person's name. This resembles situations where we see someone we vaguely know and can only recall that, say, he has a name that ends in "o" and is pretty short. Forgetting is thus not necessarily all or none and it is a function of the quality of the retrieval cue. Let us now look at some of the details of this model.

This network has two unusual aspects compared with most neural networks. First, the weights can take on only the values 0 and 1 and the learning rule can only change weights from 0 to 1 but not back (i.e., weights come into existence and stay; there is no unlearning). Second, there is feedforward inhibition from the input neurons to the output neurons: The number of active input neurons (i.e., the number of ones in the input pattern) is summed and this value is used as divisor of the net input to each output cell. This allows the network to learn both patterns with many and with few activations in the same network without too much interference. These principles are illustrated in Figure 5.1.

In Figure 5.1(a) we see how three different input–output pairs are learned by the network. To get a good view of the connection weights in this network, the input patterns have been drawn as columns of zeros and ones and the output patterns as rows. If there is a connection from, say, the third active neuron of the input pattern to the first active neuron of the output pattern, the weight of the connection will be located at the third position of the first column. Because both the input and output neuron are 1, the Hebb rule specifies that we enter a 1 here. This is done for all active inputs and outputs. For clarity, zeros are suppressed in the illustration. Note that where weights should have been strengthened twice there is still only a single 1, because in the Willshaw network that is the maximum value. The matrix of ones and zeros, though of modest size, is what we call a *distributed memory*. The reason for this is that we have stored several input–output pairs in the same set of weights. Each weight takes part in representing each of the three pattern pairs and the representation of each pair is distributed over all weights. The same principle is at work in the brain, where a single neuron or set of weights can take part in many different representations. Of course, this would not be an advantage unless we were still able to retrieve the original outputs.

In Figure 5.1(b) we see what happens if one of the learned input patterns is presented. Each activated neuron contributes to the net activation of each output neuron, but only if there is a connection with weight 1. Not all of these were necessarily learned when this pattern was presented; other patterns have caused weights to be created as well. Because of this, the net input to the six output neurons is (3 2 2 3 3 2) where the original output pattern was

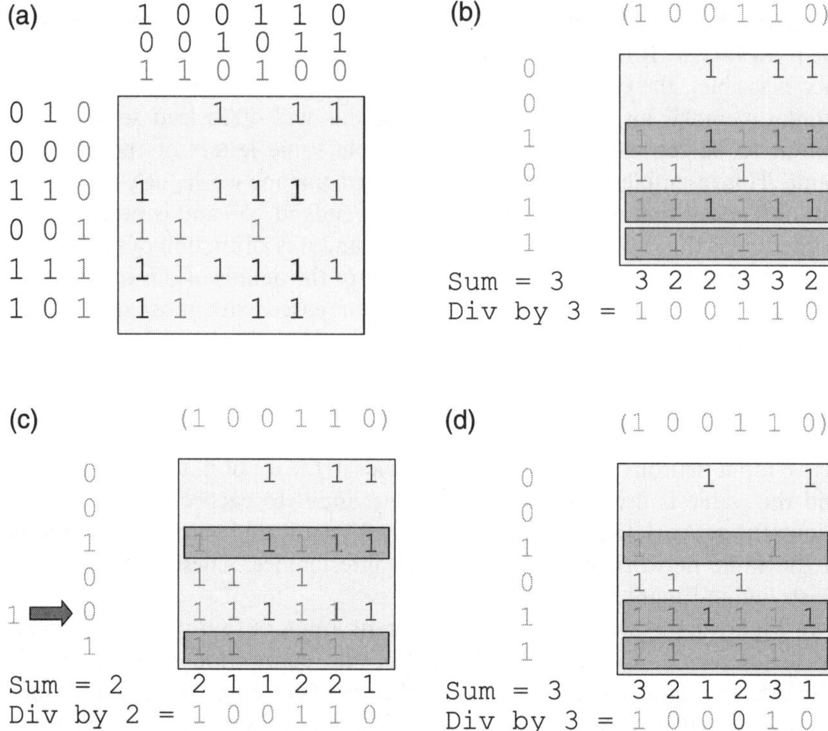

Figure 5.1 Example of learning and forgetting in a Willshaw network. (a) Three input–output pairs are learned in the network. (b) One of the output patterns is presented to the network and the output is retrieved even though three patterns have been stored using the same weights. (c) Only a partial input pattern (cue) is presented but the output is still retrieved perfectly. (d) A relatively large fraction of the weights has been removed at random. The output can still be retrieved but with errors.

(1 0 0 1 1 0). We obtain this output by using the feedforward inhibition rule of the Willshaw network: Count the number of ones in the input pattern, which is 3, and divide the net input by this. The activation rule prescribes that we use integer division here, whereby 2/3 is 0 and not 0.667.

The value of the feedforward inhibition becomes even clearer when we use a partial cue, created by randomly deactivating one of the active input neurons in the pattern (i.e., a distortion of 1/6 or about 17%). In Figure 5.1(c) we see that in this case the output is (2 1 1 2 2 1) and the number of active input neurons is 2. Integer division again gives the correct output (1 0 0 1 1 0). Clearly, there are limits to how much we can delete from the retrieval cue. Using just (0 0 0 0 0 1) as the input pattern would result in the erroneous output (1 1 0 1 1 0). Notice though that the output is not entirely wrong, it is merely distorted. The same happens when we randomly delete some of the learned connections. This is only a small example, but we would obtain the same type of result if we repeated this "simulation" with a much larger network that, for example, could store black-and-white images.

In Figure 5.1(d) about 30% of the 1s have been set to 0. The same input cue as above is used, now giving net inputs (3 2 1 2 3 1). Integer division by 3 now gives (1 0 0 0 1 0). We have a mistake at the fourth position, but again we notice that the error is in proportion to the damage. This is often called the principle of "graceful degradation": impoverished or distorted retrieval cues or perturbed (deleted) connections result in retrieval errors that are in proportion to changes in cue or weights. In many networks, quite large distortions or lesions still result in near-perfect retrieval. This is due to the distributed nature and the redundancy of the neural representations.

In summary, we see that a Willshaw network exhibits good pattern retrieval with imperfect retrieval cues and that it shows graceful degradation with very low-quality cues or with strong perturbation of the weights. These are all desirable characteristics for models of human forgetting. Most neural network models share these characteristics, making connectionism such a viable paradigm for modeling human learning and forgetting.

Attractor networks

The Willshaw model is rather limited in that information flows directly from input to output without any intermediate stages. There is also a class of models that allows more complex processing because these models possess recurrent connections. That is, any two neurons may be connected in any direction (self-connections are often prohibited). This means that there is no simple flow from input to output. We will discuss here the classic neural network paradigm (i.e., class of network models) proposed by the physicist John Hopfield (1982). He noticed that if a neural network with recurrent connections has only symmetrical connections, many analytical results from physics apply. To simplify the analyses, his 1982 model uses neural activations that are either 1 ("firing") or –1 ("no firing"). All these constraints are not biologically plausible, but many of the basic results hold when the networks are made more plausible, except that the behavior, and hence the analyses, become much more complex.

A pattern is stored in a Hopfield network by straightforward application of the Hebb rule. The activation of two connected neurons is multiplied and the product is added to the weights that connect them. For example, if one neuron is –1 and the other is 1, we add –1 to the weights. If they are both 1 (or –1), we add 1 to the weight. As in the Willshaw network, different patterns can be superimposed on the same set of weights in this manner.

Also as in the Willshaw network, we start calculation of a new activation value of some neuron by taking the sum of activations weighed by the incoming connection weights. If this net input exceeds the threshold 0, the new activation becomes 1, if it falls below zero it becomes –1 (if the net input is exactly 0, the old activation is retained). Neural activations are updated by selecting one neuron randomly and applying the threshold rule, then selecting the next, etc. This one-at-a-time random updating is not biologically plausible, but ensures that the analyses remain simple. If parallel updating is used, the results still largely hold.

The most important achievement of the Hopfield network is that it can be proven mathematically that it will always move to a stable activation pattern, such that further activation updates will no longer result in any changes in the activations. Such a stable state (i.e., configuration of activation values) is called an *attractor* because if the network is in an activation state that resembles a certain attractor, the activation state will move in that direction. An attractor can also be seen as a configuration of activations that fits the weights as well as possible. The fact that the activation rule drives the activation state to the nearest attractor is relevant because it can also be proven that patterns stored in the network by the Hebb rule each form an attractor. Thus, if a partial pattern is presented to the network, it will be completed to the full attractor state, which is the pattern stored originally.

Hopfield networks have distributed memory and exhibit both pattern completion and graceful degradation. Moreover, when several similar patterns are learned by an attractor network, it has a tendency to lose details of the originals and form a prototype. Whether this happens and to what extent the patterns will merge into a single prototype will depend on how similar they are. The mechanism by which prototypes are formed is akin to that of digging holes on the beach. Attractors can be viewed as "holes" in a type of landscape (in the language of physics, the landscape is a multidimensional energy space where attractors are points of low energy). Digging many holes very close together will cause them to partially merge.

To simplify our thinking about prototype formation, let us assume we are using activation values that are 0 or 1, instead of –1 and 1. It can easily be shown that the statements above are still true for a Hopfield network with such activations, if the learning rule is altered slightly. The variant learning rule states that if two neurons have activations 0 and 1, the weight between them is decreased. If they are both 0, nothing happens and if they are both 1, the weight is increased. Such neural networks still have attractors in the above sense and also form prototypes by merging of attractors.

Looking at it in another way, we can easily see that if two neurons A and B are active together in certain patterns, the connection between them will become quite strong due to the Hebb rule. One could view this as storage of co-occurrence statistics in the weights. For example, if one neuron represents the letter "t" and another the letter "h," their connection could be strong if the network were trained with words from the English language because these letters occur together frequently. The connection between neurons that represent, say, "q" and "x" would be weak, indicating an infrequent co-occurrence.

An interesting example that uses this idea is a study by McClelland and Rumelhart (1985). They describe a network that learns the "statistics of rooms" as a rough analogy to how people learn about rooms. What is a living room? And does it differ from a study? We acquire knowledge about rooms by being exposed to hundreds of examples. The forming of "room concepts" is not just a matter of associating features with names. After all, chairs can occur in many rooms, as do ceilings and doors. Nor is it just a simple association between features. The rooms we happen to encounter may never have had a piano, an aquarium, and a dinner table. But as soon as I am told about such a room, I will tend to fill in the rest and perhaps imagine a certain type of living room in a house. Attractor neural networks store co-occurrence statistics in their weights, but the resulting attractors are far richer, forming conceptual feature networks of their own, within the larger neural network. If part of such a feature network – an attractor – is activated, the rest of the attractor will also become activated. This property of neural networks can be used to model the formation of schemata and prototypes in human memory. When remembering, subjects tend to adjust their memory to fit their preconceived concepts, for example they report having seen books in an academic office where they had been carefully removed as part of the experiment (Brewer & Treyens, 1981).

Why is all this relevant to forgetting? We see that a natural side-effect of attractor networks is that they tend to form prototypes or concept networks and lose certain details of individual patterns in the process. From the perspective of memory psychology we might say that episodic knowledge is converted into semantic knowledge. This process tends to interfere with accurate retention of individual episodes and thus forms an important source of forgetting in neural networks.

Boltzmann Machine

Hopfield networks are deterministic in the evaluation of an activation value in the sense that a given net input always leads to the same activation (though the choice of which neuron's activation to update next is random). A variant of this is where the net input to a Hopfield neuron is translated into a *probability* of changing its activation. A neuron that receives a high net input activation will have a high probability of having activation 1, but it may also become −1. One might say that the net input is merely a "suggestion" to turn the activation to either 1 or −1. A parameter may be set for a network so that neurons tend to follow the suggestion of the net input most of the time when this parameter is close to 0; the network behaves much like a normal Hopfield network. But when this parameter is set very high, neurons will pay little attention to the net input and fire nearly randomly. Randomness like this is useful for simulating errors that subjects tend to make in psychological experiments, but it also has a deeper meaning. In analogy with physical systems, this parameter is called the network *temperature*. It plays an important role in the quality of the solutions found by a neural network, notably in the retrieval of stored patterns.

If we store many patterns in an ordinary Hopfield network, these will form attractors, as we saw above. When we present a retrieval cue by activating some of the neurons, a Hopfield network will find a nearby attractor and this is typically the pattern to be retrieved. However, Hopfield networks will not necessarily find the deepest attractor (i.e., the best-fitting stored pattern). We say that the network tends to get stuck in local minima (shallow attractors). We can often reach deeper attractors (better retrievals) if we were allowed to change neuronal activations randomly to escape from the shallow attractors. This is where the randomness in the Boltzmann Machine activation rule helps.

Boltzmann Machine networks do not stay in any attractor indefinitely. Even if they are in a deep attractor, there is a finite (but possibly extremely small) chance of shifting its activation configuration to another attractor. When we present a retrieval cue by keeping certain activations fixed (called clamping), the network will tend to keep cycling through retrievals that involve the cue. Such a mechanism may be useful for retrieving words learned in a certain context (i.e., those on a particular list). Activating the neurons that represent the "list context" will result in subsequent retrieval of words on the list. When the retrieval cue is removed (unclamped), the network will continue to cycle through all words in all lists learned, as well as through any other attractors it may have formed. This is the basis of the learning algorithm for the Boltzmann Machine (Ackley, Hinton, & Sejnowski, 1985).

In essence, the learning algorithm is not complicated. During the "offline" phase, no patterns are clamped and the network is left free to cycle through all its attractors (e.g., stored patterns). During this phase we keep track of the activations, letting the network cycle long enough so that we can be sure it has visited all attractors repeatedly. At this point, we possess reliable statistics about the "offline" behavior of the network. In the "online" learning phase, we do the same but now we clamp a group of neurons with a pattern to be learned.

Why would we go to all this trouble of collecting coactivation statistics in two different "phases"? The reason is that this approach gives us a very powerful learning algorithm in case we have a network where a group of neurons never receive input directly (i.e., they are never clamped). These neurons have the same function as the hidden layer neurons in a backpropagation network, discussed below. With the aid of additional "hidden neurons" Boltzmann Machine networks can represent very abstract regularities in the input that are relevant for complex human behavior such as speech recognition or object recognition. Having hidden neurons allows us to study the learning problem faced by the mammalian brain, where in the case of the cortex only a tiny fraction of the neurons receive direct inputs from the sensory organs (Braitenberg & Schüz, 1991). In this sense, more than 99.9% of human neurons are "hidden."

Learning algorithms such as this one give important insights into how hidden neurons might develop representations of regularities in the outside world, that is, of our knowledge of the world. In this case, the algorithm is based on comparing "online" learning, where it receives input, with "offline" learning, where it runs without input, and adjusting the connections based on the observed differences (Ackley et al., 1985). It is natural to compare these two phases with "waking" and "dreaming" (or other sleep phases). These networks thus have a natural need for a consolidation phase following initial learning during which the internal representations develop further (Káli & Dayan, 2004). This type of memory consolidation will alter the observed behavior in a way akin to the forming of prototypes, except that the emerging representations may be more general than prototypes, which tend to be mere averages of patterns. A side-effect of this internal learning process during the "offline" phase is that details of stored episodes (i.e., patterns) may be lost, and it is a form of forgetting that is functional with respect to the extraction of general knowledge. We will further discuss models of long-term memory consolidation below.

Error-correcting learning

An important class of neural network is based on providing explicit teaching signals to the output layer of neurons. This suits learning situations where we are teaching a model to learn input–output mappings. Examples are learning to pronounce text (text-to-speech) or learning lists of paired associates such as TABLE–GRASS in a typical verbal learning experiment.

Perceptron and delta rule

One of the first neural network models that was able to learn, the so-called Perceptron, was developed by Frank Rosenblatt in the late 1950s (Rosenblatt, 1958). Like the Willshaw network, the model has an input layer and an output layer with neurons that have activation values 0 or 1. A simple threshold rule is used to decide the activation state on the basis of the net input, similar to the Hopfield network. The threshold, however, is not always equal to 0 but can take any value. With these types of networks, it is often called *bias*; e.g., with a negative bias, more net input is needed to turn the activation value to 1.

Weights in a Perceptron can take any value, such as –5.4 or 0.39. Initially – before learning anything – the weights are set to small random values (e.g., uniform random from –0.3 to 0.3). The learning algorithm operates by correcting the "spontaneous" output that is produced by the network and which initially is random. By comparing the "spontaneous" output with the target or desired output, can we calculate an error signal for each output neuron (see Figure 5.2). The error specifies in what direction the spontaneous output should change. It can take only three values: –1 (activation should decrease), 1 (activation should increase), or 0 (activation is correct). In order to get the activation to decrease, the net input must be lowered. This is achieved by decreasing the weights to the neuron with a small constant

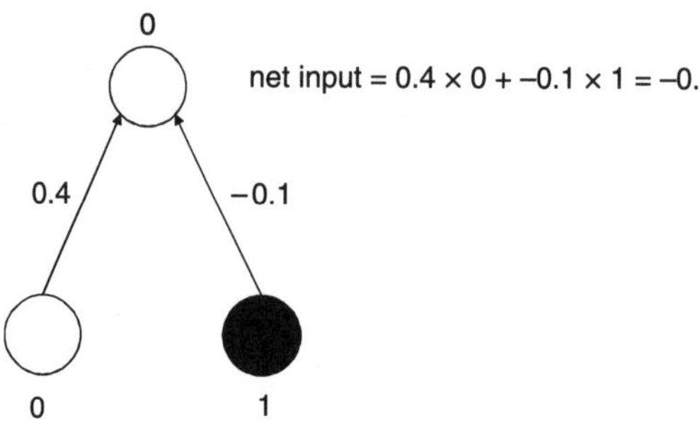

Figure 5.2 Learning in a Perceptron with an input layer of size 2 and an output layer of size 1. The spontaneous output of the current input pattern is 0 but the target output is 1. This means that the error is 1 and that the net input of 0.1 should be increased. If the weight from the activated neuron is increased from –0.1 to 0.1 the network will produce the desired output for this input pattern.

(e.g., 0.2), which is called the *learning rate*. Weights from input neurons that have activation 0 are not changed, however, because they do not contribute to the net input of the output neuron.

Learning is usually not achieved in a single run through all input–output patterns. If complex input–output mappings must be learned, it may take considerable time to find a set of weights that fits all the data. This means that it is necessary to iterate through all input–output patterns many times until the total error (summed over all output neurons and all patterns) does not decrease any more. Important is that Rosenblatt (1958) proved that *if* a pattern set can be represented by a Perceptron, the above learning rule will always find a set of weights that fits the data. The *if* is important here; this became apparent from the analyses by Minsky and Papert (1969), who proved that certain important logical functions (e.g., the exclusive OR) can never be represented by a two-layer network. At least one extra layer is necessary between the input and output to accomplish this, but it was not obvious how such a system would have to be trained because for this "hidden layer" no explicit target signals are available. This limitation squashed much of the initial enthusiasm for the Perceptron, and indeed for neural networks in general. The development of a solution to this problem, in the form of the backpropagation algorithm in 1986 that is discussed below, contributed much to the returned popularity of connectionism.

Before the development of backpropagation, Widrow and Hoff (1960) developed a version of the Perceptron that could work with output neurons that had graded activations. With this rule the difference between the target output and the spontaneous output – called *delta* for difference – is calculated and the weights are adjusted with a constant small fraction, as with the Perceptron learning rule. The effect is that learning initially proceeds very rapidly, while the delta is still large, but as the spontaneous output starts to approach the target output, it slows down to almost zero. Mathematically we have an exponential learning curve. Interestingly, in 1976 Rescorla and Wagner proposed, independently, the same learning rule for learning in animal conditioning. They were not familiar with the Widrow–Hoff learning rule that had until then mainly been used in electrical engineering, for example, to efficiently encode signals in modems.

Backpropagation

The main problem that remained to be solved was how to train the hidden layer of a multilayer Perceptron. Ideally such an algorithm would also have graded neurons because binary (0, 1) activations are a limitation in many cases. Rumelhart, Hinton, and Willams (1986) presented such an algorithm. Its activation rule use is S-shaped. With negative net input like –8.1 the activation is close to 0. With net input around 0, the activation is around 0.5, and with very high positive net input the activation value will approach 1.

The solution they offered works as follows: to obtain the error values for a neuron H in the hidden layer, the sum of error values of the output neurons is used, weighed by the weights of H to each output neuron. In other words, the weights that are normally used to calculate the input to an output neuron are now used to calculate the errors of hidden layer neurons. This is using the connections in reverse, which is why the authors called it *error-backpropagation* or backpropagation for short. The algorithm cannot just work with a single hidden layer but with any number as long as the connections are feedforward. That is, if the layers are sorted from input to output, no (recurrent) connections are allowed from higher to lower levels.[2]

Backpropagation is a powerful learning algorithm that was immediately put to the test in a set of simulations by Sejnowski and Rosenberg (1987). They trained a network to pronounce English text and called their backpropagation-based model NetTalk, a take-off of a similar rule-based algorithm called DECTalk developed by a large computer manufacturer. The model learned to pronounce most of the English words in which it was trained and also showed a good generalization to unseen words, better than DECTalk that had hand-tailored pronunciation rules. Since then, thousands of models have used backpropagation, ranging from models that explain animal conditioning to those that try to predict financial markets. A major question that experimental psychologists had was whether the learning and forgetting behavior exhibited by the backpropagation algorithm was psychologically plausible. As it turned out, it wasn't by a long shot.

Catastrophic forgetting in backpropagation

The first studies to try to assess the forgetting behavior of backpropagation gave very negative results (McCloskey & Cohen, 1989; Ratcliff, 1990), reporting catastrophic interference. After sufficient training on a not too difficult pattern set A, backpropagation would usually achieve near-perfect retrieval of the response (output pattern) when a stimulus (input pattern) is presented. We could for example model learning a list of paired associates like TABLE–GRASS in this manner. When subjects learn a second list there is little interference from the second list, unless the stimuli of list B resemble those of list A. If that is the case, what happens depends on the responses in list B (Osgood, 1949). If the responses in B are very similar to those in A (and paired in the same way), recall on list A will improve. One can view list B as an imperfect rehearsal of list A. If list B has very different responses, however, there is strong forgetting of list A as earlier stimuli are now paired with different responses. The problem with backpropagation was that it always showed very strong – "catastrophic" – forgetting, even when the second list had completely different stimuli and responses, a condition in which human subjects forget only a little as a result of learning the second list. Backpropagation thus has psychologically implausible forgetting behavior. This is not only a problem for its use in memory psychology but it also limits its application to real-world problems because it is impossible to "update" a backpropagation algorithm by training it on the latest patterns (e.g., when trying to predict the stockmarket).

Two studies (French, 1992; Murre, 1992) noticed that the hidden layer representations tend to have many activations around 0.5, which thus highly overlap even though the input patterns may not. For example, the three simple input patterns (1 0 0 0), (0 1 0 0), and (0 0 1 0) do not overlap at all. Yet, their hidden layer representations do and will often continue to do so after training. We could, for example, train the network to produce the same output pattern that was presented at the input, say with a hidden layer of four neurons. This is an easy task that the network learns quickly. But because all hidden layer representations are very similar, if a fourth pattern (0 0 0 1) is learned, the hidden layer weights will be directed to that pattern (i.e., to the fourth neuron, with target activation 1) and strong unlearning of connections to the first three neurons will occur (because their target values are 0). Thus, after training on (0 0 0 1), without rehearsal of earlier patterns the first three patterns are largely forgotten. This type of forgetting occurs in human subjects only if the stimuli (input patterns) are highly similar. If the stimuli are dissimilar, little forgetting would occur. In this case the stimuli are not similar, but the internal representations are, giving the same result. In fact, based on Osgood's (1949) review, we would expect that additional training on patterns with similar outputs would lead to an implausible *improvement* in performance on the earlier patterns, which is in fact the case (Murre, 1996a): the opposite of catastrophic forgetting, which is equally implausible from the point of view of memory psychology.

Based on this analysis, a remedy would be to somehow induce backpropagation to make its hidden layer representations less overlapping (i.e., sparse). This approach works and removes much of the catastrophe from the forgetting (French, 1992; Murre, 1992). Another approach is to rehearse the first pattern set, where it was shown with simulation studies that only a small random portion of the first set needs to be rehearsed to prevent the first set from being wiped out by learning the second (Murre, 1992). Several other successful approaches to reducing catastrophic interference have been proposed (French, 1999). We may wonder whether the simpler variants of backpropagation, lacking the troublesome hidden layer, would give more plausible results. This is indeed the case (Murre, 1996a). A Perceptron or two-layer backpropagation network gives results similar to those summarized in Osgood (1949) and does not suffer from catastrophic forgetting.

It is perhaps important here to point out that just because backpropagation shows implausible patterns of forgetting, this does not mean that all neural networks suffer from this. An early example of a neural network model that foresaw problems with strong interference due to novel learning is *adaptive resonance theory* or ART by Steven Grossberg (Carpenter & Grossberg, 1988; Grossberg, 1976). This network has two layers, where one represents the pattern to be learned or retrieved and a *category layer* where "category neurons" represent either a single pattern or a category of similar patterns. At learning, the input pattern is associated in two directions with a single category neuron. When a retrieval cue is presented to the network, the closest matching category neuron is activated. Because learned patterns may overlap in complicated ways, this is not always the best match. ART networks are able to assess the quality of the match between the currently selected category neuron and the input pattern. This is called resonance: the degree to which the feedback from the category neuron reinforces the currently activated input pattern. If there is high resonance, one could conclude that a suitable category neuron has been selected. If there is low resonance, an ART network is able to reset its category layer, suppressing already selected category neurons so that a novel categorization can take place. In this way, the system is able to cycle through various candidate category neurons until one is found with a high resonance, at which point the search process stops. If no suitable category neurons are found, a currently uncommitted category neuron is found and associated with the current input pattern. In this way, ART is able to accommodate novel patterns without too much disturbance of patterns already learned.

Summary of basic mechanisms

So far we have looked at some of the basic neural network paradigms. We have seen how feedforward networks with two layers of neurons can learn either with a Hebbian-type rule (Willshaw network) or with an error-correcting learning rule (Perceptron, Widrow–Hoff rule). More complex processing is possible in multilayer Perceptrons that use backpropagation learning or in attractor networks which have recurrent connections (i.e., the Hopfield network). A great many other types of network paradigms have been developed in the past two decades that we cannot discuss here (see, for example, introductory textbooks such as Bechtel & Abrahamsen, 1991; Ellis & Humphreys, 1999; Rumelhart & McClelland, 1986).

Because the learning and activation dynamics of neural networks may have quite different underlying principles, not all neural network have the same characteristics. Nonetheless, most neural networks can do the following:

- learn episodes (i.e., individual patterns)
- extract statistical regularities from the episodes
- form prototypes or other abstract representations
- retrieve a learned pattern on the basis of partial or distorted input
- exhibit graceful degradation of performance when weights are lesioned.

In particular, backpropagation networks can learn complex input–output mappings such as the pronunciation of English text on the basis of examples, with good generalization of this behavior to untrained words to be pronounced. Unfortunately, three-layer backpropagation networks also suffer from catastrophic interference, which makes them unsuitable for direct use as a model of learning and forgetting unless additional measures are taken. In the remainder of this chapter, we discuss connectionist models of memory that have been developed with the aim to test specific aspects of learning, consolidation, and forgetting.

Connectionist models of memory

Many researchers have built on the basic memory mechanisms of neural networks in order to study in more detail the principles that underlie human memory. We shall discuss some memory models here, with emphasis on their forgetting mechanisms. As mentioned above, short-term memory is typically modeled by the current state of the activations in a network. Short-term forgetting can then be viewed as the processes by which this state decays or gets modified by new incoming information. To model human forgetting in some interesting detail, however, it is necessary to extend this approach so that multiple items can be held in memory. One model of serial recall (Page & Norris, 1998), for example, is a neural network in which different items (e.g., words in a list) are located in different parts of the network. The ordering of the items in the list is represented by relative levels of activation, where the highest activated items are to be recalled first. Because the read-out mechanism is noisy, mistakes are made that replicate those of humans. This noisy read-out also limits the number of items that can be represented in this way, because very small differences in activation necessary to accommodate long lists would lead to many errors and hence imply an automatic limit on the capacity. Thus, as more items become active, distinctions in activation levels become lost, which leads to forgetting of weaker items.

An interesting model by Raffone and Wolters (2002) uses a different approach. Their model is based on the notion of neural synchrony. In the network models discussed so far in this chapter, there is one basic mechanism by which elements of a short-term memory item are represented as belonging to that same item, namely coactivation. For example, in a Hopfield or back-propagation network, a pattern is represented by coactivating a number of neurons. These determine the item currently "held in short-term memory." With noisy neurons this is more complicated. If a memory is represented by, say, 50 neurons, different subsets of the 50 will fire in various random combinations where the probability of any two neurons of the 50 firing together is relatively high. Thus, if we have two groups of neurons A and B, neurons in A would tend to fire together, as would those of B. When measuring two neurons in A, we would conclude that their firing is synchronized compared to a neuron in A with a neuron in B, which would not tend to fire at the same time.

The model by Raffone and Wolters (2002) is based on a more complex type of model neuron than discussed so far. It is more biologically detailed and includes among other things a refractory period: a period in which a neuron cannot fire immediately after firing. Considering again groups A and B, suppose that many neurons in A have fired, then these will be silent for a short while, giving neurons in other groups a chance to fire, say those in B. In this way, several groups of neurons can follow each other in time: A, B, C, D . . . When the refractory period is over, group A can fire again. One could view the firing groups as a short-term memory where one of the limits on the sequence is imposed by the refractory period, which is a biologically given constant. As it turns out, when biologically detailed model neurons are used (MacGregor & Oliver, 1974), a neural network model of visual memory can contain about four groups that fire in sequence, thus giving a plausible account of the observed limit on visual short-term memory of four items (Luck & Vogel, 1997). When more items are presented to this model, one of the four that is currently cycling is dropped to accommodate the new item. One could say that the model contains a visual buffer of limited capacity or a cyclic memory "loop" (Atkinson & Shiffrin, 1968; Baddeley & Hitch, 1974). Though Raffone and Wolters (2002) did not investigate the forgetting behavior systematically, we would expect similar behavior to that found by authors who have assumed the existence of such a buffer (e.g., Mensink & Raaijmakers, 1988).

Many authors have reported that memory follows a power function (Anderson & Schooler, 1991; Wixted & Ebbesen, 1991) and we might ask whether neural networks show the same behavior. Power functions are of the shape t^{-a}, where t is time (in suitable units) and $a > 0$ is the forgetting parameter. Exponential forgetting has shape a^{-t}. As time progresses, exponential forgetting will lead to a near-complete loss of memories much faster than power function forgetting.

Sikström (2002) shows through simulation and analysis how a modified

Hopfield network exhibits power function forgetting. He uses a learning rule where the weights are bounded, which has the effect that with progressive learning there is exponential forgetting in the weights. Another difference from the Hopfield network is that the model does not use a single learning rate that applies to all weights but instead each weight has its own learning rate drawn from a suitable probability distribution. In the network we will thus find both weights with a high learning rate (fast weights) and with a low learning rate (slow weights), as well as with intermediate rates. Forgetting in this model occurs through interference where new patterns will partially erase old ones. We have seen above that in a distributed memory many patterns can be superimposed on the same set of weights and that no forgetting need occur as long as the capacity of the network is not exceeded. Indeed, Sikström (2002) observes that in his model memories tend to be stored as usual in the slow weights, which keep functioning as in a Hopfield network (as long as the weight values remain away from the weight boundaries). But in the fast weights, a new pattern may easily wipe out previous information and thus these weights tend to represent mainly the most recently learned patterns. Analysis and simulations of such a model show that forgetting tends to follow a power function. Note that the additional assumptions introduced, namely bounded weights and varying learning rates, make the network model biologically more plausible, as did introducing a refractory period in the model by Raffone and Wolters (2002), where it resulted in a plausible value for the capacity of visual short-term memory. There are also connectionist models of memory that focus more directly on the neurobiology of memory, in particular on the effects of lesioning on certain brain structures thought to be crucial for storage and retrieval of long-term memory.

Instead of studying forgetting as a side-effect of noisy or decaying connections or because of interference due to new learning, some authors have developed models of long-term memory consolidation. This is an active process that occurs after initial learning and operates to safeguard certain memories from rapid forgetting. In one view, memories are first stored via the hippocampus or medial temporal lobe structures. This is a very plastic area with limited capacity, which causes fairly rapid forgetting of newly acquired memories (say, in the order of weeks or months in humans). Consolidation theories propose that memories are somehow transferred to the neocortex where they are less prone to forgetting (Alvarez & Squire, 1994; McClelland, McNaughton, & O'Reilly, 1995; Meeter & Murre, 2005; Murre, 1996b). Some authors dispute this view, which they refer to as the "standard theory of consolidation," and instead propose that memories always remain dependent on the hippocampus (Nadel & Moscovitch, 1997). Interesting that in this debate connectionist models play an important role, mainly to verify and demonstrate that the consolidation mechanisms indeed work as purported (Nadel, Samsonovitch, Ryan, & Moscovitch, 2000). We review the evidence for the different viewpoints on consolidation elsewhere (Meeter &

Murre, 2004a) and limit ourselves to a brief discussion of the two models of consolidation.

The model by McClelland et al. (1995) is based on a backpropagation network. To solve the problem of catastrophic interference they propose that, following new learning, a random proportion of the old patterns (which represent episodes) is rehearsed. This interleaved learning allows for the gradual build-up of representations in the hidden layer (artificial neocortex). The "medial temporal lobe" or MTL in this model is simply a store that holds patterns, which randomly drop out over time (forgetting from MTL). This causes the MTL store mainly to contain recent patterns. Retrieval of an episode can occur either from MTL, or if it is no longer present there from the neural network (neocortex). Lesioning the MTL of the model therefore leads primarily to a loss of recent memories, because the older memories will have been consolidated in the neural network through the interleaved learning. This is a well-known effect that occurs in a wide variety of retrograde amnesia syndromes and was first described by Ribot (1881).

There is now abundant evidence that neural processes during sleep play at least some role in the consolidation of memories (Ellenbogen, Payne, & Stickgold, 2006; Marshall & Born, 2007; Stickgold, 2005; Stickgold, James, & Hobson, 2000). There is neural evidence for replay of memories during the slow-wave sleep stage (Wilson & McNaughton, 1994) and a natural assumption is that it is this mechanism that actively consolidates memory (which has not been proven conclusively). The TraceLink model (Meeter & Murre, 2005; Murre, 1996b) implements some of the details of such a process. TraceLink is an attractor network that has a Trace system representing the neocortex and a Link system that represents the MTL. It is assumed that the Link system has a higher learning rate so that it can rapidly store associations (links) between elements of the Trace pattern, which are initially not well connected. Following learning, there is a period of simulated "slow-wave sleep" in which the network is given random activations after which the activations are cycled until the network has found an attractor. This attractor (pattern) is then strengthened in the Trace system only. The consolidation mechanism causes patterns to become stronger in the Trace system over time. At the same time there is fairly high forgetting in the Link system because of interference from newly learned patterns. If after learning the Link system (MTL) is lesioned, recent memories are lost but older memories, which have received consolidation, are retained. One of the predictions of TraceLink is that stronger patterns show much less forgetting over time than weak patterns, because the latter receive relatively little consolidation. It also predicts that forgetting is accelerated in semantic dementia because the neocortical basis is severely weakened so that normal consolidation cannot take place (Meeter & Murre, 2004b).

Concluding remarks

It will be evident from the review here that there may be many causes of forgetting in neural networks, either as a side-effect of basic learning mechanisms or because certain mechanisms of forgetting have been added deliberately to simulate specific forms of forgetting. With respect to theory formation, we might ask what the role of neural networks is. From a general point of view neural networks show us how complex systems that consist of many interacting neurons may give rise to behavior that is of interest to memory psychology. An example is the formation of prototypes. While the prototypes are forming, details of individual patterns may be lost. Rather than forcing a choice between either exemplar or prototype storage, connectionist models allow us to study the intermediate case (McClelland & Rumelhart, 1985). Moreover, this behavior will be found in most types of neural networks and it is therefore not unreasonable to assume that similar processes will take place in the nervous tissue of the neocortex. Two-layer neural networks, like the Perceptron, exhibit similar interference and transfer to humans (Osgood, 1949). Making neural network models more biologically plausible often further increases their psychological plausibility (Raffone & Wolters, 2002; Sikström, 2002). It thus seems that neural networks – especially those that remove certain biological implausibilities – share many pervasive characteristics with human memory.

Some of the connectionist models discussed here go beyond basic mechanisms. These models can be thought of as existence proofs, demonstrating that a certain set of theoretical assumptions (e.g., about memory consolidation) is sufficiently consistent and detailed to drive implementation and testing in a neural network. This is often not true of verbally stated theories, where inconsistencies and lack of crucial details may remain unnoticed in interesting-sounding but vague language. Modeling reveals these theoretical trouble spots and enforces clarity. Neural network models are less well suited to precise quantitative fitting and prediction. It is computationally demanding to run a model many times while searching for optimal combinations of parameters that best fit the data. Also, the number of parameters may be very large. We therefore see that most modelers merely show that their models exhibit certain general characteristics, such as power function forgetting or a specific type of retrograde amnesia gradient. An interesting approach is where modelers try to capture some of the essence of their neural network model in a set of equations that can be analyzed mathematically (e.g., McClelland et al., 1995; Sikström, 2002). In this way, hierarchies of models can be developed that range from low-level biological to high-level mathematical (Meeter, Jehee, & Murre, 2007). Connectionist models best fit a role in the middle. Being neither biologically detailed, nor mathematically concise, they can nonetheless provide many insights about possible mechanisms that may underlie human forgetting.

Notes

1 We will use the term "neuron" here, dropping artificial, where it is understood that the operation of neural network neurons may be a very crude abstraction of the intricacies of biological neurons.

2 The paper by Rumelhart et al. (1986) also describes an extension to the basic algorithm that does allow recurrent connections, but this algorithm is considerably more complex.

References

Ackley, D. H., Hinton, G. E., & Sejnowski, T. J. (1985). A learning algorithm for Boltzmann Machines. *Cognitive Science*, *9*, 147–169.

Alvarez, P., & Squire, L. R. (1994). Memory consolidation and the medial temporal lobe: A simple network model. *Proceedings of the National Academy of Sciences (USA)*, *91*, 7041–7045.

Anderson, J. R., & Schooler, L. J. (1991). Reflections of the environment in memory. *Psychological Science*, *2*, 396–408.

Atkinson, R. C., & Shiffrin, R. M. (1968). Human memory: A proposed system and its control processes. In K. W. Spence & J. T. Spence (Eds.), *The psychology of learning and motivation: Advances in research and theory (Vol. 2)* (pp. 89–195). New York: Academic Press.

Baddeley, A. D., & Hitch, G. (1974). Working memory. In G. A. Bower (Ed.), *The psychology of learning and motivation* (pp. 47–89). New York: Academic Press.

Bechtel, W., & Abrahamsen, A. A. (1991). *Connectionism and the mind.* Oxford: Blackwell.

Braitenberg, V., & Schüz, A. (1991). *Anatomy of the cortex: Statistics and geometry.* Berlin: Springer Verlag.

Brewer, W. F., & Treyens, J. C. (1981). Role of schemata in memory for places. *Cognitive Psychology*, *13*(2), 207–230.

Carpenter, G. A., & Grossberg, S. (1988). The ART of adaptive pattern recognition by a self-organizing neural network. *Computer*, *21*, 77–88.

Ellenbogen, J. M., Payne, J. D., & Stickgold, R. (2006). The role of sleep in declarative memory consolidation: Passive, permissive, active or none? *Current Opinion in Neurobiology*, *16*(6), 716–722.

Ellis, R., & Humphreys, G. W. (1999). *Connectionist psychology: A text with readings.* Hove, UK: Psychology Press.

French, R. M. (1992). Semi-distributed representations and catastrophic forgetting in connectionist networks. *Connection Science*, *4*, 365–377.

French, R. M. (1999). Catastrophic forgetting in connectionist networks. *Trends in the Cognitive Sciences*, *3*, 128–135.

Grossberg, S. (1976). Adaptive pattern classification and universal recoding, II: Feedback, expectation, olfaction, and illusions. *Biological Cybernetics*, *23*, 187–202.

Grossberg, S. (1987). *The adaptive brain. Volume I: Cognition, learning, reinforcement, and rhythm. Volume II: Vision, speech, language, and motor control.* Amsterdam: North-Holland.

Hebb, D. O. (1949). *The organization of behavior*. New York: Wiley.

Hopfield, J. J. (1982). Neural networks and physical systems with emergent collective computational abilities. *Proceedings of the National Academy of Sciences USA*, *79*, 2554–2558.

James, W. (1892/2001). *Psychology: The briefer course*. Mineola, NY: Dover.

Káli, S., & Dayan, P. (2004). Off-line replay maintains declarative memories in a model of hippocampal–neocortical interactions. *Nature Neuroscience*, *7*, 286–294.

Luck, S. J., & Vogel, E. K. (1997). The capacity of visual working memory for features and conjunctions. *Nature*, *390*(6657), 279.

McClelland, J. L., McNaughton, B. L., & O'Reilly, R. C. (1995). Why there are complementary learning systems in the hippocampus and neocortex: Insights from the successes and failures of connectionist models of learning and memory. *Psychological Review*, *102*, 419–457.

McClelland, J. L., & Rumelhart, D. E. (1985). Distributed memory and the representation of general and specific information. *Journal of Experimental Psychology: General*, *114*, 159–188.

McCloskey, M., & Cohen, N. J. (1989). Catastrophic interference in connectionist networks: The sequential learning problem. In G. H. Bower (Ed.), *The psychology of learning and motivation* (pp. 109–164). New York: Academic Press.

MacGregor, R. J., & Oliver, R. M. (1974). A model for repetitive firing in neurons. *Cybernetik*, *16*, 53–64.

Marshall, L., & Born, J. (2007). The contribution of sleep to hippocampus-dependent memory consolidation. *Trends in Cognitive Sciences*, *11*(10), 442–450.

Meeter, M., Jehee, J., & Murre, J. (2007). Neural models that convince: Model hierarchies and other strategies to bridge the gap between behavior and the brain. *Philosophical Psychology*, *20*(6), 749.

Meeter, M., & Murre, J. M. J. (2004a). Consolidation of long-term memory: Evidence and alternatives. *Psychological Bulletin*, *130*, 843–857.

Meeter, M., & Murre, J. M. J. (2004b). Simulating episodic memory deficits in semantic dementia with the TraceLink model. *Memory*, *12*, 272–287.

Meeter, M., & Murre, J. M. J. (2005). Tracelink: A model of consolidation and amnesia. *Cognitive Neuropsychology*, *22*(5), 559–587.

Mensink, G. J., & Raaijmakers, J. G. W. (1988). A model for interference and forgetting. *Psychological Review*, *95*, 434–455.

Minsky, M. L., & Papert, S. (1969). *Perceptrons: An introduction to computational geometry*. Cambridge, MA: MIT Press.

Murre, J. M. J. (1992). *Categorization and learning in modular neural networks*. Hillsdale, NJ: Lawrence Erlbaum Associates, Inc.

Murre, J. M. J. (1996a). Hypertransfer in neural networks. *Connection Science*, *8*(2), 249–258.

Murre, J. M. J. (1996b). TraceLink: A model of amnesia and consolidation of memory. *Hippocampus*, *6*, 675–684.

Nadel, L., & Moscovitch, M. (1997). Memory consolidation, retrograde amnesia and the hippocampal complex. *Current Opinion in Neurobiology*, *7*, 217–227.

Nadel, L., Samsonovitch, A., Ryan, L., & Moscovitch, M. (2000). Multiple trace theory of human memory: Computational, neuroimaging and neuropsychological results. *Hippocampus*, *10*, 352–368.

Osgood, C. E. (1949). The similarity paradox in human learning. *Psychological Review*, *56*, 132–143.

Page, M., & Norris, D. (1998). The primacy model: A new model of immediate serial recall. *Psychological Review*, *105*(4), 761–781.

Purves, D. (1988). *Body and brain: A trophic theory of neural connections*: Cambridge, MA: Harvard University Press.

Raffone, A., & Wolters, G. (2002). A cortical mechanism for binding in visual working memory. *Journal of Cognitive Neuroscience, 13*, 766–785.

Ratcliff, R. (1990). Connectionist models of recognition memory: Constraints imposed by learning and forgetting functions. *Psychological Review, 97*, 285–308.

Ribot, T. (1881). *Les Maladies de la mémoire*. Paris: Germer Baillare.

Rosenblatt, F. (1958). The Perceptron: A probabilistic model for information storage in the brain. *Psychological Review, 65*, 386–408.

Rumelhart, D. E., & McClelland, J. L. (Eds.). (1986). *Parallel distributed processing. Explorations in the microstructure of cognition (Vol. 1: Foundations)*. Cambridge, MA: MIT Press.

Rumelhart, D. E., Hinton, G. E., & Williams, R. J. (1986). Learning internal representations by error propagation. In D. E. Rumelhart & J. L. McClelland (Eds.), *Parallel distributed processing. Volume 1: Foundations* (pp. 318–362). Cambridge, MA: MIT Press.

Sejnowski, T. J., & Rosenberg, C. R. (1987). Parallel networks that learn to pronounce English text. *Complex Systems, 1*(1), 145–168.

Sikström, S. (2002). Forgetting curves: Implications for connectionist models. *Cognitive Psychology, 45*(1), 95–152.

Stickgold, R. (2005). Sleep-dependent memory consolidation. *Nature, 437*, 27.

Stickgold, R., James, L., & Hobson, J. A. (2000). Visual discrimination learning requires sleep after training. *Nature Neuroscience, 3*, 1237–1238.

Widrow, B., & Hoff, M. E. (1960). Adaptive switching circuits. 1960 IRE WESCON Convention Record. *New York: IRE, 4*, 96–104.

Willshaw, D. J., Buneman, O. P., & Longuet-Higgins, H. C. (1969). Non-holographic associative memory. *Nature, 222*(5197), 960–962.

Wilson, M. A., & McNaughton, B. L. (1994). Reactivation of hippocampal ensemble memories during sleep. *Science, 255*, 676–679.

Wixted, J. T., & Ebbesen, E. B. (1991). On the form of forgetting. *Psychological Science, 2*, 409–415.

6 Synaptic plasticity and the neurobiology of memory and forgetting

Flavia Valtorta

S. Raffaele Scientific Institute, Milan, Italy, and International School of Psychotherapy with Imaginative Procedures (SISPI), Milan, Italy

Fabio Benfenati

Italian Institute of Technology, Genoa, Italy, and University of Genoa, Genoa, Italy

Memory is commonly seen as a positive ability of the individual to improve performance, indispensable for survival and social success. Forgetting, on the other hand, generally has a negative connotation, which is often associated with pathological states and/or aging. This common view is also reflected in our knowledge of the underlying biological processes. While thousands of papers have elucidated the processes of learning and memory from the molecular and cellular level up to the cognitive and psychological level, relatively few data are available on the mechanisms of forgetting.

Memory and forgetting are daily processes of our lives that allow us to select from our billions of experiences those which are the most relevant for our personal history and our culture. Thus, memory and forgetting are two complementary faces of the same biological process that profoundly affect and direct our behaviour and the sense of our individuality. One could say that without forgetting memory would be completely useless.

This concept is very well exemplified in the short fantasy story "Funes el memorioso" by Jorge Luis Borges (1944, p. 55). Describing Funes, Borges says:

> Without effort, he had learned English, French, Portuguese, Latin. I suspect, nevertheless, that he was not very capable of thought. To think is to forget a difference, to generalize, to abstract. In the overly replete world of Funes there were nothing but details, almost contiguous details. . . . It occurred to me that each one of my words (each one of my gestures) would live on in his implacable memory; I was benumbed by the fear of multiplying superfluous gestures.

The inability to forget details prevents the process of generalization which is necessary for abstract thought and ultimately for making sense of our experiences.

While there is a wide consensus on the cellular bases of learning and memory, work on forgetting has primarily had a psychological focus. Therefore, relatively few data regarding the neurobiological mechanisms of forgetting are available. As memory reflects an array of temporally related processes including acquisition, consolidation, retention, retrieval and reconsolidation, a failure of any of these mechanisms could give rise to forgetting. Depending on the memory process that is affected, various types of forgetting can be envisaged:

- natural decay, resulting from the passage of time and the infrequent recall of the memory (passive natural forgetting or retention defect)
- interference, due to a conflict between the initial mechanisms of acquisition and those of the consolidation of a previously acquired memory
- retrieval failure due to changed or otherwise inadequate retrieval cues or due to specific emotions (repression)
- defect in reconsolidation, i.e., in a process needed to restabilize memories returned to a labile state upon retrieval
- forgetting as a new learning process (i.e., extinction)
- amnesia due to selective or generalized brain damage.

It should be noted that virtually all types of forgetting involve forms of explicit memory. This is mainly due to the fact that implicit memory is much more robust than explicit memory and less susceptible to forgetting, except in severe brain pathologies.

In this chapter we will briefly review the cellular bases of neural activity and synaptic plasticity, and their implications in learning and memory phenomena. We will then describe the various aspects of forgetting either as a failure of specific stages of the memory process or as distinct phenomena involving active processes triggered by environmental or pathological factors.

The synaptic basis of neural activity

> All the psychological matters that we are progressively formulating, will have to rely, one day, on an organic substrate.
>
> (S. Freud, *Entwurf einer Psychologie*, 1895)

Neurons are specialized for communication and information processing. They are highly polarized cells composed of distinct functional compartments, including the following:

(1) A *receiving domain* represented by dendrites and the cell body that capture information from other neurons at numerous (about 1000 on average) synaptic contacts.

(2) An *integration domain* represented by the initial segment of the axon (the most excitable part of the neuron) that integrates all the received information within time and space and takes the final decision of whether or not to generate an action potential.
(3) A *cable domain*, the axon, specialized for the rapid transfer of the nerve impulse.
(4) A *transmission domain*, the nerve terminal, that is specialized in transducing the all-or-none nerve impulse into a highly regulated release of a chemical messenger (neurotransmitter), for which specific receptors exist on the postsynaptic neuron (Kandel, Schwartz, & Jessell, 2000).

The specific areas of contact between neurons were named synapses (from the Greek term "tighten together") by the British physiologist Charles S. Sherrington in 1897. In chemical synapses, which account for most if not all mammalian synapses, neurotransmitters are stored in synaptic vesicles within the presynaptic terminal and are released by a process of regulated exocytosis, in which synaptic vesicles fuse with the presynaptic membrane and release their content into the synaptic cleft. Neurotransmitter release preferentially occurs at the active zone, a highly specialized area of the presynaptic membrane, and is triggered by depolarization that promotes influx of calcium (Ca^{2+}) through voltage-dependent Ca^{2+} channels (Figure 6.1). Once secreted, the neurotransmitter rapidly diffuses within the narrow synaptic cleft to reach postsynaptic receptors that bind and transduce it into an electrical and/or metabolic response of the postsynaptic neuron. Over long distances neurons can only transmit a digital stereotyped signal (the action potential) that cannot be modulated in amplitude, but only in frequency. At the synapse, however, a digital-to-analog process occurs that enables an identical signal to be transmitted across the synaptic cleft in a highly modulatable fashion (Zucker, 1996).

The efficiency of information transfer through the synapse, called *synaptic strength*, depends on the complexity of the signal transduction processes including an electrical-to-chemical transduction at the presynaptic level followed by a chemical-to-electrical/metabolic transduction at the postsynaptic level. In other words, an action potential can promote exocytosis of a variable number of synaptic vesicles, each containing a highly reproducible number of neurotransmitter molecules (the neurotransmitter *quantum*), and neurotransmitter molecules can be bound by a variable number and type of postsynaptic receptors. Thus, synaptic strength can be regulated by a variety of presynaptic and postsynaptic events and depends on three factors that can be determined experimentally, namely:

- the number of active release sites n, corresponding to the number of synaptic vesicles ready for release at the active zone
- the probability p of each vesicle to undergo fusion at the arrival of the action potential

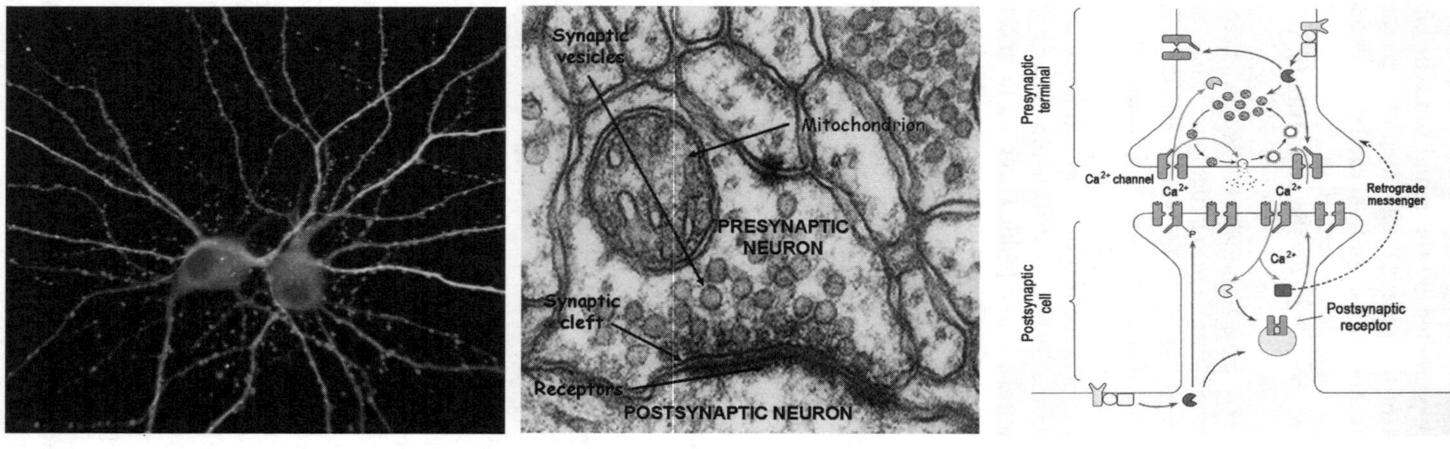

Figure 6.1 Synaptic connections among neurons. *Left panel:* Two large hippocampal neurons in culture receiving multiple synaptic inputs labelled for the presynaptic protein synaptophysin (puncta). *Middle and right panel:* Ultrastructure (courtesy of Dr Pietro De Camilli, Yale University, New Haven, CT) and schematics of a chemical synapse. The neurotransmitter is stored in synaptic vesicles which undergo an activity-dependent exo-endocytotic cycle and, once released into the synaptic cleft, binds to adjacent postsynaptic receptors. Activated postsynaptic receptors mediate biological responses in the postsynaptic cells which not only modify the electrical state of the neuron (either excitation or inhibition), but also activate signal transduction pathways affecting receptor turnover and response to the transmitter, generation of retrograde messengers or transcription/translation processes.

- the quantum content q that depends on both the number of neurotransmitter molecules per vesicle (generally a very constant value) and the number of stimulated receptors on the postsynaptic side.

These three parameters are very sensitive to the previous history of the neuron (e.g., previous patterns of stimulation), as well as to intracellular messengers and protein phosphorylation processes at both presynaptic and postsynaptic sides (see below; Greengard, Valtorta, Czernik, & Benfenati, 1993; Kandel et al., 2000; Zucker, 1996).

Synaptic plasticity and the cellular bases of learning and memory

The major and most distinctive feature of the nervous system is its astonishing ability to adapt to the environment and to improve its performance over time and experience. In 1906 this special/unique property, collectively named "plasticity", was precisely defined by Santiago Ramón y Cajal as "the property by virtue of which sustained functional changes occur in particular neuronal systems following the administration of appropriate environmental stimuli or the combination of different stimuli". Since the neural changes evoked by the stimuli can persist for a very long time, virtually for the whole life of the individual, neural plasticity could represent an attractive basis for learning and memory. Conversely, the built-in property of neural plasticity might allow experience to functionally and structurally shape the nervous system. The latter aspect, which is also a fundamental feature of neural development and maturation, was envisaged in the 3rd century BC by the Greek philosopher Epicurus, who wrote that "it's because something of the external objects penetrates in ourselves that we can identify shapes and think". It is known that neurons are generated in great excess and that only some of them, selected on the basis of the size and activity of the innervated territories, survive through development, while the others undergo programmed cell death. The selected neurons then grow processes and contact target neurons that are recognized on the basis of a mosaic of secreted and membrane-exposed signals whose expression is genetically determined. Thus, the first assembly of neuronal networks is driven by genetic factors, i.e., by the size of the physiological targets and the expression of chemotactic and/or cell adhesion "recognition" proteins whose genes are specifically transcribed and translated by the various neuronal populations (Kandel et al., 2000).

After this first gene-driven developmental period, neuronal circuits are continuously modified and shaped by experience (epigenetic development): synaptic connections that are scarcely used become weaker and weaker and eventually disappear, whereas synapses that are heavily used become stronger and stronger and eventually increase in number. As mentioned above, synaptic strength can be finely tuned over a short or even a long timescale by a combination of factors including previous activity of the network, generation of second messengers, functional changes in presynaptic and postsynaptic proteins as well as regulation of the expression of genes implicated in growth, survival and synaptic transmission. This results in changes in the efficiency of synaptic transmission that can last from a fraction of a second to minutes in the case of short-term synaptic plasticity (paired-pulse facilitation or depression, augmentation, synaptic depression, posttetanic potentiation) to hours, days and months in the case of long-term synaptic plasticity (long-term potentiation, LTP; long-term depression, LTD). These changes profoundly affect the processing carried out between input and output information and, ultimately, filter and shape the flow of information within the neural network (Figure 6.2).

Interestingly, after the cornerstone discoveries of Camillo Golgi and Santiago Ramón y Cajal (1906), but some 50 years before Donald Hebb (1949) formulated the idea of synaptic plasticity as the basis of psychological functions, Sigmund Freud (1895) proposed in his *Entwurf einer Psychologie* that the physical structure of memories consists of a long-lasting, activity-dependent modification of information transfer between neurons (Centonze, Siracusano, Calabresi, & Bernardi, 2004; Sejnowski, 1999). Freud drew attention to the synapse, which he called "contact barrier", and to the quantity of information "$Q\eta$" that passes through the synapse during the process of neural excitation, i.e., the equivalent of synaptic strength. He identified two types of communication, that of "permeable or φ neurons that behave as if they have no contact barriers" (i.e., neurons which transfer information across the synapse without resistance) and that of "impermeabile or ψ neurons which act in such a way as to permit only a difficult or partial passage of $Q\eta$". Thus, the activity of a network depends on the mosaic of facilitated and nonfacilitated barriers since, as Freud says: "$Q\eta$ in an a neuron will be directed toward a more facilitated barrier . . . and the higher $Q\eta$ during the course of excitation, the greater the facilitation" (see Figure 6.2, upper panel). Thus, memories can be represented as sequences of activity patterns distributed across a population of neurons, which in turn are associated with a different subsequent pattern of encoding. During retrieval, a memory cue may cause neural activity to evolve toward one of these activity patterns (attractor state; Hasselmo & McClelland, 1999; see Figure 6.2, lower panel).

From short-term to long-term memories

Memory consolidation, interference and forgetfulness

> I've seen things you people wouldn't believe. Attack ships on fire off the shoulder of Orion. I watched C-beams glitter in the dark near the Tannhauser gate. All those moments will be lost in time, like tears in rain.
>
> (Ridley Scott, *Blade Runner*, 1982)

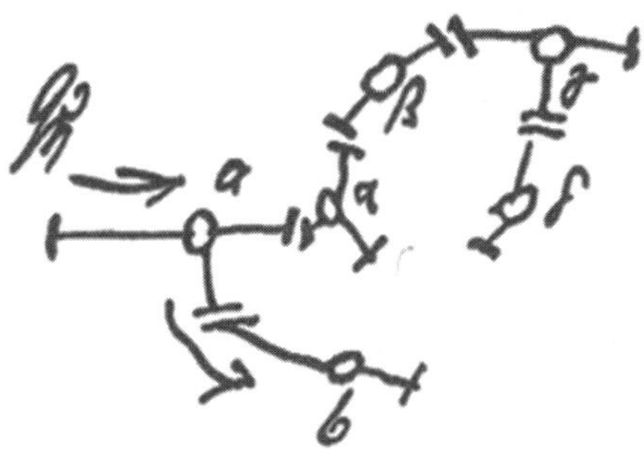

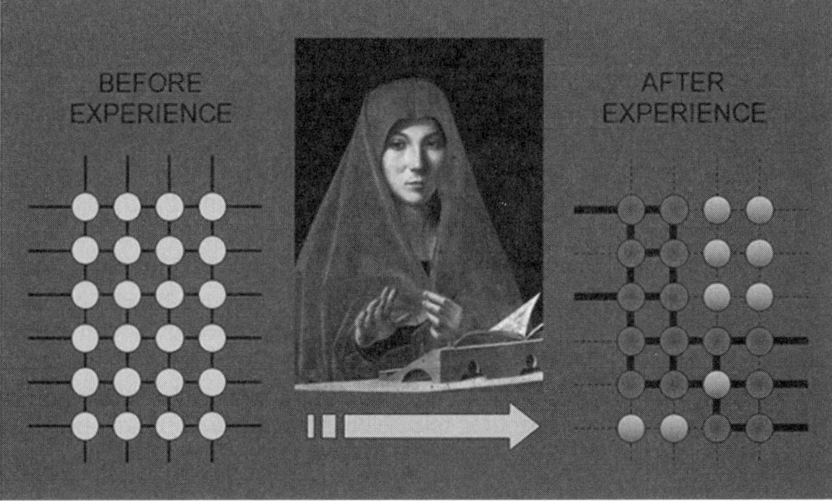

Figure 6.2 Synaptic plasticity and memory. *Upper panel:* Sigmund Freud's drawing putting forward the possibility of a change in the gain of synaptic connections in a neuronal network as the basis of learning and memory. *Lower panel:* A sensory experience (e.g., the *Annunciata* by Antonello da Messina, 1474–1475) can modify prestructured neuronal networks by changing the efficiency of transmission in selective synaptic connections, thereby modifying the flow of information within the network.

Learning induces cellular and molecular changes that facilitate or impair communication among neurons and are fundamental for memory storage. If learning brings about changes in "synaptic strength" within neuronal circuits, the persistence of these changes represents the way memories are stored. Short-term memory is believed to involve only functional changes in pre-existing neuronal networks mediated by a fine-tuning of multiple intracellular signal transductions systems. These short-lived changes can undergo either of two processes: either fade out with time (forgetfulness) or be reinforced and transformed into long-term memory by a process called memory consolidation. Forgetfulness is at least as important as consolidation. Since only a minimal part of what we perceive is useful, the brain needs a mechanism to prevent itself from being burdened by insignificant information. To be consolidated, functional changes have to be followed by gene transcription and protein synthesis that produce permanent phenotypic changes in the neuron associated with structural rearrangements in neuronal networks. Thus, consolidation of memories is abolished by mRNA and protein synthesis inhibitors. Consolidation is not a high-fidelity process: Stored memories gradually change and fade with time and only the most relevant and useful aspects are retained over time (Kandel & Pittenger, 1999; Silva & Josselyn, 2002).

Several molecular actors and biochemical processes underlie short-term memory processes. Two processes that appear to be a final common pathway are phosphorylation and dephosphorylation of synaptic proteins (Greengard et al., 1993; Greengard, 2001). These chemical reactions consist of the enzymatic incorporation of a phosphate group into a protein (either at serine, threonine or tyrosine residues) by a protein kinase, or of its removal from a phosphorylated protein by a protein phosphatase. Phosphorylation has dramatic effects on proteins' conformation, interactions, and functions. Thus, the balance between phosphorylation and dephosphorylation is tightly regulated in neurons via the activation of kinase and phosphatase enzymes by specific intracellular signalling molecules called "second messengers" (as opposed to "first or extracellular messengers" represented by action potentials and released neurotransmitters) which include cyclic AMP and Ca^{2+}. The processes involved in short-term memory include: (1) changes in the action potential–neurotransmitter release coupling at the presynaptic level, promoted by Ca^{2+} influx and phosphorylation which regulate synaptic vesicle trafficking and exocytosis; (2) increase in the cytosolic Ca^{2+} concentration at the postsynaptic level due to Ca^{2+} influx through Ca^{2+}-permeable glutamate receptors (NMDA receptors) or second messenger-activated Ca^{2+} release from intracellular stores. The increase in postsynaptic Ca^{2+}, in turn, switches on specific kinases (such as Ca^{2+}/calmodulin-dependent kinases, protein kinase C or tyrosine kinases) phosphorylating neurotransmitter receptors, or activates specific enzymes generating retrograde messengers (such as nitric oxide and arachidonic acid) that reach the presynaptic terminal and increase neurotransmitter release. The activation of the molecules involved in these signalling pathways can last for minutes and thereby represents a sort of short-term "molecular memory" (Abel & Lattal, 2001; Elgersma & Silva, 1999; Greengard et al., 1993). Notably, all reactions mediated by phosphorylation typically have half-lives that depend on the kinetics of dephosphorylation by protein phosphatases. An important role in the establishment of short-term memories is played by the balance between Ca^{2+}/calmodulin-dependent protein kinase II (CaMKII), a key enzyme in synaptic plasticity at both pre- and postsynaptic levels, and protein phosphatase 1 (PP1). Upon Ca^{2+} influx during training, CaMKII undergoes an autophosphorylation reaction that converts it into a constitutively active kinase. The "switched-on" CaMKII, however, is returned to the resting state by PP1 that thereby has an inhibitory effect on learning (Genoux, Haditsch, Knobloch, Michalon, Storm, & Mansuy 2002; Greengard, Valtorta, Czernik, & Benfenati 1993; Silva & Josselyn, 2002). Thus, the antagonistic interactions between CaMKII and PP1 represent a push–pull system that plays a fundamental role during learning as well as in the delicate balance between maintaining and forgetting stored memories (see Figure 6.3).

These purely functional changes cannot survive for long in the absence of a structural rearrangement of the neurons participating in the modulated synapse. The sustained activation of the same pathways promotes memory consolidation by affecting gene transcription and translation. Sustained stimulation leads to persistent activation of the cyclic AMP-dependent protein kinase A (PKA) and neurotrophin-dependent Erk/MAP kinase (MAPK) pathways. In turn, PKA phosphorylates and activates the transcriptional activator CREB1a, whereas MAPK phosphorylates and inactivates the transcriptional repressor CREB2. The CREB family of transcription regulators is highly conserved across evolution and represents the major switch involved in the transformation of short-term memory into long-term memory. The CREB target genes, whose transcription is regulated during consolidation, include a set of immediate-early genes (such as C/EBP or zif 268) that affect transcription of downstream genes. This results in changes, either increases or decreases, in the expression of an array of proteins involved in protein synthesis, axon growth, synaptic structure and function (Alberini, 2005; Bozon, Kelly, Josselyn, Silva, Davis, & Laroche, 2003; Kandel and Pittenger, 1999).

When synaptic strength has to be permanently potentiated (long-term potentiation, LTP), ribosomal proteins, neurotrophins, Ca^{2+}-binding proteins, proteins involved in the exo-endocytotic cycle of synaptic vesicles and neurotransmitter receptors become upregulated, whereas cell adhesion molecules that usually maintain synaptic stability become downregulated. These specific changes in protein expression favour growth of terminal axon branches and establishments of novel synaptic contacts. Opposite phenomena are believed to occur in the case of long-term depression (LTD) of synaptic strength, favouring a decrease in the number of synaptic connections and/or a decreased activity of the existing synapses. Such properties of synapses were remarkably pointed out by Donald Hebb: When an axon of cell A is near enough to excite cell B or repeatedly or consistently takes part in firing it, some growth or metabolic change takes place in one or both cells such that A's efficiency, as one of the cells firing B, is increased (Hebb, 1949, p. 62; Sejnowski, 1999). In other words, a "synaptic learning rule" exists by which synapses learn from the pattern of afferent stimulation and persistently change synaptic strength accordingly. Although LTP and LTD were originally referred to a specific type of synapse (the Schaffer collaterals-CA1 pyramidal neuron in the hippocampus for LTP and the parallel fiber-Purkinje

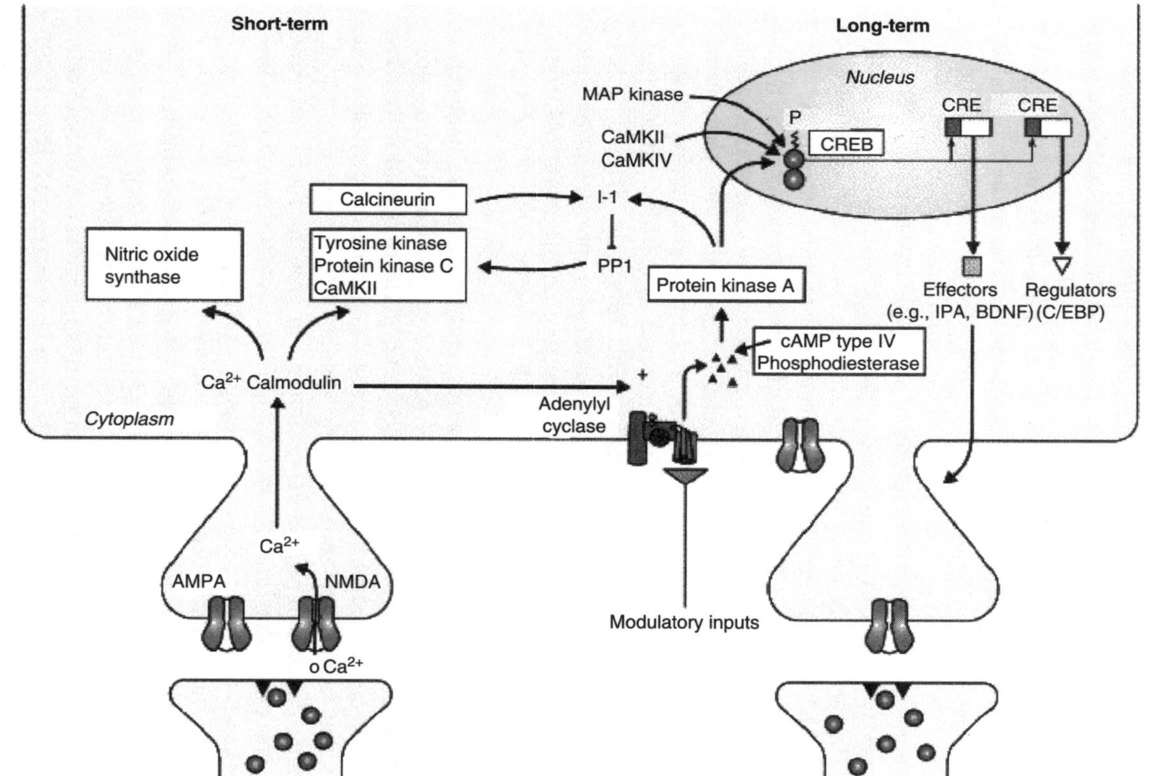

Figure 6.3 Molecular mechanisms of short-term and long-term memory. The two identified coincidence detectors, namely adenylyl cyclase and NMDA glutamate receptors, are shown. Short-term memory processes consist of short-lived functional changes in synaptic strength, while long-term memory processes involve gene transcription and synthesis of new proteins responsible for structural changes.

cell in the cerebellum for LTD), it turned out that virtually every synapse can finely tune its strength entering a potentiated or depressed state that can last for long periods of time. This synaptic learning rule is exemplified in Figure 6.4.

Multiple memory systems exist in the brain

Two major types of memory exist, one for skills and one for knowledge. The first one refers to information storage to perform various reflexive or perceptual tasks and is also referred to as nondeclarative or implicit memory because it is recalled unconsciously. The second form of memory, called declarative or explicit memory because it is recalled by a deliberate and conscious effort, concerns factual knowledge of persons, things, notions, and places. Declarative memory can be further subdivided into episodic or

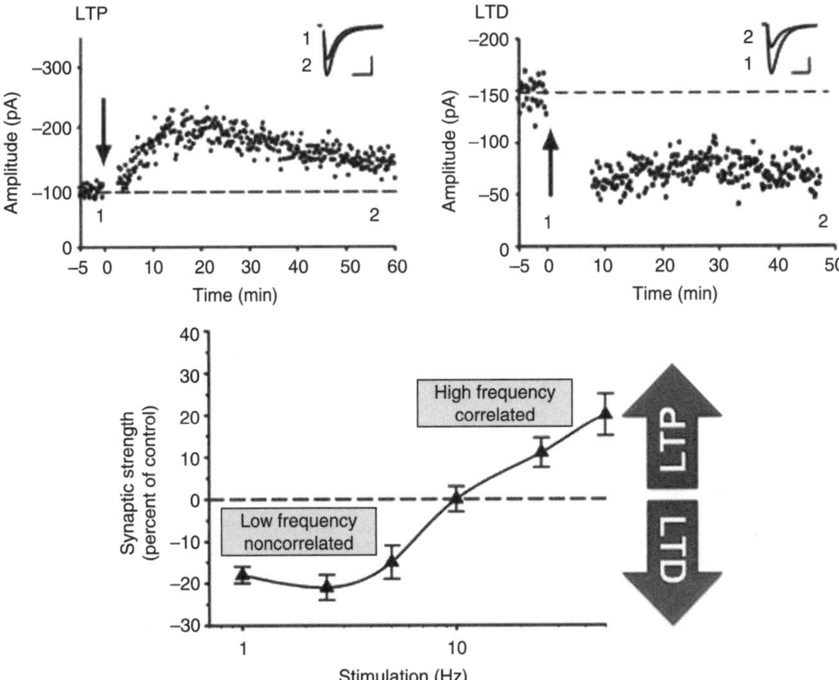

Figure 6.4 Plasticity paradigms as a "synaptic learning rule." *Upper panels:* LTP and LTD in the dentate gyrus of the hippocampus. Point plot representing the magnitude of extracellular synaptic responses (slope of field EPSP, mV/ms) in awake behaving rats evoked once every minute. *Lower panel:* Bidirectional modification of synaptic plasticity as a function of frequency and correlation of the presynaptic activity. Depending on the conditioning stimulation, different NMDA-dependent concentrations of Ca^{2+} are reached within the postsynaptic neuron which direct corresponding changes in synaptic strength.

autobiographic memory and semantic memory. Neuropsychological studies have shown that the multiple memory systems involve distinct brain areas and exhibit distinctive features. Thus, explicit memory requires an intact medial temporal lobe (hippocampus), while implicit memory systems are integrated at various levels in the central nervous system including reflex pathways, striatum, cerebellum, amygdala and neocortex. Moreover, the kinetics of the learning, consolidation and recall phases of memories are quite different. Implicit memory, for example learning to ride a bicycle, takes time and many attempts to build up, while explicit memory, such as learning a page of history or a telephone number, is more immediate and implies a smaller effort. However, while explicit memory fades relatively rapidly in the absence of recall and refreshing, implicit memory is much more robust and may last for a lifetime even in the absence of further practice (Blackemore, 1977; Kandel and Pittenger, 1999).

Mechanisms of implicit memory

The simplest paradigms of implicit memory are elementary forms of non-associative and associative behaviours, which are present in primitive animals. These paradigms have been effectively studied in molluscs, particularly the sea snail *Aplysia californica*, which has a very simple central nervous system made up of a few thousand neurons (the human brain in comparison is made up of about 10^{11}–10^{12}). *Aplysia* is able to learn specific behaviours that, upon practice, can be consolidated into long-term memories. The animal progressively learns to respond more weakly to repeated innocuous stimuli (e.g., a light tactile stimulus), a behaviour called *habituation*, and to reinforce the response to repeated noxious stimuli (e.g., a painful electrical shock), a behaviour known as *sensitization*. In both cases, the synaptic efficiency in the integration centre of a sensory-motor reflex is changed by experience, leading to an increased response of the reflex in the case of sensitization or to a reflex inhibition in the case of habituation. Both changes are integrated at the presynaptic level, mediated by changes in Ca^{2+} influx in response to the action potential. In habituation, Ca^{2+} influx is decreased into the sensory neuron terminal and the release of the neurotransmitter glutamate is accordingly decreased (synaptic depression). In sensitization, on the other hand, the activity of a facilitating serotonergic interneuron increases cyclic AMP concentration into the sensory neuron terminal, leading to PKA activation, phosphorylation of a potassium channel, lengthening of the depolarization evoked by the action potential, larger influx of Ca^{2+}, and increased glutamate release (synaptic potentiation). It is noteworthy that these two opposite forms of learning are associated with opposite changes in synaptic strength at the same integration centre of a somatic reflex arc (Kandel & Pittenger, 1999; Kandel, Schwartz, & Jessell, 2000).

Aplysia also exhibits a more complex form of associative learning, typical of higher animals, and known as classical conditioning. In this learning paradigm, the animal is given a strong and painful unconditioned stimulus (which if administered alone would produce sensitization) in association with a weak, innocuous, conditioned stimulus (which if administered alone would produce habituation). Following the repeated pairing of these two stimuli over the trials, the animal learns to associate the two stimuli and to react to the isolated conditioned stimulus with an enhanced response (greater than sensitization to the noxious stimulus). Classical conditioning is reflected in the neural circuitry as a greatly enhanced synaptic strength of the input connections between the sensory neuron and the motor neuron. In contrast to nonconditioned learning, this potentiation involves both presynaptic and postsynaptic mechanisms. The coincidence of the two stimuli is revealed by specific coincidence detectors located on both sides of the synapse. At the presynaptic level, the coincidence detector is adenylyl cyclase (the enzyme that synthesizes cyclic AMP from ATP), whose response to G protein-mediated activation is potentiated by Ca^{2+} influx and Ca^{2+}/calmodulin binding promoted by the activation of the conditioned pathway. On the postsynaptic side, the coincidence detector is the ligand- and voltage-operated glutamate NMDA receptor. This Ca^{2+} channel cannot be opened by glutamate alone because, when the postsynaptic neuron is in the resting state, the channel is blocked by Mg^{2+} ions. However, when glutamate release is associated with postsynaptic depolarization, as happens when the conditioned stimulus is paired with the unconditioned stimulus, the Mg^{2+} block is removed and the channel can open. Under these conditions, Ca^{2+} influx triggers signal transduction cascades leading to activation of protein kinases, phosphorylation of receptors, and activation of multiple enzyme cascades (Kandel & Pittenger, 1999; Kandel et al., 2000). This simple model also tells us that in all forms of memories involving association among events, the key mechanism is a coincidence detector, that is, a signal transducer that requires the convergence of at least two distinct input stimuli (e.g., G protein activation plus Ca^{2+}/calmodulin stimulation for adenylyl cyclase or glutamate release plus postsynaptic depolarization for NMDA glutamate receptors; see Figure 6.3).

Mechanisms of explicit memory

The studies on the mechanisms involved in explicit memory are more complex, as explicit memory involves conscious recall and the integration of multiple sensory inputs. Thus, these studies are not feasible in invertebrates and lower vertebrates but instead require the complexity of the mammalian nervous system. Studies addressing the molecular mechanisms of such explicit memory in mammals have profited from: (1) the possibility of manipulating the mouse genome by knocking out or overexpressing single proteins in the brain or in specific neuronal populations; (2) studying synaptic plasticity at network level (e.g., in hippocampal slices); (3) evaluating explicit memory by behavioural tests for spatial memory and object recognition. In the mouse (and man) the brain area that plays a central role in this type of conscious learning is the hippocampus. Experimental work has provided strong evidence for the involvement of the hippocampus in many kinds of explicit memory, and particularly in spatial memory. Examples are the case of HM, a patient who after bilateral hippocampectomy lost the ability to acquire new conscious memories, and functional MRI studies, which have demonstrated an activation of the medial temporal lobe in all tasks in which the subject memorizes a map or mentally rehearses an itinerary. Moreover, studies on the rodent hippocampus have revealed the existence of "place cells", whose firing is primarily controlled by the position of the animal and by distant visual cues that create an internal representation of the animal's location with respect to the surrounding environment (Colgin, Moser, and Moser, 2008). Finally, the hippocampus exhibits the most known and extensively studied form of synaptic plasticity, namely long-term potentiation (Colgin, Moser, & Moser, 2008; Kandel et al., 2000; Kandel and Pittenger, 1999; Moser & Paulsen, 2001).

A large number of studies have demonstrated that LTP is indeed a valid model of "memory storage". Hippocampal LTP can be induced by animal experience and, conversely, conscious learning is impaired under conditions in which LTP is impaired or abolished. LTP has all the features required to be the cellular mechanism of explicit memory as it is associative in nature, is triggered by the coincidence of events and can be activated by endogenous patterns of electrical activity (e.g., the Θ rhythm). The molecular mechanisms that mediate the generation of hippocampal LTP are surprisingly conserved across evolution and are closely similar to the mechanisms of associative learning identified in invertebrates. Thus, both pre- and postsynaptic mechanisms participate in the early phase of LTP expression, with a coincidence detector represented in most cases by NMDA glutamate receptors that trigger activation of multiple kinase pathways, including CaMKII, and generation of retrograde messengers. Moreover, the late phase of LTP involves activation of transcription factors (*CREB*, *C/EBPβ*, *Arc*, *c-fos*, etc.) and regulation of transcription of the target genes, and therefore it is sensitive to blockade by drugs inhibiting protein and/or mRNA synthesis (Alberini, 2005, 2008, 2009; Matynia, Kushner, & Silva, 2002; Miller & Mayford 1999; Miyashita, Kubik, Lewandowski, & Guzowski, 2008; Won & Silva, 2008).

Memory needs time to be stabilized in the hippocampus before the final storage. In fact, LTP induced by an experience is inhibited by a novel experience administered soon (within 1 hour) after the first one, whereas an LTP established for more than 1 hour is immune to this reversal mechanism (memory interference, see below). These observations suggest that the critical event in determining the retention of information may consist in the stabilization of the potentiated hippocampal synapses in order to resist the LTP reversal upon new information (Miller & Mayford, 1999). Although the hippocampus is fundamental to the acquisition of new memories, it appears to be dispensable after the memory has been fully consolidated. Although patient HM was totally unable to lay down new memories, he was still able to remember his past life preceding the bilateral ablation of the hippocampi. This indicates that permanent memories are distributed among different cortical regions according to the various perceptual features, and that these various aspects are linked so that, upon recall, the different components of a memory are bound together to reproduce the memory in its integrity. This process appears to be time-dependent and the hippocampus is still necessary to bind together the components of recent memories, whereas more remote explicit memories can be recalled independently of the hippocampus as the connections between cortical representation strengthen (Seung, 2009). It is currently believed that this memory transfer process occurs largely during sleep, particularly rapid eye movement (REM) sleep (Alberini, 2005; Kandel & Pittenger, 1999). Thus, the hippocampus may represent both the site of the imprinting of the memory and the temporary store for this trace during the progressive formation of neocortical memory representations (Hasselmo & McClelland, 1999).

Memory interference

> How is education supposed to make me feel smarter? Besides, every time I learn something new, it pushes some old stuff out of my brain. Remember when I took that home winemaking course, and I forgot how to drive?
>
> (Homer Simpson, *The Simpsons*)

A large body of behavioural and neurophysiological experiments indicates that memory consolidation is a graded process, which in order to be completed properly should not to be interfered with by other inputs from the external world. Interference is a fundamental phenomenon in the field of memory and one of the major causes of forgetting. It is believed that the acquisition of new memories causes forgetting of those old memories that are not yet fully consolidated. This occurs because of a conflict between the initial mechanisms of acquisition and those of consolidation of the previously acquired memory (retroactive interference). In both cases, interference is often achieved between similar experiences, although it may also occur between independent experiences (Colgin et al., 2008; Wixted, 2004).

The phenomenon of retroactive memory interference against an initial memory (obtained by either behavioural training or electrophysiological stimulation) can be easily demonstrated either behaviourally or electrophysiologically by the administration of subsequent interfering learning. Interference is certainly the phenomenon in which the link between hippocampal-specific behavioural learning and LTP at hippocampal synapses is very tight.

If an animal trained by task-1 is subjected to another behavioural task before the first memory has consolidated, the first memory is impaired. However, if exposure to the second memory task is sufficiently delayed, no interference with the first memory is observed (actual interference). Thus, a temporal window of retroactive interference exists that is directly related to the time needed to obtain full consolidation of the previous memory and a temporal gradient for interference is present in which the potency of the interfering learning decreases with the delay between the original and the interfering learning. Similarly, in vivo induction of LTP within this window impairs LTP associated with previous learning. Moreover, spatial memory acquired with the Morris water maze is impaired if in vivo LTP is subsequently induced by high-frequency stimulation of hippocampal electrodes (virtual interference; Miller & Mayford, 1999; Wixted, 2004).

Although less information is available on the molecular mechanisms of interference, the common interpretation is that it results from a competition for the very same molecular mechanisms underlying long-term synaptic plasticity and memory consolidation. This concept implies that amnesic drugs (such as alcohol, benzodiazepines or glutamate NMDA receptor blockers) can play opposite functions as far as consolidation and interference are concerned, depending on the time frame in which they are administered. By inhibiting long-term plasticity in the hippocampus, they usually cause anterograde amnesia for hippocampal-dependent learning. However, if applied during interfering learning they protect older, related memories against interference. Sleep, as well as rest during awake periods, is also known to passively protect memories by sheltering them from interference, although an active role for sleep on declarative memories has recently been proposed (Colgin et al., 2008; Ellenbogen, Payne, & Stickgold, 2006). Interference also has a high social impact in the information and communication technology era, and in designing new learning methods that could cope with the astonishing increase in information and interfering sensory stimulation impinging on our brains during daily life.

Memory recall and reconsolidation

In the previous section we have described that, upon new learning, a short-lived memory (short-term memory, STM) is formed that can be either stabilized over the following several hours or pruned out. If this consolidation process takes place, a long-term memory (LTM) is formed that is thought to be rather stable over time and stored as permanent modifications in the wiring of the brain in modality-specific areas. Traditionally, consolidation has been considered as an event which occurs only once in the biological history of a memory, and recall of a given memory has often been considered a good exercise against forgetting. However, it has only recently become clear that retrieval does not directly reinvigorate memories, rather it makes them return to a labile state susceptible to disruption and interference which needs further consolidation (the so-called reconsolidation process).

This process, originally proposed in the 1960s (Lewis, 1979), has only recently been studied in detail. Reconsolidation appears to be a highly dynamic process that occurs every time memories are reactivated. From a general point of view, consolidation and reconsolidation should be considered as part of the fundamental process of memory stabilization that allows a memory to be preserved, recalled, refreshed over the years. It is commonly found that memories do not remain unchanged over time, but undergo transformations in their basic elements and emotional content which have nothing to do with fading. This phenomenon implies that consolidation which is carried out soon after the salient experience cannot be the unique mechanism involved. Rather, reconsolidation provides a dynamic mechanism for updating and modifying memories while they are recalled. What is a bit counterintuitive in this general scheme of memory processes is that a stable memory goes back to a labile state when it is recalled, that is to say that memory recalling is per se an amnesic challenge. However, as memories are not printed as tracks in a compact disk, but are dynamically stored as changes in activity patterns in networks of neurons which in turn depend on modulation of synaptic strength, it is understandable that reactivation of these activity patterns during recall may change the plastic substrate of the memory, so that additional plasticity changes are needed to preserve it. Moreover, the temporal dynamics and the extent by which a memory is deconsolidated upon retrieval strongly depend on the strength of the initially consolidated trace, on the intensity of reactivation, and on the number of reactivation episodes over time. As a general rule, stronger memories are less susceptible to forgetfulness, and the stronger the reactivation the more labile the memory becomes. It is as if reactivation subtracts part of the memory body and the subtracted part has to be "rebuilt" by reconsolidation. Moreover, although every time a memory is reactivated it regresses to a labile state and needs reconsolidation, each successive reactivation task requires a progressively smaller reconsolidation. The memory therefore becomes rather stable after several cycles, and successive retrieval episodes will not disrupt the trace; the respective reconsolidation episodes will only modify it (Dudai & Eisenberg, 2004; Nader, 2003a, 2003b).

As mentioned above, consolidation (i.e., the transformation of STM into LTM) requires transcription of specific genes and protein synthesis and involves an array of highly conserved signalling pathways including Ca^{2+}, cyclic AMP, PKA, MAPK and tyrosine kinases that collectively render the memory resistant to cell turnover (see Figure 6.5). Distinct areas are engaged over time in a precise temporal and spatial sequence at both cellular and systems levels. It is well known that hippocampus-related memories are hippocampus-dependent only over a limited period and that at later times they become hippocampus-independent (remote memories), indicating that other brain regions connected to the hippocampus have undergone a sequential memory imprinting (Nader, 2003a; Nader & Hardt, 2009).

When the memory is reactivated, it regresses to an STM labile state (post-reactivation STM or PR-STM) which is again hippocampus-dependent and sensitive to interference. Thus, the memory needs to be reconsolidated in order to become "post-reactivaton" LTM (PR-LTM). However, if the memory is not reactivated, it will remain in a stable state which will slowly fade away over time. Thus, recall appears to disrupt this process of slow decay

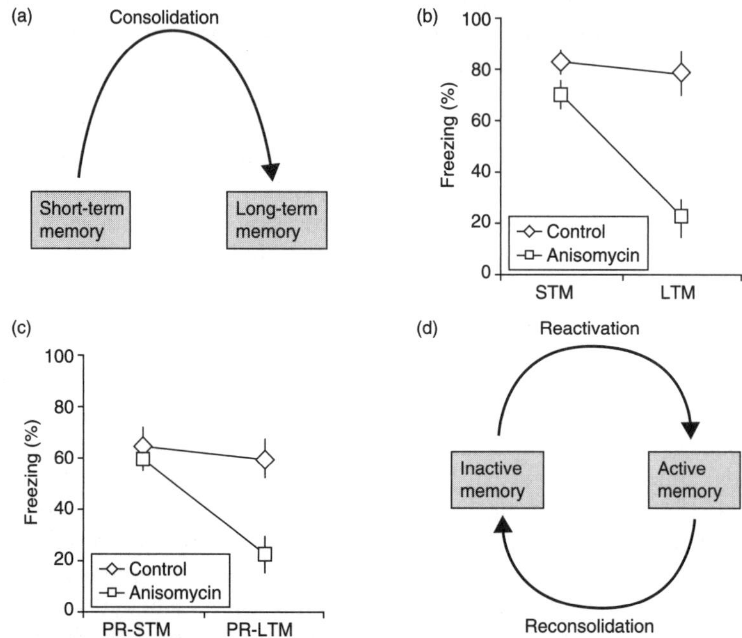

MOLECULAR SIGNATURE	BEHAVIOURAL TASK	CONSOLIDATION	RECONSOLIDATION
RNA SYNTHESIS	Classical conditioning	REQUIRED	REQUIRED
PROTEIN SYNTHESIS	Multiple tasks	REQUIRED	REQUIRED
CREB	Contextual fear conditioning	REQUIRED	REQUIRED
C/EBP	Inhibitory avoidance	REQUIRED	NOT REQUIRED
Zif268	Contextual fear conditioning	NOT REQUIRED	REQUIRED
Zif268	Object recognition	REQUIRED	REQUIRED
LRX	Object recognition	REQUIRED	REQUIRED
PKA	Conditioned taste aversion	REQUIRED	REQUIRED
CAMs	Classical conditioning	REQUIRED	REQUIRED
BDNF	Contextual fear conditioning	REQUIRED	NOT REQUIRED

Figure 6.5 Properties of consolidation and reconsolidation of memories. *Upper panel:* (a) Model of consolidation of short-term memory (STM) to long-term memory (LTM). (b) Blockade of consolidation of a fear memory by administration of anisomycin after conditioning. The treatment does not affect STM, but strongly impairs LTM. (c, d) Model of reconsolidation of LTM. LTM and post-reactivation LTM (PR-LTM) are stable traces in an inactive state. Reactivated memories return in an active, labile state which needs reconsolidation for long-term storage (PR-LTM). *Lower panel:* List of the main molecular mechanisms involved in consolidation and reconsolidation (modified from Dudai & Eisenberg, 2004).

of LTM. While the exact mechanisms of recall are not fully understood, reconsolidation has been thoroughly studied by the use of transcription or translation inhibitors (anisomycin in most studies) or of genetically altered mice lacking specific proteins involved in synaptic plasticity (see Figure 6.5). The most conservative mechanism that can be envisaged for memory reconsolidation is that this process employs the very same molecular mechanisms used for consolidation of STM and that both cellular and systems reconsolidation processes occur. Under conditions of inhibition of protein synthesis, the functional and structural changes that mediate LTM become either dysfunctional or actively removed in 4–24 hours after reactivation (Alberini, 2005; Nader & Hardt, 2009).

Reconsolidation has been found to occur in many species from invertebrates to vertebrates (including mammals) and therefore represents a highly conserved fundamental process in memory storage. A typical experiment is the following (see Figure 6.5). An animal is subjected to a classical conditioning trial and, after the memory is fully stabilized, it is exposed to the conditioning stimulus to reactivate the memory. If the animal is treated with anisomycin in the reactivation session, it exhibits an intact PR-STM, but the PR-LTM is markedly impaired. Interestingly, if the animal is not challenged for memory reactivation, protein inhibition is ineffective on the LTM acquired in the conditioning session, demonstrating that only the reactivated memory becomes sensitive to disruption, unless synthesis of new proteins is allowed. The sensitivity to protein inhibition applies only to a narrow time window. If the anisomycin "amnesic" treatment is administered several hours after reactivation it is ineffective, indicating that reconsolidation, like consolidation, is a time-dependent mechanism and that the time needed for reconsolidation is generally shorter than that needed for consolidation. This picture was observed in the case of diverse memory paradigms, including contextual or fear conditioning, passive avoidance, object recognition, taste aversion, motor sequence learning, etc. As for consolidation, reconsolidation is not demonstrated only in behavioural tasks, but also has neurophysiological correlates. It has been demonstrated that if anisomycin is given 2 hours after LTP induction, it does not affect LTP maintenance. However, if the potentiated synapses are stimulated again under conditions of protein synthesis inhibition, a short-term potentiation (PR-STP) can be observed which fails to reconsolidate in PR-LTP. As RNA or protein synthesis inhibition block both consolidation and reconsolidation, the most conservative explanation is that the two processes share the same mechanisms of synaptic rearrangement and permanent tuning of the strength of synaptic connections. Indeed, this often seems to be the case, although similarities between the two processes are not complete and important differences exist in either the molecular actors involved, or the target brain regions, or both (Alberini, 2005; Nader, 2003a; Nader & Hardt, 2009).

Differences in the brain areas implicated in reconsolidation versus consolidation were mostly revealed using local administration of nonspecific protein inhibitors or area-selective knockdown of specific proteins. Thus, protein synthesis in the dorsal hippocampus is essential for consolidation of inhibitory avoidance memory, while it is dispensable for reconsolidation. The same applies to the expression of the transcription factor C/EBPβ in the same area. These results suggest that the two processes rely on distinct brain areas. Closely similar results were obtained when protein synthesis or expression of the transcription factor c-fos were considered during consolidation and reconsolidation of a passive avoidance task. Specific amygdala circuits are recruited for consolidation, but not for reconsolidation of taste aversion, and the same applies to the recruitment of *nucleus accumbens* which is necessary for consolidation, but not for reconsolidation of appetitive memories. Again, in object recognition, MAPK is activated in distinct hippocampal circuits during consolidation and reconsolidation, respectively (Alberini, 2005).

In most cases, the very same evolutionarily conserved molecular mechanisms involving transcription factors (such as CREB, C/EBPβ, zif 268 or c-fos), signalling molecules (such as neurotrophins or cell adhesion molecules) and protein kinases (such as MAPK or PKA) are activated during both consolidation and reconsolidation, albeit in distinct areas. However, evidence exists that the molecular mechanisms of consolidation and reconsolidation are, in some cases, non-overlapping and virtually segregated. Thus, in the case of contextual fear conditioning, expression of the neurotrophin BDNF in the hippocampus is required for consolidation, but not for reconsolidation, while hippocampal expression of zif 268 is indispensable for reconsolidation, but not for consolidation (Alberini, 2005; Dudai & Eisenberg, 2004; Nader & Hardt, 2009).

In conclusion, memory recall destabilizes LTM and poses the need for memory reconsolidation. Successive cycles of reconsolidation make the memory more stable, even in the presence of successive retrievals and, at the same time, rearrange and slowly modify the trace of the memory so that the most salient and emotionally significant features are preserved or even enhanced. Consolidation and reconsolidation often occur in distinct brain regions or subregions, consistent with the idea that consolidated memories are sorted to diverse brain areas, but the molecular mechanisms involved largely overlap.

Extinction

The simplest definition of extinction is that of a progressive decrease in the conditioned response when the conditioned stimulus that elicits it is repeatedly nonreinforced. Extinction is a learning process, and is not simply due to the passage of time. Indeed, it requires exposure to the conditioned stimulus in the absence of the unconditioned stimulus. In addition, with extinction the conditioned memory is not lost, and can be revived by appropriate cues. Thus, it can be seen as a form of inhibitory learning (Konorski, 1967; Pavlov, 1927). In this respect, extinction is different from forgetting, although it involves the loss of a learned behavioural response.

Whereas from a behavioural point of view studies on extinction have been conducted since the late 19th century, scientists have only recently begun to tackle the problem of its neural and cellular bases. Neurobiological studies are guided by theoretical accounts of extinction based on psychological models. Most of our knowledge concerning the cellular and molecular mechanisms underlying extinction processes stem from studies of fear extinction. Much less is known about extinction in appetitive tasks. This is due to the fact that, in the last two decades, an impressive amount of research has been dedicated to the neural bases of fear conditioning, thus laying the ground for the study of fear extinction (LeDoux, 2000). This has also been fostered by the growing interest in the use of exposure therapies, based on extinction, for the treatment of anxiety disorders. In the classical Pavlovian fear extinction paradigm, a previously fear-conditioned individual is exposed to a fear-eliciting cue in the absence of an aversive event, thus causing a reduction in the predictive value of a conditioned stimulus concerning the occurrence of an unconditioned stimulus (Pavlov, 1927).

As far as the identification of the neural basis of fear extinction is concerned, it is now clear that there is not such a thing as a single brain structure responsible for this process. Rather, several brain areas appear to be involved, consistent with the complexity of the phenomenon (Myers & Davis, 2007; Quirk & Mueller, 2008). Among them, those whose role has been defined best are the hippocampus, the amygdala, and the prefrontal cortex. A further level of complexity stems from the observation that, within a single brain structure, extinction may be contributed to by various populations of neurons, involving different neurotransmitters or neuromodulators and, within the same cells, responses may imply the activation of multiple signal transduction pathways, as well as activators or repressors of transcription. In addition, extinction occurs in three phases: acquisition, consolidation, and retrieval. These separate phases are likely to be mediated by separate mechanisms, and possibly involve separate or partially overlapping brain areas (or different plasticity events within the same area), thus complicating the identification of the cellular and molecular bases of the phenomenon. Some of the features of extinction appear to be shared with acquisition of conditioning, whereas others are likely to be unique to extinction. It is also likely that certain features depend on the paradigm, e.g., the nature of the unconditioned or the conditioned stimulus. Thus, the brain structures involved as well as the underlying mechanisms of plasticity are likely to be different for fear extinction from extinction of appetitive behaviours.

Fear extinction is not a permanent process, and the extinguished conditioned response may reappear. Reappearance may occur spontaneously, as a function of the passage of time, or can follow re-exposure to unsignalled presentations of the unconditioned stimulus in a context-dependent manner – reinstatement or renewal (for review, see Myers & Davis, 2007). The observation that extinction tends to fade with time suggests that the inhibitory association responsible for extinction is more labile than the excitatory association characterizing conditioning (see Figure 6.6). Poor extinction retrieval could also be due to pathological phenomena, leading to defects in the consolidation or recall of extinction. Extinction is not a generalized process, being cue-specific: it depends strictly on the sensory modality and,

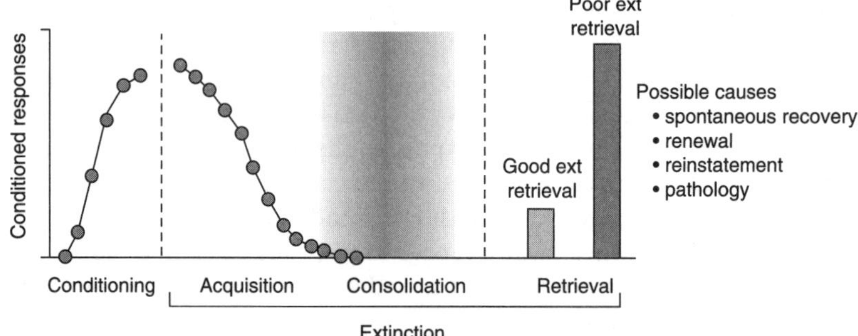

DRUG	MECHANISM OF ACTION
D-cycloserine	partial NMDAr agonist
methylene blue	metabolic enhancer
yohimbine	α2receptor antagonist
sulpiride	dopamine D2receptor antagonist
AM-4D4	cannabinoid reuptake inhibitor
WIN 55,212-2	cannabinoid receptor agonist
PEPA	AMPA receptor potentiator
dexamethasone	glucocorticoid receptor agonist
cortisol	endogenous glucocorticoid

Figure 6.6 Mechanisms of extinction. *Upper panel*: Extinction learning occurs in three phases. Acquisition is characterized by a decrease in conditioned responses to the presentation of a conditioned stimulus without the unconditioned stimulus. Consolidation is a time-dependent process during which a long-term extinction representation is formed. Retrieval of extinction occurs at a later time, when the CS is re-presented. Good extinction retrieval is characterized by low levels of conditioned responses, whereas poor extinction retrieval is characterized by high levels of conditioned responses. Poor retrieval of extinction is normally observed following renewal, reinstatement, spontaneous recovery, or under pathological conditions characterized by extinction failure (reproduced from Quirk & Mueller, 2008, with permission). *Lower panel*: Pharmacological enhancers of extinction (modified from Quirk & Mueller, 2008, with permission).

within the same sensory modality, on its physical characteristics (e.g., the frequency of a tone).

Recent studies indicate that stress may impair extinction. This is likely to be due to the detrimental effects of stress on synaptic plasticity. Indeed, chronic stress may even induce morphological alterations in neurons. It has been reported that stress reduces dendritic spines in the hippocampus and medial prefrontal cortex, while increasing spine counts in the amygdala (Vyas, Mitra, Shankaranarayana, & Chattarji, 2002). In principle, these combined effects may lead to increased conditioning and to impairment of extinction (Quirk & Mueller, 2008).

In general, it is assumed that whereas conditioning involves primarily excitatory neurotransmission, the expression of extinction is largely mediated by GABA (Harris & Westbrook, 1998 Myers & Davis, 2002, 2007, Walker & Davis, 2002). Thus, in both cases the process is characterized by synaptic strengthening between sensory pathways involving information as to the conditioned stimulus and neurons mediating execution, but the neuronal populations involved in execution obviously differ in the two cases. Consistent with this hypothesis, it has recently been reported that extinction of aversive memories is associated with disruption of long-term depression at GABAergic synapses in the basolateral amygdala (Marsicano et al., 2002).

Since extinction is a learning process, it is not surprising that the same plasticity phenomena involved in learning and memory have been found to be implicated in extinction as well. Thus, NMDA-type glutamate receptors have been found to be essential for both fear memory acquisition and extinction. In addition, a variety of intracellular signalling mechanisms have been found to modulate both processes. Extinction requires protein synthesis, similarly to other learning phenomena, suggesting that, like learning, it is associated with both functional and structural synaptic rearrangements.

Considerable interest is also given to the study of the pharmacological manipulation of extinction, with the aim of both clarifying the underlying neurotransmitters, receptors and signalling processes involved, and of developing therapeutic strategies for the treatment of anxiety disorders (and addiction). A multiplicity of drugs has been shown to enhance extinction in rodents. These include drugs acting through a variety of receptors and intracellular signalling mechanisms, from glucocorticoid receptor agonists to D_2 or α_2 receptor antagonists, to drugs acting on the endocannabinoid system. The results of the pharmacological studies are complicated by the observed differences in efficacy between systemic and targeted (e.g., by intraparenchimal injection in selected brain areas) manipulations (for review, see Myers & Davis, 2007). In the absence of a defined locus for extinction, the systemic delivery of drugs seems a reasonable approach. However, it usually leads to a limited insight into the underlying mechanisms of the observed effect, given the complexity of the mechanisms involved.

One promising agent which is also being tested in humans is D-cycloserine, a partial agonist for the NMDA receptor (Walker, Ressler, & Davis, 2002;

Yang & Lu, 2005). Given the established role of NMDA receptors in learning and extinction consolidation, the efficacy of D-cycloserine is not unexpected. However, thus far the use of D-cycloserine in humans as an adjunct to exposure therapy has given controversial results (see, e.g., Guastella, Lovibond, Dadds, Mitchell, & Richardson, 2007). Agonists of the glucocorticoid receptor have also been proposed as therapeutic tools. They might indeed have a compensatory effect, since it has been reported that patients with post-traumatic stress disorder have reduced plasma levels of cortisol. Initial clinical trials are consistent with the idea that cortisol has enhancing effects on extinction consolidation (Soravia et al., 2006).

A deluge of clinical observations implicates the endocannabinoids in learning mechanisms (Heifets & Castillo, 2009). Prolonged exposure to Δ^9-tetrahydrocannabinol (the major psychoactive component of *Cannabis sativa*) impairs learning processes. In rodents it has been demonstrated that, depending on the test, the endocannabinoids are required for either the acquisition or the extinction of memory. Experiments using antagonists for the CB1 receptor (the major receptor for cannabinoids) or CB1 receptor-deficient mice indicate an essential role of the endocannabinoid system in fear extinction. However, the converse experiments, i.e., overexpression or stimulation of CB1 receptors, did not lead to robust results, consistent with the lack of evidence for a beneficial effect of CB1 activation in humans suffering from post-traumatic stress disorder or other anxiety disorders (Lutz, 2007). It is noteworthy that endocannabinoids are well-known negative modulators of GABAergic transmission and are implicated in mediating long-term depression at inhibitory synapses (Szabo & Schlicker, 2005). Interestingly, fear extinction induces inhibitory long-term depression in the amygdala, in conjunction with an increase in the levels of endocannabinoids (Marsicano et al., 2002).

As far as intracellular signalling pathways are concerned, it has been reported that auditory fear memory training or testing preferentially activates neurons with relatively increased levels of the transcription factor CREB in the lateral amygdala (Han et al., 2007). Using transgenic mice in which cell death may be induced in a temporally and spatially restricted manner, Han et al. (2009) have recently shown that, in the same paradigm, selective deletion of neurons overexpressing CREB after learning blocks expression of the fear memory. Interesting results have been reported concerning the involvement of cyclin-dependent kinase 5 (Cdk5) in extinction consolidation (Sananbenesi et al., 2007). These authors showed that Cdk5 activity was inversely related to consolidation in a contextual fear extinction paradigm in mice. The beauty of this study, compared to analogous studies showing involvement of various signal transduction pathways in extinction, lies in the fact that the authors were able to dissect the up- and downstream signalling pathways responsible for this effect by employing a combination of approaches, from genetic manipulations to pharmacological agents. They showed that extinction reduces the activity of the small G protein Rac1 in the hippocampus, causing a redistribution of Cdk5 and its activator p^{35} to the cytosol. This results in sequestering of p^{35} from the kinase PAK-1, with the consequent activation of the latter. PAK-1 activity has previously been associated with actin rearrangement and synaptic remodelling. Thus this chain of events might well provide a molecular basis for the regulation of fear extinction.

As mentioned above, protein phosphorylation/dephosphorylation processes are critical elements for almost all synaptic plasticity phenomena. One hypothesis that has gained momentum holds that learning and forgetting are regulated by an equilibrium between the activity of protein kinases and phosphatases. Thus, protein phosphorylation would be primarily involved in learning, whereas forgetting would require protein dephosphorylation. In agreement with this hypothesis, it has recently been shown that a reduction in the brain activity of the phosphatase calcineurin makes the memory for taste aversion more resistant to extinction. Conversely, reversal of taste aversion is facilitated when calcineurin activity is high at the time of learning. Consistently, conditioned taste aversion training was found to cause a selective decrease of calcineurin activity in the amygdala. In this setting, changes in calcineurin activity are accompanied by variations in the levels of expression of the memory-related transcription factor zif268, with the consequent modification in the expression levels of a subset of proteins, raising the possibility that calcineurin is involved in memory persistence (Baumgärtel et al., 2008). Although attractive, the hypothesis that learning and forgetting are mediated by opposite changes in protein phosphorylation/dephosphorylation phenomena appears too simplistic, also in view of the fact that the intracellular signalling pathways up- and downstream protein kinases and phosphatases are intimately interconnected, with protein phosphatases regulating the activity of protein kinases and vice versa.

Repression

Repression was first described more than a century ago by Sigmund Freud (1914), who suggested that unwanted memories or instinctual drives are pushed into the unconscious. Repression is different from suppression, which is an intentional censorship of a thought. For Freud, repression was a defence mechanism – repressed memories are often traumatic in nature, but, although hidden, they continue to exert an effect on behaviour. Thus, although repression is usually listed among the forgetting phenomena, it cannot be considered real forgetting. Rather, it can be defined as a phenomenon by which unwanted memories are kept out of consciousness. However, such memories are not really forgotten, and, although they cannot be accessed at will, it is possible to retrieve them. Indeed, the whole process of Freudian psychoanalysis largely relies on strategies aimed at eluding the psychological mechanisms that make these unwanted memories inaccessible.

Although repression is a well-known phenomenon in psychoanalysis, scientists have only recently begun to unravel the psychological mechanisms which underlie it. It can be considered an active phenomenon, requiring the activation of inhibitory mechanisms of executive control for preventing memories from entering awareness (Anderson & Green, 2001). In spite of the important clinical implications of repression, its cellular and molecular bases are virtually completely unknown. The task of unravelling the plasticity phenomena underlying repression are obviously made more difficult by the near to total lack of knowledge concerning the unconscious, which is still envisaged more as an abstract concept than a real neural structure (or function).

Amnesia

> Saying who I was, on the other hand, was like turning around and finding a wall. No, not a wall; I tried to explain. It doesn't feel like something solid, it's like walking through fog . . .
>
> A thick, opaque fog, which enveloped the noises and called up shapeless phantoms . . .
>
> They left and I cried. Tears are salty. So, I still had feelings. Yes, but made fresh daily. Whatever feelings I once had were no longer mine . . . I wondered whether I had ever been religious; it was clear, whatever the answer, that I had lost my soul.
>
> (Umberto Eco, *The Mysterious Flame of Queen Loana*, 2004, pp. 7, 3, 21)

Amnesia can be distinguished from forgetting in that it is not limited to the loss of selected memories with a specific content. Rather it involves the systematic loss (or difficulty in retrieval) of a whole category of memories, more frequently pertaining to episodic memory. Amnesia is often a serious and possibly irreversible deficit of cognitive functions, engendered by brain damage and/or disfunction. Amnesia may be induced acutely (e.g., by trauma or electric shock) or be the consequence of a chronic disorder. It may be either anterograde or retrograde and may also be selective for certain types of memory.

Senescent forgetfulness

Perhaps the most common form of amnesia is (benign) senescent forgetfulness. Ageing is generally accompanied by a decline in memory, although large individual variations exist in this respect. Senescent forgetfulness may be limited to explicit memory, and appears to involve an impairment in the functioning of the hippocampus (Hedden & Gabrieli, 2004). A similar deterioration in memory with ageing is also observed in rodents, where it is accompanied by a failure in LTP in the CA1 region of the hippocampus, with selective impairment of the late, protein synthesis-dependent phase of LTP (Bach et al., 1999). However, multiple, as yet ill-defined distinct processes appear to be involved in ageing-related memory decline. Inter-individual variability in memory loss might also be ascribed to differences in the efficiency of compensatory phenomena (Buckner, 2004).

Alzheimer's disease

Alzheimer's disease (AD) is the most common cause of dementia in the elderly. It is a progressive neurodegenerative disease resulting in a decline in activities of daily living, behavioural disturbances, and cognitive impairment. In its earliest stage, the disease is characterized by a virtually pure impairment of declarative memory. Thus, the elucidation of the molecular and cellular bases of this disorder might lead to important advancements in our understanding of normal brain function, besides laying the ground for improvements in therapeutic strategies for this devastating disease.

Alzheimer's disease is characterized by distinct neuropathological changes, i.e., the accumulation of amyloid plaques and neurofibrillary tangles, as well as by inflammation and neuronal loss which, unlike in Parkinson's disease, is not limited to a single transmitter class of neurons. Neurofibrillary tangles are formed intracellularly by the abnormal aggregation of hyperphosphorylated tau, a microtubule-associated protein, whereas amyloid plaques are deposits of filamentous amyloid-β, a cleavage product of a transmembrane protein, APP (amyloid-precursor protein; for review, see Selkoe, 2001).

Most cases of AD are sporadic, but a small percentage of cases, characterized by early onset, run in families, and show a mendelian distribution. The identification of the genes whose mutation underlies the familial forms of the disease has allowed the development of a model for the aetiology of the pathological lesions which characterize the disorder. All identified genes encode for proteins which participate in the cascade of reactions involved in the degradation/accumulation of the amyloid-β peptide (Bertram & Tanzi, 2008). It has thus been put forward that accumulation of amyloid-β is the key pathogenic event which leads to neuronal death.

The central role of amyloid-β in the pathogenesis of AD is now supported by a deluge of experimental data (see Figure 6.7). However, it is becoming increasingly more evident that the toxic forms of amyloid-β are not the large aggregates which are visible under the light microscope, but rather small soluble oligomers, which have been shown to interfere with a variety of intracellular signalling cascades. Among the signalling events involved, a central role is probably played by alterations in intracellular Ca^{2+} homeostasis, known to both modulate synaptic function and activate cell death pathways (La Ferla, Green & Oddo, 2007).

Although one of the hallmarks of AD is progressive neuronal loss, amnesia precedes the loss of neurons, and is likely to reflect neuronal dysfunction rather than neuronal death. Similarly to other neurodegenerative disorders, AD is now seen primarily as a "synaptopathy", meaning that the initial defect arises from synaptic dysfunction (La Ferla & Oddo, 2005). Indeed, in AD, cognitive impairment correlates better with the loss of synapses and of synaptic proteins than with the loss of neurons or the abundance of plaques and tangles. The cascade of signalling events triggered by amyloid-β leads to modifications in synaptic activity and hence in neuronal and network function. This view may change the way we look at the disease and at therapeutic interventions, since the initial pathogenic event is no longer considered to be a reduction in the number of neurons. Rather it represents a dysfunction of the surviving neurons (although eventually massive neuronal death poses important limits), and the possible compensatory plasticity phenomena gain importance (Palop, Chin, & Mucke, 2006).

Amyloid-β oligomers have been shown to decrease neuronal excitability, to induce synaptic depression and disrupt LTP. These effects are mediated, at least in part, by a reduction in glutamate receptors of the AMPA type and by

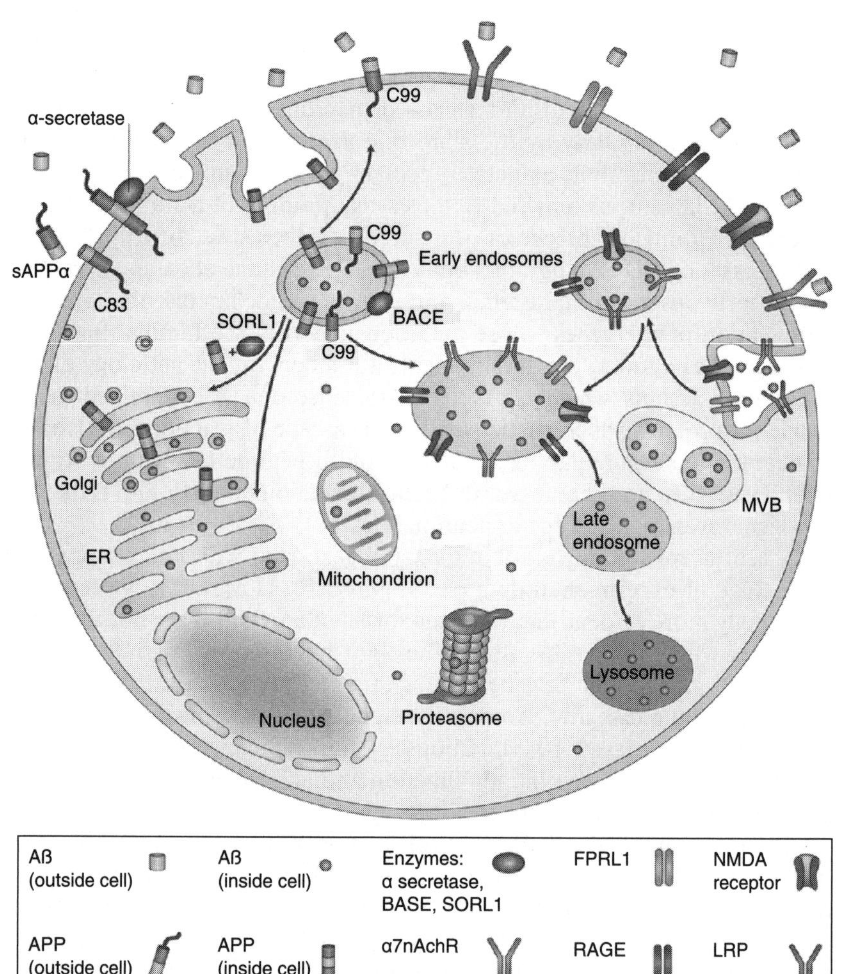

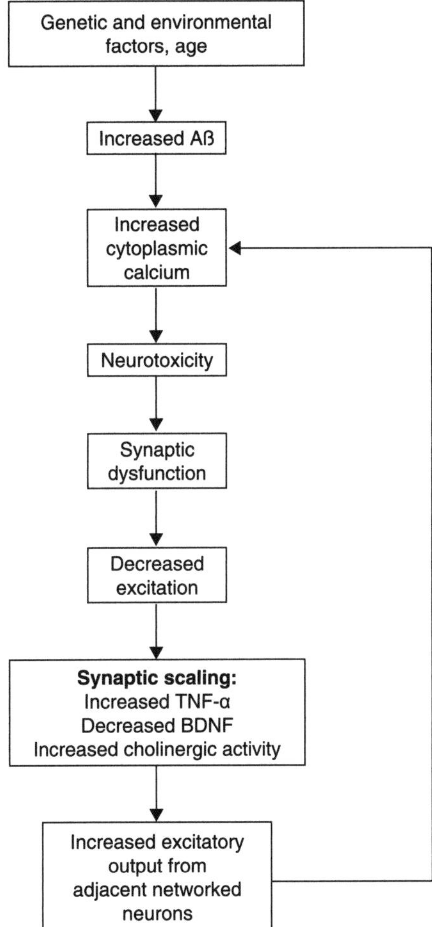

Figure 6.7 Pathogenesis of synaptic dysfunction in Alzheimer's disease. *Left panel*: Pathological effects of intraneuronal amyloid-β. Amyloid-β (Aβ), produced intracellularly or taken up from extracellular sources, has various pathological effects on cell and organelle function. Intracellular Aβ can exist as a monomeric form that further aggregates into oligomers. Any of these species may mediate pathological events in vivo, particularly within a dysfunctional neuron. Evidence suggests that intracellular Aβ may contribute to pathology by facilitating tau hyperphosphorylation, disrupting proteasome and mitochondria function, and triggering increases in calcium and reactive oxygen species which lead to synaptic dysfunction (reproduced from La Ferla et al., 2007, with permission). *Right panel*: Sequence of events linking Aβ accumulation to the synaptic dysfunction underlying pathological amnesia (reproduced from Small, 2008, with permission).

loss of dendritic spines. The reduction in synaptic activity mediated by amyloid-β is partially compensated, at a network level, by synaptic scaling, a form of synaptic plasticity that, by inducing hyperactivity in the remaining healthy neurons, allows them to maintain signal strength (Small, 2008). While synaptic scaling may help to slow down the cognitive decline in the short term, it is possible that in the long run the hyperactivity induced in the healthy neurons, by raising intracellular Ca^{2+} levels makes these neurons more susceptible to toxicity and hence contributes to the spreading of neurodegeneration.

The accumulating evidence for a causal role of amyloid-β in AD does not explain why the disease is primarily (albeit not exclusively) characterized by amnesia, and why in the early stages amnesia is confined to declarative memory. One likely possibility is that the relatively subtle changes in synaptic and network function observed in early AD affect the brain processes for which there is less redundancy and which require a higher level of integration.

Conclusions

It is clear that memory is not just an ability to store information, but the essence of our beings, the basis of our individuality and our consciousness. Each individual knows that he or she is unique, not merely because of his or her external appearance, but because of his or her personal history, behaviour, and ability to face daily life.

Learning and memory are achieved by permanently shaping neuronal circuits and interneuronal connections. These modifications are initially labile, but if they are perceived as useful and salient, then they are consolidated and eventually reconsolidated to become a stable memory. However, most of the percept is quickly discarded, in a process of selection. What we think is relevant is remembered, although it tends to fade and change with time: "Memory acts like a convergent lens in a camera obscura: it focuses everything, and the image that results from it is much more beautiful than the original" Eco, 2005, p. 25).

Forgetting is equally as important as remembering: "If we had to record and store all the stimuli we encounter, our memory would be a bedlam. So we choose, we filter" (Eco, 2005, p. 11) Unfortunately, much less attention has been devoted to the mechanisms of physiological forgetting than to the processes of learning and memory. Indeed, specific mechanisms for forgetting seem to exist, and forgetting cannot be merely considered as the "dark side of remembering".

Although many questions remain open, the astonishing progress in the field of molecular and cellular neuroscience is greatly contributing to the understanding of the exact role of gene products and signalling pathways in distinct processes of memory and forgetting, and it is likely that within a few years this knowledge will be translated into the development of novel therapeutic approaches to memory disorders. However, we share Alcino Silva's view that "The excitement of sensing that a small, but important piece of this puzzle might be within reach should not be mistaken for the naïve belief that the molecules behind memory will reduce memory to molecules" (Silva & Giese, 1994, p. 417).

References

Abel, T., & Lattal, K. M. (2001). Molecular mechanisms of memory acquisition, consolidation and retrieval. *Current Opinion in Neurobiology*, *11*, 180–187.

Alberini, C. M. (2005). Mechanisms of memory stabilization: Are consolidation and reconsolidation similar or distinct processes? *Trends in Neuroscience*, *28*, 51–56.

Alberini, C. M. (2008). The role of protein synthesis during the labile phases of memory: Revisiting the skepticism. *Neurobiology of Learning and Memory*, *89*, 234–246.

Alberini, C. M. (2009). Transcription factors in long-term memory and synaptic plasticity. *Physiological Reviews*, *89*, 121–145.

Anderson, M. C., & Green, C. (2001). Suppressing unwanted memories by executive control. *Nature*, *410*, 366–369.

Bach, M. E., Barad, M., Son, H., Zhuo, M., Lu, Y. F., Shih R., et al. (1999). Age-related defects in spatial memory are correlated with defects in the late phase of hippocampal long-term potentiation in vitro and are attenuated by drugs that enhance the cAMP signaling pathway. *Proceedings of the National Academy of Science of the USA*, *96*, 5280–5285.

Baumgärtel, K., Genoux, D., Welzl, H., Tweedie-Cullen, R. Y., Koshibu, K., Livingstone-Zatchej, M., et al. (2008). Control of the establishment of aversive memory by calcineurin and Zif268. *Nature Neuroscience*, *11*, 572–578.

Bertram, L., & Tanzi, R. E. (2008). Thirty years of Alzheimer's disease genetics: The implications of systematic meta-analyses. *Nature Reviews Neuroscience*, *9*, 768–778.

Blackemore, C. (1977). *Mechanics of the mind*. Cambridge: Cambridge University Press.

Borges, J. L. (1944). *Ficciones*. Buenos Aires: Editorial Sur.

Bozon, B., Kelly, A., Josselyn, S. A., Silva, A. J., Davis, S., & Laroche, S. (2003). MAPK, CREB and zif268 are all required for the consolidation of recognition memory. *Philosophical Transactions of the Royal Society of London B: Biological Sciences*, *358*, 805–814.

Buckner, R. L. (2004). Memory and executive function in aging and AD: Multiple factors that cause decline and reserve factors that compensate. *Neuron*, *44*, 195–208.

Centonze, D., Siracusano, A., Calabresi, P., & Bernardi, G. (2004). The project for a scientific psychology (1895): A Freudian anticipation of LTP-memory connection theory. *Brain Research Reviews*, *46*, 310–314.

Colgin, L. L., & Moser, E. I. (2006). Rewinding the memory record. *Nature*, *440*, 615–617.

Colgin, L. L., Moser, E. I., & Moser, M. B. (2008). Understanding memory through hippocampal remapping. *Trends in Neuroscience*, *31*, 469–477.

Dudai, Y., & Eisenberg, M. (2004). Rites of passage of the engram: Reconsolidation and the lingering consolidation hypothesis. *Neuron*, *44*, 93–100.

Eco, U. (2005). *The mysterious flame of Queen Loana*. Orlando, FL: Harcourt.

Elgersma, Y., & Silva, A. J. (1999). Molecular mechanisms of synaptic plasticity and memory. *Current Opinion in Neurobiology*, *9*, 209–213.

Ellenbogen, J. M., Payne, J. D., & Stickgold, R. (2006). The role of sleep in declarative memory consolidation: Passive, permissive, active or none? *Current Opinion in Neurobiology*, *16*, 716–722.

Freud, S. (1953). *The standard edition of the complete psychological works of Sigmund Freud*. London: Hogarth Press.

Genoux, D., Haditsch, U., Knobloch, M., Michalon, A., Storm, D., & Mansuy, I. M. (2002). Protein phosphatase 1 is a molecular constraint on learning and memory. *Nature*, *418*, 970–975.

Greengard, P. (2001). The neurobiology of slow synaptic transmission. *Science*, *294*, 1024–1030.

Greengard, P., Valtorta, F., Czernik, A. J., & Benfenati, F. (1993). Synaptic vesicle phosphoproteins and regulation of synaptic function. *Science*, *259*, 780–785.

Guastella, A. J., Lovibond, P. F., Dadds, M. R., Mitchell, P., & Richardson, R. (2007). A randomized controlled trial of the effect of D-cycloserine on extinction and fear conditioning in humans. *Behaviour Research and Therapy*, *45*, 663–672.

Han, J. H., Kushner, S. A., Yiu, A. P., Cole, C. J., Matynia, A., Brown, R. A., et al. (2007). Neuronal competition and selection during memory formation. *Science*, *316*, 457–460.

Han, J. H., Kushner, S. A., Yiu, A. P., Hsiang, H. L., Buch, T., Waisman, A., et al. (2009). Selective erasure of a fear memory. *Science*, *323*, 1492–1496.

Harris, J. A., & Westbrook, R. F. (1998). Evidence that GABA transmission mediates context-specific extinction of learned fear. *Psychopharmacology (Berlin)*, *140*, 105–115.

Hasselmo, M. E., & McClelland, J. L. (1999). Neural models of memory. *Current Opinion in Neurobiology*, *9*, 184–188.

Hebb, D. O. (1949). *Organization of behavior: A neuropsychological theory*. New York: Wiley.

Hedden, T., & Gabrieli, J. D. (2004). Insights into the ageing mind: A view from cognitive neuroscience. *Nature Reviews Neuroscience*, *5*, 87–96.

Heifets, B. D., & Castillo, P. E. (2009). Endocannabinoid signaling and long-term synaptic plasticity. *Annual Review of Physiology*, *71*, 283–306.

Kandel, E. R., & Pittenger, C. (1999) The past, the future and the biology of memory storage. *Philosophical Transactions of the Royal Society London B: Biological Sciences*, *354*, 2027–2052.

Kandel, E. R., Schwartz, J. H., & Jessell, T. M. (2000). *Principles of neural sciences*. Maidenhead: McGraw Hill.

Konorski, J. (1967). *Integrative activity of the brain*. Chicago, IL: University of Chicago Press.

LaFerla, F. M., Green, K. N., & Oddo, S. (2007). Intracellular amyloid-ß in Alzheimer's disease. *Nature Reviews Neuroscience*, *8*, 499–509.

LaFerla, F. M., & Oddo, S. (2005). Alzheimer's disease: Aß, tau and synaptic dysfunction. *Trends in Molecular Medicine*, *11*, 170–176.

LeDoux, J. E. (2000). Emotion circuits in the brain. *Annual Review of Neuroscience*, *23*, 155–184.

Lewis, D. J. (1979). Psychobiology of active and inactive memory, *Psychological Bulletin*, *86*, 1054–1083.

Lutz, B. (2007). The endocannabinoid system and extinction learning. *Molecular Neurobiology*, *36*, 92–101.

Marsicano, G., Wotjak, C. T., Azad, S. C., Bisogno, T., Rammes, G., Cascio, M. G., et al. (2002). The endogenous cannabinoid system controls extinction of aversive memories. *Nature*, *418*, 530–534.

Matynia, A., Kushner, S. A., & Silva, A. J. (2002). Genetic approaches to molecular and cellular cognition: A focus on LTP and learning and memory. *Annual Review of Genetics*, *36*, 687–720.

Miyashita, T., Kubik, S., Lewandowski, G., & Guzowski, J. F. (2008). Networks of neurons, networks of genes: An integrated view of memory consolidation. *Neurobiology of Learning and Memory*, *89*, 269–284.

Miller, S., & Mayford, M. (1999). Cellular and molecular mechanisms of memory: The LTP connection. *Current Opinion in Genetics & Development*, *9*, 333–337.

Moser, E. I., & Paulsen, O. (2001). New excitement in cognitive space: Between place cells and spatial memory. *Current Opinion in Neurobiology*, *11*, 745–751.

Myers, K. M., & Davis, M. (2002). Behavioral and neural analysis of extinction. *Neuron*, *36*, 567–584.

Myers, K. M., & Davis, M. (2007). Mechanisms of fear extinction. *Molecular Psychiatry*, *12*, 120–150.

Nader, K. (2003a). Memory traces unbound. *Trends in Neuroscience*, *26*, 65–72.

Nader, K. (2003b). Re-recording human memories. *Nature*, *425*, 571–572.

Nader, K., & Hardt, O. (2009). A single standard for memory: The case for reconsolidation. *Nature Reviews Neuroscience*, *10*, 224–234.

Palop, J. J., Chin, J., & Mucke, L. (2006). A network dysfunction perspective on neurodegenerative diseases. *Nature*, *443*, 768–773.

Pavlov, I. (1927). *Conditioned reflexes*. Oxford: Oxford University Press.

Quirk, G. J., & Mueller, D. (2008). Neural mechanisms of extinction learning and retrieval. *Neuropsychopharmacology*, *33*, 56–72.

Ramón y Cajal, S. (1906/1967). The structure and connexions of neurons. *Nobel lectures: Physiology or medicine, 1901–1921* (pp. 220–253). Amsterdam: Elsevier.

Sananbenesi, F., Fischer, A., Wang, X., Schrick, C., Neve, R., Radulovic, J., et al. (2007). A hippocampal Cdk5 pathway regulates extinction of contextual fear. *Nature Reviews Neuroscience*, *10*, 1012–1019.

Sejnowski, T. J. (1999). The book of Hebb. *Neuron*, *24*, 773–776.

Selkoe, D. J. (2001). Alzheimer's disease: Genes, proteins, and therapy. *Physiological Reviews*, *2*, 741–766.

Seung, H. S. (2009). Reading the book of memory: Sparse sampling versus dense mapping of connectomes. *Neuron*, *62*, 17–29.

Silva, A. J., & Giese, K. P. (1994). Plastic genes are in! *Current Opinion in Neurobiology*, *4*, 413–420.

Silva, A. J., & Josselyn, S. A. (2002). The molecules of forgetfulness. *Nature*, *418*, 929–930.

Small, D. H. (2008). Network dysfunction in Alzheimer's disease: Does synaptic scaling drive disease progression? *Trends in Molecular Medicine*, *14*, 103–108.

Soravia, L. M., Heinrichs, M., Aerni, A., Maroni, C., Schelling, G., Ehlert, U., et al. (2006). Glucocorticoids reduce phobic fear in humans. *Proceedings of the National Academy of Science of the USA*, *103*, 5585–5590.

Szabo, B., & Schlicker, E. (2005). Effects of cannabinoids on neurotransmission. *Handbook of Experimental Pharmacology*, *168*, 327–365.

Vyas, A., Mitra, R., Shankaranarayana Rao, B. S., & Chattarji S. (2002). Chronic stress induces contrasting patterns of dendritic remodeling in hippocampal and amygdaloid neurons. *Journal of Neuroscience*, *22*, 6810–6818.

Walker, D. L., Ressler, K. J., Lu, K. T., & Davis, M. (2002). Facilitation of conditioned fear extinction by systemic administration or intra-amygdala infusions of D-cycloserine as assessed with fear-potentiated startle in rats. *Journal of Neuroscience*, *22*, 2343–2351.

Walker, D. L., & Davis, M. (2002). The role of amygdala glutamate receptors in fear learning, fear-potentiated startle, and extinction. *Pharmacology Biochemistry & Behavior*, *71*, 379–392.

Wixted, J. T. (2004). The psychology and neuroscience of forgetting. *Annual Review of Psychology*, *55*, 235–269.

Won, J., & Silva, A. J. (2008). Molecular and cellular mechanisms of memory allocation in neuronetworks. *Neurobiology of Learning and Memory*, *89*, 285–292.

Yang, Y. L., & Lu, K. T. (2005). Facilitation of conditioned fear extinction by D-cycloserine is mediated by mitogen-activated protein kinase and phosphatidylinositol 3-kinase cascades and requires de novo protein synthesis in basolateral nucleus of amygdala. *Neuroscience*, *134*, 247–260.

Zucker, R. S. (1996). Exocytosis: A molecular and physiological perspective. *Neuron*, *17*, 1049–1055.

7 The functional neuroimaging of forgetting

Benjamin J. Levy, Brice A. Kuhl, and Anthony D. Wagner
Stanford University, California, USA

Forgetting is a common, often troubling, experience. Failing to remember where we left our keys, the name of a colleague, the meaning of a word we once knew, or an errand that needed to be done on the way home, can be embarrassing and, at times, quite costly. Not all instances of forgetting are unpleasant, however. More often than we realize our goal is actually to forget, rather than remember. For example, forgetting is adaptive when we move and must unlearn information that is no longer relevant, such as our old phone number and address. Similarly, workers who must repeat similar activities throughout a workday, such as a waiter who takes many similar orders in a shift, would likely be better off if they could forget the orders from earlier in the day. Thus, while many of us desire to have a perfect memory, in many ways we would be disadvantaged if we were to remember every experience.

Why do we forget? This question was once one of the most prominent topics of research on memory, with much of the original work inspired by Ebbinghaus (1885/1913), who carefully documented the rate at which he forgot nonsense syllables. Early accounts pitted the idea that memories passively decay over time against the notion that subsequent learning interferes with our prior experiences, either by disrupting the consolidation of those traces into durable memories or by interfering with our ability to retrieve them. Over time, each of these theories has experienced difficulty explaining some aspects of forgetting and, thus, none has been able to provide a unified account of forgetting. Regrettably, this has meant that the field has never settled on a cohesive theory of forgetting, with modern overviews tending to focus on describing a set of experimental results without a clear theoretical account of why forgetting occurs. Given the ubiquity of forgetting in everyday life, however, a comprehensive understanding of its causes is of prime importance to theories of memory. Perhaps the primary failing of these earlier theories was the implicit assumption that forgetting is produced by a single mechanism. Instead, forgetting may arise from a disruption to any of the events that promote successful memory. Here we propose five distinct mechanisms that produce forgetting, none of which alone is sufficient to account for all types of forgetting. In the following sections, we describe the behavioral and neuroimaging evidence supporting the existence of each of these mechanisms in order to better understand why we sometimes fail to remember past experiences.

Forgetting due to failed encoding

Perhaps the most obvious, though somewhat underappreciated, reason why we forget is because we often poorly encode events as they happen. This can be due to absent-mindedness, distraction, or any other factor that limits attention as we engage with the world. For example, forgetting where you left your keys may simply reflect a failure to pay attention to what you were doing when you set them down. Similarly, if you are distracted when introduced to a new co-worker you are unlikely to later remember that person's name. In these instances, forgetting does not arise because of the loss of information over time; rather, forgetting arises because the initial episode was never transformed into a durable memory representation. Many theories of forgetting have ignored this cause, since in these cases nothing is successfully stored in memory and, thus, nothing is ever truly lost from memory. It seems likely, though, that many of the memories that we describe as "forgotten" are attributable to failures to encode. Therefore, it is worth considering the factors that influence encoding lapses.

To understand why encoding sometimes fails, it is helpful to understand how successful encoding occurs. Functional neuroimaging studies have typically examined this issue by using the subsequent memory paradigm, where brain activity is monitored during an experience and then related to behavioral evidence about whether or not the experience is later remembered (e.g., Brewer, Zhao, Desmond, Glover, & Gabrieli, 1998; Paller, Kutas, & Mayes, 1987; Wagner et al., 1998). In this paradigm, activity during encoding trials that are subsequently remembered is compared to activity on trials that are subsequently forgotten, yielding a pattern of activity that is specifically associated with successful memory encoding.

There are now over 100 functional magnetic resonance imaging (fMRI) studies using this subsequent memory paradigm, and they have consistently revealed a network of regions that positively relate to subsequent remembering, including ventrolateral prefrontal cortex (PFC), medial temporal lobe (MTL), and dorsal parietal cortex (see Figure 7.1; for reviews see Blumenfeld & Ranganath, 2006; Davachi, 2006; Paller & Wagner, 2002; Uncapher & Wagner, 2009). One interpretation of these findings is that fronto-parietal control mechanisms are engaged during encoding to modulate processing in posterior cortical regions in a goal-directed fashion. This modulation is thought to regulate the inputs that are received by the MTL, which ultimately binds these distributed patterns of activity into durable episodic memory traces. Increased activity for subsequently remembered items presumably reflects the increased engagement of this network. According to this framework, memories may be doomed to forgetting when we fail to sufficiently engage these neural mechanisms during encoding.

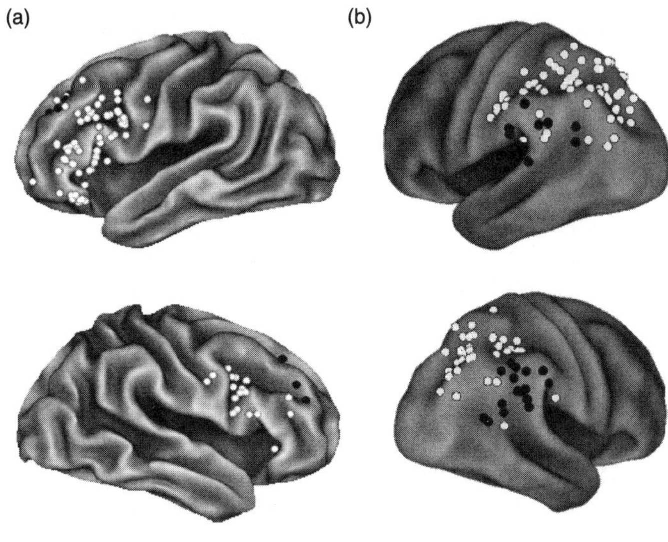

○ Remembered > Forgotten

● Forgotten > Remembered

Figure 7.1 Meta-analyses of subsequent memory effects. (a) The local maxima within PFC from 33 fMRI studies of LTM formation (from Blumenfeld & Ranganath, 2006) reveal that positive subsequent memory effects (i.e., remembered > forgotten) tend to fall within VLPFC. (b) The local maxima within parietal cortex from 93 fMRI studies of LTM formation (from Uncapher & Wagner, 2009). Positive subsequent memory effects tended to fall within intraparietal sulcus and superior parietal cortex, while negative effects appeared exclusively in inferior parietal regions.

There is considerable behavioral evidence that directing attention to specific aspects of a stimulus has a profound impact on subsequent memory, both in the likelihood that it will be remembered (Craik & Lockhart, 1972; Craik & Tulving, 1975) and the type of representation that is stored (Mitchell, Macrae, & Banaji, 2004; Morris, Bransford, & Franks, 1977; Otten, Henson, & Rugg, 2002; Otten & Rugg, 2001a; Tulving & Thomson, 1973). These findings suggest that the allocation of attention during study ultimately influences what is stored in memory. More direct evidence about the importance of attention during encoding comes from studies where subjects are given an attentionally demanding secondary task to perform during encoding. The typical finding from these studies is that doing this severely impairs later memory for those items (e.g., Craik, Govoni, Naveh-Benjamin, & Anderson, 1996), and also leads to reduced activation in fronto-parietal regions (Fletcher, Frith, Grasby, Shallice, Frackowiak, & Dolan, 1995; Iidaka, Anderson, Kapur, Cabeza, & Craik, 2000; Kensinger, Clarke, & Corkin, 2003; Shallice, Fletcher, Frith, Grasby, Frackowiak, & Dolan, 1994;

Uncapher & Rugg, 2005, 2008). The idea that goal-directed attention plays a critical role during encoding has been further elaborated by Uncapher and Wagner (2009), who recently highlighted the contribution of dorsal parietal regions, in and around the intraparietal sulcus, to positive subsequent memory effects. This region is known to be involved generally when subjects must maintain attention in a goal-directed fashion (Corbetta, Patel & Shulman, 2008; Corbetta & Shulman, 2002), suggesting that the recruitment of dorsal parietal mechanisms during successful encoding reflects the allocation of top-down attentional control toward the inputs that are to be remembered. Thus, it seems plausible that fronto-parietal neural activity observed in subsequent memory analyses at least partially reflects the allocation of attention to perceptual and conceptual representations related to the studied item.

While the evidence above suggests that unsuccessful encoding arises simply from a failure to engage top-down control, there is also evidence that subsequently forgotten trials can be associated with a distinct pattern of brain activity (e.g., Otten & Rugg, 2001b; Wagner & Davachi, 2001; for a review see Uncapher & Wagner, 2009). Specifically, increased activity in ventral lateral parietal, medial parietal, and posterior cingulate cortical areas has consistently been found to predict subsequent forgetting. This suggests that these regions play some role in producing forgetting, but the mechanism(s) through which they negatively influence learning remains unclear. One hypothesis, which focuses on activity in ventral parietal cortex, near the temporo-parietal junction (TPJ), is that this activity reflects reflexive orienting toward representations that are not related to the encoding task (Cabeza, 2008; Uncapher & Wagner, 2009). For example, if someone nearby says your name while you are being introduced to a co-worker you are likely to reflexively orient to this salient perceptual input and thus fail to attend to the name of your co-worker. This interpretation builds on a rich attention literature documenting that the ventral parietal cortex is involved in attentional capture by abrupt onsets or salient stimuli (Corbetta & Shulman, 2002; Corbetta et al., 2008). From this perspective, when subjects engage ventral parietal reflexive attention mechanisms to orient to information that is not relevant to the later memory test, they are prone to subsequently forget the to-be-encoded information. Thus, one potential mechanism by which failed encoding may arise is by distraction from task-irrelevant inputs that steal attention from the to-be-encoded items. Further work is needed to isolate this as the mechanism behind these negative subsequent memory effects.

In summary, many instances of forgetting can be explained by a disruption of event encoding. This can occur either because we fail to activate fronto-parietal control mechanisms that orient attention to the relevant dimensions of the event or because ventral parietal regions related to reflexive attentional capture are engaged by distracting, task-irrelevant information. These processes have been described as making separate contributions, but it is also possible that goal-directed control and reflexive capture interact in some competitive fashion. For example, a lapse in top-down control may set the stage for attention to be captured by irrelevant representations (e.g., Weissman, Roberts, Visscher, & Woldorff, 2006), or reflexive shifts of attention to irrelevant representations may interrupt our top-down focus of attention. Of course, failures to encode cannot explain all instances of forgetting. It is clear that in many situations we form a memory of an event and are able to recall it for some time afterwards, only to later lose that ability and be left with the distinct feeling of having forgotten something we once knew. Thus, other mechanisms are necessary to explain why and how some memories transition from memorable to forgotten.

Forgetting due to disrupted consolidation

What could cause us to forget something that we once knew? One possibility is that a memory trace, once formed, may be subject to damage or disruption. The most prominent modern version of this account focuses on disruption that occurs during consolidation – the process by which memories that are initially stored in a temporary, fragile state in the MTL are slowly "consolidated" into more durable, long-term representations distributed throughout the cortex (McGaugh, 2000; Müller & Pilzecker, 1900; Squire & Alvarez, 1995). During this initial period of consolidation – which has been argued to last anywhere from hours to years – recent memories are thought to be vulnerable to disruption from new experiences. By this account, forgetting arises because we experience new events before we have a chance to fully develop lasting traces of earlier events (Wixted, 2004, 2005).

One of the strongest forms of evidence in favor of disrupted consolidation is that damage to the MTL causes a pattern of forgetting known as temporally graded retrograde amnesia. In addition to impairments in learning new information, amnesics show forgetting of memories that were acquired before the damage occurred, even extending years prior to the onset of amnesia. Importantly, such instances of retrograde amnesia display a temporal gradient, where the most recent memories are the ones most likely to be forgotten (Ribot, 1882; Squire, Slater, & Chace, 1975; Zola-Morgan & Squire, 1990). This empirical observation led to the suggestion that memories require some period of time to consolidate (Squire, 1992).

A similar temporal gradient is observed in standard forgetting curves, motivating Wixted (2004) to propose that disrupted consolidation may account for forgetting in the healthy brain. The forgetting curve, first detailed by Ebbinghaus (1885/1913), shows that most forgetting occurs in the initial hours and days after a study episode, with more remote memories in the tail end of the curve often showing very little evidence of forgetting with the passage of additional time. Thus, in both the normal forgetting curve and in instances of MTL damage, the addition of time seems to render older memories more resistant to damage. One problem with evaluating this claim, and indeed the reason that this view might not be more widespread, is that most studies of human memory have tended to focus on fixed retention intervals that are typically well within the consolidation period. Thus, many studies of memory may simply be poorly designed to detect forgetting due to disrupted consolidation.

While the disrupted consolidation account holds promise for explaining forgetting, it has not yet translated into functional neuroimaging research. To date, fMRI studies of consolidation have focused on demonstrating that consolidation involves the transfer of memories from the MTL to cortical regions. These studies have sought to show that retrieving older memories results in less hippocampal activity, suggesting that after time these memories have been transferred to cortical sites and no longer require the hippocampus to be retrieved (e.g., Haist, Gore, & Mao, 2001; Niki & Luo, 2002; but see Addis, Moscovitch, Crawley, & McAndrews, 2004; Gilboa, Winocur, Grady, Hevenor, & Moscovitch, 2004). However, even if these studies were able to conclusively provide evidence in favor of consolidation, none of the extant studies provides any insight into whether encoding new experiences can disrupt consolidation of earlier memories.

The disrupted consolidation theory described here is only one specific instantiation of a general class of theories that posit that stored memories are vulnerable and can be damaged by new experiences. As a general account of forgetting, these disrupted storage theories share a key limitation with the failure-to-encode account described earlier: They seem to predict that forgetting should be a permanent phenomenon. If the trace was not formed or has been disrupted in some way, then it is unclear why an experience that is forgotten at one point in time should ever be remembered later. In contrast to that view, however, we often experience momentary forgetting of some fact or event, only to later have this memory come back to mind. This common experience highlights the point that transient instances of forgetting can occur even when the underlying memory trace exists. To account for such findings, we need a mechanism that can explain why forgetting can occur in one retrieval situation and not another. In the following sections we detail several factors that promote forgetting, even when a memory trace still exists.

Forgetting due to retrieval competition

One situation that is known to induce forgetting is when a retrieval cue is related to multiple associated memories, especially when alternative memories are more strongly activated than the desired memory. In these situations, the alternative traces compete for access and interfere with the ability to retrieve the desired information. Consider, for example, trying to remember the name of a particular elementary school teacher. In some situations the retrieval cues lead directly to the desired memory (e.g., the name of your second-grade teacher) and the information is retrieved almost effortlessly. At times, though, we fail to remember the name because other memories that are strongly linked to the cues (e.g., the name of your third-grade teacher) spring to mind more readily. Once we have retrieved an alternate memory it can often be difficult to move on to the desired target: The incorrect representation interferes with or blocks the ability to retrieve the desired memory. The proposal that memories compete for access and can block subsequent recall attempts has been long advanced as a primary cause of forgetting (e.g., McGeoch, 1942) and is instantiated in many modern computational models of memory as the primary mechanism by which forgetting occurs (e.g., Anderson, 1983; Mensink & Raaijmakers, 1988).

Retrieval competition is often investigated in fan effect studies (Anderson, 1974), where subjects are taught a set of propositions (e.g., "The *farmer* is in the park" and "The *doctor* is in the school"), with some items appearing in multiple propositions (e.g., "The *farmer* is in the bank"). The standard finding is that subjects are slower and less accurate at recognizing propositions when they contain items that are associated with multiple propositions. The interpretation of this effect has focused primarily on the idea that a finite amount of activation is shared between all the possible representations within a fan. Thus, when there are many possible responses it becomes more difficult to retrieve any one of them. Similarly, if one representation is strengthened, then the other representations are necessarily weakened.

Interference has also been extensively explored in the classic A–B, A–C learning paradigm (for reviews, see Anderson & Neely, 1996; Wixted, 2004). In these experiments, subjects first learn a list of A–B cue-associate word pairs (e.g., Shoe–House) and then later study a second list of word pairs. Critically, some of the pairs in this second list share a cue word with a pair from the earlier list (e.g., Shoe–Rope; A–C pairs). Thus, competition arises between the B and C terms due to their shared retrieval cue (A), thereby increasing the likelihood of forgetting. Indeed, increased retrieval failures are observed when subjects are later tested on the B or C terms. For example, forgetting of B items is much greater if it is followed by a new list of A–C pairs than a condition where entirely unrelated C–D pairs are learned (Müller & Pilzecker, 1900). Historically, the distinction between the temporal order of these interference effects has been quite influential, with the impairment of originally studied A–B pairs referred to as retroactive interference and the negative influence of past learning on acquisition of the new A–C pairs referred to as proactive interference. Many modern theories of forgetting (e.g., Mensink & Raaijmakers, 1988), however, attribute both types of interference effects to a common competition mechanism.

The ability to overcome competition is clearly important for many acts of remembering, as available retrieval cues often remind us of many things beyond the memory we wish to retrieve. A large body of neuropsychological and neuroimaging evidence indicates that overcoming retrieval competition is heavily dependent on lateral PFC. Lesion evidence has shown that PFC damage causes increased distractibility and a tendency to persevere on incorrect responses. For example, frontal lobe patients often perform as well as controls in the initial acquisition of A–B word pairs, but suffer considerable difficulty recalling the subsequently learned A–C pairs (e.g., Shimamura,

Jurica, Mangels, Gershberg, & Knight, 1995). Indeed, when presented with the A retrieval cue on the final test and asked to recall the C items, frontal lobe patients often make competition-driven errors by recalling the B items.

While lesions to lateral PFC generally result in increased susceptibility to proactive interference, it is less clear from lesion studies which specific regions within lateral PFC are critical for resolving mnemonic competition. Increased proactive interference effects have been associated with damage to both left (Moscovitch, 1982; Smith, Leonard, Crane, & Milner, 1995) and right PFC (Smith et al., 1995; Turner, Cipolotti, Yousry, & Shallice, 2007), while other studies have found relatively normal proactive interference in patients with frontal lobe damage despite impairments on other tests designed to measure frontally mediated control processes (Janowsky, Shimamura, Kritchevsky, & Squire, 1989). This variability in outcomes is perhaps not surprising, though, given the variability in the extent and location of naturally occurring lesions. Therefore, it is often difficult to draw conclusions from the lesion data other than the general implication that lateral PFC is important for resolving competition in memory.

Greater specificity regarding the role of distinct PFC subregions in resolving competition has been obtained through the higher spatial resolution afforded by positon emission topography (PET) and fMRI. The consensus from extant neuroimaging studies is that resolving interference in memory is most commonly associated with left ventrolateral PFC (VLPFC). One of the earliest neuroimaging studies of retrieval competition, where subjects underwent PET while performing a standard A–B/A–C learning paradigm (Dolan & Fletcher, 1997; for a similar fMRI result see Henson, Shallice, Josephs, & Dolan, 2002), revealed increased activity in left lateral PFC (including both VLPFC and dorsolateral prefrontal cortex, DLPFC) when subjects studied A–C items compared to when they studied entirely new word pairs (D–E pairs; see Figure 7.2). Subsequent work revealed that rearranging previously studied word pairs also leads to increased left VLPFC activity (Fletcher, Shallice, & Dolan, 2000), suggesting that lateral PFC is engaged whenever irrelevant associations have been previously learned and are no longer relevant to the current encoding task. Henson et al. (2002) elaborated on this general pattern by showing that activation in left VLPFC decreases with subsequent presentations of a word pair, suggesting that activity declines as an association is strengthened and less interference is experienced.

While the above studies revealed engagement of left VLPFC during encoding in the face of interference, similar activity is observed during interference-laden retrieval. Specifically, left VLPFC, along with anterior cingulate cortex (ACC), is engaged when subjects must retrieve A–C pairs after prior A–B learning (Henson et al., 2002). Similarly, left VLPFC engagement has been observed in studies of the fan effect, with increased VLPFC activity during high- compared to low-fan situations (Sohn, Goode, Stenger, Carter, & Anderson, 2003; Sohn, Goode, Stenger, Jung, Carter, & Anderson, 2005). More recently, Danker, Gunn, and Anderson (2008) showed that two distinct

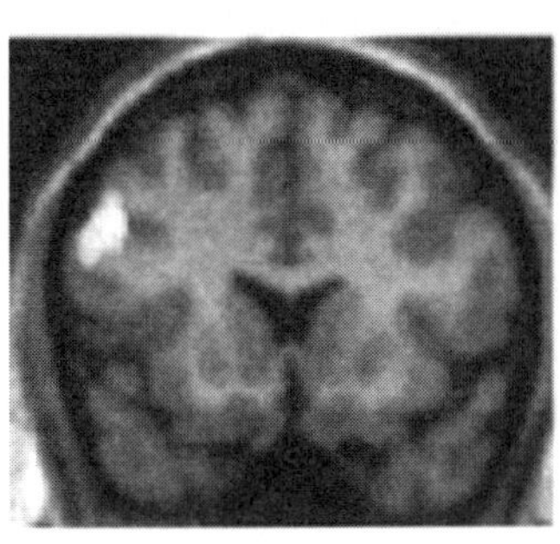

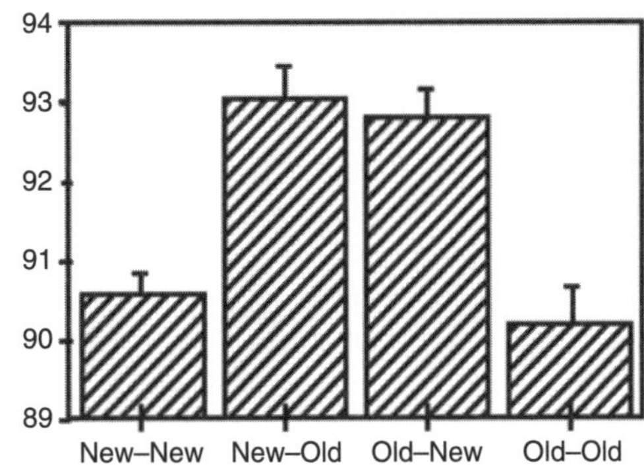

Figure 7.2 Activation in the left lateral PFC as a function of encoding condition (Dolan & Fletcher, 1997). "New–New" corresponds to encoding of a novel word pair; "New–Old" and "Old–New" correspond to a word pair in which one member of the pair is novel and the other was previously studied with a different word; "Old–Old" corresponds to a word pair that is repeated, intact. The left lateral PFC is maximally engaged (in the left panel, see the white activation overlaid on a structural image) when the word pair being encoded partially overlaps with a previous pair (i.e., when interference is present).

regions within left VLPFC respond differentially to two different aspects of controlled retrieval – manipulation of fan interference was associated with activation in left mid-VLPFC, whereas left anterior-VLPFC did not respond to the fan but was sensitive to the amount of training that was performed on the target association (see Figure 7.3 for more detail on PFC anatomy). This dissociation is consistent with the proposal that two distinct subregions in left VLPFC subserve separable processes during retrieval (Badre & Wagner, 2007). According to this model, anterior VLPFC mediates controlled retrieval of representations whenever retrieval cannot be done relatively automatically, whereas mid-VLPFC is engaged post-retrieval to resolve competition amongst active representations.

Beyond episodic memory, left mid-VLPFC is engaged in other situations that involve selection in the face of mnemonic interference. For example, activity in this region is consistently observed during semantic retrieval when one must select between multiple competing responses (e.g., Badre, Poldrack, Pare-Blagoev, Insler, & Wagner, 2005; Thompson-Schill, D'Esposito, Aguirre, & Farah, 1997; for a review, see Badre & Wagner, 2007). Critically, lesions studies have shown that damage to this region, in particular, is associated with difficulty retrieving relevant semantic representations from amongst competitors (Martin & Cheng, 2006; Metzler, 2001; Thompson-Schill, Swick, Farah, D'Esposito, Kan, & Knight, 1998). Left mid-VLPFC also plays a critical role in resolving proactive interference that accumulates over trials in working memory tasks, as revealed by functional neuroimaging (for a review, see Jonides & Nee, 2006), lesion (Thompson-Schill et al., 2002)

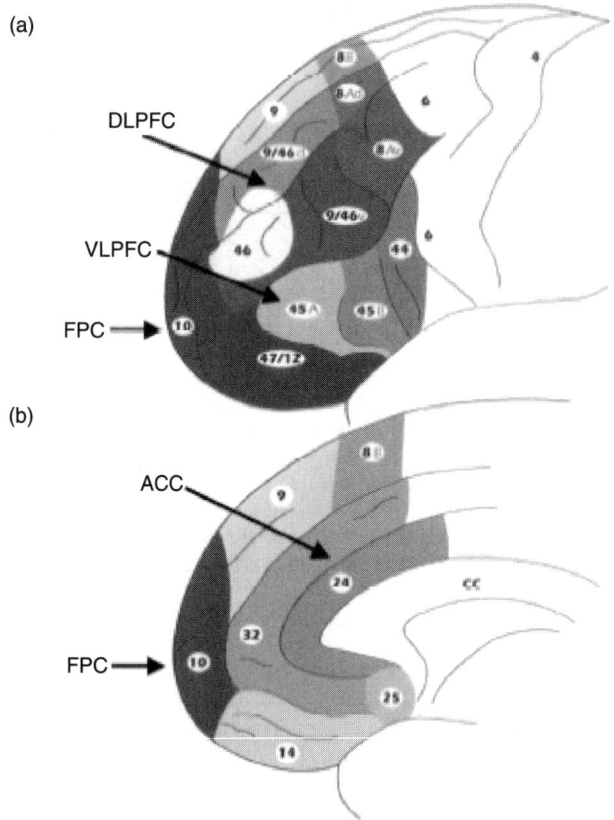

Figure 7.3 Organization of prefrontal cortex. (a) Lateral view of PFC and corresponding cytoarchitectonic areas. DLPFC corresponds to areas 46 and 9/46, while VLPFC corresponds to areas 47/12, 45, and 44. In this review, we highlight functional differences between anterior VLPFC (area 47/12) and mid-VLPFC (area 45). FPC corresponds to area 10. (b) Medial view of PFC. Medial portion of area 10 corresponds to FPC and ACC corresponds to areas 32 and 24. Adapted from Petrides and Pandya (1999).

and transcranial magnetic stimulation studies (Feredoes, Tononi, & Postle, 2006). Consideration of all the foregoing results suggests that left mid-VLPFC is critical for resolving interference across a variety of episodic, semantic, and working memory tasks.

In summary, competition can powerfully impact the likelihood of retrieval success, as inappropriate memories can dominate and preclude retrieval of desired memories. This is most evident in patients with frontal lobe damage, who suffer substantial problems selecting the most appropriate response and instead persevere on prepotent, incorrect responses. In healthy subjects, it is also clear that some instances of forgetting can be explained by mnemonic competition. For example, attempts to recall the name of an actress from a movie can often be met with frustration as names of other actresses, similar in career history or appearance, leap to mind. Recent neuroimaging work has built on general evidence from lesion studies that underscored the importance of PFC in resolving retrieval competition by specifically implicating mid-VLPFC in resolving interference amongst competing representations. Therefore, some instances of forgetting may be due to a failure to sufficiently engage mid-VLPFC in the face of competition at retrieval.

As a final point, it is worth noting that modern accounts of interference-related forgetting have tended to focus almost exclusively on competition that occurs during retrieval (but see Dolan & Fletcher, 1997; Fletcher et al., 2000; Henson et al., 2002). That is, all learned responses are assumed to be stored in memory and compete for access at the time of test. When the desired response loses the competition, forgetting occurs. However, there is evidence from the classical interference literature that is difficult to explain entirely through retrieval-stage competition. Most notably, Melton and Irwin (1940) reported substantial retroactive interference effects even under conditions where there were few overt intrusions of the interfering material and the frequency of intrusions did not relate in any sensible way to the magnitude of interference. While overt intrusions are an imperfect measure of competition (i.e., subjects could be covertly retrieving competing items), Melton and Irwin (1940) suggested that a second factor, in addition to mnemonic competition, was necessary to explain interference-related forgetting. The second factor they proposed – unlearning of the association between the cue and the interfering response – has not been supported by empirical evidence, but an influential idea that arose from their proposal is that competition elicits a second process that actively reduces competition (e.g., Anderson, 2003; Osgood, 1949; Postman, Stark, & Fraser, 1968). In the following section, we will describe the modern descendant of this idea and show how this secondary mechanism can also produce forgetting.

Forgetting as a consequence of resolving competition

While retrieval is often thwarted by strong, irrelevant memories that block access to a currently desired memory, this interference can be overcome, allowing retrieval of the initially obscured information. One account of cognitive control during retrieval has suggested that this form of conflict resolution is achieved by inhibitory processes that weaken the representations of prepotent competitors, making them less interfering and thus allowing goal-directed control over retrieval (for reviews see Anderson, 2003; Levy & Anderson, 2002). This form of control does not produce forgetting at the time of the initial retrieval – in fact, it counteracts retrieval competition and thus promotes successful remembering. Rather, the inhibition of competing memories lingers and produces forgetting later when those items become goal-relevant and thus need to be recalled. From this perspective, some instances of forgetting reflect the consequence of having resolved retrieval competition in the past. Such inhibitory processes have now been implicated in at least two distinct situations: when we wish to selectively retrieve a particular memory amongst competing alternatives; and when there is an explicit attempt to prevent a specific memory from being retrieved.

Selective retrieval

The idea that inhibition may be involved in achieving control during competitive retrieval situations has been explored in the retrieval practice paradigm (Anderson, Bjork, & Bjork, 1994), a procedure which bears many similarities to the classic retroactive interference paradigm. In a typical experiment, subjects study category–exemplar word pairs (e.g., fruit–apple, fruit–banana, drink–whiskey, drink–rum) and then engage in selective retrieval practice of some of the items from some of the categories (e.g., "fruit–a____" might be given as a cue to recall "apple"). After a delay, subjects are then asked to recall all of the exemplars they studied earlier. As would be expected, the items that were practiced during the selective retrieval practice phase (referred to as RP+ items) are recalled more often than baseline items, which were exemplars from categories that were not tested at all during the selective retrieval phase (e.g., "whiskey" or "rum", referred to as NRP items). More interestingly, items from the practiced categories that were not practiced themselves (referred to as RP– items) are recalled less often than the baseline (NRP) items (see Figure 7.4). Thus, selectively retrieving associates of a cue strengthens those items, but also weakens other unpracticed associates related to that cue. This finding, that selective retrieval can cause forgetting of competing memories, has been referred to as retrieval-induced forgetting (RIF), and it has been interpreted as evidence that inhibition is engaged

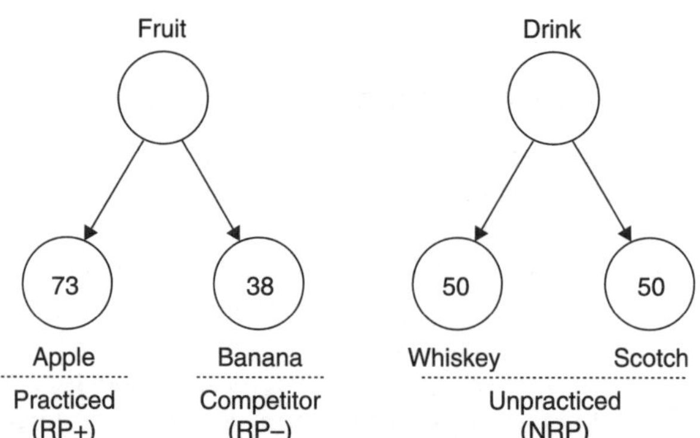

Figure 7.4 Schematic of retrieval-induced forgetting. Practiced items (RP+) are typically better remembered than baseline (NRP) or competing (RP–) items (numbers reflect percentage recall). Critically, RP– items are typically more poorly recalled than NRP items. The recall impairment for RP– items, relative to NRP items, reflects the magnitude of RIF.

during selective retrieval in order to dampen the interference from competing representations. This inhibition putatively promotes successful retrieval and indirectly produces later forgetting.

The basic RIF effect – forgetting of unpracticed items from practiced categories – is not uniquely diagnostic of inhibition. Increased retrieval competition could explain such forgetting because the practiced items are strengthened and should therefore cause even greater competition when the nonpracticed competitors are to be recalled during the final test. Several findings argue against such an interpretation, however, and support the inhibition explanation. First, RIF occurs even when items are tested with retrieval cues that were not studied earlier (e.g., "monkey–b______" for "banana"; Anderson & Bell, 2001; Anderson, Green, & McCulloch, 2000; Anderson & Spellman, 1995; Aslan, Bäuml, & Pastötter, 2007; Camp, Pecher, & Schmidt, 2005; Johnson & Anderson, 2004; Levy, McVeigh, Marful, & Anderson, 2007; MacLeod & Saunders, 2005; Saunders & MacLeod, 2006). This is inconsistent with a pure retrieval-competition explanation as there is no reason to think that the practiced items should provide competition in this situation (e.g., presenting "monkey" as a retrieval cue should not make subjects think of "apple"). Further evidence of the cue-independent nature of RIF comes from reports that memory for RP– items is also impaired on tests of recognition memory (Hicks & Starns, 2004; Spitzer & Bäuml, 2007; Starns & Hicks, 2004; Verde, 2004) and implicit lexical decision (Veling & van Knippenberg, 2004). Thus, it appears that the forgetting occurs due to weakening of the competitors, rather than simply strengthening of alternative representations. Second, RIF is strength-independent, such that the magnitude of forgetting does not depend on the degree of strengthening of the practiced memories. This directly challenges the retrieval competition account, which predicts that forgetting arises because the practiced memories are strengthened, blocking later access to the subsequently relevant competitors. This decoupling between strengthening of initial targets and impairment of competitors can be observed in situations where targets are strengthened without a corresponding impairment for competitors (Anderson et al., 1994; Bäuml, 1996, 1997; Bäuml, & Hartinger, 2002; Ciranni & Shimamura, 1999), and in situations where competitors are forgotten without clear evidence of targets being strengthened (Storm, Bjork, Bjork, & Nestojko, 2006). Third, RIF is stronger for competitors that provide more interference during initial selective retrieval (e.g., "banana" is more likely to be forgotten than "kiwi"; Anderson et al., 1994; Bäuml, 1998). This finding suggests that RIF is interference-dependent, challenging the response competition account that predicts that strong and weak competitors alike should be influenced. Taken together, these results strongly support the inhibitory account of RIF.

As discussed earlier, neuroimaging data indicate that lateral PFC is engaged when competition must be resolved during selective retrieval. On the one hand, PFC could be engaged in response to the presence of conflict or in service of resolving competition in some noninhibitory manner. On the other hand, frontal regions – or perhaps a subset of them – may directly mediate the inhibitory process that is measured by the behavioral RIF effect. Two recent fMRI studies have explored this relationship between PFC activity, retrieval competition, and inhibition (Kuhl, Dudukovic, Kahn, & Wagner, 2007; Wimber, Rutschmann, Greenlee, & Bäuml, 2009). Kuhl et al. (2007) predicted that inhibition should cause competitors to be less interfering with subsequent retrieval practice and thus successive acts of selective retrieval should require less control (i.e., recalling "apple" should make it easier to recall "apple" later due to inhibition of "banana"). Consistent with this prediction, Kuhl et al. found that lateral and medial PFC showed a pattern of decreasing activation across repeated retrieval practice trials. While intriguing, this pattern alone would be expected even from a purely noninhibitory response competition account, as successive trials should lead to strengthening of the target and therefore less control would be needed with each subsequent attempt (i.e., recalling "apple" gets easier simply because "apple" is strengthened). A second analysis, however, directly tested for a relationship between the decreases in PFC engagement and the weakening of competitor (RP–) items. This analysis revealed that two subregions within PFC – ACC and right anterior VLPFC – exhibited decreases in activation in proportion to the forgetting that competing memories suffered (see Figure 7.5). The authors argued that these decreases reflected the reduced engagement of control processes that are engaged in relation to the strength of competing memories.

The relationship between selective retrieval and competitor forgetting was also addressed by Wimber et al. (2009), in a study that directly contrasted selective retrieval with a nonselective condition where the word pairs were simply re-presented. This re-presentation condition is known to produce comparable strengthening of the practiced items yet no inhibition of competitors (Bäuml, 1996, 1997; Bäuml, & Hartinger, 2002; Ciranni & Shimamura, 1999). Since both conditions are similar in terms of strengthening, Wimber et al. reasoned that additional activity observed in the selective retrieval condition should reflect, at least in part, processes involved in inhibiting competitors. Indeed, this contrast (retrieval > re-presentation) revealed activity within lateral and medial PFC, presumably reflecting the engagement of control processes that are needed to a greater extent in the selective retrieval condition. Moreover, Wimber et al. found that the difference in activation during selective retrieval vs. re-presentation in several PFC regions – specifically, ACC and DLPFC – was correlated with behavioral evidence of competitor forgetting. The localization within ACC was highly consistent with the ACC region that Kuhl et al. found to be correlated with competitor forgetting (see Figure 7.5).

The involvement of PFC during selective retrieval is also supported by an event-related potential (ERP) study. Using a procedure similar to the one employed by Wimber et al. (2009), Johansson, Aslan, Bäuml, Gabel, and

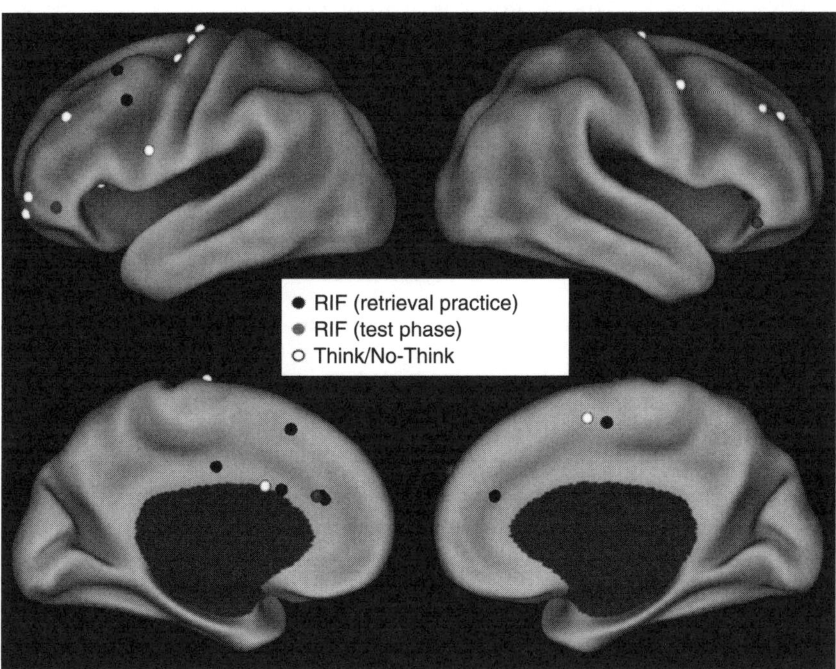

Figure 7.5 PFC regions that predict behavioral inhibition. Plotted here are the peak activations that showed a positive between-subject correlation with behavioral inhibition from six fMRI studies of inhibitory control in memory (Anderson et al., 2004; Depue et al., 2007; Kuhl et al., 2007, 2008; Wimber, Bäuml, Bergström, Markoponlos, Heinze, & Richardson-Klavehn, 2008, Wimber et al., 2009). The magnitude of behavioral inhibition was calculated for each subject based upon the difference between recall for baseline items and the putatively inhibited items (RP– items in the RIF studies and NT items in the TNT studies). This behavioral inhibition score was then regressed upon the main contrast in the study, to reveal regions which were more active for subjects who more successfully inhibited. The black foci represent correlations from the retrieval practice phase of RIF studies, while the grey foci represent correlations from the test phase of RIF studies. The white foci are from TNT phase data. In general, the RIF results tend to converge in ventral regions, with noticeable clustering in anterior VLPFC and ACC. By contrast, TNT results tend to appear more in DLPFC and frontopolar cortex. However, there are only a few studies of each type displayed here and there is considerable variability in the location of these peaks, suggesting that further work will be needed to clearly localize these effects.

Mecklinger (2007) found that selective retrieval produced an enhanced positive component, relative to the re-presentation condition, over frontal electrode sites. Importantly, this enhanced activity did not reflect strengthening of the practiced items because the two conditions yielded comparable facilitation. Rather, the magnitude of this positive frontal component during retrieval practice predicted how much forgetting subjects experienced for the competitor (RP–) items. While localization of the source of ERP components is difficult, the frontal effect observed in these studies corresponds generally with the prior fMRI findings on the involvement of PFC during selective retrieval and suggests again that the degree to which these regions are engaged relates to subsequent forgetting.

When considered alongside the retrieval competition literature, these studies suggest a tentative model of PFC functioning during selective retrieval. Left mid-VLPFC is activated during situations that feature mnemonic competition, but, to date, there is little evidence that the mechanisms subserved by this region correlate with later forgetting of competitors. This suggests that left mid-VLPFC plays a direct role in resolving competition, but not in a manner that is related to subsequent inhibition of the nonselected items. This is consistent with the idea that left mid-VLPFC is engaged post-retrieval to select amongst multiple active representations (Badre & Wagner, 2007).

In contrast to left mid-VLPFC, there is accumulating evidence that activity in DLPFC, anterior-VLPFC, and ACC are related to the forgetting that competing memories suffer (a putative result of inhibition). One interpretation of these relationships is that lateral PFC mechanisms (e.g., DLPFC and right anterior-VLPFC) guide attention toward task-relevant representations. This orienting of attention then indirectly produces inhibition of the competitors, consistent with a biased competition account (e.g., Miller & Cohen, 2001). Interestingly, a recent computational model of RIF has suggested that the weakening of competing representations could occur entirely locally within the MTL, suggesting that the role of PFC may only be involved in selecting representations and not directly involved in inhibition (Norman, Newman, & Detre, 2007). Alternatively, lateral PFC regions may implement a form of inhibitory control that directly weakens the competing representation (see Levy & Anderson, 2002). While distinguishing between these accounts is difficult, it is worth emphasizing that both accounts predict that lateral PFC regions should be engaged in relation to the strength of competing memories. Interestingly, two recent studies (Kuhl, Kahn, Dudukovic, & Wagner, 2008; Wimber et al., 2008) reported that when initially selected-against competing memories are subsequently retrieved (i.e., when they later become retrieval targets), activation is observed in anterior-VLPFC that specifically relates to the magnitude of weakening that competitors suffered. Thus, consistent with evidence from other retrieval contexts, there is strong evidence that anterior VLPFC is sensitive to the strength of information being retrieved (Badre et al., 2005; Badre & Wagner, 2007; Danker et al., 2008; Wagner, Maril, Bjork, & Schacter, 2001). The relationship between ACC and competitor forgetting is potentially consistent with other findings that implicate ACC in the detection of conflict (Botvinick, Braver, Barch, Carter, & Cohen, 2001; Braver, Barch, Gray, Molfese, & Snyder, 2001; MacDonald, Cohen, Stenger, & Carter, 2000; van Veen & Carter, 2002). That is, in the retrieval practice paradigm, competing memories may elicit conflict that is detected by ACC; as competitors are weakened, responses in ACC should decrease correspondingly. Importantly, lateral PFC may be engaged in response to ACC conflict detection, thus supporting successful target retrieval (e.g., Badre & Wagner, 2004; Bunge, Burrows, & Wagner, 2004). While this hypothesis is speculative, it is consistent with theories regarding the roles of ACC and lateral PFC in cognitive control.

Perhaps challenging the conclusions of the foregoing section, neuropsychological evidence suggests that RIF can occur even when lateral PFC functioning is compromised. Specifically, the retrieval practice paradigm has now been studied in several populations associated with frontal functional impairments, including patients with frontal lobe damage (Conway & Fthenaki, 2003), Alzheimer's patients (Moulin, Perfect, Conway, North, Jones, & James, 2002), and healthy older adults (Aslan et al., 2007; Hogge, Adam, & Collette, 2008; Moulin et al., 2002). In each study, the "frontally-impaired" group showed normal RIF, suggesting that this form of inhibition may not depend upon intact frontal functioning. However, a difficulty arises in interpreting these studies because all but one (Aslan et al., 2007) relied solely on the studied categories as cues at test. As described earlier, that type of test does not distinguish between forgetting that is produced by inhibition during the earlier retrieval practice or by retrieval competition during the final test (i.e., is the forgetting due to strengthening of "apple" or weakening of "banana"?). In fact, populations with impaired PFC function are likely to be even more vulnerable to response competition – as we discussed above – and may therefore display very robust forgetting without any contribution of inhibition per se (Anderson & Levy, 2007). Aslan et al. (2007), however, found preserved RIF in older adults using independent probes, suggesting that RIF may actually be preserved in healthy aging. It is difficult to interpret this study, however, with respect to the involvement of PFC in RIF because Aslan et al. did not ascertain whether these older adults were experiencing any frontal lobe dysfunction – indeed, their retrieval performance, in general, did not suggest any deficits. Given this limitation and the fact that earlier studies were unable to disentangle response competition from inhibition, it remains uncertain whether normal PFC functioning is a prerequisite for RIF to occur.

Stopping retrieval

Another situation that requires control over memory is when we desire to prevent a memory from coming to mind. For example, when confronted with a reminder of something upsetting (e.g., seeing someone who recently witnessed you doing something embarrassing) we often wish to avoid thinking about the unpleasant thoughts associated with that event. Similarly, the ability to focus cognition in a goal-directed manner relies on the ability to selectively prevent task-irrelevant memories from entering awareness. In these situations the focus is not on selectively retrieving alternative memories; rather, the desire is to simply stop the retrieval process itself. Recent research using the Think/No-Think (TNT) paradigm suggests that this situation also relies on inhibitory control that weakens the to-be-avoided memory, rendering it less intrusive. In a typical TNT study, participants learn a list of cue-target word pairs (e.g., ordeal–roach) and are then presented with some of the studied cue words (e.g., ordeal) and asked to either think of the associated word (roach) or prevent that word from coming to mind. After seeing these "Think" and "No-Think" cues multiple times, subjects are then asked to recall all of the words they studied earlier. If subjects are able to recruit control mechanisms to inhibit the unwanted memories on No-Think trials and if this suppression lingers, then these words should be less accessible later.

Unsurprisingly, when subjects were instructed to remember (i.e., Think condition), reminders enhanced later memory relative to baseline word pairs, which were studied initially but whose cues were not seen again during the TNT phase (see Figure 7.6). In contrast, when people try to prevent an associate from coming to mind (i.e., No-Think condition), subjects have more difficulty recalling these items than baseline items (Anderson & Green, 2001; Anderson et al., 2004; Depue, Banich, & Curran, 2006; Depue, Curran, &

(a)

			Test Phase	
	Study	TNT Phase	Same Probe	Independent Probe
No-Think	Ordeal–Roach	Ordeal	Ordeal	Insect r___
Think	Steam–Train	Steam	Steam	Vehicle t___
Baseline	Jaw–Gum		Jaw	Candy g___

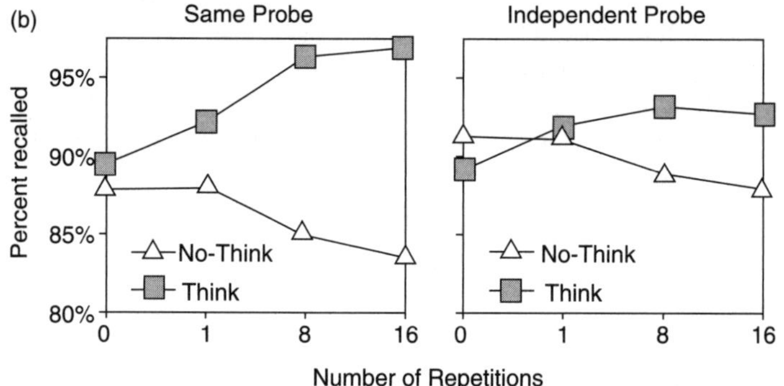

Figure 7.6 The Think/No-Think paradigm. (a) During the TNT phase, subjects are cued to think of the corresponding associate for Think items, but to avoid thinking of the response for No-Think items. (b) Final recall performance. Memory for the Think items increases as a function of repetition, while recall of the No-Think items decreases as a function of repetition. The No-Think impairment is apparent both in the Same Probe and Independent Probe tests.

Banich, 2007; Hertel & Calcaterra, 2005; Joorman, Hertel, Brozovitch, & Gotlib, 2005; Wessel, Wetzels, Jelicic, & Merckelbach, 2005; although, see Bulevich, Roediger, Balota, & Butler, 2006). Thus, avoiding a memory makes it harder to recall later even when it is desired, and this impairment is a function of the number of times that the thought has been avoided (Anderson & Green, 2001; Depue et al., 2006).

As was the case with RIF, the basic TNT forgetting effect is compatible with either an inhibitory process or a noninhibitory retrieval competition explanation. For example, subjects might generate diversionary thoughts when they see the No-Think cues. Subsequently, when presented with the same cues on the final memory test, the strengthened diversionary thoughts may come to mind and block retrieval of the original representation. Arguing against a pure noninhibitory account, however, is evidence that increased forgetting is observed even when subjects are provided with novel, extralist items as retrieval cues on the final test (e.g., "insect–r______" for "roach"; Anderson & Green, 2001). This finding of cue-independent forgetting suggests that retrieval competition from diversionary thoughts cannot account for the observed memory impairments. While this result supports the inhibitory account, it is still unclear exactly how these avoided memories are inhibited as it is compatible with at least two distinct inhibitory mechanisms. First, as described earlier, subjects may generate diversionary thoughts as a means of preventing the original word from coming to mind (Hertel & Calcaterra, 2005). Then when No-Think cues are presented again, subjects may retrieve these earlier diversionary thoughts, creating a selective retrieval situation where the original learned words suffer from RIF. Alternatively, when confronted with a reminder of an unwanted memory, subjects may engage control processes that directly target the to-be-avoided memory and inhibit this representation. At present, it is unclear which of these two inhibitory accounts best describes forgetting in the TNT paradigm.

While extant behavioral data suggest an active inhibitory process is engaged in the TNT paradigm, fMRI studies have sought more direct evidence of inhibitory control during attempts to stop retrieval. Using neutral word stimuli, Anderson et al. (2004) found that No-Think trials are associated with elevated activity, relative to Think trials, in several frontal regions, including bilateral DLPFC, VLPFC, and ACC. Depue et al. (2007) extended this study, using negatively valenced photographs (e.g., a photograph of a car crash) as the to-be-avoided memories, and observed increased activation in a similar set of right frontal regions, including DLPFC, anterior VLPFC, and frontopolar cortex. Strikingly, both Anderson et al. (2004) and Depue et al. (2007) found that the magnitude of DLPFC engagement during No-Think trials predicted the amount of behavioral inhibition that subjects displayed on the final memory test (see Figure 7.5). These data suggest that lateral PFC is engaged during attempts to stop retrieval, with DLPFC, in particular, perhaps playing a key role in producing the subsequent forgetting of these avoided memories. Stopping retrieval is, therefore, not simply a failure to engage retrieval processes; rather, activation of control-related prefrontal regions during No-Think trials suggests that subjects actively engage processes to prevent unwanted memories from coming to mind.

In addition to regions that are engaged by the No-Think task, fMRI studies have also identified regions that are less active during attempts to stop retrieval. In particular, both Anderson et al. (2004) and Depue et al. (2007) observed decreases in MTL activity during No-Think trials relative to Think trials. Decreased MTL activity during No-Think trials is not surprising, as this region is known to be active during conscious recollection (e.g., Eldridge, Knowlton, Furmanski, Bookheimer, & Engel, 2000; Kirwan & Stark, 2004) and the goal of the Think and No-Think tasks, respectively, is to engage and override conscious recollection. This difference, therefore, suggests that subjects are able to phasically regulate the activity of the MTL as necessitated by current goals, but it is unclear whether this difference is due to engagement during Think trials and/or disengagement during No-Think trials. Evidence in support of the latter explanation comes from the finding that the degree of hippocampal activity during No-Think trials is related to behavioral memory inhibition (see Anderson et al., 2004 for a description of this relationship), suggesting that the MTL modulation during No-Think trials is related to processes that produce the subsequent forgetting of the No-Think items. Taken together, it appears that attempts to stop retrieval are associated with increased lateral PFC activity and decreased MTL activity; both of these effects are related to subsequent forgetting.

Recent electrophysiological data suggest similar conclusions. Attempting to stop retrieval is associated with early frontal ERP components (Bergström, de Fockert, & Richardson-Klavehn, 2009; Mecklinger, Parra, & Waldhauser, 2009) that resemble the N2 component observed during the stopping of overt motor responses (Kok, 1986; Kopp, Matler, Goertz, & Rist, 1996). Interestingly, Hanslmayr et al. (2009) found that giving subjects advance warning about an upcoming No-Think trial led to a similar frontal negativity during the warning period, even before the cue word appeared. Critically, the magnitude of this anticipatory effect predicted subsequent forgetting, again linking frontal engagement to successful inhibition. In addition to these early frontal components, a late left parietal component is present selectively on Think trials (Bergström, et al., 2009; Bergström, Velmans, de Fockert, & Richardson-Klavehn, 2007), with the timing and topography of this component being consistent with the parietal old/new episodic memory effect that has been linked to the subjective experience of consciously recollecting a past event (e.g., Friedman & Johnson, 2000; Paller & Kutas, 1992; Rugg & Curran, 2007; Rugg, Schloerscheidt, Doyle, Cox, & Patching, 1996). Because this component is greatly reduced during the No-Think trials, these data suggest that executive control processes that stop retrieval eliminate this parietal retrieval-related component. Together, extant ERP and fMRI evidence suggests that the suppression of competing or avoided memories is associated with lateral PFC function. A fundamental objective for future research will be to determine whether PFC control processes, including those mediated by DLPFC and VLPFC, implement the stopping of conscious recollection (or the suppression of competitors in the RIF paradigm), or whether these changes in PFC processing demands reflect the benefits of suppression accomplished through other mechanisms (e.g., processes within the MTL).

Forgetting due to ineffective retrieval cues

On some occasions we forget simply because the current retrieval cues are insufficient to bring the desired experience back to mind. This general, but fundamental, observation has been made in a number of different theoretical frameworks, including the encoding specificity principle (Tulving & Thomson, 1973) and context models of memory (e.g., Estes, 1955; Howard & Kahana, 2002; Mensink & Raaijmakers, 1989). According to the encoding specificity principle, the cues present during the encoding experience will be the most effective cues for later retrieving the memory, so a shift in the cues used to guide retrieval away from those present at encoding can cause forgetting. Context models expand this focus on specific cues to explain forgetting as a mismatch between the general context of the encoding situation and that of the retrieval situation, which arises because context varies over time and this constant updating results in a drift between encoding and retrieval (Estes, 1955; Howard & Kahana, 2002; Mensink & Raaijmakers, 1989; Polyn, Norman, & Kahana, 2009). Thus, when we later wish to bring these individual bits of information back to mind, we may fail to retrieve them because the test context is sufficiently different from the original study context so as to poorly cue memory. Common to both of these accounts is the idea that forgetting can be produced when the cues used to guide retrieval are insufficiently related to the desired memory and thus fail to reinstate it. This factor is clearly relevant for understanding forgetting and clearly differs from the other mechanisms advanced here, but as of yet little functional neuroimaging data have been gathered to examine the neural contexts that produce this form of forgetting (although, see Polyn & Kahana, 2008 for a review of early work on this topic).

Conclusions

Here we have argued that forgetting has several distinct causes, rather than being produced by any single mechanism. It seems clear that there are at least five factors that contribute to forgetting of past experiences. First, forgetting can be caused by a failure to encode the initial experience. Ineffective encoding sometimes occurs because of a failure to engage fronto-parietal mechanisms that direct attention to relevant representations for encoding, or because attention is captured by task-irrelevant representations, putatively marked by engagement of ventral parietal engagement, that distract encoding-relevant resources away from to-be-remembered items. Second, intervening experiences, even those unrelated to the original event, can interfere with the MTL-dependent memory trace before it is fully consolidated. Finally, three other mechanisms focus on the retrieval dynamics created by the relationship between retrieval cues and target memories. When cues are strongly related to competing memories, failures to engage VLPFC can result in strong alternatives blocking retrieval of the desired memory. In situations where we are able to overcome such retrieval competition, however, it appears that the act of interference resolution is accomplished, at least in part, by processes that weaken the alternative memories, causing us to later forget these items. Such memory suppression is associated with activation in anterior VLPFC and DLPFC structures, revealing a relationship between cognitive control and forgetting. Lastly, forgetting can occur when the retrieval cues are simply insufficient to reinstate the desired memory.

Each mechanism proposed here accounts for critical aspects of forgetting, but is unable to explain all the data, suggesting that no one mechanism is sufficient to provide a coherent account of forgetting. It is also clear that while progress has been made in characterizing each of these forms of forgetting, many outstanding questions remain, particularly in terms of the neural mechanisms giving rise to forgetting. For example, it is clear that lateral PFC plays a crucial role during both the encoding of our experiences and during attempts to subsequently remember. Within lateral PFC, future work will need to carefully explore how PFC mechanisms involved in resolving retrieval competition (mediated by left mid-VLPFC) relate to those that correlate with later forgetting as a consequence of resolving competition. We do not wish to suggest, though, that these mechanisms will necessarily be associated with dissociable neural substrates, as many of the differences between them focus on the stage at which they operate (e.g., encoding or retrieval). For example, similar PFC regions may play a role in both failed encoding and failure to resolve interference during retrieval, but at different points in time. Finally, we emphasize that the five mechanisms proposed here likely do not constitute an exclusive list. Nevertheless, the lines of behavioral and functional neuroimaging research described herein hold promise for an increasingly specified account of why we sometimes fail to remember our past.

References

Addis, D. R., Moscovitch, M., Crawley, A. P., & McAndrews, M. P. (2004). Recollective qualities modulate hippocampal activation during autobiographical memory retrieval. *Hippocampus*, *14*, 752–762.

Anderson, J. R. (1974). Retrieval of propositional information from long-term memory. *Cognitive Psychology*, *6*, 451–474.

Anderson, J. R. (1983). *The architecture of cognition*. Cambridge, MA: Harvard University Press.

Anderson, M. C. (2003). Rethinking interference theory: Executive control and the mechanisms of forgetting. *Journal of Memory and Language*, *49*, 415–445.

Anderson, M. C., & Bell, T. A. (2001). Forgetting our facts: The role of inhibitory processes in the loss of propositional knowledge. *Journal of Experimental Psychology: General*, *130*, 544–570.

Anderson, M. C., Bjork, R. A., & Bjork, E. L. (1994). Remembering can cause forgetting: Retrieval dynamics in long-term memory. *Journal of Experimental Psychology: Learning, Memory, and Cognition*, *20*, 1063–1087.

Anderson, M. C., & Green, C. (2001). Suppressing unwanted memories by executive control. *Nature*, *410*, 366–369.

Anderson, M. C., Green, C., & McCulloch, K. C. (2000). Similarity and inhibition in long-term memory: Evidence for a two-factor theory. *Journal of Experimental Psychology: Learning, Memory, & Cognition*, *26*, 1141–1159.

Anderson, M. C., & Levy, B. J. (2007). Theoretical issues in inhibition: Insights from research on human memory. In D. Gorfein & C. MacLeod (Eds.), *The place for inhibitory processes in cognition*. Washington, DC: American Psychological Association.

Anderson, M. C. & Neely, J. H. (1996). Interference and inhibition in memory retrieval. In E. L. Bjork & R. A. Bjork (Eds.), *Memory Handbook of Perception and Cognition* (2nd ed.), (pp. 237–313). San Diego, CA: Academic Press.

Anderson, M. C., Ochsner, K., Kuhl, B., Cooper, J., Robertson, E., Gabrieli, S. W., et al. (2004). Neural systems underlying the suppression of unwanted memories. *Science*, *303*, 232–235.

Anderson, M. C., & Spellman, B. A. (1995). On the status of inhibitory mechanisms in cognition: Memory retrieval as a model case. *Psychological Review*, *102*, 68–100.

Aslan, A., Bäuml, K., & Pastötter, B. (2007). No inhibitory deficit in older adults' episodic memory. *Psychological Science*, *18*, 72–78.

Badre, D., Poldrack, R. A., Pare-Blagoev, E. J., Insler, R. Z., & Wagner, A. D. (2005). Dissociable controlled retrieval and generalized selection mechanisms in ventrolateral prefrontal cortex. *Neuron*, *47*, 907–918.

Badre, D., & Wagner, A. D. (2004). Selection, integration, and conflict monitoring: Assessing the nature and generality of prefrontal cognitive control mechanisms. *Neuron*, *41*, 473–487.

Badre, D., & Wagner, A. D. (2007). Left ventrolateral prefrontal cortex and the cognitive control of memory. *Neuropsychologia*, *45*, 2883–2901.

Bäuml, K. (1996). Revisiting an old issue: Retroactive interference as a function of the degree of original and interpolated learning. *Psychonomic Bulletin & Review*, *3*, 380–384.

Bäuml, K. (1997). The list-strength effect: Strength-dependent competition or suppression. *Psychonomic Bulletin & Review*, *4*, 260–264.

Bäuml, K. (1998). Strong items get suppressed, weak items do not: The role of item strength in output interference. *Psychonomic Bulletin & Review*, *5*, 459–463.

Bäuml, K., & Hartinger, A. (2002). On the role of item similarity in retrieval-induced forgetting. *Memory*, *10*, 215–224.

Bergström, Z., de Fockert, J., & Richardson-Klavehn, A. (2009). Event-related potential evidence that automatic retrieval can be voluntarily avoided. *Journal of Cognitive Neuroscience*, *21*, 1280–1301.

Bergström, Z. M., Velmans, M., de Fockert, J., & Richardson-Klavehn, A. (2007). ERP evidence for successful voluntary avoidance of conscious recollection. *Brain Research*, *1151*, 119–133.

Blumenfeld, R., & Ranganath, C. (2006). Dorsolateral prefrontal cortex promotes long-term memory formation through its role in working memory organization. *Journal of Neuroscience*, *26*, 916–925.

Botvinick, M. M., Braver, T. S., Barch, D. M., Carter, C. S., & Cohen, J. D. (2001). Conflict monitoring and cognitive control. *Psychological Review*, *108*, 624–652.

Braver, T. S., Barch, D. M., Gray, J. R., Molfese, D. L., & Snyder, A. (2001). Anterior cingulate cortex and response conflict: Effects of frequency, inhibition and errors. *Cerebral Cortex*, *11*, 825–836.

Brewer, J., Zhao, Z., Desmond, J., Glover, G., & Gabrieli, J. (1998). Making memories: Brain activity that predicts how well visual experience will be remembered. *Science*, *281*, 1185–1187.

Bulevich, J. B., Roediger, H. L., Balota, D. A., & Butler, A. C. (2006). Failures to find suppression of episodic memories in the Think/No-Think paradigm. *Memory & Cognition*, *34*, 1569–1577.

Bunge, S. A., Burrows, B., & Wagner, A. D. (2004). Prefrontal and hippocampal contributions to visual associative recognition: Interactions between cognitive control and episodic retrieval. *Brain and Cognition*, *56*, 141–152.

Cabeza, R. (2008). Role of parietal regions in episodic memory retrieval: The dual attentional processes hypothesis. *Neuropsychologia*, *46*, 1813–1827.

Camp, G., Pecher, D., & Schmidt, H. G. (2005). Retrieval-induced forgetting in implicit memory tests: The role of test awareness. *Psychonomic Bulletin & Review*, *12*, 490–494.

Ciranni, M. A., & Shimamura, A. P. (1999). Retrieval-induced forgetting in episodic memory. *Journal of Experimental Psychology: Learning, Memory, and Cognition*, *25*, 1403–1414.

Conway, M. A., & Fthenaki, A. (2003). Disruption of inhibitory control of memory following lesions to the frontal and temporal lobes. *Cortex*, *39*, 667–686.

Corbetta, M., Patel, G., & Shulman, G. (2008). The reorienting system of the human brain: From environment to theory of mind. *Neuron*, *58*, 306–324.

Corbetta, M., & Shulman, G. L. (2002). Control of goal-directed and stimulus-driven attention in the brain. *Nature Reviews Neuroscience*, *3*, 201–215.

Craik, F. I., Govoni, R., Naveh-Benjamin, M., & Anderson, N. D. (1996). The effects of divided attention on encoding and retrieval processes in human memory. *Journal of Experimental Psychology – General*, *125*, 159–180.

Craik, F. I. M., & Lockhart, R. S. (1972). Levels of processing: A framework for memory research. *Journal of Verbal Learning and Verbal Behavior*, *11*, 671–684.

Craik, F. I. M., & Tulving, E. (1975). Depth of processing and the retention of words in episodic memory. *Journal of Experimental Psychology: General*, *104*, 268–294.

Danker, J. F., Gunn, P., & Anderson, J. R. (2008). A rational account of memory predicts left prefrontal activation during controlled retrieval. *Cerebral Cortex*, *18*, 2674–2685.

Davachi, L. (2006). Item, context and relational episodic encoding in humans. *Current Opinion in Neurobiology*, *16*, 693–700.

Depue, B. E., Banich, M. T., & Curran, T. (2006). Suppression of emotional and non-emotional content in memory: Effects of repetition on cognitive control. *Psychological Science*, *17*, 441–447.

Depue, B. E., Curran, T., & Banich, M. T. (2007). Prefrontal regions orchestrate suppression of emotional memories via a two-phase process. *Science*, *37*, 215–219.

Dolan, R. J., & Fletcher, P. C. (1997). Dissociating prefrontal and hippocampal function in episodic memory encoding. *Nature, 388*, 582–585.

Ebbinghaus, H. (1885/1913). *Memory. A contribution to Experimental Psychology*. New York: Teachers College/Columbia University (Engl. ed.).

Eldridge, L. L., Knowlton, B. J., Furmanski, C. S., Bookheimer, S. Y., & Engel, S. A. (2000). Remembering episodes: A selective role for the hippocampus during retrieval. *Nature Neuroscience, 3*, 1149–1152.

Estes, W. K. (1955). Statistical theory of spontaneous recovery and regression. *Psychological Review, 62*, 145–154.

Feredoes, E., Tononi, G., & Postle, B. R. (2006). Direct evidence for a prefrontal contribution to the control of proactive interference in verbal working memory. *Proceedings of the National Academy of Sciences of the USA, 103*, 19530–19534.

Fletcher, P., Frith, C., Grasby, P., Shallice, T., Frackowiak, R., & Dolan, R. (1995). Brain systems for encoding and retrieval of auditory-verbal memory. An in vivo study in humans. *Brain: A Journal of Neurology, 118*, 401–416.

Fletcher, P. C., Shallice, T., & Dolan, R. J. (2000). "Sculpting the response space" – an account of left prefrontal activation at encoding. *Neuroimage, 12*, 404–417.

Friedman, D., & Johnson, R., Jr. (2000). Event-related potential (ERP) studies of memory encoding and retrieval: A selective review. *Microscopy Research and Technique, 51*, 6–28.

Gilboa, A., Winocur, G., Grady, C. L., Hevenor, S. J., & Moscovitch, M. (2004). Remembering our past: Functional neuroanatomy of recollection of recent and very remote personal events. *Cerebral Cortex, 14*, 1214–1225.

Haist, F., Gore, J. B., & Mao, H. (2001). Consolidation of human memory over decades revealed by functional magnetic resonance imaging. *Nature Neuroscience, 4*, 1139–1145.

Hanslmayr, S., Leipold, P., Pastötter, B., & Bäuml, K. (2009). Anticipatory signatures of voluntary memory suppression. *Journal of Neuroscience, 29*, 2742–2747.

Henson, R. N., Shallice, T., Josephs, O., & Dolan, R. J. (2002). Functional magnetic resonance imaging of proactive interference during spoken cued recall. *Neuroimage, 17*, 543–558.

Hertel, P. T., & Calcaterra, G. (2005). Intentional forgetting benefits from thought substitution. *Psychonomic Bulletin & Review, 12*, 484–489.

Hicks, J. L., & Starns, J. J. (2004). Retrieval-induced forgetting occurs in tests of item recognition. *Psychonomic Bulletin & Review, 11*, 125–130.

Hogge, M., Adam, S., & Collette, F. (2008). Retrieval-induced forgetting in normal ageing. *Journal of Neuropsychology, 2*, 463–476.

Howard, M. W., & Kahana, M. J. (2002). A distributed representation of temporal context. *Journal of Mathematical Psychology, 46*, 269–299.

Iidaka, T., Anderson, N. D., Kapur, S., Cabeza, R., & Craik, F. I. (2000). The effect of divided attention on encoding and retrieval in episodic memory revealed by positron emission tomography. *Journal of Cognitive Neuroscience, 12*, 267–280.

Janowsky, J. S., Shimamura, A. P., Kritchevsky, M., & Squire, L. R. (1989). Cognitive impairment following frontal lobe damage and its relevance to human amnesia. *Behavioral Neuroscience, 103*, 548–560.

Johansson, M., Aslan, A., Bäuml, K. H., Gabel, A., & Mecklinger, A. (2007). When remembering causes forgetting: Electrophysiological correlates of retrieval-induced forgetting. *Cerebral Cortex, 17*, 1335–1341.

Johnson, S. K., & Anderson, M. C. (2004). The role of inhibitory control in forgetting semantic knowledge. *Psychological Science, 15*, 448–453.

Jonides, J., & Nee, D. E. (2006). Brain mechanisms of proactive interference in working memory. *Neuroscience, 139*, 181–193.

Joorman, J., Hertel, P. T., Brozovich, F., & Gotlib, I. H. (2005). Remembering the good, forgetting the bad: Intentional forgetting of emotional material in depression. *Journal of Abnormal Psychology, 114*, 640–648.

Kensinger, E., Clarke, R., & Corkin, S. (2003). What neural correlates underlie successful encoding and retrieval? A functional magnetic resonance imaging study using a divided attention paradigm. *Journal of Neuroscience, 23*, 2407–2415.

Kirwan, C. B., & Stark, C. E. (2004). Medial temporal lobe activation during encoding and retrieval of novel face-name pairs. *Hippocampus, 14*, 919–930.

Kok, A. (1986). Effects of degradation of visual stimuli on components of the event-related potentials (ERP) in go/no-go reaction tasks. *Biological Psychology, 23*, 21–38.

Kopp, B., Matler, U., Goertz, R., & Rist, F. (1996). N2, P3, and the lateralized readiness potential in a go/no-go task involving selective response priming. *Electroencephalography and Clinical Neurophysiology, 99*, 19–27.

Kuhl, B. A., Dudukovic, N. M., Kahn, I. & Wagner, A. D. (2007). Decreased demands on cognitive control following memory suppression reveal benefits of forgetting. *Nature Neuroscience, 10*, 908–914.

Kuhl, B. A., Kahn, I., Dudukovic, N. M., & Wagner, A. D. (2008). Overcoming suppression in order to remember: Contributions from anterior cingulate and ventrolateral prefrontal cortex. *Cognitive, Behavioral, and Affective Neuroscience, 8*, 211–221.

Levy, B. J., & Anderson, M. C. (2002). Inhibitory processes and the control of memory retrieval. *Trends in Cognitive Sciences, 6*, 299–305.

Levy, B. J., McVeigh, N. D., Marful, A., & Anderson, M. C. (2007). Inhibiting your native language: The role of retrieval-induced forgetting during second-language acquisition. *Psychological Science, 18*, 29–34.

MacDonald, A. W., III, Cohen, J. D., Stenger, V. A., & Carter, C. S. (2000). Dissociating the role of the dorsolateral prefrontal and anterior cingulate cortex in cognitive control. *Science, 288*, 1835–1838.

McGaugh, J. L. (2000). Memory: A century of consolidation. *Science, 287*, 248–251.

McGeoch, J. A. (1942). *The psychology of human learning: An introduction*. New York: Longmans, Green and Co.

MacLeod, M. D., & Saunders, J. (2005). The role of inhibitory control in the production of misinformation effects. *Journal of Experimental Psychology: Learning, Memory & Cognition, 31*, 964–979.

Martin, R. C., & Cheng, Y. (2006). Selection demands versus association strength in the verb generation task. *Psychonomic Bulletin & Review, 13*, 396–401.

Mecklinger, A., Parra, M., & Waldhauser, G. T. (2009). ERP correlates of intentional forgetting. *Brain Research, 1255*, 132–147.

Melton, A. W., & Irwin, J. M. (1940). The influence of degree of interpolated learning on retroactive inhibition and the overt transfer of specific responses. *American Journal of Psychology, 3*, 173–203.

Mensink, G., & Raaijmakers, J. G. (1988). A model for interference and forgetting. *Psychological Review, 95*, 434–455.

Mensink, G. J., & Raaijmakers, J. G. W. (1989). A model for contextual fluctuation. *Journal of Mathematical Psychology*, *33*, 172–186.

Metzler, C. (2001). Effects of left frontal lesions on the selection of context-appropriate meanings. *Neuropsychology*, *15*, 315–328.

Miller, E. K., & Cohen, J. D. (2001). An integrative theory of prefrontal cortex function. *Annual Review of Neuroscience*, *24*, 167–202.

Mitchell, J., Macrae, C., & Banaji, M. (2004). Encoding-specific effects of social cognition on the neural correlates of subsequent memory. *Journal of Neuroscience*, *24*, 4912–4917.

Morris, C. D., Bransford, J. D., & Franks, J. J. (1977). Levels of processing versus transfer appropriate processing. *Journal of Verbal Learning and Verbal Behavior*, *16*, 519–533.

Moscovitch, M. (1982). Multiple dissociations of function in amnesia. In L. Cermak (Ed.), *Human memory and amnesia* (pp. 337–370). Hillsdale, NJ: Lawrence Erlbaum Associates, Inc.

Moulin, C. J. A., Perfect, T. J., Conway, M. A., North, A. S., Jones, R. W., & James, N. (2002). Retrieval-induced forgetting in Alzheimer's disease. *Neuropsychologia*, *40*, 862–867.

Müller, G. E., & Pilzecker, A. (1900). Experimentalle Beitrage zur Lehre com Gedachtnis. *Zeitschrift für Psychologie*, *1*, 1–300.

Niki, K., & Luo, J. (2002). An fMRI study on the time-limited role of the medial temporal lobe in long-term topographical autobiographic memory. *Journal of Cognitive Neuroscience*, *14*, 500–507.

Norman, K. A., Newman, E. L., & Detre, G. (2007). A neural network model of retrieval-induced forgetting. *Psychological Review*, *114*, 887–953.

Osgood, C. E. (1949). The similarity paradox in human learning: A resolution. *Psychological Review*, *56*, 132–143.

Otten, L., Henson, R., & Rugg, M. (2002). State-related and item-related neural correlates of successful memory encoding. *Nature Neuroscience*, *5*, 1339–1344.

Otten, L., & Rugg, M. (2001a). Task-dependency of the neural correlates of episodic encoding as measured by fMRI. *Cerebral Cortex*, *11*, 1150–1160.

Otten, L., & Rugg, M. (2001b). When more means less: Neural activity related to unsuccessful memory encoding. *Current Biology*, *11*, 1528–1530.

Paller, K. A., & Kutas, M. (1992). Brain potentials during memory retrieval provide neurophysiological support for the distinction between conscious recollection and priming. *Journal of Cognitive Neuroscience*, *4*, 375–391.

Paller, K. A., Kutas, M., & Mayes, A. R. (1987). Neural correlates of encoding in an incidental learning paradigm. *Electroencephalography and Clinical Neurophysiology*, *67*, 360–371.

Paller, K., & Wagner, A. (2002). Observing the transformation of experience into memory. *Trends in Cognitive Sciences*, *6*, 93–102.

Petrides, M., & Pandya, D. N. (1999). Dorsolateral prefrontal cortex: Comparative cytoarchitectonic analysis in the human and the macaque brain and corticocortical connection patterns. *European Journal of Neuroscience*, *11*, 1011–1036.

Polyn, S. M., & Kahana, M. J. (2008). Memory search and the neural representation of context. *Trends in Cognitive Sciences*, *12*, 24–30.

Polyn, S. M., Norman, K. A., & Kahana, M. J. (2009). A context maintenance and retrieval model of organizational processes in free recall. *Psychological Review*, *116*, 129–156.

Postman, L., Stark, K., & Fraser, J. (1968). Temporal changes in interference. *Journal of Verbal Learning & Verbal Behavior*, *7*, 672–694.

Ribot, T. (1882). *The diseases of memory: An essay in the positive psychology* (W. H. Smith, Trans.). London: Kegan Paul, Trench, & Co.

Rugg, M. D., & Curran, T. (2007). Event-related potentials and recognition memory. *Trends in Cognitive Sciences*, *11*, 251–257.

Rugg, M. D., Schloerscheidt, A. M., Doyle, M. C., Cox, C. J., & Patching, G. R. (1996). Event-related potentials and the recollection of associative information. *Cognitive Brain Research*, *4*, 297–304.

Saunders, J., & MacLeod, M. D. (2006). Can inhibition resolve retrieval competition through the control of spreading activation? *Memory & Cognition*, *34*, 307–322.

Shallice, T., Fletcher, P., Frith, C., Grasby, P., Frackowiak, R., & Dolan, R. (1994). Brain regions associated with acquisition and retrieval of verbal episodic memory. *Nature*, *368*, 633–635.

Shimamura, A. P., Jurica, P. J., Mangels, J. A., Gershberg, F. B., & Knight, R. T. (1995). Susceptibility to memory interference effects following frontal lobe damage: Findings from tests of paired-associate learning. *Journal of Cognitive Neuroscience*, *7*, 144–152.

Smith, M. L., Leonard, G., Crane, J., & Milner, B. (1995). The effects of frontal- or temporal-lobe lesions on susceptibility to interference in spatial memory. *Neuropsychologia*, *33*, 275–285.

Sohn, M. H., Goode, A., Stenger, V. A., Carter, C. S., & Anderson, J. R. (2003). Competition and representation during memory retrieval: Roles of the prefrontal cortex and the posterior parietal cortex. *Proceedings of the National Academy of Sciences of the USA*, *100*, 7412–7417.

Sohn, M. H., Goode, A., Stenger, V. A., Jung, K. J., Carter, C. S., & Anderson, J. R. (2005). An information-processing model of three cortical regions: Evidence in episodic memory retrieval. *Neuroimage*, *25*, 21–33.

Spitzer, B., & Bäuml, K.-H. (2007). Retrieval-induced forgetting in item recognition: Evidence for a reduction in general memory strength. *Journal of Experimental Psychology: Learning, Memory, and Cognition*, *33*, 863–875.

Squire, L. R. (1992). Memory and the hippocampus: A synthesis from findings with rats, monkeys, and humans. *Psychological Review*, *99*, 195–231.

Squire, L. R., & Alvarez, P. (1995). Retrograde amnesia and memory consolidation: A neurobiological perspective. *Current Opinion in Neurobiology*, *5*, 169–177.

Squire, L. R., Slater, P. C., & Chace, P. M. (1975). Retrograde amnesia: Temporal gradient in very long-term memory following electroconvulsive therapy. *Science*, *187*, 77–79.

Starns, J. J., & Hicks, J. L. (2004). Episodic generation can cause semantic forgetting: Retrieval-induced forgetting of false memories. *Memory & Cognition*, *32*, 602–609.

Storm, B. C., Bjork, E. L., Bjork, R. A., & Nestojko, J. F. (2006). Is retrieval a necessary condition for retrieval-induced forgetting? *Psychonomic Bulletin & Review*, *13*, 1023–1027.

Thompson-Schill, S. L., D'Esposito, M., Aguirre, G. K., & Farah, M. J. (1997). Role of left inferior prefrontal cortex in retrieval of semantic knowledge: A reevaluation. *Proceedings of the National Academy of Sciences of the USA*, *94*, 14792–14797.

Thompson-Schill, S. L., Jonides, J., Marshuetz, C., Smith, E. E., D'Esposito, M., Kan, I. P., et al. (2002). Effects of frontal lobe damage on interference effects in working memory. *Cognitive, Affective, & Behavioral Neuroscience*, *2*, 109–120.

Thompson-Schill, S. L., Swick, D., Farah, M. J., D'Esposito, M., Kan, I. P., & Knight, R. T. (1998). Verb generation in patients with focal frontal lesions: A neuropsychological test of neuroimaging findings. *Proceedings of the National Academy of Sciences of the USA*, *95*, 15855–15860.

Tulving, E., & Thomson, D. M. (1973). Encoding specificity and retrieval processes in episodic memory. *Psychological Review*, *80*, 352–373.

Turner, M. S., Cipolotti, L., Yousry, T., & Shallice, T. (2007). Qualitatively different memory impairments across frontal lobe subgroups. *Neuropsychologia*, *45*, 1540–1552.

Uncapher, M., & Rugg, M. (2005). Effects of divided attention on fMRI correlates of memory encoding. *Journal of Cognitive Neuroscience*, *17*, 1923–1935.

Uncapher, M., & Rugg, M. (2008). Fractionation of the component processes underlying successful episodic encoding: A combined fMRI and divided attention study. *Journal of Cognitive Neuroscience*, *20*, 240–254.

Uncapher, M., & Wagner, A. D. (2009). Posterior parietal cortex and episodic encoding: Insights from fMRI subsequent memory effects and dual attention theory. *Neurobiology of Learning & Memory*, *91*, 139–154.

van Veen, V., & Carter, C. S. (2002). The anterior cingulate as a conflict monitor: fMRI and ERP studies. *Physiology & Behavior*, *77*, 477–482.

Veling, H., & Van Knippenberg, A. (2004). Remembering can cause inhibition: Retrieval-induced inhibition as a cue independent process. *Journal of Experimental Psychology: Learning, Memory, & Cognition*, *30*, 315–318.

Verde, M. F. (2004). The retrieval practice effect in associative recognition. *Memory & Cognition*, *32*, 1265–1272.

Wagner, A., & Davachi, L. (2001). Cognitive neuroscience: Forgetting of things past. *Current Biology*, *11*, R964–967.

Wagner, A. D., Maril, A., Bjork, R. A., & Schacter, D. L. (2001). Prefrontal contributions to executive control: fMRI evidence for functional distinctions within lateral prefrontal cortex. *Neuroimage*, *14*, 1337–1347.

Wagner, A., Schacter, D., Rotte, M., Koutstaal, W., Maril, A., Dale, A., et al. (1998). Building memories: Remembering and forgetting of verbal experiences as predicted by brain activity. *Science*, *281*, 1188–1191.

Weissman, D. H., Roberts, K. C., Visscher, K. M., & Woldorff, M. G. (2006). The neural bases of momentary lapses in attention. *Nature Neuroscience*, *9*, 971–978.

Wessel, I., Wetzels, S., Jelicic, M., & Merckelbach, H. (2005). Dissociation and memory suppression: A comparison of high and low dissociative individuals' performance on the Think-No Think task. *Personality and Individual Differences*, *39*, 1461–1470.

Wimber, M., Bäuml, K., Bergström, Z., Markopoulos, G., Heinze, H., & Richardson-Klavehn, A. (2008). Neural markers of inhibition in human memory retrieval. *Journal of Neuroscience*, *28*, 13419–13427.

Wimber, M., Rutschmann, R. M., Greenlee, M. W., & Bäuml, K. (2009). Retrieval from episodic memory: Neural mechanisms of interference resolution. *Journal of Cognitive Neuroscience*, *21*, 538–549.

Wixted, J. T. (2004). The psychology and neuroscience of forgetting. *Annual Review of Psychology*, *55*, 235–269.

Wixted, J. T. (2005). A theory about why we forget what we once knew. *Current Directions in Psychological Science*, *14*, 6–9.

Zola-Morgan, S., & Squire, L. R. (1990). The primate hippocampal formation: Evidence for a time-limited role in memory storage. *Science*, *250*, 288–290.

8 Sleep and forgetting

*Philippe Peigneux**
Université Libre de Bruxelles, Brussels, Belgium, and University of Liège, Liège, Belgium

Remy Schmitz and Charline Urbain*
Université Libre de Bruxelles, Brussels, Belgium

Introduction

Why do we sleep? Even after decades of investigation, this simple question remains an open issue. Indeed, there is no single answer, and complementary functional hypotheses have been suggested. For instance, it has been proposed that we sleep in order to preserve energy (Berger & Phillips, 1995), to keep cerebral thermoregulation constant (McGinty & Szymusiak, 1990), to detoxify neural cells (Inoue, Honda, & Komoda, 1995), to restore tissues (Adam & Oswald, 1977), and to preserve genetically programmed behavioural patterns (Jouvet, 1991). An additional hypothesis of interest is that sleep aids the long-term storage of memories recently acquired during wakefulness, and thus that it helps to prevent forgetting. Quintilien raised a similar idea in the 1st century AD (see Dudai, 2004). However, it was not until the beginning of the 20th century that this hypothesis was tested empirically. The first known experimental study on this matter was performed by Jenkins and Dallenbach in 1924. They showed that the classical Ebbinghaus forgetting curve for nonsense syllables was markedly dampened if the time between learning and recall was spent asleep, as opposed to time spent in the waking state. However, according to these authors and their immediate successors (e.g., Newman, 1939; Van Ormer, 1933), sleep merely had a passive role in the prevention of oblivion, by protecting novel memories from the intrusion of interfering information arising during wakefulness.

A more active role for sleep was advocated 50 years later by the Nobel Prize recipient Francis Crick, who proposed with Mitchison (1983) that sleep allows us to forget undesirable memories. In their view, which is rooted in the connectionism framework, memories are specific configurations of synaptic strengths within neuronal network assemblies, and learning can be defined as the ongoing modification of these synaptic strengths. According to Crick and

* Philippe Peigneux and Remy Schmitz are joint first authors of this chapter.

Mitchison, cortical activity bursts that occur during the rapid-eye-movement (REM) stage of sleep serve to wipe out weak connections, which are randomly created during wakefulness. These bursts are said to clean out the brain of all unwanted, feeble memories and eventually leaving room for the efficient storage and organization of the remaining material within memory. However, others have claimed that rather than supporting an oblivion function, sleep actually promotes consolidation of novel information in long-term memory systems (see for reviews Maquet, 2001; Peigneux, Laureys, Delbeuck, & Maquet, 2001; Rauchs, Desgranges, Foret, & Eustache, 2005). Although these two conceptions may appear to be complementary facets of the same coin in that relevant information ends up being consolidated, they describe a different phenomenon. Indeed, the forgetting hypothesis implies that all residues of the preceding day are processed during REM sleep, during which unwanted memories are actively filtered and erased from memory. The consolidation hypothesis on the other hand suggests that information is acquired and preprocessed during wakefulness, and that only relevant information is further consolidated during subsequent sleep. Positive evidence favouring a selective consolidation function for sleep essentially comes from studies showing that cerebral structures engaged during task practice are activated again during posttraining sleep (Maquet et al., 2000; Peigneux et al., 2004). This finding suggests an ongoing reprocessing of associated memories, albeit only when the learned material is sufficiently structured during wakefulness (Peigneux et al., 2003). In addition, interindividual differences in learning-related cerebral activity during the learning episode also predict the occurrence of subsequent sleep-dependent changes in performance (Albouy et al., 2008).

The consolidation hypothesis has acquired an increasingly dominant status in the field of cognitive neurosciences: the assumption being that sleep works to preserve and consolidate recently acquired memories. It should be noted that Crick and Mitchison (1983) themselves acknowledged the possibility of such a consolidating role for sleep, but thought it more specific to non-REM (NREM) sleep, a further main stage of sleep. Still, this does not entirely prevent us from considering forgetting as a complementary side of the consolidating coin. If particular memories are strengthened during sleep they should be more likely to be retrieved than those memories that are not strengthened during sleep. This in turn means that unconsolidated memories should be more likely to be forgotten than consolidated memories. As highlighted by Wixted (2004), most recent studies investigating sleep and memory are rooted in a neurobiological framework. This may have incited authors to present their results in terms of a sleep-dependent gain or stabilization of performance as opposed to in terms of a decrease in forgetting, the very hypothesis put forward by the aforementioned 20th-century experimental psychologists.

In the present chapter, we describe behavioural and neurophysiological studies supporting the hypothesis that sleep exerts a positive impact on long-term retention in declarative memory, either by consolidating relevant memories or by actively erasing unwanted day residues. We do not aim to be comprehensive, but rather to illustrate the complex relationships between posttraining sleep, forgetting, and information storage in long-term memory. We specifically focus on hippocampus-dependent spatial navigation and word pair learning, two representative activities underlying the declarative memory system. Hippocampus-dependent spatial navigation has been studied in both animals and humans and may be considered the evolutionary precursor of human verbal episodic memory (O'Keefe, Burgess, Donnett, Jeffery, & Maguire, 1998), in that specific relationships between distinct elements have to be created in both the spatial and verbal domain. We go on to introduce the novel but still scarce literature suggesting modulatory effects of emotion on sleep-dependent processes of memory consolidation in man. For the interested reader, sleep-dependent learning effects that have been also largely observed in the framework of other memory systems are reviewed elsewhere (see e.g., Maquet et al., 2003; Peigneux et al., 2001; Rauchs et al., 2005; Smith, 2001; Walker & Stickgold, 2006).

Sleep and memory are both split phenomena

Different sleep states

Sleep can be defined operationally according to the presence or absence of various behavioural criteria (Tobler, 1995). Sleeping individuals are, by and large, in apparent physical quiescence. They adopt a typical body posture that can vary in relation to ambient temperature. Enhancement of excitability and reactivity thresholds are also present during sleep (Muzet, 1995), together with rapid reversibility between wakefulness and sleep stages. Sleep itself is under regulation of a homeostatic process, i.e., the accumulated sleep pressure due to time spent awake, which is itself modulated by circadian (24 h cycle) and ultradian (90-min cycle) factors (Borbely, Hayaishi, Sejnowski, & Altman, 2000). Most importantly, sleep is not a unitary phenomenon. Rather, it encompasses two main states characterized by specific polygraphic patterns (see Figure 8.1; Aserinsky & Kleitman, 1953; Rechtschaffen & Kales, 1968; Silber et al., 2007): (1) rapid eye movement (REM) sleep, and (2) non-REM (NREM) sleep.

Hallmarks of REM sleep are occasional bursts of rapid horizontal and vertical ocular movements, loss of muscular tone, and a desynchronized electroencephalographic (EEG) activity which is similar to that recorded during wakefulness. Given this similarity, REM sleep is also sometimes referred to as "paradoxical" sleep. The converse stage is NREM sleep. In humans, NREM sleep can be subdivided into four main stages characterized by an increasingly slow and ample electroencephalographic activity with diminished but preserved muscle tone and no or slow rolling eye movements. Stage 1 refers to the transition from the waking activity (8–11 Hz) to the other NREM sleep

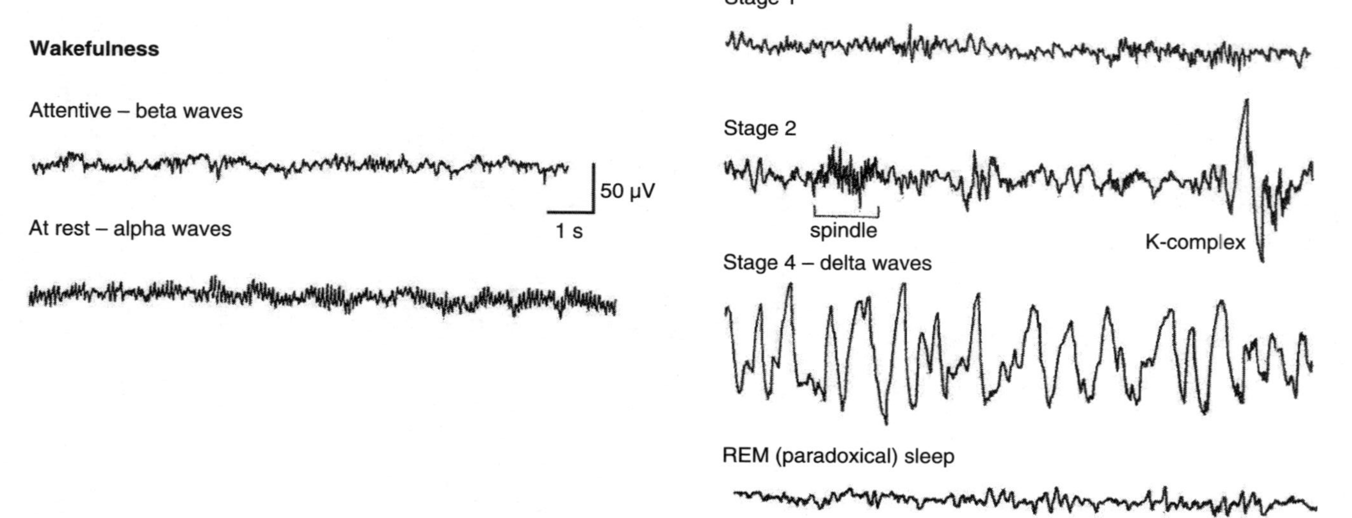

Figure 8.1 Typical electroencephalographic (EEG) recordings during the different states of sleep and wakefulness, characterized by specific oscillation frequencies (e.g., beta 15–30 Hz, alpha 8–12 Hz and delta 0.5–4 Hz) and the shape of the graph elements (e.g., spindle and K-complex).

stages. Because of its mixed EEG activity, studies investigating the link between sleep and memory usually do not take account of this transitional stage. Stage 2, also known as light NREM sleep, is characterized by slow background EEG activity, on which spindles are superimposed. Spindles are bursts of rapid activity in the sigma range (11–16 Hz) that are most often preceded by brief high-voltage peaks known as K-complexes. Stages 3 and 4 are ordinarily gathered together under the label of slow-wave sleep, characterized by a dominant proportion of delta waves (1–4 Hz) and slow-wave activity (SWA) below 1 Hz. REM and NREM sleep states are subtended by partially distinct functional neuroanatomical networks (Maquet, 2000). During the course of a normal night, REM–NREM alternation cycles run over an ultradian rhythm of about 90 minutes in man, NREM sleep always preceding REM sleep. Due to the close relationship between SWA and sleep pressure dissipation (i.e., the homeostatic process, see Borbely et al., 2000), the first half of the night is particularly rich in slow-wave activity (about 80% of time), whereas REM sleep proportion increases over the second half of the night to alternate with stage 2 of NREM sleep (Hartmann, 1966) (see Figure 8.2). Finally, the neurotransmitters balance also varies among the different stages of sleep (Pace-Schott & Hobson, 2002). As compared to wakefulness in which all levels are high, cholinergic activity is drastically diminished during NREM sleep; serotoninergic and noradrenergic activities are also decreased but to a lesser extent. During REM sleep, cholinergic tone is high, even more so than during wakefulness, and serotoninergic and noradrenergic systems are strongly inhibited. These elements show that sleep cannot be seen as a simple "nonwaking" state in which the brain merely shuts off after daytime activity.

Different memory states

Like sleep, memory is a multidimensional construct. It is said to consist of a short-term memory system and a long-term memory system. Long-term memory is commonly subdivided into: (1) declarative memory, in which information is easily accessible to verbal description, and encoding and/or retrieval is usually carried out explicitly; (2) nondeclarative or procedural memory, in which memories are not easily accessible to verbal description and can be acquired and re-expressed implicitly (Squire & Knowlton, 1995). Declarative memory further comprises episodic and semantic memory components. Dissociations between declarative and nondeclarative memory systems were brought to light with the henceforth famous patient HM who underwent bilateral resection of the internal side of the temporal lobe (Scoville & Milner, 1957). Like neurologically intact controls, HM was able to improve through daily practice on a mirror drawing task. However, his forgetting in the declarative memory domain was so dramatic that he was unable to remember having practised this task previously, or even having met the experimenter the day before (Milner, 1962). Conversely, other patients with striatal, cerebellar, or

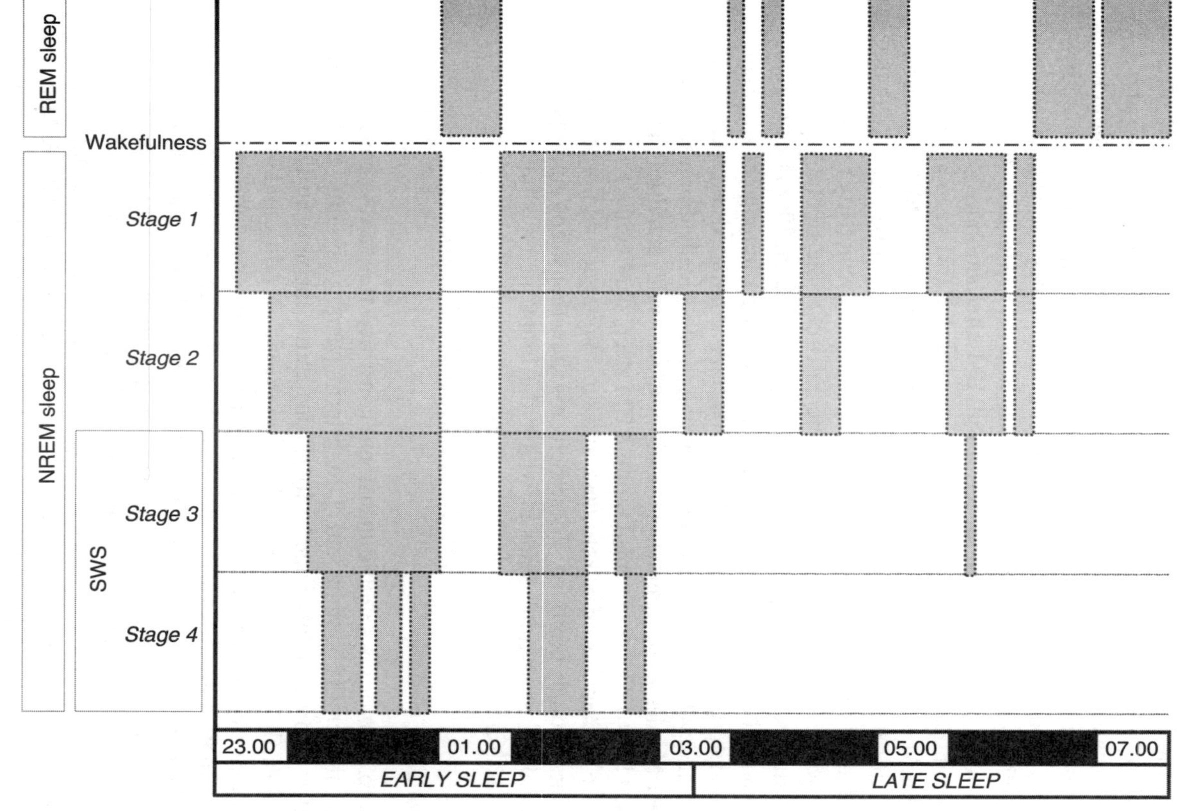

Figure 8.2 Distribution of the different sleep stages (vertical axis) during the course of a normal night (from 23.00 to 7.00, horizontal axis). The dashed bars below the dotted line represent the depth of NREM sleep. Stages 3 and 4 of NREM sleep are usually grouped together under the label of slow-wave sleep (SWS). The dashed bars above the dotted line depict REM (paradoxical) sleep. Note that SWS appears predominantly during the first half of the night (early sleep), whereas REM sleep is particularly present during the second half (late night). Periods of wakefulness occur in the absence of dashed bars around the dotted line.

motor cortex lesions may exhibit preserved declarative memory accompanied by deficits in the procedural memory domain (Squire, 2004). Other types of associative learning such as motor and fear conditioning have been found to rely on cerebellum and amygdala structures respectively (LaBar & Cabeza, 2006; Medina, Repa, Mauk, & LeDoux, 2002). Altogether, these data indicate that, in both humans and animals, memory consists of various subsystems, which are subtended by distinct neuroanatomical substrates and are relatively independent (see Squire & Kandel, 1999, for a review).

Combining sleep and memory states

Given that both sleep and memory are multidimensional in that they contain various stages/systems, each with specific neuroanatomical substrates, it is likely that not all memories benefit to the same extent from all sleep components.

As mentioned above, sleep-dependent memory consolidation has become a dominant view in the last decades (Peigneux et al., 2001; Rauchs et al., 2005; Walker & Stickgold, 2006). Within this framework, consolidation is defined as a set of processes whereby memory traces become more stable and resistant to interference with the passage of time, even in the absence of further practice (Dudai, 2004; McGaugh, 2000). The underlying idea is that recently acquired memories are labile and temporally stored in the brain, thus prone to forgetting. These labile memories are progressively integrated within long-term memory stores with the passage of time, thus making them more robust and resistant to interference (McClelland, McNaughton, & O'Reilly, 1995). Human and animal evidence suggests that declarative memory traces are initially encoded within the hippocampus and the surrounding medial temporal lobe, and then gradually transferred to neocortical areas in the form of distributed representations (Frankland & Bontempi, 2005). Sleep is hypothesized to actively participate in this offline process of memory consolidation by allowing replay and recoding of newly encoded material in the brain, and by promoting hippocampo-neocortical transfer (Marshall & Born, 2007) at various levels of integration from gene to behaviour (Hobson & Pace-Schott, 2002; Walker & Stickgold, 2004).

Experimental paradigms

Several paradigms have been used to probe the role of sleep in memory consolidation. These paradigms examine: (1) the effects of postlearning sleep deprivation on memory; (2) the differential effect of early vs. late sleep periods on specific memories; (3) the effect of learning on posttraining sleep parameters. Direct stimulation during sleep will not be reviewed here (see Peigneux et al., 2001; Rauchs et al., 2005).

In the postlearning sleep deprivation paradigm, participants have to learn novel material during wakefulness. Half of the participants are then allowed to sleep normally during the following night, whereas the other half are kept awake all night (total sleep deprivation), or awoken at each occurrence of a specific stage of sleep (selective sleep deprivation). Memory for the learned material is subsequently tested in both groups. In the case of total sleep deprivation, participants are allowed two recovery nights before testing to avoid the confounding effect of a sleep deprivation state on memory retrieval processes. Moreover, it is good practice to test subjects at the same time of day as the learning episode to control for circadian confounds on performance (Schmidt, Collette, Cajochen, & Peigneux, 2007). The underlying hypothesis in this paradigm is that sleep deprivation will alter the processes of consolidation normally at work during the first postlearning night, therefore leading to performance deterioration (i.e., higher forgetting rates) and possible changes in memory retrieval-related cerebral activity in sleep-deprived participants, as compared to participants who slept normally on the posttraining night. Deprivation is organized on the first posttraining night since immediate posttraining periods of sleep have been shown most crucial for sleep-dependent memory consolidation processes (Gais, Lucas, & Born, 2006).

The early/late sleep paradigm (Ekstrand, 1967) is a variant of the sleep deprivation paradigm that takes into account the peculiarities of the internal architecture of sleep. As discussed above, NREM sleep proportionally predominates during the first half of the night whereas REM sleep is more prominent during the second half (Figure 8.2). In the early/late sleep paradigm participants encode the novel material just before or after the first half of a night of sleep (e.g., 22:00 or 02:00), and are then tested after the first (e.g., 02:00) or the second half (e.g., 06:00) of the night respectively. In this way it is possible to compare the respective effects of NREM and REM sleep-dominant periods on the consolidation of specific memory material. An additional advantage of this paradigm is that it avoids the confounding effects of factors known to disturb memory consolidation: (1) stress-related deprivation (Siegel, 2001); (2) repeated awakenings from particular sleep stages (i.e., selective sleep deprivation paradigm) that disorganize the sleep architecture (Ficca, Lombardo, Rossi, & Salzarulo, 2000). In order to minimize circadian confounds, results in the early and late sleep groups are usually compared to control situations, in which participants are kept awake during equivalent periods of time during the night.

Finally, evidence for a relationship between posttraining sleep and overnight memory consolidation processes can also be gleaned from the finding that novel learning during daytime exerts a measurable influence on postlearning sleep parameters, e.g., duration or latency of sleep episodes, spindle activity, spectral power in a specific frequency range, hormonal levels, gene expression, reactivation of neuronal activity observed during the learning episode, etc., and that these parameters are associated with subsequent modifications in performance (see below for a detailed description). The underlying rationale is that neurophysiological correlates of newly learned material are tuned during the posttraining night and reflect memory reorganization processes during sleep.

Sleep-dependent learning in spatial environments

Finding our way in novel and familiar environments is an essential cognitive ability for both humans and animals. Cell recording studies in rodents were the first to suggest a replay of spatial learning-related activity in place cells during subsequent sleep. Place cells are hippocampal neurons that fire selectively when rodents actively explore specific spatial locations, thereby allowing the animal to create a mental map of the environment (Burgess, Barry, & O'Keefe, 2007). Animal studies have shown that place cells activated during prior learning tend to fire again during subsequent sleep (Pavlides & Winson, 1989) following a similar temporal discharge pattern (Skaggs & McNaughton, 1996), and preserving coactivation profiles within the hippocampus (Wilson & McNaughton, 1994). Additionally, robust correlations of neuronal discharges between the hippocampus and neocortical areas during NREM sleep (Sirota, Csicsvari, Buhl, & Buzsaki, 2003) have been proposed to coordinate the progressive transfer of long-term memories to neocortical areas (Buzsaki, 1986).

Investigation of sleep-dependent processes of consolidation for spatial navigation memories in humans have corroborated and extended animal findings. In a recent positron emission tomography (PET) study (Peigneux et al. 2004), participants were scanned while they had to learn to find their way in a virtual maze. Successful navigation performance during this task was associated with increased hippocampal activity, an activity which was actually re-expressed, or reactivated, during the subsequent posttraining NREM sleep. Moreover, a positive correlation was reported between the amplitude of hippocampal activation in NREM sleep and the overnight gain of performance in navigation. This correlation suggests that learning-dependent modulation in hippocampal activity during human sleep reflects the offline processing of recent episodic and spatial memory traces which eventually leads to the plastic changes underlying the subsequent improvement in performance.

Behavioural deprivation studies have further demonstrated that subjects allowed to sleep during the posttraining night are better at finding their way or at recognizing correct sequences of landmarks in real (Ferrara et al., 2006) or virtual (Ferrara et al., 2008) navigation settings than sleep-deprived subjects. It should be highlighted that cerebral reorganization during sleep need not necessarily be associated with detectable improvement in performance. Indeed, Orban et al. (2006) and Rauchs et al. (2008) have shown that despite similar performance levels three days postlearning, the sleep status in the posttraining night preconditions access to distinct cerebral networks during memory retrieval. In sleep-deprived participants, performance was associated with activity in the same hippocampal network that had been active during learning on day 1. In contrast, in participants who had been allowed to sleep, performance was associated with activity in subcortical striatal regions involved in routine behaviour (Bohbot, Iaria, & Petrides, 2004), suggesting an automation of navigation behaviour after sleep. Overall, behavioural and neuroimaging studies have shown that sleep helps to prevent forgetting of spatially organized material in both man and animal.

Verbal associative memory: forestalling forgetting with sleep

The learning of verbal associations has been extensively used in sleep research under the assumption that these tasks are good models of declarative memory (but see Peigneux et al. 2001 for a discussion). In the most widely used paradigm, participants have to memorize word pairs (e.g., car–parrot) in the learning phase. Following a delay interval, which is spent either asleep or awake, the first word of the pair is presented as a cue, and the second word must be recalled (e.g., car–?). In this task, forgetting is a function of both the sleep status in the postlearning night and the time of the day when learning takes place (Gais et al., 2006). Indeed, forgetting at retest is higher when participants are sleep deprived during the night following learning than if they are allowed to sleep. This occurs even if testing takes place three days postlearning, i.e., in the presence of two recovery nights in order to avoid the negative effects of sleep deprivation on recollection processes. Interestingly, forgetting is further reduced in sleeping subjects when learning takes place within two hours before sleep onset, as compared to learning in the morning. This finding strengthens the hypothesis that sleep consolidates newly acquired information at the retention level achieved at the end of the day (Marshall & Born, 2007). Thus, retention of word pairs follows the Ebbinghaus forgetting curve throughout the learning day. After intervening sleep, however, recall clock time (8 am vs. 8 pm) and duration of retention from study to recall (24 h vs. 48 h) no longer affect forgetting levels, suggesting that verbal information has been consolidated in memory in a stable manner (Gais et al., 2006). Interestingly, posttraining sleep is mostly beneficial for associations that are not yet firmly established. Indeed, there was no detectable effect of posttraining sleep on memory consolidation when subjects had already reached high accuracy levels at the end of the learning session (e.g., 90%). In contrast, overnight forgetting was reduced via sleep in those subjects whose initial accuracy levels were lower (e.g., 60%) (Drosopoulos, Schulze, Fischer, & Born, 2007). Again, the lack of behavioural benefit of sleep in the participants with high pre-sleeping accuracy levels need not automatically translate into an absence of sleep-related differences in the underlying brain activity (see the aforementioned spatial navigation studies by Orban et al., 2006; Rauchs et al., 2008). Indeed, functional magnetic resonance imaging (fMRI) work has shown that when subjects are tested 2 days following encoding, successful recall of words is associated with higher hippocampal activity and strengthened relationships between the hippocampus and the medial prefrontal cortex (mPFC) in subjects who slept during the posttraining night than those who were sleep deprived. Six months later, recollection of learned word pairs activated the mPFC more when the word pairs were encoded before sleep, suggesting that sleep leads to long-lasting changes in the representation of memories at the cerebral level (Gais et al., 2007).

A specific role of NREM sleep for declarative memory consolidation?

Studies using the early/late sleep paradigm (Ekstrand, 1967) described above have repeatedly shown that it is primarily the first part of the night (i.e., the part which is richer in NREM sleep) that minimizes forgetting of paired-associate word lists. The second part of the night (i.e., the part which is richer in REM sleep) has no specific impact on declarative memory consolidation (Ekstrand, 1967; Fowler, Sullivan, & Ekstrand, 1973; Plihal & Born, 1997; Yaroush, Sullivan, & Ekstrand, 1971). It should be noted that a short (around 60-min) diurnal nap (usually essentially composed of NREM sleep) has the same beneficial effect on performance on this declarative memory task (Gorfine, Yeshurun, & Zisapel, 2007; Mednick, Cai, Kanady, & Drummond, 2008; Schabus, Hoedlmoser, Pecherstorfer, & Klosch, 2005; Tucker et al., 2006). Extending these studies, EEG recordings have shown that the learning of difficult associations between pairs of words increases spindle activity during subsequent naps (Schmidt et al., 2006). Spindles are a hallmark of stage 2 NREM sleep, thought to be especially important for memory consolidation processes because they promote cortical plasticity (Destexhe and Sejnowski, 2001). Sleep-dependent overnight improvements in performance have consistently shown to be positively correlated with bursts of spindle activity during posttraining NREM sleep (Gais, Molle, Helms, & Born, 2002; Schabus et al., 2004; Schabus et al., 2008) or, after a 60-min nap, with theta band activity in stage 2 sleep (Schabus et al., 2005). Additionally, EEG coherence has been reported to increase after declarative learning during NREM sleep in the frequency band of slow oscillations below 1 Hz, which additionally modulates the temporal pattern of spindle activity (Molle, Marshall, Gais, & Born, 2004). Conversely, artificial enhancement of slow oscillations by means of transcranial magnetic stimulation during NREM sleep increases recall performance on the next day above levels achieved after a normal night of sleep (Marshall, Helgadottir, Molle, & Born, 2006). Even though NREM sleep undeniably exerts positive and specific effects upon memory, it must be noted that preservation of NREM–REM cycles is also crucial to prevent forgetting over a night of sleep. Indeed, even when the amount of slow-wave sleep is kept constant, disruption of the sleep architecture by means of repeated awakenings results in deficits in overnight memory performance (Ficca et al., 2000).

At the neurochemical level, modification of the normal balance between neurotransmitters in sleep can also disrupt subsequent recall of word pairs

(Gais & Born, 2004; Plihal & Born, 1999; Plihal, Pietrowsky, & Born, 1999; Rasch, Born, & Gais, 2006). Indeed, artificial prevention of the normal reduction of cholinergic levels during NREM sleep restores forgetting by blocking the beneficial effect of sleep on memory consolidation (Gais & Born, 2004; Plihal & Born, 1999; Plihal et al., 1999). Pharmacological manipulations suggest that high cholinergic levels during wakefulness are necessary for memory encoding, whereas the natural shift towards minimal cholinergic levels during slow-wave sleep (SWS) would tune the brain for optimal declarative memory consolidation during a period with no need for new memory encoding (Rasch et al., 2006). Notwithstanding, minimal cortisol levels remain necessary since administration of a cortisol suppressor disrupts slow-wave sleep and impairs subsequent performance for text recall (Wagner, Degirmenci, Drosopoulos, Perras, & Born, 2005). Overall, psychopharmacological studies have indicated that optimal levels of acetylcholine and cortisol during NREM sleep are necessary conditions for the hampering of forgetting.

Susceptibility to retroactive interference and sleep

Finally, another way to probe the beneficial effect of sleep on memory is to test newly learned associations' resistance to interference (Drosopoulos et al., 2007; Ekstrand, 1967; Ellenbogen, Hulbert, Stickgold, Dinges, & Thompson-Schill, 2006). In the classical A–B, A–C paradigm, subjects have to learn a list of word pairs in which each specific cue word (A) is associated with a target word (B). Subsequently, a second list must be learned in which each cue word of the first list (A) is associated with a novel target word (C). Typically, performance deteriorates when the first list is recalled after the second one has been learned. Using the A–B, A–C paradigm, Ellenbogen et al. (2006) showed that recall of the first learned list was subject to retroactive interference when a period of wakefulness intervened between the learning of the first list and the learning of the second, interfering list. Conversely, retroactive interference effects were strongly diminished when subjects were allowed to sleep between learning the first list and the second list (the second list was presented the next morning). These results suggest that memories are consolidated during sleep and are consequently less susceptible to disruption. Additional data have shown that when the first and the second, interfering lists are learned on the same day, both lists are equally well recalled if subjects are allowed to sleep during the posttraining night, but not when they are sleep deprived. This finding suggests that sleep may provide recovery from retroactive interference induced at encoding (Drosopoulos et al., 2007). Further studies including independent replications are needed to confirm the generality of these effects.

Emotion and declarative memories

Emotionally arousing memories are generally more resistant to forgetting (McGaugh, 2004; Phelps, 2006). Their special status in memory consolidation processes is likely to be due to the involvement of the amygdala, in addition to the participation of the classical hippocampo-neocortical network (LaBar & Cabeza, 2006). Only a few studies have investigated the role of sleep in the consolidation of emotional declarative memories. These studies have used texts (Wagner et al., 2005; Wagner, Gais, & Born, 2001; Wagner, Hallschmid, Rasch, & Born, 2006), pictures (Atienza & Cantero, 2008; Hu, Stylos-Allan, & Walker, 2006; Nishida, Pearsall, Buckner, & Walker, 2009; Yoo, Gujar, Hu, Jolesz, & Walker, 2007), scenes (Payne, Stickgold, Swanberg, & Kensinger, 2008), and faces (Wagner, Kashyap, Diekelmann, & Born, 2007).

One of the first studies to investigate this topic (Wagner et al., 2001) relied on the idea that REM sleep should be more beneficial to emotional memories because of a particularly high activity in the amygdala during this stage of sleep (Maquet & Franck, 1997), and because of the presence of REM sleep disruption in affective disorders (Benca et al., 1997). Using the early/late sleep paradigm, Wagner et al. (2001) found that forgetting levels were lower after posttraining REM sleep than wakefulness for emotional texts, but not for neutral ones. In a follow-up study conducted 4 years later, retention of emotional texts was higher when a period of sleep (either REM or NREM sleep) was present the night after learning (Wagner et al., 2006), showing a robust effect of posttraining sleep for consolidation of emotional material. It should be noticed that, in the early/late paradigm, subjects tested after the first part of the night (richer in NREM sleep) are allowed to sleep during the second part (richer in REM sleep). This additional contribution of REM sleep may explain the absence of sleep stage effect 4 years later. Contrary to the effects observed for neutral texts, cortisol suppression during REM sleep actually protected emotional texts from being forgotten, and even boosted recall performance (Wagner et al., 2005). In this context, naturally high levels of cortisol during REM sleep have been hypothesized to protect individuals from overconsolidation of emotional memories acquired during wakefulness. Finally, facilitation of emotional memory after a 90-min nap was associated with REM sleep parameters including its amount and latency, and increases in the theta band power (Nishida et al., 2009). Nonetheless, it should be noted that the links between REM sleep and emotional memories are not entirely unequivocal. Indeed, accuracy of emotional face recognition was associated with NREM sleep duration, whereas response speed (deemed a marker of implicit memory by the authors) was predicted by the amount of REM sleep (Wagner et al., 2007).

The time course of memory consolidation for negative scenes was recently investigated in a study in which subjects were exposed to negative or neutral scenes, and in which the background or the central object could change between exposition and testing phases (Payne et al., 2008). Results revealed time- and sleep-dependent effects for negative scenes only. Participants' retention was better for the central objects than the backgrounds of negative scenes when tested after 30 minutes. When tested after 12 hours of wakefulness, both scenes and backgrounds were forgotten, although central objects were still better remembered than scene backgrounds. However, when the same period contained an intervening period of sleep, forgetting was neutralized for negative central objects, but not for scene backgrounds, suggesting that sleep helps for the long-term storage of emotionally relevant information contained in a scene.

Finally, inconsistent data have suggested that recollection and familiarity of emotional material may be differentially affected by posttraining sleep. Whereas several studies have found a sleep-related improvement in response familiarity and recollection measures (Hu et al., 2006), others have found a selective enhancement for recollection (Atienza & Cantero, 2008) or recognition (Wagner et al., 2007), or no effect of posttraining sleep on either dimension of memory (Sterpenich et al., 2007). It should be noted, however, that the latter study did elucidate sleep-related changes in cerebral activity underlying performance during recollection of memories. Hippocampal and mPFC activations were more strongly associated during recollection of emotional material when participants were allowed to sleep following learning than when they were sleep deprived. When sleep-deprived memory recollection was associated with activity in amygdala and occipital regions (Sterpenich et al., 2007). These results suggest that sleep allows emotional memories to be digested and integrated into the long-term memory store within the classical neocortical network, since when sleep is prevented after presentation of emotional material, the brain persists in showing emotional reactions when confronted again with the same arousing material.

Conclusions

Mounting evidence suggest a functional link between sleep and memory. Although sleep was initially seen as a purely passive shield against forgetting (Jenkins & Dallenbach, 1924), its active implication in memory consolidation is nowadays widely recognized. After an early proposal that the active role of sleep resides in the fact that it promotes forgetting of irrelevant information (Crick & Mitchison, 1983), actual evidence favours the converse hypothesis that sleep helps the consolidation of recently acquired and significant memories. At the behavioural level, the first postlearning night is the most important time point at which sleep appears to be necessary to minimize forgetting in the long term. Additionally, the reduction of retroactive interference effects when sleep episodes intervene between learning and exposure to the interfering material provides supplementary evidence for a role of sleep in the consolidation of newly acquired memories. Although the preservation of the NREM–REM cycles is also important, both behavioural, neuroimaging, and psychopharmacological data converge to assign a preponderant role of NREM sleep stages in consolidating processes for declarative memories. For instance, precisely balanced, optimal levels of hormones and neurotransmitters concentration are necessary during NREM sleep to fix memories and counteract forgetting. Interestingly, fMRI studies have also yielded sleep-dependent, covert, neural modifications without overt changes at the behavioural level. Therefore, even without any change in performance, sleep shapes the neural network activated when evoking memories during subsequent wakefulness, and allows a better integration and processing of the recently learned information. Additionally, the emotional valence of the learning material has a profound influence on forgetting, which is partly due to the specificity of the cerebral network dedicated to emotional memory. Because of links between amygdala function and REM sleep, the consolidation of emotional memories has often been thought a specific REM sleep role. Even though the as yet scarce literature tends to validate this hypothesis, the link between REM sleep and emotional memory is far from being unambiguous, and a complementary participation of NREM sleep cannot be excluded at this point in time.

Although the field is still in its infancy and in need of further developments, it is now worth remembering that although sleep may have been considered a state of oblivion, it actually plays a significant role in the processes that allow us to counteract forgetting and enhance reminiscence functions.

Acknowledgements

RS is Research Fellow at the Fonds National de la Recherche Scientifique (FNRS) of Belgium. CU is supported by a PhD grant at the Université Libre de Bruxelles (ULB) from the Frisque Foundation. We thank an anonymous reviewer for careful reading and constructive comments on a previous version of this manuscript.

References

Adam, K., & Oswald, I. (1977). Sleep is for tissue restoration. *Journal of the Royal College of Physicians of London*, *11*(4), 376–388.

Albouy, G., Sterpenich, V., Balteau, E., Vandewalle, G., Desseilles, M., Dang-Vu, T., et al. (2008). Both the hippocampus and striatum are involved in consolidation of motor sequence memory. *Neuron*, *58*(2), 261–272.

Aserinsky, E., & Kleitman, N. (1953). Regularly occurring periods of eye motility, and concomitant phenomena, during sleep. *Science*, *118*(3062), 273–274.

Atienza, M., & Cantero, J. L. (2008). Modulatory effects of emotion and sleep on recollection and familiarity. *Journal of Sleep Research*, *17*(3), 285–294.

Benca, R. M., Okawa, M., Uchiyama, M., Ozaki, S., Nakajima, T., Shibui, K., et al. (1997). Sleep and mood disorders. *Sleep Medicine Reviews*, *1*(1), 45–56.

Berger, R. J., & Phillips, N. H. (1995). Energy conservation and sleep. *Behavioural Brain Research*, *69*(1–2), 65–73.

Bohbot, V. D., Iaria, G., & Petrides, M. (2004). Hippocampal function and spatial memory: Evidence from functional neuroimaging in healthy participants and performance of patients with medial temporal lobe resections. *Neuropsychology*, *18*(3), 418–425.

Borbely, A. A., Hayaishi, O., Sejnowski, T. J., & Altman, J. S. (Eds.). (2000). *The regulation of sleep*. Strasbourg: Human Frontier Science Program.

Burgess, N., Barry, C., & O'Keefe, J. (2007). An oscillatory interference model of grid cell firing. *Hippocampus*, *17*(9), 801–812.

Buzsaki, G. (1986). Hippocampal sharp waves: Their origin and significance. *Brain Research*, *398*(2), 242–252.

Crick, F., & Mitchison, G. (1983). The function of dream sleep. *Nature*, *304*(5922), 111–114.

Destexhe, A., & Sejnowski, T. J. (2001). *Thalamocortical assemblies: How ion channels, single neurons, and large-scale networks organize sleep oscillations*. Oxford: Oxford University Press.

Drosopoulos, S., Schulze, C., Fischer, S., & Born, J. (2007). Sleep's function in the spontaneous recovery and consolidation of memories. *Journal of Experimental Psychology: General*, *136*(2), 169–183.

Dudai, Y. (2004). The neurobiology of consolidations, or, how stable is the engram? *Annual Review of Psychology*, *55*, 51–86.

Ekstrand, B. R. (1967). Effect of sleep on memory. *Journal of Experimental Psychology*, *75*(1), 64–72.

Ellenbogen, J. M., Hulbert, J. C., Stickgold, R., Dinges, D. F., & Thompson-Schill, S. L. (2006). Interfering with theories of sleep and memory: Sleep, declarative memory, and associative interference. *Current Biology*, *16*(13), 1290–1294.

Ferrara, M., Iaria, G., De Gennaro, L., Guariglia, C., Curcio, G., Tempesta, D., et al. (2006). The role of sleep in the consolidation of route learning in humans: A behavioural study. *Brain Research Bulletin*, *71*(1–3), 4–9.

Ferrara, M., Iaria, G., Tempesta, D., Curcio, G., Moroni, F., Marzano, C., et al. (2008). Sleep to find your way: The role of sleep in the consolidation of memory for navigation in humans. *Hippocampus*, *18*(8), 844–851.

Ficca, G., Lombardo, P., Rossi, L., & Salzarulo, P. (2000). Morning recall of verbal material depends on prior sleep organization. *Behavioural Brain Research*, *112*(1–2), 159–163.

Fowler, M. J., Sullivan, M. J., & Ekstrand, B. R. (1973). Sleep and memory. *Science*, *179*(70), 302–304.

Frankland, P. W., & Bontempi, B. (2005). The organization of recent and remote memories. *Nature Reviews Neuroscience*, *6*(2), 119–130.

Gais, S., Albouy, G., Boly, M., Dang-Vu, T. T., Darsaud, A., Desseilles, M., et al. (2007). Sleep transforms the cerebral trace of declarative memories. *Proceedings of the National Academy of Sciences of the USA*, *104*(47), 18768–18783.

Gais, S., & Born, J. (2004). Low acetylcholine during slow-wave sleep is critical for declarative memory consolidation. *Proceedings of the National Academy of Sciences of the USA*, *101*(7), 2140–2144.

Gais, S., Lucas, B., & Born, J. (2006). Sleep after learning aids memory recall. *Learning and Memory*, *13*(3), 259–262.

Gais, S., Molle, M., Helms, K., & Born, J. (2002). Learning-dependent increases in sleep spindle density. *Journal of Neuroscience*, *22*(15), 6830–6834.

Gorfine, T., Yeshurun, Y., & Zisapel, N. (2007). Nap and melatonin-induced changes in hippocampal activation and their role in verbal memory consolidation. *Journal of Pineal Research*, *43*(4), 336–342.

Hartmann, E. (1966). Mechanism underlying the sleep-dream cycle. *Nature*, *212*(5062), 648–650.

Hobson, J. A., & Pace-Schott, E. F. (2002). The cognitive neuroscience of sleep: Neuronal systems, consciousness and learning. *Nature Reviews Neuroscience*, *3*(9), 679–693.

Hu, P., Stylos-Allan, M., & Walker, M. P. (2006). Sleep facilitates consolidation of emotional declarative memory. *Psychological Science*, *17*(10), 891–898.

Inoue, S., Honda, K., & Komoda, Y. (1995). Sleep as neuronal detoxification and restitution. *Behavioural Brain Research*, *69*(1–2), 91–96.

Jenkins, J. G., & Dallenbach, K. M. (1924). Obliviscence during sleep and waking. *American Journal of Psychology*, *35*(4), 605–612.

Jouvet, M. (1991). Paradoxical sleep: Is it the guardian of psychological individualism? *Canadian Journal of Psychology*, *45*(2), 148–168.

LaBar, K. S., & Cabeza, R. (2006). Cognitive neuroscience of emotional memory. *Nature Reviews Neuroscience*, *7*(1), 54–64.

McClelland, J. L., McNaughton, B. L., & O'Reilly, R. C. (1995). Why there are complementary learning systems in the hippocampus and neocortex: Insights from the successes and failures of connectionist models of learning and memory. *Psychological Review*, *102*(3), 419–457.

McGaugh, J. L. (2000). Memory – a century of consolidation. *Science*, *287*(5451), 248–251.

McGaugh, J. L. (2004). The amygdala modulates the consolidation of memories of emotionally arousing experiences. *Annual Review of Neuroscience*, *27*, 1–28.

McGinty, D., & Szymusiak, R. (1990). Keeping cool: A hypothesis about the mechanisms and functions of slow-wave sleep. *Trends in Neurosciences*, *13*(12), 480–487.

Maquet, P. (2000). Functional neuroimaging of normal human sleep by positron emission tomography. *Journal of Sleep Research*, *9*(3), 207–231.

Maquet, P. (2001). The role of sleep in learning and memory. *Science*, *294*(5544), 1048–1052.

Maquet, P., & Franck, G. (1997). REM sleep and amygdala. *Molecular Psychiatry*, *2*(3), 195–196.

Maquet, P., Laureys, S., Peigneux, P., Fuchs, S., Petiau, C., Phillips, C., et al. (2000). Experience-dependent changes in cerebral activation during human REM sleep. *Nature Neuroscience*, *3*(8), 831–836.

Maquet, P., Laureys, S., Perrin, F., Ruby, P., Melchior, G., Boly, M., et al. (2003). Festina lente: Evidences for fast and slow learning processes and a role for sleep in human motor skill learning. *Learning and Memory*, *10*(4), 237–239.

Marshall, L., & Born, J. (2007). The contribution of sleep to hippocampus-dependent memory consolidation. *Trends in Cognitive Sciences*, *11*(10), 442–450.

Marshall, L., Helgadottir, H., Molle, M., & Born, J. (2006). Boosting slow oscillations during sleep potentiates memory. *Nature*, *444*(7119), 610–613.

Medina, J. F., Repa, J. C., Mauk, M. D., & LeDoux, J. E. (2002). Parallels between cerebellum- and amygdala-dependent conditioning. *Nature Reviews Neuroscience*, *3*(2), 122–131.

Mednick, S. C., Cai, D. J., Kanady, J., & Drummond, S. P. (2008). Comparing the benefits of caffeine, naps and placebo on verbal, motor and perceptual memory. *Behavioural Brain Research*, *193*(1), 79–86.

Milner, B. (1962). Les troubles de la mémoire accompagnant des lésions hippocampiques bilatérales. In P. Passouant (Ed.), *Physiologie de l'hippocampe* (pp. 257–272). Paris: Centre National de la Recherche Scientifique.

Molle, M., Marshall, L., Gais, S., & Born, J. (2004). Learning increases human electroencephalographic coherence during subsequent slow sleep oscillations. *Proceedings of the National Academy of Sciences of the USA, 101*(38), 13963–13968.

Muzet, A. (1995). Réactivité de l'homme endormi. In O. Benoit & J. Foret (Eds.), *Le Sommeil humain* (pp. 77–83). Paris: Masson.

Newman, E. B. (1939). Forgetting of meaningful material during sleep and waking. *American Journal of Psychology, 52*, 65–71.

Nishida, M., Pearsall, J., Buckner, R. L., & Walker, M. P. (2009). REM sleep, prefrontal theta, and the consolidation of human emotional memory. *Cerebral Cortex, 19*(5), 1158–1166.

O'Keefe, J., Burgess, N., Donnett, J. G., Jeffery, K. J., & Maguire, E. A. (1998). Place cells, navigational accuracy, and the human hippocampus. *Philosophical Transactions of the Royal Society of London, 353*(1373), 1333–1340.

Orban, P., Rauchs, G., Balteau, E., Degueldre, C., Luxen, A., Maquet, P., et al. (2006). Sleep after spatial learning promotes covert reorganization of brain activity. *Proceedings of the National Academy of Sciences of the USA, 103*(18), 7124–7129.

Pace-Schott, E. F., & Hobson, J. A. (2002). The neurobiology of sleep: Genetics, cellular physiology and subcortical networks. *Nature Reviews Neuroscience, 3*(8), 591–605.

Pavlides, C., & Winson, J. (1989). Influences of hippocampal place cell firing in the awake state on the activity of these cells during subsequent sleep episodes. *Journal of Neuroscience, 9*(8), 2907–2918.

Payne, J. D., Stickgold, R., Swanberg, K., & Kensinger, E. A. (2008). Sleep preferentially enhances memory for emotional components of scenes. *Psychological Science, 19*(8), 781–788.

Peigneux, P., Laureys, S., Delbeuck, X., & Maquet, P. (2001). Sleeping brain, learning brain. The role of sleep for memory systems. *Neuroreport, 12*(18), A111–124.

Peigneux, P., Laureys, S., Fuchs, S., Collette, F., Perrin, F., Reggers, J., et al. (2004). Are spatial memories strengthened in the human hippocampus during slow wave sleep? *Neuron, 44*(3), 535–545.

Peigneux, P., Laureys, S., Fuchs, S., Destrebecqz, A., Collette, F., Delbeuck, X., et al. (2003). Learned material content and acquisition level modulate cerebral reactivation during posttraining rapid-eye-movements sleep. *Neuroimage, 20*(1), 125–134.

Phelps, E. A. (2006). Emotion and cognition: Insights from studies of the human amygdala. *Annual Review of Psychology, 57*, 27–53.

Plihal, W., & Born, J. (1997). Effects of early and late nocturnal sleep on declarative and procedural memory. *Journal of Cognitive Neuroscience, 9*(4), 534–547.

Plihal, W., & Born, J. (1999). Memory consolidation in human sleep depends on inhibition of glucocorticoid release. *Neuroreport, 10*(13), 2741–2747.

Plihal, W., Pietrowsky, R., & Born, J. (1999). Dexamethasone blocks sleep induced improvement of declarative memory. *Psychoneuroendocrinology, 24*(3), 313–331.

Rasch, B. H., Born, J., & Gais, S. (2006). Combined blockade of cholinergic receptors shifts the brain from stimulus encoding to memory consolidation. *Journal of Cognitive Neuroscience, 18*(5), 793–802.

Rauchs, G., Desgranges, B., Foret, J., & Eustache, F. (2005). The relationships between memory systems and sleep stages. *Journal of Sleep Research*, *14*(2), 123–140.

Rauchs, G., Orban, P., Schmidt, C., Albouy, G., Balteau, E., Degueldre, C., et al. (2008). Sleep modulates the neural substrates of both spatial and contextual memory consolidation. *PLoS ONE*, *3*(8), e2949.

Rechtschaffen, A., & Kales, A. (1968). *A manual of standardized terminology, techniques and scoring system for sleep stages of human subjects*. Bethesda, MA: US Department of Health.

Schabus, M., Gruber, G., Parapatics, S., Sauter, C., Klosch, G., Anderer, P., et al. (2004). Sleep spindles and their significance for declarative memory consolidation. *Sleep*, *27*(8), 1479–1485.

Schabus, M., Hoedlmoser, K., Pecherstorfer, T., Anderer, P., Gruber, G., Parapatics, S., et al. (2008). Interindividual sleep spindle differences and their relation to learning-related enhancements. *Brain Research*, *1191*, 127–135.

Schabus, M., Hoedlmoser, K., Pecherstorfer, T., & Klosch, G. (2005). Influence of midday naps on declarative memory performance and motivation. *Somnologie*, *9*(3), 148–153.

Schmidt, C., Collette, F., Cajochen, C., & Peigneux, P. (2007). A time to think: Circadian rhythms in human cognition. *Cognitive Neuropsychology*, *24*(7), 755–789.

Schmidt, C., Peigneux, P., Muto, V., Schenkel, M., Knoblauch, V., Munch, M., et al. (2006). Encoding difficulty promotes postlearning changes in sleep spindle activity during napping. *Journal of Neuroscience*, *26*(35), 8976–8982.

Scoville, W. B., & Milner, B. (1957). Loss of recent memory after bilateral hippocampal lesions. *Journal of Neurology, Neurosurgery, and Psychiatry*, *20*(1), 11–21.

Siegel, J. M. (2001). The REM sleep-memory consolidation hypothesis. *Science*, *294*(5544), 1058–1063.

Silber, M. H., Ancoli-Israel, S., Bonnet, M. H., Chokroverty, S., Grigg-Damberger, M. M., Hirshkowitz, M., et al. (2007). The visual scoring of sleep in adults. *Journal of Clinical and Sleep Medicine*, *3*(2), 121–131.

Sirota, A., Csicsvari, J., Buhl, D., & Buzsaki, G. (2003). Communication between neocortex and hippocampus during sleep in rodents. *Proceedings of the National Academy of Sciences of the USA*, *100*(4), 2065–2069.

Skaggs, W. E., & McNaughton, B. L. (1996). Replay of neuronal firing sequences in rat hippocampus during sleep following spatial experience. *Science*, *271*(5257), 1870–1873.

Smith, C. (2001). Sleep states and memory processes in humans: procedural versus declarative memory systems. *Sleep Medicine Reviews*, *5*(6), 491–506.

Squire, L. R. (2004). Memory systems of the brain: A brief history and current perspective. *Neurobiology of Learning and Memory*, *82*(3), 171–177.

Squire, L. R., & Kandel, E. R. (1999). *Memory. From mind to molecules*. New York: Freeman.

Squire, L. R., & Knowlton, B. J. (1995). Memory, hippocampus, and brain systems. In M. S. Gazzaniga (Ed.), *The cognitive neurosciences* (pp. 825–837). Cambridge, MA: MIT Press.

Sterpenich, V., Albouy, G., Boly, M., Vandewalle, G., Darsaud, A., Balteau, E., et al. (2007). Sleep-related hippocampo-cortical interplay during emotional memory recollection. *PLoS Biology*, *5*(11), e282.

Tobler, I. (1995). Is sleep fundamentally different between mammalian species? *Behavioural Brain Research*, *69*(1–2), 35–41.

Tucker, M. A., Hirota, Y., Wamsley, E. J., Lau, H., Chaklader, A., & Fishbein, W. (2006). A daytime nap containing solely non-REM sleep enhances declarative but not procedural memory. *Neurobiology of Learning and Memory*, *86*(2), 241–247.

Van Ormer, E. B. (1933). Sleep and retention. *Psychological Bulletin*, *30*, 415–439.

Wagner, U., Degirmenci, M., Drosopoulos, S., Perras, B., & Born, J. (2005). Effects of cortisol suppression on sleep-associated consolidation of neutral and emotional memory. *Biological Psychiatry*, *58*(11), 885–893.

Wagner, U., Gais, S., & Born, J. (2001). Emotional memory formation is enhanced across sleep intervals with high amounts of rapid eye movement sleep. *Learning and Memory*, *8*(2), 112–119.

Wagner, U., Hallschmid, M., Rasch, B., & Born, J. (2006). Brief sleep after learning keeps emotional memories alive for years. *Biological Psychiatry*, *60*(7), 788–790.

Wagner, U., Kashyap, N., Diekelmann, S., & Born, J. (2007). The impact of post-learning sleep vs. wakefulness on recognition memory for faces with different facial expressions. *Neurobiology of Learning and Memory*, *87*(4), 679–687.

Walker, M. P., & Stickgold, R. (2004). Sleep-dependent learning and memory consolidation. *Neuron*, *44*(1), 121–133.

Walker, M. P., & Stickgold, R. (2006). Sleep, memory, and plasticity. *Annual Review of Psychology*, *57*, 139–166.

Wilson, M. A., & McNaughton, B. L. (1994). Reactivation of hippocampal ensemble memories during sleep. *Science*, *265*(5172), 676–679.

Wixted, J. T. (2004). The psychology and neuroscience of forgetting. *Annual Review of Psychology*, *55*, 235–269.

Yaroush, R., Sullivan, M. J., & Ekstrand, B. R. (1971). Effect of sleep on memory. II. Differential effect of the first and second half of the night. *Journal of Experimental Psychology*, *88*(3), 361–366.

Yoo, S. S., Gujar, N., Hu, P., Jolesz, F. A., & Walker, M. P. (2007). The human emotional brain without sleep – a prefrontal amygdala disconnection. *Current Biology*, *17*(20), R877–878.

9 Forgetting due to retroactive interference in amnesia

Findings and implications

Michaela Dewar
University of Edinburgh, UK

Nelson Cowan
University of Missouri-Columbia, USA

Sergio Della Sala
University of Edinburgh, UK

Imagine the improbable. A man with a dense anterograde amnesia is lying in bed at night, at home, watching television while his wife, who generally strives to be at his side, steps out of the room to take a shower. During that time, there is a power failure and both the man and his wife are left in the dark and the silence, separated for all of 7 minutes while she gropes around for her towel, glasses, and so on. She is worried because he might have time to become disoriented, forget what he was doing, and come looking for her. When she finally makes it back to the bedroom, it is still dark and her husband, who hears her coming, states, "I was just watching a show about dog tricks." The wife is astounded, as her husband has not remembered anything for this long since before his stroke.

This is a fictional scenario but we have been recently confronted with data even more astounding than this (Cowan, Beschin, & Della Sala, 2004; Della Sala, Cowan, Beschin, & Perini, 2005; Dewar, Fernandez Garcia, Cowan & Della Sala, 2009). What follows is a description of what we have found, and our attempt to reconcile it with other evidence on the nature of amnesia and the memory system. We believe that there are profound implications.

Anterograde amnesia

Envisage a life in which all currently perceived and experienced information and events fade away as soon as they are no longer the focus of your attention. Life would be spent in the here and now; nothing would remain for more than a few seconds. Currently perceived information, such as this paragraph, or the librarian who may have just given you this book, would appear entirely novel if encountered again, even after the briefest of delays. The philosopher

Friedrich Nietzsche (1844–1900) tried to see the bright side of such plight, arguing that: "The advantage of a bad memory is that one enjoys several times the same good things for the first time."

However, for people who have suffered anterograde amnesia as a consequence of head injury, illness or a degenerative disease (e.g., Alzheimer's disease, AD), such forgetting is a most debilitating condition. This is perhaps most evocatively displayed by Clive Wearing, a professional musician who in his forties was left densely amnesic following viral encephalitis. Clive's amnesia was so severe that he repeatedly stated that he had only just now recovered consciousness. Even if his wife left his room for only a few minutes he would greet her on her return with great emotion, as if they had not seen each other for a very long time. Patients like Clive are clearly stuck in a moment, seemingly unable to retain anything for more than a few seconds. Is such severe forgetting inevitable though? Our recent work indicates that it need not be.

Studies on retroactive interference in anterograde amnesia

Cowan et al. (2004) presented 6 densely amnesic patients with a list of 15 words, which they were asked to recall immediately afterwards as well as after a 10-minute delay. This delay interval either simulated a standard memory assessment in that it was filled with further cognitive tasks, or it remained unfilled, meaning that the patient was left alone in a quiet, darkened testing room. Remarkably, 4 of the 6 patients showed substantially greater retention of the word list material that had been reproduced in immediate recall following the unfilled (49%) than the filled delay (14%). The data were even more astonishing when the delay was increased to 1 hour, and when short stories were used instead of word lists. When the retention period was filled with cognitive tasks, one patient recalled just 27% of what was recalled an hour earlier and the other 5 patients recalled nothing. When the retention period was spent in the quiet, dark room, however, the patient who had recalled 27% in delayed recall now went up to 63% in delayed recall. What is more amazing is that 3 patients who had recalled 0% with a task-filled retention interval now went up to 85%, 90%, and 78% in the absence of cognitive tasks. On average, these 4 patients (the same 4 as in the word list trials) went from 7% retention over a task-filled hour to an astounding 79% retention over an hour with no stimulation (see Figure 9.1).

Why some patients benefited from the minimization of interference while others did not is unclear, but differences in lesion loci and aetiology are likely candidates (Cowan et al., 2004). In order to minimize individual differences in aetiology and lesion loci, Della Sala et al. (2005) replicated Cowan et al.'s (2004) prose memory study with a sample of patients diagnosed with amnestic mild cognitive impairment (aMCI) (Petersen, Smith, Waring, Ivnik, Tangalos, & Kokmen, 1999). Such patients present with a degenerative isolated anterograde amnesia, which is often a harbinger of Alzheimer's

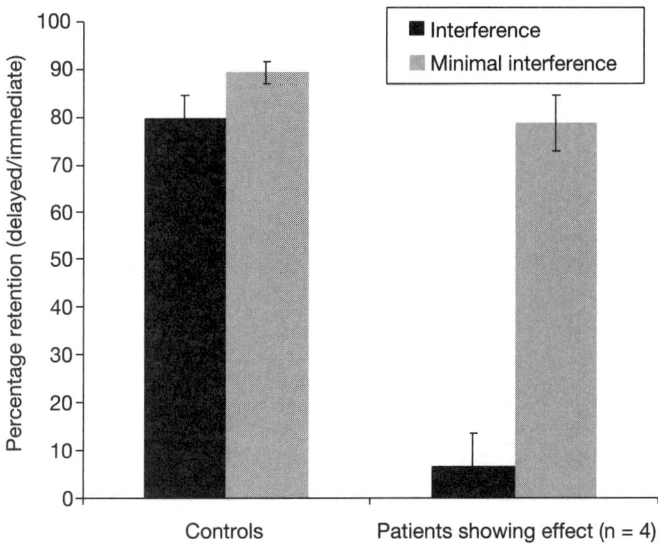

Figure 9.1 Mean percentage retention (delayed recall/immediate recall) of story material for 4 severely amnesic patients and 6 controls following a 1-hour delay interval, which was either filled with cognitive tasks (*retroactive interference*) or was spent alone in the quiet, darkened testing room (*minimal retroactive interference*). While the amnesic patients performed extremely poorly following the retroactive interference delay, all 4 showed remarkably high story retention following the minimal retroactive interference delay. Two further amnesic patients were tested but retained no story material in either delay condition. (Error bars = Standard error of the mean.) (Cowan et al., 2004)

disease. Again patients performed significantly better following the unfilled (55%) than the filled delay interval (20%). (Age- and education-matched controls showed a group mean percentage retention of 80% following the filled and 89% following the unfilled condition.) This is shown in Figure 9.2.

These remarkable findings clearly demonstrate that at least some amnesic patients can retain new information for much longer than is typically assumed if the time following learning is devoid of further information. This in turn suggests that forgetting in amnesia might be largely attributed to retroactive interference, i.e., the interference generated by material and tasks that follow new learning.

Can these novel findings be readily accounted for by existing cognitive theories of forgetting and models of memory? It seems not.

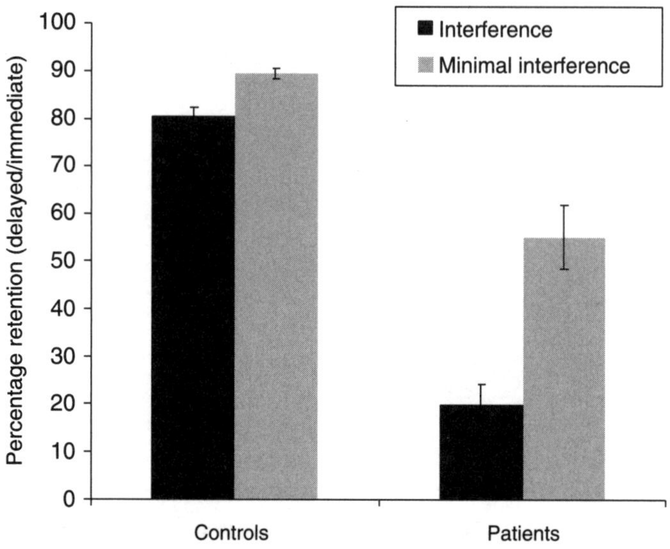

Figure 9.2 Mean percentage retention (delayed recall/immediate recall) of story material for 10 patients diagnosed with amnestic mild cognitive impairment (aMCI), a frequent harbinger of Alzheimer's disease, and 10 controls, following a 1-hour delay interval. The amnesic patients retained much more story material when the delay interval was spent alone in the quiet, darkened testing room (*minimal retroactive interference*) than when it was filled with cognitive tasks (*retroactive interference*). (Error bars = Standard error of the mean.) (Della Sala et al., 2005)

Existing cognitive theories of amnesia

The standard dual store account

Anterograde amnesia has been traditionally interpreted within a two-store model of memory, in which new information is passed from a temporary short-term memory (STM) store to a permanent long-term memory (LTM) store (Aktinson & Shiffrin, 1968). Amnesic patients are said to have intact STM but no new LTM, meaning that they are entirely reliant upon STM for retention of new information. However, in neurologically intact people as well as amnesic patients information in STM is said to decay rapidly (~ 30 seconds) unless it is maintained within consciousness, e.g., via explicit rehearsal. This traditional model is illustrated in Figure 9.3.

With this in mind, could it be that minimizing retroactive interference simply allows amnesic patients to consciously maintain new information within STM, thus effectively protecting it from STM decay? It is known already that amnesic patients, including the famous patient HM, can retain new information such as a three-figure number or a pair of unrelated words for longer than usual (several minutes) if they are not

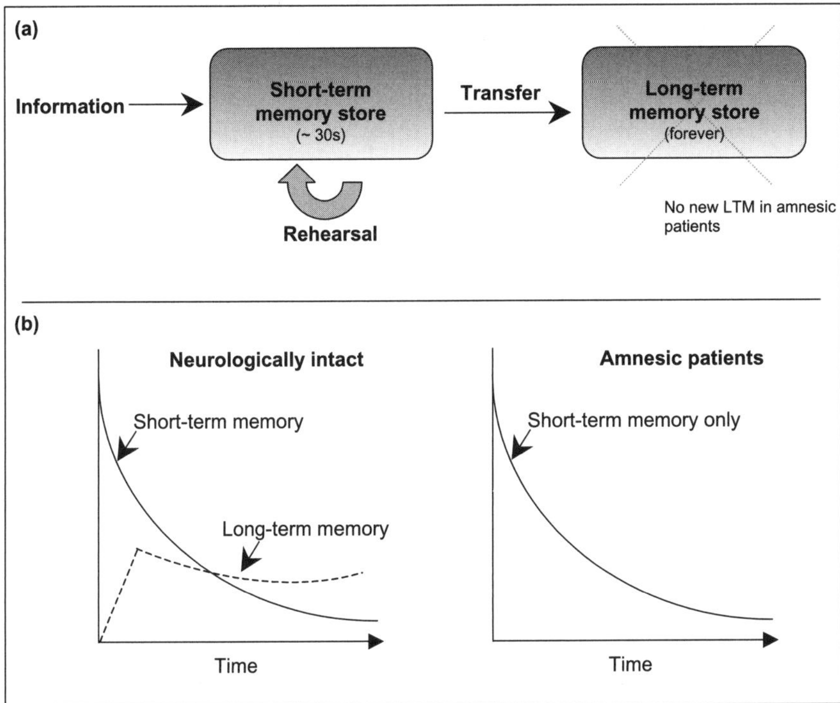

Figure 9.3 The traditional two-store model of memory (adapted from Aktinson & Shiffrin, 1968). New information is said to be transferred from a temporary short-term memory store to a permanent long-term memory store (a). Amnesic patients are postulated to have intact short-term memory but no new long-term memory. They are thus said to rely exclusively upon short-term memory for retention of new material. However, material within short-term memory decays rapidly (~30s) unless it is actively maintained within consciousness (e.g., via explicit rehearsal) (b).

distracted from such information (Milner, 1968; Ogden, 1996; Scoville & Milner, 1957).

However, several findings by Cowan et al. (2004) and Della Sala et al. (2005) speak against such a conscious rehearsal account of the data. First, the initial delayed recall came as a surprise, meaning that participants had little or no incentive to consciously rehearse the material for up to an hour, yet that did not lead to poorer recall than later trials. Moreover, two patients were observed to be sleeping through at least part of the retention interval with minimal retroactive interference, yet benefited from minimal retroactive interference as much as on other trials, and as much as other patients did.

Even stronger evidence against a mere conscious rehearsal account of the minimal retroactive interference-induced memory enhancement in amnesic patients comes from our subsequent work (Dewar et al., 2009). We hypothesized that if the augmented retention following minimal retroactive interference in amnesic patients were solely the result of continuous STM maintenance based on rehearsal, with no additional LTM memory processing, amnesic patients should forget to-be-retained material as soon as retroactive interference interrupts rehearsal, irrespective of the prior duration of such rehearsal. If, on the other hand, a period of minimal retroactive interference allowed for some enhanced LTM processing in amnesic patients, some memory retention may persist even in the presence of retroactive interference, provided that such retroactive interference is preceded by a sufficient period of minimal retroactive interference (see Figure 9.4).

We presented 12 patients with aMCI and 12 age and IQ matched controls with a list of 15 words, which they were asked to recall immediately following word list presentation, and again after a 9-minute delay. This delay was either entirely unfilled (as in Cowan et al., 2004 and Della Sala et al., 2005), or it was filled with a 3-minute rehearsal-blocking interference task (naming presented line drawings). The critical manipulation was the temporal placement of this retroactive interference task within the otherwise unfilled delay. Retroactive

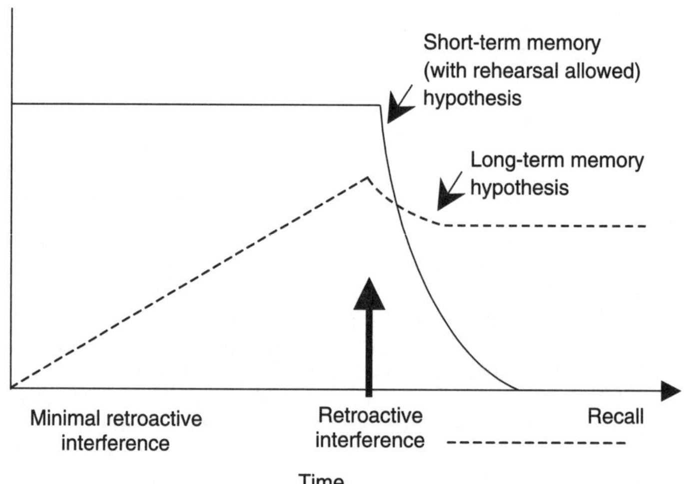

Figure 9.4 The benefit of minimal retroactive interference. Predictions made by a short-term memory hypothesis and a long-term memory hypothesis of the phenomenon. The short-term memory hypothesis predicts that a period of minimal retroactive interference allows amnesic patients to consciously maintain new information within their intact short-term memory. This new information, however, decays rapidly from short-term memory as soon as such conscious maintenance is interrupted via retroactive interference, leading to very poor retention. The long-term memory hypothesis, on the other hand, predicts that a period of minimal retroactive interference enhances long-term memory processing of the new material in amnesic patients. This enhanced processing is predicted to render new material less susceptible to subsequent retroactive interference. Some retention should therefore persist in the presence of retroactive interference, so long as this retroactive interference is preceded by a period of minimal retroactive interference.

interference was either placed in the first (early retroactive interference), the middle (mid-retroactive interference) or the last (late retroactive interference) portion of the delay.

As predicted from our previous retroactive interference work, the patients performed significantly better than usual when no retroactive interference was present during the delay interval. Most importantly, the patients also retained significantly more word list material when retroactive interference was delayed by 6 minutes (late retroactive interference) than when it was delayed by only 3 minutes (mid-retroactive interference), or when it occurred at the very beginning of the delay interval (early retroactive interference) (see Figure 9.5). All 12 patients showed the improvement from the early to the late condition, and 8 patients showed the improvement from the mid to the late condition, indicating that these findings were very robust indeed. Most remarkable was the finding that 8 of the tested patients recalled nothing when retroactive interference occurred at the start of the delay, yet they recalled between 30% and 70% when retroactive interference was delayed by 6 minutes.

These striking findings of an effect of the temporal placement of retroactive interference clearly conflict with an account of the minimal retroactive interference-induced memory enhancement in amnesia based only on STM with rehearsal. The early, mid and late interference conditions all included the same amount of rehearsal-disrupting interference. Mere rehearsal, in the absence of any LTM processing, should have thus only led to improved memory in the condition in which no interference was present. Memory performance in the early, mid and late conditions should have been equally poor.

Further evidence against such an STM-with-rehearsal notion comes from an unpublished case study on a 72-year-old highly educated patient who, as a consequence of limbic encephalitis, was left severely amnesic (Dewar, Cowan, & Della Sala, unpublished). This patient, PB (not his real initials), was entirely unable to recall a previously presented story following a 10-minute delay filled with a simple tone detection task. In striking contrast, when the delay was unfilled, PB was able to recall 66% of what he had repeated back 10 minutes before. Remarkably, he could still recall most of this information after a further 5-minute delay, during which we engaged him in a casual conversation entirely unrelated to the story. Indeed, we found that PB continued to be able to recall some of the story material following a further few of these short conversation-filled delays, a finding that resulted in much amazement in both himself and his wife. It would have certainly been near to impossible for PB to have continuously maintained the story material within consciousness while engaging in such unrelated conversations. Nonetheless, he was able to remember some new information.

The above findings indicate a clear incompatibility between our data and the standard two-store theory of forgetting in amnesia. Indeed, our data imply that some LTM functioning is spared in a number of amnesic patients, and that it is a LTM process, not merely STM maintenance, that is enhanced when retroactive interference is minimal.

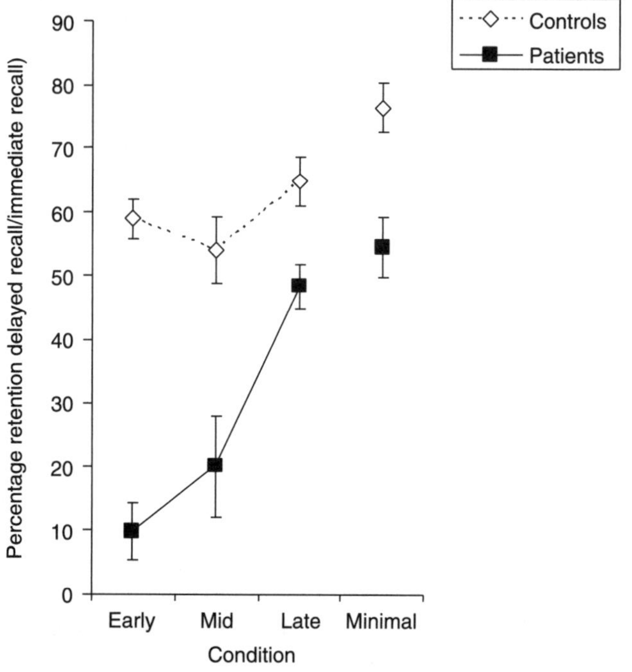

Figure 9.5 Mean percentage retention (delayed recall/immediate recall) of a word list for 12 severely amnesic patients (diagnosed with amnestic mild cognitive impairment) and 12 controls following a 9-minute delay interval, in which retroactive interference occurred either in the first 3 minutes (early), the middle 3 minutes (mid) or the last 3 minutes (late). An entirely unfilled delay (minimal) was also included. In line with a long-term memory hypothesis the patients were able to retain some word list material following retroactive interference, provided that this retroactive interference was preceded by at least 6 minutes of minimal retroactive interference (see early and mid vs. late conditions). According to a short-term memory hypothesis of the benefit of minimal retroactive interference patients should have only shown improved retention in the entirely unfilled (minimal) condition. Memory performance in the early, mid and late conditions should have been equally poor. The results strongly suggest that minimal retroactive interference enhances long-term memory in amnesic patients. (Dewar et al., 2009)

Long-term memory interference in amnesia

Which LTM process might minimal retroactive interference enhance in amnesic patients? There are two key possibilities. It may be the case that new information can reach LTM in amnesic patients but that their memory retrieval is greatly impaired, and thus that minimal retroactive interference facilitates LTM retrieval. Alternatively, it could be that minimal retroactive interference enhances an impaired LTM formation (consolidation) process in amnesic patients. Both assume that at least some new LTM formation is possible in amnesic patients, thus conflicting with the standard cognitive theory of amnesia. We will discuss these two possibilities in turn.

Retrieval interference

Memory retrieval is essentially driven by retrieval cues, which activate the memory traces that best match that cue. Such cues can be explicit in that they aid a conscious memory search. For example, on being asked what one did for one's birthday 4 years ago, various memory traces matching "my birthday" will be activated and help one narrow down the search. Retrieval cues can also be implicit, relating to context (e.g., environmental factors and internal states). The powerful effect which such implicit retrieval cues can have on memory is beautifully illustrated by Marcel Proust who, upon tasting madeleine crumbs in his tea, is taken on a vivid and emotion-filled time travel back to his boyhood when his aunt indulged him with such treats on Sunday mornings.

Memories are said to be retrieved best if the encoding context matches the retrieval context closely, i.e., when features such as location, auditory, and visual information present at initial encoding are also present at retrieval (Tulving & Thomson, 1973). This was perhaps most famously demonstrated by Godden and Baddeley (1975), who showed that deep-sea divers learning a list of words under water recalled these better when under water than on land, and vice versa.

If a particular retrieval cue activates two or more memory traces, these memory traces are said to compete for retrieval, thus effectively inhibiting each other. In the above birthday example, it is possible that memory traces from a birthday party 2 years before and 7 years before interfere with the to-be-recalled birthday 4 years before. In the lab such retrieval interference can be induced experimentally via the presentation of two or more stimuli which are similar and/or share a retrieval cue (Dewar et al., 2007; Postman & Alpner, 1946; Skaggs, 1933; Wixted, 2004). For example, two subsequently presented lists of word pairs, which share a common cue word, such as *tree*–glass (List 1) and *tree*–train (List 2) tend to produce interference at retrieval when the cue (*tree*) is presented. Moreover, similar items learned in the same context are also more likely to interfere at retrieval when this context is also present during retrieval (Anderson & Bjork, 1994; Mensink & Raaijmakers, 1988).

Might minimal retroactive interference enhance retrieval in amnesic patients by keeping competing memory traces at bay? Such a hypothesis would imply that amnesic patients can form new memories but struggle to retrieve these when competing memory traces are present.

Research has shown that some patients with subtle memory impairment associated with executive dysfunction, who have difficulty planning their behaviours to meet their goals, present with such problems exactly (e.g.,

Baldo & Shimamura, 2002; Shimamura, Jurica, Mangels, Gershberg, & Knight, 1995). For example, Shimamura et al. (1995) report that in their dysexecutive patients the learning of a list of paired associates such as *lion–hunter* interfered substantially with the subsequent learning of a second list of paired associates, in which the cue word matched that of the first list, e.g., *lion–circus*. Their work hints that such increased interference also occurs in dysexecutive patients when to-be-retained information is followed by highly similar material (i.e., similar retroactive interference).

In the 1970s Warrington and Weiskrantz (1970, 1974) also proposed such a hypothesis for anterograde amnesia. However, they soon rejected this theory for various reasons, one being the lack of a benefit from a reduction of potentially competing memory traces (Warrington & Weiskrantz, 1978). Two decades later, Mayes, Isaac, Holdstock, Carriga, Gummer, and Roberts (1994) examined the effects of 12 minutes of similar retroactive interference (photos of faces) versus 12 minutes of unrelated retroactive interference (conversation and other activities that did not contain faces) on the retention of photos of faces in amnesic patients and also failed to find any evidence for a benefit from the reduction of competing memory traces (similar retroactive interference).

Unlike these studies, our own retroactive interference material bears little close resemblance to the to-be-retained material used in our studies. Therefore, if the observed minimal retroactive interference-induced memory enhancement were the sole product of a reduction of competing memory traces (i.e., similar retroactive interference), one would predict that our retroactive interference material would be ineffectual, and that amnesic patients therefore would perform similarly in our filled and unfilled conditions. This clearly is not the case, though.

Perhaps the threshold for similarity of memory traces is lower in amnesic patients than it is in neurologically intact people, meaning that memory traces need not be very similar for a substantial retrieval interference to occur in amnesia. But how might one account for the fact that the same material poses a greater detrimental effect on retrieval when placed at the beginning of the delay than at the end of the delay, as in the Dewar et al. (in press) data?

One could argue that the placement of the interfering material affects the context of that material. Mensink and Raaijmakers (1988) suggest that contexts fluctuate over time. Such contextual fluctuation might result in greater contextual overlap between to-be-retained material and immediately following retroactive interference stimuli than between to-be-retained material and delayed retroactive interference stimuli. Indeed, work in the immediate recall domain suggests that list items which are temporally isolated from other list items are retrieved more easily than list items that are in close temporal proximity to other list items (see Chapter 4). Importantly, however, with a contextual fluctuation conception one would also predict a larger contextual overlap between the retrieval context and the retroactive interference occurring at the end of the delay than between the retrieval context and earlier retroactive interference. Thus, both early and late retroactive interference would be predicted to interfere somewhat with retrieval, more than mid-retroactive interference. Indeed, work on neurologically intact individuals on similar retroactive interference has elucidated such an "inverted U" response pattern exactly (e.g., Newton & Wickens 1956; Postman & Alpner, 1946; see Wixted, 2004 for a review). However, such was not the case in the study by Dewar et al. (2009).

Moreover, retrieval interference often results in the emergence of intrusions (i.e., falsely activated memory traces) during recall of to-be-recalled material. If retroactive interference occurring early in the delay interval led to more retrieval interference than did retroactive interference occurring later in the delay, one might expect a larger number of intrusions in the former than latter condition. However, Dewar et al. (2009) did not find that. Instead, the average number of such intrusions was extremely low in all conditions (< 1) and did not differ from that of controls.

On a more observational note it should be highlighted that patients with anterograde amnesia are typically able to retrieve memories normally from a long time ago. Unless the mechanisms for retrieval of such retrograde memory differ from those of anterograde memory, any retrieval difficulties should manifest themselves during retrieval of both types of memory (cf., Curran & Schacter, 2000; Squire, 1980, 1982, 2006; Wilson, 1987).

While we do not for one moment doubt that forgetting can be induced by retrieval interference, a retrieval interference hypothesis currently appears to be unable to provide an adequate account of the amnesia data summarized here.

In order to derive a better-fitting account for our data we might well need to move away from traditional cognitive memory models and incorporate what pharmacological and behavioural neuroscience work has revealed about a physiological phenomenon, memory consolidation.

Consolidation interference

The term "consolidation" was coined over a century ago by the experimental psychologist Georg Müller (see Figure 9.6) and medical student Alfons Pilzecker (Dewar, Cowan, & Della Sala, 2007; Lüer, 2007; Müller & Pilzecker, 1900; Wixted, 2004). The term comes from the Latin word *consolidare*, meaning "to make solid" (from *cum* + *solidus* "solid"). Consolidation has been mostly ignored within modern psychology, with a few notable exceptions (e.g., Bosshardt et al., 2005a, 2005b; Gaskel & Dumay, 2003). It has, however, proven to be a popular and widely researched process within neuroscience and psychopharmacology, where it is defined as "the progressive postacquisition stabilization of long-term memory" and "the memory phase(s) during which such presumed stabilization takes place" (Dudai, 2004, p. 52).

The first clinical evidence for consolidation came from observations made by Théodule Armand Ribot (1881, 1882), who reported that brain injury had

Figure 9.6 Georg Elias Müller (1850–1934).

a more detrimental effect on recent than remote premorbid memories. Such finding has been replicated extensively during the last century and today is known as "temporally graded retrograde amnesia". One of the first explanations for such temporally graded retrograde amnesia can be gleaned from Burnham (1903):

> The fixing of an impression depends upon a physiological process. It takes time for an impression to become so fixed that it can be reproduced after a long time interval; for it to become part of a permanent store of memory considerable time may be necessary. This we may suppose is not merely a process of making a permanent impression upon the nerve cells, but also a process of association, of organization of the new impressions with the old ones . . . Now suppose a shock occurs which arrests these physiological processes in the nervous tissue. What will be the result? Not only will the mind be a blank for the period of insensibility following the shock, but no impressions will be remembered which were not already at the time of the accident sufficiently well organized to make their persistence for a considerable interval possible. Hence the amnesia will be "retroactive".
>
> (Burnham, 1903, pp. 128–129)

He goes on to state: "The essential characteristic of these cases of retroactive amnesia is that the memory is lost because it was never fully organized" (Burnham, 1903, p. 129).

These early clinical findings and hypotheses clearly indicate that the formation of memories takes time and cannot be compared to the instantaneous long-term "memorizing" of files by a computer. Thus, while a personal computer is capable of "memorizing" documents such as this very book within milliseconds, our brains require time, up to many years, to consolidate the often highly complex information and episodes which we perceive and experience.

More recent evidence for a consolidation process comes from animal neuroscience work on protein synthesis inhibitors. Protein synthesis inhibitors, typically antibiotics or toxins, interfere with the neural processes associated with memory formation in animals (Agranoff, Davis, & Brink, 1966; Dudai, 2004) (see Chapter 6). Retention of recently learned material is low if a protein synthesis inhibitor is introduced shortly following learning, but improves steadily with augmenting delay in the introduction of the protein synthesis inhibitor (see Figure 9.7). Such reduction in interference susceptibility over time clearly indicates that memories strengthen as a function of time. Importantly, such "temporal gradient" of interference is also found when interference is behavioural as opposed to pharmacological. Izquierdo, Schröder, Netto, and Medina (1999), for example, trained rats not to step off a platform by administering a mild shock if they did so. The rats were subsequently allowed to explore a novel environment for 2 minutes either 1 hour or 6 hours following learning. When tested 24 hours following initial learning, memory was found to be impaired in those rats who had explored the new environment 1 hour postlearning, but not in those who had explored the new environment 6 hours postlearning.

Interestingly, such temporal gradient of "behavioural" interference has also been reported in neurologically intact humans. In their aforementioned pioneer work on consolidation and retroactive interference, Müller and Pilzecker (1900) presented participants with a to-be-retained syllable list. Either 17 seconds or 6 minutes following the learning of the to-be-retained syllable list the participants were presented with a new syllable list. The participants' retention increased from 28% in the 17-second condition to 49% in the 6-minute condition. Müller and Pilzecker argued that the first syllable list could consolidate thoroughly during the 6-minute interval, thus being less susceptible to the subsequent interfering effect of the interpolated syllable list. They therefore reasoned that new memory traces are initially fragile and vulnerable to retroactive interference but strengthen, i.e., consolidate, over time (Dewar et al., 2007).

Further behavioural work on such consolidation interference hypothesis was undertaken by Skaggs (1925). He presented participants with a chessboard containing five chessmen, whose positions the participant had to remember after a 5-minute delay. During this delay simple algebra problems were interpolated at one of 4 onset times. In keeping with the consolidation

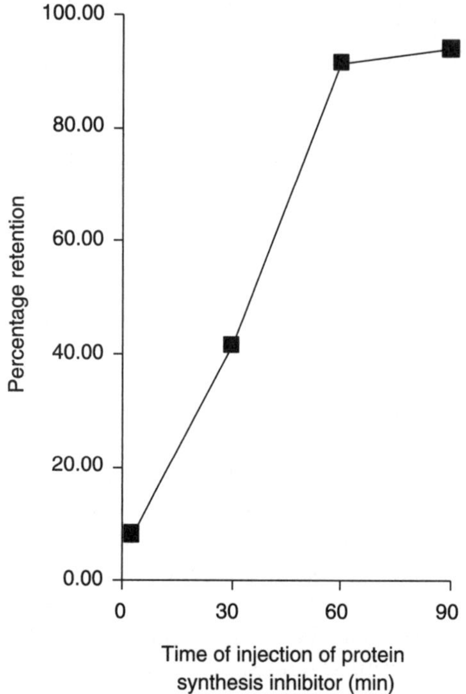

Figure 9.7 Percentage retention as a function of time of injection of a protein synthesis inhibitor (puromycin) in the goldfish. Goldfish were placed at one end of a shuttle box tank, which was divided into two sections by an underwater barrier. The fish were trained to swim across the barrier whenever a light was flashed within the section of the tank that they were placed in. The training was achieved via administration of an electric shock. When the protein synthesis inhibitor was injected immediately following training, the goldfish showed near to no retention of the task following a delay interval (i.e., their performance reverted to that of naive, untrained fish). However, when the time of injection of the protein synthesis inhibitor was delayed, the goldfish showed some retention of the task. Indeed, their retention increased with augmenting temporal delay in the injection of the protein synthesis inhibitor, revealing a reduction in interference susceptibility and thus a strengthening of the memory trace over time. (Figure adapted from Agranoff et al., 1966; see also Dudai, 2004.)

interference hypothesis, the average number of errors was highest when the interpolated task occurred immediately following learning but levelled thereafter.

It should be highlighted that interference stimuli need not be similar to to-be-retained material for a consolidation interference effect to occur. Such was not only elucidated by the aforementioned study by Skaggs (1925), but also by pioneer work by Müller and Pilzecker (1900), as well as more recent work by ourselves (Dewar et al., 2007; see also Wixted, 2004 for a review). Such a finding is important given that modern psychologists tend to define retroactive interference in terms of interference by subsequent similar information (Dewar et al., 2007; Wixted, 2004).

Taken together, these behavioural and pharmacological findings strongly suggest that various kinds of interference, occurring immediately or shortly following the learning of to-be-retained information, have a detrimental effect on the consolidation of the to-be-retained material in neurologically intact neural systems.

The aforementioned findings of a temporal gradient of retroactive interference in amnesic patients by Dewar et al. (2009) are in close accordance with such data. This suggests that: (a) minimal retroactive interference may allow for enhanced memory consolidation in at least some amnesic patients; (b) that forgetting in at least some amnesic patients might well be the result of a disruption of memory consolidation by retroactive interference.

Unlike protein synthesis inhibitors, "behavioural" retroactive interference, such as the one applied in the reported studies, is of course the norm in everyday life, and neurologically intact individuals are easily able to consolidate new memories in the midst of such interfering information. In amnesic patients, however, this ability seems to have broken down.

The reasons behind such potential breakdown in normal consolidation ability in amnesic patients remain to be examined. One possibility is that resources required for the consolidation of new memory traces are greatly reduced in amnesic patients, presumably due to lesions to, or degeneration of, vital memory structures (i.e., medial temporal lobe/hippocampus). Wixted (2004) maintains that in neurologically intact individuals the resources required for consolidation are not infinite. He hypothesizes that when to-be-retained stimuli are followed by further information, resources have to be divided between the processing of the to-be-retained stimuli and the processing of further information. This division of resources is hypothesized to lead to the small reduction in retention that is observed in neurologically intact individuals when performance following a filled delay is compared with that following an unfilled delay.

In amnesic patients who do not benefit from the removal of postlearning material, consolidation resources may be entirely absent or too few to allow for any consolidation, even when new learning is followed by an unfilled interval. In amnesic patients who do benefit from the removal of new postlearning material, consolidation resources may be greatly depleted, but not absent. A considerable depletion of such consolidation resources could render the consolidation mechanism unable to process more than a few memory traces at any one time. Newly learned information may thus not be consolidated properly if further information, competing for greatly restricted resources, follows immediately. If, however, the onset of further information is delayed, there may be sufficient resources for the newly learned information to be adequately strengthened. Of course the absence or delaying of new presented material in unfilled delay intervals does not imply that no new events are consolidated during such intervals. After testing, neurologically intact individuals remember well that they were left alone in a dark quiet room during this interval, even if they were never asked to try and remember such episodic information. As highlighted by Martin (1999), such memory demonstrates that any new events are automatically processed in the intact brain, irrespective of whether or not participants are asked to remember them. This processing of the unfilled delay episode in normals would also be expected to occur, at least in part, in those amnesic patients in whom some consolidation function is spared. Perhaps it is interference from such information that explains why even in unfilled conditions amnesic patients retain less new information than do controls.

Irrespective of whether or not this is the case, the possibility of at least some enhanced consolidation in amnesic patients following minimal retroactive interference is clearly an exciting prospect. Does this interpretation imply that amnesic patients can form new permanent long-term memories if care is taken to reduce any retroactive interference immediately following new learning?

So far we have been unable to find sound evidence for durable long-term memory (following several months) for specific material learned prior to minimal retroactive interference in the lab, even when cues were provided. Of course, even neurologically intact people tend to struggle somewhat when trying to recall details as specific as experimental stimuli after several months. A better indication of retention may thus be a more general episodic memory test of the original test session. Neurologically intact individuals tend to remember well that they attended a testing session (Martin, 1999). They may even be able to recall something specific about the laboratory or the experimenter.

What about amnesic patients? Preliminary data suggest that, when explicitly asked, some patients do indeed state that they can remember general information such as taking part in the study. When phoned a year after initial testing, one of our severely amnesic patients freely recalled that there had been an "English doctor". This memory was clearly not a mere intelligent guess. The patient was Italian and tested at his local Italian hospital where "English doctors" are rather seldom found. However, on the day of testing the team of experimenters did indeed include a visiting UK psychologist. Whether this lasting memory was the result of minimal retroactive interference or some other entirely unrelated factor can of course not be deduced from this observation. Further work is thus necessary to examine whether or not minimal retroactive interference can lead to memory traces that persist over long durations as predicted by the consolidation theory.

Would a failure to reveal such long-term memory go against a consolidation theory of the minimal retroactive interference-induced memory enhancement? Not necessarily. Neuroscience research suggests that there are in fact two types of consolidation, a fast and short-lived kind of consolidation (as initially proposed by Müller & Pilzecker, 1900) as well as a slow and long-lived kind of consolidation. Dudai (2004) refers to such fast and slow kinds of consolidation as "synaptic" and "systems" consolidation respectively (see Chapter 6). Minimal retroactive interference might enhance both kinds of consolidation, or it might enhance only synaptic consolidation.

In short, *synaptic consolidation*, which has been the focus of molecular research, refers to a fast and short strengthening process, taking place in synapses and neurons immediately following encoding (Dudai, 2004; Dudai & Morris, 2000). Such consolidation is, as Dudai puts it, "universal" (Dudai, 2004, p. 56) in that it has been identified in all species. Synaptic consolidation is alleged to render new memories resistant to interference by distraction, drugs, seizures, and lesions within a matter of seconds to hours (Dudai, 2004). Moreover, it is frequently associated with long-term potentiation (LTP; Bliss & Lomo, 1973; see Lynch, 2004 and Morris, 2003 for reviews), which is a long-lasting strengthening of the synapses (i.e., the connections) between two neurons that are simultaneously active, and takes place within the hippocampus. The main evidence for synaptic consolidation comes from the aforementioned findings of a temporal gradient of the detrimental effect of protein synthesis inhibitors.

Systems consolidation refers to a much slower type of memory strengthening: a "progressive reorganisation of memory traces throughout the brain" (Dudai & Morris, 2000, p. 149) that can last years (Dudai, 2004). Such a process is assumed to take place between the medial temporal lobe (MTL) structures/hippocampus and the neocortex, by way of repeated activation of the memory trace, either implicitly (e.g., during sleep) or explicitly via retrieval/rehearsal (Dudai, 2004). While the standard consolidation account holds time per se responsible for the strengthening of such LTM, a newer theory, termed "multiple trace theory" (Nadel & Moscovitch, 1997), posits that it is the number of reactivations of a memory trace that determines its relative strength. Evidence for systems consolidation comes from the elucidation of temporally graded retrograde amnesia (i.e., the larger apparent effect of brain lesion on recent than distant pre-morbid memories) in neurological patients. To date it is unknown whether systems consolidation occurs in parallel to or as a consequence of synaptic consolidation (Dudai, 2004).

While the bulk of evidence for such division of consolidation processes comes from neuroscience, some behavioural evidence is beginning to emerge from the neuropsychological investigation of temporal lobe epilepsy and transient epileptic amnesia. This work has revealed that some epilepsy patients show normal retention of new information following short filled delays (around 30 minutes) but abnormally low retention following longer delays of weeks (Blake, Wroe, Breen, & McCarthy, 2000; Butler, Grahan, Hodges, Kapur, Wardlaw, & Zeman 2007; Kapur, Millar, Colbourn, Abbot, Kennedy, & Docherty, 1997; Manes, Graham, Zeman, de Lujan Calcagno, & Hodges, 2005; Mayes, 2003; O'Connor, Sieggreen, Ahern, Schomer, & Mesulam, 1997; Zeman, Boniface, & Hodges, 1998; see also Chapter 10).

On a purely observational note, there also seems to be evidence from everyday life for such division of consolidation processes. For example, on leaving a new art gallery following a longish and enjoyable browse, we tend to remember where we parked our car. However, we do not usually remember such information following a few days or weeks. Similarly, when visiting a city abroad, we will probably remember which bus to catch to get us from the airport to our hotel and back, but we are unlikely to remember such information once we have returned to our day-to-day business at home. Yet there are other events and pieces of information that we tend to remember for a long time, and possibly forever.

To return to amnesia and retroactive interference: this standard consolidation model makes various predictions as to how and for how long minimal retroactive interference may enhance memory in amnesic patients. Given the findings of minimal retroactive interference-induced memory enhancement over short delays (i.e., up to an hour), it may be that synaptic consolidation is impaired but not entirely defective, and that it benefits hugely from an absence of retroactive interference in those amnesic patients who show some memory enhancement.

Systems consolidation may be entirely defective or unresponsive to minimal retroactive interference occurring immediately following learning, meaning that any memory enhancement would be short-lived in amnesic patients. Alternatively, systems consolidation may also benefit from minimal retroactive interference, either directly at the time of minimal retroactive interference (if the processes act in parallel), or indirectly because material has been adequately strengthened by synaptic consolidation for further processing (if the processes occur serially).

In patients who do not show any minimal retroactive interference-induced memory enhancement, both consolidation types would be predicted to be defective.

Criticisms of the consolidation theory

Like any theory, the consolidation theory is not free of opponents and sceptics. In particular, advocates of retrieval models of forgetting and amnesia have criticized the consolidation theory for its apparent inability to account for instances of memory recovery following longer delays or cues (cf., Spear & Riccio, 1994). Given that we have not yet administered any further extensive free recall or cued recall tests as part of our amnesia retroactive interference work, it is unknown whether any of the previously nonrecalled material may have been retrievable by our patients under such conditions. Moreover, a null finding in such tests still could not remove all doubt in this regard. Also, a positive finding would not necessarily speak against a consolidation account of our data (Dewar et al., 2009). Retroactive interference may not block all consolidation of newly learned material in amnesic patients. It could simply lead to a greatly weakened memory trace that is only retrievable via specific reminders or contextual cues (cf., Dudai, 2004; Squire, 2006). Indeed, Dudai (2004) as well as Miller and Matzel (2006) have argued that perhaps we should not simply consider consolidation as the strengthening of a memory trace per se, but also as the strengthening of that memory trace's retrieval cues. When viewed in this way, consolidation not only strengthens a memory trace but also renders it more retrievable (Dudai, 2004; Miller & Matzel, 2006). Therefore, retroactive interference may not only weaken a memory trace, but it may also make it less retrievable in the future.

If a memory trace has been sufficiently consolidated it should presumably be resistant to all future interference. However, animal work has shown this not to be the case. Reactivation of an apparently stable memory trace via appropriate external retrieval cues can, in some cases, render the memory trace susceptible to immediately following interference again (e.g., Lewis, Bregman, & Mahan, 1972; Misanin, Miller, & Lewis, 1968, see also Sara, 2000 for a review). At first glance these findings appear to be incompatible with a theory that holds that memories become immune to interference over time. However, in recent years it has been proposed that memory traces might not be simply consolidated once, but that they can also be "reconsolidated" (Nader, Schafe, & LeDoux, 2000; Sara, 2000) on various future occasions. Such reconsolidation appears necessary for the modification of existing memory traces and the integration of existing memory traces with new memory traces (Dudai, 2004; Nader et al., 2000; see also Hupbach, Gomez, Hardt, & Nadel, 2007 for work on reconsolidation in neurologically intact people). Nader et al. (2000) thus suggest that it is not simply new, but "active" memory traces which are rendered fragile and in need of strengthening. While previously stable memory traces may, at times, become damaged via interference, the resulting vulnerability to interference might, as Dudai (2004) nicely puts it, simply be "the price paid for modifiability" (p. 75). Moreover, as argued by Dudai (2004), we are not generally at risk of pharmacologically induced reconsolidation blockers (i.e., large doses of protein synthesis inhibitors) and should thus be relative safe from any substantial memory corruption.

Nonetheless, given the apparent high vulnerability to behavioural retroactive interference in some amnesic patients, it is possible that such behavioural retroactive interference could also be highly detrimental to the reconsolidation of recently retrieved retrievable (i.e., retrograde) memory in such patients.

A revised cognitive model of forgetting

Given our findings and consideration of existing cognitive and neuroscience theories, we propose a revised model of forgetting. In a nutshell, we propose a cognitive model containing an *intermediate memory/consolidation* stage. This is illustrated in Figure 9.8. We hypothesize that currently attended (and interpreted) information is temporarily held in STM which might act as a funnel,

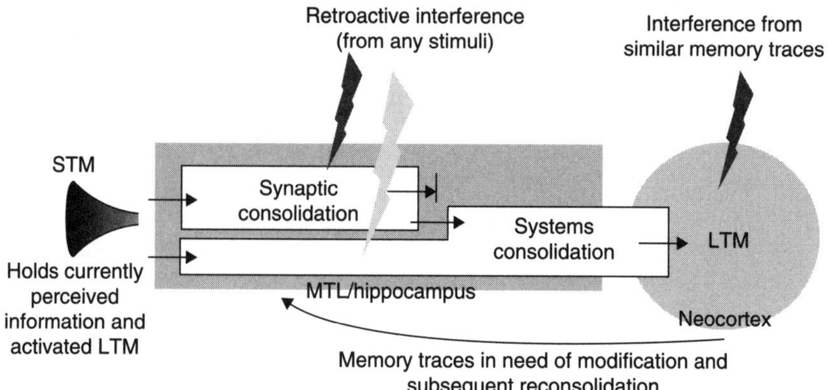

Figure 9.8 A revised cognitive model of forgetting. Currently attended (and interpreted) information is temporarily held in STM, which might act as a funnel, enabling a synaptic consolidation process (probably within the hippocampus) to rapidly strengthen and bind memory for currently relevant stimuli. This consolidation process allows for only the short-term retention of new information (minutes to hours). Additional or subsequent systems consolidation is required for this new information to become an enduring memory trace. In neurologically intact individuals synaptic consolidation is mildly susceptible to interference by any subsequent material. The same might be true for systems consolidation. Items within the long-term memory store are mildly susceptible to interference by competing memory traces (retrieval interference) or to interference with reconsolidation. In patients with anterograde amnesia synaptic consolidation is hypothesized to be highly susceptible to interference by any subsequent material. It remains to be established whether this might also be the case for systems consolidation.

allowing a synaptic consolidation process (probably within the hippocampus) to rapidly strengthen and bind memory for currently relevant stimuli. This synaptic consolidation process is likely to be capacity limited in that it can only maintain or process a limited number of items at any one time. As a consequence this type of consolidation presumably only allows us to remember new information for minutes to hours. An activated and temporarily strengthened memory trace can either be further strengthened by systems consolidation (via implicit or explicit rehearsal and reactivation), or it is simply displaced from the "intermediate memory" generated by synaptic consolidation.

Whether a memory trace is consolidated further may depend on the importance placed upon it, and thus perhaps on the amount of rehearsal/reactivation. It may also depend on other factors such as emotional salience (cf., McGaugh, 2000).

Synaptic consolidation is predicted to be susceptible to retroactive interference (by which we mean interference from any new stimuli). Systems consolidation may also be susceptible to retroactive interference. However, it remains to be established whether systems consolidation occurs in parallel to or as a consequence of synaptic consolidation.

Items that are successfully consolidated and stored in LTM may be forgotten temporarily via retrieval interference (by competing memory traces) or interference with reconsolidation (cf., Nader et al., 2000). Patients with executive dysfunction are hypothesized to be especially susceptible to retrieval interference.

In neurologically intact humans the effects of retroactive interference are predicted to be mild, yet significant when compared to minimal retroactive interference (cf., Dewar et al., 2007; Müller & Pilzecker, 1900; Skaggs, 1925). However, in patients with anterograde amnesia, retroactive interference is predicted to be highly detrimental to synaptic consolidation (as well as perhaps to systems consolidation). In such patients minimal retroactive interference is therefore hypothesized to lead to enhanced synaptic consolidation. It remains to be established whether systems consolidation also benefits from minimal retroactive interference in amnesic patients.

Summary and conclusions

To summarize, the amnesia research reported and discussed in this chapter demonstrates that at least some amnesic patients can retain new information for much longer than is typically assumed if the period that follows new learning is devoid of further material. This minimal retroactive interference-induced memory improvement appears to underlie enhanced memory consolidation. Thus, it strongly appears that at least some patients with anterograde amnesia are in actual fact (still) able to consolidate new information, but that a high susceptibility to retroactive interference impairs such process substantially. Whether minimal retroactive interference leads to a long-term benefit in amnesic patients remains to be established, and is likely to be dependent upon the functioning of systems consolidation.

The reported data and interpretation have important implications. On a practical note, the findings strongly indicate that some patients with anterograde amnesia may be more capable of forming new LTM traces than previously assumed. Future research on minimal retroactive interference could thus lead to fruitful memory training techniques.

With respect to theoretical implications, the reported work clearly highlights the necessity for modern psychology to follow in the footsteps of both Müller and Pilzecker (1900) and contemporary neuroscience and (re-)incorporate an intermediate consolidation stage into its standard two-stage model of memory.

Acknowledgements

Michaela Dewar is currently supported by an Alzheimer's Research Trust postdoctoral Research Fellowship.

References

Agranoff, B. W., Davis, R. E., & Brink, J. J. (1966). Chemical studies on memory fixation in goldfish. *Brain Research*, *1*, 303–309.

Anderson, M. C., & Bjork, R. A. (1994). Mechanisms of inhibition in long-term memory: A new taxonomy. In D. Dagenbach & T. Carrn (Eds.), *Inhibitory processes in attention, memory and language* (pp. 265–326). London: Academic Press.

Atkinson, R. C., & Shiffrin, R. M. (1968). Human memory: A proposed system and its control processes. In K. W. Spence & J. T. Spence (Eds.), *The psychology of learning and motivation* (pp. 89–195). London: Academic Press.

Baldo, J. V., & Shimamura, A. P. (2002). Frontal lobes and memory. In A. Baddeley, M. D. Kopelman, & B. A. Wilson (Eds.), *The handbook of memory disorders* (2nd ed.). Chichester: Wiley.

Blake, R. V., Wroe, S. J., Breen, E. K., & McCarthy, R. A. (2000). Accelerated forgetting in patients with epilepsy. Evidence for an impairment in memory consolidation. *Brain*, *123*, 472–483.

Bliss, T. V. P., & Lomo, T. (1973). Long-lasting potentiation of synaptic transmission in the dentate area of the anaesthetized rabbit following stimulation of the perforant path. *Journal of Physiology*, *232*, 331–356.

Bosshardt, S., Degonda, N., Schmidt, C. F., Boesiger, P., Nitsch, R. M., Hock, C., et al. (2005a). One month of human memory consolidation enhances retrieval-related hippocampal activity. *Hippocampus*, *15*, 1026–1040.

Bosshardt, S., Schmidt, C. F., Jaermann, T., Degonda, N., Boesiger, P., Nitsch, R. M., et al. (2005b). Effects of memory consolidation on human hippocampal activity during retrieval. *Cortex*, *41*, 486–498.

Burnham, W. H. (1903). Retroactive amnesia: Illustractive cases and tentative explanation. *American Journal of Psychology*, *14*, 118–132.

Butler, C. R., Graham, K. S., Hodges, J. R., Kapur, N., Wardlaw, J. M., & Zeman, A. Z. J. (2007). The syndrome of transient epileptic amnesia. *Annals of Neurology*, *61*, 587–598.

Cowan, N., Beschin, N., & Della Sala, S. (2004). Verbal recall in amnesiacs under conditions of diminished retroactive interference. *Brain*, *27*, 825–834.

Curran, T., & Schacter, D. L. (2000). Amnesia II: Cognitive neuropsychological issues. In M. J. Farah & T. E. Feinberg (Eds.), *Patient-based approaches to cognitive neuroscience* (pp. 291–299). Cambridge, MA: MIT Press.

Della Sala, S., Cowan, N., Beschin, N., & Perini M. (2005). Just lying there, remembering: Improving recall of prose in amnesic patients with mild cognitive impairment by minimizing retroactive interference. *Memory*, *13*, 435–440.

Dewar, M. T., Cowan, N., & Della Sala, S. (2007). Forgetting due to retroactive interference: A fusion of Müller and Pilzecker's (1900) early insights into forgetting and recent research on anterograde amnesia. *Cortex*, *43*, 616–634.

Dewar, M., Fernandez Garcia, Y., Cowan, N., & Della Sala, S. (2009). Delaying interference enhances memory consolidation in amnesic patients. *Neuropsychology*, *23*, 627–634.

Dudai, Y. (2004). The neurobiology of consolidation, or, how stable is the engram? *Annual Review of Psychology*, *55*, 51–86.

Dudai, Y., & Morris, R. G. M. (2000). To consolidate or not to consolidate: What are the questions? In J. J. Bolhuis (Ed.), *Brain, perception, memory. Advances in cognitive sciences* (pp. 149–162). Oxford: Oxford University Press.

Gaskel, M. G., & Dumay, N. (2003). Lexical competition and the acquisition of novel words. *Cognition, 89*, 105–132.

Godden, D. R., & Baddeley, A. (1975). Context-dependent memory in two natural environments: On land and underwater. *British Journal of Psychology, 66*, 325–331.

Hupbach, A., Gomez, R., Hardt, O., & Nadel, L. (2007). Reconsolidation of episodic memories: A subtle reminder triggers integration of new information. *Learning & Memory, 14*, 47–53.

Izquierdo, I., Schröder, N., Netto, C. A., & Medina, J. H. (1999). Novelty causes time-dependent retrograde amnesia for one-trial avoidance in rats through NMDA receptor- and CaMKII-dependent mechanisms in the hippocampus. *European Journal of Neuroscience, 11*, 3323–3328.

Kapur, N., Millar, J., Colbourn, C., Abbot, P., Kennedy, P., & Docherty, T. (1997). Very long-term amnesia in association with temporal lobe epilepsy: Evidence for multiple-stage consolidation processes. *Brain and Cognition, 35*, 58–70.

Lewis, D., Bregman, N. J., & Mahan, J. (1972). Cue-dependent amnesia in rats. *Journal of Comparative and Physiological Psychology, 81*, 243–247.

Lüer, G. (2007). Georg Elias Müller (1850–1934): A founder of experimental memory research in psychology. *Cortex, 43*, 579–582.

Lynch, M. A. (2004). Long-term potentiation and memory. *Physiological Reviews, 84*, 87–136.

Manes, F., Graham, K. S., Zeman, A., de Lujan Calcagno, M., & Hodges, J. R. (2005). Autobiographical amnesia and accelerated forgetting in transient epileptic amnesia. *Journal of Neurology, Neurosurgery & Psychiatry, 76*, 1387–1391.

Martin, A. (1999). Automatic activation of the medial temporal lobe during encoding: Lateralized influences of meaning and novelty. *Hippocampus, 9*, 62–70.

McGaugh, J. L. (2000). Memory – a century of consolidation. *Science, 287*, 248–251.

Mayes, A. R., Downes, J. J., Symons, V., & Shoqeirat, M. (1994). Do amnesics forget faces pathologically fast? *Cortex, 30*, 543–563.

Mayes, A. R., Isaac, C. L., Holdstock, J. S., Cariga, P., Gummer, A., & Roberts, N. (2003). Long-term amnesia: A review and detailed illustrative case study. *Cortex, 39*, 567–603.

Mensink, G. J., & Raaijmakers, J. G. W. (1988). A model for interference and forgetting. *Psychological Review, 95*, 434–455.

Miller, R., & Matzel, L. D. (2006). Retrieval failure versus memory loss in experimental amnesia: Definitions and processes. *Learning and Memory, 13*, 491–497.

Milner, B. (1968). Disorders of memory after brain lesions in man. *Neuropsychologia, 6*, 175–179.

Misanin, J. R., Miller, R. R., & Lewis, D. J. (1968). Retrograde amnesia produced by electroconvulsive shock after reactivation of consolidated memory trace. *Science, 160*, 554–555.

Morris, R. G. M. (2003). Long-term potentiation and memory. *Philosophical Transactions of the Royal Society of London, B, 358*, 643–647.

Müller, G. E., & Pilzecker, A. (1900). Experimentelle Beiträge zur Lehre vom Gedächtniss. *Zeitschrift für Psychologie. Ergänzungsband 1*: 1–300.

Nadel, L., & Moscovitch, M. (1997). Memory consolidation, retrograde amnesia and the hippocampal complex. *Current Opinion in Neurobiology, 7*, 217–227.

Nader, K., Schafe, G. E., & LeDoux, J. E (2000). Fear memories require protein synthesis in the amygdala for reconsolidation after retrieval. *Nature*, *406*, 722–726.

Newton, J. M., & Wickens, D. D. (1956). Retroactive inhibition as a function of the temporal position of the interpolated learning. *Journal of Experimental Psychology*, *51*, 149–154.

O'Connor, M., Sieggreen, M. A., Ahern, G., Schomer, D., & Mesulam, M. (1997). Accelerated forgetting in association with temporal lobe epilepsy and paraneoplastic encephalitis. *Brain and Cognition*, *35*, 71–84.

Odgen, J. (1996). Marooned in the moment. In J. Odgen (Ed.), *Fractured minds. A case-study approach to clinical neuropsychology* (pp. 41–58). Oxford: Oxford University Press.

Petersen, R. C., Smith, G. E., Waring, S. C., Ivnik, R. J., Tangalos, E. G., & Kokmen, E. (1999). Mild cognitive impairment. Clinical characterization and outcome. *Archives of Neurology*, *56*, 303–308.

Postman, L., & Alpner, T. G. (1946). Retroactive inhibition as a function of the time of interpolation of the inhibitor between learning and recall. *American Journal of Psychology*, *59*, 439–449.

Proust, M. (2004). *Swann's way. In search of lost time*. Harmondsworth: Penguin.

Ribot, T. (1881). *Les Maladies de la mémoire* [Diseases of memory]. New York: Appleton-Century-Crofts.

Ribot, T. (1982). *Diseases of memory: An essay in positive psychology*. London: Kegan Paul, Trench.

Sara, S. J. (2000). Retrieval and reconsolidation: Toward a neurobiology of remembering. *Learning and Memory*, *7*, 73–84.

Scoville, W. B., & Milner, B. (1957). Loss of recent memory after bilateral hippocampal lesions. *Journal of Neurology, Neurosurgery and Psychiatry*, *20*, 11–21.

Shimamura, A. P., Jurica, P. J., Mangels, J. A., Gershberg, F. B., & Knight, R. T. (1995). Susceptibility to memory interference effects following frontal lobe damage: Findings from tests of paired-associate learning. *Journal of Cognitive Neuroscience*, *7*, 144–152.

Spear, N. E., & Riccio, D. C. (1994). *Memory: Phenomena and principles*. Needham Heights, MA: Allyn & Bacon.

Squire, L. R. (1980). Specifying the defect in human amnesia: Storage, retrieval and semantics. *Neuropsycholgia*, *18*, 368–372.

Squire, L. R. (1982). The neuropsychology of human memory. *Annual Review of Neuroscience*, *5*, 241–273.

Squire, L. R. (2006). Lost forever or temporarily misplaced? The long debate about the nature of memory impairment. *Learning & Memory*, *13*, 522–529.

Skaggs, E. B. (1925). Further studies in retroactive inhibition. *Psychological Monographs, Whole No. 161*, 1–60.

Skaggs, E. B. (1933). A discussion on the temporal point of interpolation and degree of retroactive inhibition. *Journal of Comparative Psychology*, *16*, 411–414.

Tulving, E., & Thomson, D. M. (1973). Encoding specificity and retrieval processes in episodic memory. *Psychological Review*, *80*, 352–373.

Warrington, E. K., & Weiskrantz, L. (1970). Amnesic syndrome: Consolidation or retrieval? *Nature*, *288*, 628–630.

Warrington, E. K., & Weiskrantz, L. (1974). The effect of prior learning on subsequent retention in amnesic patients. *Neuropsychologia*, *12*, 419–428.

Warrington, E. K., & Weiskrantz, L. (1978). Further analysis of the prior learning effect in amnesic patients. *Neuropsychologia, 16*, 169–177.
Wilson, B. A. (1987). *Rehabilitation of memory*. New York: Guilford Press.
Wixted, J. T. (2004). The psychology and neuroscience of forgetting. *Annual Review of Psychology*, *55*, 235–269.
Zeman, A. Z. J., Boniface, S., & Hodges, R. (1998). Transient epileptic amnesia: A description of the clinical and neuropsychological features in 10 cases and a review of the literature. *Journal of Neurology, Neurosurgery & Psychiatry*, *64*, 435–443.

10 Accelerated long-term forgetting

Christopher Butler
University of Oxford, Oxford, UK

Nils Muhlert and Adam Zeman
Peninsula Medical School, Plymouth, UK

The study of patients with neurological disease has contributed much to our understanding of human memory. Recently, a novel pattern of forgetting has been described, typically amongst patients with epilepsy, in which information may apparently be learnt and remembered normally at first, but is forgotten at an accelerated rate over subsequent days to weeks. This phenomenon, termed accelerated long-term forgetting (ALF), is clinically important and may provide insights into the mechanisms underlying memory consolidation. Work on ALF is still at an early stage. In this chapter, we introduce the concept with examples from the literature, discuss its clinical and theoretical implications, highlight some important methodological considerations regarding its investigation, and propose avenues for future research.

Descriptions of ALF

The phenomenon of ALF is perhaps best introduced with some descriptions of individual cases. In a recent systematic review (Butler & Zeman, 2008b), we identified nine case reports of patients in whom memory retention after standard delays was considered to be in the normal range (in comparison with published norms or matched control subjects), but in whom testing after extended delays revealed clear impairment. These cases are summarized in Table 10.1. Three examples are described below.

Case 1

We have recently reported the case of a 54-year-old university professor who described difficulty remembering new information for more than a few days (Butler & Zeman, 2008a). On one occasion, for example, he went to the cinema and the following day related his disappointment in the film to his daughter. However, one week later he was no longer able to recall anything of the evening's events. Three weeks after returning from an academic meeting in Milan, he wrote in his journal:

Table 10.1 Individual case studies of accelerated long-term forgetting (ALF)

Authors (year)	*Initials of patient*	*Age*	*Sex*	*Seizures*	*Seizure side*	*Aetiology*	*Structural pathology on brain imaging*	*Non-memory impairment*	*Memory impairment at 30 mins?*	*First delay at which ALF found*	*Remote memory impairment*
Cases											
De Renzi and Lucchelli (1993)	PI	26	M	No	–	Possible hypoxia	None	No	No	15 d	Yes
Kapur et al. (1996)	SP	50	F	GTC	n/d	CHI	Bilat TL	Naming ↓	Recog mem ↓ (mild)	6 wk	Yes
O'Connor et al. (1997)	JT	42	M	CPS	bilat	Paraneoplastic LE	MTL bilat	No	No	24 hr	Yes
Kapur et al. (1997)	PA	62	F	CPS	L	Unknown	L HC (subtle)	No	No	6 wk	Yes
Lucchelli and Spinnler (1998)	GB	65	M	CPS	L	Unknown	No	No	Verbal ↓ (mild)	7 d	Yes
Mayes et al. (2003)	JL	46	F	CHI → CPS	n/d	CHI	Bilat TL; HC normal	Fear perc ↓	Recog mem ↓ (mild)	3 wk	Yes
Manning et al. (2006)	JR	54	M	CPS → GTC	L	HS	L HS (postop)	No	No	30 hr	Yes
Cronel-Ohayon et al. (2007)	JE	18	M	CPS	L	MTL dysplasia	L AG (postop)	No	Yes (mild)	7 d	Yes
Butler and Zeman (2008)	NR	54	M	TEA	L	Unknown	L HC (subtle)	No	No	7 d	Yes

Key: AG = amygdala; ALF = accelerated long-term forgetting; Bilat = bilateral; CHI = closed head injury; CPS = complex partial seizures; GTC = generalized tonic-clonic seizure; HC = hippocampus; HS = hippocampal sclerosis; L = left; LE = limbic encephalitis; (M)TL = (medial) temporal lobe; n/d = not discussed; R = right; TEA = transient epileptic amnesia.

> I remember almost nothing that went on at the meeting . . . I don't remember any of the talks! I am also completely unable to remember anything about the conference banquet, even though I know there must have been a conference banquet somewhere at some point. I mentioned this to [his wife] and she told me that I had described a very elegant restaurant with grape vines as a roof over the outdoor terrace.

In addition to this accelerated forgetting, the patient gradually began to notice that his recollection of many remote, salient, personal events, such as family holidays and weddings from the past 20 to 30 years had become "very sketchy or completely absent".

Over the previous 4 years, he had also experienced a number of episodes of transient amnesia, all of which occurred upon waking and lasted about 30 minutes. Magnetic resonance imaging (MRI) brain imaging was unremarkable, but an electroencephalogram (EEG) revealed epileptiform activity over the left temporal region. During one amnesic attack that persisted over several days, he was admitted to hospital. Magnetic resonance (MR) and positron emission tomography (PET) imaging revealed changes in the left hippocampus, suggestive of an active seizure focus (Figure 10.1a, b). A diagnosis of transient epileptic amnesia (TEA) (see below) was made and the amnesic attacks ceased on anticonvulsant medication. Nevertheless, the patient's interictal memory difficulties persisted. His performance on a variety of standard neuropsychological tests revealed well-preserved anterograde memory for both verbal and nonverbal material over a 30-minute delay, as well as normal language and executive function. However, after an extended interval of 1 week, his recall for a learned story and set of designs was markedly

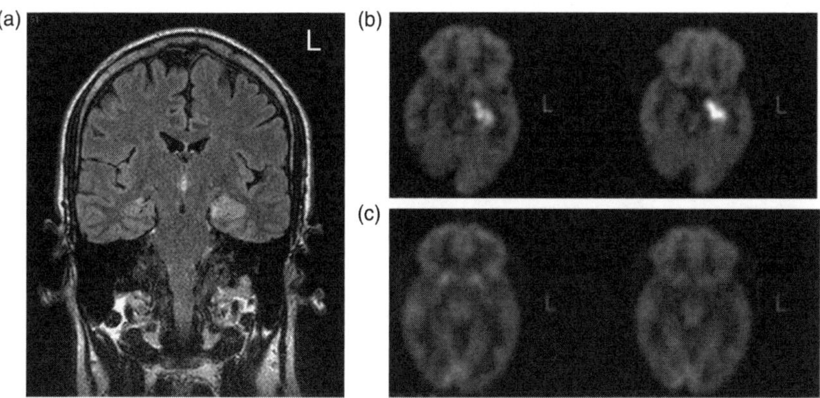

Figure 10.1 (a) FLAIR MRI scanning during a prolonged amnesic episode revealed hyperintensity in the left hippocampus. (b) FDG-PET scanning during the same episode showed hypermetabolism localized to the left anterior hippocampus. (c) This region had returned to normal 1 month later. (Reproduced with the permission of Nature Publishing Group.)

impaired (Figure 10.2). Despite these difficulties, he continued with academic and teaching commitments, publishing 8 papers as first author in the 4 years following the onset of his amnesic attacks, and gaining a promotion from associate to full professor. Nevertheless, he commented:

> My productivity is certainly affected by this, inasmuch as I also have trouble remembering the contents of any papers I've read lately – or even papers that I have written! Reading my own work has become a lot like reading someone else's work, and I waste a good deal of time going back over the same ground.

Repeat neuroimaging revealed mild atrophy restricted to the left hippocampus, but was otherwise unremarkable.

Case 2

O'Connor and colleagues (Ahern et al., 1994; O'Connor, Sieggreen, Ahern, Schomer, & Mesulam, 1997) report the case of a 42-year-old man, JT, with paraneoplastic limbic encephalitis secondary to a testicular neoplasm. His initial presentation was with memory problems, but he soon developed symptoms of focal epilepsy including brief periods of unresponsiveness, olfactory hallucinations, oro-alimentary automatisms, and transient anxiety attacks. EEG revealed bitemporal epileptiform discharges, and serial MRI demonstrated progressive T2 high signal and atrophy in the antero-medial temporal lobes bilaterally. JT had dramatically accelerated forgetting of recent events, including the death of a close friend. His performance on standard tests of intelligence, memory, attention, language, and visuospatial perception was excellent. However, when taught a list of words to 100% accuracy, his ability to recall them declined rapidly between 2 and 24 hours later, following a number of witnessed seizures. His performance on the same test was greatly improved, although still not to the level of a control subject, when his seizures were partially treated by paraldehyde. JT also had evidence of a patchy loss of autobiographical memories and amnesia for public events from across his life span.

Case 3

Mayes, Isaac, Holdstock, Cariga, Gummer, and Roberts (2003) describe the case of JL, a 46-year-old woman, whose memory trouble began at the age of 18 when she developed temporal lobe epilepsy (TLE) following a closed head injury. She experienced 20 to 30 complex partial seizures per month despite treatment with two anticonvulsants. MRI scanning revealed bilateral damage to the anterolateral temporal lobes, more pronounced in the left hemisphere, as well as to the right amygdala, perirhinal and orbitofrontal cortices. JL's full-scale intelligence quotient (IQ) was 122. Performance on a wide

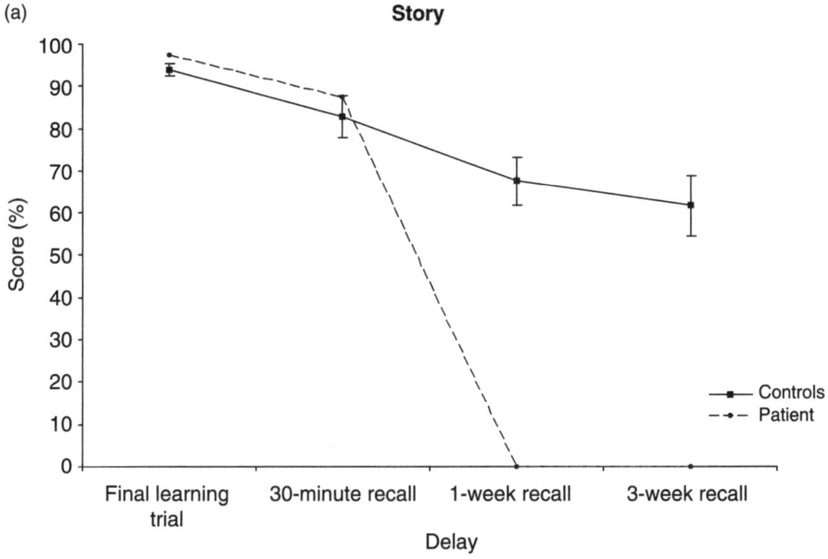

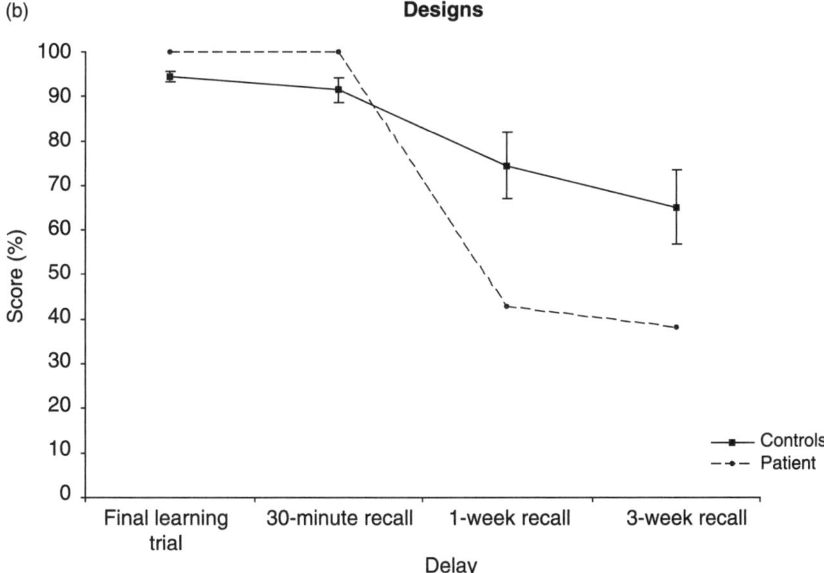

Figure 10.2 The patient's long-term recall of a learned **(a)** story and **(b)** set of designs is shown compared to performance of 24 healthy control subjects. Despite normal learning and 30-minute retention, he demonstrates accelerated forgetting over longer intervals.

range of standard neuropsychological tests was normal, save some subtle impairment on difficult visual recognition memory tasks. Recall and recognition of verbal and visual material, not learned to criterion, was within the normal range at delays of 20 seconds and 30 minutes but grossly impaired at 3 weeks. In addition, several tests revealed impairment in JL's autobiographical memory for events that occurred during both the pre- and post-morbid periods.

Definition

In this chapter, we use the term accelerated long-term forgetting (ALF) to describe the phenomenon in which forgetting over extended intervals is disproportionate to that observed over standard neuropsychological testing delays of up to 30 minutes (henceforth "standard delays"). The precise definition of what is "disproportionate" in this context remains to be established. In some cases, particularly those in which memory at standard delays is clearly normal, the demonstration of ALF is relatively uncontroversial. However, the situation may be less straightforward when patients already show some impairment at standard delays. It is possible that ALF is neurologically and cognitively heterogeneous. Therefore, as will become clear in what follows, refinement of the concept is likely to be required, especially if it is to be applied in research studies involving larger groups of subjects.

Other authors have referred to the phenomenon in question as long-term amnesia (LTA) (Kapur, Millar, Colbourn, Abbott, Kennedy, & Docherty, 1997; Kapur, Scholey, Moore, Barker, Brice, & Thompson, 1996; Mayes et al., 2003) or accelerated forgetting (Bell & Giovagnoli, 2007; Blake, Wroe, Breen, & McCarthy, 2000). Our adoption of the term ALF is intended to distinguish the disorder from the amnesic syndrome and to include cases in which long-term memory may be deficient but not completely absent. Furthermore, the term ALF acknowledges that clinically there is, and mechanistically there may be, a distinction between this type of forgetting and the rapid early forgetting that occurs in other neurological conditions.

Characteristics of ALF

A number of features stand out in the cases of ALF listed in Table 10.1. Of the nine patients, all but one (De Renzi & Lucchelli, 1993) had TLE. Where pathology was visible on brain imaging, it was restricted to the temporal lobes in all cases but one (Mayes et al., 2003), in which the right orbitofrontal cortex was also affected. Neuropsychological testing using standard instruments revealed normal or near normal performance in both memory and nonmemory domains in all patients. However, in addition to ALF, all patients showed disruption of remote memory, often for events that occurred many years prior to the onset of their memory difficulties. In striking contrast with classically amnesic individuals, these patients maintained active, independent lives and several remained in employment. These cases raise interesting questions of both clinical and theoretical importance:

- What is the best way of detecting ALF?
- What types of memory does it affect?
- Over what timescale does it occur?
- Does ALF occur only among patients with epilepsy or also in other types of neurological disorder?
- Can it help to explain why many patients with epilepsy complain of poor memory despite performing well on standard neuropsychological tests?
- In patients with epilepsy, is it primarily due to seizure activity, whether clinical or subclinical, or to the underlying structural pathology?
- Does it respond to treatment with anticonvulsant medication?
- Does the fundamental cognitive problem occur at the time of memory acquisition or during subsequent memory processing?
- If the latter, what can ALF teach us about mechanisms of long-term memory consolidation?

Firm answers to most of these questions are, as yet, unavailable. However, the investigation of ALF is gaining momentum: besides the 9 case reports listed in Table 10.1, a further 11 studies have examined very long-term anterograde memory in neurological patients at a group level (see Table 10.2). These studies have been reviewed in depth in two recent publications (Bell & Giovagnoli, 2007; Butler & Zeman, 2008b).

Timescale

Given the current lack of knowledge about the timescale of ALF, investigators have chosen the delay at which to assess very long-term forgetting pragmatically – e.g., to coincide with follow-up clinic appointments (Blake et al., 2000) – or after a period deemed long enough for memory consolidation to take place (Mameniskiene, Jatuzis, Kaubrys, & Budrys, 2006). Thus the intervals have ranged from 24 hours (Bell et al., 2005; Holdstock, Mayes, Isaac, Gong, & Roberts, 2002; Martin, Loring, Meador, Lee, Thrash, & Arena, 1991; O'Connor et al., 1997) to 8 weeks (Blake et al., 2000). The rate of ALF appears to differ across these studies. In certain case reports, memory was normal after delays of up to 4 hours (De Renzi & Lucchelli, 1993) and even 24 hours (Holdstock et al., 2002; Lucchelli & Spinnler, 1998), whilst these same patients showed impaired memory following delays of 1 week (Lucchelli & Spinnler, 1998), 13 days (De Renzi & Lucchelli, 1993), or 3 weeks (Holdstock et al., 2002). In contrast to the patients described by Lucchelli and Spinnler (1998) and Holdstock et al. (2002), O'Connor et al. (1997) report the case of a patient who demonstrated accelerated forgetting over a 24-hour delay after experiencing several seizures. The group studies have also demonstrated ALF after a variety of delays including 24 hours (Martin et al., 1991), 1 week

Table 10.2 Group studies of accelerated long-term forgetting (ALF) in patients with epilepsy

Authors (year)	*Number of patients*	*Age mean (SD)*	*Sex ratio*	*Seizure type*	*Seizure lateralization*	*Structural pathology on brain imaging*	*Non-memory impairment*	*Memory impairment at 30 min?*	*First long delay (ALF found?)*	*Remote memory impairment*
Series										
Martin et al. (1991)	21	31 (7.5)	10 M	TLE	13 L; 8 R	6 postop	IQ ↓	No	24 hr (+)	n/d
Giovagnoli et al. (1995)	24	38 (11.6)	14 M	TLE	12 L; 12 R	No	No	No	2 wk (–)	n/d
Helmstaedter et al. (1998)	55	27	27 M	TLE	28 L; 27 R	45 TL lesion	IQ ↓	Yes	1 wk (+)	n/d
Blake et al. (2000)	21	34 (8.7)	7 M	14 TLE; 7 other	11 L; 10 R	HS 5/14	No	No	8 wk (+)	n/d
Bell et al. (2005)	42	37 (11.4)	14 M	TLE	22 L; 20 R	No	IQ ↓	Yes	24 hr (–)	n/d
Bell (2006)	25	39 (10.0)	10 M	TLE	11 L; 6 R; 2 B	6 postop	IQ ↓	Yes	2 wk (–)	n/d
Manes et al. (2005)	7	57 (8.1)	6 M	TEA	n/d	No	No	No	6 wk (+)	yes
Mameniskiene et al. (2006)	70	33 (9.5)	29 M	TLE	n/d	11 TL lesion	n/d	Yes	4 wk (+)	n/d
Butler et al. (2007)	24	68 (8.7)	14 M	TEA	n/d	No	No	No	1 wk (+)	yes
Davidson et al. (2007)	21	11.5	7 M	IGE	–	n/d	No	No	1 wk (+)	n/d

Key: ALF = accelerated long-term forgetting; B = bilateral; HS = hippocampal sclerosis; IGE = idiopathic generalized epilepsy; IQ = intelligence quotient; L = left; n/d = not discussed; R = right; SD = standard deviation; TEA = transient epileptic amnesia; TL = temporal lobe; TLE = temporal lobe epilepsy; + = ALF detected; – = ALF not detected.

(Butler, Graham, Hodges, Kapur, Wardlaw, & Zeman, 2007), 4 weeks (Mameniskiene et al., 2006), and 8 weeks (Blake et al., 2000).

The use of a single very long-term delay does not give much information about forgetting rates. In order to define the forgetting curve in ALF, multiple probes are needed. In a study of patients with TEA, Butler et al. (2007) assessed forgetting following delays of 30 minutes, 1 week and 3 weeks. While patients who reported memory difficulties were performing near floor at the 3-week delay, the greatest forgetting was seen between 30 minutes and 1 week. In summary, although there appears to be some variability in the degree of forgetting reported over a 24-hour interval, ALF is generally identified over delays of 1 to several weeks. It is possible that the rate at which ALF occurs varies according to, *inter alia*, the underlying pathology, its severity, and the type of material used in the memory test. Future research using multiple delays to assess ALF may provide a more accurate indication of the timescale of ALF.

Types of memory affected

ALF can affect declarative memory for both verbal and nonverbal material. It has been identified using list learning tests, story recall, story recognition, complex figure recall, complex figure recognition, visual design recall, visual design recognition, and word position tests. Two group studies of patients with epilepsy have found ALF for both verbal and nonverbal material (Butler, Graham, Hodges, Kapur, Wardlaw, & Zeman, 2007; Mameniskiene, Jatuzis, Kaubrys, & Budrys, 2006). As with other forms of memory impairment in epilepsy (Hermann, Seidenberg, Schoenfeld, & Davies, 1997), ALF may differentially affect memory for verbal and nonverbal material according to the laterality of pathology. For example, Blake et al. (2000) found ALF for verbal material only amongst patients with a left-sided seizure focus. Jokeit, Daamen, Zang, Janszky, and Ebner (2001) investigated a group of patients undergoing videotelemetry for presurgical evaluation of TLE, and found that forgetting of word position over a 24-hour period was accelerated only amongst patients who experienced a seizure of left-hemisphere onset during the test interval.

Several studies have investigated whether ALF affects both recall and recognition memory. Most found ALF for both, across a range of study materials including a story (Blake et al., 2000; Kapur et al., 1997; Manes, Graham, Zeman, de Lujan Calcagno, & Hodges, 2005; Mayes et al., 2003), a complex figure (Mayes et al., 2003), and a series of visual designs (Kapur et al., 1997). Although one study found evidence for ALF on recall but not recognition of a word list (Martin et al., 1991), the general finding that recall and recognition can be affected by ALF suggests that memories may be lost, rather than being difficult to retrieve.

To date, there is no clear evidence regarding whether or not ALF may also affect nondeclarative memories. None of the studies listed in Tables 10.1 or

10.2 examined procedural memory, priming or conditioned response memory. The apparent link to temporal lobe pathology in the majority of these cases suggests that delayed nondeclarative memory retention should be intact.

It is striking that, in addition to their ALF, all the patients listed in Table 10.1 also showed impairment of memory for remote events, and often for events that occurred many years before the apparent onset of their memory disturbance. This retrograde amnesia may be patchy or affect all life periods equally, rather than showing the temporal gradient usually found after damage to the medial temporal lobes (Squire, 1997). Such impairment has also been demonstrated at the group level in patients with TEA (Butler et al., 2007; Manes et al., 2005). The relationship between ALF and remote memory impairment remains unclear. Kopelman (1985) has suggested that the amnesia for very remote autobiographical events seen in patients with TEA may reflect long-standing impairment of anterograde memory due to subclinical seizure activity predating the clinical onset of epilepsy. This hypothesis is yet to be formally tested, but does not explain why patients should lose memories which they clearly once possessed (as attested by witnesses). It also cannot explain remote memory impairment in cases of ALF resulting from a clear pathological insult, such as that described by Kapur et al. (1996). Even if ALF does not directly cause the extensive, apparently retrograde amnesia with which it is often associated, the two may have a common pathophysiological origin that results in selective disruption of very long-term memory traces. Elucidation of the causes of ALF and remote memory impairment may shed light on theoretical models of human memory.

In what clinical contexts does ALF occur?

The high prevalence of epilepsy amongst the case reports listed in Table 10.1 prompts the question of whether there is a general association of ALF with epilepsy or certain subtypes of epilepsy. The studies that have investigated this issue (see Table 10.2) have not produced entirely consistent results. For example, as detailed below, some have found ALF in TLE and others have not. This heterogeneity is likely to derive, at least in part, from differences in the way of defining ALF, the patient populations studied, and the neuropsychological methods used. Methodological issues related to the investigation of ALF are explored in the penultimate section of this chapter and in Butler and Zeman (2008b).

Seven studies have investigated patients with "typical" TLE, that is, temporal lobe seizures that begin in the first two or three decades of life, are not due to any clear-cut episode of brain injury, and are not associated with structural pathology other than, in some cases, hippocampal sclerosis. Of these studies, four (Blake et al., 2000; Helmstaedter, Hauff, & Elger, 1998; Mameniskiene et al., 2006; Martin et al., 1991) found evidence of ALF and three (Bell, 2006; Bell et al., 2005; Giovagnoli, Casazza, & Avanzini, 1995) did not. Bell (2006) notes that those studies which have demonstrated ALF in

TLE have either used "atypical" memory tests, specifically ones that involve numerous presentations of the test material, or tested "atypical" patients, that is patients with onset of TLE in later life or as a result of a clear pathological insult. All the case reports of ALF fall into this latter camp. Bell claims that, in patients with "typical" TLE, standard memory tests over standard intervals are sufficient to demonstrate impairment when present, and that no accelerated forgetting of the material occurs over longer delays of up to two weeks. However, there are methodological problems with studies on both sides of the debate and the issue of whether ALF occurs widely in TLE is not yet resolved.

Two studies (Butler et al., 2007; Manes et al., 2005) have focused upon TEA, a form of TLE in which complaints of ALF are particularly common. In TEA, the principal manifestation of seizures is recurrent episodes of isolated amnesia. These episodes typically begin in middle to old age, are relatively brief, often occur upon waking, and usually respond well to anticonvulsant medication. Case 1, described at the start of the chapter, illustrates the principal features of TEA. Patients with TEA generally perform in the normal range on standard tests of memory, but show ALF over delays of 1 to 8 weeks.

One study examined long-term forgetting in children with idiopathic generalized epilepsy (IGE; Davidson, Dorris, O'Regan, & Zuberi, 2007). Compared with controls, patients showed impairment of recall for a story after a delay of 1 week, despite having normal recall at 30 minutes. No recognition memory deficit was found. Importantly, patients took more trials to reach the learning criterion, and controlling for this abolished the long-term recall differences. Davidson and colleagues conclude that ALF in IGE is due to an impairment of memory encoding that renders long-term retrieval processes less effective.

Does ALF occur outwith the context of epilepsy? There is very little evidence either way. Several studies have demonstrated a similar phenomenon in patients undergoing electroconvulsive therapy (ECT) for treatment of depression (Lewis & Kopelman, 1998; Squire, 1981). However, ECT involves causing brief, generalized, seizure-like brain activity with externally applied electrodes, so the associated ALF may be caused by the same mechanisms as in epilepsy. One study (Manes et al., 2008) has found evidence of ALF over a 6-week delay in a small group of older patients with subjective complaints of memory dysfunction but no evidence of impairment at standard delays. The authors raise the possibility that ALF might, in some cases, reflect mild damage to memory systems outside the medial temporal lobes, such as the retrosplenial cortex, and be a harbinger of neurodegenerative disease. This idea needs to be tested in larger groups of patients.

Clinical relevance of ALF

If ALF does occur more widely in neurological disease than in a few isolated cases, there are some important clinical implications. ALF may help to explain complaints of poor memory in patients who perform normally on standard memory tests, which typically assess retention of information over delays of up to 30 minutes. This mismatch between subjective and objective memory performance is common in TLE. It is often thought to be due to an alteration of the perception of memory performance resulting from anxiety or depression (Elixhauser, Leidy, Meador, Means, & Willian, 1999; Piazzini, Canevini, Maggiori, & Canger, 2001). However, it remains possible that the patient is detecting real memory failures that are invisible to standard neuropsychological instruments. There is some evidence to suggest that this may be the case. In the group of TLE patients studied by Blake et al. (2000), subjective memory ratings correlated with very long-term forgetting rates. In TEA, patients' perception of everyday memory failures is unrelated to memory performance at standard delays, but correlates independently with mood and recall at a 3-week delay (Butler et al., 2009).

The possibility that ALF may be treatable is a second clinically important issue. A few reports suggest that, in patients with epilepsy, ALF may respond to anticonvulsant medication, at least partially (O'Connor et al., 1997). Temporal lobectomy in patients with medically refractory epilepsy has also been shown to improve certain types of memory function (Voltzenlogel, Despres, Vignal, Kehrli, & Manning, 2007), although ALF has not been investigated in this context. However, anticonvulsant therapy, at least at doses intended to maximize seizure control, does not abolish ALF: the patients with TEA studied by Butler et al. (2007) showed ALF despite abolition of their seizures by medication. Prospective treatment trials are necessary to address this important clinical question. These would be facilitated by the development of standardized neuropsychological tests capable of detecting ALF.

The pathophysiology of ALF

Several mechanisms may be hypothesized to underlie ALF: (1) clinical or subclinical seizure activity; (2) structural brain pathology; (3) an adverse effect of anticonvulsant medication; (4) psychological mechanisms.

Seizures

Patients with TEA sometimes report that seizures "wipe out" memories of preceding events, and feel that their memory abilities improve once seizures are controlled with anticonvulsant therapy. O'Connor et al. (1997) document such an improvement in a single case of temporal lobe epilepsy. Mameniskiene et al. (2006) found a positive correlation between long-term forgetting and both (1) manifest seizures during the experimental period; and (2) subclinical epileptiform EEG activity. Importantly, however, ALF may be documented even once overt seizures have been completely controlled with medication (Butler et al., 2007).

In a study directly addressing the question of whether incident seizures accelerate forgetting, Bergin, Thompson, Fish, and Shorvon (1995) tested immediate, 30-minute and 48-hour memory for verbal and nonverbal material in 58 patients undergoing videotelemetry for the investigation of medically refractory partial seizures. No difference was found in long-term forgetting between patients who did and did not have seizures during the study period. This important result does not, however, rule out a negative influence of seizures upon anterograde memory. Features such as the timing, duration, and anatomical focus of seizures may play an important role. Jokeit et al. (2001) examined memory over 24 hours for verbal material in a small group of patients (n = 10) undergoing videotelemetry. They found a difference in long-term recall between days with and without seizures, but this was restricted to the group of patients with a left temporal lobe seizure focus. A further source of evidence comes from studies that document an improvement in verbal memory scores in patients following right temporal lobectomy (Martin et al., 1998; Novelly et al., 1984). This finding suggests that a seizure focus in one hippocampus can negatively affect function in distant brain regions.

As mentioned above, the question of whether transient impairment of neuronal function can disrupt very long-term memory has also been addressed in patients undergoing ECT for depression, a procedure known to induce anterograde and retrograde amnesia. Squire (1981) investigated recognition memory for pictures and sentences at intervals of 10 minutes, 30 minutes and 30 hours in patients on 2 occasions: 2 hours and 4 months after ECT. The subjects therefore acted as their own controls. Initial acquisition was matched by using longer stimulus presentation on the earlier occasion. Picture forgetting was significantly more rapid when the subjects had recently received ECT. On the other hand, patients with diencephalic amnesia (Korsakoff's syndrome) and a patient with chronic medial temporal lobe amnesia did not show accelerated forgetting when initial acquisition was matched to a group of healthy control subjects. These findings were replicated and extended by Lewis and Kopelman (1998), who included a group of depressed patients not undergoing ECT. Accelerated forgetting was again found solely in the post-ECT group and could therefore not be attributed to depression per se. Transient impairment of brain function also underlies post-traumatic amnesia (PTA). Levin, High, and Eisenberg (1988), investigating recognition memory for photographs, found accelerated forgetting over 32 hours in head injury patients in PTA, compared with head injury patients who had recovered from PTA.

Structural brain pathology

Structural damage or hypometabolism within the temporal lobes was present in all but one (Lucchelli & Spinnler, 1998) of the published cases of ALF. This raises the possibility that temporal lobe damage alone may sometimes account for ALF. In contrast, many of the group studies found ALF in patients with no obvious lesions on MRI. Neuroimaging evidence of structural lesions was found in 3 of the 9 patients with left TLE who showed ALF in Blake et al. (2000); 11 of the 70 patients who showed ALF in Mameniskiene et al. (2006); 3 of the 10 patients with ALF in Manes et al. (2005); and none of the 24 patients who showed ALF in Butler et al. (2007). In sum, of the 113 patients with ALF and structural neuroimaging included in these group studies, only 17 had identifiable structural brain abnormalities. We have recently used manual and automated volumetric MRI techniques in a large group of patients with TEA to investigate the neural basis of ALF (Butler et al., 2009). Whilst patients showed subtle hippocampal volume loss compared with controls, and this loss correlated with memory performance across standard delays, no correlation was observed between grey matter volumes in the hippocampus or any other brain region and very long-term forgetting. The evidence from group studies, therefore, in support of a role for structural pathology in causing ALF is, thus far, relatively weak.

It is possible that the imaging methods used are insufficiently sensitive to detect the relevant structural abnormalities. In TLE, diffusion tensor imaging has been used to demonstrate reduced functional connectivity within the parahippocampal gyrus ipsilateral to the seizure focus (Yogarajah et al., 2008). MR spectroscopy shows loss of neuronal integrity within the hippocampus (Sawrie, Martin, Knowlton, Faught, Gilliam, & Kuzniecky, 2001) and throughout the brain (e.g., Mueller et al., 2002). These techniques can reveal pathology in tissue which otherwise appears normal, and may offer better correlations with memory performance than volume measurements (Sawrie et al., 2001). Their application in patients with ALF may, therefore, uncover more subtle, correlated structural abnormalities.

Some authors have questioned whether ALF represents a "mild" form of the amnesic syndrome typically associated with severe damage to the medial temporal lobes (Mayes et al., 2003). If so, one would predict that forgetting should be dramatically accelerated in amnesic patients. A number of studies have addressed this issue and results have been mixed (see Isaac & Mayes, 1999a for a review). One early investigation suggested that accelerated forgetting was a feature of amnesia caused by medial temporal lobe lesions but not diencephalic lesions (Huppert & Piercy, 1979). However, this finding was later found not to be replicable (Freed, Corkin, & Cohen, 1987). Isaac and Mayes (1999a, 1999b) conclude that forgetting in the amnesic syndrome is accelerated over the first 10 minutes but only for certain types of material – specifically free recall of prose and semantically related words. They interpret this as reflecting impairment of early consolidation processes due to medial temporal lobe damage. Beyond 10 minutes, forgetting rates have been measured in patients with anoxic brain damage (McKee & Squire, 1992), Alzheimer's disease (Kopelman, 1985) and head injury after recovery from post-traumatic amnesia (Levin et al., 1988), and have been found to be normal. Accelerated forgetting over longer periods has been reported in healthy older subjects by some authors (Davis, Small, Stern, Mayeux, Feldstein, &

Keller, 2003; Huppert & Kopelman, 1989), but not others (Petersen, Smith, Kokmen, Ivnik, & Tangalos, 1992).

If ALF is essentially due to a mild form of hippocampal amnesia, one might also predict a subtle degree of memory impairment over standard testing intervals. The observation that some patients perform normally on standard tests yet exhibit ALF appears to argue against the existence of any defect in acquisition and initial retention of declarative memories. It could be, however, that standard tests are insufficiently sensitive, and that more detailed neuropsychological testing may uncover a mild deficit in these stages of memory processing.

Anticonvulsant medication

There is good evidence that antiepileptic drugs (AEDs) can have a negative impact upon cognition, although the field is fraught with methodological difficulties (Kwan & Brodie, 2001; Motamedi & Meador, 2004). The most commonly observed effects are slowed mental processing and reduced attention, and these are most marked with high doses and polytherapy. However, a specific impact on memory has been reported in several studies. Some newer drugs may have a better cognitive profile (Motamedi & Meador, 2003). The specific question of whether anticonvulsants can accelerate shorter-term forgetting has been addressed in a single, retrospective study (Jokeit, Kramer, & Ebner, 2005). Amongst 162 patients with medically refractory epilepsy, higher serum levels of AED were associated with greater forgetting of both verbal and visual material over a 30-minute delay after controlling for potentially confounding variables such as IQ, age, duration of epilepsy, and seizure frequency.

Whilst it remains possible that the ALF observed in some studies reviewed above is a direct result of treatment with anticonvulsants, it seems unlikely to be the sole cause for a number of reasons: first, patients with TEA complain of ALF prior to initiation of therapy; second, patients with TEA usually report that their memory improves once treatment is started (Butler et al., 2007; Zeman, Boniface, & Hodges, 1998); third, the forgetting observed by Blake et al. (2000) was specific to the group of patients with left temporal lobe epilepsy; and fourth, the doses of anticonvulsants used in TEA patients, those who complain most profoundly of ALF, are generally low.

Psychosocial factors

Markowitsch, Kessler, Kalbe, and Herholz (1999) describe the interesting case of a patient who developed a severe and focal anterograde memory deficit following a whiplash injury, despite no evidence of brain injury on detailed neuroimaging. Immediate recall was normal for a variety of material types, but recall performance declined rapidly and was at floor after a delay of 2 hours. The patient's amnesia is described as "functional", and suggests that an apparent consolidation deficit may, in some cases, be a result of psychogenic mechanisms. As mentioned above, the disparity between subjective reports of memory difficulty amongst patients with epilepsy and their performance on neuropsychological tests (Corcoran & Thompson, 1992) has been attributed to disturbances of mood and poor self-esteem (Elixhauser et al., 1999; Giovagnoli et al., 1997). It is undoubtedly important to take such factors into account when investigating cognitive function in epilepsy. However, they are unlikely to play a major causal role in ALF. Three studies (Blake et al., 2000; Butler et al., 2007; Mameniskiene et al., 2006) assessed mood using the Hospital Anxiety and Depression Scale and found no correlation with very long-term memory performance. Furthermore, Lewis and Kopelman (1998) did not find accelerated forgetting in a group of depressed patients.

In conclusion, the pathophysiological origins of ALF are, as yet, unknown. Structural abnormalities, seizure activity, and even other forms of neural disturbance may act together to produce the phenomenon. Future work using electrophysiology, neuroimaging, and therapeutic interventions will help to clarify the situation.

ALF in relation to theoretical models of memory and memory consolidation

The combination of normal or near normal performance on standard memory tests which probe recall or recognition at around 30 minutes and markedly impaired performance at longer delays suggests that patients with ALF have a disorder of memory consolidation rather than memory acquisition. While the possibility that there may be a subtle disorder of acquisition in patients with ALF – such that the memories formed are abnormally fragile – requires further investigation, we shall assume in this theoretical section that ALF opens a window on to processes underlying long-term memory consolidation.

The concept of long-term memory consolidation originated from observations of a temporal gradient in retrograde amnesia following a discrete episode of brain injury (Ribot, 1882). Older memories appear resistant to disruption, particularly in the context of medial temporal lobe damage. This resistance is thought to be conferred by a process of "slow" or "systems" consolidation, the neurobiological details of which are debated. According to what has become known as the "standard theory of consolidation" (e.g., Alvarez & Squire, 1994), memories are dependent upon the MTL in the initial stages after learning, but their traces are gradually reorganized over time to become supported entirely by the neocortex. Accordingly, synaptic plasticity in the hippocampus has been shown to support rapid, one-trial learning (e.g., McNaughton & Morris, 1987), whereas learning in the neocortex is slower. Computational studies have demonstrated the adaptive advantages of this system, which allows regularities in the environment that are repeatedly experienced to be incorporated into existing knowledge in a way that prevents existing memory traces from being destabilized by new learning (McClelland & McNaughton, 1995).

Over the past decade, the standard theory of consolidation has faced a sustained challenge from proponents of the alternative multiple trace theory (MTT; Moscovitch & Nadel, 1998; Moscovitch, Nadel, Winocur, Gilboa, & Rosenbaum, 2006; Nadel & Moscovitch, 1997). This theory is particularly concerned with "episodic" memories – memories for unique, personally experienced events that are embedded in a specific spatial and temporal context, and whose recollection is associated with a feeling of reliving the past or "autonoetic consciousness" (Tulving, 2002; Wheeler, Stuss, & Tulving, 1997). The originators of the MTT were motivated by observations that, in some patients, highly focal hippocampal damage may result in a retrograde loss of episodic memories that extends back over decades or even across the entire life span. The MTT proposes that the hippocampus never relinquishes its role in the storage of an episodic memory trace. Furthermore, each time an episodic memory is retrieved, it is subsequently re-encoded, leading to the establishment of multiple traces mediated by hippocampal-neocortical neural ensembles. Older, often recollected memories will therefore be more likely to survive partial hippocampal damage, a consequence that could explain the temporal gradient seen in some amnesic patients. With regard to semantic memories, free of temporal and spatial specificity and not associated with autonoetic consciousness, the MTT is in accord with the standard theory: through as yet undefined processes of consolidation, semantic memory traces gradually come to be supported solely by the neocortex.

As with neuropsychological studies, the evidence for hippocampal involvement in recent and remote memories from functional neuroimaging studies is mixed. Some studies find increased hippocampal activity for recent but not remote episodic memories (Fink, Markowitsch, Reinkemeier, Bruckbauer, Kessler, & Heiss, 1995; Piefke, Weiss, Zilles, Markowitsch, & Fink, 2003), in line with the standard model, whereas others find hippocampal activations regardless of memory age (Gilboa, Winocur, Grady, Hevenor & Moscovitch, 2004; Maguire, Henson, Mummery & Frith, 2001; Maguire & Frith, 2003; Piolino, Giffard-Quillon, Desgranges, Che'telat, Baron, & Eustache, 2004; Rekkas & Constable, 2005).

When assessing both episodic and semantic memories, it is difficult to ensure that older memories and more recent memories are matched for personal significance and vividness (Addis, Moscovitch, Crawley, & McAndrews, 2004). Thus, the validity of retrospective memory tests can be affected by the unregulated nature of memorable events. Some studies have attempted to control for these confounds by presenting stimuli to participants and measuring activity after varying long-term delays. Although this is unfeasible over delays of decades, studies have assessed changes in patterns of activation over delays of days and months.

Takashima et al. (2006) presented participants with 320 pictures and assessed recognition for those pictures after 1 day, 2 days, 1 month, and

3 months. They found evidence for decreasing hippocampal activity as time passed after learning. A previous study had found no evidence for changes in MTL activity when participants were recognizing pictures presented 30 minutes, 1 day or 1 week prior to scanning (Stark & Squire, 2000). In contrast, other studies have reported greater hippocampal activity when participants recognize word pairs that were learned 1 day compared with 10 minutes before scanning (Bosshardt et al., 2005a), as well as 1 month compared with 1 day before scanning (Bosshardt et al., 2005b). Bosshardt and colleagues interpreted their findings as supporting the MTT, with increased hippocampal activity over time reflecting the proliferation of memory traces during consolidation. Squire and Bayley (2007), however, argue that the current evidence is in keeping with the standard model of consolidation.

The phenomenon of ALF has the potential to provide new insights into slow consolidation in long-term memory systems. Importantly, ALF allows slow consolidation to be investigated in an anterograde fashion, allowing greater experimental control than traditional methods.

ALF may result from structural damage or from the interfering effects of abnormal electrical activity caused by seizure activity. If structural damage causes ALF, then this would suggest that the damaged regions are necessary for consolidation to occur. In contrast, if seizures cause ALF, then this may indicate that seizure activity in particular areas of the brain can lead to erasure of consolidated memories, or disruption of ongoing consolidation processes.

As discussed earlier, ALF has been reported following damage both to the medial temporal lobes (Kapur et al., 1997) and to the neocortex of the anterior and lateral temporal lobes (Mayes et al., 2003). ALF resulting from medial temporal damage can be accounted for either by the standard model of consolidation or by the MTT, as both models predict that the MTL is initially involved in the support and retrieval of long-term memories. Although the standard model predicts that the neocortex becomes capable of supporting and retrieving memories independently of the MTL, this process is thought to take many months or years. Were ALF to result from neocortical damage, however, it would pose a challenge to the MTT, as this model does not predict a gradual transfer of information to the neocortex over time.

In animals, patterns of memory loss similar to those seen in ALF can be observed following damage to particular brain structures. Remondes and Schuman (2004) found that rats who received lesions to hippocampal inputs following training on a spatial memory task demonstrated normal spatial memory following a delay of 24 hours, but impaired spatial memory following a delay of 4 weeks. Similar patterns of forgetting have been reported in transgenic rats with abnormal neocortical plasticity (Hayashi et al., 2004). Furthermore, the timescale over which memory loss occurs appears to differ following disruption of specific temporal lobe structures. For instance, blocking NMDA glutamate receptors in rats can cause amnesia for a training episode (Izquierdo & Medina, 1995). Administration of substances to the hippocampus or amygdala causes amnesia for that task when given immediately after training, but not 90 minutes after training, whereas administration to the entorhinal cortex causes amnesia when given between 90 and 180 minutes after training, but not immediately after or 360 minutes after training (Ferreira, Da Silva, Medina, & Izquierdo, 1992). As well as indicating the time-limited roles in memory consolidation of specific structures, these studies suggest that ALF might result from damage outwith the hippocampus.

These animal studies may also help to account for differences in the timescale of ALF. As discussed earlier, some studies found evidence for ALF over a 24-hour delay (Martin et al., 1991; O'Connor et al., 1997), whereas others found intact memory at 24 hours, but impaired memory over longer delays (Holdstock et al., 2002; Lucchelli & Spinnler, 1998). Hippocampal volume loss has been found to correlate with memory deficits over 30-minute delays (e.g., Baxendale et al., 1998), but not 1-week delays (Butler et al., 2009). The timescale of ALF may therefore relate to structural damage on a hippocampal-neocortical axis, with damage closer to the hippocampus causing memory loss over delays of 24 hours, whereas damage close to or within anterolateral neocortical structures leads to forgetting over longer delays (e.g., Holdstock et al., 2002). Future work with sensitive MRI techniques may help to explore this possibility.

ALF and sleep

The close association between amnesic attacks and waking in TEA raises the intriguing question of whether subclinical, nocturnal epileptiform activity might disturb sleep-dependent memory consolidation processes (Ellenbogen, Hulbert, Stickgold, Dinges, & Thompson-Schill, 2006; Walker, 2005; Walker & Stickgold, 2006).

Sleep has been linked to the consolidation and enhancement of memories, although this topic remains controversial. As many patients with TEA have episodes of amnesia upon awakening (Butler et al., 2007), sleep processes may also be abnormal. Consolidation of declarative memories in particular has been shown to depend upon deeper stages of sleep (slow-wave sleep, SWS; Stickgold & Walker, 2005). Peigneux et al. (2004) provide evidence for the link between SWS sleep and declarative memory consolidation. They trained healthy participants on a spatial memory task and then measured regional cerebral blood flow while they slept in a PET scanner. Post-sleep improvement on the task correlated with the amount of hippocampal and parahippocampal activity during SWS sleep. In some cases, improvements in memory can be identified even following short sleep periods. Tucker, Hirota, Wamsley, Lau, Chaklader, and Fishbein (2006) presented two groups of participants with a set of paired associates. One group was allowed a short nap after seeing the pictures, whereas the second group spent the same period in quiet rest. When tested after these delays, participants who had slept recalled significantly more word pairs than the rest group. These results suggest a link between brain processes that occur during sleep and consolidation over long delays.

It is not yet known whether sleep processes are disrupted in patients with ALF. Impaired consolidation has been demonstrated in patients with reductions in the amount of delta wave activity during sleep (Göder et al., 2004) and in healthy participants after inducing abnormalities in acetylcholine levels (Gais & Born, 2004). Consolidation may also be affected by cortisol levels during sleep (see Payne & Nadel, 2008). Exploration of these processes in patients with ALF could help to clarify the contribution of sleep to memory consolidation.

Methodological issues relating to ALF

The assessment of long-term forgetting encounters a number of methodological challenges beyond the purely pragmatic issue of arranging to test the subject on several different occasions. In this section, we highlight these challenges and some potential solutions.

First, patient and control groups should be matched as carefully as possible for demographic and nonmemory cognitive variables to isolate the phenomenon of interest. Although careful matching is key to any case-control study, several published studies of ALF in epilepsy have failed to achieve it. ALF is most convincingly demonstrated when patients exhibit normal initial learning and 30-minute recall, but clear impairment at longer delays. In cases where patients are already impaired over short delays, a number of techniques may be used to assess long-term forgetting rates:

(1) Using a variety of the technique introduced by Huppert and Piercy (1978), the experimenter can modulate exposure to the study material to ensure that patients and control subjects reach the same initial level of learning. As Bell, Fine, Dow, Seidenberg, and Hermann (2005) have observed, this "over-learning" method may mask early forgetting with a ceiling effect. An alternative is to use a "selective reminding" technique, in which only nonremembered items are represented at each learning trial.
(2) Individual patients and controls may be matched for learning on a case-by-case basis. This method, however, risks producing nonrepresentative results if "upper range" patients are matched with "lower range" control subjects.
(3) Differing acquisition levels may be accepted and the overall shape of the forgetting curves compared. The problem which arises here is that there is no widely accepted model of how variations in initial learning level affect forgetting over time (Rubin & Wenzel, 1996).

The choice of study material is likely to be important. Relative impairments in verbal and nonverbal memory depend, in other contexts, on the laterality of the seizure focus. Also, forgetting may be different for semantically related (e.g., a story) and unrelated (e.g., a word list) material (Isaac & Mayes, 1999a, 1999b).

Rehearsal of the material between test sessions may confound results. In some studies of ALF, subjects have been forewarned about the delayed tests whereas in others they have not. The material used will also influence this: a story is more likely to be rehearsed than a large number of meaningless visual designs.

The length of the interval between testing sessions may determine whether or not ALF is found – the underlying mechanisms may operate over 24 hours or several weeks. An interval should be chosen at which control subjects perform at neither ceiling nor floor.

The nature of the retrieval task – free recall, cued recall, or recognition – may be important. Davidson et al. (2007) suggest that their failure to find a deficit in recognition memory at an extended delay implies that ALF in their patients was due to a problem with memory retrieval rather than storage.

When the same material is probed at several time intervals, memories are presumably re-encoded to some degree at each probe. This in itself is likely to alter the time course of forgetting. One way of avoiding this problem is to test distinct subsets of the originally learned material at each interval.

Future work

The above discussion has highlighted several prominent clinical, psychological, and pathophysiological questions about ALF. Clinically, it is important to discover how widespread the phenomenon is in neurological disease and whether it can be treated. A battery of standardized neuropsychological tests for ALF therefore needs to be developed. Psychological questions abound and include:

- Is ALF a truly distinct cognitive phenomenon, or is it a mild version of the amnesic syndrome?
- Are learning and early retention really intact in patients with ALF?
- What is the time frame of ALF, and what types of memory does it affect?

Work on the pathophysiology of ALF should address the relationships between (subclinical) seizure activity, sleep, and long-term forgetting. Neuroimaging techniques such as MR spectroscopy and diffusion tensor imaging may uncover structural correlates that have thus far been elusive.

Conclusions

In this chapter, we have described the phenomenon of ALF, a relatively recently recognized pathological form of forgetting, in which material is initially remembered normally but is forgotten at an excessively rapid rate over subsequent days to weeks. ALF is dramatically illustrated by a number of published case reports, but is also recognized to occur in larger groups of patients, particularly those with TEA and other types of TLE. The phenomenon is clinically important as it may go undetected by standard neuropsychological tests of memory. It is also of potential importance to models of long-term memory consolidation. Research on ALF faces a number of methodological challenges that will need to be addressed in future work.

Acknowledgements

The authors gratefully acknowledge the support of the Patrick Berthoud Charitable Trust, the Health Foundation and the Great Western Research Initiative.

References

Addis, D. R., Moscovitch, M., Crawley, A. P., & McAndrews, M. P. (2004). Recollective qualities modulate hippocampal activation during autobiographical memory retrieval. *Hippocampus*, *14*, 752–762.

Ahern, G. L., O'Connor, M., Dalmau, J., Coleman, A., Posner, J. B., Schomer, D. L., et al. (1994). Paraneoplastic temporal lobe epilepsy with testicular neoplasm and atypical amnesia. *Neurology*, *44*(7), 1270–1274.

Alvarez, P., & Squire, L. R. (1994). Memory consolidation and the medial temporal lobe: A simple network model. *Proceedings of the National Academy of Sciences*, *91*(15), 7041–7045.

Baxendale, S. A., Paesschen, W., Thompson, P. J., et al. (1998). The relationship between quantitative MRI and neuropsychological functioning in temporal lobe epilepsy. *Epilepsia*, *39*, 158–166.

Bell, B. D. (2006). WMS-III logical memory performance after a two-week delay in temporal lobe epilepsy and control groups. *Journal of Clinical and Experimental Neuropsychology*, *28*(8), 1435–1443.

Bell, B. D., Fine, J., Dow, C., Seidenberg, M., & Hermann, B. P. (2005). Temporal lobe epilepsy and the selective reminding test: The conventional 30-minute delay suffices. *Psychological Assessment*, *17*(1), 103–109.

Bell, B. D., & Giovagnoli, A. R. (2007). Recent innovative studies of memory in temporal lobe epilepsy. *Neuropsychology Review*, *17*(4), 455–476.

Bergin, P. S., Thompson, P. J., Fish, D. R., & Shorvon, S. D. (1995). The effect of seizures on memory for recently learned material. *Neurology*, *45*(2), 236–240.

Blake, R. V., Wroe, S. J., Breen, E. K., & McCarthy, R. A. (2000). Accelerated forgetting in patients with epilepsy: Evidence for an impairment in memory consolidation. *Brain*, *123 Pt 3*, 472–483.

Bosshardt, S., Degonda, N., Schmidt, C. F., Boesiger, P., Nitsch, R. M., Hock, C., et al. (2005b). One month of human memory consolidation enhances retrieval-related hippocampal activity. *Hippocampus*, *15*, 1026–1040.

Bosshardt, S., Schmidt, C. F., Jaermann, T., Degonda, N., Boesiger, P., Nitsch, R. M., et al. (2005a). Effects of memory consolidation on human hippocampal activity during retrieval. *Cortex*, *41*, 486–498.

Butler, C. R., Bhaduri, A., Acosta-Cabronero, J., Nestor, P. J., Kapur, N., Graham, K. S., et al. (2009). Transient epileptic amnesia: Regional brain atrophy and its relationship to memory deficits. *Brain*, *132*(2), 357–368.

Butler, C. R., Graham, K. S., Hodges, J. R., Kapur, N., Wardlaw, J. M., & Zeman, A. Z. (2007). The syndrome of transient epileptic amnesia. *Annals of Neurology*, *61*(6), 587–598.

Butler, C. R., & Zeman, A. (2008a). A case of transient epileptic amnesia with radiological localization. *Nature Clinical Practice Neurology*, *4*(9), 516–521.

Butler, C. R., & Zeman, A. Z. (2008b). Recent insights into the impairment of memory in epilepsy: Transient epileptic amnesia, accelerated long-term forgetting and remote memory impairment. *Brain*, *131*(9), 2243–2263.

Corcoran, R., & Thompson, P. (1992). Memory failure in epilepsy: Retrospective reports and prospective recordings. *Seizure*, *1*(1), 37–42.

Cronel-Ohayon, S., Zesiger, P., Davidoff, V., Boni, A., Roulet, E., & Deonna, T. (2006). Deficit in memory consolidation (abnormal forgetting rate) in childhood temporal lobe epilepsy. Pre and postoperative long-term observation. *Neuropediatrics*, *37*(6), 317–324.

Davidson, M., Dorris, L., O'Regan, M., & Zuberi, S. M. (2007). Memory consolidation and accelerated forgetting in children with idiopathic generalized epilepsy. *Epilepsy & Behavior*, *11*(3), 394–400.

Davis, H. P., Small, S. A., Stern, Y., Mayeux, R., Feldstein, S. N., & Keller, F. R. (2003). Acquisition, recall, and forgetting of verbal information in long-term memory by young, middle-aged, and elderly individuals. *Cortex*, *39*(4–5), 1063–1091.

De Renzi, E., & Lucchelli, F. (1993). Dense retrograde amnesia, intact learning capability and abnormal forgetting rate: A consolidation deficit? *Cortex*, *29*(3), 449–466.

Elixhauser, A., Leidy, N. K., Meador, K., Means, E., & Willian, M. K. (1999). The relationship between memory performance, perceived cognitive function, and mood in patients with epilepsy. *Epilepsy Research*, *37*(1), 13–24.

Ellenbogen, J. M., Hulbert, J. C., Stickgold, R., Dinges, D. F., & Thompson-Schill, S. L. (2006). Interfering with theories of sleep and memory: Sleep, declarative memory, and associative interference. *Current Biology*, *16*(13), 1290–1294.

Ferreira, M. B. C., Da Silva, R. C., Medina, J. H., & Izquierdo, I. (1992). Late posttraining memory processing by entorhinal cortex: Involvement of NMDA and GABA receptors. *Pharmacology, Biochemistry and Behavior*, *41*, 767–771.

Fink, G. R., Markowitsch, H. J., Reinkemeier, M., Bruckbauer, T., Kessler, J., & Heiss, W. D. (1995). Cerebral representation of one's own past: Neural networks involved in autobiographical memory. *Journal of Neuroscience*, *16*, 4275–4282.

Freed, D. M., Corkin, S., & Cohen, N. J. (1987). Forgetting in HM: A second look. *Neuropsychologia*, *25*(3), 461–471.

Gais, S., & Born, J. (2004). Low acetylcholine during slow-wave sleep is critical for declarative memory consolidation. *Proceedings of the National Academy of Sciences*, *101*(7), 2140–2144.

Gilboa, A., Winocur, G., Grady, C. L., Hevenor, S. J., & Moscovitch, M. (2004). Remembering our past: Functional neuroanatomy of recollection of recent and very remote personal events. *Cerebral Cortex*, *14*(11), 1214–1225.

Giovagnoli, A. R., Casazza, M., & Avanzini, G. (1995). Visual learning on a selective reminding procedure and delayed recall in patients with temporal lobe epilepsy. *Epilepsia*, *36*(7), 704–711.

Giovagnoli, A. R., Mascheroni, S., & Avanzini, G. (1997). Self-reporting of everyday memory in patients with epilepsy: Relation to neuropsychological, clinical, pathological and treatment factors. *Epilepsy Research*, *28*(2), 119–128.

Göder, R., Boigs, M., Braun, S., Friege, L., Fritzer, G., Aldenhoff, J. B., et al. (2004). Impairment of visuospatial memory is associated with decreased slow wave sleep in schizophrenia. *Journal of Psychiatric Research*, *38*, 591–599.

Hayashi, M. L., Choi, S. Y., Rao, B. S. S., Jung, H. Y., Lee, H. K., Zhang, D., et al. (2004). Altered cortical synaptic morphology and impaired memory consolidation in forebrain-specific dominant-negative PAK transgenic mice. *Neuron*, *42*, 773–787.

Helmstaedter, C., Hauff, M., & Elger, C. E. (1998). Ecological validity of list-learning tests and self-reported memory in healthy individuals and those with temporal lobe epilepsy. *Journal of Clinical and Experimental Neuropsychology*, *20*(3), 365–375.

Hermann, B. P., Seidenberg, M., Schoenfeld, J., & Davies, K. (1997). Neuropsychological characteristics of the syndrome of mesial temporal lobe epilepsy. *Archives of Neurology*, *54*(4), 369–376.

Holdstock, J. S., Mayes, A. R., Isaac, C. L., Gong, Q., & Roberts, N. (2002). Differential involvement of the hippocampus and temporal lobe cortices in rapid and slow learning of new semantic information. *Neuropsychologia*, *40*, 748–768.

Huppert, F. A., & Kopelman, M. D. (1989). Rates of forgetting in normal ageing: A comparison with dementia. *Neuropsychologia*, *27*(6), 849–860.

Huppert, F. A., & Piercy, M. (1978). Dissociation between learning and remembering in organic amnesia. *Nature*, *275*(5678), 317–318.

Huppert, F. A., & Piercy, M. (1979). Normal and abnormal forgetting in organic amnesia: Effect of locus of lesion. *Cortex*, *15*(3), 385–390.

Isaac, C. L., & Mayes, A. R. (1999a). Rate of forgetting in amnesia: I. Recall and recognition of prose. *Journal of Experimental Psychology: Learning, Memory, & Cognition*, *25*(4), 942–962.

Isaac, C. L., & Mayes, A. R. (1999b). Rate of forgetting in amnesia: II. Recall and recognition of word lists at different levels of organization. *Journal of Experimental Psychology: Learning, Memory, & Cognition*, *25*(4), 963–977.

Izquierdo, I., & Medina, J. H. (1995). Correlation between the pharmacology of long-term potentiation and the pharmacology of memory. *Neurobiology of Learning and Memory*, *63*, 19–32.

Jokeit, H., Daamen, M., Zang, H., Janszky, J., & Ebner, A. (2001). Seizures accelerate forgetting in patients with left-sided temporal lobe epilepsy. *Neurology*, *57*(1), 125–126.

Jokeit, H., Kramer, G., & Ebner, A. (2005). Do antiepileptic drugs accelerate forgetting? *Epilepsy Behavior*, *6*(3), 430–432.

Kapur, N., Millar, J., Colbourn, C., Abbott, P., Kennedy, P., & Docherty, T. (1997). Very long-term amnesia in association with temporal lobe epilepsy: Evidence for multiple-stage consolidation processes. *Brain & Cognition*, *35*(1), 58–70.

Kapur, N., Scholey, K., Moore, E., Barker, S., Brice, J., & Thompson, S. (1996). Long-term retention deficits in two cases of disproportionate retrograde amnesia. *Journal of Cognitive Neuroscience*, *8*(5), 416–434.

Kopelman, M. D. (1985). Rates of forgetting in Alzheimer-type dementia and Korsakoff's syndrome. *Neuropsychologia*, *23*(5), 623–638.

Kwan, P., & Brodie, M. J. (2001). Neuropsychological effects of epilepsy and antiepileptic drugs. *The Lancet*, *357*(9251), 216–222.

Levin, H. S., High, W. M., Jr., & Eisenberg, H. M. (1988). Learning and forgetting during posttraumatic amnesia in head injured patients. *Journal of Neurology, Neurosurgery & Psychiatry*, *51*(1), 14–20.

Lewis, P., & Kopelman, M. D. (1998). Forgetting rates in neuropsychiatric disorders. *Journal of Neurology, Neurosurgery & Psychiatry*, *65*(6), 890–898.

Lucchelli, F., & Spinnler, H. (1998). Ephemeral new traces and evaporated remote engrams: A form of neocortical temporal lobe amnesia? A preliminary case report. *Neurocase*, *4*, 447–459.

McClelland, J. L., & McNaughton, B. L. (1995). Why there are complementary learning systems in the hippocampus and neocortex: Insights from the successes and failures of connectionist models of learning and memory. *Psychological Review*, *102*, 419–457.

McKee, R. D., & Squire, L. R. (1992). Equivalent forgetting rates in long-term memory for diencephalic and medial temporal lobe amnesia. *Journal of Neuroscience*, *12*(10), 3765–3772.

McNaughton, B. L., & Morris, R. G. M. (1987). Hippocampal synaptic enhancement and information storage within a distributed memory system. *Trends in Neurosciences*, *10*, 408–415.

Maguire, E. A., & Frith, C. D. (2003). Lateral asymmetry in the hippocampal response to the remoteness of autobiographical memories. *Journal of Neuroscience*, *23*, 5302–5307.

Maguire, E. A., Henson, R. N. A., Mummery, C. J., & Frith, C. D. (2001). Activity in prefrontal cortex, but not hippocampus, varies parametrically with the increasing remoteness of memories. *Neuroreport*, *12*, 441–444.

Mameniskiene, R., Jatuzis, D., Kaubrys, G., & Budrys, V. (2006). The decay of memory between delayed and long-term recall in patients with temporal lobe epilepsy. *Epilepsy Behavior*, *8*(1), 278–288.

Manes, F., Graham, K. S., Zeman, A., de Lujan Calcagno, M., & Hodges, J. R. (2005). Autobiographical amnesia and accelerated forgetting in transient epileptic amnesia. *Journal of Neurology, Neurosurgery & Psychiatry*, *76*(10), 1387–1391.

Manes, F., Serrano, C., Calcagno, M., Cardozo, J., & Hodges, J. (2008). Accelerated forgetting in subjects with memory complaints. *Journal of Neurology*, *255*(7), 1067–1070.

Manning, L., Voltzenlogel, V., Chassagnon, S., Hirsch, E., Kehrli, P., & Maitrot, D. (2006). Selective memory impairment for public events associated with accelerated forgetting in a patient with left temporal lobe epilepsy. *Revue Neurologique*, *162*(2), 222–228.

Markowitsch, H. J., Kessler, J., Kalbe, E., & Herholz, K. (1999). Functional amnesia and memory consolidation: A case of severe and persistent anterograde amnesia with rapid forgetting following whiplash injury. *Neurocase*, *5*(3), 189–200.

Martin, R. C., Loring, D. W., Meador, K. J., Lee, G. P., Thrash, N., & Arena, J. G. (1991). Impaired long-term retention despite normal verbal learning in patients with temporal lobe dysfunction. *Neuropsychology*, *5*(1), 3–12.

Martin, R. C., Sawrie, S. M., Roth, D. L., Gilliam, F. G., Faught, E., Morawetz, R. B., et al. (1998). Individual memory change after anterior temporal lobectomy: A base rate analysis using regression-based outcome methodology. *Epilepsia*, *39*(10), 1075–1082.

Mayes, A. R., Isaac, C. L., Holdstock, J. S., Cariga, P., Gummer, A., & Roberts, N. (2003). Long-term amnesia: A review and detailed illustrative case study. *Cortex*, *39*(4–5), 567–603.

Moscovitch, M., & Nadel, L. (1998). Consolidation and the hippocampal complex revisited: In defense of the multiple-trace model. *Current Opinion in Neurobiology*, *8*(2), 297–300.

Moscovitch, M., Nadel, L., Winocur, G., Gilboa, A., & Rosenbaum, R. S. (2006). The cognitive neuroscience of remote episodic, semantic and spatial memory. *Current Opinion in Neurobiology*, *16*(2), 179–190.

Motamedi, G., & Meador, K. (2003). Epilepsy and cognition. *Epilepsy & Behavior*, *4*(Supplement 2), 25–38.

Motamedi, G. K., & Meador, K. J. (2004). Antiepileptic drugs and memory. *Epilepsy & Behavior*, *5*(4), 435–439.

Mueller, S. G., Suhy, J., Laxer, K. D., Flenniken, D. L., Axelrad, J., Capizzano, A. A., et al. (2002). Reduced extrahippocampal NAA in mesial temporal lobe epilepsy. *Epilepsia*, *43*(10), 1210–1216.

Nadel, L., & Moscovitch, M. (1997). Memory consolidation, retrograde amnesia and the hippocampal complex. *Current Opinion in Neurobiology*, *7*(2), 217–227.

Novelly, R. A., Augustine, E. A., Mattson, R. H., Glaser, G. H., WIlliamson, P. D., Spencer, D. D., et al. (1984). Selective memory improvement and impairment in temporal lobectomy for epilepsy. *Annals of Neurology*, *15*(1), 64–67.

O'Connor, M., Sieggreen, M. A., Ahern, G., Schomer, D., & Mesulam, M. (1997). Accelerated forgetting in association with temporal lobe epilepsy and paraneoplastic encephalitis. *Brain & Cognition*, *35*(1), 71–84.

Payne, J. D., & Nadel, L. (2008). Sleep, dreams, and memory consolidation: The role of the stress hormone cortisol. *Learning & Memory*, *11*, 671–678.

Peigneux, P., Laureys, S., Fuchs, S., Collette, F., Perrin, F., Reggers, J., et al. (2004). Are spatial memories strengthened in the human hippocampus during slow wave sleep? *Neuron*, *44*, 535–545.

Petersen, R. C., Smith, G., Kokmen, E., Ivnik, R. J., & Tangalos, E. G. (1992). Memory function in normal aging. *Neurology*, *42*(2), 396–401.

Piazzini, A., Canevini, M. P., Maggiori, G., & Canger, R. (2001). The perception of memory failures in patients with epilepsy. *European Journal of Neurology*, *8*(6), 613–620.

Piefke, M., Weiss, P. H., Zilles, K., Markowitsch, H., & Fink, G. R. (2003). Differential remoteness and emotional tone modulate the neural correlates of autobiographical memory. *Brain*, *126*(3), 650–668.

Piolino, P., Giffard-Quillon, G., Desgranges, B., Che'telat, G., Baron, J.-C., & Eustache, F. (2004). Autobiographical memory and autonoetic consciousness: Triple dissociation in neurodegenerative diseases. *Brain*, *126*, 2203–2219.

Rekkas, P. V., & Constable, R. T. (2005). Evidence that autobiographical memory retrieval does not become independent of the hippocampus: An fMRI study contrasting very recent with remote events. *Journal of Cognitive Neuroscience*, *17*, 1950–1961.

Remondes, M., & Schuman, E. M. (2004). Role for a cortical input to hippocampal area CA1 in the consolidation of long-term memory. *Nature*, *431*, 699–703.

Ribot, T. A. (1882). *Diseases of memory*. New York: Appleton-Century-Crofts.

Rubin, D. C., & Wenzel, A. E. (1996). One hundred years of forgetting: A quantitative description of retention. *Psychological Review*, *103*(4), 734–760.

Sawrie, S. M., Martin, R. C., Knowlton, R., Faught, E., Gilliam, F., & Kuzniecky, R. (2001). Relationships among hippocampal volumetry, proton magnetic resonance spectroscopy, and verbal memory in temporal lobe epilepsy. *Epilepsia*, *42*(11), 1403–1407.

Squire, L. R. (1981). Two forms of human amnesia: An analysis of forgetting. *Journal of Neuroscience*, *1*(6), 635–640.

Squire, L. R. (1997). Amnesia, memory and brain systems. *Philosophical Transactions of the Royal Society London B: Biological Sciences*, *352*(1362), 1663–1673.

Squire, L. R., & Bayley, P. J. (2007). The neuroscience of remote memory. *Current Opinion in Neurobiology*, *17*, 185–196.

Stark, C. E. L., & Squire, L. R. (2000). fMRI activity in the medial temporal lobe during recognition memory as a function of study-test interval. *Hippocampus*, *10*, 329–337.

Stickgold, R., & Walker, M. P. (2005). Memory consolidation and reconsolidation: What is the role of sleep? *Trends in Neurosciences*, *28*(8), 408–415.

Takashima, A., Petersson, K. M., Rutters, F., Tendolkar, I., Jensen, O., Zwarts, M. J., et al. (2006). Declarative memory consolidation in humans: A prospective functional magnetic resonance imaging study. *Proceedings of the National Academy of the Sciences*, *103*(3), 756–761.

Tucker, M. A., Hirota, Y., Wamsley, E. J., Lau, H., Chaklader, A., & Fishbein, W. (2006). A daytime nap containing solely non-REM sleep enhances declarative but not procedural memory. *Neurobiology of Learning and Memory*, *86*, 241–247.

Tulving, E. (2002). Episodic memory: From mind to brain. *Annual Review of Psychology*, *53*(1), 1–25.

Voltzenlogel, V., Despres, O., Vignal, J.-P., Kehrli, P., & Manning, L. (2007). One-year postoperative autobiographical memory following unilateral temporal lobectomy for control of intractable epilepsy. *Epilepsia*, *48*(3), 605–608.

Walker, M. P. (2005). A refined model of sleep and the time course of memory formation. *Behavioral and Brain Sciences*, *28*(01), 51–64.

Walker, M. P., & Stickgold, R. (2006). Sleep, memory, and plasticity. *Annual Review of Psychology*, *57*, 139–166.

Wheeler, M. A., Stuss, D. T., & Tulving, E. (1997). Toward a theory of episodic memory: The frontal lobes and autonoetic consciousness. *Psychological Bulletin*, *121*(3), 331–354.

Yogarajah, M., Powell, H. W. R., Parker, G. J. M., Alexander, D. C., Thompson, P. J., Symms, M. R., et al. (2008). Tractography of the parahippocampal gyrus and material specific memory impairment in unilateral temporal lobe epilepsy. *NeuroImage*, *40*(4), 1755–1764.

Zeman, A. Z. J., Boniface, S. J., & Hodges, J. R. (1998). Transient epileptic amnesia: A description of the clinical and neuropsychological features in 10 cases and a review of the literature. *Journal of Neurology, Neurosurgery & Psychiatry*, *64*(4), 435–443.

11 Aspects of forgetting in psychogenic amnesia

Matthias Brand

University of Bielefeld, Bielefeld, Germany, and University of Duisburg-Essen, Duisburg, Germany

Hans J. Markowitsch

University of Bielefeld, Bielefeld, Germany

Introduction

Memory disorders (amnesias) are the most common syndrome following brain damage or dysfunction and may have severe consequences for patients. In particular, the loss of autobiographical memories may fundamentally alter normal, everyday life for the patient and his or her relatives.

Retrograde amnesia can be caused by specific or more general structural brain damage. However, the phenomenon of impaired retrieval of recent or remote autobiographical memories can also occur in the absence of structural damage to the brain, at least as far as structural abnormalities are detectable with current brain imaging techniques (computed tomography, CT; magnet resonance tomography, MRT). Those conditions are referred to as psychogenic amnesia, also known as dissociative or functional amnesia. Even though this syndrome has been well known for a long time (see Markowitsch & Brand, 2010), new insights into this rare form of forgetting have been emerging since potential neural correlates of psychogenic amnesia have been investigated using modern functional neuroimaging methods.

What is psychogenic amnesia?

Neuropsychological symptoms

Psychogenic amnesia is characterized by retrograde memory impairments, primarily affecting autobiographical-episodic memory, in the absence of overt brain damage or a known neurological causation (Brandt & van Gorp, 2006; Kopelman, 2000; Markowitsch, 2003b). Although impaired recall of autobiographical events is the most prominent symptom in psychogenic amnesia, deficits in retrieving personal facts (i.e., personal non-context-based semantic information) and general semantic (non-personal) knowledge can also occur (Barbarotto, Laiacona, & Cocchini, 1996; Fujiwara et al., 2008; Kritchevsky, Chang, & Squire, 2004). In addition, anterograde memory deficits can accompany the retrograde amnesia (Kritchevsky et al., 2004; Markowitsch, Kessler, Van der Ven, Weber-Luxenburger, & Heiss, 1998). However, in the majority of patients with psychogenic amnesia, anterograde memory functions are preserved to a large extent (Brand et al., in press; De Renzi, Lucchelli, Muggia, & Spinnler, 1997; Glisky, Ryan, Reminger, Hardt, Hayes, & Hupbach, 2004). On the other hand, anterograde amnesia with preserved retrograde memory can also be a consequence of psychological stress (Kumar, Rao, Sunny, & Gangadhar, 2007), although such cases are very rare. In conclusion, the autobiographical-episodic memory domain is more frequently and severely affected than the semantic domain and anterograde memory. Even in cases with both autobiographical-episodic and semantic memory impairments accompanied by anterograde reductions, the cardinal symptom is retrograde amnesia for personal events (Brandt & van Gorp, 2006; Fujiwara et al., 2008; Markowitsch, 2003b).

Psychogenic amnesia may affect memories from across the whole life span or just those from a specific time period or with a specific content. For instance, some patients "forget" events which happened within a clear time window, for example within the last 6 years (see case AMN described by Markowitsch et al., 1998), or within the last 13 years before the critical incident (see case GH in Fujiwara et al., 2008). With regard to the content of memories, the amnesia may affect all autobiographical memories, or distinct contents such as family- or business-related events.

Executive dysfunction is found in some cases of psychogenic amnesia. For example, in a recent study of 14 patients, we found deficits in executive function in 4 patients, of whom 3 performed more than 2 standard deviations below the control mean (Brand et al., 2009). These patients also had more pronounced retrograde memory deficits than those with normal executive functioning. This result further supports the view that executive functions may co-vary with successful retrieval of autobiographical-episodic memories, as has been proposed by Kopelman (2000; see also Glisky et al., 2004).

It has been suggested by Kopelman (2000) that severe precipitating stress and emotional alterations such as depression or emotional instability and additional former transient amnesia of organic origin elevate the probability of developing psychogenic amnesia. Moreover, he argued that this most likely occurs in interaction with executive dysfunctioning leading to inhibition of retrieval of autobiographical memories. On the basis of Kopelman's suggestions, Fujiwara and Markowitsch (2004) argued that executive control – or supervisory attentional system (Norman & Shallice, 1986) – is engaged in holding unwanted or stressful memories out of self-awareness or autonoëtic consciousness. This may lead to a kind of overload of the executive system and may reduce frontal capacities necessary for successful retrieval of other nonstressful personal memories in psychogenic amnesia. In line with this argumentation are studies that have linked the prefrontal cortex – which is crucially engaged in a network fundamental for executive functioning (Elliott, 2003; Fuster, 2006; Kane & Engle, 2002; Roberts, Robbins, & Weiskrantz,

1998) – to retrieval mode and retrieval effort (Buckner, 2003; Lepage, Ghaffar, Nyberg, & Tulving, 2000; Rugg, Otten, & Henson, 2002; Velanova, Jacoby, Wheeler, McAvoy, Petersen, & Buckner, 2003). The link between stress and frontal lobe dysfunctions has also been shown in patients with mild head trauma accompanied by former psychological trauma (Raskin, 1997) and in victims of violence (Stein, Kennedy, & Twamley, 2002). The involvement of frontal lobe dysfunctions in psychogenic amnesia has also been discussed in the study by Tramoni, Aubert-Khalfa, Guye, Ranjeva, Felician, and Ceccaldi (2009). In accordance with these findings and the aforementioned hypothesis, executive reductions in patients with psychogenic amnesia observed in standard neuropsychological executive tasks (see comments above) may be caused by an overload of the frontal system which is overstrained by its function in keeping traumatic memories away from the self. This executive overload may contribute to the more general retrograde memory deficit frequently observed in psychogenic amnesia (Brand et al., 2009).

Beyond these standard neuropsychological domains, emotional processing and theory-of-mind functions (i.e., perspective taking, understanding other people's mental states) may also be commonly deteriorated in psychogenic amnesia as revealed in the multicase study by Fujiwara et al. (2008). In 3 of 4 patients in whom theory-of-mind functions were examined by the "Reading the Mind in the Eyes Test" (Baron-Cohen, Wheelwright, Hill, Raste, & Plumb, 2001), deficits in processing the facial emotional expression of other people have been found. In addition, personality changes and a sum of psychological-psychiatric symptoms have also been reported in a considerably high proportion of patients with psychogenic amnesia (e.g., Fujiwara et al., 2008; Kritchevsky et al., 2004).

Case histories of psychogenic amnesia: two examples

Markowitsch et al. (1998) describe the case of a 23-year-old male, AMN, with psychogenic amnesia for events from the 6 years preceding the triggering incident. AMN witnessed a fire in his house and developed both retrograde and anterograde amnesia afterwards. An organic aetiology of his amnesic state was excluded by extensive neurological and neuroradiological examinations. Although no structural brain changes were identified, neural correlates of the amnesia were demonstrated using positron emission tomography ([^{18}F]-fluorodeoxyglucose-PET, [FDG-PET]). Temporo-frontal as well as diencephalic regions were hypometabolic and the extent of the metabolic changes was comparable to that of a patient who suffered from retrograde amnesia of clear organic causation (hypoxia). In the course of extensive psychotherapeutic interventions, AMN reported a traumatic experience at the age of 4 years when he witnessed a man dying in a burning car. Accordingly, the fire in his house at the age of 23 years may be seen as a retraumatization which was most likely associated with an excessive release of glucocorticoids (stress hormones). As described in the next paragraph, a massive release of stress hormones is assumed to block the retrieval of autobiographical memories (O'Brien, 1997) due to dysregulation of hippocampal functioning.

An example of a patient who suffered from psychogenic fugue (e.g., Loewenstein, 1996; Serra, Fadda, Buccione, Caltagirone, & Carlesimo, 2007), also named "*Wanderlust*" (see Markowitsch & Brand, 2010), has been reported by Markowitsch, Fink, Thöne, Kessler, and Heiss (1997a). The 37-year-old male patient left his house in the morning to buy rolls for breakfast. Instead of coming home afterwards, he continued cycling for 5 days along the river Rhine. A subsequent neuroradiological examination revealed no signs of brain abnormalities. He nevertheless persistently suffered from amnesia for personal events prior to the fugue's onset. In a PET investigation measuring cerebral blood flow (^{15}O-PET) during retrieval attempt of autobiographical-episodic memories, left hemispheric regions were activated predominantly while in normal healthy subjects the respective right hemispheric areas are activated (Fink, Markowitsch, Reinkemeier, Bruckbauer, Kessler, & Heiss, 1996). The PET findings in the patient with fugue reported by Markowitsch et al. (1997a) may therefore indicate that he processed his own biography neutrally and in a verbal way which is comparable to the way healthy individuals imagine events which are unrelated to their biographies (Fink et al., 1996).

These two examples illustrate that symptoms and case histories can vary substantially across patients. Nonetheless, we have found massive stress or stressful life events prior to the onset of amnesia in most of the patients (e.g., Brand et al., in press).

Stress and autobiographical memory retrieval

Subjectively perceived negative stress and/or stress with a very high intensity can negatively influence the retrieval of autobiographical memories substantially by changing neural functioning. Although short-term and positive stress may enhance neural plasticity, a long-term and massive release of stress hormones (i.e., glucocorticoids such as cortisol) may result in decreased synaptic plasticity and even cell death (Bremner, 1999, 2007; Porter & Landfield, 1998; Raz & Rodrigue, 2006; Susman, 2006; Szeszko et al., 2006; see also the critical review by Jelicic & Merckelbach, 2004). The negative impact of stress on recall of memories has been consistently demonstrated by a series of studies that used either pharmacological or psychological interventions to induce stress (Buss, Wolf, Witt, & Hellhammer, 2004; Kuhlmann, Kirschbaum, & Wolf, 2005a; Kuhlmann, Piel, & Wolf, 2005b).

The covariation between stress and brain dysregulation can be seen impressively in patients with posttraumatic stress disorder (PTSD). In such patients, volume reductions and functional alterations in the region of the hippocampal formation have been reported (Bremner, 2007; Bremner et al., 2003; Li, Chen, Lin, Zhang, He, & Lin, 2006; Shin et al., 2004). In addition, other limbic structures such as the amygdala as well as parts of the prefrontal cortex were also shown to be structurally or functionally changed in patients with PTSD (Bremner, Elzinga, Schmahl, & Vermetten, 2008; Driessen et al., 2004; Shin et al., 2005). Autobiographical memory reductions associated with PTSD, in particular over-generalized memory and intrusive memories (Moore & Zoellner, 2007; Speckens, Ehlers, Hackmann, Ruths, & Clark, 2007), are most likely related to the aforementioned dysregulation within a limbic-prefrontal network (Bremner et al., 2008).

Moreover, reductions in autobiographical memory retrieval integrity have also been reported for other psychological and psychiatric disorders in addition to patients with selective brain damage to limbic or prefrontal areas. For instance, patients with depression commonly suffer from less specific autobiographical memories compared with healthy subjects (Van Vreeswijk & De Wilde, 2004). Instead of narrating temporally and contextually distinctive episodes, patients with depression tend to report summaries of repeated occasions (Barnhofer, de Jong-Meyer, Kleinpass, & Nikesch, 2002; Williams, 1996; Williams et al., 2007). This pattern can also be found in patients with schizophrenia and other psychological disorders and it is most likely related to reduced perspective taking and social cognition (Corcoran & Frith, 2003).

Likewise, patients with head injury or other types of brain dysfunction frequently show deficits in autobiographical memory retrieval (see the review by Brand & Markowitsch, 2008). However, even in patients with a clear organic causation of the amnesic syndrome, psychological factors (e.g., stress) contribute to symptom severity and the course of the amnesia (Kapur, 1999; for a detailed discussion of organic and psychogenic factors associated with amnesia see Markowitsch, 1996a). In summary, massive and/or long-lasting stress is most likely linked to structural and functional changes of limbic and prefrontal integrity which may result in specific deterioration of autobiographical memory retrieval.

Neuroimaging studies in psychogenic amnesia: a synthesis

In the last two decades several case reports have been published in which potential neural correlates of forgetting autobiographical memories in psychogenic amnesia were investigated. These reports have substantially increased our knowledge about the brain–memory association in this rare amnesic condition. Nevertheless, it is still a challenge to draw from the results of single case studies a consistent neural pattern of psychogenic amnesia, given the major differences among the utilized methods and parameters (e.g., glucose utilization and cerebral blood flow measured by PET or blood oxygen level dependent signals examined with functional magnetic resonance imaging, fMRI). Furthermore, in some studies general functional brain status has been investigated while in other studies neural correlates of retrieval attempt in psychogenic amnesia have been measured using different experimental paradigms, for example sentences or pictures describing autobiographical events that happened prior to the onset of amnesia (see the comments on methodological issues concerning functional imaging investigations in psychogenic amnesia in the review by Brand & Markowitsch, 2009).

Considering these important limitations, there are nevertheless two regions which are commonly reported as characteristically dysregulated in patients with psychogenic amnesia: the medial temporal lobes (see Figure 11.1), in particular the hippocampal formation, and parts of the prefrontal lobes, primarily the ventral section (e.g., Brand et al., 2009; Costello, Fletcher, Dolan, Frith, & Shallice, 1998; Lucchelli, Muggia, & Spinnler, 1995; Markowitsch, 1996a; Markowitsch et al., 1997a, 1998; Piolino et al., 2005; Sellal, Manning, Seegmuller, Scheiber, & Schoenfelder, 2002). Most likely, there is a dominance of right hemispheric functional prefrontal changes (Brand et al., 2009; Tramoni et al., 2009), although this has not been shown in all studies. There is also evidence for normal brain functioning (at least in a resting state glucose utilization investigation) (Dalla Barba, Mantovan, Ferruzza, & Denes, 1997; De Renzi & Lucchelli, 1993; De Renzi, Lucchelli, Muggia, & Spinnler, 1995;

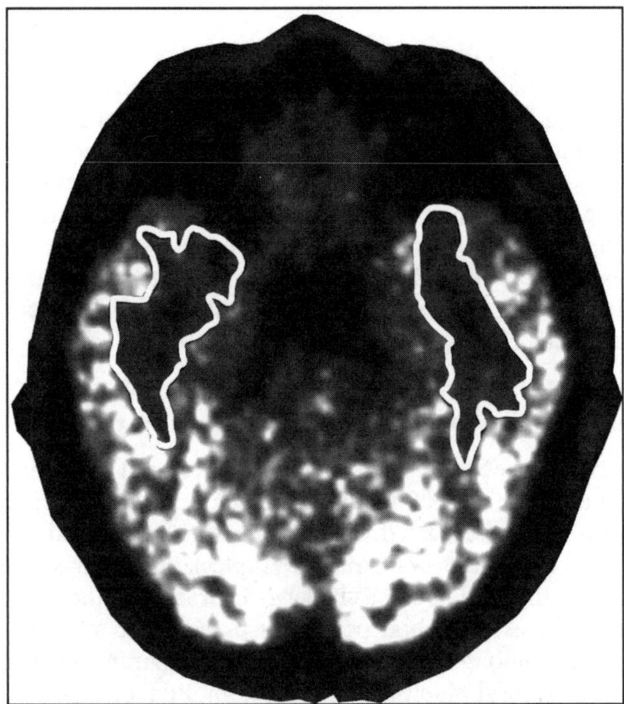

Figure 11.1 A horizontal view of an examination with FDG-PET in a male patient with psychogenic amnesia. Reduced glucose utilization (hypometabolism) can be seen within the medial temporal lobe in both hemispheres (framed). The other brain regions showed normal metabolism.

Kessler, Markowitsch, Huber, Kalbe, Weber-Luxenburger, & Kock, 1997; Markowitsch, Kessler, Kalbe, & Herholz, 1999a; Markowitsch, Kessler, Russ, Frölich, Schneider, & Maurer, 1999b; Reinvang & Gjerstad, 1998). In addition to these somewhat disparate findings, recent studies that examined neural reactions to retrieval attempt in psychogenic amnesia emphasized the role of the medial temporal lobes and the prefrontal cortex. For instance, it has been demonstrated that those regions critically involved in retrieval of autobiographical memories in healthy subjects (e.g., Fink et al., 1996; Piefke, Weiss, Zilles, Markowitsch, & Fink, 2003; Piolino, Giffard-Quillon, Desgranges, Chetelat, Baron, & Eustache, 2004; Viard et al., 2007) are not activated when patients with psychogenic amnesia are confronted with stimuli representing information to trigger the remembering of autobiographical episodes (Botzung, Denkova, & Manning, 2007; Fujiwara et al., 2004; Markowitsch et al., 1997a; Markowitsch, Thiel, Kessler, von Stockhausen, & Heiss, 1997b; Reinhold, Kühnel, Brand, & Markowitsch, 2006; Yasuno et al., 2000; see the review by Brand & Markowitsch, 2009).

Previous findings with respect to functional brain changes in patients with psychogenic amnesia, as summarized above, support the view that a clear distinction between "organic" and "nonorganic" amnesia does not adequately represent the amnesic syndromes. In addition, amnesic symptoms in patients in whom an "organic" causation is relatively evidenced are also frequently influenced or at least moderated by "psychological" factors such as stress. Moreover, dissociative disorders (e.g., dissociative identity disorder) and other psychological-psychiatric symptoms can be developed following traumatic brain injury (Cantagallo, Grassi, & Della Sala, 1999). Taking these results together, we argue that, in all types of amnesia, an interaction between psychological and organic factors is responsible for the memory loss (Barbarotto et al., 1996; Brand & Markowitsch, 2009; Markowitsch, 1996a, 1996b). Most likely, amnesias can be organized in a continuum between "organic" and "psychological" causation, but – generally – in all amnesias psychological aspects are important to take into account and – on the other hand – brain changes can be demonstrated using functional imaging techniques even in the absence of structural brain damage.

Psychogenic amnesia: a stable condition?

The amnesic symptoms of the patient AMN described by Markowitsch et al. (1998) and summarized above had an impressive course. Within 12 months after onset of amnesia, both retrograde and anterograde memory impairments recovered almost completely. A second FDG-PET scan showed that recovery from amnesia was accompanied by a normalization of the metabolic rate of glucose (Markowitsch, Kessler, Van der Ven, Weber-Luxenburger, & Heiss, 2000) indicating that functional brain changes linked to memory impairments in patients with psychogenic amnesia are dynamic and can potentially normalize in correspondence with regains of memory functions (see also Yasuno et al., 2000). Evidence for recovery from retrograde amnesia of psychogenic causation also comes from other case descriptions. For example, the very young patient AB in the study by Fujiwara et al. (2008), who had isolated autobiographical-episodic memory loss, also recovered from amnesic symptoms in the course of the investigation. On the other hand, there are also patients with psychogenic amnesia, either anterograde or retrograde, who stayed amnesic for a very long time without signs of recovery (Markowitsch, 2003a; Reinhold et al., 2006).

Given that psychogenic amnesia is a very rare phenomenon and – to the authors' best knowledge – no group study is available so far that has addressed the course of the amnesic symptoms, no evidence-based prognosis can be formulated. On the basis of the case studies which have done a follow-up investigation, it seems likely that young patients relative to older patients and those who have less severe amnesic symptoms have the highest chance of recovery. In addition, those patients without severe additional cognitive reductions (e.g., within the executive functions domain) and no anterograde amnesia accompanying the retrograde memory impairments are more likely to get their personal memories back. However, these speculations must be evaluated by long-term studies (see comments below).

Conclusion

Psychogenic amnesia is a condition that is characterized by severe impairments in remembering episodes from the personal past. Although inconsistent across patients, psychogenic amnesia can be accompanied by retrograde memory reductions with respect to personal facts or general semantic information as well as by anterograde amnesia, executive dysfunctions, and abnormal emotional processing. Neuroimaging investigations point to an involvement of limbic (hippocampal) and prefrontal dysfunctioning in this amnesic condition. Future studies are needed to explore the brain correlates of psychogenic amnesia in larger samples of patients using the same methodological approaches. From our point of view, future studies with patients having psychogenic amnesia should consequently incorporate an extensive neuropsychological test battery assessing all main domains (anterograde memory, executive functions, emotion processing, attention, etc.) beyond the elaborative testing of the patients' retrograde memory. When examining the core symptoms of retrograde amnesia, it is absolutely necessary to differentiate between autobiographical-episodic, autobiographical-semantic and general semantic memory. All these facets of retrograde memory should be investigated extensively in patients with psychogenic amnesia. In addition, it also seems worth including personality inventories and other psychological-psychiatric instruments for the assessment of the patients' psychological background. Functional neuroimaging investigations should focus on both general brain changes (e.g., using resting-state techniques) and functional brain abnormalities during retrieval attempt. Moreover, single-case and group studies are needed that address the course of psychogenic amnesia in order to derive hypotheses on mechanisms of recovery from autobiographical memory loss. Considering these approaches, future studies will successfully contribute to a better understanding of the spectacular phenomenon of psychogenic amnesia.

Acknowledgements

Our research was supported by the German Research Council and the European Commission (FP6–043460).

References

Barbarotto, R., Laiacona, M., & Cocchini, G. (1996). A case of simulated, psychogenic or focal pure retrograde amnesia: Did an entire life become unconscious? *Neuropsychologia*, *34*, 575–585.

Barnhofer, T., de Jong-Meyer, R., Kleinpass, A., & Nikesch, S. (2002). Specificity of autobiographical memories in depression: An analysis of retrieval processes in a think-aloud task. *British Journal of Clinical Psychology*, *41*, 411–416.

Baron-Cohen, S., Wheelwright, S., Hill, J., Raste, Y., & Plumb, I. (2001). The "Reading the Mind in the Eyes" Test revised version: A study with normal adults, and adults with Asperger syndrome or high-functioning autism. *Journal of Child Psychology and Psychiatry*, *42*, 241–251.

Botzung, A., Denkova, E., & Manning, L. (2007). Psychogenic memory deficits associated with functional cerebral changes: An FMRI study. *Neurocase*, *13*, 378–384.

Brand, M., Eggers, C., Reinhold, N., Fujiwara, E., Kessler, J., Heiss, W.-D., et al. (in press). Functional brain imaging in fourteen patients with psychogenic amnesia reveals right inferolateral prefrontal hypometabolism. *Psychiatry Research: Neuroimaging*.

Brand, M., & Markowitsch, H. J. (2008). The role of the prefrontal cortex in episodic memory. In E. Dere, J. P. Huston, & A. Easton (Eds.), *Handbook of episodic memory* (pp. 317–341). Amsterdam: Elsevier.

Brand, M., & Markowitsch, H. J. (2009). Environmental influences on autobiographical memory: The mnestic block syndrome. In L. Bäckman & L. Nyberg (Eds.), *Memory, aging, and brain: A Festschrift in honour of Lars Goran-Nilsson* (pp. 229–264). Hove, UK: Psychology Press.

Brandt, J., & van Gorp, W. G. (2006). Functional ("psychogenic") amnesia. *Seminars in Neurology*, *26*, 331–340.

Bremner, J. D. (1999). Does stress damage the brain? *Biological Psychiatry*, *45*, 797–805.

Bremner, J. D. (2007). Traumatic stress: Effects on the brain. *Dialogues in Clinical Neuroscience*, *8*, 445–461.

Bremner, J. D., Elzinga, B., Schmahl, C., & Vermetten, E. (2008). Structural and functional plasticity of the human brain in posttraumatic stress disorder. *Progress in Brain Research*, *167*, 171–186.

Bremner, J. D., Vythilingam, M., Vermetten, E., Southwick, S. M., McGlashan, T., Nazeer, A., et al. (2003). MRI and PET study of deficits in hippocampal structure and function in women with childhood sexual abuse and posttraumatic stress disorder. *American Journal of Psychiatry*, *160*, 924–932.

Buckner, R. L. (2003). Functional-anatomic correlates of control processes in memory. *Journal of Neuroscience*, *23*, 3999–4004.

Buss, C., Wolf, O. T., Witt, J., & Hellhammer, D. H. (2004). Autobiographic memory impairment following acute cortisol administration. *Psychoneuroendocrinology*, *29*, 1093–1096.

Cantagallo, A., Grassi, L., & Della Sala, S. (1999). Dissociative disorder after traumatic brain injury. *Brain Injury*, *13*, 219–228.

Corcoran, R., & Frith, C. D. (2003). Autobiographical memory and theory of mind: Evidence of a relationship in schizophrenia. *Psychological Medicine*, *33*, 897–905.

Costello, A., Fletcher, P. C., Dolan, R. J., Frith, C. D., & Shallice, T. (1998). The origins of forgetting in a case of isolated retrograde amnesia following a haemorrhage: Evidence from functional imaging. *Neurocase*, *4*, 437–446.

Dalla Barba, G., Mantovan, M. C., Ferruzza, E., & Denes, G. (1997). Remembering and knowing the past: A case study of isolated retrograde amnesia. *Cortex*, *33*, 143–154.

De Renzi, E., & Lucchelli, F. (1993). Dense retrograde amnesia, intact learning capability and abnormal forgetting rate: A consolidation deficit? *Cortex*, *29*, 449–466.

De Renzi, E., Lucchelli, F., Muggia, S., & Spinnler, H. (1995). Persistent retrograde amnesia following a minor trauma. *Cortex*, *31*, 531–542.

De Renzi, E., Lucchelli, F., Muggia, S., & Spinnler, H. (1997). Is memory without anatomical damage tantamount to a psychogenic deficit? The case of pure retrograde amnesia. *Neuropsychologia*, *35*, 781–794.

Driessen, M., Beblo, T., Mertens, M., Piefke, M., Rullkoetter, N., Silva-Saavedra, A., et al. (2004). Posttraumatic stress disorder and fMRI activation patterns of traumatic memory in patients with borderline personality disorder. *Biological Psychiatry*, *55*, 603–611.

Elliott, R. (2003). Executive functions and their disorders. *British Medical Bulletin*, *65*, 49–59.

Fink, G. R., Markowitsch, H. J., Reinkemeier, M., Bruckbauer, T., Kessler, J., & Heiss, W.-D. (1996). Cerebral representation of one's own past: Neural networks involved in autobiographical memory. *Journal of Neuroscience*, *16*, 4275–4282.

Fujiwara, E., Brand, M., Kracht, L., Kessler, J., Diebel, A., Netz, J., et al. (2008). Functional retrograde amnesia: A multiple case study. *Cortex*, *44*, 29–45.

Fujiwara, E., & Markowitsch, H. J. (2004). Das mnestische Blockadesyndrom – hirnphysiologische Korrelate von Angst und Stress. In G. Schiepek (Ed.), *Neurobiologie der Psychotherapie* (pp. 186–212). Stuttgart: Schattauer.

Fujiwara, E., Piefke, M., Lux, S., Fink, G. R., Kessler, J., Kracht, L., et al. (2004). Brain correlates of functional retrograde amnesia in three patients. *Brain and Cognition*, *54*, 135–136.

Fuster, J. M. (2006). The cognit: A network model of cortical representation. *International Journal of Psychophysiology*, *60*, 125–132.

Glisky, E. L., Ryan, L., Reminger, S., Hardt, O., Hayes, S. M., & Hupbach, A. (2004). A case of psychogenic fugue: I understand, aber ich verstehe nichts. *Neuropsychologia*, *42*, 1132–1147.

Jelicic, M., & Merckelbach, H. (2004). Traumatic stress, brain changes, and memory deficits: A critical note. *Journal of Nervous and Mental Disease*, *192*, 548–553.

Kane, M. J., & Engle, R. W. (2002). The role of prefrontal cortex in working-memory capacity, executive attention, and general fluid intelligence: An individual-differences perspective. *Psychonomic Bulletin and Review*, *9*, 637–671.

Kapur, N. (1999). Syndromes of retrograde amnesia: A conceptual and empirical synthesis. *Psychological Bulletin*, *125*, 800–825.

Kessler, J., Markowitsch, H. J., Huber, M., Kalbe, E., Weber-Luxenburger, G., & Kock, P. (1997). Massive and persistent anterograde amnesia in the absence of detectable brain damage: Anterograde psychogenic amnesia or gross reduction in sustained effort? *Journal of Clinical and Experimental Neuropsychology*, *19*, 604–614.

Kopelman, M. D. (2000). Focal retrograde amnesia and the attribution of causality: An exceptionally critical review. *Cognitive Neuropsychology*, *17*, 585–621.

Kritchevsky, M., Chang, J., & Squire, L. R. (2004). Functional amnesia: Clinical description and neuropsychological profile of 10 cases. *Learning and Memory*, *11*, 213–226.

Kuhlmann, S., Kirschbaum, C., & Wolf, O. T. (2005a). Effects of oral cortisol treatment in healthy young women on memory retrieval of negative and neutral words. *Neurobiology of Learning and Memory*, *83*, 158–162.

Kuhlmann, S., Piel, M., & Wolf, O. T. (2005b). Impaired memory retrieval after psychosocial stress in healthy young men. *Journal of Neuroscience*, *25*, 2977–2982.

Kumar, S., Rao, S. L., Sunny, B., & Gangadhar, B. N. (2007). Widespread cognitive impairment in psychogenic anterograde amnesia. *Psychiatry and Clinical Neurosciences*, *61*, 583–586.

Lepage, M., Ghaffar, O., Nyberg, L., & Tulving, E. (2000). Prefrontal cortex and episodic memory retrieval mode. *Proceedings of the National Academy of Sciences of the USA*, *97*, 506–511.

Li, L., Chen, S., Liu, J., Zhang, J., He, Z., & Lin, X. (2006). Magnetic resonance imaging and magnetic resonance spectroscopy study of deficits in hippocampal structure in fire victims with recent-onset posttraumatic stress disorder. *Canadian Journal of Psychiatry*, *51*, 431–437.

Loewenstein, R. J. (1996). Dissociative amnesia and dissociative fugue. In L. K. Michelson & W. J. Ray (Eds.), *Handbook of dissociation: Theoretical, empirical, and clinical perspectives*. New York: Plenum Press.

Lucchelli, F., Muggia, S., & Spinnler, H. (1995). The "Petites Madeleines" phenomenon in two amnesic patients. Sudden recovery of forgotten memories. *Brain*, *118*, 167–183.

Markowitsch, H. J. (1996a). Organic and psychogenic retrograde amnesia: Two sides of the same coin? *Neurocase*, *2*, 357–371.

Markowitsch, H. J. (1996b). Retrograde amnesia: Similarities between organic and psychogenic forms. *Neurology, Psychiatry and Brain Research*, *4*, 1–8.

Markowitsch, H. J. (2003a). Memory: Disturbances and therapy. In T. Brandt, L. Caplan, J. Dichgans, H. C. Diener, & C. Kennard (Eds.), *Neurological disorders, course and treatment* (2nd ed., pp. 287–302). San Diego: Academic Press.

Markowitsch, H. J. (2003b). Psychogenic amnesia. *NeuroImage*, *20*, S132–S138.

Markowitsch, H. J., & Brand, M. (2009). Forgetting – an historical perspective. In S. Della Sala (Ed.), *Forgetting*. Hove, UK: Psychology Press.

Markowitsch, H. J., Fink, G. R., Thöne, A., Kessler, J., & Heiss, W.-D. (1997a). A PET study of persistent psychogenic amnesia covering the whole life span. *Cognitive Neuropsychiatry*, *2*, 135–158.

Markowitsch, H. J., Kessler, J., Kalbe, E., & Herholz, K. (1999a). Functional amnesia and memory consolidation. A case of persistent anterograde amnesia with rapid forgetting following whiplash injury. *Neurocase*, *5*, 189–200.

Markowitsch, H. J., Kessler, J., Russ, M. O., Frölich, L., Schneider, B., & Maurer, K. (1999b). Mnestic block syndrome. *Cortex*, *35*, 219–230.

Markowitsch, H. J., Kessler, J., Van der Ven, C., Weber-Luxenburger, G., & Heiss, W.-D. (1998). Psychic trauma causing grossly reduced brain metabolism and cognitive deterioration. *Neuropsychologia*, *36*, 77–82.

Markowitsch, H. J., Kessler, J., Weber-Luxenburger, G., Van der Ven, C., Albers, M., & Heiss, W. D. (2000). Neuroimaging and behavioral correlates of recovery from mnestic block syndrome and other cognitive deteriorations. *Neuropsychiatry, Neuropsychology, and Behavioral Neurology*, *13*, 60–66.

Markowitsch, H. J., Thiel, A., Kessler, J., von Stockhausen, H.-M., & Heiss, W.-D. (1997b). Ecphorizing semi-conscious episodic information via the right temporopolar cortex – a PET study. *Neurocase*, *3*, 445–449.

Moore, S. A., & Zoellner, L. A. (2007). Overgeneral autobiographical memory and traumatic events: An evaluative review. *Psychological Bulletin*, *133*, 419–437.

Norman, D. A., & Shallice, T. (1986). Attention to action: Willed and automatic control of behavior. In R. J. Davidson, G. E. Schwartz, & D. Shapiro (Eds.), *Consciousness and self-regulation* (pp. 1–18). New York: Plenum Press.

O'Brien, J. T. (1997). The "glucocorticoid cascade" hypothesis in man. *British Journal of Psychiatry*, *170*, 199–201.

Piefke, M., Weiss, P. H., Zilles, K., Markowitsch, H. J., & Fink, G. R. (2003). Differential remoteness and emotional tone modulate the neural correlates of autobiographical memory. *Brain*, *126*, 650–668.

Piolino, P., Giffard-Quillon, G., Desgranges, B., Chetelat, G., Baron, J. C., & Eustache, F. (2004). Re-experiencing old memories via hippocampus: A PET study of autobiographical memory. *NeuroImage*, *22*, 1371–1383.

Piolino, P., Hannequin, D., Desgranges, B., Girard, C., Beaunieux, H., Giffard, B., et al. (2005). Right ventral frontal hypometabolism and abnormal sense of self in a case of disproportionate retrograde amnesia. *Cognitive Neuropsychology*, *22*, 1005–1034.

Porter, N., & Landfield, P. W. (1998). Stress hormones and brain ageing: Adding injury to insult. *Nature Neuroscience*, *1*, 3–4.

Raskin, S. A. (1997). The relationship between sexual abuse and mild traumatic brain injury. *Brain Injury*, *11*, 587–603.

Raz, N., & Rodrigue, K. M. (2006). Differential aging of the brain: Patterns, cognitive correlates and modifiers. *Neuroscience and Biobehavioral Reviews*, *30*, 730–748.

Reinhold, N., Kühnel, S., Brand, M., & Markowitsch, H. J. (2006). Functional brain imaging in memory and memory disorders. *Current Medical Imaging Reviews*, *2*, 35–57.

Reinvang, I., & Gjerstad, L. (1998). Focal retrograde amnesia associated with vascular headache. *Neuropsychologia*, *36*, 1335–1341.

Roberts, A. C., Robbins, T. W., & Weiskrantz, L. (Eds.). (1998). *The prefrontal cortex. Executive and cognitive functions*. Oxford: Oxford University Press.

Rugg, M. D., Otten, L. J., & Henson, R. N. A. (2002). The neural basis of episodic memory: Evidence from functional neuroimaging. *Philosophical Transactions of the Royal Society of London, Series B, Biological Sciences*, *357*, 1097–1110.

Sellal, F., Manning, L., Seegmuller, C., Scheiber, C., & Schoenfelder, F. (2002). Pure retrograde amnesia following mild head trauma: A neuropsychological and metabolic study. *Cortex*, *38*, 499–509.

Serra, L., Fadda, L., Buccione, I., Caltagirone, C., & Carlesimo, G. A. (2007). Psychogenic and organic amnesia. A multidimensional assessment of clinical, neuroradiological, neuropsychological and psychopathological features. *Behavioural Neurology*, *18*, 53–64.

Shin, L. M., Shin, P. S., Heckers, S., Krangel, T. S., Macklin, M. L., Orr, S. P., et al. (2004). Hippocampal function in posttraumatic stress disorder. *Hippocampus*, *14*, 292–300.

Shin, L. M., Wright, C. I., Cannistraro, P. A., Wedig, M. M., McMullin, K., Martis, B., et al. (2005). A functional magnetic resonance imaging study of amygdala and medial prefrontal cortex responses to overtly presented fearful faces in posttraumatic stress disorder. *Archives of General Psychiatry*, *62*, 273–281.

Speckens, A. E., Ehlers, A., Hackmann, A., Ruths, F. A., & Clark, D. M. (2007). Intrusive memories and rumination in patients with post-traumatic stress disorder: A phenomenological comparison. *Memory*, *15*, 249–257.

Stein, M. B., Kennedy, C. M., & Twamley, E. W. (2002). Neuropsychological function in female victims of intimate partner violence with and without posttraumatic stress disorder. *Biological Psychiatry*, *52*, 1079–1088.

Susman, E. J. (2006). Psychobiology of persistent antisocial behavior: Stress, early vulnerabilities and the attenuation hypothesis. *Neuroscience and Biobehavioral Reviews*, *30*, 376–389.

Szeszko, P. R., Betensky, J. D., Mentschel, C., Gunduz-Bruce, H., Lencz, T., Ashtari, M., et al. (2006). Increased stress and smaller anterior hippocampal volume. *NeuroReport*, *17*, 1825–1828.

Tramoni, E., Aubert-Khalfa, S., Guye, M., Ranjeva, J. P., Felician, O., & Ceccaldi, M. (2009). Hypo-retrieval and hyper-suppression mechanisms in functional amnesia. *Neuropsychologia*, *47*, 611–624.

Van Vreeswijk, M. F., & De Wilde, E. J. (2004). Autobiographical memory specificity, psychopathology, depressed mood and the use of the Autobiographical Memory Test: A meta-analysis. *Behavioural Research and Therapy*, *42*, 731–743.

Velanova, K., Jacoby, L. L., Wheeler, M. E., McAvoy, M. P., Petersen, S. E., & Buckner, R. L. (2003). Functional-anatomic correlates of sustained and transient processing components engaged during controlled retrieval. *Journal of Neuroscience*, *23*, 8460–8470.

Viard, A., Piolino, P., Desgranges, B., Chételat, G., Lebreton, K., Landeau, B., et al. (2007). Hippocampal activation for autobiographical memories over the entire lifetime in healthy aged subjects: An fMRI study. *Cerebral Cortex*, *17*, 2453–2467.

Williams, J. M. G. (1996). Depression and the specificity of autobiographcial memory. In D. C. Rubin (Ed.), *Remembering our past* (pp. 244–267). New York: Cambridge University Press.

Williams, J. M. G., Barnhofer, T., Crane, C., Hermans, D., Raes, F., Watkins, E., et al. (2007). Autobiographical memory specificity and emotional disorder. *Psychological Bulletin*, *133*, 122–148.

Yasuno, F., Nishikawa, T., Nakagawa, Y., Ikejiri, Y., Tokunaga, H., Mizuta, I., et al. (2000). Functional anatomical study of psychogenic amnesia. *Psychiatry Research*, *99*, 43–57.

12 Autobiographical forgetting, social forgetting, and situated forgetting

Forgetting in context

Celia B. Harris, John Sutton, and Amanda J. Barnier

Macquarie University, Sydney, Australia

Introduction

We have a striking ability to alter our psychological access to past experiences. Consider the following case. Andrew "Nicky" Barr, OBE, MC, DFC (1915–2006), was one of Australia's most decorated World War II fighter pilots. He was the top ace of the Western Desert's 3 Squadron, the pre-eminent fighter squadron in the Middle East, flying P-40 Kittyhawks over Africa. From October 1941, when Nicky Barr's war began, he flew 22 missions and shot down 8 enemy planes in his first 35 operational hours. He was shot down 3 times, once 25 miles behind enemy lines while trying to rescue a downed pilot. He escaped from prisoner-of-war camps four times, once jumping out of a train as it travelled from Italy into Austria. His wife Dot, whom he married only weeks before the war, waited for him at home. She was told on at least three occasions that he was missing in action or dead.

For 50 years, Nicky Barr never spoke publicly, and rarely privately, of his war-time experiences. He was very much a forgotten and forgetting hero (for further details, see Dornan, 2002). In his first public interview in 2002 on the Australian television documentary programme *Australian Story*, Nicky explained his 50-year silence by saying:

> I think my reluctance [to talk] comes from a very definite desire to forget all about the war as quickly as I could. I was concerned about how the regurgitating of all the things that I didn't like, things I wasn't very proud about, the things I had to do in order to survive – how that would really impact on us . . . We found we couldn't quite cope . . . the memories got on top. I didn't need to go through the business of discussing all my adventures . . . some of the things should have stayed forgotten.

Forgetting the past has received a great deal of attention in recent years, both inside and outside psychology (e.g., Connerton, 2008; Erdelyi, 2006; Golding & MacLeod, 1998; McNally, 2005; Schacter, 1996). While the events Barr strove to forget are extraordinary (at least to a generation who has not lived through war), his desire to forget is not. Functioning in our day-to-day lives involves, or perhaps even requires, forgetting. We forget and remember events from our past in a goal-directed, strategic way (Bjork, Bjork, & Anderson, 1998; Conway, 2005). Bjork et al. (1998) defined goal-directed forgetting as "forgetting that serves some implicit or explicit personal need" (p. 103). Despite this definition, forgetting is often equated with failure (see also Cubelli, this volume, Chapter 3). This is probably because of the influence of the computer metaphor of human memory, which sees human information processing as a sequence of steps where information is encoded, stored, and then retrieved. By this view, recall is expected to be perfect or verbatim, just as a computer can output on command completely and accurately the contents saved in its memory system. But for human memory, this is neither plausible nor functional. Rather, it may be functional to forget certain information that is irrelevant, redundant, out of date, damaging, or distressing (see also Markowistch & Brand, this volume, Chapter 11).

In this chapter, we focus on autobiographical memory, which relates to events and experiences in our personal past. We focus in particular on autobiographical forgetting. Autobiographical remembering and forgetting serve a range of functions, especially in maintaining our identity (Conway, 2005; Nelson, 2003) and guiding our behaviour into the future (Pillemer, 2003). In this chapter, we also extend our discussion of forgetting to social memory, which occurs in conversation or community with other people. We focus in particular on social forgetting – both what is not recalled during joint remembering and what is forgotten subsequent to joint memory activities. Social remembering and forgetting serve a range of functions, such as establishing and maintaining relationships, teaching or entertaining others (Alea & Bluck, 2003), and supporting group identity (Sahdra & Ross, 2007).

Although remembering and forgetting may be functional for individuals, groups or societies, across each of these levels different (and possibly competing) functions may be more or less important. For example, in recent years younger Australians have become increasingly involved in commemorating our wartime heroes, especially on ANZAC Day (April 25, which is the anniversary of Australian and New Zealand troops landing on the Turkish peninsula at Gallipoli in World War I) and especially as the last of our World War I veterans pass away. Commentators have noted a swell in the social or national desire to remember these events and individuals. Attendance at ANZAC Day ceremonies has surged, descendants of servicemen are marching in greater numbers in ANZAC Day parades, and each year more and more young Australians make the journey to Turkey to pay their respects at the site of the Gallipoli landing (Wilson, 2008). This contrasts with the individual desire of many veterans, such as Nicky Barr, to forget their wartime experiences. Some war veterans, for instance, avoided ANZAC Day marches and ceremonies entirely (see the case of Marcel Caux; "Marcel Caux, 105",

2004). In other words, an individual's goal to forget may be threatened by a broader goal to remember (or vice versa).

Forgetting may occur for a number of reasons (see Cubelli, this volume, Chapter 3; Levy, Kuhl & Wagner, this volume, Chapter 7). In this chapter, we focus on the inability to retrieve information that has been successfully stored in memory. That is, we assume that both encoding and storage were successful, and that forgetting occurs at the retrieval stage. When a particular memory has been encoded and stored successfully but cannot be retrieved, there are at least two possible reasons: reduced memory accessibility and/or reduced memory availability (Tulving & Pearlstone, 1966; see also Kihlstrom & Barnhardt, 1993). Memories that are both available and accessible can be consciously brought to awareness, and can be indexed by explicit memory tests (tests which involve the conscious, intentional recall of target material; Schacter, 1987). Memories that are available but not currently accessible remain outside awareness but can influence ongoing behaviour, and can be indexed by implicit memory tests (tests which do not require conscious recall but where prior learning can aid performance, e.g., priming; Schacter, 1987). Although memories may be inaccessible in a particular context or on a particular recall occasion, they may become accessible in another context, with repeated retrieval attempts or with an appropriate cue (Rubin, 2007). Memories that are neither available nor accessible do not influence either conscious or unconscious processing, so that the likelihood of recalling these memories is low and they may be effectively lost over time.

Adopting a functional view of autobiographical memory (Conway, 2005), in this chapter we consider research that has extended studies of remembering and forgetting to a broad range of "memory cases" (Barnier, Sutton, Harris, & Wilson, 2008). We describe experimental paradigms for studying goal-directed forgetting in the laboratory, and review research extending these paradigms towards more autobiographical remembering and forgetting, and towards more social remembering and forgetting. Finally, we link these experimental findings to interdisciplinary work from social science and philosophy on autobiographical forgetting and social forgetting.

Autobiographical memory: forgetting the personal past

The self-memory system

Autobiographical memories are our recollections of specific episodes from the past. Tulving (2002) described autobiographical remembering as "mental time travel", in which we relive the best, the worst, and the everyday occurrences of our lives. In the absence of significant disruption, we remember many things from our past. However, autobiographical memory is selective. We tend to remember events that place us in a good light, support our current self-image, or promote ongoing activities. And we try to forget – with varying success – memories of experiences that undermine the current self, contradict our beliefs, plans, and goals, and increase anxiety or other negative emotions (Conway, 2005; Conway & Pleydell-Pearce, 2000).

Conway (2005; Conway & Pleydell-Pearce, 2000) proposed the self-memory system (SMS) to describe the structure of autobiographical memory and the relationship between autobiographical memory and self-identity. In the SMS, people's knowledge about their lives is organized hierarchically across three levels of increasing specificity: lifetime periods (e.g., when I was in high school), general events (e.g., going to maths class), and event-specific knowledge (e.g., the day I had our final maths exam). A specific autobiographical memory is generated by a stable pattern of activation across all three levels of knowledge. However, the construction of this pattern of activation is constrained by executive control processes that coordinate access to the knowledge base and modulate output from it (Conway, 2005; Conway & Pleydell-Pearce, 2000). These control processes are termed the "working self". The working self can facilitate or inhibit retrieval of certain memories depending on current goals. In the SMS, goals influence the encoding, storage, and retrieval of information to determine the content and accessibility of autobiographical memories (Conway, 2005).

Conway (2005; Conway, Singer, & Tagini, 2004) identified two fundamental principles underlying autobiographical memory. The first is "coherence", which refers to the need to maintain an integrated and consistent sense of one's life experiences. The second is "correspondence", which refers to the need for episodic memory to correspond with reality. These principles are not mutually exclusive. Rather, a balance between them is required for a functioning autobiographical memory system. This distinction between coherence and correspondence is not new. Bartlett (1932) emphasized that the purpose of remembering, particularly in a social context, is to share our impressions with others, so people are likely to construct and embellish upon their memories rather than generate a strictly accurate representation of what happened. Conway (2005) argued that over time, in long-term memory, coherence takes precedence over correspondence.

One main idea from the SMS is that what is remembered from our lives, and what in turn is forgotten, is determined by our current working self (the image of ourselves we have at any given time). As noted above, autobiographical memories that are consistent with the goals and values of our working self are prioritized for remembering, whereas memories that conflict with our working self are likely to be forgotten (Barnier, Conway, Mayoh, Speyer, Avizmil, & Harris, 2007; Conway, 2005; Conway & Pleydell-Pearce, 2000). Within the SMS model then, autobiographical forgetting is a goal-directed, executive process, where certain memories are actively gated from consciousness. Those memories that are irrelevant, inconsistent with current identity goals, or upsetting are particularly likely to be forgotten.

Studying autobiographical forgetting

Research within different traditions and paradigms supports the view that certain kinds of memories are forgotten in apparently goal-directed ways. For instance, diary studies have suggested that, but people are more likely to forget events about themselves that are negative rather than positive, they are more likely to forget events about others that are positive rather than negative (Thompson, Skowronski, Larsen, & Betz, 1996; Walker, Skowronski, & Thompson, 2003). Also, people tend to organize their life story in terms of well-remembered turning points (Thorne, 2000), and forget events that are inconsistent with their current goals and motivations (Habermas & Bluck, 2000). In the clinical domain, some people with posttraumatic stress disorder deliberately and persistently try to forget memories of their trauma (Brewin, 1998), people with functional amnesia forget whole chunks or even their entire autobiographical history following a traumatic experience (Kihlstrom & Schacter, 1995), and people with a repressive coping style (low reported anxiety but high defensiveness) are much more likely to forget negative childhood events than nonrepressors and will actively suppress negative life events whether instructed to or not (Barnier, Levin, & Maher, 2004; Myers & Brewin, 1994).

In the next section, we review three major experimental paradigms of goal-directed forgetting: retrieval-induced forgetting (RIF; Anderson, Bjork, & Bjork, 1994), directed forgetting (DF; Bjork, 1970; Bjork et al., 1998), and Think/No-think (Anderson & Green, 2001). Directed forgetting is claimed to operate at the level of accessibility, temporarily reducing access to the memory. Retrieval-induced forgetting and Think/No-think are claimed to operate on availability, degrading the memory representation itself (for a review of these paradigms and their claims, see Anderson 2005). Each of these paradigms has been adopted and extended to explore the functional nature of memory, for example by using emotional words as stimuli or by examining specific clinical populations. Studies of clinical populations are important because it has been suggested that people with certain disorders develop memory biases that can maintain their illnesses; that is, their functional remembering and forgetting becomes dysfunctional (Starr & Moulds, 2006). Each of these paradigms has been extended also (to varying degrees) to study the forgetting of autobiographical memories. Studies involving autobiographical material are important because they index the extent to which these paradigms can tell us about everyday remembering and forgetting.

Retrieval-induced forgetting

The retrieval-induced forgetting (RIF) paradigm developed by Anderson et al. (1994; see also Anderson, 2005) models the kind of forgetting that occurs unconsciously in response to competition between memories, by practising some memories at the expense of others. Imagine the woman who thinks of her wedding day, and consistently remembers the things that went according to, rather than contrary to, her careful plans. After repeated rehearsals of the things that went right, she is less likely to remember the things that went wrong. Hence, retrieval-induced forgetting avoids cluttering memory with information that is unwanted, redundant or out of date.

In the standard paradigm, participants learn a set of category–exemplar pairs, such as "fruit–apple", "fruit–banana", "instrument–flute", and "instrument–violin". Participants are then presented with the cue "fruit–a" a number of times, and practise retrieving "apple" repeatedly when presented with this cue. Finally, participants are presented with the categories (fruit, instrument) and asked to recall all the exemplars for each one (see Figure 12.1). Typically, participants are less likely to recall "banana" than they are to remember "flute" or "violin". This is the RIF effect: retrieval practice reduces recall of unpractised exemplars from the practised category, relative to exemplars from an unpractised category. It has been suggested that when presented with "fruit–a" all the fruit exemplars are activated to some extent, and so successful retrieval practice of "apple" requires the inhibition of the competing, irrelevant fruit exemplar "banana". This means that "banana" is subsequently more difficult to recall than noncompeting irrelevant information (like flute, violin), which was not activated during retrieval practice (see Bjork et al., 1998; see also Levy Kuhl, & Wagner, this volume, Chapter 7). It has been argued that RIF impairs both memory accessibility and availability. This is supported by evidence showing that recall of unpractised, related exemplars is still inhibited when tested with a novel, independent cue (Anderson, 2005; Anderson & Spellman, 1995; but see MacLeod, Dodd, Sheard, Wilson, & Bibi, 2003 for a non-inhibitory account).

RIF is considered an automatic, inevitable consequence of practising one piece of information at the expense of another. But researchers have examined whether RIF effects are influenced by motivation. Generally, this has taken the form of comparing RIF for emotional (positive or negative) material with RIF for unemotional material (the standard paradigm uses neutral word pairs). The logic is that people might be motivated to forget certain types of information (e.g., negative information), and so might show greater RIF for these words. Alternatively, people might have difficulty forgetting such information (e.g., in certain clinical populations), and so RIF may not occur for emotional material. In other words, are RIF effects

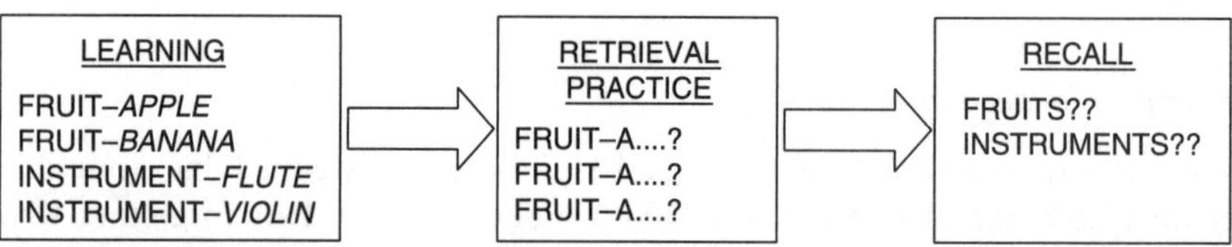

Figure 12.1 The retrieval-induced forgetting procedure (Anderson et al., 1994).

selective consistent with the functional view of remembering and forgetting? For example, Moulds and Kandris (2006) investigated RIF of negative and neutral words in high and low dysphoric participants (dysphoria is a measure of negative mood, and is used as an analogue for depression in nonclinical samples). In general, high dysphoric participants tend to recall more negative than positive memories (Mineka & Nugent, 1995). However, Moulds and Kandris (2006) found that both high and low dysphoric participants showed RIF for neutral but not negative words; that is, in both groups negative words were not forgotten. Similarly, Kuhbandner, Bäuml, and Stiedl (in press) examined RIF for negative pictures and found that the more intensely negative the picture was, the less likely participants were to show RIF for it; this was particularly so for participants in a negative mood. Relatedly, Amir, Coles, Brigidi, and Foa (2001) found that people with generalized social phobia showed RIF for nonsocial words and positive social words, but not for negative social words. In other words they had difficulty forgetting words that were particularly relevant to their phobia (category–exemplar pairs included, for example, dating–rejection, dating–clumsy, conversation–babble, conversation–silence). Taken together, these results suggest that motivational factors do influence forgetting in the RIF paradigm. Emotionally negative material may be less likely forgotten, and individual memory biases can moderate the effects of retrieval practice. What then might this predict for RIF of autobiographical memories, which are not only emotional, but meaningful, complex, and self-relevant?

Macrae and Roseveare (2002) suggested that the personal relevance of the information to be remembered vs. forgotten might influence RIF. In their study, participants learned a list of "gift" words by either imagining themselves purchasing the gift ("self" condition) or imagining another person purchasing the gift ("other" condition). Interestingly, whereas participants in the other condition showed a standard RIF effect, participants in the self condition did not; that is, participants did not forget the gifts they imagined themselves buying, even when these gifts competed for retrieval with practised items. Macrae and Roseveare (2002) argued that self-relevant material might be protected from RIF. Given that autobiographical memories are by definition self-relevant (Conway, 2005), are they susceptible to RIF? Is RIF a good model of autobiographical forgetting?

To test this, Barnier, Hung, and Conway (2004a) adapted the RIF paradigm to examine forgetting of positive, neutral, and negative autobiographical memories. In their procedure, participants elicited four memories to each of a number of cues such as "happy", "tidy" and "sickness". Subsequently, participants practised retrieving half their memories in response to half the cues, before being asked to remember all the memories for each cue. Barnier et al. (2004a) found an overall RIF effect. Participants were less likely to recall unpractised memories that competed with practised memories than they were to recall baseline memories. That is, retrieval practice resulted in forgetting of competing, irrelevant autobiographical memories. However, in contrast to

RIF research using words and other simple materials, Barnier et al. (2004a) found that emotional valence of the memories did not influence the RIF effect. Rather, independent of retrieval practice, participants were simply less likely to elicit and more likely to forget emotional than unemotional memories.

In a follow-up study, Wessel and Hauer (2006) replicated Barnier et al.'s (2004a) finding of RIF for autobiographical memories. But unlike Barnier et al., however, they found RIF for negative but not positive memories. This suggests that negative memories are sometimes forgotten in the RIF paradigm. It may be that manipulating memory valence – positive vs. negative. vs. neutral – does not fully capture memory biases (see Barnier et al., 2007), and that more subtle manipulations (such as whether memories are personally significant or not and whether memories are self-defining or not) may be required to determine when retrieval practice leads to forgetting of autobiographical memories.

Directed forgetting

The directed forgetting (DF) paradigm models the type of forgetting that occurs when we are explicitly instructed that certain information is unnecessary or unwanted (Bjork et al., 1998). This can occur when old information is updated with new, competing information. Imagine a jury is presented with one set of facts about a defendant, but then promptly told by a judge to forget this information and to focus on a new set of facts instead.

In the standard list-method directed forgetting (DF) paradigm, participants study two lists of words (list 1 and list 2). After studying list 1, half the participants are told to forget list 1 items, and half are told to remember list 1 items. Both groups are told to remember list 2 items, which are subsequently presented (see Figure 12.2). Participants told to forget list 1 items recall fewer items from this list than participants told to remember list 1 items: this is the DF effect (Bjork et al., 1998). Notably, competition between to-be-forgotten (list 1) material and to-be-remembered (list 2) material is necessary for DF; there is no forgetting in the absence of list 2 learning (Bjork et al., 1998). DF impairs explicit memory while leaving implicit memory intact, as demonstrated by Basden, Basden, and Gargano (1993) using a word stem completion task. Also, DF can be abolished using a recognition test rather than a recall test (Basden et al., 1993; Bjork et al., 1998). Thus, it has been argued that DF impairs memory accessibility, but not availability, since these items

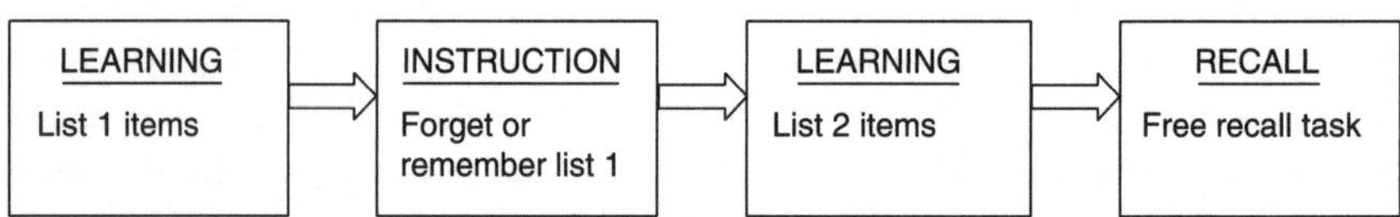

Figure 12.2 The list-method directed forgetting procedure (Bjork, 1970).

can still be recalled given sufficient cues, as in a recognition task (but see Sahakyan & Delaney, 2005, for an alternative, non-inhibitory account of DF).

Like the RIF paradigm, researchers have examined whether DF effects are influenced by motivation. Again, this has generally taken the form of comparing DF for emotional (positive or negative) material with DF for unemotional material (for a review, see Koutstaal & Schacter, 1997). Are DF effects selective consistent with the functional view of remembering and forgetting? To test this Payne and Corrigan (2007), for example, examined DF of emotional and neutral pictures, and found a DF effect for neutral pictures but not for emotional pictures; that is, emotional stimuli were not forgotten. In contrast, Wessel and Merckelbach (2006) found DF effects for both emotional and unemotional words. But as Payne and Corrigan (2007) argued, this might be because words are unlikely to elicit emotional responses in a normal population. Laying aside questions about the stimuli, Payne and Corrigan's (2007) findings, as well as some RIF findings, suggest that emotional material – particularly negative material – might be resistant to forgetting. This conclusion is consistent with the functional, selective view of remembering and forgetting outlined above, although it remains controversial whether and why negative material would be particularly resistant to forgetting (Anderson & Levy, 2002; Brewin, 1998; Erdelyi, 2006; Kihlstrom, 2002, 2006; McNally, 2005).

Like RIF, much research on DF has focused on clinical populations. For example, Geraerts, Smeets, Jelicic, Merckelbach, and van Heerdan (2006) compared DF of neutral words with DF of words associated with child sexual abuse in either participants who had reported continuous memories of abuse, participants who recovered memories of abuse, and control participants. Unexpectedly, all participants demonstrated less forgetting (no or reduced DF effects) for abuse-related words. This is similar to Payne and Corrigan's finding (2007), which suggested that emotional material may be immune to DF. In contrast, other researchers have reported that certain populations show more forgetting (greater DF effects) of negative material. For example, Moulds and Bryant (2002) examined patients with acute stress disorder. They found that these patients forgot more trauma-related words when given a forget instruction than controls (Moulds & Bryant, 2002). Myers, Brewin, and Power (1998) examined individuals with a repressive coping style (individuals characterized by low reported anxiety and high defensiveness). They found that repressive copers forgot more negative material when given a forget instruction than nonrepressors (Myers et al., 1998). Similarly Myers and Derakshan (2004) found that repressive copers forgot more negative words when given a forget instruction than nonrepressors, but only when they rated the words for self-descriptiveness; when they rated them for other-descriptiveness there was no difference.

Taken together, these findings suggest that DF effects are selective. Some research suggests that DF operates on all kinds of material, other research suggests that DF does not operate on emotional material, and still other research suggests that DF operates particularly for emotional material, and may depend on individuals' memory biases. Although, as suggested above for RIF, memory valence may not fully capture motivational effects on forgetting in the DF paradigm, these findings lead us to ask how DF (like RIF) might influence autobiographical memories.

Joslyn and Oakes (2005) conducted a diary study to examine this. They asked participants to record 10 events from their lives each week over a 2-week period. After 1 week, half the participants were told that the first week was for practice (experiment 1), or that the first week memories were for a different experiment (experiment 2). Finally, participants were asked to recall all the events they had recorded from both weeks. Joslyn and Oakes (2005) reported a significant DF effect: participants in the forget condition recalled fewer week 1 memories than participants in the remember condition. This effect occurred for positive and negative events, and for high-intensity and low-intensity events (Joslyn & Oakes, 2005). In a closer adaptation of the original DF procedure, Barnier et al. (2007) also examined directed forgetting of autobiographical memories. In our adaptation, participants elicited autobiographical memories in response to cue words such as "happy" and "sickness". Halfway through the words, participants were either told to forget or remember the first list, before eliciting memories for a second set of cues (list 2). Barnier et al. (2007) found a DF effect for positive, negative, and neutral autobiographical memories, although unemotional memories were more likely to be forgotten overall than emotional memories. This contrasts with Barnier et al.'s (2004a) findings for RIF, where emotional memories were more likely to be forgotten overall than unemotional memories. Again, more targeted manipulations, such as whether memories are personally significant or not and whether memories are self-defining or not, might help us to better understand these different patterns for emotional and unemotional memories (as well as emotional and unemotional simple material) and better capture the goal-directed nature of remembering and forgetting.

Think/No-think

The Think/No-think paradigm models the kind of forgetting that occurs when we intentionally suppress or avoid remembering in response to strong reminders of a particular event (Anderson & Green, 2001; Levy & Anderson, 2002). Imagine a man who associates a particular song with an unhappy love affair. Each time he hears the song, he tries to avoid thinking of the failed relationship, and over time he remembers less.

In this paradigm, participants learn a series of cue-target pairs (e.g., "ambition–ballet", "ordeal–roach", "fuss–poodle"). Subsequently, in the Think/No-think phase, participants are presented with some of the cue words again. In this phase, for half the cues (e.g., "ambition") participants recall the associated target, and for half the cues (e.g., "ordeal") participants avoid letting the target come into their mind (see Figure 12.3). On a final cued recall

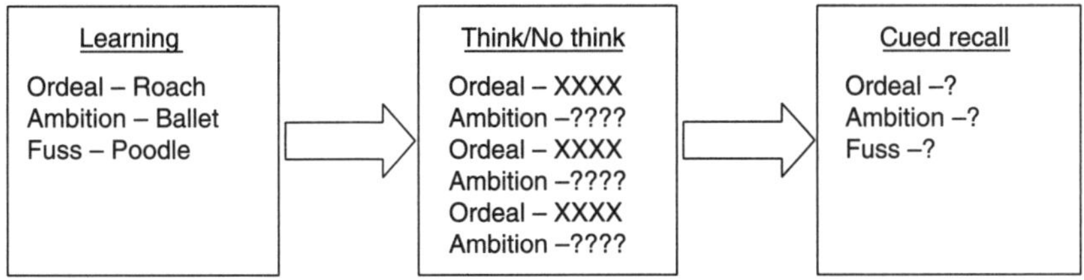

Figure 12.3 The think/no-think procedure (Anderson & Green, 2001).

test, Anderson and Green (2001) found that participants recalled fewer targets that they suppressed (e.g., "roach") than baseline targets (items that did not appear at all in the Think/No-think phase, e.g., "poodle"). They concluded that this procedure might model Freudian repression, by showing that deliberate attempts to suppress may result in forgetting (Anderson & Levy, 2002; but see Kihlstrom, 2002; see also Erdelyi, 2006; Kihlstrom, 2006). TNT has been argued to impair both memory accessibility and availability. This is supported by evidence that participants show poorer recall for suppressed items even when recall is cued with a novel cue (e.g., "insect" for "roach"; Anderson & Green, 2001).

While some researchers have replicated the forgetting effect following suppression in this paradigm (for review, see Levy & Anderson, 2008), others have had difficulty. For example, across three attempted replications with increasingly precise adherence to Anderson and Green's (2001) original procedure, Bulevich, Roediger, Balota, and Butler (2006) failed to find a TNT effect. It is worth noting that, compared to RIF and DF, the magnitude of the TNT effect is quite small (Anderson & Green, 2001; Levy & Anderson, 2008). Hertel and Calcaterra (2005) argued that the use of particular strategies during suppression may predict successful forgetting in TNT. They replicated the TNT effect only when participants used the strategy of thinking about an alternative word during suppression, either because they were instructed to do so or did so spontaneously (but see Levy & Anderson, 2008).

Like RIF and DF, some researchers have examined motivational influences on TNT; does TNT differentially impact recall of emotional material? Depue, Banich, and Curran (2006) compared TNT for negative and neutral stimuli, and found stronger forgetting effects for negative stimuli. They argued that cognitive control processes may be activated more strongly for emotional information. Although this finding is consistent with a functional view of forgetting, it contrasts with the mixed findings for emotional material in the RIF and DF paradigms. Also, like RIF and DF, other researchers have focused on whether specific populations might show stronger or weaker TNT effects. For example, Joormann, Hertel, LeMoult, and Gotlib (2009) examined TNT of positive and negative words in depressed and nondepressed participants. They found that, while nondepressed participants forgot positive and negative words they had suppressed, depressed participants did not show forgetting of negative words. However, when trained to think of an alternative word during suppression (as in Hertel & Calcaterra, 2005), depressed participants successfully forgot negative words. These results suggest that both motivations and strategies may determine the success of suppression in the TNT paradigm.

As with RIF and DF, we have explored whether TNT influences autobiographical memories, using a similar adaptation. In a series of experiments that adapted the TNT procedure to autobiographical memories (similar to our adaptations of RIF and DF), we asked participants to generate autobiographical memories in response to cue words. Then, participants were presented with some of the words, half of which they responded to by recalling the associated memory, and half of which they avoided by suppressing the associated memory. To date, we have conducted five experiments. In the first, participants completed three suppression cycles during the TNT phase. In the second, participants completed 12 suppression cycles. In the third, we instructed participants to think about an alternative memory during suppression (as in Hertel & Calcaterra, 2005). In the fourth, we introduced competition between the memories: participants elicited 6 memories to each of 6 cues (as in the RIF paradigm, see Barnier et al., 2004a), so that the respond memories directly competed for recall with the unwanted avoid memories via a shared cue. In our final experiment, we combined 12 suppression trials, a distraction condition, and a cue structure that created competition between the memories, plus a delay between memory elicitation and the TNT phase to reduce overall recall. We also asked participants about their life experiences, particularly about their exposure to trauma and attempts to suppress memories of this trauma in their daily lives (as suggested by Levy & Anderson, 2008). We have had difficulty finding a robust TNT effect. Overall, participants remember their autobiographical events despite repeated attempts to suppress (their memory performance is mostly at ceiling). However, introducing competition between the memories decreased memory overall and may have aided suppression (at least for a subset of participants), and in our most recent experiment there is some indication that trauma exposure may predict suppression success (Levy & Anderson, 2008).

Results with TNT are interesting in the light of work in the related "thought suppression" paradigm (Wegner, Schneider, Carter, & White, 1987). In our lab, in a thought suppression study comparing repressive copers and nonrepressors, we found that nonrepressors were able to suppress positive memories during a suppression period, but experienced a rebound effect following suppression; they were unable to suppress negative memories at all (Barnier et al., 2004b). In other words, nonrepressors' initial suppression success, at least for positive memories, did not result in later forgetting, which contrasts with findings from the TNT paradigm. However, repressive copers were particularly successful in suppressing negative events, even when they were not instructed to do so (Barnier et al., 2004b; see also Geraerts, Merckelbach, Jelicic, & Smeets, 2006), and they showed no rebound effect (but see Geraerts et al., 2006). This is similar to findings from the TNT paradigm. Thus, it remains unclear when and why suppression (whether in TNT or thought suppression) might result in successful forgetting of autobiographical memories.

Conclusion

Based on this review, it is clear that the effects of RIF, DF, and TNT paradigms extend from the simple materials used to develop the original methodologies, to emotional words and sometimes to autobiographical memories. However, as the material increases in complexity (emotionality and personal meaningfulness), so do the effects. These paradigms can be argued to model different mechanisms of goal-directed forgetting and provide good laboratory analogues for everyday, real-world forgetting. As noted above, one assumption of a functional view of memory is that people might try to forget upsetting memories. In general, results across these paradigms suggest that sometimes people remember more emotional than unemotional material, sometimes they remember as much, and sometimes they forget more emotional material than unemotional. This implies that in remembering and forgetting the past, people are not just influenced by the simple valence of a piece of information or of an event. It is likely there are other dimensions predicting its self-relevance, and thus, whether it is prioritized for remembering or forgetting.

Social forgetting: forgetting with others

While memory is motivated by individual goals such as maintaining a positive identity, it is also motivated by social goals such as promoting group cohesion, enhancing relationships, negotiating the meaning of shared experiences, and planning joint action or projects (Alea & Bluck, 2003; Barnier, et al., 2008). For instance, consider the following excerpts from interviews with two long-married couples whom we asked (both individually and jointly) to describe their autobiographical memories and their remembering practices. One couple, married for 35 years, remembered together in a genuinely shared way, dynamically constructing the past, and often speaking directly to each other rather than to the interviewers. In his individual interview, the husband described the role of remembering in their relationship:

Interviewer: How often do you talk about the past together with [wife]?
Husband: A lot. We're big talkers. That has always been a big point of our lives, still is!

In contrast, another couple, who had recently experienced marital difficulties, did not seem to jointly remember in an efficient manner. The wife, in her individual interview, described how recent difficulties in their relationship had resulted in less day-to-day reminiscing with her husband:

Interviewer: Do you tend to reminisce together?
Wife: Not as much as we used to.
Interviewer: Okay, so it's kind of changed you think.
Wife: Yeah, I do. Yeah, there were some circumstances that changed it, a couple of years ago, which were really not, not happy for me, and not happy for him.

Insights from these interviews support our view that studying social influences on remembering and forgetting is a natural extension of the functional approach to autobiographical memory.

We are likely to discuss a whole range of events with others: recent and distant, significant and mundane, shared and unshared. However, just as individual autobiographical memory is selective and goal directed, social memory is also likely to be selective, depending on the norms and values of the group that might prioritize certain items for retrieval and others for forgetting. The social context might also shape what is remembered and what is forgotten more subtly, by dictating the appropriate style and contents of recall, the social dynamics of who speaks when and whose recollections are given the most weight, and the purpose of remembering (Weldon & Bellinger, 1997). According to Schudson (1995, p. 360), people remember "collectively, publicly and interactively", in the sense that remembering occurs for a particular audience and with input from that audience. Listeners' responses can guide what is recalled during conversation (Pasupathi, 2001), and recalling selectively in a social context can shape subsequent individual memory (Tversky & Marsh, 2000). Based on these ideas, autobiographical memory has been labelled "relational" (Campbell, 2003). It originates with an individual's experience of an event but is maintained, shaped, and elaborated through interaction with others (Hayne & MacDonald, 2003), as well as through individual identity goals.

In terms of forgetting, the selective nature of social remembering suggests that information that conflicts not just with individual goals, but also with social goals, is unlikely to be recalled during conversation. Fivush (2004) described "silencing", the self- or other-censorship that can occur when recalling the past with others. She argued that this silencing during social interaction can cause subsequent forgetting of material that was not mentioned during the conversation (Fivush, 2004). Thus, social influence may cause forgetting, particularly of memories that conflict with the group's goals. An alternative (but not conflicting) view is that social influence may reduce forgetting by providing social support for memory, and we elaborate further on this later in the chapter. We do not focus on social influences on misremembering, which have been extensively studied and are covered in detail elsewhere (see Loftus, 2005 for a review).

Studying social forgetting

Social aspects of remembering and forgetting have received a great deal of attention from psychologists, at least since Bartlett's (1932) *Remembering*. In the developmental domain, researchers have focused on how parents talk to children about the past and teach them the narrative structures of autobiographical remembering (Reese & Fivush, 2008). In the forensic domain, researchers have examined how eyewitnesses influence each other's memories, and whether interactions between witnesses can distort later testimony (Paterson & Kemp, 2006). In the organizational domain, researchers have focused on how groups coordinate performance to enhance workplace productivity (Brandon & Hollingshead, 2004). In contrast, cognitive psychology has traditionally been more individualistic in its approach to studying memory, and it is only relatively recently that cognitive, experimental paradigms have been developed to examine how remembering with others is different from remembering alone. Below, we review two major experimental paradigms that have been used to study social forgetting in the laboratory. The first is socially shared retrieval-induced forgetting (SS-RIF), which is an extension of the RIF paradigm into a social context (Cuc, Koppel, & Hirst, 2007). The second is collaborative recall, which was developed to directly measure how what is remembered and forgotten in a group compares to what is remembered and forgotten by the same number of individuals recalling alone (Weldon & Bellinger, 1997). These paradigms demonstrate the ways in which individual and social processes combine to influence both remembering and forgetting.

Socially shared retrieval-induced forgetting (SS-RIF)

The RIF paradigm (described in the previous section) has been extended to examine forgetting in a social context. This paradigm models the kind of forgetting that is the result of selective remembering in conversation with others. Imagine a politician who repeatedly directs her audience's attention to her successful, popular policies, and avoids mentioning her unpopular policies and scandals. She might hope that this would cause her listeners to subsequently forget her misdeeds. Cuc et al. (2007) argued that the selective remembering that happens in a conversation (where only information consistent with conversational goals is mentioned; Tversky & Marsh, 2000) is a form of retrieval practice that should result in forgetting of unpractised, related information.

To test this, Cuc et al. (2007) replicated the standard RIF procedure of Anderson et al. (1994) but introduced a "listener" who observed the "speaker's" retrieval practice and monitored them for either accuracy or fluency. Speakers showed RIF as expected. Most importantly, listeners showed RIF as well but only when they monitored the speaker's accuracy, presumably because this encouraged listeners to perform the retrieval practice themselves as they observed the speaker. To examine whether SS-RIF might also operate in a natural discussion, where participants were not explicitly instructed to monitor for accuracy and where the role of speaker and listener shifted back and forth, in a second experiment Cuc et al. (2007) modified the SS-RIF procedure so that the retrieval practice phase consisted of a free-flowing conversation between two participants. They found that both speaker and listener showed RIF (Cuc et al., 2007; see also Stone, Barnier, Sutton & Hirst, 2010). Thus, SS-RIF appears to be one plausible explanation for forgetting in social interactions, and in our lab we are currently extending this effect to autobiographical memories. This research suggests that the content of a conversation could be shaped either intentionally or unintentionally to induce forgetting of unwanted information. In this way, social interaction could lead to individual forgetting (Hirst & Manier, 2008).

Collaborative recall

Another major experimental paradigm used to measure the impact of recalling the past with others is collaborative recall (Basden, Basden, Bryber, & Thomas, 1997; Blumen & Rajaram, 2008; Finlay, Hitch, & Meudell, 2000; Weldon & Bellinger, 1997), which was designed to assess the "costs and benefits" of remembering in a group (Basden, Basden, & Henry, 2000; for review, see Harris, Paterson, & Kemp, 2008). Collaborative recall models the kind of remembering and forgetting that occurs around the dinner table when a family reminisces about the last holiday they took together. In this paradigm, the recall performance of collaborative groups (people recalling together) is compared to the recall performance of nominal groups (the pooled recall of the same number of individuals recalling alone; see Figure 12.4). We might assume that recalling with others should help our individual performance, but the opposite is true. Research on collaborative recall has consistently demonstrated that collaborative groups recall less than nominal groups; this effect is termed "collaborative inhibition" (Basden et al., 2000; Weldon & Bellinger, 1997).

The best-supported explanation for collaborative inhibition is the retrieval strategy disruption hypothesis: recalling information in a group disrupts each individual's retrieval strategies, making them less efficient (Basden et al., 1997). That is, recalling with others results in each individual forgetting items that they would have been able to recall alone. Evidence for this account comes from research showing that collaborative inhibition is abolished when each group member is responsible for recalling a different part of a categorized list (Basden et al., 1997). Also, collaborative inhibition is abolished when recall is cued (Finlay et al., 2000), when group members are forced to organize their recall by category (and hence, presumably, use the same retrieval strategies, Basden et al., 1997), or when group members are unable to hear or see the items recalled by other group members (Wright & Klumpp, 2004).

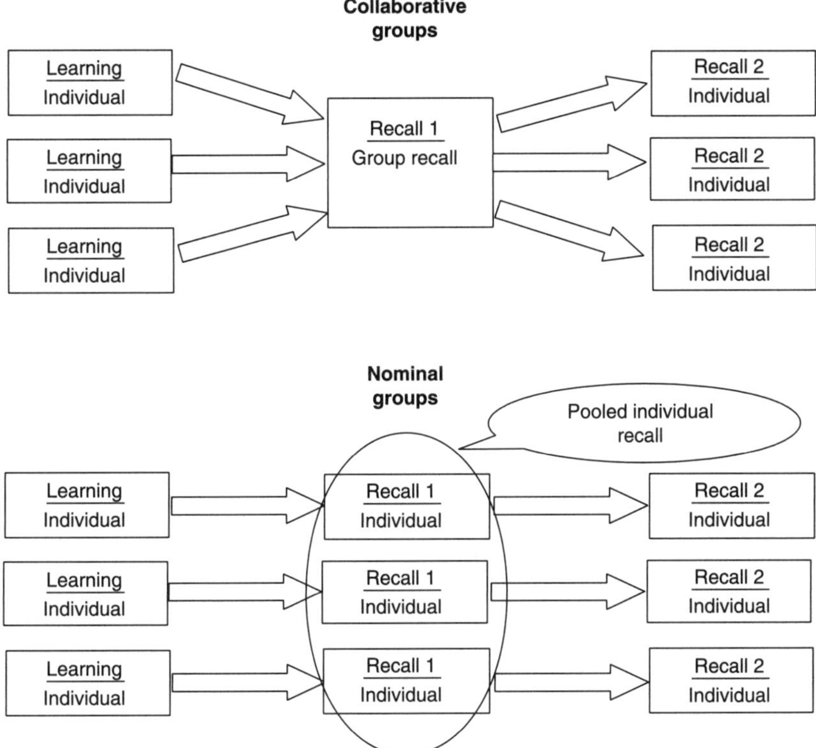

Figure 12.4 The collaborative recall procedure (Basden et al., 2000).

Essentially, collaborative inhibition is abolished when individuals in a group remember not as a group but as individuals, that is, when the group cannot hinder, but also cannot help, recall.

Collaboration has ongoing influences on individual memory. Prior collaboration results in an inhibition of hypermnesia; participants who have collaborated are subsequently more likely to recall items mentioned in the collaboration, but less likely to recall new items from the original list (Basden et al., 2000). That is, collaboration shapes subsequent individual recall, both in terms of remembering (mentioned items) and forgetting (unmentioned items). Interestingly, recent results from our lab suggest that collaboration can improve accuracy (if not amount recalled), both during collaboration and on subsequent individual tests, but only when collaborating groups are instructed to reach a consensus about each item recalled (Harris, Barnier, & Sutton, submitted).

Much like standard RIF, DF, and TNT, most of the research on collaborative recall has focused on relatively neutral material. If remembering with others does influence what we remember and forget, we might expect this influence to operate particularly for important or emotional memories, when recalling with our social groups (e.g., family, friends) or when recalling shared events. In terms of emotional events, Yaron-Antar and Nachson (2006) examined whether collaboration impaired recall of the details of the assassination of Israeli Prime Minister Rabin: it still did; collaborative groups still showed collaborative inhibition. In terms of recalling with our social groups, studies of whether collaborative inhibition is reduced or abolished when in groups of acquaintances have yielded mixed results. Andersson and Rönnberg (1995) reported less collaborative inhibition for groups of friends, while Gould, Osborne, Krein, and Mortenson (2002) reported no difference between married and unacquainted dyads. Other aspects of the group, apart from familiarity, may also be important in determining the outcomes of collaboration. Social and motivational factors – such as whether the interaction is face to face or electronic, and the perceived output level of the group – impact the amount remembered and forgotten by the individuals in a group (Ekeocha & Brennen, 2008; Reysen, 2003). Notably, in a recent study of collaboration between expert pilots, who are skilled at communicating in order to perform tasks together, Meade, Nokes, and Morrow (2009) found facilitation not inhibition. In terms of shared and unshared events, we recently conducted a study of collaborative recall among friends and strangers, who encoded information either together or individually. Our results suggest that when information is encoded individually, collaboration results in inhibition for both groups of strangers and groups of friends. But when information is encoded as a group, collaboration results in no inhibition for groups of strangers or groups of friends (Harris, Barnier, & Sutton, 2009).

In an extension of the collaborative recall paradigm to memory for personal experiences, we examined how conversation about a shared, significant event might shape memory for and feelings about that event (Harris, Barnier, Sutton, & Keil, 2010). Following the sudden death of the Australian celebrity, "Crocodile Hunter" Steve Irwin, we asked participants to come to the lab and either discuss their memories for hearing of Irwin's death in a group of three, or to spend time thinking about their memory alone. We indexed participants' memories for and feelings about the event on 3 occasions – before the discussion phase, 1 week later, and 1 month later. We found that, during discussion, references to personally being upset by Irwin's death were silenced. Consider the following excerpt from a group conversation between a female participant (K) and two male participants (M and E):

K: I know people that cried when they were watching the memorial service when Bindi was doing her speech.
M: Yeah, that was really sad! I don't know anybody who actually cried . . .
E: Did you cry?
K: Can't say that I did.
E: Do you know anybody that cares at all?
M: I don't think a lot of people . . .

K: I think people feel bad for him. A lot of people.
E: People die every day.

This excerpt illustrates the process of negotiation that occurred during conversations, such that personal emotion was silenced. This silencing influenced subsequent memory – participants who discussed their memory reduced their ratings of how upset they had been when they heard the news, relative to participants who thought about the event alone. In this case, discussion resulted in forgetting of emotion, rather than the factual details of the event. While the collaborative recall paradigm suggests that remembering with others results in forgetting, our research suggests that this forgetting is targeted – that collaboration may result in forgetting of specific aspects of an event depending on the group norms that emerge during discussion (Harris et al., 2010). That is, social motivations, such as fitting into a group of peers or agreeing with others, can drive what is remembered and forgotten, even for emotional events that are well remembered (cf., Fivush, 2004).

Conclusion

Overall, research on SS-RIF and collaborative recall suggests that a range of individual and social factors can influence what is remembered and what is forgotten when people talk about the past together. This research highlights that laboratory paradigms of individual and social forgetting can be extended to examine more complex questions about ways in which our social interactions influence what we remember and what we forget.

Situated forgetting: forgetting in context

As mainstream cognitive psychology has moved towards the functional (constructive, motivated, selective) view of remembering that we have described, it has increasingly stressed the central role of the "context" in determining what is remembered vs. forgotten. So far we have highlighted two aspects of the remembering context that might influence forgetting: individual motivations and goals, and social motivations and goals. In this section, we discuss a view of forgetting where context plays an even more pivotal role: situated forgetting. Over the past 20 years, philosophers of cognitive science have proposed that human cognitive processing is "hybrid": including not only the individual brain and body, but also the environment with its social and technological resources. This view has been labelled as "situated", "distributed", "extended" or "embedded" cognition, proposing that an individual's neural system does not act in causal isolation from its environmental and social context (see Barnier et al., 2008).

Distributed cognition and situated forgetting

Within the situated cognition framework, the human brain is seen as embedded in and extended into its world (Clark & Chalmers, 1998; Wheeler, 2005), where it rarely performs cognitive operations in isolation. Rather, intelligent action is conceptualized as the outcome of the cooperation or "coupling" of neural, bodily, and external systems in complex webs of "continuous reciprocal causation" (Clark, 1997, pp. 163–166). Applying this framework to memory, philosophers argue that humans augment their relatively unstable individual memories, which are not typically stored as discrete, fully formed units but as distributed representations, with more stable external "scaffolding" (Sutton, 2009; Wilson, 2005). They form temporarily integrated larger cognitive systems that incorporate distinct, but complementary, internal and external components. As Andy Clark puts it: "our brains make the world smart so that we can be dumb in peace" (Clark, 1997, p. 180). Memory systems are seen as extending the natural, technological, and social environment. This approach builds on Bartlett's (1932) work on remembering as the context-dependent compiling of materials from changing "interest-carried traces"; Vygotsky's (1978) analysis of how children's memory is transformed as they incorporate the ability to use artificial signs and cultural operations; and Halbwachs' (1980) stress on "the necessity of an affective community" in structuring and maintaining memory. A rich interdisciplinary literature now seeks to update and implement these ideas (Bloch, 1998; Connerton, 1989; Donald, 1991; Hirst & Manier, 2008; Middleton & Brown, 2005; Nelson & Fivush, 2004; Olick, 1999; Rowlands, 1999; Rubin, 1995; Welzer & Markowitsch, 2005; Wertsch, 2002; Zerubavel, 2003).

Most discussions of situated or distributed cognition have focused on the way an individual's memory system might extend to incorporate various technologies. For instance, an abstract artist may work incessantly with a sketchpad because imagining an artwork in the mind's eye will not successfully allow the perception, creation, and transformation of the right aesthetic patterns (van Leeuwen, Verstijnen, & Hekkert, 1999). The sketchpad isn't just a convenient storage bin for pre-existing visual images: the ongoing externalizing and reperceiving is an intrinsic part of artistic cognition itself (Clark, 2001). Other frequently cited examples include the tools and objects used to process orders in a café, the notes and records used to write an academic paper, or the use of particular glasses by bartenders in remembering cocktail orders (Beach, 1988; Clark, 1997; Hutchins, 1995; Kirsh, 2006).

In this context, forgetting can be seen as complementary to remembering. The storage of information which is less self-relevant or which is computationally costly might be offloaded on to the world, so that individuals can safely forget some information that they would have to hold internally if the environment was less structured or stable. Nevertheless, it is fair to say that researchers' focus has generally been on how situated memory, memory extended beyond the brain, can reduce forgetting. There has been less discussion of ways in which the use of objects may promote forgetting of material that is redundant, unnecessary, or unwanted. However, the functional approach to remembering and forgetting recognizes that what and how we forget is as important as what and how we remember. More work could be done to identify how people use technological resources to manage the balance between remembering and forgetting.

An individual's memory is also situated more broadly in their physical and cultural environment. Broader cultural symbols – such as museums, memorials, and monuments – may serve to shape and support an individual's memory, which is seen in these interdisciplinary literatures as notoriously fallible. These external objects are considered relatively stable and secure supplements to our internal storage systems. By this view, because neural processes are active, constructive, and selective, we rely on information outsourced to more enduring and unchanging cultural symbols (Clark, 1998; Donald, 1998). Similar to the research on memory-supporting technologies, research has focused mostly on how cultural symbols promote remembering, with less discussion of the balance between remembering and forgetting.

There are some notable exceptions, however, which promise an interesting integration of approaches to forgetting from the social sciences and from cognitive psychology (Connerton, 2008; Erdelyi, 2008; Singer & Conway, 2008; Wessel & Moulds, 2008). Objects that act as cultural symbols are not always intended to persist unchanged, and even those that are intended to last may not do so (Bowker 2005; Kwint 1999; Malafouris 2004; Sutton 2008). By preserving or highlighting certain features of the past, or rendering others open to dispute or renegotiation, cultural symbols can act as agents of forgetting. This is most obvious in cases of "repressive erasure" (Connerton 2008, pp. 60–61) such as the politically motivated airbrushing of a person from a photograph (e.g., the case of Vladimír Clementis described by Kundera, 1980). But objects can also play more subtle roles in encouraging forgetting. In certain African and Melanesian cultures, for example, some artifacts and structures "are made only to be abandoned immediately to decay", ephemeral monuments which may be the means by which "the members of the society get rid of what they no longer need or wish to remember" (Forty, 1999, pp. 4–5). In the Melanesian society described by Küchler (1999), an elaborate memorial device called a "malangann" is carved after someone's death. But instead of being installed as a permanent physical reminder, it stands on the grave for one night only before being abandoned or destroyed. Likewise, while places, buildings, or other physical locations do often support remembering, acting as key features of the cognitive (and affective and social) environment in which we reinstate or reconstruct the past, geographical sites too are vulnerable to change, reinterpretation, or erasure (Casey, 1987, 1992). In many projects of "urban renewal", for example, the physical destruction of existing communities is accompanied by a loss of the memories and traditions of the neighbourhoods in question, leaving only partial clues in a landscape of scars (Klein, 1997).

Socially situated forgetting and transactive memory

In our own work, we particularly focus on one form of situated or extended memory: how memory is shared among people in social groups. We investigate how small groups influence individual memory and how this reliance on the group may, in turn, lead to collective memory that is more than the sum of individual memories. Social influences on memory can be seen as so pervasive that some have argued that memory is inherently social and individual memory does not exist. For instance, Halbwachs (1980) suggested that even when we are superficially alone, we carry our groups with us, so that nothing much like memory at all would be left if all the social contexts of autobiographical remembering were truly stripped away. This view may seem extreme, especially to cognitive psychologists, but it draws our attention to theoretical accounts that try to reconcile individual and social memory, and within which we might place our laboratory studies of forgetting (see also Barnier, et al., 2008; Sutton, 2009; Tollefsen, 2006; Wilson, 2005).

For example, some theorists highlight the specific social and narrative environments in which we first learn to think and talk about the past. These environments, each with their own norms and dynamics, influence the subsequent selection principles and style of our own spontaneous remembering (Nelson & Fivush, 2004; Reese, 2002). Other theorists argue that as adults "sharing memories is our default" (Campbell, 2008, p. 43; Sutton, 2009). Where there is a rich shared history of joint actions in a couple or a small group, this history of interactions and negotiations dictates what is most commonly and comfortably forgotten or passed over, and in what contexts. The common ground on which successful communication within a dyad or group rests is itself partly constituted by shared memories, and in turn underlies the members' ongoing ways of thinking about the past whether together or alone.

The theory of transactive memory developed by Wegner and colleagues emphasizes the potential benefits of sharing memories, and gives rise to a clear picture of the interpersonal dimensions of forgetting. A transactive memory system is a combination of the information held by the individuals in a group, and the communication processes that occur between them. Transactive memory is a real property of the group, not merely the sum of its component members, because information is often transformed as it is encoded, modified, and retrieved across the distributed but coordinated system (Wegner, 1986; Wegner, Giuliano, & Hertel, 1985; Tollefsen, 2006). For example, as a couple struggle to recall information about something they did together years before, they may exchange suggestions (often partial or idiosyncratic) in an iterative process of interactive cueing which may, in the extreme, be the only way that either of them could have produced the item sought (Wegner et al., 1985, p. 257). Consider the following exchange from one of our own interviews with a couple who jointly discussed their honeymoon 40 years before.

Wife: And we went to two shows, can you remember what they were called?
Husband: We did. One was a musical, or were they both? I don't . . . no . . . one . . .
Wife: John Hanson was in it.
Husband: *Desert Song*.
Wife: *Desert Song*, that's it, I couldn't remember what it was called, but yes, I knew John Hanson was in it.
Husband: Yes.

This is a particularly striking example because neither member of the couple can remember the name of the show individually (they have both forgotten). Yet through a process of communicative cross-cueing the couple as a group can recall this information. Thus, the other person in such a long-standing and successful transactive system is a crucial component of the retrieval context.

Transactive memory theory focuses on the way in which socially shared remembering supports memory, and by extension protects against forgetting. One application of transactive memory to problems of forgetting is in the arena of social-cognitive supports for memory in ageing (Dixon, 1996). In transactive memory theory, the fact that I do not store certain detailed memories internally does not equate to memory failure, since the relevant information might still be accessible given the right reliable remembering environment, such as being in the company of my spouse (as in the example described above). "I forget" does not entail "we forget". As long as I retain sufficient "labelling" information about the location of the information, and as long as the external storage is in fact available, retrieval success can be achieved within the context of a broader transactive system. What would look like a failure of individual memory, particularly when people are tested in isolation from their usual contexts and supports, can in fact be a functional, computationally efficient distributed system (Wegner, 1986, p. 189).

Notably, transactive memory theory predicts that changes or disruptions to the remembering system should result in forgetting for the people who make up the group. This is the case in the breakdown of intimate relationships, for example, when an individual can no longer "count on access to a wide range of storage in their partner" and when their partner is no longer around to reinstate the settings of to-be-recalled experience (Wegner, 1986, p. 201). Further, one "loses access to the differentiated portion of transactive memory held by the other", so that in the extreme "because transactive retrieval is no longer possible, there will be entire realms of one's experience that merely slip away, unrecognized in their departure, and never to be retrieved again" (Wegner et al., 1985, p. 273). This theory also predicts that a decline in cognitive function in one partner, perhaps due to ageing or disease, could result in reduced memory performance in both members of the couple, unless they update their transactive system based on new strategies to overcome the deficit.

Despite its origins in the study of intimate couples, transactive memory theory has arguably had its greatest influence in organizational psychology and small group research (Austin, 2003; Peltokorpi, 2008). In this context, change to the remembering system occurs when there is turnover in the personnel in teams or small groups, where a departing team member may remove knowledge from the whole transactive system. For example, Lewis and colleagues argued that groups tend to retain an earlier transactive memory system, developed by former members of the group, even when the distribution of expertise and knowledge has changed or needs to change; this ineffective transactive system would result in forgetting by the group. They suggest, however, that the negative effects of failing to update the transactive system can be overcome when group members are instructed to reflect on who knows what; that is, when they reflect on the nature and distribution of collective knowledge (Lewis, Belliveau, Herndon, & Keller, 2007).

It is interesting to note here that work on the socially situated and embedded nature of remembering, including the theory of transactive memory, emphasizes the benefits of shared remembering. Shared remembering is seen as a way of reducing forgetting by sharing the cognitive load between members of a stable social group, and thus improving joint memory performance consistent with their shared goals. However, in laboratory work, such as the work on collaborative recall reviewed above, shared remembering appears to be detrimental to the individual. Individuals who remember in groups show collaborative inhibition (at least in terms of amount recalled; accuracy of recall may be boosted; Harris et al., 2008). How should we reconcile these laboratory findings and work on socially situated memory? Perhaps work in the laboratory does not yet fully capture the richly shared remembering that is the focus of other disciplines (see Barnier et al., 2008). For instance, transactive memory theory predicts that the benefits of remembering with others might only emerge over time in stable groups (see also Tollefsen, 2006). Future work needs to investigate a broader range of remembering cases in the laboratory. Just as RIF, DF, and TNT have moved from neutral words to more emotional and complex personal memories, SS-RIF and collaborative recall could move to study more real-world groups and their memories.

Final thoughts

In this chapter, we have focused on ways in which individuals and groups manage their memories. We have adopted a functional approach (Conway, 2005), which suggests that both remembering and forgetting are important and adaptive for individuals and groups. What is remembered vs. forgotten at any particular time is driven by a range of individual and social goals and motivations. For individuals and groups alike, the goals and motivations that influence access to memories of the past may compete and need to be balanced. Think back to the case of Nicky Barr, who reluctantly recalled long-past, distressing wartime experiences for a television interview, after years of trying to forget them. He described the personal cost of remembering these events. But was there a broader, cultural benefit of not letting him forget, of persuading him to let us commemorate his heroic actions? Equally, for many years, as individual Indigenous Australians remembered the trauma of being forcibly removed from their families as members of the Stolen Generation, there seemed to be a national climate of forgetting these events. This seemed to change when the Australian Government formally apologized for past wrongs in February 2008, signalling that we could now all "remember" (National Inquiry into the Separation of Aboriginal and Torres Strait Islander Children from their Families, 1997). The functional, selective, constructive account of memory described above views neither remembering nor forgetting as intrinsically better; both serve important roles for individuals, groups, and societies.

In this chapter, we have walked through forgetting, from the individual, to individuals in groups, and finally to groups themselves. We have reviewed experimental paradigms and findings as well as broader theoretical views of social memory, situated cognition and transactive memory, hopefully to give the sense that the forgetting that we as individuals experience lies on a continuum with the forgetting that happens between couples, families, members of community groups, and even nations. The challenge is to identify ways to investigate the processes that underlie these forms of forgetting and how they are related. We believe that laboratory paradigms from cognitive psychology can be extended to map a full range of remembering cases within a broader interdisciplinary framework (Barnier et al., 2008). We believe that a picture of remembering and forgetting as functional and selective can unify our understanding of both autobiographical and social memory. These forms of memory alike serve, drive, and reflect the goals and motivations of individuals and groups.

References

Alea, N., & Bluck, S. (2003). Why are you telling me that? A conceptual model of the social function of autobiographical memory. *Memory*, *11*(2), 165–178.

Amir, N., Coles, M. E., Brigidi, B., & Foa, E. B. (2001). The effect of practice on recall of emotional information in individuals with generalized social phobia. *Journal of Abnormal Psychology*, *110*, 76–82.

Anderson, M. C. (2005). The role of inhibitory control in forgetting unwanted memories: A consideration of three methods. In C. MacLeod & B. Uttl (Eds.), *Dynamic cognitive processes* (pp. 159–190). Tokyo: Springer-Verlag.

Anderson, M. C., Bjork, R. A., & Bjork, E. L. (1994). Remembering can cause forgetting: Retrieval dynamics in long-term memory. *Journal of Experimental Psychology: Learning, Memory, & Cognition*, *20*, 1063–1087.

Anderson, M. C., & Green, C. (2001). Suppressing unwanted memories by executive control. *Nature*, *410*, 366–369.

Anderson, M. C., & Levy, B. (2002). Repression can (and should) be studied empirically. *Trends in Cognitive Sciences*, *6*, 502–503.

Anderson, M. C., & Spellman, B. A. (1995). On the status of inhibitory mechanisms in cognition: Memory retrieval as a model case. *Psychological Review*, *102*, 68–100.

Andersson, J., & Rönnberg, J. (1995). Recall suffers from collaboration: Joint recall effects of friendship and task complexity. *Applied Cognitive Psychology*, *9*, 273–287.

Austin, J. R. (2003). Transactive memory in organizational groups: The effects of content, consensus, specialization, and accuracy on group performance. *Journal of Applied Psychology*, *88*, 866–878.

Barnier, A. J., Conway, M. A., Mayoh, L., Speyer, J., Avizmil, O., & Harris, C. B. (2007). Directed forgetting of recently recalled autobiographical memories. *Journal of Experimental Psychology: General*, *136*, 301–322.

Barnier, A. J., Hung, L., & Conway, M. A. (2004a). Retrieval-induced forgetting of autobiographical episodes. *Cognition & Emotion*, *18*, 457–477.

Barnier, A. J., Levin, K., & Maher, A. (2004b). Suppressing thoughts of past events: Are repressive copers good suppressors? *Cognition and Emotion*, *18*, 513–531.

Barnier, A. J., Sutton, J., Harris, C. B., & Wilson, R. A. (2008). A conceptual and empirical framework for the social distribution of cognition: The case of memory. *Cognitive Systems Research*, *9*, 33–51.

Bartlett, F. C. (1932). *Remembering: A study in experimental and social psychology*. Cambridge: Cambridge University Press.

Basden, B. H., Basden, D. R., Bryber, S., & Thomas, R. L. III (1997). A comparison of group and individual remembering: Does collaboration disrupt retrieval strategies? *Journal of Experimental Psychology: Learning, Memory and Cognition*, *23*, 1176–1189.

Basden, B. H., Basden, D. R., & Gargano, G. J. (1993). Directed forgetting in implicit and explicit memory tests: A comparison of methods. *Journal of Experimental Psychology: Learning, Memory, and Cognition*, *19*, 603–616.

Basden, B. H., Basden, D. R., & Henry, S. (2000). Costs and benefits of collaborative remembering. *Applied Cognitive Psychology*, *14*, 497–507.

Beach, K. (1988). The role of external mnemonic symbols in acquiring an occupation. In M. M. Gruneberg & R. N. Sykes (Eds.), *Practical aspects of memory* (pp. 342–346). New York: Wiley.

Bjork, R. A. (1970). Positive forgetting: The noninterference of items intentionally forgotten. *Journal of Verbal Learning and Verbal Behavior*, *9*, 255–268.

Bjork, R. A., Bjork, E. L., & Anderson, M. C. (1998). Varieties of goal-directed forgetting. In J. M. Golding & C. M. MacLeod (Eds.), *Intentional forgetting: Interdisciplinary approaches* (pp. 103–137). Mahwah, NJ: Lawrence Erlbaum Associates, Inc.

Bloch, M. (1998). *How we think they think: Anthropological approaches to cognition, memory, and literacy*. Boulder, CO: Westview Press.

Blumen, H. M., & Rajaram, S. (2008). Re-exposure and retrieval disruption during group collaboration as well as repeated retrieval influence later individual recall. *Memory*, *16*, 231–244.

Bowker. G. (2005). *Memory practices in the sciences*. Cambridge, MA: MIT Press.

Brandon, D. P., & Hollingshead, A. B. (2004). Transactive memory systems in organizations: Matching tasks, expertise and people. *Organization Science*, *15*, 633–644.

Brewin, C. R. (1998). Intrusive autobiographical memories in depression and post-traumatic stress disorder. *Applied Cognitive Psychology*, *12*, 359–370.

Bulevich, J. B., Roediger, H. L. III, Balota, D. A., & Butler, A. C. (2006). Failures to find suppression of episodic memories in the think/no-think paradigm. *Memory and Cognition, 34*, 1569–1577.

Campbell, S. (2003). *Relational remembering: Rethinking the memory wars*. Lanham, MD: Rowman and Littlefield.

Campbell, S. (2008). The second voice. *Memory Studies, 1*, 41–48.

Casey, E. S. (1987). *Remembering: A phenomenological study*. Bloomington, IN: Indiana University Press.

Casey, E. S. (1992). Forgetting remembered. *Man and World, 25*, 281–311.

Clark, A. (1997). *Being there: Putting brain, body, and world together again*. Cambridge, MA: MIT Press.

Clark, A. (1998). Author's response: Review symposium on *Being There*. *Metascience, 7*, 95–103.

Clark, A. (2001). *Mindware: An introduction to the philosophy of cognitive science*. Oxford: Oxford University Press.

Clark, A., & Chalmers, D. (1998). The extended mind. *Analysis, 58*, 7–19.

Connerton, P. (1989). *How societies remember*. Cambridge: Cambridge University Press.

Connerton, P. (2008). Seven types of forgetting. *Memory Studies, 1*, 59–71.

Conway, M. A. (2005). Memory and the self. *Journal of Memory and Language, 53*, 594–628.

Conway, M. A., & Pleydell-Pearce, C. W. (2000). The construction of autobiographical memories in the self-memory system. *Psychological Review, 107*, 261–288.

Conway, M. A., Singer, J. A., & Tagini, A. (2004). The self and autobiographical memory: Correspondence and coherence. *Social Cognition, 22*, 491–529.

Cuc, A., Koppel, J., & Hirst, W. (2007). Silence is not golden: A case for socially shared retrieval-induced forgetting. *Psychological Science, 18*, 727–733.

Depue, B. E., Banich, M. T., & Curran, T. (2006). Suppression of emotional and nonemotional content in memory: Effects of repetition on cognitive control. *Psychological Science, 17*, 441–447.

Dixon, R. A. (1996). Collaborative memory and aging. In D. J. Herrman, M. K. Johnson, C. L. McEvoy, C. Herzog, & P. Hertel (Eds.), *Basic and applied memory research: Theory in context* (pp. 359–383). Mahwah, NJ: Lawrence Erlbaum Associates, Inc.

Donald, M. (1991). *Origins of the modern mind: Three stages in the evolution of culture and cognition*. Cambridge, MA: Harvard University Press.

Donald, M. (1998). Material culture and cognition. In C. Renfrew & C. Scarre (Eds.), *Cognition and material culture: The archaeology of symbolic storage* (pp. 181–187). Cambridge: McDonald Institute for Archaeological Research.

Dornan, P. (2002). *Nicky Barr: An Australian air ace*. Sydney: Allen & Unwin.

Ekeocha, J. O., & Brennen, S. E. (2008). Collaborative recall in face-to-face and electronic groups. *Memory, 16*, 245–261.

Erdelyi, M. (2006). The unified theory of repression. *Behavioral and Brain Sciences, 29*, 499–511.

Erdelyi, M. (2008). Forgetting and remembering in psychology: Commentary on Paul Connerton's "Seven Types of Forgetting" (2008). *Memory Studies, 1*, 273–278.

Finlay, F., Hitch, G. J., & Meudell, P. (2000). Mutual inhibition in collaborative recall: Evidence for a retrieval-based account. *Journal of Experimental Psychology: Learning, Memory and Cognition, 26*(6), 1556–1567.

Fitzgerald, J. M. (1992). Autobiographical memory and conceptualisations of the self.

In M. A. Conway, D. C. Rubin, H. Spinnler, & W. A. Wagenaar (Eds.), *Theoretical perspectives on autobiographical memory* (pp. 99–114). Netherlands: Kluwer.

Fivush, R. (2004). Voice and silence: A feminist model of autobiographical memory. In J. Lucariello, J. A. Hudson, R. Fivush, & P. J. Bauer (Eds.), *The development of the mediated mind: Sociocultural context and cognitive development*. Mahwah, NJ: Lawrence Erlbaum Associates, Inc.

Forty, A. (1999). Introduction: The art of forgetting. In A. Forty & S. Küchler (Eds.), *The art of forgetting* (pp. 1–18). Oxford: Berg.

Geraerts, E., Merckelbach, H., Jelicic, M., & Smeets, E. (2006). Long term consequences of suppression of intrusive thoughts and repressive coping. *Behaviour Research and Therapy*, *44*, 1451–1460

Geraerts, E., Smeets, E., Jelicic, M., Merckelbach, H., & van Heerdan, J. (2006). Retrieval inhibition of trauma-related words in women reporting repressed or recovered memories of childhood sexual abuse. *Behaviour Research and Therapy*, *44*, 1129–1136.

Golding, J. M., & MacLeod, C. M. (Eds.) (1998). *Intentional forgetting: Interdisciplinary approaches*. Mahwah, NJ: Lawrence Erlbaum Associates, Inc.

Gould, O. N., Osborn, C., Krein, H., & Mortenson, M. (2002). Collaborative recall in married and unacquainted dyads. *International Journal of Behavioral Development*, *26*(1), 36–44.

Habermas, T., & Bluck, S. (2000). Getting a life: The emergence of the life story in adolescence. *Psychological Bulletin*, *126*, 748–769.

Halbwachs, M. (1980). *The collective memory*. F. J. Ditter and V. Y. Ditter (Trans), M. Douglas (Ed.). New York: Harper and Row.

Harris, C. B., Barnier, A. J., & Sutton, J. (2009). Is collaborative inhibition inevitable? Invited paper presented in A. Memon (Chair), "Interpersonal Dimensions of Remembering: Memory Performance and Biases in a Social Context", Symposium at the 21st Annual Convention of the Association for Psychological Science, Marriot Hotel, San Francisco, California, USA.

Harris, C. B., Barnier, A. J., & Sutton, J. (submitted). Minimal vs. interactive collaboration: Costs and benefits of remembering with others.

Harris, C. B., Barnier, A. J., Sutton, J., & Keil, P. G. (2010). How did you feel when "The Crocodile Hunter" died? Silencing in conversation influences memory for a shared national event. *Memory*, 185–197.

Harris, C. B., Paterson, H. M., & Kemp, R. I. (2008). Collaborative recall and collective memory: What happens when we remember together? *Memory*, *16*, 213–230.

Hayne, H., & MacDonald, S. (2003). The socialization of autobiographical memory in children and adults: The role of culture and gender. In R. Fivush & C. A. Haden (Eds.), *Autobiographical memory and the construction of a narrative self: Developmental and cultural perspectives* (pp. 99–120). Mahwah, NJ: Lawrence Erlbaum Associates, Inc.

Hertel, P. T., & Calcaterra, G. (2005). Intentional forgetting benefits from thought substitution. *Psychonomic Bulletin & Review*, *12*, 484–489.

Hirst, W., & Manier, D. (2008). Towards a psychology of collective memory. *Memory*, *16*, 183–200.

Hutchins, E. (1995). *Cognition in the wild*. Cambridge, MA: MIT Press.

Joormann, J., Hertel, P. T., LeMoult, J., & Gotlib, I. H. (2009). Training forgetting of negative material in depression. *Journal of Abnormal Psychology*, *118*, 34–43.

Joslyn, S. L., & Oakes, M. A. (2005). Directed forgetting of autobiographical events. *Memory and Cognition, 33*, 577–587.

Kihlstrom, J. F. (2002). No need for repression. *Trends in Cognitive Sciences, 6*, 502.

Kihlstrom, J. F. (2006). Repression: A unified theory of will-o-the-wisp. *Behavioral and Brain Sciences, 29*, 523.

Kihlstrom, J. F., & Barnhardt, T. M. (1993). The self regulation of memory: For better and for worse, with and without hypnosis. In D. M. Wegner and J. Pennebaker (Eds.), *Handbook of mental control* (pp. 88–125). Englewood Cliffs, NJ: Prentice Hall.

Kihlstrom, J. F., & Schacter, D. L. (1995). Functional disorders of autobiographical memory. In A. D. Baddeley, B. A. Wilson, & F. N. Watts (Eds.), *Handbook of memory disorders* (pp. 337–364). Chichester: Wiley.

Kirsh, D. (2006). Distributed cognition: A methodological note, *Pragmatics and Cognition, 14*, 249–262.

Klein, N. M. (1997). *The history of forgetting: Los Angeles and the erasure of memory*. London: Verso.

Koutstaal, W., & Schacter, D. L. (1997). Intentional forgetting and voluntary thought suppression: Two potential methods for coping with childhood trauma. In L. J. Dickstein, M. B. Riba, & J. M. Oldham (Eds.), *Review of Psychiatry: Vol. 16* (pp. II-79–II-121). Washington, DC: American Psychiatric Press.

Küchler, S. (1999). The place of memory. In A. Forty & S. Küchler (Eds.), *The art of forgetting* (pp. 55–72). Oxford: Berg.

Kuhbandner, C., Bäuml, K.-H., & Stiedl, F. C. (in press). Retrieval-induced forgetting of negative stimuli: The role of emotional intensity. *Cognition and Emotion.*

Kundera, M. (1980). *The book of laughter and forgetting*. Harmondsworth: Penguin.

Kwint, M. (1999). Introduction: The physical past. In M. Kwint, C. Breward, & J. Aynsley (Eds.), *Material memories* (pp. 1–16). Oxford: Berg.

Levy, B. J., & Anderson, M. C. (2002). Inhibitory processes and the control of memory retrieval. *Trends in Cognitive Sciences, 6*, 299–305.

Levy, B. J., & Anderson, M. C. (2008). Individual differences in the suppression of unwanted memories: The executive deficit hypothesis. *Acta Psychologica, 127*, 623–635.

Lewis, K., Belliveau, M., Herndon, B., & Keller, J. (2007). Group cognition, membership change, and performance: Investigating the benefits and detriments of collective knowledge. *Organizational Behavior and Human Decision Processes, 103*, 159–178.

Loftus, E. F. (2005). Planting misinformation in the human mind: A 30-year investigation of the malleability of memory. *Learning and Memory, 12*, 361–366.

MacLeod, C. M., Dodd, M. D., Sheard, E. D., Wilson, D. E., & Bibi, U. (2003). In opposition to inhibition. In B. H. Ross (Ed.), *The psychology of learning and motivation* (pp. 163–214). San Diego, CA: Academic Press.

McNally, R. J. (2005). *Remembering trauma*. Cambridge, MA: Harvard University Press.

Macrae, C. N., & Roseveare, T. A. (2002). I was always on my mind: The self and temporary forgetting. *Psychonomic Bulletin & Review, 9*, 611–614.

Malafouris, L. (2004). The cognitive basis of material engagement: Where brain, body and culture conflate. In E. DeMarrais, C. Gosden, & C. Renfrew (Eds.), *Rethinking materiality: The engagement of mind with the material* world (pp. 53–62). Cambridge: McDonald Institute for Archaeological Research.

Marcel Caux, 105. (2004, 25 April). *The Age*. Retrieved April 14, 2009, from http://www.theage.com.au/articles/2004/04/24/1082719676658.html.

Meade, M. L., Nokes, T. J., & Morrow, D. G. (2009). Expertise promotes facilitation on a collaborative memory task. *Memory, 17*, 39–48.

Middleton, D., & Brown, S. D. (2005). *The social psychology of experience: Studies in remembering and forgetting*. London: Sage.

Mineka, S., & Nugent, K. (1995). Mood-congruent biases in anxiety and depression. In D. L. Schacter (Ed.), *Memory distortion: How minds, brains and societies reconstruct the past*. Cambridge, MA: Harvard University Press.

Moulds, M. L., & Bryant, R. A. (2002). Directed forgetting in acute stress disorder. *Journal of Abnormal Psychology, 111*, 175–179.

Moulds, M. L., & Kandris, E. (2006). The effect of practice on recall of negative material in dysphoria. *Journal of Affective Disorders, 91*, 269–272.

Myers, L. B., & Brewin, C. R. (1994). Recall of early experience and the repressive coping style. *Journal of Abnormal Psychology, 103*, 288–292.

Myers, L. B., Brewin, C. R., & Power, M. J. (1998). Repressive coping and the directed forgetting of emotional material. *Journal of Abnormal Psychology, 107*, 141–148.

Myers, L. B., & Derakshan, N. (2004). To forget or not to forget: What do repressors forget and when do they forget? *Cognition and Emotion, 18*, 495–511.

National Inquiry into the Separation of Aboriginal and Torres Strait Islander Children from their Families (1997). *Bringing them home: Report of the national inquiry into the separation of Aboriginal and Torres Strait Islander children from their families*. Retrieved April 14 2009, from http://www.hreoc.gov.au/pdf/social_justice/bringing_them_home_report.pdf.

Nelson, K. (2003). Self and social functions: Individual autobiographical memory and collective narrative. *Memory, 11*, 125–136.

Nelson, K., & Fivush, R. (2004). The emergence of autobiographical memory: A social cultural developmental theory. *Psychological Review, 111*, 486–511.

Olick, J. (1999). Collective memory: The two cultures. *Sociological Theory, 17*, 333–348.

Pasupathi, M. (2001). The social construction of the personal past and its implications for adult development. *Psychological Bulletin, 127*(5), 651–672.

Paterson, H., & Kemp, R. (2006). Comparing methods of encountering postevent information: The power of co-witness suggestion. *Applied Cognitive Psychology, 20*, 1083–1099.

Payne, B. K., & Corrigan, E. (2007). Emotional constraints on intentional forgetting. *Journal of Experimental Social Psychology, 43*, 780–786.

Peltokorpi, V. (2008). Transactive memory systems. *Review of General Psychology, 12*, 378–394.

Pillemer, D. B. (2003). Directive functions of autobiographical memory: The guiding power of the specific episode. *Memory, 11*, 193–202.

Reese, E. (2002). A model of the origins of autobiographical memory. In J. W. Fagen & H. Hayne (Eds.), *Progress in infancy research, Vol.* 2 (pp. 215–260). Hillsdale, NJ: Lawrence Erlbaum Associates, Inc.

Reese, E., & Fivush, R. (2008). The development of collective remembering. *Memory, 16*, 202–212.

Reysen, M. B. (2003). The effects of social pressure on group recall. *Memory & Cognition, 31*, 1163–1168.

Rowlands, M. (1999). *The body in mind: Understanding cognitive processes*. Cambridge: Cambridge University Press.

Rubin, D. C. (1995). *Memory in oral traditions: The cognitive psychology of epic, ballads, and counting-out rhymes*. Oxford: Oxford University Press.

Rubin, D. C. (2007). Forgetting: Its role in the science of memory. In H. L. Roediger III, Y. Dudai, & S. M. Fitzpatrick (Eds.), *Science of memory: Concepts* (pp. 325–328). Oxford: Oxford University Press.

Sahakyan, L., & Delaney, P. F. (2005). Directed forgetting in incidental learning and recognition testing: Support for a two factor account. *Journal of Experimental Psychology: Learning, Memory & Cognition, 31*(4), 789–801.

Sahdra, B., & Ross, M. (2007). Group identification and historical memory. *Personality and Social Psychology Bulletin*, *33*, 384–395.

Schacter, D. L. (1987). Implicit memory: History and current status. *Journal of Experimental Psychology: Learning, Memory, and Cognition*, *13*, 501–518.

Schacter, D. L. (1996). *Searching for memory: The brain, the mind, and the past*. New York: Basic Books.

Schudson, M. (1995). Dynamics of distortion in collective memory. In D. L. Schacter (Ed.), *Memory distortions: How minds, brains and societies reconstruct the past* (pp. 346–364). Cambridge, MA: Harvard University Press.

Singer, J. A., & Conway, M. A. (2008). Should we forget forgetting? *Memory Studies*, *1*, 279–285.

Starr, S., & Moulds, M. L. (2006). The role of negative interpretations of intrusive memories in depression. *Journal of Affective Disorders*, *93*, 125–132.

Stone, C., Barnier, A. J., Sutton, J., & Hirst, W. (2010). Building consensus about the past: Schema-consistency and integration in socially-shared retrieval-induced forgetting and the consequences for joint recall, *Memory*, *18*, 170–184.

Sutton, J. (2008). Material agency, skills, and history: Distributed cognition and the archaeology of memory. In C. Knappett & L. Malafouris (Eds.), *Material agency: Towards a non-anthropocentric approach* (pp. 37–55). New York: Springer.

Sutton, J. (2009). Remembering. In P. Robbins & M. Aydede (Eds.), *The Cambridge handbook of situated cognition* (pp. 217–235). Cambridge: Cambridge University Press.

Thompson, C. P., Skowronski, J. J., Larsen, S. F., & Betz, A. (1996). *Autobiographical memory: Remembering what and remembering when*. Mahwah, NJ: Lawrence Erlbaum Associates, Inc.

Thorne, A. (2000). Personal memory telling and personality development. *Personality & Social Psychology Review*, *4*, 45–56.

Tollefsen, D. P. (2006). From extended mind to collective mind. *Cognitive Systems Research*, *7*, 140–150.

Tulving, E. (2002). Episodic memory: From mind to brain. *Annual Review of Psychology*, *53*, 1–25

Tulving, E., & Pearlstone, Z. (1966). Availability versus accessibility of information in memory for words. *Journal of Verbal Learning and Verbal Behavior*, *5*, 381–391.

Tversky, B. & Marsh, E. J. (2000). Biased retellings of events yield biased memories. *Cognitive Psychology*, *40*, 1–38

van Leeuwen, C., Verstijnen, I. M., & Hekkert, P. (1999). Common unconscious dynamics underly uncommon conscious effect: A case study in the iterative nature of perception and creation. In J. S. Jordan (Ed.), *Modeling consciousness across the disciplines*. Lanham, MD: University Press of America.

Vygotsky, L. (1978). *Mind in society: The development of higher psychological processes*. Cambridge, MA: Harvard University Press.

Walker, W. R., Skowronski, J. J., & Thompson, C. P. (2003). Life is pleasant – and memory helps to keep it that way! *Review of General Psychology*, *7*, 203–210.

Wegner, D. M. (1986). Transactive memory: A contemporary analysis of the group mind. In B. Mullen & G. R. Goethals (Eds.), *Theories of group behaviour* (pp. 185–208). New York: Springer-Verlag.

Wegner, D. M., Giuliano, T., & Hertel, P. T. (1985). Cognitive interdependence in close relationships. In W. Ickes (Ed.), *Compatible and incompatible relationships* (pp. 253–276). New York: Springer-Verlag.

Wegner, D. M., Schneider, D. J., Carter, S. R. III, & White, T. L. (1987). Paradoxical effects of thought suppression. *Journal of Personality and Social Psychology*, *53*, 636–647.

Weldon, M. S., & Bellinger, K. D. (1997). Collective memory: Collaborative and individual processes in remembering. *Journal of Experimental Psychology: Learning, Memory and Cognition, 23(5)*, 1160–1175.

Welzer, H., & Markowitsch, H. J. (2005). Towards a bio-psycho-social model of autobiographical memory. *Memory*, *13*, 63–78.

Wertsch, J. V. (2002). *Voices of collective remembering*. Cambridge: Cambridge University Press.

Wessel, I., & Hauer, B. (2006). Retrieval-induced forgetting of autobiographical memory details. *Cognition and Emotion*, *20*, 430–447.

Wessel, I., & Merckelbach, H. (2006). Forgetting "murder" is not harder than forgetting "circle": Listwise-directed forgetting of emotional words. *Cognition and Emotion*, *20*, 129–137.

Wessel, I., & Moulds, M. (2008). How many types of forgetting? Comments on Connerton (2008). *Memory Studies*, *1*, 287–294.

Wheeler, M. (2005). *Reconstructing the cognitive world: The next step.* Cambridge, MA: MIT Press.

Wilson, P. (2008, April 25). War pilgrims flock to the corner of a foreign field. *The Australian*. Retrieved April 14, 2009, from http://www.theaustralian.news.com.au/story/0,25197,23595543–22242,00.html.

Wilson, R. A. (2005). Collective memory, group minds, and the extended mind thesis. *Cognitive Processing*, *6*, 227–236.

Wright, D. B., & Klumpp, A. (2004). Collaborative inhibition is due to the product, not the process, of recalling in groups. *Psychonomic Bulletin and Review*, *11*, 1080–1083.

Yaron-Antar, A., & Nachson, I. (2006). Collaborative remembering of emotional events: The case of Rabin's assassination. *Memory*, *14*, 46–56.

Zerubavel, E. (2003). *Time maps: Collective memory and the social shape of the past*. Chicago: University of Chicago Press.

13 The role of retroactive interference and consolidation in everyday forgetting

John T. Wixted

University of California, San Diego, USA

As the previous chapters in this book make abundantly clear, the subject of forgetting is as multifaceted as it is enigmatic. Why, exactly, do we forget? As noted by Levy, Kuhl, and Wagner (this volume, Chapter 7) we often use the term "forget" to refer to the inability to retrieve information that we failed to encode in the first place. Thus, for example, I might say that I forgot where I placed my keys, but the truth may be that I set them down without ever taking note of the fact that I put them on the kitchen counter. Although such absent-mindedness is an interesting issue in its own right, when experimental psychologists and cognitive neuroscientists study forgetting, they usually study the loss of information that was encoded, as shown by the fact that the information was once retrievable from long-term memory. What is it about the passage of time that renders once retrievable information ever more difficult to remember? That is the question I consider in this chapter.

The time course of forgetting was first experimentally addressed by Ebbinghaus (1885), who used himself as a subject and memorized lists of nonsense syllables until they could be perfectly recited. Later, after varying delays of up to 31 days, he relearned those same lists and measured how much less time was needed to learn them again relative to the time required to learn them in the first place. If 10 minutes were needed to learn the lists initially, but only 4 minutes were needed to learn them again after a delay of 6 hours, then his memory was such that 60% savings had been achieved. As the retention interval increased, savings decreased, which is to say that forgetting occurred with the passage of time. When his famous savings function was plotted out over 31 days, what we now know as the prototypical forgetting function was revealed (Figure 13.1).

The form of forgetting

The mathematical form of the Ebbinghaus savings function is something close to a power law, which, in general terms, is to say that it declines rapidly at first but declines at a slower rate as time goes on (Wixted & Ebbesen, 1991). Although not widely appreciated, that property of forgetting is consistent with Jost's (1897) law of forgetting (Wixted, 2004a). Jost's second law states

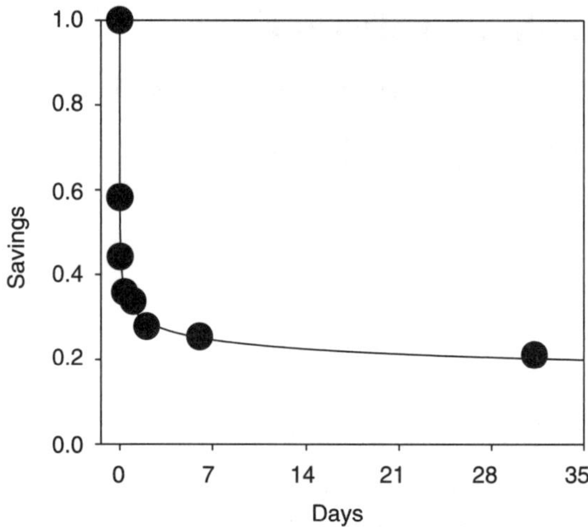

Figure 13.1 The Ebbinghaus (1885) savings data. The solid curve represents the least squares fit of the 3-parameter Wickelgren power law, $m = \lambda(1 + \beta t)^{-\psi}$, where m is memory strength, and t is time (i.e., the retention interval). The equation has 3 parameters: λ is the state of long-term memory at $t = 0$ (i.e., the degree of learning), ψ is the rate of forgetting, and β is a scaling parameter.

that if two memories have the same strength but different ages (i.e., if one memory was formed more recently than the other), the younger trace will lose strength more rapidly than the older one. In light of Jost's law, Herbert Simon (1966) suggested that forgetting may not be exponential in form. By definition, the exponential requires a constant rate of forgetting over time, which would mean that the rate of forgetting is independent of the age of the trace. In practice, they are not independent because as the trace ages, the rate of forgetting slows.

Armed with nothing but a slide rule and the forgetting data he had collected on himself, Ebbinghaus (1885) argued that forgetting was a 3-parameter logarithmic function of time. Much later, Wickelgren (1974) instead suggested a 3-parameter power function of time to characterize the course of forgetting, but the behavior of these two mathematical functions is nearly identical, and it is hard to imagine that the slight differences between them are important. Figure 13.1 shows a fit of the 3-parameter Wickelgren power function to the Ebbinghaus savings data (Wixted & Carpenter, 2007). This figure is, essentially, a depiction of the basic result that needs to be explained by any theory of forgetting. Ebbinghaus learned his lists to perfection, but as time passed the information that was once retrievable from long-term memory became less retrievable (at an ever-decelerating rate). Why? Although natural decay may play some role (e.g., Bailey & Chen 1989), interference theory offers the most interesting and nuanced account of forgetting.

A variety of interference theories

Interference as cue-overload

In the field of psychology, the story of interference has almost always focused on the retrieval cue, which makes sense in light of the critical role played by retrieval cues in episodic memory. One of Endel Tulving's great insights was that episodic memory is cue dependent (e.g., Tulving & Pearlstone, 1966). Although countless episodic memories are encoded in one's brain, they are typically all in a quiescent state, and they simply cannot be called to mind at will. Instead, it is the retrieval cue (and only the retrieval cue) that activates an episodic memory (one at a time). If the right retrieval cue does not come along, the corresponding memory trace might as well not even be there as it will never be retrieved again.

What is the "right" retrieval cue? Tulving's principle of *encoding specificity* (Tulving & Thomson, 1973) offers a compelling answer, and it states that a retrieval cue will be effective in activating an episodic memory trace only to the extent that the cue was encoded along with the to-be-remembered material. Thus, for example, if I study the word pair "glue–chair," then "glue" will later be an effective retrieval cue for the occurrence of "chair" on the study list. By contrast, a cue like "table," though highly associated with the word "chair," will not be effective in retrieving that same memory. It may prompt retrieval of the word "chair" from semantic memory, but it will not call to mind the episode of having studied that word on a list just minutes ago.

In light of the undeniably cue-dependent nature of episodic memory, it makes sense that powerful interference effects can be achieved by influencing properties of the retrieval cue. In fact, traditional interference theory, which has dominated thinking in psychology from the 1930s on, basically holds that the more items associated with a retrieval cue, the less effective that cue will be in retrieving a particular memory (Watkins & Watkins, 1975). The cue-overload principle applies to both retroactive interference (interference caused by subsequent learning) and proactive interference (interference caused by prior learning). If, for example, in addition to learning "glue–chair" I also learn "glue–model," then the ability of "glue" to retrieve either one of the two memories it subserves ("chair" and "model") will be diminished. This holds true whether "glue–model" was learned before "glue–chair" (a case of proactive interference), or after (a case of retroactive interference). A retrieval cue that has been encoded along with many memories is, for some reason, less effective than a retrieval cue that has been encoded with only one memory. This principle accounts for why it can be difficult to remember a prior episode when many similar episodes have also been experienced (because similar information tends to be subserved by the same retrieval cue).

Although cue-overload interference effects can be powerful in the laboratory and in real life (e.g., when trying to remember the names of the many students in your class), there is some question as to whether it offers a complete account – or even the central account – of everyday forgetting. In the 1960s, one of the leading interference theorists of the day, Benton Underwood, set out to demonstrate that cue-overload interference – in particular, proactive interference – not only produces powerful effects in the laboratory but also accounts for forgetting in the real world. Proactive interference was, at the time, the dominant account of forgetting, even though it is more intuitive to assume that forgetting is caused by retroactive interference (i.e., interference caused by subsequent learning). The dominance of the less intuitive proactive interference account was due in no small part to Underwood's (1957) classic paper showing that, for lists learned to one perfect recitation, the amount of forgetting over a 24-hour period (which varied from 20% to 80% across studies) was almost fully accounted for by the number of previous similar lists which the subjects in each experiment had learned. This was an ingenious observation, and it was understandably regarded as a major insight into the understanding of why we forget. However, Underwood's later efforts to show that proactive interference is not only a powerful force in the experimental laboratory but is also a powerful force in everyday forgetting were as surprising to him as they were disappointing. His every attempt to show that proactive interference plays a significant role in forgetting outside of the laboratory instead suggested otherwise (e.g., Underwood & Ekstrand, 1966, 1967; Underwood & Postman, 1960). As a result, the major advocate of the proactive interference account of forgetting eventually came to question its significance (Underwood, 1983).

What about retroactive interference? Is it possible that the main cause of forgetting is the overloading of a retrieval cue in the days, weeks and months after learning occurs? The suggestion that retroactive interference of some kind plays an important role came early in the last century when Jenkins and Dallenbach (1924) showed that a period of sleep after learning results in less forgetting than a similar period of wakefulness. When sleeping, one is presumably not overloading retrieval cues that might be associated with items learned on a list prior to sleep, but the same may not be true of the waking state.

Underwood (1957) himself did not find it plausible that the subsequent learning of similar material following the learning of a target list in the laboratory could possibly account for the degree of forgetting that is observed over a period as short as 24 hours (about 20% of the list when no prior similar lists are learned). Thus, he attributed that amount of forgetting to the prior real-life learning that the subject brought to the laboratory. That is, although it seemed unlikely that subjects would, in the course of 24 hours of normal living, overload retrieval cues that happen to have been used on a list in the laboratory, it was very likely that similar cues had been encountered in the years prior to arriving in the laboratory. But this idea introduced a new puzzle: If all forgetting outside of the laboratory is due to proactive interference (even when no previous lists were learned in the laboratory), why would sleep after learning be helpful? Underwood (1957) speculated that, for some reason, the recovery of previously learned information (the presumed mechanism of proactive interference) was suspended during sleep. However, this idea was challenged when Underwood's student, Bruce Ekstrand, had subjects learn both an interfering list and a target list just prior to a night of sleep. Compared to a control group, memory for both lists was enhanced (Ekstrand, 1967). Thus, the presumed mechanism of PI (recovery of previously learned information) was enhanced, not retarded, by sleep. Even so, memory for the target list was enhanced as well.

Interference as trace degradation

By the early 1970s, interference theory had largely run its course and seemed to be making little headway (Tulving & Madigan, 1970). Another one of Underwood's students, Geoffrey Keppel, argued that similarity-based interference might not be the cause of most everyday forgetting and that nonspecific retroactive interference may be the major cause instead (Keppel, 1968). Somehow, it seemed that even the learning of unrelated material (which would presumably not overload a relevant retrieval cue) causes retroactive interference.

The distinction between cue-overload retroactive interference and nonspecific retroactive interference is, from my point of view, critical. This distinction has been largely ignored by the field of experimental psychology (which has focused almost exclusively on similarity-based, cue-overload interference), and it has sometimes been obscured by researchers working in related fields. Consider, for example, learning a to-be-remembered list of 10 A–B paired associates and then, an hour later, learning an interfering list of 10 A–C paired associates (which have the same cue words as the A–B list but different response words). According to the cue-overload idea, the only retroactive interference of any consequence is the interference caused by the learning of that A–C list an hour after the A–B list was learned. Moreover, the mechanism of interference involves the overloading of the retrieval cues (i.e., the A words), which renders them less effective at the time of retrieval. By contrast, the nonspecific retroactive interference idea, as further elaborated in my prior work (Wixted, 2004b), holds that interference is also caused by the encoding of new memories (even unrelated ones) during the course of that hour. The fact that new memories would be formed during that hour is clear from the fact that the subjects in any such experiment would not be amnesic for events that took place between the learning of the A–B list and the learning of the A–C list an hour later. Instead, their memories of that time would be clear, which would mean that memories were formed, and the formation of those additional memories may also serve as an interfering force. Moreover, the mechanism of interference caused by the subsequent encoding of unrelated memories does not involve cue overload but may instead involve *trace degradation*. That is, newly encoded memories have a damaging effect on previously encoded memories. Indeed, this kind of interference – by virtue of being constantly applied during waking hours – may be a greater contributor to everyday forgetting than cue-overload interference.

A role for consolidation

In 1900, the German experimental psychologist Georg Elias Müller published a monograph with his student Alfons Pilzecker in which a new theory of forgetting was proposed, one that included a role for consolidation. In its essentials, Müller's theory of forgetting is the theory I readvocated in Wixted (2004b) and will develop in more detail in the pages that follow. Müller and Pilzecker (1900) introduced numerous experimental innovations in the study of memory and forgetting, as described in some detail by Lechner, Squire, and Byrne (1999). Their basic method involved asking subjects to memorize a list of paired-associate nonsense syllables. To investigate why forgetting occurred, Müller and Pilzecker (1900) also presented subjects with a second, interfering list of pairs to memorize before memory for the first was tested. The cues for the two lists were different, so in today's notation this would be an A–B, C–D design. They found that the interpolated list reduced memory for the target list compared to a control group that was not exposed to an interpolated list. In light of that result, they introduced the concept of retroactive inhibition. Critically, they found the point of interpolation of the interfering list within the retention interval mattered such that an interfering list presented soon after learning had a more disruptive effect on retention than one presented later in the retention interval. This led them to propose that memories require time to consolidate and that retroactive interference is a force that works against the retention of newly formed memories.

Müller and Pilzecker (1900) advocated a trace degradation account – not a cue-overload account – of retroactive interference. According to this idea, newly memorized information degrades previously memorized but not-yet-consolidated information, and the interference occurs at the level of physiology. As such, it does not matter whether the interfering material is similar to the studied material. To test this, Müller and Pilzecker (1900) had subjects learn paired associates followed by interpolated lists of unrelated pictures. Still, a definite interfering effect was observed.

From the early 1930s until the present day, experimental psychologists largely rejected this way of thinking as the cue-overload view of interference came to dominate. This was partly due to the fact that the temporal gradient obtained by Müller and Pilzecker (1900) is not easy to replicate (Wixted, 2004a, 2004b), and one reason for that may be that awake humans never stop making memories. As such, in a typical experiment, interfering material naturally occurs throughout the retention interval (i.e., the subject makes new memories continuously), so it does not matter when the nominally interfering material arranged by the experimenter is presented. For example, following study of an A–B list, the presentation of an A–C list will impair memory for the original list compared to the presentation of a C–D interfering list due to cue overload, but it will not matter much if the A–C list occurs early or late in the retention interval (e.g., Wickelgren, 1974). This result might create the impression that interference does not have a temporal gradient, that consolidation is not relevant, and that cue overload (not trace degradation) is what matters most. However, in any such experiment, retroactive interference of the trace degradation variety would be equated in the two conditions because, in both conditions, memories would be formed continuously throughout the retention interval. Additional interference would be added by the experimenter using a cue-overload manipulation, but that effect would not be time dependent (at least not in the same way). As described later, a different story emerges when steps are taken to temporarily stop the process of memory formation to see what effect that has on previously formed memories in humans.

A multidisciplinary inquiry into retroactive interference and consolidation

The case in favor of a generalized (nonspecific) retroactive interference account of forgetting that includes a role for consolidation emerges most clearly when several separate literatures are considered simultaneously. These include work on: (a) the cellular processes associated with the formation of memories in the hippocampus; (b) the effect of sleep on episodic memory (beyond what Jenkins & Dallenbach, 1924 established long ago); (c) the effect of pharmacological agents (such as alcohol and benzodiazepines) on episodic memory. Based on a review of behavioral evidence, Brown and Lewandowsky (this volume, Chapter 4) present an argument against the idea that consolidation can help to explain forgetting. In that regard, they join a long and almost unbroken chain of distinguished experimental psychologists dating back to the 1930s. My own view has been heavily influenced by the cellular and molecular evidence reviewed next, which I construe as elucidating the biological mechanisms of the consolidation process that experimental psychologists have long been reluctant to embrace.

In many ways, the account I present parallels the case made by Dewar, Cowan, and Della Sala (this volume, Chapter 9). They offer evidence suggesting that in patients with amnestic mild cognitive impairment (aMCI), consolidation resources are limited, which makes the trace degrading effects of retroactive interference especially pronounced. The evidence I consider below suggests that, in a less pronounced way, the trace degrading effects of retroactive interference on partially consolidated memory traces also accounts for much of what unimpaired individuals forget in everyday life.

The cellular basis of memory formation in the hippocampus

The hippocampus is one of several structures in the medial temporal lobe (MTL) that is known to play a critical role in the formation of new memories (see also Valtorta & Benfenati, this volume, Chapter 6). The importance of these structures became clear when the famous patient HM received a bilateral medial temporal lobe resection in an effort to control his epileptic seizures (Scoville & Milner, 1957). Although successful in that regard, HM was also unexpectedly left with a profound case of anterograde amnesia (i.e., the inability to form new memories from that point on). Another outcome – one that may be relevant to the story of forgetting – was that HM also exhibited temporally graded retrograde amnesia (Scoville & Milner, 1957; Squire, 2009). That is, memories that were formed prior to surgery were also somewhat impaired, and the degree of impairment was greater for memories that had been formed just prior to surgery than for memories that were encoded well before. Indeed, HM's oldest memories were largely intact.

The temporal gradient of retrograde amnesia that is sometimes associated with head injury was noted long ago by Ribot (1881/1882), but he had no way of knowing what brain structures were centrally involved in this phenomenon. The experience of HM made it clear that the relevant structures reside in the MTL, and more recent studies in animals and humans have shown that the temporal gradient of retrograde amnesia is evident even when bilateral lesions are limited to the hippocampus (Squire, Clark, & Knowlton, 2001). These findings suggest a role for the consolidation of memories, but, as noted by Dewar et al. (this volume, Chapter 9), it is important to distinguish between two kinds of consolidation, namely, systems consolidation and synaptic consolidation (McGaugh, 2000).

Systems consolidation and forgetting

The fact that retrograde amnesia is temporally graded has long been taken to suggest that memories require time to consolidate (Zola-Morgan & Squire, 1990). That is, when a memory is initially formed, it is dependent on the hippocampus. As a result, hippocampal damage impairs those recently formed memories, and retrograde amnesia is observed. Eventually, however, through a little-understood process of *systems consolidation*, memories become independent of the hippocampus as they are consolidated elsewhere in the neocortex (McGaugh, 2000). At that point, hippocampal damage no longer has any effect on those memories. This process is thought to require days or weeks in rats, weeks or months in monkeys, and perhaps years in humans (Squire et al., 2001).

The mechanism that underlies systems consolidation is not known, but a leading candidate is neural replay. Specifically, cells that fire together in the rat hippocampus during the learning of a behavioral task tend to become coactive again during sleep and during periods of quiet wakefulness (Wilson & McNaughton, 1994). Analogously, Peigneux, Schmitz, and Urbain (this volume, Chapter 8; see also Peigneux et al., 2004) describe intriguing, one-of-a-kind neuroimaging evidence in humans showing that hippocampal areas that are activated during route learning in a virtual town are activated again during subsequent slow-wave sleep. Recently, Ji and Wilson (2007) reported that hippocampal replay during slow-wave sleep in rats was coordinated with firing patterns in the visual cortex (consistent with the idea that this process underlies the redistribution of memories) and that it occurred 5 to 10 times faster than the firing sequences occurred during the waking state. Through repeated epochs of accelerated coactivation, this neural playback may be the mechanism that eventually creates an independent ensemble of interconnected areas that were active during the encoding experience (Hoffman & McNaughton, 2002).

Is it conceivable that memories also become less vulnerable to the trace-degrading forces of retroactive interference as they become less dependent on the hippocampus (not just less vulnerable to hippocampal damage)? That is, are the neural representations of memories that are consolidated elsewhere in the neocortex less likely to be degraded when new memories are formed in the hippocampus? Not much is known about that, but it seems reasonable to suppose that it is true. It also seems to follow from a theory proposed by McClelland, McNaughton, and O'Reilly (1995) according to which memories are initially encoded in hippocampal circuits and are slowly integrated with prior knowledge represented in the neocortex. Memories that are eventually distributed in the neocortex through a process that slowly interleaves them with pre-existing knowledge would presumably be less vulnerable to subsequent slow changes in neocortical synapses associated with new learning. Whether or not that is the case, as described next, it seems clear that memory traces do become less vulnerable to the damaging forces of new memory formation even during the period of time in which they are still largely dependent on the hippocampus because of a second kind of consolidation process that unfolds in that structure on a shorter time scale.

Synaptic consolidation and forgetting

A second kind of consolidation takes place over a matter of hours and days when a memory is formed in the hippocampus (McGaugh, 2000), and this form of consolidation seems particularly relevant to the physiological processes that Müller and Pilzecker (1900) had in mind. This kind of consolidation – *synaptic consolidation* – occurs at the level of neurons (Izquierdo, Schröder, Netto, & Medina, 2006). The leading model of the initial stages of memory formation at the level of neurons in the hippocampus is long-term potentiation (LTP; Martin, Grimwood, & Morris, 2000). LTP is a relatively long-lasting enhancement of synaptic efficacy that is induced by a *tetanus* (a brief burst of high-frequency electrical stimulation) delivered to presynaptic neurons in the hippocampus (Bliss & Collingridge, 1993). Before the tetanus, a single test pulse of electrical stimulation applied to the presynaptic neuron elicits a certain baseline response in the postsynaptic neuron, but after the tetanus that same test pulse elicits a greater response. The enhanced reactivity typically lasts hours or days (and sometimes weeks), so it presumably does not represent the way in which memories are permanently coded. Still, LTP is readily induced in hippocampal neurons, and it is the leading candidate for modeling the neural basis of initial memory formation (Whitlock, Heynen, Schuler, & Bear, 2006). In this model, the tetanus is analogous to the effect of a behavioral experience, and the enhanced efficacy of the synapse is analogous to the memory of that experience.

Although LTP looks like neural memory for an experience (albeit an artificial experience consisting of a train of electrical impulses), what reason is there to believe that a similar process plays a role in real memories? The induction of LTP in hippocampal neurons involves the opening of calcium channels in postsynaptic NMDA receptors (Bliss & Collingridge, 1993). When those receptors are blocked by an NMDA antagonist, high-frequency stimulation fails to induce LTP. Perhaps not coincidentally, NMDA antagonists have often been shown to impair the learning of hippocampus-dependent tasks in animals (e.g., Morris, 1989; Morris, Anderson, Lynch, & Baudry, 1986), as if an LTP-like process plays an important role in the formation of new episodic memories. A recent and rather remarkable study suggests that the encoding of actual memories (not just an artificial train of electrical pulses) also gives rise to LTP in the hippocampus (Whitlock et al., 2006).

An important consideration for understanding the time-related effects of retroactive interference is that LTP is thought to have at least two stages: early-stage LTP, which does not involve protein synthesis (and during which time LTP is vulnerable to interference), and late-stage LTP, which does involve protein synthesis associated with morphological changes in dendritic spines and synapses (and after which the LTP is less vulnerable to interference). Late-stage LTP, which occurs approximately 4–5 hours after the induction of LTP, can be prevented by protein synthesis inhibitors (Abel, Nguyen, Barad, Deuel, Kandel, & Bourtchouladze, 1997; Frey, Krug, Reymann, & Matthies, 1988). Perhaps not coincidentally, protein synthesis inhibitors prevent the consolidation of new learning on hippocampus-dependent tasks as well (Davis & Squire, 1984).

The fact that protein synthesis inhibitors do not block learning (even when administered before training), but do accelerate forgetting by preventing consolidation (Davis & Squire, 1984), may be related to the accelerated forgetting in temporal lobe epilepsy patients, as summarized by Butler, Muhlert, and Zeman (this volume, Chapter 10). Like experimental animals exposed to protein synthesis inhibitors, those patients can sometimes remember normally after short delays (e.g., 30 minutes) and then exhibit profound forgetting after a delay of 24 hours. Conceivably (indeed, seemingly), these patients lack the late-phase LTP mechanisms required to stabilize memory traces that are initially encoded in the hippocampus.

In any case, the important point for purposes of understanding how and why normal forgetting occurs is that LTP exhibits all of the characteristics envisioned by Müller and Pilzecker (1900). In their own work, Müller and Pilzecker (1900) used an original learning phase (L1) followed by an interfering learning phase (L2) followed by a memory test for the original list (T1). Holding the retention interval between L1 and T1 constant, they essentially showed that L1-L2—T1 yields greater interference than L1—L2-T (where the dashes represent units of time). In experimental animals, memories formed in the hippocampus and LTP induced in the hippocampus both exhibit a similar temporal gradient with respect to retroactive interference (Izquierdo et al., 1999; Xu, Anwyl, & Rowan, 1998). Whether L1 and L2 both involve hippocampus-dependent learning tasks (e.g., L1 = one-trial inhibitory avoidance learning, L2 = exploration of a novel environment), as reported by Izquierdo et al. (1999), or one involves the induction of LTP (L1) while the other involves exposure to a learning task (L2), as reported by Xu et al. (1998), the same pattern emerges. Specifically, L2 interferes with L1 if the time between them is relatively short (e.g., 1 hour) but not when the time between them is relatively long (e.g., 6 or more hours). Moreover, if an NMDA antagonist is infused into the hippocampus prior to L2 (thereby blocking the induction of interfering LTP that might be associated with the learning of a potentially interfering task), no interference effect is observed even when the L1–L2 temporal interval is short.

As indicated earlier, the temporal gradient of interference that is readily observed in experimental animals and that was observed by Müller and Pilzecker (1900) and a few others long ago (e.g., Skaggs, 1925) is usually hard to obtain in humans. The reason may be that awake humans never stop making memories, so the interfering force that one would like to bring to a standstill is always in action. In experimental rats and mice, by contrast, memory formation in the hippocampus may occur primarily when the animal is exposed to a specific learning task, such as exposure to a novel environment. Although it is not easy to keep humans from forming new memories when they are awake in order to test for evidence of temporally graded retroactive interference, sleep and amnesia-inducing drugs can be used for this purpose.

Sleep-induced retrograde facilitation

It is already well known that less forgetting occurs during sleep than during a comparable period of wakefulness (Jenkins & Dallenbach, 1924). That is, a temporary period of anterograde amnesia (e.g., a few hours of sleep) confers a benefit on recently formed memories compared to remaining awake. The benefit consists of less forgetting when memory is later tested, and this phenomenon could be termed *retrograde facilitation*. This term is not typically used in the sleep literature, but it is often used in the psychopharmacology literature that will be considered later in this chapter. Using the same term for the effect of sleep on memory helps to draw attention to the fact that the same phenomenon is observed whether a temporary period of anterograde amnesia is induced by sleep or by pharmacological agents such as alcohol and benzodiazepines.

Retrograde facilitation refers to the fact that following a postlearning intervention (e.g., a period of sleep after learning or the administration of an amnestic drug after learning), performance is better relative to a control group (e.g., no sleep or no drug after learning). The enhanced performance of the experimental group compared to that of the control group usually reflects less forgetting in the former compared to the latter. This is the pattern reported by Jenkins and Dallenbach (1924) in their classic sleep study, and in many other sleep studies (e.g., Ekstrand, 1967, 1972; Gais et al., 2006; Phihal & Born, 1997). Because that basic result is clearly established, the question of interest is whether or not the effect exhibits a temporal gradient (as a consolidation account would predict).

Temporal gradient of sleep-induced retrograde facilitation

If memories need time to consolidate in order to become hardened against the damaging forces of new memory formation, and if sleep provides a window of time for such consolidation to unfold in the absence of interference, then sleep soon after learning should confer more protection than sleep that is delayed. This can be tested by holding the retention interval between learning (L1) and test (T1) constant (e.g., at 24 hours), with the location of sleep (S) within that retention interval varied. That is, using the notation introduced earlier, L1-S—T1 should confer greater protection than L1—S-T1. If a temporal gradient is observed (i.e., if memory performance at T1 is greater in the first condition than the second), it would suggest that sleep does more than simply subtract out a period of retroactive interference that would otherwise occur. Instead, it would raise the possibility that sleep also allows a process of consolidation to unfold relatively unfettered.

Is a temporal gradient of retrograde facilitation observed in sleep studies? The answer is yes, and the relevant finding was reported long ago by Ekstrand (1972), who deserves to be recognized as a pioneer in the investigation of the effect of sleep on episodic memory. Ekstrand (1972) tested memory for paired-associate words following a 24-hour retention interval in which subjects slept either during the 8 hours that followed list presentation or during the 8 hours that preceded the recall test. That is, he used a design that might be represented as L1-S—T1 vs. L1—S-T1. In the immediate sleep condition (in which L1 occurred at night, just before sleep), he found that 81% of the items were recalled 24 hours later; in the delayed sleep condition (in which L1 occurred in the morning), only 66% were recalled. In other words, a clear temporal gradient of retrograde facilitation was observed, one that is the mirror image of the temporal gradient of retroactive interference reported by Müller and Pilzecker (1900).

More recent sleep studies have reinforced the idea that the temporal gradient of retrograde facilitation is a real phenomenon, and they have addressed various confounds that could have accounted for the results that Ekstrand (1972) obtained. Gais et al. (2006), for example, replicated the Ekstrand (1972) design and included several other conditions to rule out time-of-day or circadian rhythm confounds. Talamini, Nieuwenhuis, Takashima, and Jensen (2008) conducted a conceptually similar study and again showed that cued recall for face–location associations after 24 hours is significantly higher when sleep occurs shortly after learning than when it is delayed. The temporal gradient associated with sleep, like the LTP and animal learning research described earlier, is consistent with the notion that when memory formation is temporarily halted, recently formed and still fragile memories are protected from interference and are given a chance to become hardened against the forces of retroactive interference that they will later encounter.

Sleep and LTP

The synaptic consolidation interpretation of the temporal gradient of sleep-induced retrograde facilitation is supported by a consideration of the effects of sleep on LTP. During sleep, some new memories are formed, but this occurs almost exclusively during rapid eye movement (REM) sleep. These memories of our dreams do not seem to be normal (e.g., they seem to fade rapidly), but they clearly do occur. Just as clearly, memories are not formed during other stages of sleep, especially slow-wave sleep. This is true despite the fact that mental activity occurs during slow-wave sleep (Pivik & Foulkes, 1968). If memories occur during REM sleep (but not during non-REM sleep), does that mean that LTP can be induced in the hippocampus during REM sleep (but not during non-REM sleep)? And does it also mean that REM sleep is not particularly protective of recently formed memories (because REM memories serve as an interfering force), whereas non-REM sleep is? The answer to both questions appears to be yes.

In experiments performed on sleeping rats, Jones Leonard, McNaughton, and Barnes (1987) showed that LTP can be induced during REM sleep but not during slow-wave sleep. Whereas slow-wave sleep inhibits the induction of LTP, it does not disrupt the maintenance of previously induced LTP (Bramham & Srebo, 1989). In that sense, slow-wave sleep is like the NMDA antagonists discussed earlier (i.e., they block the induction of new LTP but not the maintenance of previously induced LTP). By contrast, with regard to synaptic plasticity in the hippocampus, REM sleep is similar to the awake state (i.e., LTP can be induced during REM). Based on findings like these, one might reasonably speculate that it is not sleep, per se, that is protective of recently formed memories. Instead, slow-wave sleep (during which the formation of new memories is prevented) should specifically confer that protection because it is during that stage of sleep that prior memories are protected from interference that might otherwise occur (thereby giving them a chance to consolidate before they encounter interference from new learning).

Once again, Ekstrand and colleagues (Ekstrand, 1972; Yaroush et al., 1971) performed the pioneering experiment that addressed this question. These researchers took advantage of the fact that most REM sleep occurs in the second half of the night, whereas most non-REM sleep occurs in the first half. Some subjects in this experiment learned a list, went to sleep immediately, and were awakened 4 hours later for a test of recall. These subjects experienced mostly slow-wave sleep during the 4-hour retention interval. Others slept for 4 hours, were awakened to learn a list, slept for another 4 hours, and then took a recall test. These subjects experienced mostly REM sleep during the 4-hour retention interval. The control (i.e., awake) subjects learned a list during the day and were tested for recall 4 hours later. The subjects all learned the initial list to a similar degree, but the results showed that 4 hours of mostly non-REM sleep facilitated delayed recall relative to the other two conditions, which did not differ from each other (i.e., REM sleep did not facilitate memory). Barrett and Ekstrand (1972) reported similar results in a study that controlled for time-of-day and circadian rhythm confounds, and the effect was later replicated in studies by Phihal & Born (1997, 1999).

Fowler, Sullivan, and Ekstrand (1973) argued that this pattern of results is not easy to reconcile with an interference-reduction explanation because both the REM and non-REM conditions involve equivalent amounts of sleep and, therefore, equivalent reductions in interference. Although one might be tempted to argue that mental activity during REM sleep (i.e., dreaming) causes interference, whereas the absence of mental activity during non-REM sleep might result in a reduction of interference, Fowler et al. (1973) argued that this idea is weakened by "ample evidence of a great deal of mental activity during the non-rapid eye movement (non-REM) stages" (p. 304). However, what the synaptic plasticity literature suggests is that mental activity during non-REM sleep might not matter because LTP cannot be induced under those conditions. As such, despite the significant mental activity that occurs, potentially interfering memories might not be formed during slow-wave sleep. This makes the interference-reduction explanation of why non-REM sleep is particularly protective of declarative memory more plausible than it seemed to Fowler et al. (1972).

The benefits of slow-wave sleep for declarative memory are interpretable in terms of what is known about synaptic consolidation and the stabilization of LTP, but, as noted earlier, a mechanism suspected of playing a role in systems consolidation (neural replay) also tends to occur during slow-wave sleep (Wilson & McNaughton, 1994). Neural reply has been observed during REM sleep as well, but in that case it occurs at a rate that is similar to the neuron firing that occurred during learning (Louie & Wilson, 2001) and thus may simply reflect dreaming. The neural replay that occurs during slow-wave sleep occurs at a rate 5–10 times faster than it did during the waking state (e.g., Ji & Wilson, 2007) and thus may reflect a biological consolidation process separate from mental activity. It is simply not known whether a systems consolidation process like this, which is usually thought to train the neocortex over months and years in humans, contributes to the hardening of a memory trace during a retention interval of 24 hours or less, but it might.

Phihal and Born (1997, 1999), who replicated the beneficial effect of slow-wave sleep over REM sleep in the protection of recently formed declarative memories, also confirmed earlier work by Karni, Tanne, Rubenstein, Askenasy, and Sagi (1994) showing that the opposite pattern applies to the retention of non-hippocampus-dependent *procedural* memories (i.e., procedural memories benefit from REM sleep but not from non-REM sleep). Thus, in that respect, the sleep-related consolidation of procedural memories appears to differ from the sleep-related consolidation of declarative memories. Indeed, they differ in another important way as well. Unlike declarative memories, the sleep-related facilitation of procedural memory does not consist simply of less forgetting (as is typically true of studies on declarative memory). Instead, it often consists of an absolute enhancement in the level of performance over and above what was evident at the end of training. This offline improvement in learning is often called "consolidation" (e.g., Walker, 2005), but, used in that sense, the term does not necessarily refer to systems consolidation (with traces becoming independent of the hippocampus), or synaptic consolidation (with traces becoming stabilized in the hippocampus). It is not clear why these differences between procedural and declarative memories exist. However, it is clear that declarative memories differentially benefit from slow-wave sleep (not REM sleep), and it seems reasonable to suppose that this occurs because, during slow-wave sleep, new memories are not being formed.

Drug-induced retrograde facilitation

NMDA antagonists (in rats) and slow-wave sleep (in humans) are not the only ways to induce a temporary period of anterograde amnesia. In sufficient quantities, alcohol and benzodiazepines do the same. Moreover, like NMDA antagonists and slow-wave sleep, these drugs not only induce anterograde amnesia, but they also inhibit the induction of LTP in the hippocampus, and they result in retrograde facilitation. More specifically, memories formed prior to drug intake (like memories formed prior to sleep) are forgotten to a lesser degree than memories formed prior to placebo.

Because alcohol (Givens & McMahon 1995; Roberto, Nelson, Ur, & Gruol, 2002; Sinclair & Lo 1986) and benzodiazepines (Del Cerro, Jung, & Lynch, 1992; Evans & Viola-McCabe 1996) have been shown to block the induction of LTP in the hippocampus, it makes sense that these drugs would induce anterograde amnesia. Although it blocks the induction of LTP, alcohol does not impair the maintenance of hippocampal LTP induced one hour prior to drug administration (Givens & McMahon, 1995). In that sense, alcohol is like slow-wave sleep and NMDA antagonists. Benzodiazepines presumably do not impair the maintenance of previously induced LTP either, but this has not yet been specifically tested.

By limiting the formation of new memories, alcohol and benzodiazepines may protect memories that were formed just prior to drug intake. While protected from the trace-degrading force of new memory formation, it is possible that these memories are allowed to consolidate in a way that hardens them against the interference they will later encounter when new memories are once again formed. Thus, less forgetting should be observed than would otherwise be the case. Indeed, numerous studies have reported that even though alcohol induces amnesia for information studied under the influence of the drug, it actually results in improved memory for material studied just prior to consumption (e.g., Bruce & Pihl, 1997; Lamberty, Beckwith, & Petros, 1990; Mann, Cho-Young, & Vogel-Sprott, 1984; Parker, Birnbaum, Weingartner, Hartley, Stillman, & Wyatt, 1980; Parker, Morihisa, Wyatt, Schwartz, Weingartner, & Stillman, 1981). Similar findings have been frequently reported for benzodiazepines such as diazepam and triazolam (Coenen & Van Luijtelaar, 1997; Fillmore, Kelly, Rush, & Hays, 2001; Ghoneim, Hinrichs, & Mewaldt, 1984; Hinrichs, Ghoneim, & Mewaldt, 1984; Weingartner, Sirocco, Curran, & Wolkowitz, 1995). This retrograde facilitation looks very much like the effect of sleep on episodic memory (as noted by Coenen & Van Luijtelaar, 1997).

The psychopharmacology literature has considered a variety of explanations for retrograde facilitation and has not settled on any one of them. Indeed, a review of this literature instead reveals widespread disagreement. As with sleep, it is sometimes suggested that alcohol induces retrograde facilitation because it somehow directly enhances the consolidation process (Parker et al., 1980, 1981) or directly enhances the retrieval process (Weingartner et al., 1995). However, it seems odd to suppose that an agent that boosts consolidation or retrieval would cause anterograde amnesia. Instead, it seems more likely that any enhancement of consolidation or retrieval would, if anything, yield anterograde facilitation in addition to retrograde facilitation. For example, glucose, like alcohol and NMDA inhibitors, has repeatedly been shown to cause retrograde facilitation (Manning et al., 1992; Sünram-Lea, Foster, Durlach, & Perez, 2002). However, unlike alcohol and NMDA inhibitors (and slow-wave sleep), glucose does not inhibit the induction of LTP in the hippocampus (Kamal, Spoelstra, Biessels, Urban, & Gispen, 1999). Moreover, glucose does not cause anterograde amnesia when taken before learning. Instead, it causes anterograde facilitation (Manning, Parsons, & Gold, 1992; Sünram-Lea et al., 2002). It therefore seems reasonable to suppose that glucose leads to retrograde facilitation because it somehow boosts the consolidation process after learning, not because it blocks new learning. Similarly, amphetamine results in both anterograde facilitation and retrograde facilitation (Soetens, Casaer, D'Hooge, & Hueting, 1995). Like glucose, this drug also does not inhibit the induction of LTP in the hippocampus (Dommett, Henderson, Westwell, & Greenfield, 2008), and its effects are also thought to be due to an enhancement of the consolidation process (McGaugh, 2000). By contrast, alcohol and benzodiazepines do block the induction of LTP and do cause anterograde amnesia. As such, they should protect memories formed just before drug intake from the interfering forces of new memory formation (which is why they, too, result in retrograde facilitation).

Psychopharmacology researchers who argue in favor of an enhanced consolidation or enhanced retrieval interpretation of retrograde facilitation have interpreted a particular pattern of results as weighing against an interference-reduction explanation. This pattern involves the apparent equating of retroactive interference across conditions, but retrograde facilitation is observed anyway. For example, in some studies, no formal interfering list was presented to either the drug group or the placebo control group. If no interfering list was presented, and if one assumes that, as a result, no interference occurred in the placebo control condition, how could reduced interference explain retrograde facilitation? This is one reason why Parker et al. (1981) favored an enhanced consolidation interpretation. In other studies, an interfering list similar to the pre-drug study list was presented to both the drug group and the placebo group during the retention interval, but the drug group somehow managed to learn the interfering list as well as the control group despite being under the influence of the amnesia-inducing drug (File, Fluck, & Joyce, 1999; Weingartner et al., 1995). Even so, retrograde facilitation was observed. Again, they argued, if interference was equated across groups, how could reduced interference explain retrograde facilitation for the drug group?

The reasoning used in these studies appears to have been based on a cue-overload view of retroactive interference. That is, the authors adopted the view that retroactive interference for a list of words is caused by the subsequent learning of a similar list of words (and not by anything else). However, the reduced interference that may account for retroactive facilitation is, I argue, the interference caused by a reduced rate of memory formation in general in the hours after the drug is administered, not by reduced memory for one similar interfering list that was studied for, say, 60 seconds during the several-hour period in which subjects were under the influence of the drug. Under the influence of an amnesia-inducing drug, memories will be formed at a reduced rate even if no formal interfering list is presented, and memories are likely to be formed at a reduced rate even if, for one particular list, the drug group manages to learn it as well as the control group. Indeed, clear evidence for this can be seen in Weingartner et al. (1995). Subjects in the triazolam condition of that experiment learned an interfering list that was similar to the pre-drug study list as well as placebo controls did, yet they exhibited retrograde facilitation anyway. However, on other unrelated memory tasks that the triazolam group completed while under the influence of the drug (e.g., sentences learned and recalled under the influence of the drug), memory was clearly impaired. Thus, the overall rate of memory formation in the hours following drug administration was undoubtedly impaired, and it seems reasonable to suppose that this generally reduced rate of memory formation is why retrograde facilitation was observed.

By creating a period of anterograde amnesia shortly after learning, alcohol and benzodiazepines are (like slow-wave sleep) assumed to: (a) protect these fragile memories from trace degradation during an especially vulnerable period; and (b) allow the process of synaptic consolidation to unfold such that the once fragile memories become resistant to interference by the time new memories are once again encoded. If this interpretation is correct, then a temporal gradient of drug-induced retrograde facilitation should be observed (as it is in sleep).

Temporal gradient of drug-induced retrograde facilitation

Is a temporal gradient of retrograde facilitation observed when amnesia-inducing drugs are used? To date, the answer is no, but only two studies have looked for it, and neither was designed in a way that was likely to reveal any temporal gradient that might exist. Mueller, Lisman, and Spear (1983) had subjects learn two lists of words prior to ingesting alcohol. A consolidation account would predict that the more recently learned list should exhibit greater retrograde facilitation, but the enhancement effect was the same for both lists. As such, they argued that consolidation does not play a role in alcohol-induced retrograde facilitation and that reduced interference is the probable explanation. However, the lists were learned closely together in time, and a greater separation is almost surely needed. Tyson and Schirmuly (1994), also using alcohol, reported a similar result for lists learned 40 minutes apart. No temporal gradient was observed but, again, there is reason to believe that the interval between lists was too short. Indeed, in a sleep study, Ekstrand (1967) presented two successive lists close together in time prior to sleep and found that, although memory for both lists was enhanced, memory for the first list (not the second) was differentially enhanced.

Studies that have shown a temporal gradient using NMDA antagonists or sleep used temporal intervals substantially greater than 40 minutes. Usually, even the shorter of the two temporal intervals is longer than that. Xu et al. (1998), for example, induced hippocampal LTP in rats and then exposed the animals to an interfering novel environment either 1 hour or 24 hours later. LTP was abolished in the 1-hour group but was unaffected in the 24-hour group. As the authors point out, this is consistent with the fact that the maintenance of LTP is divided into two phases, an early phase (1 to 3 hours after induction) and a late phase (more than 3 hours after induction). The late phase, but not the early phase, is dependent on protein synthesis and may involve morphological changes to hippocampal neurons (Bliss & Collingridge, 1993). It seems reasonable to assume that memories that make it to that stage may be hardened against the forces of retroactive interference. Thus, the study by Tyson and Schirmuly (1994) involved two temporal intervals that both fell within the early phase of LTP, and it is not clear that a temporal gradient would be expected under those conditions.

Other studies reviewed above suggested that a temporal gradient also involved temporal intervals much longer than 40 minutes. Izquierdo et al. (1999), for example, found that an interfering task presented 1 hour after inhibitory avoidance training hindered later memory for that training, but no such effect was observed if the interfering task was presented 6 hours after inhibitory avoidance training. Similarly, sleep studies have shown that sleep just after learning is more protective than sleep that is delayed by 12 hours. The point is that these temporal gradients have all involved delays that are 1 hour or longer (even for the short delay). Müller and Pilzecker (1900) were able to obtain a temporal gradient of interference when the study list and interfering list were separated by a matter of minutes, and it is somewhat ironic that the mechanisms now thought to underlie the consolidation process that they envisioned long ago would not clearly predict that a temporal gradient of interference would be observed. Although they did observe one, and Dewar, Fernandez Garcia, Cowan, and Della Sala (in press) observed one over a similar timescale using patients with mild cognitive impairment (who may suffer from particularly depleted consolidation resources), most research suggests that a larger timescale may be necessary to reliably observe the effect (and related retrograde facilitation effects) in intact organisms.

Whether a temporal gradient of retrograde facilitation for alcohol or benzodiazepines would be observed using longer temporal intervals (e.g., 1 hour vs. 6 hours after learning) is unknown. If a temporal gradient is ultimately observed, the simplest explanation would be the same one that applies to the various other procedures that (a) block the induction of LTP in the hippocampus and (b) yield a temporal gradient of retrograde facilitation.

Temporal gradients of retrograde amnesia and retrograde facilitation

As indicated earlier, bilateral lesions of the hippocampus often yield temporally graded retrograde amnesia, and this phenomenon has long been taken as evidence that memories consolidate and become less dependent on the hippocampus with the passage of time (McGaugh, 2000; Squire & Alvarez, 1995). Usually, this phenomenon is not tied to a theory of forgetting, but the point I am making here is that it probably should be. In this regard, it is useful to conceptualize the hippocampus as performing two jobs: (1) encoding new memories and (2) consolidating recently formed memories. Hippocampal lesions bring an abrupt end to both activities, resulting in both anterograde amnesia (because the first job is disrupted) and temporally graded retrograde amnesia (because the second job is disrupted as well). By contrast, glucose and amphetamines effectively do the reverse by enhancing both hippocampal activities and resulting in both anterograde facilitation and retrograde facilitation.

Other circumstances can be conceptualized as inhibiting the first job (encoding new memories) without impairing the second (consolidating recently formed memories). These circumstances include slow-wave sleep, the use of NMDA antagonists and, perhaps, the administration of alcohol and benzodiazepines. All of these block the induction of hippocampal LTP and induce anterograde amnesia. In rats and mice, a state of quiet wakefulness in a familiar environment may also be sufficient to release the hippocampus from the job of encoding new memories (though this seems unlikely in humans, who form new memories whenever awake). In each case, the consolidation of recently formed memories may proceed in a more efficient manner than it otherwise would because, when released from job 1, the hippocampus performs job 2.

Consolidation is an often ill-defined term, so it is important to be clear about how the term is used here. When not encoding new memories, the hippocampus is assumed to be released to engage in both synaptic consolidation (involving the stabilization of recently induced LTP) and systems consolidation (perhaps involving coordinated neural replay). When the hippocampus is engaged in the task of forming new memories, both kinds of consolidation processes may instead be hindered in one way or another. In everyday life, the freedom to consolidate comes on a regular basis in the form of nightly slow-wave sleep (and, for some animals, during certain periods of wakefulness as well). During slow-wave sleep, synaptic plasticity in the hippocampus is inhibited, which allows recently established memories to stabilize (i.e., synaptic consolidation can proceed unfettered) and, perhaps, sets the occasion for coordinated neural replay (i.e., systems consolidation can proceed as well). The same may happen when synaptic plasticity is diminished while the animal is awake but not in motion (e.g., Karlsson & Frank, 2009). Indeed, with respect to neural replay and systems consolidation, a similar idea was proposed long ago by Buzsaki (1989). More recently, Hoffman and McNaughton (2002) put it this way:

> Consistent with the former prediction, neural ensembles in the rat hippocampus and neocortex show memory trace reactivation during "offline periods" of quiet wakefulness, slow-wave sleep, and in some cases REM (rapid eye movement) sleep.
>
> (pp. 2070–2071)

The idea that neural replay spontaneously occurs during offline periods has been advanced to account for the fact that memories eventually become independent of the hippocampus. However, the idea that memories become less dependent on the hippocampus as a result of systems consolidation says nothing about how and why *forgetting* occurs. Instead, it speaks to the issue of why memories eventually become unaffected by hippocampal lesions. Whether systems consolidation also hardens them against the interfering force of new memory formation is not known, but it seems reasonable to suppose that it does.

In addition to hardening memories against the forces of retroactive interference, systems consolidation may also directly enhance the learning of declarative memories in the same way that REM sleep often promotes the enhanced learning of procedural memories. However, it is rare that an actual improvement of declarative memory performance is observed following slow-wave sleep. Instead, sleep usually forestalls forgetting. Still, there is reason to believe that reactivation of memories during slow-wave sleep might be able to enhance declarative memories as well. For example, an intriguing study by Rasch, Buchel, Gais, and Born (2007) showed that cuing recently formed odor-associated memories by odor re-exposure during slow-wave sleep (but not during REM sleep) prompted hippocampal activation and increased retention performance after sleep. This result raises the possibility that a reactivation process during slow-wave sleep has the capacity to improve declarative memories in addition to (possibly) hardening them against retroactive interference.

Retroactive interference and everyday forgetting

The preceding considerations suggest a general theory of forgetting according to which nonspecific retroactive interference associated with the formation of new memories degrades previously formed memories (more so the more recently those previous memories were formed). Humans form memories all day long every day, and the constant application of this interfering force may have a large cumulative effect on what we later retain. The interference caused by the formation of new memories presumably has its greatest effect on recently formed memories because they have not yet become hardened against the corrupting influence of new memories (i.e., they have not yet consolidated in that sense).

Villarreal, Haddad, and Derrick (2002) performed an interesting experiment that illustrates the cumulative effect of retroactive interference associated with the everyday life of a laboratory rat. In this experiment, hippocampal LTP was induced in rats via implanted electrodes, and the magnitude of LTP was assessed for the next 6 days. Some rats received an NMDA receptor antagonist each day (a treatment that should prevent the further induction of LTP that might be associated with natural memory formation), whereas control rats received a water vehicle. No explicit retroactively interfering task was arranged in this experiment, so any interference that occurred was presumably due to the formation of memories associated with normal events in the life of a laboratory rat. Although such memories likely occur at a very low rate in rats housed in a familiar environment, they presumably do occur and, when they do, they presumably have a cumulative degrading effect on recently formed memories. The results of this experiment revealed that LTP decayed back to baseline for the control rats over the next several days but remained elevated for the experimental subjects. Thus, it seems that LTP was protected in the experimental rats because the subsequent LTP that would have been induced by the formation of new memories was prevented by the NMDA antagonist. When the NMDA antagonist was no longer administered (after day 6), LTP in the experimental rats began to decay as well. Thus, even LTP that has substantially consolidated (i.e., late-phase LTP) is vulnerable to cumulative retroactive interference, though it is less vulnerable than newly induced LTP. Villarreal et al. (2002) also showed that very similar protective effects of an NMDA antagonist were observed when a spatial learning task was used (instead of inducing LTP) and memory performance was tested after a delay (instead of monitoring the maintenance of LTP).

The point is just that retroactive interference resulting from the formation of new memories may be a constantly applied, cumulative force that operates whenever a rat (or a human) is awake. Humans presumably make memories at a high rate, and it is hard to prevent that from happening (though it can be done using sleep or amnesia-inducing drugs). The rat hippocampus is presumably less taxed when in a familiar environment, but even that can be altered by enriching its environment. In a study by Abraham, Logan, Greenwood, and Dragunow (2002), LTP was induced in the hippocampus of rats, and the animals were then housed in their familiar home cage for 2 weeks. In this low-interference environment, LTP decayed, but it did so gradually (presumably because new memories were formed at a low rate – an explicitly arranged interfering task would have been needed to reverse it more quickly). In the following week, some of these animals were exposed to a more complex environment involving a larger cage, multiple objects, and other animals for 14 hours per day. Exposure to this environment for several days resulted in complete reversal of the previously induced LTP (presumably because the rate of new memory formation was substantially increased), whereas LTP in the control animals continued its very gradual decay.

All of these findings are consistent with the idea that the formation of new memories has a degrading effect on recently established memories (or recently established LTP). Over time, memories consolidate and become more resistant to such interference, but during that time they are confronted with – and degraded by – the interference associated with the encoding of other memories. Returning once again to the classic forgetting function presented by Ebbinghaus (1885), nonspecific retroactive interference associated with the formation of new memories may explain why forgetting occurs rapidly at first but occurs at an ever-slowing rate as time passes (Figure 13.1). As time passes, surviving memories become more resistant to the constantly applied, interfering force of new memory formation.

This way of thinking could also help to explain why forgetting functions have the shape they do even when plotted over a 50-year period. Bahrick (1984) reported long-term forgetting data for Spanish learned in high school. The data from various subtests in this study were aggregated (following Hintzman, 1990) and then fit with the same 3-parameter power function that accurately described the Ebbinghaus savings data. The averaged data are somewhat variable, but the form of forgetting over 50 years (Figure 13.2) looks much like the form of forgetting over 31 days (Figure 13.1). On both timescales, memories weaken rapidly at first and then weaken at an ever slower rate as time passes.

Bahrick (1984) proposed the concept of "permastore" to account for the shape of the 50-year retention function. According to this idea, memories start off in a somewhat labile state but then enter a different, more permanent

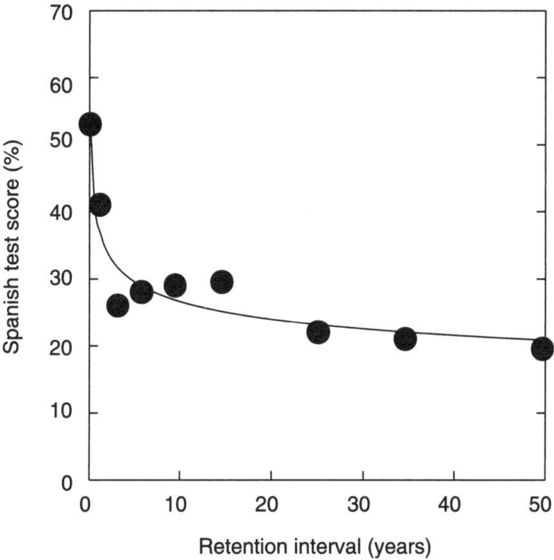

Figure 13.2 Retention of Spanish learned in high school, as reported by Bahrick (1984). The solid curve represents the least squares fit of the 3-parameter Wickelgren power law (defined in the caption for Figure 13.1).

state some years later. He implied that memories that had not yet transitioned into permastore were vulnerable to interference, whereas memories that had were essentially invulnerable. The consolidation account of forgetting that I have presented here is much the same, except that it does not envision a discontinuous transition into a qualitatively different state. Instead, memories continuously harden against the forces of interference as a result of synaptic and systems consolidation – perhaps reaching some maximum state of resistance after several years (after which they are still vulnerable to interference, just much less so than they were before). In addition, in the account I have described (and that Müller and Pilzecker described long ago), the interfering force against which memories harden over time is that associated with the formation of new memories – a process that degrades previously established memories, whether or not those previously established memories are related to the subsequently formed memories.

With all of the credit that Müller and Pilzecker (1900) justifiably receive for introducing the theory of consolidation (Lechner, Squire, & Byrne, 1999; McGaugh, 2000), it is sometimes forgotten that theirs was a theory of interference and forgetting, not a theory about how memories eventually become less dependent on one brain structure and more dependent on another. They were, after all, experimental psychologists, not neuroscientists. More than 100 years and thousands of studies later, their theory of forgetting is still standing.

References

Abel, T., Nguyen, P. V., Barad, M., Deuel, T A., Kandel, E. R., & Bourtchouladze, R. (1997). Genetic demonstration of a role for PKA in the late phase of LTP and in hippocampus-based long-term memory. *Cell, 88*, 615–626.

Abraham, W. C., Logan, B., Greenwood, J. M., & Dragunow, M. (2002). Induction and experience-dependent consolidation of stable long-term potentiation lasting months in the hippocampus. *Journal of Neuroscience, 22*, 9626–9634.

Bahrick, H. P. (1984). Semantic memory content in permastore: Fifty years of memory for Spanish learning in school. *Journal of Experimental Psychology: General, 113*, 1–29.

Bailey, C. H., & Chen, M. (1989). Time course of structural changes at identified sensory neuron synapses during long-term sensitization in *Aplysia. Journal of Neuroscience, 9*, 1774–1780.

Barrett, T. R., & Ekstrand, B. R. (1972). Effect of sleep on memory: III. Controlling for time-of-day effects. *Journal of Experimental Psychology, 96*, 321–327.

Bliss, T.V.P., & Collingridge, G. L. (1993). A synaptic model of memory: Long-term potentiation in the hippocampus. *Nature, 361*, 31–39.

Bramham, C. R., & Srebo, B. (1989). Synaptic plasticity in the hippocampus is modulated by behavioral state. *Brain Research, 493*, 74–86.

Bruce, K. R., & Pihl, R. O. (1997). Forget "drinking to forget": Enhanced consolidation of emotionally charged memory by alcohol. *Experimental and Clinical Psychopharmacology, 5*, 242–250.

Buzsaki, G. (1989). A two-stage model of memory trace formation: A role for "noisy" brain states. *Neuroscience, 31*, 551–570.

Coenen, A. M. L., & Van Luijtelaar, E. L. J. M. (1997). Effects of benzodiazepines, sleep and sleep deprivation on vigilance and memory. *Acta Neurologica Belgica, 97*, 123–129.

Davis, H. P., & Squire, L. R. (1984). Protein synthesis and memory: A review. *Psychological Bulletin, 96*, 518–559.

Del Cerro, S., Jung, M., & Lynch, L. (1992). Benzodiazepines block long-term potentiation in slices of hippocampus and piriform cortex. *Neuroscience, 49*, 1–6.

Dewar, M., Fernandez Garcia, Y., Cowan, N., & Della Sala, S. (in press). Delaying interference enhances memory consolidation in amnesic patients. *Neuropsychology*.

Dommett, E. J., Henderson, E. L., Westwell, M. S., & Greenfield, S. A. (2008). Methylphenidate amplifies long-term plasticity in the hippocampus via noradrenergic mechanisms. *Learning & Memory, 15*, 580–586.

Ebbinghaus, H. (1885). *Über das Gedchtnis. Untersuchungen zur experimentellen Psychologie*. Leipzig: Duncker & Humblot. English edition: Ebbinghaus, H. (1913). *Memory. A contribution to experimental psychology*. New York: Teachers College, Columbia University.

Ekstrand, B. R. (1967). The effect of sleep on memory. *Journal of Experimental Psychology, 75*, 64–72.

Ekstrand, B. R. (1972). To sleep, perchance to dream (about why we forget). In C. P. Duncan, L. Sechrest, & A. W. Melton (Eds.), *Human memory: Festschrift for Benton J. Underwood* (pp. 59–82). New York: Appelton-Century-Crofts.

Evans, M. S., & Viola-McCabe, K. E. (1996). Midazolam inhibits long-term potentiation through modulation of $GABA_A$ receptors. *Neuropharmacology, 35*, 347–357.

File, S. E., Fluck, E., & Joyce, E. M. (1999). Conditions under which lorazepam can facilitate retrieval. *Journal of Clinical Psychopharmacology, 19*, 349–353.

Fillmore, M. T., Kelly, T. H., Rush, C. R., & Hays, L. (2001). Retrograde facilitation of memory by triazolam: Effects on automatic processes. *Psychopharmacology, 158*, 314–321.

Fowler, M. J., Sullivan, M. J., & Ekstrand, B. R. (1973). Sleep and memory. *Science, 179*, 302–304.

Frey, U., Krug, M., Reymann, K. G., & Matthies, H. (1988). Anisomycin, an inhibitor of protein synthesis, blocks late phases of LTP phenomena in the hippocampal CA1 region in vitro. *Brain Research, 452*, 57–65.

Gais, S., Lucas, B., & Born, J. (2006). Sleep after learning aids memory recall. *Learning & Memory, 13*, 259–262.

Ghoneim, M. M., Hinrichs, J. V., & Mewaldt, S. P. (1984). Dose-response analysis of the behavioral effects of diazepam: I. Learning and memory. *Psychopharmacology, 82*, 291–295.

Givens, B., & McMahon, K. (1995). Ethanol suppresses the induction of long-term potentiation in vivo. *Brain Research, 688*, 27–33.

Hinrichs, J. V., Ghoneim, M. M., & Mewaldt, S. P. (1984). Diazepam and memory: Retrograde facilitation produced by interference reduction. *Psychopharmacology, 84*, 158–162.

Hintzman, D. (1990). *Permastore or grade inflation? Adjusting Bahrick's data for changes in academic standards.* (Tech. Rep. No. 90–15.) Eugene: University of Oregon, Institute of Cognitive and Decision Sciences.

Hoffman, K. L., & McNaughton, B. L. (2002). Coordinated reactivation of distributed memory traces in primate neocortex. *Science, 297*, 2070–2073.

Izquierdo, I., Schröder, N., Netto, C. A., & Medina, J. H. (1999). Novelty causes time-dependent retrograde amnesia for one-trial avoidance in rats through NMDA receptor- and CaMKII-dependent mechanisms in the hippocampus. *European Journal of Neuroscience, 11*, 3323–3328.

Jenkins, J. G., & Dallenbach, K. M. (1924). Oblivescence during sleep and waking. *American Journal of Psychology, 35*, 605–612.

Ji, D., & Wilson, M. A. (2007). Coordinated memory replay in the visual cortex and hippocampus during sleep. *Nature Neuroscience, 10*, 100–107.

Jones Leonard, B., McNaughton, B. L., & Barnes, C. A. (1987). Suppression of hippocampal synaptic activity during slow-wave sleep. *Brain Research, 425*, 174–177.

Jost, A. (1897). Die Assoziationsfestigkeit in ihrer Abhängigkeit von der Verteilung der Wiederholungen [The strength of associations in their dependence on the distribution of repetitions]. *Zeitschrift für Psychologie und Physiologie der Sinnesorgane, 16*, 436–472.

Kamal, A., Spoelstra, K., Biessels, G., Urban, I. J. A., & Gispen, W. H. (1999). Effects of changes in glucose concentration on synaptic plasticity in hippocampal slices. *Brain Research, 824*, 238–242.

Karlsson, M. P., & Frank, L. M. (2009). Awake replay of remote experiences in the hippocampus. *Nature Neuroscience, 12*, 913–920.

Karni, A., Tanne, D., Rubenstein, B. S., Askenasy, J. J. M., & Sagi, D. (1994). Dependence on REM sleep of overnight improvement of a perceptual skill. *Science, 265*, 679–682.

Keppel, G. (1968). Retroactive and proactive inhibition. In T. R. Dixon & D. L.

Horton (Eds.), *Verbal behavior and general behavior theory* (pp. 172–213). Englewood Cliffs, NJ: Prentice-Hall.

Lamberty, G. J., Beckwith, B. E., & Petros, T. V. (1990). Posttrial treatment with ethanol enhances recall of prose narratives. *Physiology & Behavior*, *48*, 653–658.

Lechner, H. A., Squire, L. R., & Byrne, J. H. (1999). 100 years of consolidation – Remembering Müller and Pilzecker. *Learning & Memory*, *6*, 77–87.

Louie, K., & Wilson, M. A. (2001). Temporally structured replay of awake hippocampal ensemble activity during rapid eye movement sleep. *Neuron*, *29*, 145–156.

McClelland, J. L., McNaughton, B. L., & O'Reilly, R. C. (1995). Why there are complementary learning systems in the hippocampus and neocortex: Insights from the successes and failures of connectionist models of learning and memory. *Psychological Review*, *102*, 419–457.

McGaugh, J. L. (2000). Memory: A century of consolidation. *Science*, *287*, 248–251.

Mann, R. E., Cho-Young, & Vogel-Sprott, M. (1984). Retrograde enhancement by alcohol of delayed free recall performance. *Pharmacology, Biochemistry & Behavior*, *20*, 639–642.

Manning, C. A., Parsons, M. W., & Gold, P. E. (1992). Anterograde and retrograde enhancement of 24-h memory by glucose in elderly humans. *Behavioral & Neural Biology*, *58*, 125–130.

Martin, S. J., Grimwood, P. D., & Morris, R. G. M. (2000). Synaptic plasticity and memory: An evaluation of the hypothesis. *Annual Review of Neuroscience*, *23*, 649–711.

Morris, R. G. M. (1989). Synaptic plasticity and learning: Selective impairment of learning in rats and blockade of long-term potentiation in vivo by the N-methyl-D-aspartate receptor antagonist AP5. *Journal of Neuroscience*, *9*, 3040–3057.

Morris, R. G. M., Anderson, E., Lynch, G. S., & Baudry, M. (1986). Selective impairment of learning and blockade of long-term potentiation by an N-methyl-D-aspartate receptor antagonist, AP5. *Nature 319*, 774–776.

Mueller, C. W., Lisman, S. A., & Spear, N. E. (1983). Alcohol enhancement of human memory: Tests of consolidation and interference hypotheses. *Psychopharmacology*, *80*, 226–230.

Müller, G. E. & Pilzecker, A. (1900). Experimentelle Beiträge zur Lehre vom Gedächtnis. Ergänzungsband [Experimental contributions to the science of memory]. *Zeitschrift für Psychologie*, *1*, 1–300.

Parker, E. S., Birnbaum, I. M., Weingartner, H., Hartley, J. T., Stillman, R. C., & Wyatt, R. J. (1980). Retrograde enhancement of human memory with alcohol. *Psychopharmacology*, *69*, 219–222.

Parker, E. S., Morihisa, J. M., Wyatt, R. J., Schwartz, B. L., Weingartner, H., & Stillman, R. C. (1981). The alcohol facilitation effect on memory: A dose-response study. *Psychopharmacology*, *74*, 88–92.

Peigneux, P., Laureys, S., Fuchs, S., Collette, F., Perrin, F., Reggers, J., et al. (2004). Are spatial memories strengthened in the human hippocampus during slow-wave sleep? *Neuron*, *44*, 535–545.

Phihal, W., & Born, J. (1997). Effects of early and late nocturnal sleep on declarative and procedural memory. *Journal of Cognitive Neuroscience*, *9*, 534–547.

Phihal, W., & Born, J. (1999). Effects of early and late nocturnal sleep on priming and spatial memory. *Psychophysiology*, *36*, 571–582.

Pivik, T., & Foulkes, D. (1968). NREM mentation: Relation to personality, orientation time, and time of night. *Journal of Consulting and Clinical Psychology, 32*, 144–151.

Rasch, B., Buchel, C., Gais, S., & Born, J. (2007). Odor cues during slow-wave sleep prompt declarative memory consolidation. *Science, 315*, 1426–1429.

Ribot, T. (1881). *Les Maladies de la mémoire* [Diseases of memory]. New York: Appleton-Century-Crofts.

Ribot, T. (1882). *Diseases of memory: An essay in positive psychology*. London: Kegan Paul, Trench & Co.

Roberto, M., Nelson, T. E., Ur, C. L., & Gruol, D. L. (2002). Long-term potentiation in the rat hippocampus is reversibly depressed by chronic intermittent ethanol exposure. *Journal of Neurophysiology, 87*, 2385–2397.

Scoville, W. B., & Milner, B. (1957). Loss of recent memory after bilateral hippocampal lesions. *Journal of Neurology, Neurosurgery and Psychiatry, 20*, 11–21.

Simon, H. A. (1966). A note on Jost's Law and exponential forgetting. *Psychometrika, 31*, 505–506.

Sinclair, J. G., & Lo, G. F. (1986). Ethanol blocks tetanic and calcium-induced long-term potentiation in the hippocampal slice. *General Pharmacology, 17*, 231–233.

Skaggs, E. B. (1925). Further studies in retroactive inhibition. *Psychological Monographs (Whole No. 161), 34*, 1–60.

Soetens, E., Casaer, S., D'Hooge, R., & Hueting, J. E. (1995). Effect of amphetamine on long-term retention of verbal material. *Psychopharmacology, 119*, 155–162.

Squire, L. R. (2009). The legacy of patient H.M. for neuroscience. *Neuron, 61*, 6–9.

Squire, L. R., & Alvarez, P. (1995). Retrograde amnesia and memory consolidation: A neurobiological perspective. *Current Opinion in Neurobiology, 5*, 169–177.

Squire, L. R., Clark, R. E., & Knowlton, B. J. (2001). Retrograde amnesia. *Hippocampus, 11*, 50–55.

Sünram-Lea, S. I., Foster, J. K., Durlach, P., & Perez, C. (2002). The effect of retrograde and anterograde glucose administration on memory performance in healthy young adults. *Behavioural Brain Research, 134*, 505–516.

Talamini L. M., Nieuwenhuis, I. L., Takashima A., & Jensen O. (2008). Sleep directly following learning benefits consolidation of spatial associative memory. *Learning & Memory, 15*, 233–237.

Tulving, E., & Madigan, S. A. (1970). Memory and verbal learning. *Annual Review of Psychology, 21*, 437–484.

Tulving, E., & Pearlstone, Z. (1966). Availability versus accessibility of information in memory for words. *Journal of Verbal Learning & Verbal Behavior, 5*, 381–391.

Tulving, E., & Thomson, D. M. (1973). Encoding specificity and retrieval processes in episodic memory. *Psychological Review, 80*, 352–373.

Tyson, P., & Schirmuly, M. (1994). Memory enhancement after drinking ethanol: Consolidation, interference, or response bias? *Psychology and Behavior, 56*, 933–937.

Underwood, B. J. (1957). Interference and forgetting. *Psychological Review, 64*, 49–60.

Underwood, B. J. (1983). *Attributes of memory*. Glenview, IL: Scott, Foresman and Company.

Underwood, B. J., & Ekstrand, B. R. (1966). An analysis of some shortcomings in the interference theory of forgetting. *Psychological Review, 73*, 540–549.

Underwood, B. J., & Ekstrand, B. R. (1967). Studies of distributed practice: XXIV.

Differentiation and proactive inhibition. *Journal of Experimental Psychology, 74*, 574–580.

Underwood, B. J., & Postman, L. (1960). Extraexperimental sources of interference in forgetting. *Psychological Review, 67*, 73–95.

Villarreal, D. M., Do, V., Haddad, E., & Derrick, B. E. (2002). NMDA receptor antagonists sustain LTP and spatial memory: Active processes mediate LTP decay. *Nature Neuroscience, 5*, 48–52.

Walker, M. P. (2005). A refined model of sleep and the time course of memory formation. *Behavioral and Brain Sciences, 28*, 51–104.

Watkins, C., & Watkins, M. J. (1975). Buildup of proactive inhibition as a cue-overload effect. *Journal of Experimental Psychology: Human Learning & Memory, 1*, 442–452.

Weingartner, H. J., Sirocco, K., Curran, V., & Wolkowitz, O. (1995). Memory facilitation following the administration of the benzodiazepine triazolam. *Experimental and Clinical Psychopharmacology, 3*, 298–303.

Whitlock J. R., Heynen A. J., Schuler M. G., & Bear M. F. (2006). Learning induces long-term potentiation in the hippocampus. *Science, 313*, 1058–1059.

Wickelgren, W. A. (1974). Single-trace fragility theory of memory dynamics. *Memory & Cognition, 2*, 775–780.

Wilson, M. A., & McNaughton, B. L. (1994). Reactivation of hippocampal ensemble memories during sleep. *Science, 265*, 676–679.

Wixted, J. T. (2004a). On common ground: Jost's (1897) law of forgetting and Ribot's (1881) law of retrograde amnesia. *Psychological Review, 111*, 864–879.

Wixted, J. T. (2004b). The psychology and neuroscience of forgetting. *Annual Review of Psychology, 55*, 235–269.

Wixted, J. T., & Carpenter, S. K. (2007). The Wickelgren power law and the Ebbinghaus savings function. *Psychological Science, 18*, 133–134.

Wixted, J. T., & Ebbesen, E. (1991). On the form of forgetting. *Psychological Science, 2*, 409–415.

Xu, L., Anwyl, R., & Rowan, M. J. (1998). Spatial exploration induces a persistent reversal of long-term potentiation in rat hippocampus. *Nature, 394*, 891–894.

Yaroush, R., Sullivan, M. J., & Ekstrand, B. R. (1971). The effect of sleep on memory: II. Differential effect of the first and second half of the night. *Journal of Experimental Psychology, 88*, 361–366.

Zola-Morgan, S., & Squire, L. R. (1990). The primate hippocampal formation: Evidence for a time-limited role in memory storage. *Science, 250*, 288–290.

Author index

Page references in *italic* refer to where an author or their team leader is only referred to in a figure caption or a table. Names in the index include research team members who may not actually appear by name in the text.

Abbot, P., 201, *212*, 216, 219, 228
Abel, T., 108, 294
Abeles, M., 28
Abraham, W. C., 306
Abrahamsen, A. A., 92
Ackley, D. H., 86, 87
Acosta-Cabronero, J., *218*, 222, 224, 229
Adam, K., 165
Adam, S., 151
Addis, D. R., 140, 227
Aerni, A., 124
Agranoff, B. W., 197, *198*
Aguirre, G. K., 143
Ahern, G., 201, *212*, 214, 217, 222, 229
Alberini, C. M., 109, 114, 115, 119, 120
Albers, M., 245
Albouy, G., 166, 173, 175, 178
Aldenhoff, J. B., 230
Alea, N., 254, 265
Alexander, D. C., 224
Alin, L. H., 65
Almeida, Q. J., 41
Alpner, T. G., 193, 195
Altman, J. S., 167
Alvarez, P., 94, 139, 226, 303
Amir, N., 259
Ancoli-Israel, S., 167
Anderer, P., 175
Anderson, E., 293
Anderson, J. R., 55, 93, 141, 143, 150
Anderson, M. C., 14, 17–18, 126, 141, 145, 146, 147, *149*, 150, 151, 152, 153, 154, 193, 254, 257, 258, 260, 261, 262–263, 264, 267
Anderson, N. D., 137
Andersson, J., 270
Angell, E. B., 28
Anshel, M. H., 41
Antuono, P., 69
Anwyl, R., 295
Arbuckle, T. Y., 14
Arena, J. G., 217, *218*, 219, 220, 229
Aserinsky, E., 167
Ashkenazi, A., 50
Ashtari, M., 242
Askenasy, J. J. M., 299
Aslan, A., 147, 149, 151
Atienza, M., 177, 178
Atkinson, R. C., xiii, 51, 93, 188, *189*
Aubert-Khalfa, S., 241, 244
Augustine, E. A., 223
Austin, J. R., 276
Avanzini, G., *218*, 220, 226
Avizmil, O., 256, 260, 262
Avons, S. E., 54, 61
Axelrad, J., 224
Azad, S. C., 123, 124
Azam, M., 28

Bach, M. E., 126
Baddeley, A. D., 51, 52, 93, 193
Badre, D., 143, 150, 151
Bahrick, H. P., 6, 41, 306–307
Bahrick, P. O., 41
Bailey, C. H., 286
Baldo, J. V., 194
Balota, D. A., 153, 263
Balteau, E., 166, 173, 174, 178
Banaji, M., 137
Banich, M. T., 23, *149*, 152, 153, 154, 263
Barad, M., 126, 294
Barbarotto, R., 239, 245
Barch, D. M., 150
Barker, S., *212*, 216, 220
Barnes, C. A., 297
Barnhardt, T. M., 255
Barnhofer, T., 243
Barnier, A. J., 255, 256, 257, 259–260, 262, 264, 265, 268, 269, 270–271, 274, 276, 277
Baron, J.-C., 227, 245

Baron-Cohen, S., 241
Barrett, T. R., 298
Barrouillet, P., 54
Barry, C., 173
Bartlett, F. C., 38, 256, 267, 272
Bartolo, A., 41
Basden, B. H., 260, 268, 269
Basden, D. R., 260, 268, 269
Baudry, M., 293
Bauer, J., 27
Baumgärtel, K., 125
Bäuml, K. H., 147, 148, *149*, 149, 150, 151, 154, 259
Baxendale, S. A., 229
Bayley, P. J., 228
Beach, K., 272
Bear, M. F., 294
Beaunieux, H., 244
Beblo, T., 243
Bechtel, W., 92
Bechterew, W. von, 28
Becker, J., 7, 8
Beckwith, B. E., 300
Bell, B. D., 216, 217, *218*, 220–221, 230
Bell, T. A., 147
Bellinger, K. D., 266, 267, 268
Belliveau, M., 276
Benca, R. M., 177
Benfenati, F., 105, 108, 109
Berger, R. J., 165
Bergin, P. S., 223
Bergström, Z., *149*, 150, 154
Berman, M. G., 52, 53
Bernardi, G., 106
Bernardin, S., 54
Bertram, L., 127
Beschin, N., 42, 53, 185, 186, *187*, *188*, 189, 190
Betensky, J. D., 242
Betz, A., 257
Bhaduri, A., *218*, 222, 224, 229
Bhatarah, P., 50
Bibi, U., 258
Biessels, G., 300
Bireta, T. J., 54
Birnbaum, I. M., 300
Bisogno, T., 123, 124
Bjork, E. L., 9, 14, 17, 146, 147, *149*, 254, 257, 258, 260, 267
Bjork, R. A., 9, 14, 17, 60, 61, 146, 147, *149*, 150, 193, 254, 257, 258, 260, 267
Black, S. E., 41
Blackemore, C., 112
Blake, R. V., 201, 216, 217, *218*, 219, 220, 222, 224, 225, 226
Bliss, T. V. P., 201, 293, 302
Bloch, M., 272
Bluck, S., 254, 257, 265
Blumen, H. M., 268
Blumenfeld, R., 136, *137*
Boesiger, P., 195, 228
Bohbot, V. D., 174
Boigs, M., 230
Boly, M., 167, 175, 178
Bomb, P., 53
Boni, A., *212*
Boniface, S., 201, 225
Bonnet, M. H., 167
Bontempi, B., 171
Bookheimer, S. Y., 154
Boon, J C. W., 42
Borbely, A. A., 167, 169
Borges, J. L., xiii, 26, 36, 101
Born, J., 65, 68, 95, 171, 172, 174, 175, 176, 177, 178, 230, 296–297, 298–299, 305
Bortsutzkya, S., 42
Boscolo, G., 41
Bosshardt, S., 195, 228
Botvinick, M. M., 50, 150
Botzung, A., 245
Bourtchouladze, R., 294
Bowker, G., 273
Bozon, B., 109
Brainerd, C. J., 41
Braitenberg, V., 86
Bramham, C. R., 297
Brand, M., 29, 30, 42, 239, 240, 241, 242, 243, 244, 245, 246
Brandon, D. P., 267
Brandt, J., 239, 240
Bransford, J. D., 137
Braun, S., 230
Braver, T. S., 150
Breen, E. K., 201, 216, 217, *218*, 219, 220, 222, 224, 225, 226
Bregman, L. E., 28
Bregman, N. J., 203
Bremner, J. D., 242, 243
Brennen, S., 270
Breuer, J., 26, 27
Brewer, J., 136
Brewer, W. F., 42, 85
Brewin, C. R., 257, 261
Brice, J., *212*, 216, 220
Brigidi, B., 259
Brink, J. J., 197, *198*
Broadbent, D. E., 38
Brodie, M. J., 225
Brodmann, K., 27
Brown, A. S., 67
Brown, G. D. A., 49, 50, 52–53, 53, 54, 55–59, 61, 62, 65, 67, 69, 70nn2–3
Brown, J., 14
Brown, P., 41
Brown, R. A., 124
Brown, S. D., 272
Brown, W., 9
Brozovich, F., 153
Bruce, K. R., 300
Bruckbauer, T., 227, 242, 245
Bryant, R. A., 261

Bryber, S., 268
Buccione, I., 242
Buch, T., 124
Buchanan, M., 51
Büchel, C., 305
Buckner, R. L., 177, 241
Budrys, V., 217, *218*, 219, 220, 224, 226
Buhl, D., 173
Bulevich, J. B., 153, 263
Buneman, O. P., 80
Bunge, S. A., 151
Burgess, N., 50, 51, 69, 167, 173
Burgl, G., 28
Burnett, C. T., 28
Burnham, W. H., 196–197
Burrows, B., 151
Buss, C., 242
Butler, A. C., 153, 263
Butler, C. R., 201, 211, *212*, 217, *218*, 219, 220, 221, 222, 224, 226, 229
Buzsaki, G., 173, 304
Byrne, J. H., 290, 307

Cabeza, R., 137, 138, 171, 177
Cahill, L., 17, 24
Cai, D. J., 175
Cajochen, C., 172
Calabresi, P., 106
Calcagno, M., 221
Calcaterra, G., 153, 263, 264
Caltagirone, C., 242
Camos, V., 54
Camp, G., 147
Campbell, S., 266, 274
Canevini, M. P., 222
Canger, R., 222
Cannistraro, P. A., 243
Cantagallo, A., 245
Cantero, J. L., 177, 178
Capizzano, A. A., 224
Caplan, D., 54
Caramazza, A., 41
Cardozo, J., 221
Cariga, P., 194, *212*, 214, 216, 219, 224, 228
Carlesimo, G. A., 242
Carpenter, G. A., 91
Carpenter, S. K., 5, 286
Carter, C. S., 143, 150
Carter, S. R., 264
Casaer, S., 300
Casazza, M., *218*, 220
Cascio, M. G., 123, 124
Casey, E. S., 273
Castel, A. D., 42
Castillo, P. E., 124
Caughey, J. B., 9
Ceccaldi, M., 241, 244
Centonze, D., 106
Cervantes, M. de, 26
Chace, P. M., 139
Chaklader, A., 175, 229–230
Challis, B. H., 7
Chalmers, D., 272
Chang, J., 239, 240, 241
Charcot, J. M., 26
Chase, W. G., 42
Chassagnon, S., *212*
Chater, N., 49, 50, 55–59, 62, 65, 67
Chattarji, S., 123
Chechile, R. A., 55
Chen, M., 286
Chen, S., 242
Cheng, Y., 143
Che'telat, G., 227
Chetelat, G., 245
Chin, J., 128
Choi, S. Y., 228
Chokroverty, S., 167
Cho-Young, J., 300
Cipolotti, L., 142
Ciranni, M. A., 147, 148
Clark, A., 272, 273
Clark, D. M., 243
Clark, R. E., 68, 292
Clarke, R., 137
Clifasefi, S. L., 42
Cocchini, G., 239, 245
Coenen, A. M., 300
Cohen, G., 35
Cohen, J. D., 150
Cohen, N. J., 89, 224
Colbourn, C., 201, *212*, 216, 219, 228
Cole, C. J., 124
Coleman, A., 214
Coles, M. E., 259
Colgin, L. L., 114, 115, 116
Collette, F., 151, 166, 172, 173, 229, 292
Collingridge, G. L., 293, 302
Connerton, P., 253, 272, 273
Constable, R. T., 227
Conway, M. A., 35, 151, 254, 255, 256, 259–260, 262, 264, 273, 276
Cook, R. G., 61
Cooper, J., 152, 153, 154
Corbetta, M., 138
Corcoran, R., 226, 243
Corkin, S., 137, 224
Corrigan, E., 261
Costello, A., 244
Cowan, N., 42, 50, 53, 63, 64, 65, 185, 186, *187*, *188*, 189, 190, 191, *192*, 193, 194, 195, 197, 199, 202, 205, 303
Cowles, E., 28
Cox, C. J., 154
Craik, F. I. M., 137
Crane, C., 243
Crane, J., 142
Crawley, A. P., 140, 227
Crick, F., 165–166, 178
Cronen-Ohayon, S., *212*

Crowder, R. G., 6, 11, 12, 49
Crutch, S. J., 41
Csicsvari, J., 173
Cubelli, R., 40, 41
Cuc, A., 267, 268
Curcio, G., 173
Curran, T., 23, *149*, 152, 153, 154, 195, 263
Curran, V., 300, 301
Czernik, A. J., 105, 108, 109

Da Silva, R. C., 229
Daaman, M., 219, 223
Dadds, M. R., 124
Dale, A., 136
Dalfen, A. K., 28
Dalla Barba, G., 244
Dallenbach, K. M., 9, *10*, 12, 51, 65, 165, 178, 288, 291, 295, 296
Dalmau, J., 214
Dana, C. L., 28
Dang-Vu, T. T., 166, 175
Danker, J. F., 143, 150
Dante Alighieri, 26
Darley, J. M., 35
Darsaud, A., 175, 178
Darwin, C. J., 6
Davachi, L., 136, 138
Davelaar, E. J., 50
Davidhoff, V., *212*
Davidson, M., *218*, 221, 231
Davies, G. M., 42
Davies, K., 219
Davis, H. P., 224, 294
Davis, M., 2–3, 121, 123
Davis, R. E., 197, *198*
Davis, S., 109
Dayan, P., 87
De Fockert, J., 154
De Gennaro, L., 173
De Jong-Meyer, R., 243
De Lujan Calcagno, M., 201, *218*, 219, 220, 221, 224
De Renzi, E., *212*, 216, 217, 240, 244
De Wilde, E. J., 243
Degirmenci, M., 176, 177
Degonda, N., 195, 228
Degueldre, C., 173, 174
Del Cerro, S., 299
Delaney, P. F., 261
Delbeuck, X., 166, 167, 171, 174
Della Sala, S., 40, 41, 42, 50, 53, 63, 64, 65, 185, 186, *187*, *188*, 189, 190, 191, *192*, 193, 194, 195, 197, 199, 202, 205, 303
Denes, G., 244
Denkova, E., 245
Depue, B. E., 23, *149*, 152, 153, 154, 263
Derakshan, N., 261
Derrick, B. E., 305–306
Descartes, R., 26
Desgranges, B., 166, 167, 171, 227, 244, 245
Desmond, J., 136
D'Esposito, M., 143
Despres, O., 222
Desseilles, M., 166, 175
Destexhe, A., 175
Destrebecqz, A., 166
Detre, G., 150
Deuel, T. A., 294
Dewar, M., 42, 50, 63, 64, 65, 185, 189, 191, *192*, 193, 194, 195, 197, 199, 202, 205, 303
D'Hooge, R., 300
Diebel, A., 29, 239, 240, 241, 246
Diekelmann, S., 177, 178
Dinges, D. F., 65, 176, 229
Dixon, R. A., 275
Do, V., 305–306
Docherty, T., 201, 216, 219, 228
Dodd, M. D., 258
Dolan, R. J., 137, 142, *143*, 145, 244
Dommett, E. J., 300
Donald, M., 272
Donath, J., 27, 28
Donnett, J. G., 167
Dornan, P., 253
Dorris, L., *218*, 221, 231
Dorsett, S. I., 29
Dow, C., 217, *218*, 220, 230
Doyle, M. C., 154
Draaisma, D., 37
Dragunow, M., 306
Driessen, M., 243
Droscopoulos, S., 174, 176, 177
Drummond, S. P., 175
Dudai, Y., 16, 35, 117, *118*, 120, 165, 171, 195, 197, 201, 203
Dudukovic, N. M., 148, *149*, 150
Dumay, N., 195
Dumont, C., 43
Duncan, M., 52–53, 67, 70nn2–3
Durlach, P., 300

Earhard, M., 15
Ebbesen, E. B., 55, 93, 285
Ebbinghaus, H., 4–5, 7, 36, 135, 139, 285, 286, 306
Ebner, A., 219, 223, 225
Eco, U., 126, 130
Eggers, C., 240, 241, 242, 244
Ehlers, A., 243
Ehlert, U., 124
Einstein, G. O., 42
Eisenberg, H. M., 223, 224
Eisenberg, M., 117, *118*, 120
Ekeocha, J. O., 270
Ekstrand, B. R., 65, 66, 172, 175, 176, 288, 289, 296, 297, 298, 302
Eldridge, L. L., 154
Elger, C. E., *218*, 220
Elgersma, Y., 108
Elixhauser, A., 222, 226

Ellenbogen, J. M., 65, 95, 116, 176, 229
Elliott, E. M., 53
Ellis, R., 92
Elzinger, B., 243
Engel, S. A., 154
Engle, R. W., 240
Epicurus, 105
Erdelyi, M., 253, 261, 263, 273
Erdelyi, M. H., 7, 8, 17
Estes, W. K., 155
Eustache, F., 166, 167, 171, 227, 245
Evans, M. S., 299

Fadda, L., 242
Farah, M. J., 143
Farrell, S., 50, 69
Faught, E., 223, 224
Feinstein, A., 28
Feldstein, S. N., 224
Felician, O., 241, 244
Feredoes, E., 144
Fernandez Garcia, Y., 185, 189, *192*, 194, 195, 199, 202, 303
Ferrara, M., 173
Ferreira, M. B. C., 229
Feruzza, E., 244
Ficca, G., 172, 175
File, S. E., 301
Fillmore, M. T., 300
Fine, J., 217, *218*, 220, 230
Fink, G. R., 227, 242, 244, 245
Finlay, F., 268
Fischer, A., 124
Fischer, C. E., 28
Fischer, S., 174, 176
Fish, D. R., 223
Fishbein, W., 175, 229–230
Fitzpatrick, S. M., 35
Fivush, R., 266, 267, 271, 272, 274
Flatau, G., 28
Flenniken, D. L., 224
Fletcher, P., 137, 142, *143*, 145, 244
Flexser, A. J., 15
Fluck, E., 301
Foa, E. B., 259
Forel, A., 28
Foret, J., 166, 167, 171
Forty, A., 273
Foster, J. K., 50, 300
Foulkes, D., 297
Fowler, M. J., 175, 298
Frackowiak, R., 137
Franczak, M., 69
Frank, G., 177
Frank, L. M., 304
Frankland, P. W., 171
Franks, J. J., 137
Franz, S. I., 28
Fraser, J., 145
Frederick the Great, 26
Freed, D. M., 224
Freeman, R., 65
French, R. M., 90, 91
Freud, S., 16, 26, 27, 102, 106, *107*, 125
Freund, C. S., 26
Freund, J. S., 65
Frey, U., 294
Friedman, D., 154
Friege, L., 230
Frith, C. D., 137, 227, 243, 244
Fritzer, G., 230
Frölich, L., 245
Fthenaki, A., 151
Fuchs, S., 166, 173, 229, 292
Fujiwara, E., 29, 42, 239, 240, 241, 242, 244, 245, 246
Fukutake, T., 41
Furmanski, C. S., 154
Fuster, J. M., 240

Gabel, A., 149
Gabrieli, J. D., 126, 136
Gabrieli, S. W., 152, 153, 154
Gainotti, G., 43
Gais, S., 65, 68, 172, 174, 175, 176, 177, 230, 296–297, 305
Gangadhar, B. N., 240
Ganser, S. J., 28
Garcia, Y. F., 64, 65
Gargano, G. J., 260
Garrett, M. F., 41
Garry, M., 42
Gaskell, M. G., 195
Gazzaniger, M. S., 39
Geiger, S. M., 52, 65
Genoux, D., 109, 125
Gentile, A., 65
Geraerts, E., 261, 264
Gershberg, F. B., 142, 194
Ghaffar, O., 241
Ghoneim, M. M., 300
Giese, K. P., 131
Giffard, B., 244
Giffard-Quillon, G., 227, 245
Gilboa, A., 140, 227
Gillespie, R. D., 28
Gilliam, F. G., 223, 224
Gillund, G., 50
Giovagnoli, A. R., 216, 217, *218*, 220, 226
Girard, C., 244
Gispen, W. H., 300
Giuliano, T., 274, 275
Givens, B., 299
Gjerstad, L., 245
Glaser, G. H., 223
Glisky, E. L., 240
Glover, G., 136
Gluckberg, S., 35
Godden, D. R., 193
Göder, R., 230

Goertz, R., 154
Goethe, J. W. von, 26
Gold, P. E., 300
Golding, J. M., 253
Golgi, C., 106
Gong, Q., 217, 229
Goode, A., 143
Goodhart, S. P., 28
Gordon, A., 28, 29
Gordon, B., 41
Gore, J. B., 140
Gorfine, T., 175
Goshen-Gottstein, Y., 50
Gotlib, I. H., 153, 263
Gould, O. N., 270
Govoni, R., 137
Grady, C. L., 140, 227
Graf, P., 38
Graham, K. S., 201, *218*, 219, 220, 221, 222, 224, 226, 229
Grasby, P., 137
Grass, G., 23
Grassi, L., 245
Gray, J. R., 150
Green, C., 126, 147, 152, 153, 257, 262, 263
Green, K. N., 127, *128*
Greenfield, S. A., 300
Greengard, P., 105, 108, 109
Greenlee, M. W., 148, 149
Greenwood, J. M., 306
Grigg-Damberger, M. M., 167
Grimwood, P. D., 293
Grossberg, S., 77, 78, 91
Gruber, G., 175
Gruol, D. L., 299
Guariglia, C., 173
Guastella, A. J., 124
Gujar, N., 177
Gummer, A., 194, *212*, 214, 216, 219, 224, 228
Gunduz-Bruce, H., 242
Gunn, P., 143, 150
Guye, M., 241, 244
Guynn, M. J., 3, 15, 42
Guzowski, J. F., 114

Haarmann, H. J., 50
Habermas, T., 257
Hackmann, A., 243
Haddad, E., 305–306
Haditsch, U., 109
Haist, F., 140
Halbwachs, M., 272, 274
Hallschmid, M., 177
Han, J. H., 124
Hannequin, D., 244
Hanslmayr, S., 154
Hardt, O., 117, 119, 120, 240
Harris, C. B., 255, 256, 260, 262, 265, 268, 269, 270–271, 274, 276, 277
Harris, J. A., 123
Hart, J., 41
Hartinger, A., 147, 148
Hartley, J. T., 300
Hartmann, E., 169
Hashimoto, R., 43
Hasselmo, M. E., 106, 115
Hauer, B., 260
Hauff, M., *218*, 220
Hayaishi, O., 167, 169
Hayashi, M. L., 228
Hayes, S. M., 240
Hayne, H., 266
Hays, L., 300
He, Z., 242
Heath, M., 41
Hebb, D. O., 80, 106, 109
Heckers, S., 242
Hedden, T., 126
Heifets, B. D., 124
Heilbronner, K., 28
Heilman, K. M., 41
Heine, R., 26, 27
Heinrichs, M., 124
Heinze, H., *149*, 150
Heiss, W.-D., 29, 227, 240, 241, 242, 244, 245
Heitman, J. L., 42
Hekkert, P., 272
Helgadottir, H., 175
Hellhammer, D. H., 242
Hellwig, K. A., 61
Helms, K., 175
Helmstaedter, C., *218*, 220
Henderson, E. L., 300
Henry, S., 268, 269
Henson, R., 50, 137, 142, 145, 227, 241
Herholz, K., 29, 225, 245
Hering, E., 23
Hermann, B. P., 217, *218*, 219, 220, 230
Hermans, D., 243
Herndon, B., 276
Hertel, P. T., 153, 263, 264, 274, 275
Hevenor, S. J., 140, 227
Hey, J., 26, 28
Heymans, G., 28
Heynen, A., 294
Hicks, J. L., 147
High, W. M. Jr., 223, 224
Hill, J., 241
Hinrichs, J. V., 300
Hinton, G. E., 86, 87, 89, 96n2
Hinton, S., 6, 55
Hintzman, D., 306
Hirota, Y., 175, 229–230
Hirsch, E., *212*
Hirshkowitz, M., 167
Hirst, W., 267, 268, 272
Hismjatullina, A., 53
Hitch, G. J., 50, 51, 69, 93, 268
Hoad, T. F., 35
Hobson, J. A., 95, 169, 171

Hoche, A. E., 27
Hock, C., 195, 228
Hodges, J., 221
Hodges, J. R., 201, *218*, 219, 220, 221, 222, 224, 225, 226, 229
Hodges, R., 201
Hoedlmoser, K., 175
Hoff, M. E., 88
Hoffman, K. L., 293, 304
Hogge, M., 151
Holdstock, J. S., 194, *212*, 214, 216, 217, 219, 224, 228, 229
Hollingshead, A. B., 267
Homer, 26
Honda, K., 165
Hopfield, J. J., 83
Howard, M. W., 50, 155
Hsiang, H. L., 124
Hu, P., 177, 178
Huber, M., 244
Hudjetz, A., 53
Hueting, J. E., 300
Hulbert, J. C., 65, 176, 229
Hulme, C., 50, 69
Humphreys, G. W., 41, 92
Hung, L., 259–260, 264
Hupbach, A., 240
Huppert, F. A., 224, 225, 230
Hutchins, E., 272

Iaria, G., 173, 174
Iidaka, T., 137
Ikejiri, Y., 245, 246
Inoue, S., 165
Insler, R. Z., 143, 150
Irwin, J. M., 11, 145
Isaac, C. L., 194, *212*, 214, 216, 217, 219, 224, 228, 229, 231
Ivnick, R. J., 186, 225
Ivry, R. B., 39
Izquierdo, I., 197, 228, 229, 293, 295, 302

Jacoby, L. L., 241
Jaermann, T., 195, 228
James, L., 95
James, N., 151
James, W., 36, 80
Janet, P., 26, 27, 28
Janowski, J. S., 142
Janszky, J., 219, 223
Jatuzis, D., 217, *218*, 219, 220, 224, 226
Jeffery, K. J., 167
Jehee, J., 96
Jelicic, M., 153, 242, 261, 264
Jenkins, J. G., 9, 12, 51, 65, 165, 178, 288, 291, 295, 296
Jensen, O., 227–228, 297
Jessell, T. M., 103, 105, 112, 113, 114
Ji, D., 293, 298
Joanette, Y., 43
Johansson, M., 149
Johnson, R., Jr., 154
Johnson, S. K., 147
Jokeit, H., 219, 223, 225
Jolesz, F. A., 177
Jones, R. W., 151
Jones Leonard, B., 297
Jonides, J., 52, 53, 143
Joorman, J., 153, 263
Josephs, O., 142, 145
Joslyn, S. L., 262
Josselyn, S. A., 108, 109
Jost, A., 285
Jouvet, M., 165
Joyce, E. M., 301
Jung, C. G., 26, 28
Jung, H. Y., 228
Jung, K. J., 143
Jung, M., 299
Jurica, P. J., 142, 194

Kahana, M. J., 50, 155
Kahn, I., 148, *149*, 150
Kalbe, E., 29, 225, 244, 245
Kales, A., 167
Káli, S., 87
Kamal, A., 300
Kan, I. P., 143
Kanady, J., 175
Kandel, E. R., 103, 105, 108, 109, 112, 113, 114, 115, 171, 294
Kandris, E., 259
Kane, M. J., 240
Kant, I., 26
Kapur, N., 201, *212*, 216, *218*, 219, 220, 221, 222, 224, 226, 228, 229, 243
Kapur, S., 137
Karlsson, M. P., 304
Karni, A., 299
Karpicke, J. D., 7, 14
Kashyap, N., 177, 178
Kaubrys, G., 217, *218*, 219, 220, 224, 226
Kehrli, P., *212*, 222
Keil, P. J., 270–271
Keller, F. R., 225
Keller, J., 276
Kellner, 28
Kelly, A., 109
Kelly, T. H., 300
Kemp, R. I., 267, 268, 276
Kendrick, D. F., 61
Kennedy, C. M., 241
Kennedy, P., 201, *212*, 216, 219, 228
Kensinger, E. A., 137, 177
Keppel, G., 36, 65, 289
Kerr, J. R., 61
Kessler, J., 29, 225, 227, 239, 240, 241, 242, 244, 245, 246
Kieras, D. E., 54
Kihlstrom, J. F., 255, 257, 261, 263

Kincaid, J. P., 65
Kinchla, R. A., 35
Kirschbaum, C., 242
Kirsh, D., 272
Kirwan, C. B., 154
Klein, N. M., 273
Kleinpass, A., 243
Kleitman, N., 167
Klosch, G., 175
Klumpp, A., 268
Knight, R. T., 142, 143, 194
Knoblauch, V., 175
Knobloch, M., 109
Knoedler, A. J., 61
Knowlton, B. J., 154, 169, 292
Knowlton, R., 224
Kock, P., 245
Köhler, F., 27
Köhler, W., 2
Kok, A., 154
Kokmen, E., 186, 225
Komoda, Y., 165
Konorski, J., 120
Kopelman, M. D., 220, 221, 223, 224, 225, 226, 239, 240
Kopp, B., 154
Koppel, J., 267, 268
Korsnes, M. S., 61
Koshibu, K., 125
Koutstaal, W., 136, 261
Kracht, L., 29, 239, 240, 241, 245, 246
Kramer, G., 225
Krangel, T. S., 242
Krein, H., 270
Kritchevsky, M., 142, 239, 240, 241
Krug, M., 294
Kubik, S., 114
Küchler, S., 273
Kuhbander, C., 259
Kuhl, B. A., 148, *149*, 150, 152, 153, 154
Kuhlmann, S., 242
Kühnel, S., 245, 246
Kumar, S., 240
Kundera, M., 273
Kushner, S. A., 114, 124
Kutas, M., 136, 154
Kuzniecky, R., 224
Kwan, P., 225
Kwint, M., 273

LaBar, K. S., 171, 177
Ladowsky-Brooks, R. L., 28
LaFerla, F. M., 127, *128*
Laiacona, M., 239, 245
Lamberty, G. J., 300
Landeau, B., 245
Landfield, P. W., 242
Langnickel, R., 30
Laroche, S., 109
Larsen, S. F., 257
Lattal, K. M., 108
Lau, H., 175, 229–230
Laughlin, H. P., 28, 29
Laureys, S., 166, 167, 171, 173, 174, 229, 292
Laxer, K. D., 224
Lebreton, K., 245
Lechner, H. A., 290, 307
LeDoux, J. E., 121, 171, 203, 205
Lee, G. P., 217, *218*, 219, 220, 229
Lee, H. K., 228
Leidy, N. K., 222, 226
Leipold, P., 154
Lemmo, M., 43
LeMoult, J., 263
Lencz, T., 242
Leonard, G., 142
Lepage, M., 241
Levin, H. S., 223, 224
Levin, K., 257, 264
Levy, B., 145, 147, 150, 151, 261, 262, 263, 264
Lewandowski, G., 114
Lewandowsky, S., 50, 52–53, 54, 65, 67, 69, 70nn2–3
Lewis, D. J., 116, 203
Lewis, K., 276
Lewis, P., 221, 223, 226
Lewis, R. L., 52, 53
Li, L., 242
Lin, X., 242
Lindsay, P. H., 38
Lisman, S. A., 302
Liu, J., 242
Livingstone-Zatchej, M., 125
Lo, G. F., 299
Lockhart, R. S., 137
Loess, H., 65
Loewenstein, R. J., 242
Loftus, E. F., 3, 13, 42, 266
Loftus, G. R., 3
Logan, B., 306
Lombardo, P., 172, 175
Lomo, T., 201
Long, D. L., 42
Longuet-Higgins, H. C., 80
Loring, D. W., 217, *218*, 219, 220, 229
Louie, K., 298
Lovatt, P., 54
Lovibond, P. F., 124
Lu, K. T., 123, 124
Lu, Y. F., 126
Lucas, B., 172, 174, 296–297
Lucchelli, F., *212*, 217, 223, 229, 240, 244
Luck, S. J., 93
Lücke, 26, 28
Lüer, G., 195
Lundholm, H., 27
Luo, J., 140
Luria, A. R., 17, 23, 36
Lux, S., 245
Luxen, A., 173, 174

Lynch, G. S., 293
Lynch, L., 299
Lynch, M. A., 201

MacDonald, A. W., 150
MacDonald, S., 266
MacGregor, R. J., 93
Mack, L., 41
Macklin, M. L., 242
MacLeod, C. M., 253, 258
MacLeod, M. D., 147
Macrae, C., 137, 259
Madigan, S. A., 289
Maggiori, G., 222
Magnussen, S., 61
Maguire, E. A., 167, 227
Mahan, J., 203
Maher, A., 257, 264
Maitrot, D., *212*
Malafouris, L., 273
Mameniskiene, R., 217, *218*, 219, 220, 224, 226
Manes, F., 201, *218*, 219, 220, 221, 224
Mangels, J. A., 142, 194
Mangun, G. R., 39
Manier, D., 268, 272
Mann, R. E., 300
Manning, C. A., 300
Manning, L., *212*, 222, 244, 245
Mansuy, I. M., 109
Mantovan, M. C., 244
Mao, H., 140
Maquet, P., 166, 167, 169, 171, 173, 174, 177
Marchetti, C., 41
Maril, A., 136, 150
Markopoulos, G., *149*, 150
Markowitsch, H. J., 24, 29, 30, 42, 225, 227, 239, 240, 241, 242, 243, 244, 245, 246, 272
Maroni, C., 124
Marsh, E. J., 266, 267
Marshall, L., 95, 171, 174, 175
Marshuetz, C., 143
Marsicano, G., 123, 124
Martin, A., 200
Martin, R. C., 143, 217, *218*, 219, 220, 223, 224, 229
Martin, S. J., 293
Martis, B., 243
Marzano, C., 173
Mascheroni, S., 226
Masterson, J., 54
Matler, U., 154
Matthies, 28
Matthies, H., 294
Mattson, R. H., 223
Matynia, A., 114, 124
Matzel, L. D., 203
Mauk, M. D., 171
Maurer, K., 245
Mayes, A. R., 136, 194, *212*, 214, 216, 217, 219, 224, 228, 229, 231
Mayeux, R., 224
Mayford, M., 114, 116
Maylor, E. A., 62
Mayoh, L., 256, 260, 262
McAndrews, M. P., 140, 227
McAvoy, M. P., 241
McCabe, D. P., 42
McCarthy, R. A., 201, 216, 217, *218*, 219, 220, 222, 224, 225, 226
McClelland, J. L., 50, 77, 84–85, 92, 94, 95, 96, 106, 115, 171, 227, 293
McCloskey, M., 13, 89
McCormack, T., 65, 67
McCulloch, K. C., 147
McDaniel, M. A., 42
McElree, B., 6
McGaugh, J. L., 17, 24, 139, 171, 177, 204, 292, 293, 300, 303, 307
McGeoch, J. A., 9, 10, 15, 141
McGinty, D., 165
McGlashan, T., 242
McKee, R. D., 224
McMahon, K., 299
McMillan, C. T., 43
McMullin, K., 243
McNally, R. J., 253, 261
McNaughton, B. L., 50, 94, 95, 96, 171, 173, 226, 227, 292, 293, 297, 298, 304
McVeigh, N. D., 147
Meade, M. L., 270
Meador, K. J., 217, *218*, 219, 220, 222, 225, 226, 229
Means, E., 222, 226
Mecklinger, A., 149, 154
Medina, J. F., 171
Medina, J. H., 197, 228, 229, 293, 295, 302
Mednick, S. C., 175
Meeter, M., 50, 65, 67, 94, 95, 96
Melchior, G., 167
Melton, A. W., 2, 11, 49, 145
Mensink, G. J., 93, 141, 193, 194
Mensink, G. M., 155
Mentschel, C., 242
Merckelbach, H., 153, 242, 261, 264
Mertens, M., 243
Merton, R. K., 2
Mesulam, M., 201, *212*, 214, 217, 222, 229
Metzler, C., 143
Meudell, P., 268
Mewaldt, S. P., 300
Meyer, A., 28
Meyer D. E., 54
Michalon, A., 109
Middleton, D., 272
Millar, J., 201, *212*, 216, 219, 228
Miller, E. K., 150
Miller, R., 203
Miller, S., 69, 114, 116

Milner, B., 142, 169, 189, 292
Milton, J., 26
Mineka, S., 259
Minsky, M. L., 88
Misanin, J. R., 203
Mitchell, J., 137
Mitchell, P., 124
Mitchell, S. W., 27
Mitchison, G., 165–166, 178
Mitra, R., 123
Miyashita, T., 114
Miyazawa, Y., 43
Mizuta, I., 245, 246
Molfese, D. L., 150
Molle, M., 175
Moore, E., *212*, 216, 220
Moore, S. A., 243
Morawetz, R. B., 223
Mörchen, 28
Morihisa, J. M., 300, 301
Morin, C., 65
Moroni, F., 173
Morris, C. D., 137
Morris, R. G. M., 201, 226, 293
Morrow, D. G., 270
Mortenson, M., 270
Moscovitch, M., 42, 70n4, 94, 140, 142, 201, 227
Moser, E. I., 114, 115, 116
Moser, M. B., 114, 115, 116
Motamedi, G. K., 225
Moulds, M. L., 257, 259, 261, 273
Moulin, C. J. A., 151
Mucke, L., 128
Mueller, C. W., 302
Mueller, D., 121, *122*, 123
Mueller, S. G., 224
Mueller, S. T., 54
Muggia, S., 240, 244
Müller, G. E., 139, 141, 195, *196*, 197, 198, 201, 205, 290, 293, 294–295, 296, 303, 307
Mummery, C. J., 227
Munch, M., 175
Murre, J. M. J., 50, 65, 67, 90–91, 94, 95, 96
Muto, V., 175
Muzet, A., 167
Myers, K. M., 121, 123
Myers, L. B., 257, 261

Naccache, L., 43–44
Nachson, I., 270
Nadel, L., 16, 70n4, 94, 201, 227, 230
Nader, K., 117, 119, 120, 203, 205
Nairne, J. S., 1, 17
Nakagawa, Y., 245, 246
Nakajima, T., 177
Nakano, I., 43
Naveh-Benjamin, M., 137
Nazeer, A., 242
Neath, I., 49, 50, 54, 55–59, 61, 62, 65, 67
Nee, D. E., 143
Neely, J. H., 141
Neisser, U., 12–13
Nelson, K., 254, 272, 274
Nelson, T. E., 299
Nestojko, J. F., 147
Nestor, P. J., *218*, 222, 224, 229
Netto, C. A., 197, 293, 295, 302
Netz, J., 29, 239, 240, 241, 246
Neve, R., 124
Newman, E. B., 165
Newman, E. L., 150
Newton, J. M., 195
Nguyen, P. V., 294
Nicolas, S., 35
Nielson, K. A., 69
Nietzsche, F. W., 1, 3, 4, 186
Nieuwenhuis, I. L., 297
Nikesch, S., 243
Niki, K., 140
Nimmo, L. M., 65, 67, 70n3
Nishida, M., 177
Nishikawa, T., 245, 246
Nitsch, R. M., 195, 228
Nokes, T. J., 270
Norman, D. A., 38, 240
Norman, K. A., 39, 50, 150, 155
Norris, D., 50, 51, 78, 92
North, A. S., 151
Novelly, R. A., 223
Nugent, K., 259
Nugent, L. D., 53
Nyberg, L., 241

Oakes, M. A., 262
Obayashi, T., 43
Oberauer, K., 50, 52, 53, 54, 69
O'Brien, J. T., 242
Ochsner, K., 152, 153, 154
O'Connor, M., 201, *212*, 214, 217, 222, 229
Oddo, S., 127, *128*
Ogden, J., 189
Okawa, M., 177
O'Keefe, J., 167, 173
Olick, J., 272
Oliver, R. M., 93
Orban, P., 173, 174
O'Regan, M., *218*, 221, 231
O'Reilly, R. C., 50, 94, 95, 96, 171, 293
Orr, S. P., 242
Osborn, C., 270
Osgood, C. E., 96, 145
Oswald, I., 165
Otten, L. J., 137, 138, 241
Ovid, 26
Ozaki, S., 177

Pace-Schott, E. F., 169, 171
Paesschen, W., 229
Page, M. P. A., 50, 51, 78, 92

Paller, K. A., 136, 154
Palmer, J. C., 13
Palop, J. J., 128
Pandeirada, J. N. S., 1, 17
Pandya, D. N., *144*
Papert, S., 88
Parapatics, S., 175
Pare-Blagoev, E. J., 143, 150
Parker, E. S., 17, 24, 300, 301
Parker, G. J. M., 224
Parkin, A. J., 39, 43
Parra, M., 154
Parsons, M. W., 300
Pastötter, B., 147, 151, 154
Pasupathi, M., 266
Patching, G. R., 154
Patel, G., 138
Paterson, H. M., 267, 268, 276
Paulsen, O., 114
Pavlides, C., 173
Pavlov, I., 120, 121
Payne, B. K., 261
Payne, D. G., 7, 8
Payne, J. D., 95, 116, 177, 230
Pearlstone, Z., 3–4, 9, 255, 287
Pearsall, J., 177
Pecher, D., 147
Pecherstorfer, T., 175
Peigneux. P., 166, 167, 171, 172, 173, 174, 175, 229, 292
Peltokorpi, V., 276
Perez, C., 300
Perfect, T. J., 151
Perini, M., 53, 185, 186, *188*, 189, 190
Perras, B., 176, 177
Perrin, F., 166, 167, 173, 229, 292
Petersen, R. C., 186, 225
Petersen, S. E., 241
Peterson, L. R., 6, 65
Peterson, M. J., 6
Petersson, K. M., 227–228
Petiau, C., 166
Petrides, M., *144*, 174
Petros, T. V., 300
Phelps, E. A., 177
Phihal, W., 296, 298–299
Phillips, C., 166
Phillips, N. H., 165
Piazzini, A., 222
Pick, A., 26, 28
Piefke, M., 227, 243, 245
Piel, M., 242
Piercy, M., 224, 230
Pietrowsky, R., 175, 176
Pihl, R. O., 300
Pillemer, D. B., 254
Pillon, A., 41
Pilzecker, A., 139, 141, 195, 197, 198, 201, 205, 290, 293, 294–295, 296, 303, 307
Piolino, P., 227, 244, 245
Pittenger, C., 108, 109, 112, 113, 114, 115
Pivik, T., 297
Plato, 26, 37
Plaut, D. C., 50
Pleydell-Pearce, C. W., 256
Plihal, W., 175, 176
Plumb, I., 241
Poldrack, R. A., 143, 150
Polyn, S. M., 50, 155
Poon, L. W., 36
Porter, N., 242
Portrat, S., 54
Posner, J. B., 214
Postle, B. R., 144
Postman, L., 12, 145, 193, 195, 288
Powell, H. W. R., 224
Power, M. J., 261
Prat, C. S., 42
Preece, T., 50, 69
Prince, M., 27, 28
Proust, M., 193
Purves, D., 79

Quintilien, 165
Quirk, G. J., 121, *122*, 123

Raaijmakers, J. G. W., 50, 93, 141, 155, 193, 194
Radulovic, J., 124
Radvansky, G. A., 35
Raecke, J., 28
Raes,F., 243
Raffone, A., 92–93, 94, 96
Rahal, T. A., 36
Rajaram, S., 268
Rammes, G., 123, 124
Ramon y Cajal, S., 105, 106
Ranganath, C., 136, *137*
Ranjeva, J. P., 241, 244
Rao, B. S. S., 228
Rao, S. L., 240
Rasch, B. H., 65, 68, 176, 177, 305
Raskin, S. A., 241
Raste, Y., 241
Ratcliff, R., 89
Rauchs, G., 166, 167, 171, 173, 174
Raz, N., 242
Rechtschaffen, A., 167
Reemtsma, J. P., 23
Reese, E., 267, 274
Reggers, J., 166, 173, 229, 292
Reinhold, N., 240, 241, 242, 244, 245, 246
Reinkemeier, M., 227, 242, 245
Reinvang, I., 61, 245
Rekkas, P. V., 227
Reminger, S., 240
Remondes, M., 228
Repa, J. C., 171
Rescorla, R. A., 88–89
Ressler, K. J., 123

Reymann, K. G., 294
Reyna, V. F., 41
Reysen, M. B., 270
Ribot, T., 36, 95, 139, 195–196, 226, 292
Riccio, D. C., 202
Richardson, R., 124
Richardson-Klavehn, A., *149*, 150, 154
Rist, F., 154
Robbins, T. W., 240
Roberto, M., 299
Roberts, A. C., 240
Roberts, K. C., 139
Roberts, N., 194, *212*, 214, 216, 217, 219, 224, 228, 229
Robertson, E., 152, 153, 154
Rochon, E., 54
Rodrigue, K. M., 242
Roediger, H. L., 3, 7, 8, 9, 13, 14, 15, 35, 42, 153, 263
Rönnberg, J., 270
Rosenbaum, R. S., 227
Rosenberg, C. R., 89
Rosenblatt, F., 79–80, 87, 88
Roseveare, T. A., 259
Ross, M., 254
Rossi, L., 172, 175
Roth, D. L., 223
Rothi, L. J. G., 41
Rotte, M., 136
Roulet, E., *212*
Rowan, M. J., 295
Rowlands, M., 272
Roy, E. A., 41
Rubenstein, B. S., 299
Rubin, D. C., 5, 6, 36, 38, 55, 58, 230, 255, 272
Ruby, P., 167
Rugg, M. D., 137, 138, 154
Rullkoetter, N., 243
Rumelhart, D. E., 77, 84–85, 89, 92, 96, 96n2
Rush, C. R., 300
Russ, M. O., 245
Ruths, F. A., 243
Rutschmann, R. M., 148, *149*
Rutters, F., 227–228
Ryan, L., 94, 240

Sacchett, C., 41
Sagi, D., 299
Sahakyan, L., 261
Sahdra, B., 254
Sala, S., 245
Salts, J. S., 53
Salzarulo, P., 172, 175
Samson, D., 41
Samsonovitch, A., 94
Sananbenesi, F., 124
Sands, S. F., 61
Santiago, H. C., 61
Sara, S. J., 16, 203
Sartre, J.-P., 26
Saunders, J., 147
Sauter, C., 175
Sawrie, S. M., 223, 224
Schacter, D. L., 4, 35, 38, 39, 41, 43, 136, 150, 195, 253, 255, 257, 261
Schafe, G. E., 203, 205
Scheiber, C., 244
Schelling, G., 124
Schenkel, M., 175
Schilder, P., 28
Schirmuly, M., 302
Schlicker, E., 124
Schloerscheidt, A. M., 154
Schmahl, C., 243
Schmidt, C. F., 172, 173, 175, 195, 228
Schmidt, H. G., 147
Schneider, B., 245
Schneider, D. J., 264
Schoenfelder, F., 244
Schoenfield, J., 219
Scholey, K., *212*, 216, 220
Schomer, D. L., 201, *212*, 214, 217, 222, 229
Schooler, B. A., 17–18
Schooler, L. J., 55, 93
Schreiber, F. R., 29
Schrick, C., 124
Schröder, N., 197, 293, 295, 302
Schudson, M., 266
Schuler, M. G., 294
Schultze, E., 28
Schulze, C., 174, 176
Schuman, E. M., 228
Schüz, A., 86
Schwartz, B. L., 300, 301
Schwartz, J. H., 103, 105, 112, 113, 114
Scott, R., 106
Scoville, W. B., 169, 189, 292
Sederberg, P. B., 50
Seegmuller, C., 244
Seidenberg, M., 69, 217, *218*, 219, 220, 230
Seidl, O., 27
Sejnowski, T. J., 86, 87, 89, 106, 109, 167, 169, 175
Selkoe, D. J., 127
Sellal, F., 244
Serra, L., 242
Serrano, C., 221
Seung, H. S., 115
Seymour, T. L., 54
Shabus, M., 175
Shallice, T., 137, 142, 145, 240, 244
Shankaranarayana Rao, B. S., 123
Sheard, E. D., 258
Shelton, J. R., 41
Sherrington, C. S., 103
Shibui, K., 177
Shiffrin, R. M., 50, 51, 93, 188, *189*
Shih, R., 126
Shimamura, A. P., 142, 147, 148, 194
Shin, L. M., 242, 243

Shin, P. S., 242
Shorvon, S. D., 223
Shulman, G. L., 138
Sidis, B., 28
Siegel, J. M., 172
Sieggreen, M. A., 201, *212*, 214, 217, 222, 229
Sikström, S., 55, 93–94, 96
Silber, M. H., 167
Sills, D. L., 2
Silva, A. J., 69, 108, 109, 114, 131
Silva-Saavedra, A., 243
Simon, H. A., 42, 286
Sinclair, J. G., 299
Singer, J. A., 256, 273
Siracusano, A., 106
Sirocco, K., 300, 301
Sirota, A., 173
Ska, B., 43
Skaggs, E. B., 193, 197–198, 205, 295
Skaggs, W. E., 173
Skowronski, J. J., 257
Slamecka, N. J., 6
Slater, P. C., 139
Small, D. H., *129*, 130
Small, S. A., 224
Smeets, E., 261, 264
Smith, C., 167
Smith, E. E., 143
Smith, G. E., 186, 225
Smith, M. L., 142
Snyder, A., 150
Soetens, E., 300
Sohn, M. H., 143
Son, H., 126
Soravia, L. M., 124
Southwick, S. M., 242
Spear, N. E., 202, 302
Speckens, A. E., 243
Spellman, B. A., 14, 147, 258
Spencer, D. D., 223
Sperling, G., 6
Speyer, J., 256, 260, 262
Spilich, G. J., 42
Spinnler, H., *212*, 217, 223, 229, 240, 244
Spitzer, B., 147
Spoelstra, K., 300
Squire, L. R., 38, 39, 43, 68, 94, 139, 142, 169, 171, 195, 203, 220, 221, 223, 224, 226, 228, 239, 240, 241, 290, 292, 294, 303, 307
Srebo, B., 297
Stark, C. E. L., 68, 154, 228
Stark, K., 145
Starns, J. J., 147
Starr, S., 257
Stein, M. B., 241
Stenger, V. A., 143, 150
Stern, Y., 224
Sterpenich, V., 166, 178
Stertz, G., 28
Steyvers, M., 50
Stickgold, R., 65, 95, 116, 167, 171, 176, 177, 229
Stiedl, F. C., 259
Stier, E., 28
Stillman, R. C., 300, 301
Stone, C., 268
Storm, B. C., 147
Storm, D., 109
Stuss, D. T., 227
Stylos-Allan, M., 177, 178
Suhy, J., 224
Sullivan, M. J., 175, 297, 298
Sunny, B., 240
Sünram-Lea, S. I., 300
Surprenant, A. M., 54
Susman, E. J., 242
Sutton, J., 255, 265, 268, 269, 270–271, 272, 273, 274, 276, 277
Swanberg, K., 177
Swick, D., 143
Symms, M. R., 224
Szabo, B., 124
Szesko. P. R., 242
Szymusiak, R., 165

Tagini, A., 256
Takashima, A., 227–228, 297
Talamini, L. M., 297
Tan, L., 50
Tanaka, Y., 43
Tangalos, E. G., 186, 225
Tanne, D., 299
Tanzi, R. E., 127
Tempesta, D., 173
Tendolkar, I., 227–228
Thiel, A., 245
Thomas, R. L., 268
Thompson, C. P., 257
Thompson, P. J., 223, 224, 226, 229
Thompson, S., *212*, 216, 220
Thompson-Schill, S. L., 65, 143, 176, 229
Thomson, D. M., 3, 15, 42, 137, 155, 193, 287
Thomson, N., 51
Thöne, A., 242, 244, 245
Thorne, A., 257
Thorpe, L. A., 7, 8
Thrash, N., 217, *218*, 219, 220, 229
Tobler, I., 167
Tokunaga, H., 245, 246
Tollefsen, D. P., 274, 276
Tononi, G., 144
Tourette, G. de la, 27
Tramoni, E., 241, 244
Treyens, J. C., 42, 85
Tucker, M. A., 175, 229–230
Tulving, E., 2, 3, 9, 14, 15, 35, 38, 42, 137, 155, 193, 227, 241, 255, 287, 289
Turner, M. S., 142
Turvey, M. T., 6
Tversky, B., 266, 267

Twamley, E. W., 241
Tweedie-Cullen, R. Y., 125
Tyson, P., 302

Uchiyama, M., 177
Uncapher, M., 136, 137, 138
Underwood, B. J., 1, 8, 12, 36, 65, 288–289
Ur, C. L., 299
Urban, I. J. A., 300
Usher, M., 50

Vallar, G., 52
Valtora, F., 105, 108, 109
Van der Ven, C., 29, 240, 244, 245
Van Gorp, W. G., 239, 240
Van Heerdan, J., 261
Van Knippenberg, A., 147
Van Leeuwen, C., 272
Van Luijtelaar, E. L. J. M., 300
Van Ormer, E. B., 165
Van Veen, V., 150
Van Vreeswijk, M. F., 243
Vandewalle, G., 166, 178
Velanova, K., 241
Veling, H., 147
Velmans, M., 154
Verde, M. F., 147
Verfaellie, M., 41
Vermetten, E., 242, 243
Verstijnen, I. M., 272
Vesonder, G. T., 42
Viard, A., 245
Vignal, J.-P., 222
Villareal, D. M., 305–306
Viola-McCabe, K. E., 299
Visscher, K. M., 139
Vogel, E. K., 93
Vogel-Sprott, M., 300
Voltzenlogel, V., *212*, 222
Von Stockhausen, H.-M., 245
Voss, J. F., 42
Vousden, J. I., 50
Vyas, A., 123
Vygotsky, L., 272
Vythilingam, M., 242

Wagner, A. D., 136, 138, 143, 148, *149*, 150, 151
Wagner, A. R., 88–89
Wagner, U., 176, 177, 178
Waisman, A., 124
Waldhauser, G. T., 154
Walker, D. L., 123
Walker, M. P., 167, 171, 177, 178, 229, 299
Wamsley, E. J., 175, 229–230
Wang, X., 124
Ward, G., 50, 61
Wardlaw, J. M., 201, 219, 220, 221, 222, 224, 226, 229
Waring, S. C., 186
Warrington, E. K., 41, 194
Waters, G. S., 54
Watkins, C., 287
Watkins, E., 243
Watkins, M. J., 15, 287
Watkins, O. C., 15
Waugh, N. C., 65
Wearing, C., 186
Weber-Luxenburger, G., 29, 240, 244, 245
Wechsler, D., 37
Wedig, M. M., 243
Wegner, D. M., 264, 274, 275
Weiner, B., 2
Weingartner, H., 300
Weingartner, H. J., 300, 301
Weinrich, H., 24–26
Weiskrantz, L., 194, 240
Weiss, P. H., 227, 245
Weissman, D. H., 139
Weldon, M. S., 266, 267, 268
Welzl, H., 125, 272
Wenzel, A. E., 5, 6, 55, 58, 230
Wessel, I., 153, 260, 261, 273
Westbrook, R. F., 123
Westwell, M. S., 300
Westwood, D., 41
Wetzels, S., 153
Wheeler, M. A., 8, 43, 227, 272
Wheeler, M. E., 241
Wheelwright, S., 241
White, T. L., 264
Whitlock, J. R., 294
Wickelgren, W. A., 286, 291
Wickens, D. D., 65, 195
Wickens, T. D., 55, 58
Widrow, B., 88
Williams, J. M. G., 243
Williams, R. J., 89, 96n2
Williamson, P. D., 223
Willian, M. K., 222, 226
Willshaw, D. J., 80
Wilson, A., 28
Wilson, B. A., 195
Wilson, D. E., 258
Wilson, M. A., 95, 173, 292, 293, 298
Wilson, P., 254
Wilson, R. A., 255, 265, 271, 272, 274, 276, 277
Wiltgen, B. J., 69
Wimber, M., 148, 149, *149*, 150
Winocur, G., 140, 227
Winograd, E., 39
Winson, J., 173
Witt, J., 242
Wittlinger, R. P., 41
Wixted, J. T., 5, 12, 29, 36, 50, 55, 65, 93, 115, 139, 141, 166, 193, 195, 199, 285, 286, 289
Woldorff, M. G., 139
Wolf, O. T., 242

Wolkowitz, O., 300, 301
Woltär, O., 28
Wolters, G., 92–93, 94, 96
Won, J., 114
Woodard, J. L., 69
Wotjak, C. T., 123, 124
Wright, A. A., 61
Wright, C. I., 243
Wright, D. B., 268
Wright, T., 65, 67, 70n3
Wrisberg, C. A., 41
Wroe, S. J., 201, 216, 217, *218*, 219, 220, 222, 224, 225, 226
Wyatt, R. J., 300, 301

Xu, L., 295

Yang, Y. L., 124
Yaron-Antar, A., 270
Yaroush, R., 175, 297
Yasuno, F., 245, 246
Yeshurun, Y., 175
Yiu, A. P., 124
Yogarajah, M., 224
Yoo, S. S., 177
Yousry, T., 142

Zang, H., 219, 223
Zaragoza, M., 13
Zeman, A. Z., 201, 211, *212*, 217, *218*, 219, 220, 221, 222, 224, 225, 226, 229
Zerubavel, E., 272
Zesiger, P., *212*
Zhang, D., 228
Zhang, J., 242
Zhao, Z., 136
Zhuo, M., 126
Zilles, K., 227, 245
Zingerle, H., 26, 28
Zisapel, N., 175
Zoellner, L. A., 243
Zola, S. M., 39
Zola-Morgan, S., 38, 139, 292
Zuberi, S. M., *218*, 221, 231
Zucker, R. S., 103, 105
Zwarts, M. J., 227–228

Subject index

Page references in *italic* refer to where subjects may be found only in tables or in figures and their captions.

Accelerated long-term forgetting (ALF), 211–232
and the amnesic syndrome, 224–225, 231
anticonvulsant medication, 225
case studies, 211–216
characteristics, 216–217
clinical contexts of occurrence, 220–221
clinical relevance, 221–222
definition, 216
future work, 231
group study list in patients with epilepsy, *218*
methodological issues, 230–231
pathophysiology, 222–226
psychosocial factors, 225–226
in relation to models of memory and consolidation, 226–229
seizures and, 222–223
sleep and, 229–230
structural brain pathology, 223–225
timescale, 217–219
types of memory affected, 219–220
Acquisition of memory *see* Memory encoding/acquisition
Activations (pulse signals of artificial neurons), 77–79, 293
activation rule, 82, 84, 86, 89
activation state, 78, 84, 87
activation value, 78, 79, 83–84, 85, 87, 89
backpropagation and, 90
coactivation, 86, 93
Hopfield networks, 83–84
in a Perceptron, 87–88, 89
Adaptive reasons/necessity for forgetting, 17–18, 23, 30, 36, 101–102, 108, 135
Adaptive resonance theory (ART), 91
Adenylyl cyclase, *110*, 113
Alcohol, 116, 291, 295, 299–300, 301–302, 303
ALF *see* Accelerated long-term forgetting
Alzheimer's disease (AD), 127–130
Amnesias
accelerated long-term forgetting and the amnesic syndrome, 224–225, 231
see also Accelerated long-term forgetting (ALF)
Alzheimer's disease, 127–130
anterograde *see* Anterograde amnesia
consolidation interference in, 195–203
dissociative *see* Psychogenic amnesias
distinction between amnesia and forgetting in everyday life, 35–36
dual store account, 188–192
existing cognitive theories of amnesia, 188–192
forgetting due to retroactive interference in amnesia, 185–205 *see also* Retroactive interference (RI)
functional *see* Psychogenic amnesias
hysterical, 26–27
long-term memory interference in amnesia, 192–203
neurobiology, 126–130 *see also* Neurobiology of memory and forgetting
psychogenic *see* Psychogenic amnesias
retrieval interference in, 193–195
retrograde *see* Retrograde amnesia
senescent forgetfulness, 126–127
transient epileptic amnesia (TEA), *212*, 213, *218*, 219, 220, 221, 222, 224, 225, 229
Amygdala, 29, 112, 120, 121, 123, 124, 125, 242–243
and accelerated long-term forgetting, *212*, 214, 229
emotional memories and, 177
hippocampalamygdalar dysfunction, 29–30
and sleep, 177, 178, 179
Anisomycin, *118*, 119
Anterograde amnesia, 42, 185–186, 292, 295, 303

amnesic drugs and, 116
drug-induced retrograde facilitation and, 300, 301
dual store account, 188–192
recovery from, 245
relationship to retrograde amnesia, *24*
retrieval interference, 193–195
stress and, 240
studies on retroactive interference in, 186–188
Anterograde memory, 24, 213, 223, 240, 245
deficits, 220, 225, 239–240, 245
see also Anterograde amnesia
Anticonvulsant medication, 225
Aplysia californica, 112
ART (adaptive resonance theory), 91
Articulation
duration, 54
of an irrelevant word, 53
Attractor networks, 83–85
Boltzmann Machine, 85–87
Autobiographic memory *see* Episodic-autobiographic memory
Autobiographical forgetting, 256–265
directed forgetting, 260–262
researching, 257
retrieval-induced forgetting, 257–260
Think/No-think paradigm, 262–265

Backpropagation, 89
catastrophic forgetting in, 89–91
Barr, Andrew "Nicky", 253–254, 276
Behavioural deprivation studies, 173–174
Benzodiazepines, 116, 291, 295, 299, 300, 301–302, 303
Blocking, 41, 147, 156
NMDA *see* NMDA antagonists
of rehearsal, 52–53, 190
Boltzmann Machine, 85–87
Brain damaged patients, 41, 42, 43, 195–196
dissociative disorders, 245
psychogenic amnesia, 243
structural brain pathology in ALF patients, 223–225, 228

CA^{2+} influx, 103, *104*, 108–109, *111*, 112, 113, 117, 127, 130
Calcineurin, 125
Calcium ion CA^{2+} *see* CA^{2+} influx
Calmodulin-dependent protein kinase II (CaMKII), 108–109, 113, 114
Catastrophic forgetting, in backpropagation, 89–91
Catastrophic interference, 89–91, 92, 94–95
Caux, Marcel, 254
CBI receptors, 124
Cell adhesion molecules, 109, 120
Cell adhesion proteins, 105
Cholinergic levels, 169, 176
Classical conditioning, 38, *39*, 112–113
Coactivation, 86, 93
hippocampal, 173, 293
Cognitive biases, 41–42
Collaborative inhibition, 268–269, 270, 276
Collaborative recall, 268–271
Collective memory, 273–276
Commission errors, 43
Confabulations, 42
Connectionist models of forgetting, 77–92, 95–96
activations as STM and weights as LTM, 77–79
attractor networks, 83–85
backpropagation, 89–91, 92
Boltzmann Machine, 85–87
catastrophic forgetting in backpropagation, 89–91
error-correcting learning, 87–91
Hebbian learning, 80–87
learning in neural networks, 79–80
and of memory, 92–95
Perceptron and delta rule, 87–89
Willshaw model, 80–83
Connectionist models of memory, 92–95
Consolidation, 16, 50–51, 63–69, 70n4
accelerated long-term forgetting and, 226–229
and amnesics, 116
blockade of consolidation of a fear memory, *118*
Boltzmann Machine networks, 87
cognitive model of forgetting, with intermediate memory/consolidation stage, 203–205
criticisms of the theory, 202–203
and the effects of sleep on memory, 65–66, 229–230
emotional memories and, 176–178
extinction and, *122*
forgetting due to disrupted consolidation, 139–140
and the form of the forgetting curve, 55, 61–62
interference in amnesia, 195–203
long-term memory consolidation, 226–227
see also Systems consolidation
mechanisms, 68, 69, 94, 95, 199
molecular mechanisms of, *118*
neurobiology of, 107–111
origin of term, 195
properties of memories, *118*
and reconsolidation, 16, 116–120
see also Reconsolidation
retroactive interference and, 63–65, 290–305
and retrograde amnesia, 67–69
and sleep, 65–66, 95, 166, 171–174, 175–176, 229–230
standard theory of, 94, 226–227

synaptic (fast and short-lived), 200, 201, 202, 204–205, 292, 293–295, 297, 301–302, 304
systems (slow and long-lived) consolidation, 201, 202, 204–205, 226, 292–293, 298–299, 304, 307
and the temporal gradient of retroactive interference, 63–65
and the temporal gradients of retrograde amnesia and retrograde facilitation, 303–305
Cortisol, 124, 176, 177, 230, 242
CREB transcription regulators, 109, 114, 120, 124
Cue overload
interference as cue-overload, 287–289
retroactive interference and, 288–289
theory, 15
see also Proactive interference
Cues *see* Retrieval cues
Cultural symbols, 273
Cyclic adenosine monophosphate (cAMP), 108, 112, 113, 117
cAMP-dependent PKA, 109, 117
Cyclin-dependent kinase 5 (Cdk5), 124–125

D-cycloserine, 123–124
Decay, 50
reinterpreting evidence against forgetting due to, 51–54
theory, 9–10
word-length effect and, 53–54
Declarative memory *see* Explicit/declarative memory
DECTalk, 89
Definitions of forgetting, 2–9, 35
as complete loss from storage, 2–3
as loss of information over time, 4–6
as retrieval failure, 3–4, 9
Delta rule, 88
Depersonalization, 28
Dephosphorylation of protein, 108, 125
Depression
autobiographic memory in, 243
effects of ECT in, 223
long-term (LTD), 106, 109–111
Think/No-think procedure with depressed patients, 263–264
Directed forgetting (DF), 260–262
Dissociation, 23
brain regions and, 43, 143
between declarative and nondeclarative memory systems, 169
dissociative disorders, 29, 245
"dissociative reactions", 28
Dissociative amnesias *see* Psychogenic amnesias
Dissociative identity disorder, 29, 245
Distributed cognition, 271–273
Dorsett, Sybil Isabel, 29
Drugs
anterograde amnesia and, 116
anticonvulsant medication, 225
drug-induced retrograde facilitation, 299–303
extinction and, 123–124
"forgetting" drugs, 23
Dual store account of anterograde amnesia, 188–192

Ebbinghaus savings function, 285–286
Emotional biases, 41–42
Emotional memories, 176–178
Encoding of memory *see* Memory encoding/acquisition
Encoding specificity principle, 15, 155, 287
Endocannabinoids, 124
Epilepsy
accelerated forgetting in *see* Accelerated long-term forgetting (ALF)
anticonvulsant medication, 225
consolidation processes and, 201
idiopathic generated (IGE), *212*, *218*, 221
multiple personality disorders and, 28
temporal lobe (TLE), 214, 216, *218*, 219, 220–221, 222, 224
transient epileptic amnesia (TEA), *212*, 213, *218*, 219, 220, 221, 222, 224, 225, 229
Episodic-autobiographic memory, 24, 30, 38, 39, 43
autobiographical forgetting *see* Autobiographical forgetting
coherence, 256
correspondence, 256
as cue dependent, 287
multiple trace theory and episodic memories, 227
psychogenic amnesia and *see* Psychogenic amnesias
PTSD and, 243
retrieval phase, 42
the self-memory system, 255–256
stress and autobiographical memory retrieval, 242–243
Erk/MAP kinase (MAPK), 109, 117, 120
Error-correcting learning, 87–91
Everyday forgetting
and the cellular basis of memory formation in the hippocampus, 291–295
distinction between amnesia and, 35–36
the form of forgetting, 285–286
interference theories and, 287–291
and retrograde facilitation, 295–303
role of retroactive interference and consolidation in, 285–307
and the temporal gradients of retrograde amnesia and retrograde facilitation, 303–305
Exchange errors, 37, 41

Executive dysfunction, 193, 205, 240–241
Exocytosis, 103, 108
Explicit/declarative memory, 38–39, 43, 102, 111–112
  accelerated long-term forgetting and, 219
  and the brain, 112
  dissociation with nondeclarative memory systems, 169
  emotion and, 176–178
  mechanisms of, 113–115
  slow wave sleep and, 298–299
    see also Episodic-autobiographic memory; Semantic memory
Exposure therapies, 121, 124
Extinction, 120–125
Eyewitness memory, 13, 267

"Fause reconnaissance", 28
Fear extinction, 121, 124–125
Forgetting, autobiographical *see* Autobiographical forgetting
Forgetting, definitions of *see* Definitions of forgetting
Forgetting, directed (DF), 260–262
Forgetting, disorders of *see* Accelerated long-term forgetting (ALF); Amnesias
Forgetting, everyday *see* Everyday forgetting
Forgetting, mechanisms of *see* Mechanisms of forgetting
Forgetting, neurobiology of *see* Neurobiology of memory and forgetting
Forgetting, situated *see* Situated forgetting
Forgetting, social *see* Social forgetting
Forgetting, theories of *see* Theories of forgetting
Forgetting, value of, 17–18, 23, 30, 36, 101–102, 108, 135
Forgetting curves, 4–8, 36
  with accelerated long-term forgetting, 219
    see also Accelerated long-term forgetting (ALF)
  memory models and the form of the forgetting curve, 54–59
"Forgetting" drugs, 23
Forward serial recall, 65, 70n3
Frequency of use of memories, 41
Frontal lobe dysfunctions, 241
Functional amnesias *see* Psychogenic amnesias
Functional neuroimaging
  in forgetting as a consequence of resolving competition, 145–155
  in forgetting due to disrupted consolidation, 139–140
  in forgetting due to failed encoding, 136–139
  in forgetting due to ineffective retrieval cues, 155
  in forgetting due to retrieval competition, 140–145
  in psychogenic amnesia, 243–245
  in selective retrieval, 146–151
  in stopping retrieval, 151–155
Fuzzy Trace Theory, 40

GABA, 123
Ganser syndrome, 26, 28
Generalization process, 101–102
Glutamate, 112, 113
  AMPA type receptors, 128
  NMDA receptor blockers *see* NMDA antagonists
  NMDA receptors, 108, *110*, 113, 114, 123–124, 294
Graceful degradation, 83, 84

Habituation, 112
Hebb rule, 79–80, 83, 84
Hebbian learning, 80–87
  attractor networks, 83–85
  Boltzmann Machine, 85–87
  Willshaw model, 80–83
"Hidden neurons", 86
Hippocampalamygdalar dysfunction, 29–30
Hippocampus
  cellular basis of memory formation in, 291–295
  consolidation and, 94, 117, 120, 140, 226
  explicit memory and, 112, 114–115
  extinction and, 121, 123, 124–125
  hippocampus-dependent spatial navigation, 173–174
  lesions involving, 42, 292, 303, 304
  long-term potentiation and, 293–295
  place cells, 114, 173
  retrograde amnesia and, 292–293
  senescent forgetfulness and, 126
  sleep and, 173–175, 178, 293
  and synaptic consolidation and forgetting, 293–295
  and systems consolidation and forgetting, 292–293
  and the temporal gradients of retrograde amnesia and retrograde facilitation, 303–305
HM, amnesiac patient, 39, 114, 169, 188, 292
Hopfield networks, 83–86, 93–94
Hypermnesia, 8–9, 269
Hypnosis, 27
Hysterical amnesia, 26–27

Ideomotor apraxia, 41
Idiopathic generated epilepsy (IGE), *212*, *218*, 221
Implicit/nondeclarative memory, 38–39, 43, 102, 111, 112
  accelerated long-term forgetting and, 219–220
  and the central nervous system, 112–113
  dissociation with declarative memory systems, 169
  mechanisms of, 112–113

Input interference, 14–15
Interference
  and amnesics, 116
  catastrophic, 89–91, 92, 94–95
  consolidation interference in amnesia, 195–203
  as cue-overload, 287–289
  input interference, 14–15
  long-term memory interference in amnesia, 192–203
  neurobiology, 115–116
  output interference, 14–15
  proactive, 10, 11–13, 65, 288–289
    see also Cue overload theory
  retrieval interference in amnesia, 193–195
  retroactive *see* Retroactive interference
  and the SIMPLE model, 57–58, 65
  temporal gradient of, 63–65, 116, 197, 199, 290–291, 295, 302–303
  theory, 10–15
  as trace degradation, 289–290, 291
Intermediate memory, 203–204

Jost's Second Law, 55, 58, 285–286
Judaism, 43–44

Learning
  in Boltzmann Machine networks, 86–87
  cellular basis of, 105–111, 226
    see also Neurobiology of memory and forgetting
  classical conditioning, 38, *39*, 112–113
  error-correcting, 87–91
  extinction, 120–125
  Hebbian, 80–87
  interleaved, 94–95 *see also* Rehearsal
  in neural networks, 79–91
  in a Perceptron, 87–89
  rate, 87, 93–94, 95
  sleep-dependent learning in spatial environments, 173–174
  stages of learning/memory process, 2
    see also Memory encoding/acquisition; Memory retrieval; Memory storage
  "synaptic learning rule", 109–111
  in Willshaw network, 80–83
Lethe (goddess), 26
Limb apraxia, 41
Long-term depression (LTD), 106, 109–111
Long-term memory (LTM), 119
  consolidation interference in amnesia, 195–203
  and the dual store account of amnesia, 190–192
  interference in amnesia, 192–203
  long-term memory consolidation, 226–227 *see also* Systems consolidation
  molecular mechanisms of, *110*
  neurobiological transfer from short-term memory, 106–111
  post-reactivation (PR-LTM), 117, *118*
  retrieval interference in amnesia, 193–195
Long-term memory systems (LTS), 24, *25*
  a new taxonomy, 40–42, 43
  Squire's taxonomy, 38–39, 43
    see also Episodic-autobiographic memory; Priming; Procedural memory; Semantic memory
Long-term potentiation (LTP), 106, 109–111, 114–116, 119, 126, 128, 201
  and drug-induced retrograde facilitation, 299–300, 302–303
  and retroactive interference, 305–306
  sleep and, 297–299
  and synaptic consolidation and forgetting, 293–295
LTD (long-term depression), 106, 109–111
LTM *see* Long-term memory
LTP *see* Long-term potentiation
LTS *see* Long-term memory systems

MAPK (Erk/MAP kinase), 109, 117, 120
Mechanisms of forgetting, 135–156
  competition resolution, 145–155
  consolidation disruption, 139–140
  encoding failure, 136–139
  retrieval competition, 140–145
  retrieval cue ineffectuality, 155
Medial temporal lobe (MTL), 95, 136, 139–140, 150, 154, 201, *212*, 226, 228, 245, 291–292
    see also Hippocampus
Memorists, 36
Memory ability, 23–24
  neurobiology of *see* Neurobiology of memory and forgetting
  relationship between memory and forgetting, 36–44
    see also Recall; Remembering
Memory categorization/states, 24, *25*, 38–39, 111–112
  anterograde memory *see* Anterograde memory
  autobiographic memory *see* Episodic-autobiographic memory
  collective/transactive memory, 273–276
  combining sleep and memory states, 171
  declarative memory *see* Explicit/declarative memory
  episodic memory *see* Episodic-autobiographic memory
  explicit memory *see* Explicit/declarative memory
  implicit memory *see* Implicit/nondeclarative memory
  intermediate memory, 203–204
  long-term memory *see* Long-term memory (LTM)

a new taxonomy of memory, 40–42, 43
nondeclarative memory *see* Implicit/nondeclarative memory
perceptual memory, *25*
procedural memory *see* Procedural memory
prospective memory, 39, 42
recognition memory, 61, 62, 147, 216, 219, 223, 231
reconstructive memory, 40–42, 43
reproductive memory, 40–41, 42, 43
retrograde memory *see* Retrograde memory
short-term memory *see* Short-term memory (STM)
spatial memory, 113, 114, 116, 173, 228, 229
subsystems and states, 169–171
unconscious memories, 16–17
Memory consolidation *see* Consolidation
Memory disorders *see* Accelerated long-term forgetting (ALF); Amnesias
Memory encoding/acquisition, 2, 3, 42
cellular basis of memory formation in the hippocampus, 291–295
see also Neurobiology of memory and forgetting
encoding specificity principle, 15, 155, 287
extinction and, *122*
forgetting and the encoding phase, 38, 42
forgetting due to failed encoding, 136–139
long-term potentiation and, 293–295
in multidimensional space, 56
Memory errors, 13, 37–38, 41–43
Memory improvement techniques, 23
Memory models
accelerated long-term forgetting and, 226–229
connectionist, 92–95
and consolidation, 50–51
forgetting in, 49–69
and the STS/LTS distinction, 49–50
Memory of eyewitnesses, 13, 267
Memory retrieval
autobiographic memory in psychological disorders, 243
cues for *see* Retrieval cues
extinction and, *122*
forgetting as a consequence of resolving competition, 145–155
forgetting as retrieval failure, 3–4, 9
forgetting due to ineffective retrieval cues, 155
forgetting due to retrieval competition, 140–145
retrieval interference in amnesia, 193–195
retrieval phase of episodic memory, 42
retrieval-induced forgetting *see* Retrieval-induced forgetting (RIF)
selective retrieval, 146–151, 153
stopping retrieval, 151–155
stress and autobiographical memory retrieval, 242–243
theories, 15
transactive, 273–276
see also Recall
Memory states *see* Memory categorization/states
Memory storage, forgetting as complete loss from, 2–3
Memory timeline, 62–63
see also Forgetting curves
Misattribution errors, 41–42
Mnemosyne, 26
"Molecular memory", 108
Monitoring failures, 41–42
MTL *see* Medial temporal lobe
Multiple personality disorders, 28–29
Multiple trace theory (MTT), 201, 227, 228

National Inquiry into the Separation of Aboriginal and Torres Strait Islander Children form their Families, 277
Neocortex, 94, 96, 112, 201, 226–227, 228, 292, 293, 298
NetTalk, 89
Neural network learning, 79–91
error-correcting learning, 87–91
Hebbian learning, 80–87
Neural network models *see* Connectionist models of forgetting; Connectionist models of memory
Neural replay, 292–293, 298, 304
see also Systems consolidation
Neurobiology of memory and forgetting, 101–131
Alzheimer's disease, 127–130
amnesia, 126–130
cellular basis of memory formation in the hippocampus, 291–295
consolidation, 106–111
extinction, 120–125
long-term potentiation *see* Long-term potentiation (LTP)
mechanisms of explicit memory, 113–115
mechanisms of implicit memory, 112–113
memory interference, 115–116
multiple memory systems in the brain, 111–112
recall and reconsolidation, 116–120
repression, 125–126
senescent forgetfulness, 126–127
from short-term to long-term memories, 106–116
synaptic basis of neural activity, 102–105
synaptic consolidation, 293–295, 297
see also Synaptic consolidation
synaptic plasticity and the cellular bases of learning and memory, 105–106, 226
systems consolidation, 292–293
see also Systems consolidation

Neuroimaging, functional *see* Functional neuroimaging
Neurotransmitters, 103–105, 108, 109, 112, 121
  sleep and, 169, 175–176, 178
Neurotrophins, 109, 120
NMDA antagonists, 116, 228, 294, 295, 299, 302, 303, 305–306
NMDA glutamate receptors, 108, *110*, 113, 114, 123–124, 294
Nonassociative learning, 38, *39*
Nondeclarative memory *see* Implicit/nondeclarative memory
NREM (non-rapid-eye-movement) sleep, 166, 167–169, *170*, 172, 173, 177, 298
  and declarative memory consolidation, 175–176

Omission errors, 42–43
Output interference, 14–15

PAK-1 kinase, 125
Parallel distributed processing models *see* Connectionist models of forgetting; Connectionist models of memory
Parietal cortex, 136, *137*, 138
Pattern completion, 84
Perceptron, 87–89, 91
Perceptual memory, *25*
Permastore, 306–307
PFC *see* Prefrontal cortex
Phosphorylation of protein, 108–109, 112, 113, 125, 127, *129*
PKA (protein kinase A), 109, 112, 117, 120
Place cells, 114, 173
Postlearning sleep deprivation, 171–172
Posttraumatic stress disorder (PTSD), 242–243
Power functions, 5–6, 55, 59, 93, 94, 285–286, 306, *307*
Prefrontal cortex (PFC), 136, *137*, 141–145, 147–151, 153–155, 156, 245
  sleep and, 175, 178
Primacy: recency to primacy shift, 59–63
Priming, *25*, 38, 39, 220, 255
PR-LTM (post-reactivation LTM), 117, *118*, 119
Proactive interference, 10, 11–13, 65, 288–289
  see also Cue overload theory
Procedural memory, *25*, 38, 39, 41, 42, 43, 169, 171, 220, 299
Prospective memory, 39, 42
Protein dephosphorylation, 108, 125
Protein kinase A (PKA), 109, 112, 117, 120
Protein phosphorylation, 108–109, 112, 113, 125, 127, *129*
Protein synthesis inhibitors, 119, 197, *198*, 201, 294
Prototype formation, 84–85, 87, 92, 96
PR-STM (post-reactivation STM), 117, 119
Psychogenic amnesias, 27–30, 239–247
  case studies, 241–242
  fugue states, 28
  Ganser syndrome, 26, 28
  multiple personality disorders, 28–29
  neuroimaging studies, 243–245
  neuropsychological symptoms, 239–241
  stability, 245–246
  stress and autobiographical memory retrieval, 242–243
PTSD (posttraumatic stress disorder), 242–243

Rapid-eye-movement sleep *see* REM (rapid-eye-movement) sleep
Recall
  accelerated long-term forgetting and, 211–216, 219, 225
  collaborative, 268–271
  compressed timeline for immediate and delayed, 62–63
  determined by similarity, 57–59
  forward serial, 65, 70n3
  neurobiology of reconsolidation and, 116–120
  sleep, LTP and, 298
  trials, 7–8, 52–53, 298
Recency gradient, 61, 68, 69
Recency to primacy shift, 59–63
Recognition memory, 61, 62, 147, 216, 219, 223, 231
Reconsolidation, 16, 203
  molecular mechanisms of, *118*
  neurobiology of recall and, 116–120
  properties of memories, *118*
Reconstructive memory, 40–42, 43
Rehearsal, 54, 188–191, 201, 204, 231, 258
  backpropagation and, 90–91
  blocking of, 52–53, 190
  compensatory, 52–53
  interleaved learning, 94–95
Relearning, 41
REM (rapid-eye-movement) sleep, 115, 166, 169, *170*, 172, 177, 297–299, 304–305
  EEG, *168*
Remembering, 36, 38
  capacity, 17
  commandment of, 43–44
  false, 13, 37–38 *see also* Memory errors
    see also Memory ability; Memory retrieval; Recall
Reminiscence, 8–9, 179
Repetition, 44
Repression, 16–17, 125–126
  repressive erasure, 273
    see also Suppression
Reproductive memory, 40–41, 42, 43
Response competition, 11, 12, 147–148, 151
Retention, 52–53
  epilepsy and, 201

retention/forgetting curves *see* Forgetting curves
with retroactive interference in anterograde amnesia, 186–192
sleep and, 65–66
Retrieval *see* Memory retrieval
Retrieval cues, 3, 4, 193
competition and, 140–145
cue overload, 15, 287–289
forgetting due to ineffective retrieval cues, 155
interactive cueing, 274–275
interference as cue-overload, 287–289
Willshaw model, 81, *82*, 83
Retrieval-induced forgetting (RIF), 14–15, *146*, 147, 148, *149*, 150–151, 153
autobiographical forgetting, 257–260
socially shared (SS-RIF), 267–268
Retroactive interference (RI), 10–11, 42
consolidation and, 63–65, 290–305
consolidation and the temporal gradient of, 63–65
as cue-overload, 288–289
and the dual store account of anterograde amnesia, 188–192
and everyday forgetting, 305–307
forgetting due to RI in amnesia, 185–205
neurobiology, 115–116
studies on RI in anterograde amnesia, 186–188
susceptibility to RI and sleep, 176
temporal gradient of, 63–65, 197, 199, 296
as trace degradation, 289–290, 291
Retrograde amnesia
consolidation and, 67–69, 139
disrupted consolidation and temporally graded retrograde amnesia, 139
hippocampus and, 292–293
psychogenic amnesia and, 246
recovery from, 245–246
relationship to anterograde amnesia, *24*
temporal gradients of retrograde facilitation and, 303–305
temporally graded, 196–197, 201, 292, 295, 303–305
Retrograde facilitation
drug-induced, 299–303
and the effects of sleep on LTP, 297–299
sleep-induced, 295–299
temporal gradient of drug-induced, 302–303
temporal gradient of sleep-induced, 296–297
temporal gradients of retrograde amnesia and, 303–305
Retrograde memory, 24, 246
deficits, 240, 241 *see also* Retrograde amnesia
Reynolds, Mary, 27
Ribosomal proteins, 109
Ribot gradient, 67
RIF *see* Retrieval-induced forgetting

Sea snail, *Aplysia californica*, 112
Second messengers, 106, 108
Seizures, 222–223
Selective retrieval, 146–151, 153
Self-memory system (SMS), 255–256
Semantic knowledge/schemata, 42
Semantic memory, *25*, 38, 39, 41, 43, 67, 112, 169, 227, 240, 246, 287
Senescent forgetfulness, 126–127
Sensitization, 112
Shereshevskii, Solomon, 36
Short-term memory (STM)
blockade of consolidation, *118*
consolidation *see* Consolidation
and the dual store account of amnesia, 188–192
molecular mechanisms of, *110*
"molecular memory", 108
neurobiological transfer to long-term memory, 106–111
post-reactivation (PR-STM), 117, 119
Short-term memory systems (STS)
forgetting in, 36
STS vs. LTS, 49–50
"Silencing", 266, 270–271
see also Collaborative inhibition
Similarity–distance metric, 56–57
Simonides, 26
SIMPLE (Scale Invariant Memory, Perception and LEarning) model, 55–59, 62, 65, 67–69, 70n3
Situated forgetting, 271–276
distributed cognition and, 271–273
socially situated forgetting and transactive memory, 273–276
Sleep
and accelerated long-term forgetting, 229–230
amygdala and, 177, 178, 179
behavioural deprivation studies, 173–174
combining sleep and memory states, 171
consolidation and, 65–66, 95, 166, 171–174, 175–176, 229–230
early/late sleep paradigm, 172
effects on memory, 65–66, 116
emotional memories and, 177–178
experimental paradigms of role in consolidation, 171–173
forestalling forgetting with sleep: verbal associative memory, 174–176
and forgetting, 165–179, 229–230, 288
hippocampus and, 173–175, 178, 293
long-term potentiation and, 297–299
neurotransmitters and, 169, 175–176, 178
non-REM *see* NREM (non-rapid-eye-movement) sleep
postlearning sleep deprivation, 171–172

protection from interference, 116
REM *see* REM (rapid-eye-movement) sleep
sleep-dependent learning in spatial environments, 173–174
slow wave sleep, 95, 169, *170*, 176, 229, 293, 297–299, 298, 303, 304–305
states/stages, 167–169, *170 see also* NREM (non-rapid-eye-movement) sleep; REM (rapid-eye-movement) sleep
susceptibility to retroactive interference and, 176
Sleep-induced retrograde facilitation, 295–299
LTP and, 297–299
temporal gradient of, 296–297
Slow wave sleep (SWS), 95, 169, *170*, 176, 229, 293, 297–299, 298, 303, 304–305
Social forgetting, 265–271
collaborative recall, 268–271
researching, 267
socially shared retrieval-induced forgetting (SS-RIF), 267–268
Somnambulism, 28
Spatial memory, 113, 114, 116, 173, 228, 229
Spontaneous recovery, 8, 41, *122*
SS-RIF (socially shared retrieval-induced forgetting), 267–268
STM *see* Short-term memory
Storage *see* Memory storage
Stress
anterograde amnesia and, 240
and autobiographical memory retrieval, 242–243
extinction and, 123
and frontal lobe dysfunctions, 241
hormones, 29
posttraumatic stress disorder, 242–243
psychogenic amnesia and, 240, 242–243
STS *see* Short-term memory systems
Substitution errors, 41
see also Exchange errors
Suggestibility, 41–42
Suppression, 125, 154–155, 156, 257
and the Think/No-think paradigm, 152, 262–265
see also Repression
Sybil (film), 29
Synapses
artificial, in neural network models *see* Connectionist models of forgetting; Connectionist models of memory
and consolidation, 106–111
see also Synaptic consolidation
and decay, 30, 77
long-term synaptic plasticity, 106, 116
origin of term, 103
short-term synaptic plasticity, 106
synaptic basis of neural activity, 102–105
synaptic consolidation *see* Synaptic consolidation
synaptic dysfunction, 127–128, *129*
"synaptic learning rule", 109–111
synaptic plasticity and the cellular bases of learning and memory, 105–106, 226
synaptic plasticity and the neurobiology of memory and forgetting, 101–131
synaptic plasticity inhibited during slow wave sleep, 304
synaptic strength, 103–106, 107, 109–113, 117, 123, 165
synaptic transmission, 106, *107*
Synaptic consolidation, 201, 202, 204–205, 292, 293–295, 297, 301–302, 304
"Systematic" forgetting, 26
Systems consolidation, 201, 202, 204–205, 226, 292–293, 298–299, 304, 307
neural replay, 292–293, 298, 304

TEA *see* Transient epileptic amnesia
Temporal decay of memory *see* Decay
Temporal distinctiveness models, 51, 62–63, 64, 65, 66
SIMPLE, 55–59, 62, 65, 67–69, 70n3
Temporal isolation, 65, 67, 70n3
Temporal lobe epilepsy (TLE), 214, 216, *218*, 219, 220–221, 222, 224
Temporally graded retrograde amnesia, 196–197, 201, 292, 295, 303–305
Themistocles, 26
Theories of forgetting
adaptive reasons *see* Adaptive reasons/necessity for forgetting
cognitive model, revised, 203–205
connectionist models *see* Connectionist models of forgetting
consolidation *see* Consolidation
cue overload theory, 15
decay theory, 9–10
dual store account of anterograde amnesia, 188–192
Ebbinghaus savings function, 285–286
forgetting due to retroactive interference in amnesia, 185–205
forgetting in memory models, 49–69
historical perspective on, 23–30
interference theory, 10–15
see also Interference; Retroactive interference (RI)
Jost's Second Law, 55, 58, 285–286
neurobiological *see* Neurobiology of memory and forgetting
a new taxonomy of memory and forgetting, 35–44
origins of investigating forgetting, 24–26
power functions and, 5–6, 55, 59, 93, 94, 285–286, 306, *307*
repression, 16–17
retrieval theories, 15
retrieval-induced forgetting *see* Retrieval-induced forgetting (RIF)

retroactive interference and consolidation, role in everyday forgetting, 285–307
see also Consolidation; Retroactive interference (RI)
temporal distinctiveness models
see Temporal distinctiveness models
see also Amnesias
Think/No-think (TNT) paradigm, 152–154, 262–265
Time-based resource sharing (TBRS) model, 54
TLE *see* Temporal lobe epilepsy
TNT (Think/No-think) studies, 152–154
Trace degradation, 289–290, 291
TraceLink model, 95
Trance, 28
Transactive memory, 273–276
Transient epileptic amnesia (TEA), *212*, 213, *218*, 219, 220, 221, 222, 224, 225, 229
Unconscious memories, 16–17
Unlearning, 11, 145
of connections to neurons, 90

Verbal associative memory, 174–176
and NREM sleep role for declarative memory consolidation, 175–176
and susceptibility to retroactive interference and sleep, 176

Wearing, Clive, 186
Weights, 78–79, 80, 92
attractor networks, 83–85
backpropagation and, 89–90
Hopfield networks, 83, 93–94
in a Perceptron, 87–89
Willshaw model, 80–81, *82*, 83
Willshaw networks, 80–83
Word-length effect (WLE), 53–54